FROM IKARIA TO THE STARS

BY THE SAME AUTHOR

ANCIENT HISTORY AND BIOGRAPHY
Alexander the Great (1970)
The Year of Salamis, 480–479 B.C. (1970) [updated as *The Greco-Persian Wars* (1996)]
Armada from Athens: The Failure of the Sicilian Expedition, 415–413 B.C. (1971)
A Concise History of Ancient Greece to the Close of the Classical Era (1973)
The Parthenon (1973)
Alexander of Macedon, 356–323 B.C.: A Historical Biography (1974, reprinted 1992)
Alexander to Actium: The Historical Evolution of the Hellenistic Age (1990, rev. ed. 1993)

ESSAYS
Essays in Antiquity (1960)
The Shadow of the Parthenon (1972)
Classical Bearings (1989)

TRANSLATIONS AND COMMENTARIES
Juvenal: The Sixteen Satires (1967; 3d ed. 1998)
Ovid: The Erotic Poems (1982)
Ovid: The Poems of Exile (1994)
Apollonios Rhodios: The Argonautika (1997)

FROM IKARIA
TO THE STARS

Classical Mythification,
Ancient and Modern

Peter Green

UNIVERSITY OF TEXAS PRESS

AUSTIN

This book has been supported by an endowment dedicated to classics and the ancient world and funded by the Areté Foundation; the Gladys Krieble Delmas Foundation; the Dougherty Foundation; the James R. Dougherty, Jr. Foundation; the Rachael and Ben Vaughan Foundation; and the National Endowment for the Humanities. The endowment has also benefited from gifts by Mark and Jo Ann Finley, Lucy Shoe Meritt, the late Anne Byrd Nalle, and other individual donors.

First edition, 2004

Requests for permission to reproduce material from this work should be sent to Permissions, University of Texas Press, P.O. Box 7819, Austin, TX 78713-7819.

⊗ The paper used in this book meets the minimum requirements of ANSI/NISO Z39.48-1992 (R1997) (Permanence of Paper).

Library of Congress Cataloging-in-Publication Data
Green, Peter, 1924-
From Ikaria to the stars : classical mythification, ancient and modern / Peter Green.— 1st ed.
    p.   cm.
Includes bibliographical references and index.
ISBN 0-292-70230-2 (hardcover : alk. paper)
1. Mythology, Classical.   2. Myth.   I. Title.
BL723.G74   2004
292.1′3—dc22
2003019707

Carin's, again, with love

μάλιστα δέ τ' ἔκλυον αὐτοί

CONTENTS

Acknowledgments *ix*

Abbreviations *x*

Introduction *1*

1

"These Fragments Have I Shored against My Ruins": Apollonius Rhodius
and the Social Revalidation of Myth for a New Age *5*

2

The Flight-Plan of Daedalus *40*

3

Works and Days 1–285: Hesiod's Invisible Audience *47*

4

Athenian History and Historians in the Fifth Century B.C. *67*

5

The Metamorphosis of the Barbarian:
Athenian Panhellenism in a Changing World *104*

6

Text and Context in the Matter of Xenophon's Exile *133*

7

Rebooking the Flute-Girls: A Fresh Look at the Chronological Evidence
for the Fall of Athens and the Eight-Month Rule of the Thirty *144*

8

A Variety of Greek Appetites *160*

9

Alexander's Alexandria   *172*

10

The Muses' Birdcage, Then and Now   *197*

11

How Political Was the Stoa?   *210*

12

Ancient Ethics, Modern Therapy   *222*

13

Getting to Be a Star: The Politics of Catasterism   *234*

14

The Innocence of Procris: Ovid *AA* 3.687–746   *250*

15

Magic and the Principle of Apparent Causality in
Pliny's *Natural History*   *264*

Appendix A
Tanglewood Tales for the Yuppies   *281*

Appendix B
Homer for the Kiddies   *288*

Bibliography   *297*

Index   *307*

ACKNOWLEDGMENTS

Acknowledgments for permission to reprint material included in this volume are due to: the University of California Press for Chapter 1; *Échos du Monde Classique/Classical Views* for Chapter 2; the University of Oklahoma Press for Chapter 5; Oxford University Press for Chapter 6; the *Ancient History Bulletin* for Chapter 7; the *Times Literary Supplement* for Chapter 8 and some material in Chapter 4; the Getty Museum Press for Chapter 9; *Arion* for Chapters 10 and 17; *Ancient Philosophy* for Chapter 11; the *New Republic* for Chapters 12 and 16; *Fenway Court* and the Trustees of the Isabella Stewart Gardner Museum for Chapter 13; the *Classical Journal* and the Executive Committee of the Classical Association of the Midwest and South for Chapter 14.

This also seems to me an appropriate place to record my indebtedness to the superb, and superbly wide-ranging, holdings, in classics and the humanities generally, of the Main Library in the University of Iowa; to Chris Africa, its resourceful and ever-helpful Classics Bibliographer; and to the devoted staff of its Interlibrary Loan Service, who consistently found me, with quite dazzling speed and efficiency, those few *recherché* titles I needed that were not in the system. To all the above, my grateful thanks. But my greatest debt of all, on this occasion more than most—and she knows why—is to my wife, for whom the dedication of this book is, like the exchange of armor between Diomedes and Glaukos, χάλκεα χρυσείων, bronze for gold.

All translations are mine unless otherwise indicated.

ABBREVIATIONS

Books and Journals

AAA	*Athens Annals of Archaeology*
ABSA	*Annual of the British School at Athens*
AHB	*Ancient History Bulletin*
AHR	*American Historical Review*
AJAH	*American Journal of Ancient History*
AJPh	*American Journal of Philology*
AncW	*Ancient World*
Ant. Class.	*L'Antiquité classique*
BHM	*Bulletin of the History of Medicine*
BICS	*Bulletin of the Institute of Classical Studies*, University of London
CAH	*Cambridge Ancient History*
CCC	*Civiltà classica e Cristiana*
Chron. d'Ég.	*Chronique d'Égypte.*
CIL	*Corpus inscriptionum Latinarum* (Berlin, 1863–)
Class. et Med.	*Classica et medievalia*
CJ	*Classical Journal*
CPh	*Classical Philology*
CQ	*Classical Quarterly*
CR	*Classical Review*
Daremberg-Saglio	C. Daremberg and E. Saglio, *Dictionnaire des Antiquités grecques et romaines* (Paris, 1877–1919)
D-K	H. Diels and W. Kranz, *Die Fragmente der Vorsokratiker,* 12th ed., 3 vols. (Dublin and Zürich, 1966)
EMC/CV	*Échos du Monde Classique/Classical Views*
FGrH	F. Jacoby, *Fragmente der griechischen Historiker* (Berlin and Leiden, 1923–58)

FHG	K. and Th. Müller, *Fragmenta Historicorum Graecorum* (Paris, 1841–85)
GHI	M. N. Tod, *A Selection of Greek Historical Inscriptions*, vol. 2, *From 403–323 B.C.* (Oxford, 1948)
GMPT	H. D. Betz, *The Greek Magical Papyri in Translation, Including the Demotic Spells*, vol. 1, *Texts*, 2d ed. (Chicago, 1992)
Gomme-Andrewes-Dover	A. W. Gomme, A. Andrewes, and K. J. Dover, *A Historical Commentary on Thucydides*, vol. 4 (Oxford, 1970)
GRByS	*Greek, Roman and Byzantine Studies*
Hippocr.	*Hippocratic Corpus*
HSCP	*Harvard Studies in Classical Philology*
HThR	*Harvard Theological Review*
IG	*Inscriptiones Graecae* (Berlin, 1873–)
JAW	[Bursian's] *Jahresbericht über die Fortschritte der Klassichen Altertumswissenschaft* (Berlin, 1873–1944/55)
JEA	*Journal of Egyptian Archaeology*
JHS	*Journal of Hellenic Studies*
K-R-S	G. S. Kirk, J. E. Raven, and M. Schofield, *The Presocratic Philosophers: A Critical History with a Selection of Texts*, 2d ed. (Cambridge, 1983)
LIMC	*Lexicon Iconographicum Mythologiae Classicae*, var. edd. (Zürich and Munich), vol. 1: 1981; vol. 2: 1984; vol. 3: 1986; vol. 4: 1988; vol. 5: 1990; vol. 6: 1992; vol. 7: 1994
L-P	E. Lobel and D. L. Page, *Poetarum Lesbiorum Fragmenta* (Oxford, 1955)
Meiggs-Lewis	R. Meiggs and D. M. Lewis, *Greek Historical Inscriptions to the End of the Fifth Century B.C.* (Oxford, 1969)
Mus. Helv.	*Museum Helveticum*
OCD [2,3]	*The Oxford Classical Dictionary* (Oxford, 2d ed.: 1970; 3d ed.: 1996)
OGIS	W. Dittenberger, *Orientis Graecae Inscriptiones Selectae*, 2 vols. (Leipzig, 1903–5)
PDM	*Papyri demoticae magicae* (see also *GMPT*)
PGM	K. Preisendanz, *Papyri Graecae Magicae: Die*

	griechischen Zauberpapyri, 2 vols., 2d ed. (Stuttgart, 1973–74)
Philol.	*Philologus*
PMG	D. L. Page, *Poetae Melici Graeci* (Oxford, 1962)
PWK	A. Pauly, G. Wissowa, W. Kroll, K. Ziegler, *Real-Encyclopädie der classischen Altertumswissenschaft*, 83 vols. (Stuttgart, 1894–1980)
REG	*Revue des études grecques*
RhM	*Rheinisches Museum*
SLG	D. L. Page, *Supplementum Lyricis Graecis* (Oxford, 1974)
Suppl. Mag.	*Supplementum Magicum*
SVF	J. von Arnim, *Stoicorum Veterum Fragmenta*, 4 vols. (Leipzig, 1902–24)
TAPhA	*Transactions and Proceedings of the American Philological Association*
YClS	*Yale Classical Studies*
ZPE	*Zeitschrift für Papyrologie und Epigraphik*

Ancient Sources

Ael.	Claudius Aelianus, A.D. 165/70–230/5
	Hellenized Roman essayist
	VH = Varia Historia
Aesch.	Aeschylus, 525/4–456 B.C.
	Athenian tragedian
	Pers. = The Persians
Aeschin.	Aeschines, c. 397–c. 322 B.C.
	Athenian orator
Alciphr.	Alciphron, ?2d–3d century A.D.
	Greek sophist and writer
	Ep. Amat. = Epistulae Amatoriae
Amm. Marc.	Ammianus Marcellinus, c. A.D. 330–395
	Roman historian
Andoc.	Andocides, c. 440–c. 390 B.C.
	Athenian aristocrat and politician
Ant. Lib.	Antoninus Liberalis, ?2d century A.D.
	Mythographer
AP	*Anthologia Palatina*

Apollod.

Apollodorus, c. 180–c. 110 B.C.
Mythographer
    Epit. = *Epitome*

App.

Appianos [Appian] of Alexandria, 2d century A.D.
Greek historian
    B.C. = *Bella Civilia*
    Mithr. = *Mithridaticum [Bellum]*

Ap. Rhod.

Apollonius Rhodius, c. 300–c. 230 B.C.
Alexandrian epic poet
    Arg. = *Argonautika*

Arat.

Aratus of Soli, c. 315–240 B.C.
Didactic poet
    Phaen. = *Phaenomena*

Arist.

Aristotle of Stagira, 384–322 B.C.
Greek philosopher
    Ath. Pol. = Ἀθηναίων Πολιτεία
    Eth. Nic. = *Ethica Nicomachea*
    Met. = *Meteorologica*
    Metaph. = *Metaphysica*
    Oecon. = *Oeconomica*
    Poet. = *Poetica*
    Pol. = *Politica*
    Probl. = *Problemata*
    Rhet. = *Rhetorica*

Aristoph.

Aristophanes, c. 450–c. 385 B.C.
Athenian comic playwright
    Ach. = *Acharnians*
    Eccles. = *Ecclesiazusae*
    Kn. = *Knights*
    Plut. = *Plutus*
    Thesm. = *Thesmophoriazusae*

Arrian

L. Flavius Arrianus, c. A.D. 86–160
Romanized Greek historian
    Anab. = *Anabasis*
    τὰ μετὰ Ἀλέξ = τὰ μετὰ Ἀλέξανδρον
    (*Affairs after Alexander*)

Athen.

Athenaeus of Naucratis, fl. c. A.D. 200
Belle-lettrist
    Deipnos. = *Deipnosophistae*

Aug.	St. Augustine of Hippo, A.D. 354–430
	Christian apologist
	Civ. Dei = *Civitas Dei*
Caes.	C. Julius Caesar, 100–44 B.C.
	Roman statesman and historian
	Bell. Alex. = *Bellum Alexandrinum*
Callim.	Callimachus of Cyrene, ?310–?240 B.C.
	Alexandrian poet and scholar
	H. = *Hymn*
Cato	M. Porcius Cato, 234–149 B.C.
	Roman statesman and writer
	De Agr. = *De Agri Cultura*
Catull.	C. Valerius Catullus, c. 84–c. 54 B.C.
	Roman lyric and elegiac poet
Cels.	A. Cornelius Celsus, early 1st cent. A.D.
	Medical writer
	De Med. = *De Medicina*
Cic.	M. Tullius Cicero, 106–43 B.C.
	Roman orator and writer
	Att. = *Epistulae ad Atticum*
	De Div. = *De Divinatione*
	De Fin. = *De Finibus Bonorum et Malorum*
	De Rep. = *De Republica*
	Fam. = *Epistulae ad Familiares*
	ND = *De Natura Deorum*
Clem. Alex.	T. Flavius Clemens Alexandrinus [Clement of Alexandria], c. A.D. 150–c. 215
	Christian theologian
	Protrept. = *Protrepticus*
	Strom. = *Stromateis*
Curt.	Q. Curtius Rufus, fl. c. A.D. 50
	Roman historian
Dem.	Demosthenes, 384–322 B.C.
	Athenian orator
dieg.	diegesis [narrative résumé]
Dio Cass.	L.(?) Cassius Dio, c. A.D. 164–c. 230
	Romanized Greek historian
Dio Chrys.	Dio Chrysostomus [Cocceianus], c. A.D. 40/50–c. 110

Greek orator

Diod. Sic.　　　Diodorus Siculus of Agyrium, 1st century B.C.

Greek historian

Diog. Laert.　　Diogenes Laertius, ?early 3d century A.D.

Greek biographer

Dion. Hal.　　　Dionysius Halicarnassensis, c. 50 B.C.–c. A.D. 20

Greek critic and historian

　　　　Ant. Rom. = *Antiquitates Romanae*

　　　　Ep. ad Pomp. = *Epistula ad Gnaeum Pompeium*

　　　　Isocr. = *De Isocrate*

　　　　Lys. = *De Lysia*

Eur.　　　　　　Euripides, c. 480–406/5 B.C.

Athenian tragedian

　　　　Alc. = *Alcestis*

　　　　Andr. = *Andromache*

　　　　Elect. = *Electra*

　　　　Hel. = *Helena*

　　　　Heraclid. = *Heraclidae*

　　　　Hipp. = *Hippolytus*

　　　　IA = *Iphigenia Aulidensis*

　　　　IT = *Iphigenia Taurensis*

　　　　Med. = *Medea*

　　　　Orest. = *Orestes*

　　　　Phoen. = *Phoenissae*

　　　　Suppl. = *Supplices*

　　　　Tro. = *Troades*

Euseb.　　　　　Eusebius of Caesarea, c. A.D. 260–340

Christian chronographer

　　　　Praep. Ev. = *Praeparatio Evangelica*

Eustath.　　　　Eustathius, 12th century A.D.

Archbishop of Thessalonike and Homeric scholar

Galen　　　　　　Galen of Pergamon, A.D. 129–c. 210

Greek medical writer

　　　　Comm. in Hipp. Epidem. = *Commentarium in*
　　　　Hippocratis Epidemias

Hdt.　　　　　　Herodotus Halicarnassensis, c. 485–c. 425 B.C.

Greek historian

Herod.　　　　　Herodas [?Herondas], fl. c. 250 B.C.

Alexandrian mime-writer

	Mim. = *Mimiamboi*
Hes.	Hesiod(us) of Ascra, fl. c. 700 B.C.
	Greek epic/didactic poet
	Theog. = *Theogony*
	WD = *Works & Days*
Hesych.	Hesychius of Alexandria, ?5th century A.D.
	Lexicographer
HHAphr	*Homeric Hymn to Aphrodite*
HHDem	*Homeric Hymn to Demeter*
Hippocr.	Hippocrates of Cos, ?c. 470–?400 B.C.
	Greek medical writer
	Aph. = *Aphorisms*
	Aër = *Airs, Waters, Places*
	Art. = *De Arte* (*The Art [of Medicine]*)
	Morb. Sacr. = *De Morbo Sacro*
	(*The Sacred Disease*)
	Reg. = *A Regimen for Health*
	VM = *De Vetere Medicina* (*On Ancient Medicine*)
Hom.	Homer(us), ?late 8th century B.C.
	Greek epic poet
	Il. = *Iliad*
	Od. = *Odyssey*
Hygin.	Hyginus (*not* C. Julius Hyginus the librarian),
	?2d century A.D.
	Mythographer
	Astron. = *Astronomica*
	Fab. = *Fabulae* (*Genealogiae*)
Hyp.	Hypereides, 389–322 B.C.
	Athenian orator and statesman
	c. Dem. = *contra Demosthenem*
	(speech *Against Demosthenes*)
Isocr.	Isocrates, 436–338 B.C.
	Athenian orator and rhetorician
	Ep. = *Epistulae*
	Nicocl. = *Ad Nicoclem*
	Orat. = *Orationes*
	Panegyr. = *Panegyricus*
John Chrysost.	John [Joannes] Chrysostomus, c. A.D. 354–407
	Bishop of Constantinople

Joseph.	Flavius Josephus, A.D. 37/8–c. 100
	Romanized Jewish historian
	AJ = Antiquitates Judaicae
	BJ = Bellum Judaicum
Jul. Obs.	Julius Obsequens, 4th/5th century A.D.
	Compiler of Roman prodigies
Just.	M. Iunianus Iustinus, ?3d or 4th century A.D.
	Historical epitomator
Juv.	D. Iunius Iuuenalis, c. A.D. 55–c. 138
	Roman satirist
	Sat. = Saturae
Lactant.	L. Caelius Firmianus or Lactantius,
	c. A.D. 240–c. 320
	Christian apologist
	ID = De Ira Dei
Livy	T. Livius Patavinus, 59 B.C.–A.D. 17
	Roman historian
Lucan	M. Annaeus Lucanus, A.D. 39–65
	Roman epic poet
	BC = Bellum Civile
Lys.	Lysias, ?459/8–c. 380 B.C.
	Athenian metic and speechwriter
Nep.	Cornelius Nepos, c. 110–24 B.C.
	Roman biographer
	Eum. = Eumenes
	Lys. = Lysander
Nicand.	Nicander of Colophon, fl. c. 130 B.C.
	Hellenistic didactic poet
Nic. Damasc.	Nicolaus of Damascus, c. 64 B.C.–c. A.D. 10
	Scholar and historian
	Vit. Caes. Aug. = Vita Caesaris Augusti
Ovid	Publius Ovidius Naso, 43 B.C.–A.D. 17/8
	Roman elegiac and epic poet
	AA = Ars Amatoria
	Am. = Amores
	Fast. = Fasti
	Met. = Metamorphoses
	RA = Remedia Amoris
Oxy. Pap.	*Oxyrhynchus Papyri*

Pal.   Palaiphatos, fl. late 4th century B.C.
Mythographer
Περὶ ἀπίστων (*On Incredible Things*)

Paus.   Pausanias of Magnesia-ad-Sipylum, fl. c. A.D. 150
Greek travel-writer

Philod.   Philodemus of Gadara, c. 110–c. 40/35 B.C.
Greek critic, epigrammatist, and philosopher

Philostr.   L. Flavius Philostratus, c. A.D. 180–c. 245
Second Sophistic writer
     Heroic. = *Heroicus*
     Vit. Soph. = *Vitae Sophistarum*
     (*Lives of the Sophists*)

Pind.   Pindar(os) of Cynoscephalae (Boeotia),
518–?438 B.C.
Greek lyric poet
     Isthm. = *Isthmian*
     Nem. = *Nemean*
     Ol. = *Olympian*
     Pyth. = *Pythian*
     (= the four categories of his Epinician
     [Victory] *Odes*)

Plat.   Plato, c. 429–347 B.C.
Athenian philosopher
     Crat. = *Cratylus*
     Epin. = *Epinomis*
     Epp. = *Epistulae*
     Gorg. = *Gorgias*
     Phaedr. = *Phaedrus*
     Phileb. = *Philebus*
     Rep. = *Republic*
     Soph. = *Sophist*
     Theaet. = *Theaetetus*
     Tim. = *Timaeus*

Plin.   C. Plinius Secundus, c. A.D. 23–70
Roman polymath and encyclopedist
     NH = *Natural History* (*Historia Naturalis*)

Plut.   L.(?) Mestrius Plutarch(us) of Chaeronea,
c. A.D. 45–c. 125
Greek essayist and biographer
     Ag. = *Agis*

Ages. = *Agesilaus*
Alcib. = *Alcibiades*
Alex. = *Alexander*
Apothegm. Lacon. = *Apothegmata Laconica*
(*Sayings of Spartans*)
Artax. = *Artaxerxes*
Caes. = *Caesar*
Cim. = *Cimon*
Cleom. = *Cleomenes*
Comp. = *Comparatio*
Demetr. = *Demetrius*
Eum. = *Eumenes*
Lycurg. = *Lycurgus*
Lys. = *Lysander*
Mor. = *Moralia*
Nic. = *Nicias*
Per. = *Pericles*
Pomp. = *Pompeius*
Pyrrh. = *Pyrrhus*
Rom. = *Romulus*
Sol. = *Solon*
Them. = *Themistocles*
Thes. = *Theseus*

Pollux — Julius Pollux of Naucratis, 2d cent. A.D.
Scholar and rhetorician
Onom. = *Onomasticon*

Polyaen. — Polyaenus, 2d cent. A.D.
Military writer

Polyb. — Polybius of Megalopolis, c. 200–c. 118 B.C.
Romanized Greek historian

Porph. — Porphyry of Tyre, A.D. 234–c. 305
Scholar and philosopher
De Abst. = *De Abstinentia*

Ps.-Call. — Pseudo-Callisthenes = The "Alexander Romance,"
dates uncertain

Ptol. — Claudius Ptolemaeus of Alexandria, late 2d century
A.D.
Mathematician and astronomer
Tetrab. = *Tetrabiblos* (*Astrological Influences,*
ἀποτελεσματικά)

schol.	scholium or scholia
Sen.	L. Annaeus Seneca ("the Elder," *E*),
	c. 50 B.C.–A.D. 40
	Rhetorician
	L. Annaeus Seneca ("the Younger," *Y*),
	c. 4 B.C.–A.D. 65
	Man of letters, imperial minister
	Controv. = *Controversiae* (*E*)
	De Prov. = *De Providentia* (*Y*)
	Ep. Mor. = *Epistulae Morales* (*Y*)
	NQ = *Naturales Quaestiones* (*Y*)
Sext. Emp.	Sextus Empiricus, 2d cent. A.D.
	Philosopher and medical writer
	Math. = *Adversus Mathematicos*
	(*Against the Professors*)
Soph.	Sophocles, 496/5–406/5 B.C.
	Athenian tragedian
	El. = *Electra*
	Scyth. = *Scythae*
Stob.	Joannes Stobaeus ("John of Stobi"), 5th century A.D.
	Anthologist
	Flor. = *Florilegium*
Strabo	Strabo of Amaseia, c. 64 B.C.–c. A.D. 25
	Romanized Greek geographer
Steph. Byz.	Stephanus of Byzantium, 5th century A.D.
	Greek grammarian
Suet.	G. Suetonius Tranquillus, c. A.D. 70–c. 130
	Roman imperial civil servant and biographer
	Cal. = *Caligula*
	De Gramm. = *De Grammaticis*
	Div. Aug. = *Divus Augustus*
	Div. Jul. = *Divus Julius*
	Div. Vesp. = *Divus Vespasianus*
	Tib. = *Tiberius*
Tac.	Cornelius Tacitus, c. A.D. 56–?120
	Roman historian and consular
	Ann. = *Annales*
Tert.	Q. Septimius Florens Tertullianus of Carthage,
	c. A.D. 160–c. 240
	Rhetorician and theologian

	De Anim. = *De Anima*
test.	testimonium or testimonia
Theocr.	Theocritus of Syracuse, early 3d century B.C.
	Alexandrian pastoral poet
	Id. = *Idyll*
Theophr.	Theophrastus of Eresos (Lesbos), 371–287 B.C.
	Greek philosopher and botanist
	HP = *Historia Plantarum*
Thuc.	Thucydides, c. 460–c. 395 B.C.
	Athenian historian
Tzetzes	Johannes Tzetzes, 12th century A.D.
	"A copious, careless, quarrelsome Byzantine
	polymath" (*OCD*³ 1568)
	Chil. = *Chiliades* (*Histories*)
Val. Max.	Valerius Maximus, early 1st century A.D.
	Roman anthologist
Varro	M. Terentius Varro of Reate, 116–27 B.C.
	Roman scholar and writer
	RR = *De Re Rustica*
Vell. Pat.	Velleius Paterculus, 20/19 B.C.–c. A.D. 40
	Roman historian
Virg.	P. Vergilius Maro, 70–19 B.C.
	Roman epic and pastoral poet
	Aen. = *Aeneid*
	Ecl. = *Eclogues*
	Georg. = *Georgics*
Vitruv.	Vitruvius Pollio, ?50 B.C.–?A.D. 20
	Roman architect and military engineer
Xen.	Xenophon, c. 430–350 B.C.
	Athenian general and historian.
	Anab. = *Anabasis*
	Hell. = *Hellenica*
	Lac. = *Respublica Lacedaemoniorum*
	Mem. = *Memorabilia*
Zenob.	Zenobius, 2d century A.D.
	Sophist and paroemiographer
Zonar.	Johannes Zonaras, 12th century A.D.
	Byzantine historian
	Epit. = *Epitome*

FROM IKARIA TO THE STARS

INTRODUCTION

My attitude to myth—primarily, but not exclusively, of the Greek variety—
has always been private, idiosyncratic, and out of step with current intellectual trends. As a child I found immense pleasure in Andrew Lang's *Tales of
Troy and Greece*, which nudged me in the direction of the great narrative epic
cycles: the voyage of the Argonauts, the Trojan War (including much matter
not in Homer), the fratricidal battles over Thebes. These were reinforced by
early discovery of Malory's *Morte d'Arthur*, Tennyson's *Idylls of the King*, and
William Morris's *Sigurd the Volsung*. I thus became acclimatized, very young,
to the creative paradoxes of that no-man's-land where myth and history inter-
mingle. To the more psychological and static aspects of myth, from Oedipus's
incest to various *outré* forms of metamorphosis, I was, and remain, relatively
indifferent. To me the ancient myths that matter have always had a grounding
in the actual past, have always retained a sense of diachronic actuality. One
of the most enjoyable academic tasks I have ever had was directing Elizabeth
Vandiver's doctoral dissertation, now published as *Heroes in Herodotus: The
Interaction of Myth and History* (Frankfurt a.M., 1991): this was familiar and
well-loved territory. No accident, either, that Herodotus early became, and
has always remained, by a long way my favorite ancient historian.

   Yet during over a quarter of a century as an active professor of classics I
never once lectured on myth, and in fact took very great care to avoid doing
so. I was attracted neither by the prospect of retailing a collection of exotic,
and intermittently improper, *Tanglewood Tales* for the benefit of indifferent (or
presentist) undergraduates (see Appendix A), nor by the various theoretical
banners—Freudian, sociological, Marxist, even art-historical—under which
the same material was currently being rehashed for uplift by my trendier colleagues. As MacNeice noted, "There ain't no universals in this man's town":
early research on Greco-Roman magic had driven home to me the futility of
going for *parti pris* general definitions. When my onetime teacher Geoffrey
Kirk remarked, in *The Nature of Greek Myth* (Cambridge, 1974), on the way
in which our understanding of Greek myth had been seriously distorted, not

I

only by "learned Hegelian speculations," but also "by the primitivism of Sir Edward Tylor and Lucien Lévy-Bruhl, the naïve comparatism of Sir James Frazer, the sociological exaggerations of Durkheim, Jane Harrison and the early Cornford, the ponderous neo-Kantian epistemology of Cassirer and the romantic functionalism of Lévi-Strauss" (286), I couldn't have been more delighted. Freud, too, I thought, having recently slogged my way through Philip Slater's *The Glory of Hera* (Boston, 1968): the historical reductionism of Eva Keuls's *The Reign of the Phallus* (New York, 1985) was still to come.

These two books, of course, and many more like them, served as a useful reminder that the mythification of the ancient world not only extended far beyond what was commonly thought of as the corpus of myth (roughly congruent with what Apollodorus included in his round-up), but has been going on non-stop ever since. The systematic deconstruction of actuality, truth, and objectivism popular among intellectuals since World War II (sometimes for highly personal reasons) has, of course, sharpened such awareness to a preternatural degree. From *Rashomon* (1951) on, art has reinforced the same conclusion: not only are there many perceptions of truth (something no one would deny), but, because of this, it follows that objective truth is a mere chimera. This fallacy is on a par with the grotesque human egotism apparent in the old limerick about the sycamore tree: that thinkers should seriously consider the possibility that when there wasn't someone around in the quad to look at it, it simply didn't exist. Such perceptions have, of course, spilled over into our thinking about myth, and have been strongly reinforced by propaganda techniques inherited from totalitarianism.

An easy, and obvious, example of this is the so-called Holocaust Myth, which embodies all the worst features to be found in these postwar developments. In particular, it demonstrates, in extreme form, both motive and technique for the rejection of objective fact as such. It so happens that the Holocaust was uncomfortably well-documented, not least by horrified Allied troops equipped with cine-cameras. But latter-day nationalists, racists, and totalitarians, to whom this public fact was totally unacceptable, had to find ways to reject it; and the first need was to relativize factuality as such, to create instead a smorgasbord of competing "truths," which in fact were no more than assertive opinions writ large. The entire history of our cultural evolution, from the heroic myths of the Mycenaean Age onward, shows a fascinating run-up to this kind of mass wishful-thinking: humankind, as Eliot noted, cannot bear very much reality, and has never been slow to rewrite the record by way of self-justification. Sometimes, as with Zeno's attempt, in his *Politeia*, to legislate social change by simple fiat (see p. 220), the attempt is naive, not to say childlike. More often it is complex and unconscious.

But in all cases, I think, what we see is a pursuit of some kind of truth, from an unknown absolute to the self-generated preferential dogma that nowadays is clearly the most popular version. What I find really astonishing—and, as a professional historian, should long since have accepted—is just how widespread this process is, how radically it invades every human record of the past, and how easy it is to neglect its influence. My heightened consciousness in this matter was caused, in the first instance, by the very considerable research required for the essay with which this book opens. The stubborn persistence of myth for centuries in the face of rational criticism, its retention (whether consciously or not) by whole areas of intellectual thought, the devices, from allegory to historicism, used to "save the appearances"—all this made me sit up and take notice. It wasn't a case of my having innocently posited a clear and direct transition from *mythos* to *logos:* leave that to German *Idealismus.* But I hadn't, until I really started digging, gauged the fierce intensity of the *need* for myth in the human psyche, of any age, or sensed the variety of motives dictating that need. Couple it with the intellectual passion for aprioristic universal theories, and to a very great extent the vagaries of deconstruction and postmodernism begin to explain themselves.

Having reached this point, I began to reconsider other topics I had explored in recent years, but now, specifically, with a view to isolating their potential mythic content. The result, again, surprised me. Rather like Molière's M. Jourdain, who found he had been speaking prose for over forty years without knowing it, I discovered that, again and again, I had been drawn to analyze individual instances of what (taking a leaf from William James) I suppose could be termed the variations of mythic experience. It didn't happen every time, of course; but in at least half the filed items I examined it formed a prominent leitmotif of my investigation.

Why did Daedalus turn east at Delos instead of continuing north to northwest, and why (equally intriguingly) had no one ever been bothered by the discrepancy? Just who was it that Hesiod was addressing in the beginning of the *Works and Days*, and how did this relate to early awareness of self and the use of autobiography and fiction in poetry? How much were the deep differences between Herodoteans and Thucydideans a matter of temperament rather than logic, and could a preference for inductive rather than deductive reasoning, not to mention a distaste for the banausic, be subsumed under that heading? What, exactly, does a phenomenon such as Panhellenism tell us about ethnic stereotypes, and the way they're adapted to meet changing circumstances? What causes the remarkable skepticism of scholars in the face of exciting or attractive new evidence? Why do some theories, *per contra* (e.g., that of the so-called penetrationists), catch on with all the virulent infectiousness of an epidemic? What was in Alexander's mind when he built Alexandria, and why have so many Alexandrias of the mind been propagated ever since? What factor is it that has so strikingly led scholars to aporia when faced with the deification, much less the catasteral enskyment, of ancient rulers? Why should the Stoa be saddled with the myth of democracy, or myth-as-literature with the documentary fallacy? Was magic effective or affective, designed for control or performance?

These are among the problems discussed in the essays that follow. I cannot pretend to have solved all the questions that I ask. But (as we are so often reminded nowadays) perhaps it is at least as important to ask the questions as to expect conclusive, or even wholly rational, answers. Between *mythos* and *logos* there is no clearly delimited and specific distinction (though the differences are, I think, greater than Kirk allowed), no boundary-line to be established simply by taking thought. Least of all can we trace an orderly progression from "mythic thought" (εἴ ποτ᾽ ἔην γε—perhaps itself a chimera?) to rational philosophic discourse.

Volumes of collected essays, we're told, need to justify themselves, preferably by presenting a unified thesis. We know today that non-rational (or, better, quasi-rational) modes of thought and perception have a far greater place, still, in our world than was conceivable even fifty years ago. But we also know (as I began by pointing out) that mythic expression as a vehicle for individual rewriting of the truth—on the erroneous assumption that *all* we have for a *Rashomon* situation are the accounts given, that there *is no actual truth* beyond their truths—has taken on some dangerous qualities in the last few decades. If this book throws even a little light on the first, and succeeds to any degree in combating the second, my efforts will, I feel, have been well worthwhile.

Finally, it may strike others, as it has often struck me, that modern attempts to rewrite or reinterpret the past can have their unintentionally comic side. Thus, as a species of light relief after more serious analysis, I have added two appendices, on the more risible aspects of the vulgarization of classical myth for profit and entertainment.

I

"These Fragments Have I Shored against My Ruins": Apollonius Rhodius and the Social Revalidation of Myth for a New Age

These mythes or current stories, the spontaneous and earliest growth of the Grecian mind, constituted at the same time the entire intellectual stock of the age to which they belonged. They are the common root of all those different ramifications into which the mental activity of the Greeks subsequently diverged; containing, as it were, the preface and germ of the positive history and philosophy, the dogmatic theology and the professed romance, which we shall hereafter trace each in its separate development. They furnished aliment to the curiosity, and solution to the vague doubts and aspirations, of the age; they explained the origin of those customs and standing peculiarities with which men were familiar; they impressed moral lessons, awakened patriotic sympathies, and exhibited in detail the shadowy, but anxious, presentiments of the vulgar as to the agency of the gods; moreover they satisfied that craving for adventure and appetite for the marvellous, which has in modern times become the province of fiction proper.

G. GROTE, *A History of Greece* (1888 ed.), 1:309

ALMOST THE ONLY undebated aspect of Greek myth is its extraordinarily long-enduring significance. When the Homeric epics were first conceived, Jason's ship *Argo* was already πᾶσι μέλουσα,[1] a familiar public topic,[2] and Nilsson's correlation of the major cycles of myth with known Mycenaean sites (a theory that has withstood much criticism)[3] took the kernel at least of

---

Note: Originally published in *Hellenistic Constructs: Essays in Culture, History and Historiography,* ed. P. Cartledge, P. Garnsey, and E. Gruen (Berkeley, 1997), 35–71.

1. Hom. *Od.* 12.70. The debate as to whether the epithet should be treated as one word or two goes back to Aristarchus's day: see Dräger 1993, 14 and n. 7 for a conspectus of scholarship.

2. Schol. ad loc. (Dindorf II 535.6 f.): ἐπίθετον τῆς Ἀργοῦς ἀπὸ τοῦ πᾶσιν ἐν ἐπιμελείᾳ εἶναι διὰ τοῦ κλέους.

3. See Vermeule's remarks in Nilsson 1972, vii–xiii, and Nilsson's own arguments, with especial relevance for the present discussion, in ch. 2, §7, 127–58.

this material back into the Aegean Bronze Age. But it was not only of great antiquity: it seemed indestructible. Hellenistic Alexandria made an industry out of it. *Graecia capta* found Rome equally receptive: Tiberius's obsessive passion for the arcana of mythology was notorious.[4] Revealing, too: the questions with which he tried to floor the grammarians ("Who was Hecuba's mother? What name did Achilles go under when disguised as a girl? What songs did the Sirens sing?") all tacitly assume the possibility of eliciting a truthful answer, that is, they concede the fundamental *historicity* of myth.

My prime interest is, broadly speaking, historical. What did the Greeks themselves value about myth? How much, and in what way, did those values change between Mycenaean and Greco-Roman times? What factors—social, psychological, geographical, intellectual, literary, scientific—were ultimately responsible? Because of the variety and complexity of the Greek mythic tradition, not to mention perennial, and endemic, scholarly disagreements over its interpretation, I have chosen to use as a test case one particular myth, that of the Argonauts, and restrict my study of its evolution to the period between Homer and Apollonius Rhodius. This has several advantages. The Argonaut myth is one, primarily, of heroic *action:* despite its accretion of magic and *Märchen* (cf. Buxton 1994, 75–76), it falls essentially into the historicizing category—with a background eloquent of early trade, the foundation of colonies, Mediterranean exploration, genealogical links with the heroic past, the commemoration of that past for its κλέος, its renown, and its use as an empowering model of conduct, a validation, a guide to Greek individual and public identity. Further, it possesses three key narratives, one archaic (Pindar's Fourth *Pythian*) and two Hellenistic (Apollonius's *Argonautika*, and the *Argonautai* of Dionysios Skytobrachion, summarized at length by Diodorus) to use as indices of change. Last, by cutting my study short in the mid-third century, I can for the most part avoid the mythically complicating intrusion of the Roman factor.[5]

The social mutation of myth, in its wider context, forms one facet of what is perhaps the most influential factor in all Greek history: the rapid expansion of rational knowledge generated by the so-called Greek miracle, the sixth-century B.C. intellectual breakthrough in Ionia, and the ongoing conflict this created between new perceptions and old beliefs, setting heart against head,

---

4. Suet. *Tib.* 70.3: maxime tamen curauit notitiam historiae fabularis usque ad ineptias atque derisum; nam et grammaticos . . . eius modi fere quaestionibus experiebatur: "quae mater Hecubae, quod Achilli nomen inter uirgines fuisset, quid Sirenes cantare sint solitae."

5. Cf. A. D. Momigliano, *On Pagans, Jews and Christians* (Middletown, Conn., 1987), 264–88.

tribe against polis, what Gilbert Murray called the Inherited Conglomerate[6] against innovative thought (often labeled "secular," but in fact rather "anti-Olympian": not the same thing at all). The degree to which, at all levels, the strands of past belief and future reason remained in acute conflict, not merely between intellectuals and the masses, but *within individuals,* supplying (for example) the terrible tension that dominates such plays as Sophocles' *Ajax* or *Antigone,* is central to any understanding of Greek society.

The deep and instinctive conservatism of all but the most progressive Greek intellectual thinking—τιμιώτατον γὰρ τὸ πρεσβύτατον, said Aristotle, "what's oldest is most valuable" (*Met.* A3, 983b32)—has often elicited comment,[7] but its impact on mythic historiography has not, I think, been fully appreciated. This obsession with the past, above all the heroic past, was ubiquitous and intense. To an overwhelming extent, the past and everything it stood for had been *better,* and it was not only Homer's heroes[8] who thought so. Plato, Isocrates, Aristotle all shared the same outlook: when they attacked witnesses to that lost world, it was for misrepresenting it.[9] Thus challenges to the validity of the myths in which its essence was enshrined could not but arouse intense antagonism, confusion, and distress.

Efforts at reconciliation, with all the redefining and reinterpretation of evidence that these entail, were made, and made in good faith. Criticism certainly existed, but on almost every occasion aimed to remove false accretions, not to deny the ultimate truth or kernel of the myth as such. In particular, the *historical existence* of the Heroic Age, however the truth of that claim be defined (cf. Veyne 1988, chs. 1, 7), remained an article of faith, not merely in Apollonius's day—when we find an exact contemporary (264/3) working out the chronology of such events as Deukalion's Flood (1528), the Amazon campaign against Athens (1256), and the beginning of the Trojan War (1218)[10]—

---

6. G. Murray, *Greek Studies* (Oxford, 1947), 66–67, cited by Dodds 1951, 179.

7. Most strikingly by Van Groningen 1953, 1–12, who surveys our sources from Homer to Aristotle. For the status quo as the economic ideal, cf. A. E. Samuel, *From Athens to Alexandria: Hellenism and Social Goals in Ptolemaic Egypt* (Louvain, 1983), 123, and Green 1993, 363–67, 374–75.

8. E.g., *Il.* 1.260–61; 5.302, 447; *Od.* 8.223.

9. Plat. *Phileb.* 16C: Socrates speaks of οἱ μὲν παλαιοί, κρείττονες ἡμῶν καὶ ἐγγυτέρω θεῶν οἰκοῦντες. Isocrates, as Van Groningen comments (1953, 7), "places everything which he thinks desirable in the past; the Athens of former days was exemplary; only imitations of the forefathers can bring real prosperity . . . with him 'the excellency of the fathers' becomes a synonym of the fathers themselves." For ἡ τῶν προγόνων ἀρετή, see Isocr. 12.5, 15.76. For the spirit of emulating the past, cf. 5.113–14; 6.12–13, 98; 7.84; 8.93; 12.137; 15.114; and in general, *Orat.* 4 and 7. Aristotle believed that "antiquity appears to be a near approach to what is by nature," *Rhet.* 2.9.9, 1387a16 (trans. Van Groningen).

10. The Marmor Parium (*FGrH* 239 §§4, 21, 23: cf. Dowden 1992, 51–52).

but as late as the third century A.D., when the rationalizing Eusebius, similarly, provides specific dates for such events as Laios's rape of Chrysippos (1303)[!] and (with at least antiquarian interest for the present discussion) the voyage of the Argonauts (1264).[11] From the very beginning, the mythic past was firmly situated in historical time, its basic events accepted as fact, its heroic protagonists linked both to the prior "age of origins" and to the purely human era that succeeded it (Brillante 1990, 101–2).

The "age of heroes" was seen as remote (and hence difficult of access), but no less real than contemporary history, and similarly located in time and place. The main attitude conveyed by the "age of origins," on the other hand, as reflected in Hesiod and his successors, is neither moral nor foundational, but a huge, and characteristic, sense of relief at having moved from the nothingness of monsters and chaos to a world of reasoned order, identifiable existence. Further, those ancient genealogical links that constituted one of the chief reasons for the importance attached to the mythical past also, as Rosalind Thomas points out, largely ignored the centuries intervening between heroic ancestor and present-day (alleged) descendant.[12] While oral memory extended back only about three generations, mythic memory jumped the gap to what Kipling in his *Just-So Stories*, with exquisite accuracy, termed the "high and far-off times." Compared with the Egyptians, of course (cf. Hdt. 2.143),[13] the Greeks were mere Balkan parvenus; and indeed there is something oddly makeshift about their "age of origins."

Nevertheless, makeshift or not, the Greek mythic tradition certainly filled a need, satisfying the aspirations and emotions of endless generations. In what way, we well may ask, did it achieve this end? Buxton has recently outlined four general categories that (with one striking exception) do appear to cover the most important functions that myth performed for its Greek adherents.[14]

---

11. See *Eusebi Chronicorum Canonum Quae Supersunt*, ed. A. Schoene, H. Petermann, and E. Roediger (Berlin, 1866) (reprinted Dublin and Zürich, 1967), 2:44–47. Eusebius dated to the "years after Abraham." It has been calculated that 1 Abr. = 2016 B.C.: see E. J. Bickerman, *Chronology of the Ancient World*, 2d ed. (London, 1983), 87–88. Cf. Veyne 1998, 111.

12. Thomas 1989, 177–78: her whole section "Genealogy and the Genealogists" (173–95) is of great interest in this context.

13. Herodotus's anecdote on the snubbing of Hekataios by Egyptian priests may, in detail, be *ben trovato* rather than strictly true, but the significance lies in its being told by a Greek. For a good analysis, see Alan B. Lloyd's *Herodotus Book Two: Commentary 99–182* (Leiden and New York, 1988), 107–8. The ambivalent Greek attitude to Egyptian antiquity and the sheer *size* of Egyptian temples, strange beasts, etc. is betrayed by their vocabulary: such words as κροκόδειλος, πυραμίς, ὀβελίσκος, στροῦθος, used to signify "crocodile," "pyramid," "obelisk," or "ostrich," originally meant, respectively, "house-lizard," "honey-cake" (pyramidally shaped), "little spit," and "sparrow."

14. Buxton 1994, ch. 9, "The Actors' Perceptions," 169–81.

1. The preservation of great deeds from the heroic past, what Homer described (*Il.* 9.189) as κλέα ἀνδρῶν, the deeds of heroes, and Hesiod (*Theog.* 100) as κλεῖα προτέρων ἀνθρώπων, the deeds of former men. This constitutes the primary purpose of early epic and remains a prominent ideal for Herodotus, Pindar, and the orators.

2. The didactic and educational function, the furnishing of mythical παραδείγματα, "moral exemplars, cautionary tales and formulation in gnomic utterance of moral, and indeed of technical, wisdom" (Heath 1987, 47). The source of such guidance was universally assumed to lie in the heroic past. But that past was also attacked by progressive moralists. Archaic primitivism and bluntness was becoming an embarrassment.

3. The element of *entertainment*, achieved in particular by playing on the emotions (θέλγω, τέρπω) with the retelling of famous *gestes*. This attitude, of course, also attracted the censure of serious moralists, Stoics in particular.[15]

4. "The role of myths in explaining the present in terms of its origins" (Buxton 1994, 177). Such appeals to the past for authorization or empowerment could, and did, operate to powerful effect not only in foundation-cum-charter myths and genealogical stemmata, backing up territorial or family claims, but also—an overlap, I think, with category 2—in moral decisions or personal conduct.

We find here no mention, as a fifth category, of what might be thought the most important of all, that is, religion.[16] Buxton does recognize (145) the brute and crucial fact that archaic Greek divinities, as portrayed in myth, "are neither good nor evil, but powerful," an *aperçu* that applies even to Zeus;[17] that their motives are petty and personal, their relations with one another "based on a combination of violence, deception, negotiation and reciprocity" (146). But (like so many) he shies away from the unpalatable implications of all this by treating an essentially religious phenomenon as not in fact religious (by his definition) at all, though it is precisely here that we find the archetypal layer of stubborn and irrational belief that formed the living core of Greek

---

15. Strabo, summing up much earlier Hellenistic thinking about myth at the opening of his *Geography*—see in particular 1.1.10, C.7, 1.2.3, C.15–16, 1.2.8–10, C.19–21—scathingly dismisses Eratosthenes' argument that a poet should aim to provide pleasure rather than instruction (ψυχαγωγίας, οὐ διδασκαλίας): 1.2.3, C.15, ad init., repeated at 1.1.10, C.7, ad fin.

16. I do not propose here to enter into yet another argument, at this point, of "what I think religion is," which would be wholly irrelevant to my present purpose: my concern is with what, on the evidence, *the Greeks* took to be, and did about, *their* religion.

17. Cf. M. P. Nilsson, "Die Griechengötter und die Gerechtigkeit," in *Opuscula Selecta* (Lund, 1951–60), 3:303–21, esp. 315, tellingly cited by Buxton (1994, 145 n. 1).

myth, and fought so protracted a battle against the inroads of knowledge and reason.

The evidence suggests a world where Chaos, the Unknown, still looms dauntingly near;[18] where μίασμα, religious pollution, is as real, and lethal, as bubonic plague; where gods wholly devoid of moral sense, immortal and narcissistic, subject the world to their unpredictable and arbitrary whims; where human virtue and good intentions count for nothing in the divine scheme of things. Knowledge of natural functions (e.g., rain, thunder, lightning) is limited, and the gods' powers (since the unknown is automatically seen as an instrumental perquisite of divinity) correspondingly enhanced, thus intensifying helplessness or human shiftlessness (ἀμηχανία), which not only survives, well documented, in the lyric poetry of the period,[19] but also, of course, appears—not, I would argue, by accident—as a prominent leitmotif in Apollonius's portrayal of Jason. This grim archetypal scenario forms the imprinted legacy of centuries: elements of it persist, uncomfortable ghosts, throughout Greco-Roman history.

The atavistic phenomena and attitudes outlined above came under sustained attack on several fronts, all directly connected with the expansion of knowledge, the development of *logos* at the expense of *mythos*. To begin with, for centuries Greek geographical knowledge had been virtually limited to the eastern half of the Mediterranean, and even there not all that far into the hinterland: Greeks, as Socrates remarks in the *Phaedo* (109B), stuck to the coast like frogs around a pond. The Black Sea—something to which the myth of the Clashing Rocks bears eloquent witness—was largely ἄπειρον, "boundless," as far as Aegean Greeks were concerned, until the eighth century B.C. at the very earliest,[20] while Colchis, so prominent in the Argonaut myth, and referred to in the earliest literature, shows no real physical traces of Greek presence until c. 550 (Braund 1994, 92–93). The chronological time-lag between lit-

---

18. C. Geertz, "Religion as a Culture System," in *Anthropological Approaches to the Study of Religion*, ed. M. Banton (London, 1966), 14, cites Suzanne Langer as arguing that Man "can adapt himself somehow to anything his imagination can cope with; but he cannot deal with Chaos," and goes on to isolate three points at which Chaos seriously threatens man's integrity: "At the limits of his analytic capacities, at the limits of his powers of endurance, and at the limits of his moral insight." I owe this reference to Gould (1985, 5).

19. Snell 1975, 72–75, cf. 102: "Die Hilflosigkeit ist ein wesentliches Motiv der frühgriechischen persönlichen Lyrik, das der Dichter dazu führt, von ihrem Innern, ihrer Seele, von der Tiefe ihres Empfindens zu sprechen."

20. Boardman 1980, 240. E. H. Minns, *Scythians and Greeks* (Cambridge, 1913), 9, refers to the trepidation with which Greeks long contemplated a Black Sea voyage.

erary and archaeological evidence indicates a period when myth could still flourish unchecked.

It was, of course, the great outburst of colonization and trade from the late eighth century onward that radically expanded Greek physical knowledge of the whole Mediterranean basin. Very soon the journeys traditionally taken by Odysseus and the *Argo* became regular shipping routes, which posed an interesting problem of how to accommodate various mythic wonders (θαύματα). As the boundaries of knowledge spread, travelers' tales were steadily forced further and further toward the still-unexplored periphery.[21] The geographical map began to slough off its original symbolic form and bend mythic belief to physical fact. Nothing, perhaps, had so profound an impact on the *Weltanschauung* of the archaic era as Herodotus's flat rejection, thrice repeated,[22] of the stream of Ocean.

One significant by-product of this geographical expansion was a more skeptical attitude, at least among a minority, to the kind of primaeval θαύματα involving disregard for the normal laws of nature: three-headed dogs, firebreathing brazen bulls, winged horses or heroes, the Chimaira, and so on. Yet they all turn up again in Pliny's *Natural History* (7.9–32), to survive, recycled, in medieval bestiaries and the *Travels of Sir John Mandeville*. This is significant. We sometimes assume that *logos*, when it comes, will always be welcome, that *mythos* is awaiting enlightenment. It was not so then; it is not so now. Heart and head remain in stubborn opposition. *Mythos* persists against all odds.[23]

But the growth of knowledge altered more than external and visible facts;

21. Cf. Nestle 1942, 132: "Und auch die Welt war eine andere geworden: je mehr sich durch kolonisatorische Unternehmungen in 8. und 7. Jahrhundert und durch Entdeckungsfahrten, wie die des Skylax von Karyanda von der Indusmündung bis ins Rote Meer, der geographische Horizont erweitert hatte, desto mehr mußten die Märchenländer und ihre Fabulistik, wie sie etwa noch das Arimaspenepos des Aristeas von Prokonnesos beherrschte, zurückweichen und fragwürdig werden."

22. Hdt. 2.23, 4.8, 4.36. The last of these passages is the most interesting, since it also contains a brisk dismissal of the (largely symbolic) Anaximandran map. The persistence of geographical myth, however, can be judged from the fact that though Herodotus correctly identified the Caspian as an inland sea rather than an inlet of Ocean (1.203), thus replacing water by land as an eastern boundary, it was not long before the old view was reinstated, largely as the result of propaganda on behalf of Alexander (Romm 1992, 34, 42–43).

23. Paul Veyne himself provides a remarkable instance of this (1988, 87): "For my part, I hold ghosts to be simple fictions but perceive their truth nevertheless. I am almost neurotically afraid of them, and the months I spent sorting through the papers of a dead friend were an extended nightmare. At the very moment I type these pages I feel the hairs stand up on the back of my neck." An interesting "bridge from myth in history to myth versus history" is provided by Herodotus's account (9.26–28) of the dispute between Athens and Tegea, at the battle of Plataia in 479, over which should have precedence of position in the front line. Mythic antecedents are justified by the historian's anachronistic rhetorical topoi. See Cartledge 1993, 28.

in several fundamental ways it transformed Greek social, moral, and even religious attitudes. What had been almost totally lacking still in the Archaic Age was any developed sense of *individual moral responsibility*, in heaven as on earth. Tribal authoritarianism had ruled through power, as Hesiod's ancient fable of the Hawk and the Nightingale, with its Near Eastern associations, starkly demonstrates;[24] it was the drive toward civilized urbanism, combined with written law-codes and a growing taste for ἰσονομία, "equality under the law," that made men look askance at arbitrary conduct of any sort. The virtues of cooperation militated against heroic egotism. Town life softened outspokenness, produced in time the middle-class virtues of euphemism — "dirty talk" (αἰσχρολογία) is a term not found before the fourth century[25] — and domestic respectability.[26] Divine behavior, being rooted in archaic religious and mythic tradition, was getting further and further out of step with human conduct.

The central function of myth in validating genealogies and territorial claims also meant, inevitably, that political propaganda, including on occasion the forgery of documents and interpolation of traditional texts, would not seldom influence the evolution of a mythic tradition. An ingenious but decidedly *parti pris* reworking of myth by the epic poet Eumelos attempted, as we shall see, to transfer Medeia's ancestry to Corinth. What becomes clear from such incidents is the overriding centrality of myth to the *self-definition and self-esteem* of any family or polis.[27]

Lastly, the spread of literacy, and the beginning of efforts (first visible in Hesiod) to systematize and categorize the vast heterogeneous body of Hel-

---

24. Hes. *WD* 202–12. For this fable's Sumerian, Babylonian, and other Near Eastern antecedents, see Walcot 1966, 90, and West 1978, 204–5. It is interesting how modern scholars, these two included, so often understate (to put it mildly) the bleak amorality here, which anticipates by centuries the attitude of the Athenians in the Melian Dialogue (Thuc. 5.89, cf. 105.2): ἐπισταμένους πρὸς εἰδότας ὅτι δίκαια μὲν ἐν τῷ ἀνθρωπείῳ λόγῳ ἀπὸ τῆς ἴσης ἀνάγκης κρίνεται, δυνατὰ δὲ οἱ προύχοντες πράσσουσι καὶ οἱ ἀσθενεῖς ξυγχωποῦσιν.

25. Xen. *Lac.* 5.6; Arist. *Eth. Nic.* 1128a23.

26. This trait was so marked in Athens as to become a topic for derisive outsider jokes: see Plut. *Sol.* 15.2–3.: Ἃ δ' οὖν οἱ νεώτεροι τοὺς Ἀθηναίους λέγουσι τὰς τῶν πραγμάτων δυσχερείας ὀνόμασι χρηστοῖς καὶ φιλανθρώποις ἐπικαλύπτοντας ἀστείως ὑποκορίζεσθαι, τὰς μὲν πόρνας ἑταίρας, τοὺς δὲ φόρους συντάξεις, φυλακὰς δὲ τὰς φρουρὰς τῶν πόλεων, οἴκημα δὲ τὸ δεσμωτήριον καλοῦντας.

27. Wickersham, to his credit, sees this very clearly, when he talks (23–24) of "the centrality of myth to a polis' self-concept, and how all its myths are interwoven. The historical loss of Salamis changed Megara's and everyone's view of what it meant to be Megara. Megara became not only a city that did not now have Salamis, but one that perhaps never really did. A way had to be found to reconnect, or else the loss would be compounded; all the rest of the myths predicated upon Megarian kinship with Ajax and possession of Salamis were shaken."

lenic myth, meant that any would-be mythographer was going to be confronted by a bewildering range of independent local variants. We hear a good deal nowadays about Greek mythology's "tolerance of plurality . . . the compatibility of alternatives is basic to Greek mythology" (Buxton 1994, 177, 179). But what seems to me far more likely than a state of affairs that found conflicting plurality natural (can this ever in fact have happened?) is a growing confusion caused by improved communications, which progressively broke down the barriers between hitherto isolated enclaves, and thus released a variety of irreconcilable variant myths into common circulation. Since all traditions commanded respect, contradictory voices had somehow to be accommodated.

Historians and mythographers, faced with such attacks, set themselves to "save the appearances" (σῴζειν τὰ φαινόμενα) by either explaining away or reinterpreting those elements of each *mythos* which seemed incompatible with the rational demands of *logos*. To this end they developed two interpretative methods, rationalization and allegory, each justifying apparently impossible, undesirable, or irreconcilable characters and events by explaining that they were not in fact what they appeared to be. In this sense there is comparatively little difference between historical misinterpretation or symbol: Zeus can just as easily be anaxagorized in the form of Νοῦς ("Mind") as euhemerized into a dead king deified for his achievements on earth. The distinction lies in the attitude to the past that each approach implies: the one embraces inner, the other outer, reality. While rationalization trawls for historical reality distorted by misunderstanding, poetic vision, or propaganda, allegory seeks an abstract inner truth independent of any specific or physical condition, the hidden verity beneath the surface of things.

Allegory, despite its inherent inanities, was there to stay.[28] The idea spread like wildfire: its main usefulness for the modern historian is to demonstrate just how firm a grip the myths still had on society, that they were felt worth thus rescuing at all costs. Rationalizing critics sought different targets. Where allegory chiefly concerned itself with sanitizing the *repugnant or undesirable*— divine adulteries, mutual violence, or similar improprieties liable to shock or reduce veneration in the human observer—rationalization, finding such activities only too credible (if not necessarily desirable), preferred to con-

---

28. Buxton 1994, 73, sketches its *Nachleben* from Boccaccio (the Danaïds' endless and futile pouring out of liquid = a warning against male sexual indulgence!) through Vico (the Theban Spartoi = "protagonists in an early class struggle") to Max Müller's "theory that Greek myths are disguised accounts of celestial phenomena" and, in our own day, the Jungian pattern of psychic archetypes.

centrate on the *physically or historically impossible*.[29] "By discarding the over-mythical," Dikaiarchos pronounced, "one reduces it, through reason, to natural reality."[30] Prodikos and Euhemeros at one stroke solved the awkward divine-human nexus by explaining away the Olympians, and demi-gods like Heracles, as great kings and leaders in the "high and far-off times" who had been deified by their grateful subjects,[31] thus firmly anchoring them in historical time and at a human level.

Far from dislodging the mythic world, in fact, rationalization made a remarkably thorough job of historicizing it. Modern historiographical concerns remained virtually non-existent through antiquity. Even Herodotus and Thucydides, in their opening chapters (Dowden 1992, 46), see early myth as "distorted remnants of history." The Greco-Roman period might usher in a deeper skepticism,[32] with Lucretius complaining that centaurs could never have existed "with a double nature and twin body, compounded from members of different species" (*duplici natura et corpore bino / ex alienigenis membris compacta*),[33] but rationalization of such species, plainly *contra naturam*, had been going on for centuries. This industry was associated with the name of Palaiphatos, possibly a student of Aristotle.[34] Most of the "Palaiphatan" rationalizing glosses that have come down to us follow a regular pattern: e.g., the Chimaira (Pal. xxviii) was really a volcanic mountain in Anatolia, the flanks of which were haunted by a lion and a serpent. Far-fetched though his efforts to save the mythic phenomena were, Palaiphatos remains perhaps antiquity's most eloquent witness to the truth that even die-hard skeptics wanted no

29. Feeney (1991, 36) points out, interestingly (though he does not suggest, and I am not sure, what the significance might be) that for Homer the "rationalizing angle" is very rare in the *Iliad* scholia, being largely confined to those of the *Odyssey* and to Eustathius.

30. Quoted by Porph. *De Abst.* 4.1.2 (ed. M. Patillon, A. P. Segonds, and L. Brisson [Paris, 1995] = Müller *FHG* 2.225 = fr. 49 Wehrli): τὸ δὲ λίαν μυθικὸν ἀφέντας εἰς τὸ διὰ τοῦ λόγου φυσικὸν ἀνάγειν. The Budé editors translate this as "laissant ce qui est trop légendaire, restituer la réalité en se fondant sur la raison."

31. The subject is vast, and I can no more than touch on it here. For Prodikos as anticipating Euhemeros, see Henrichs 1975, 1976, and 1984, 340–41. For the fragments of Euhemeros (updating *FGrH* 63), see now Winiarczyk 1991 (bib.). There is no satisfactory monograph: there are useful comments in the introduction and commentary of the Italian edition of G. Vallauri, *Euemero di Messene* (Turin, 1956). See also Fraser 1972, 1:289–95; Feeney 1991, 31–32; Henrichs 1984, 346–49; Buffière 1956, 245–48; Dowden 1992, 50.

32. See the apt examples (Philostr. *Heroic.* 7.9; Cic. *ND* 3.16.40, *De Div.* 2.57.117; Paus. 1.30.3) cited by Veyne 1988, 71–72, and add the stern remarks of Dion. Hal. *Ant. Rom.* 2.20.1–2.

33. 5.879–80. William Empson wittily reworked this as the beginning of his poem "Invitation to Juno," *Collected Poems* (London, 1955), 5: "Lucretius could not credit centaurs; / such bicycle he deemed asynchronous."

34. Festa 1902, xxxiii–xlvi: his argument that the four Suda entries s.v. Παλαίφατος (= *FGrH* 44 T 1–4) all in fact refer to the same person is highly convincing.

more than to purge myth of its factually or morally unacceptable accretions: basic faith in its fundamental historicity remained unshaken until far into the Christian era.

In many ways the Argonaut myth is an ideal example to test against these findings. It is extremely ancient; the many features from *Märchen* it contains give it an archetypal validity; it preserves great deeds from the heroic past; despite the carping of some modern critics, it is compulsively entertaining; and it lays down an empowering pattern for explorative colonizing ventures and embodies key instances of divine intrusion in human affairs at moments of crisis. All five categories of myth are thus covered in it. The basic structure of the narrative was established early, and remained constant enough to give identifiable significance to such exceptions as are found.[35] Since its geographical venue is an Unknown that becomes, in course of time, thoroughly explored, and indeed absorbed into the known world, the οἰκουμένη, we can measure the value placed on the Unknown per se by observing what steps are taken, between the Archaic and the Hellenistic periods, to preserve it. The myth also has its quota of paranormal θαύματα: How far are these modified to meet the standards of a more critical age? It offers ample opportunity for political propaganda: Do such considerations change the substance of the myth in any fundamental sense? To what extent, by Apollonius's day, have allegory or rationalization modified it? Last, and perhaps most important, how far, and in what way, do changing moral, social, and religious assumptions affect the myth's interpretation? In particular, what can we learn from comparing, say, Pindar's Fourth *Pythian* of 462 B.C. with the third-century epic by Apollonius—or, perhaps as important, Apollonius's version with the more or less contemporary[36] account by Dionysios Skytobrachion?

Beye (1982, 42) skillfully isolates the universal folktale motifs incorporated in the Medeia-Aiëtes-Jason narrative, which he describes as "a commonplace around the world":[37] "A young prince comes to the home of a hostile

---

35. Cf. Hunter 1989, 12-14.

36. Until recently it was taken for granted, on the basis of Suet. *De Gramm.* 7, that Dionysios Skytobrachion was very slightly older than M. Antonius Gnipho, and thus active in the early decades of the first century B.C. Rusten, however (1982, 85-92), argues very persuasively, beginning with the evidence of P. Hibeh 2.186, for a date in the mid-*third* century, "the period between 270 (the approximate day the θεοὶ ἀδελφοί were introduced) and 220 B.C." If he is right (and I am convinced he is), then Skytobrachion and Apollonius were contemporaries, a fact with significant implications for their respective versions of the Argonauts' quest.

37. See Andrew Lang, *Custom and Myth* (London, 1885), 87-102. Buxton (1994, 75-76) points out further details: Jason (like Heracles, Bellerophon, and Perseus) is sent out on his seemingly im-

being who puts him to severe trials in which he is helped by the daughter of his host. After succeeding at the imposed task, he elopes with the girl and is pursued. They elude their pursuer by throwing things in his wake which must be collected." (This of course is the precise category into which the story of Theseus, Minos, and Ariadne also falls: it is no accident that Apollonius mischievously makes Jason use it [3.998–1004, 1074–76] to allay Medeia's fears.) The references in Homer and Hesiod are casual enough to assume widespread familiarity. In the *Iliad*, Iolkos is ruled by Pelias's grandson Eumelos (2.711–15), and Lemnos by a son of Jason and Hypsipyle (7.467–69). The *Odyssey* knows Tyro as mother of Pelias (by Poseidon) and Aison (by Kretheus) (11.253–59); Aiëtes and his sister Circe are referred to (10.135–39; for the genealogy, cf. Hes. *Theog.* 956–62), and Circe is located on the island of Aiaia (10.135, 12.3–4: still in the lands of the dawn). Circe herself (12.59–72)—not only Aiëtes' sister but, thus, Medeia's aunt—describes the *Argo* to Odysseus as πᾶσι μέλουσα (70), and explains how, because of Hera's love for Jason (72), this vessel alone escaped the Wandering Rocks (*Πλαγκταί*) during the Argonauts' voyage home from Aiëtes' realm.

The Hesiodic fragments contain various references, for example to Jason's education by Cheiron, to Phrixos, Helle, and the Ram, and to Phineus's delivery from the Harpies by the Boreads,[38] which indicate general familiarity with the standard narrative. One important fragment (241 Merkelbach-West) gives a clearly early return route for the *Argo*, familiar to Hekataios (*FGrH* 1 F 18a) and utilized still by Pindar (*Pyth.* 4.251–52), from the Black Sea by way of the Phasis River (first mentioned at Hes. *Theog.* 340), from which the Argonauts debouch into Ocean, returning eventually to Libya and the Mediterranean; but after Herodotus's rejection of Ocean as a geographical entity, the general pressure to rewrite this part of the journey became, eventually, irresistible.[39]

possible quest because his presence threatens a ruler's authority. After winning through, to maturity as well as success, he returns (like Orestes or Odysseus) to "a household disrupted through usurpation." It is also true that Medeia shows a quite remarkable talent throughout for *disrupting households* (in Colchis, Iolkos, Corinth, and Athens): on this, cf. J. O. de G. Hanson, "The Secret of Medea's Success," *Greece & Rome* 12 (1965): 54–61. Remove Medeia, and we have another familiar variant (Meuli 1921, 3–4 and n. 1): the hero whose efforts to win a prize are aided by companions with an assortment of magical talents. Functionally, Medeia replaces these; yet the companions remain—significantly diminished, but still stronger, more individualized figures (Beye 1982, 43) than "the mostly faceless, forlorn, weak, and cowardly men who tag along after Odysseus." When we compare *Odyssey* and *Argonautika*, this is a point worth remembering.

38. Frs. 38–42, 68–69, 150–51, 156 Merkelbach-West. Other references collected by Braswell 1988, 8–10.

39. Vian and Delage 1981, 16–20. Antimachos, however, c. 400, still stuck to the Ocean route, thus demonstrating that for some, the power of tradition could eclipse even demonstrable physical proof: frs. 64–65 Wyss (p. 35) = schol. Ap. Rhod. 4.259 and 1153, with Wyss's note on fr. 65.

The *Theogony* (992-1002) gives the whole myth in capsule form: Jason's accomplishment of the challenge set by Pelias in his arrogance (ὑβριστής), his return to Iolkos with Aiëtes' daughter Medeia, their marriage, the birth of a son Medeios—and the fulfillment of great Zeus's design, μεγάλου δὲ Διὸς νόος ἐξετελεῖτο.

One point that emerges very clearly, from this and other evidence,[40] is that Medeia *was originally an immortal goddess*, a fact important not only for the interpretation of our later literary sources, but also for explaining one otherwise odd aspect of the iconographic tradition. A number of Attic vases, as well as two Etruscan mirrors, dating from c. 500 to the late fourth century, unmistakably portray Medeia rejuvenating not, as we might expect, the aged Aison, but Jason himself.[41] The reason is not far to seek. Medeia, being herself an immortal (ἀθάνατος), is anxious not to fall into the same trap as did Eos with Priam's brother Tithonos, for whom she won from Zeus immortality but not youth, leaving him a withered yet indestructible husk, a kind of semi-human cicada.[42] The irony, when we reflect on Medeia's later attitude to Jason, is palpable.

As has often been pointed out,[43] there is no direct correlation between the literary and the visual interpretations of myth. Literary motifs tend to be ignored by artists—who, on the other hand, will often pick up visually promising episodes omitted from the surviving literary record, a salutary reminder of the patchy nature of our evidence. It follows that any social or mythical conclusions drawn from iconography are highly uncertain, except within very broad limits, and this should be borne in mind when considering what follows. Many identifications, too, are speculative in the extreme. For example, what *may* be the earliest illustration of the Argonaut legend, on a Late Geometric Theban vase dated c. 735-710, shows a male figure and a female figure holding hands at the stern of what looks like a schematized pentekonter (thirty-

40. See schol. Eur. *Med.* 9, citing Mousaios; cf. M. L. West, *Hesiod: Theogony* (Oxford, 1966), 429: "Medea's place in this catalogue means that she is immortal." Note her attachment to Achilles in Elysion (Ibycus fr. 10; Simonides fr. 53). See also *LIMC* s.v. "Medeia" 386, and Jessen 1896, 743-44.

41. *LIMC* s.v. "Iason" nos. 58-64. It might be argued that the inscription on the hydria of c. 470 (no. 62), *ΙΑΣΩΝ*, was simply a careless reversal for *ΑΙΣΩΝ*; but this would explain neither the prevalence of the motif elsewhere, nor the clear reference to it by both Pherecydes and Simonides (*PMG* fr. 548, citing the *argumentum* to Euripides' *Medea*, repeated in schol. Aristoph. *Kn.* 1321).

42. See *HHAphr* 218-38, with Hom. *Il.* 20.237, *Od.* 5.1-2; for the tradition of Tithonos being eventually turned into a cicada, see Hellanikos *FGrH* 4 F 140, and in general Gantz 1993, 36-37.

43. See, e.g., Boardman 1974, 215-16; 1975, 223-24; 1989, 222. For what follows, in addition to the relevant articles in *LIMC*, see Vojatzi 1982, 28-94; Braswell 1988, 19-23; and Schefold 1989, 15-39; 1993, 261-69.

nine rowers actually visible). Jason and Medeia about to board the *Argo?* It would be encouraging to believe so. But the scene has also been interpreted as the rape of Helen by Paris (Hampe), or as the *departure* of the *Argo*, so that the woman then becomes Hypsipyle or Hera (Morrison and Williams); or even as "an everyday event . . . the captain just stepping on board after saying good-bye to his wife" (Wilamowitz).[44] If the *Argo* was really πᾶσι μέλουσα in this period—if, indeed, as we have every reason to suppose, all the main mythic cycles were flourishing—then we can only suppose that, for whatever reason,[45] the urge to represent them visually had not yet developed to any significant extent, though between 700 and c. 580 one or two subjects did get treated, for example, the flight of the Harpies, and Medeia's magical rejuvenation of Aison and others by boiling them in a cauldron.[46]

When we move into the sixth and early fifth centuries, we find two items of archaic visual evidence concerning the Argonaut myth that are both significant and surprising, since they point to a far earlier genesis for the "Hellenistic" elements in Apollonios's epic—specifically, the erotic motif and the concept of Jason as shiftless, ἀμήχανος—than has hitherto been supposed. The first is the representation of Jason and Medeia on the famous Chest of Kypselos, a Corinthian votive offering at Olympia no longer extant, but seen

---

44. J. S. Morrison and R. T. Williams, *Greek Oared Ships, 900–322 B.C.* (Cambridge, 1968), 29, with pl. 4e; B. I. Nadel, "The Euxine Pontos as Seen by the Greeks," *Epigraphica* 53 (1991): 272 with n. 19; G. S. Kirk, "Ships on Geometric Vases," *ABSA* 44 (1949): 149–50 (citing Hampe and Wilamowitz) with pl. 40. It is hard to argue with Kirk's flat assertion that not one Geometric representation is definitely identifiable with any episode from heroic saga or epic.

45. I am not persuaded by Schefold's argument (1989, 9), "Daß die Sagen von den Argonauten und von Theben erst gegen 600 eine epische Fassung erhielten, die vorbildlich geworden ist," as an explanation for the comparative absence of illustrative material prior to this date. That Eumelos of Corinth initiated such epic treatment for the Argonaut legend is pure speculation, and that artists were incapable of portraying episodes from myth without a *vorbildlich* epic to show them the way is nonsense.

46. The seventh century offers a meager crop of possibilities: items asterisked (*) indicate dubious or speculative identifications; a double asterisk (**) doubles the improbability (when *LIMC* says "Deutung unsicher," this is normally an understatement). All references are to *LIMC*; all dates are approximate within a range of two decades; figures are of item nos., not page nos. 700: *Medeia or Hera with Jason (s.v. "Hera," 450: Perachora relief). 660: *Hypsipyle episode (s.v. "Argonautai," 30: Boeotian pithos relief). 650: ?Medeia dealing with three-headed [!] serpent (s.v. "Medeia," 2: Etruscan amphora). 640: **Boreads (s.v. "Boreadai," 28, 34: Aeginetan pyxis, Spartan seal-ring). 630: Medeia (named) rejuvenating a man (unnamed) in a cauldron (s.v. "Medeia," 1: Etruscan olpe). 620: Harpies (named) in flight, pursued (?by Boreads) (s.v. "Harpyiai," 1: Attic BF). 610: *Jason being disgorged from serpent's mouth [see above] (s.v. "Iason," 30, 31: Corinthian aryballoi). 600: **Boreads (s.v. "Boreadai," 29: Tanagra alabastron). 600: *Jason with head in serpent's jaws (s.v. "Iason," 77: Attic BF lekythos). I am particularly doubtful about the Boreads: any kind of winged demon is liable to be thus labeled by someone.

and described by Pausanias, and datable to c. 580/70 B.C.: "Jason is standing to the right of Medeia, who is seated on a throne, with Aphrodite on her
left. An inscription above them reads: 'Jason marries Medeia, as Aphrodite
commands.'"[47] The erotic motif, far from being a Hellenistic, or even a Euripidean, addition, is there from the beginning.

As for the ἀμηχανία, the shiftlessness, we have already (above, p. 10) seen
that as a characteristic feature of archaic literature; but in Jason's case it acquires powerful support from the visual record. A famous red-figure cup by
Douris, c. 480–70 B.C., often reproduced,[48] shows Jason being disgorged, passive and flaccid, by the guardian serpent while Athena looks on, very much in
charge, and the Fleece hangs in the background. It is a commonplace that we
have here "a version of the myth unknown in the literary tradition" (Braswell
1988, 21); on the other hand, in both Corinthian (late seventh century) and
Etruscan (early to mid-fifth century) art we find this incident portrayed: it was
clearly both traditional and widespread.[49] Could there be a more eloquent expression of ἀμηχανία? Hardly. Do we have here an early, "monstrous" strand
of the legend? Almost certainly. Is this what explains the literary silence? If
so, what audience, in the years after Marathon, would enjoy the *visual* evidence of discomfiture, but balk at its *verbal* representation? We also have to
consider, in the same context, a column-krater of c. 470/60, showing "a remarkably puny Jason" (Braswell 1988, 21) reaching up for the Fleece, watched
by Athena and an unidentified, but tall and heroic, male figure.[50] The tradition of inadequacy, so clear in Apollonius, seems now, like his central erotic
motif, to have a well-established earlier, indeed archaic, precedent.

There is little more of value, in the present context, that can be drawn
from the iconographic tradition. Most positive preferences can be explained
in terms of illustrative suitability; arguments *ex silentio* (e.g., why does no artist exploit the drama of Jason's first one-sandaled encounter with Pelias before
the Pompeian wall-painters?[51]) lack force when the surviving evidence is so

---

47. Paus. 5.18.3: Μηδείας δὲ ἐπὶ θρόνου καθημένης Ἰάσων ἐν δεξιᾷ, τῇ δὲ Ἀφροδίτῃ
παρέστηκε· γέγραπται δὲ καὶ ἐπίγραμμα ἐπ' αὐτοῖς· Μήδειαν Ἰάσων γαμέει, κέλεται δ'
Ἀφροδίτα.

48. E.g., Boardman 1975, no. 288; Schefold 1989, 31, no. 14; Green 1993, 211, fig. 78.

49. *LIMC* s.v. "Iason," 632 (nos. 30–35).

50. *LIMC* s.v. "Iason," 632–33 (no. 36 = "Argonautai" no. 12, and thus cited by Braswell 1988,
21). Radermacher's suggestion (1943, 169) that this New York vase-painting can be dismissed as
"eine Parodie des Abenteuers im Drama, vielleicht Satyrspiel" I find less than convincing.

51. Schefold 1989, 21 uses Pompeii III-436 (from IX 5, 18) to illustrate this scene. The dangers are beautifully illustrated by *LIMC* "Iason," B.2. The relevant scene on this mid-fourth century calyx-krater was, until recently, identified as a scene from Euripides' *Sthenoboea*. New argu-

fragmentary.[52] The *Argo* and its crew are portrayed as early as 570, and fairly frequently thereafter. Popular scenes include Phrixos either being carried by or sacrificing the ram; the Harpies assailing Phineus and being pursued by the Boreads (though this motif, like the portrayal of monsters in general, ends earlier than most);[53] Jason (with or without Medeia and her box of *pharmaka*) snatching the Fleece from the serpent, or, rather less often, taming the fiery bulls; Amykos boxing, or being punished for his brutality (but not, as most literary sources have it, killed in combat).[54] Variants abound. On one early column-krater (*LIMC* s.v. "Iason," 7: c. 570), Jason (appropriately, given the etymology of his name) appears to be healing Phineus's blindness: no literary source mentions this. In two late-fifth-century kraters, Talos is shown being subdued by the Dioscuri (again, unconnected with this episode in any known literary source), though Medeia also seems to be "hexing" him, as in the version by Apollonius (4.1638–75).[55] The most exploited scene of all, at first sight

ments claim it shows Jason's arrival in Iolkos while Pelias is sacrificing to Poseidon. What (to quote *LIMC*'s accurate description) do we in fact *see*? "A half-draped youth wearing a pilos leans on a staff before an old man who is in the act of pouring from a phiale; at l. a woman peers from an open doorway." Are we seriously asked to make a confident identification from evidence such as this?

52. There is, for example, a single surviving bronze group that *may* portray Euphemos and Triton (the copy of a work *probably* executed in the mid-third century B.C.: Curtius ap. *LIMC* s.v. "Argonautai," 37). Even if this attribution should be correct, its relationship (if any) to Pind. *Pyth.* 4.28–49 and Ap. Rhod. 4.1547–85, 1731–64 (cf. Hdt. 4.179) remains quite uncertain, despite the confidence of Schefold (1989, 36–37, with pl. 18), Braswell (1988, 90), and Vojatzi (1982, 157 n. 398). Reasonable doubts expressed by Herter, *JAW* [Bursian] 285 ([1944/45] 1956): 398.

53. Even so, though the bulk of the Gorgons, Chimairas, and hero-versus-monster duels are gone by soon after 530 (Boardman 1975, 223), the Harpies-Phineus-Boreads theme survives until the closing years of the fifth century: see *LIMC* s.v. "Phineus I," 11.

54. I am not including here representations either of the Calydonian boar-hunt or of the funeral games for Pelias, both of which fall outside the limits of this survey. The same is true of the iconography of Circe (all referring to the *Odyssey*), and that of Peleus and Thetis: though their relationship is referred to by Apollonius (4.805–9, 816–17, 865–84), it is in no way integral to the Argonaut myth. *Argo* and the Argonauts: *LIMC* s.v. "Argonautai," 1, 2 (cf. Schefold 1993, 263–64 pl. 283 for this relief from the Sikyonian treasury at Delphi, c. 570), 3–11, 17 [570–230 B.C.]. Phrixos and the ram: *LIMC* 1–16, 20–2745–48, 51, app. a–b, d–g [560–250 B.C.]. The Harpies and Phineus: *LIMC* s.v. "Harpyiai," 1–3, 8–26, 28; s.v. "Phineus I," 1–16, 18–22 [570–400 B.C.]. Jason and the Serpent/Fleece: *LIMC* s.v. "Iason," 22–24, 36–42, cf. 57 [470–310 B.C.]. Jason and the bulls: ibid., 15–17 [440–320 B.C.]. Amykos: *LIMC* s.v. "Amykos," 1–15, 17 [430–250 B.C.]. The authors vouching for his death include Ap. Rhod. 2.90–97, Apollod. 1.9.20, Hygin. *Fab.* 17. Theocr. 22.120–34 has Polydeukes stop short (but not far) of killing him, merely exacting a promise from him "never again deliberately to be a vexation to strangers" (134). The leitmotif of Amykos being tied to a tree is sometimes supposed to derive (on no real evidence) from Sophocles' lost play *Amykos:* Beckel, *LIMC* s.v. "Amykos," p. 741.

55. *LIMC* s.v. "Talos I," nos. 4–5, well illustrated in Schefold 1989, pls. 17b and 18, pp. 35–36. See also M. Robertson, "The Death of Talos," *JHS* 97 (1977): 158–60, for the depiction of Medeia's

surprisingly, has to do with the golden apples of the Hesperides; but the reason for this may be no more than the involvement in it of that ever-popular figure, Heracles.[56]

Our literary sources show that the main lines of the Argonaut myth were established early, but that this did nothing to prevent considerable variation of detail, whether through local preference or social evolution. The iconographic tradition precisely confirms such a finding. It also suggests that one of the sharpest divergences was that between written and visual interpretation. Yet both, we should never forget, were supported by an oral tradition: the *anecdotal* nature of early Greek illustrative art makes this very clear. In other words, the visual record preserves something of a subliterary, vernacular, and archaic handing-down of myth that writers—by and large well-educated, morally progressive, and attuned to the new polis morality—found an increasing embarrassment, and thus preferred to ignore. Jason ignominiously swallowed and then disgorged by the serpent offers a classic instance of this.[57]

The earliest stratum of the Argonauts' journey, as we have seen, took them into the Unknown. "In general," Strabo says (1.2.10, C.21), "the men of that time [Homer's contemporaries] regarded the Pontic Sea as though it were another Ocean, and thought that those who sailed thither were going off the map (ἐκτοπίζειν) as surely as those who ventured far beyond the Pillars [of Herakles]." The business of accommodating the myth to geographical exploration began early. Other aspects of the "high and far-off times" could, as we shall see, be accepted, even if not reconcilable with current realities: the heroes might indeed have walked with gods, conquered monsters now extinct, possessed—innately or by magic (the latter still, of course, flourishing)—superhuman powers. But their world, the stage on which their *gestes* took place, was

---

use of the evil eye; and M. Dickie, "Talos Bewitched: Magic, Atomic Theory and Paradoxography in Apollonius' *Argonautika* 4.1638–1688," in *Papers of the Leeds International Latin Seminar,* vol. 6 (1990): *Roman Poetry and Drama, Greek Epic, Comedy, Rhetoric,* ed. F. Cairns and M. Heath (Leeds, 1990), 267–96. Ap. Rhod. schol. 1646–48 suggests that Apollonius's version of Talos's death derived from Sophocles' lost play *Daidalos.* Apollod. 1.9.26 mentions several other versions: that Medeia drove him mad with her *pharmaka* (note the presence of her *pyxis* in the Ruvo krater), and then removed the nail or plug that held in his life-giving ichor; or, alternatively, that Talos was shot in the ankle by Poias.

56. *LIMC* s.v. "Hesperides," 1–5a (solo), 6–8 (with Heracles: alarmed), 24–46 (with Heracles: calm), 54–62 (with other heroes or deities), 64–66 (misc. dub.) [570–250 B.C.].

57. The motif recurs elsewhere (e.g., in Indian, Irish, and Icelandic folk tradition) as well as, most obviously, in the Biblical story of Jonah, and seems to belong to the basic stock of giant-and-dragon *Märchen:* see J. G. Frazer, *Folklore in the Old Testament* (London, 1918), 3:82.

fixed and immutable. All that changed was the degree of human knowledge concerning it, the proportion of Unknown to Known. The huge colonizing expansion between the eighth and the sixth centuries, from the western Mediterranean to the furthest shores of the Black Sea,[58] filled gaps in the Hellenes' *mappa mundi* with irrefutable geographical realities very different from the quasi-symbolic and largely imaginary constructs of early saga. This proved the mythic tradition's most vulnerable feature, and in the Argonaut legend it played a large and crucial part.

About Aiaia and Colchis there was nothing to be done. As early as Mimnermos's day (frs. 11, 11a West) they had become, as the eastern kingdom of Aiëtes son of Helios, a fixture: it was from Aiaia, Aiëtes' city, in Mimnermos's text uncompromisingly located by the stream of Ocean, that Jason brought back "the great Fleece" (μέγα κῶας: our first surviving reference to it).[59] The Argonauts' outward route was now immutable. In consequence, two things happened: both Colchis and the Clashing Rocks lost their original significance as part of a *rite de passage* into the kind of fairyland Odysseus describes for the Phaeacians,[60] and in the course of time Aiaia's earlier association with Ocean was quietly abandoned. (Pindar is the last writer—a few years before Herodotus—to use Ocean as part of the Argonauts' route, or to regard the Pillars as a liminal barrier.[61]) The filling up of the Mediterranean map brought about some interesting relocations. Plausible but unfamiliar geography became much sought after. South Italy, Sicily, and the West in general were obvious targets. Though for Homer, Circe is located in the East (*Od.* 12.3-4), by Hesiod's day (*Theog.* 1011-15) she is already the mother, by Odysseus, of two sons, Agrios and Latinos, who rule over the Tyrrhenians: Aiaia is very soon located off the Italian coast, midway between Rome and Naples. An ingenious—and scandalous—anecdote explained Circe's move: she had poisoned the king, her husband, and needed to take a *very* long trip in a hurry.[62]

---

58. Boardman 1980, chs. 5-6, 161-266, provides an excellent general survey.

59. Both quotations are preserved by Strabo (1.2.40, C. 46-47), and his Augustan comments are revealing in themselves. Homer, he argues, mixes history and myth. For Strabo, the characters and events of the Argonaut legend are unquestioningly assumed to be historical: it is only Ocean that belongs to myth. After all, he says, the voyage explored was made in "familiar and populous regions" (ἐν γνωρίμοις τόποις καὶ εὐανδροῦσι), which of course by Strabo's day Colchis had become: hence the appropriate epithet for the *Argo* of πᾶσι μέλουσα, most inappropriate in the case of Ocean!

60. Beye 1982, 43-44; J. Lindsay, *The Clashing Rocks* (London, 1965), 7-37.

61. See *Ol.* 3.43-45, where, discussing the Ἡρακλέος σταλᾶν, he writes, with extraordinary passion and emphasis: τὸ πόρσω δ' ἔστι σοφοῖς ἄβατον ἄβατον κἀσόφοις. οὔ νιν διώξω· κεινὸς εἴην.

62. Vian and Delage 1980, 122; Hunter 1989, 133.

Thus Pindar's Fourth *Pythian*, composed (like the Fifth) in 462 B.C. to honor the chariot victory by Arcesilas IV, king of Cyrene, at Delphi, stands at a critical point in the transmission of the Argonaut myth, on the very edge of the final opening up of the whole Mediterranean world. There are, in fact, several highly interesting features in it from the viewpoint of my present discussion.[63] To begin with, it has been politically adapted to the needs of Pindar's patron. When Eumelos of Corinth did the same thing earlier for his city, manufacturing a local ancestry for Aiëtes and Medeia,[64] the changes were not incorporated into the general tradition, and impressed only an assortment of German scholars.[65] But with Euphemos (already commemorated on the Chest of Kypselos as a charioteer, Paus. 5.17.4) and the clod of earth symbolizing the colonization of Cyrene from Thera, the Argonauts are firmly and permanently linked to North Africa: Battos I, seventeenth in descent from Euphemos, was the founder, and Arcesilas IV, Pindar's patron, his eighth successor.[66] The loss of the clod described by Medeia during the course of her Pindaric prophecy (*Pyth.* 4.38–49) provides an explanation for the delay in colonization.

Thus at one level, the affirmation of genealogy, Pindar's use of the Argonaut myth performs a central and traditional function. We may note, however, that in his eagerness to pay Arcesilas the proper degree of respect, he at one point alters the basic narrative in a manner as embarrassing as it is ludicrous: he places the landfall on Lemnos, and the subsequent mass impregnation of the Λαμνιᾶν ἀνδροφόνων, the murderous Lemnian wives, not during the Argonauts' outward voyage,[67] but on their return from Colchis, with Medeia very much in evidence. The idea of Jason's bride fuming in jealousy while her husband dealt with Hypsipyle (even though a fair anticipation of coming events in Corinth) bothered critics in antiquity and has spawned some unlikely theories among modern scholars.[68] With exemplary common sense,

---

63. Segal (1986, 8) nicely summarizes its main ingredients: "Pindar brings together in a tour de force epic adventure, foundation legends, love, magic, family conflict, and cosmogonic myths."

64. For a brilliant analysis of Eumelos's appropriative scheme, see Huxley 1969, ch. 5, "Eumelos, the Early *Argonautika* and Related Epics," 60–84, and cf. Beye 1982, 46.

65. E.g., Friedländer 1914, 313–17; Radermacher 1943, 227–29; Lesky 1932, 43–50. Dräger 1993, 2–11, cf. 24–30, comes as a welcome contrast.

66. See F. Chamoux, *Cyrène sous la monarchie des Battiades* (Paris, 1953), 115–210. Hdt. 4.159–65 has an account of the first six Battiad kings. Cf. Braswell 1988, 89–90 and 153.

67. As all other accounts seem to have done: see Apollod. 1.9.17 with Frazer's note ad loc., 1921, 98–99.

68. See schol. Pind. *Pyth.* 4.252, and cf. Braswell 1988, 347. As Beye remarks (1982, 47), "Scholars who worry about Medea's virtue when she travels alone with the crew in Apollonius's fourth book narrative must find this assault on her sensibilities impossibly trying." But he himself is not

Braswell (1988, 348) explains what Pindar is about. His patron's heroic pedigree must be the climax of the narrative; equally important, "the claim of the Euphemids to Libyan sovereignty would be psychologically (if not logically) stronger if Euphemus' natural son had been sired after his father's receipt of the symbol [the clod of earth] rather than before." Royal flattery, in short, easily outclassed dramatic realism, and sharp literary critics were probably not thick on the ground in fifth-century Cyrene.

Medeia's centrality to the myth was undeniable, and seems to have caused Pindar some problems. As Segal says (1986, 6), "She at once brings into the story the atmosphere of a fabulous world close to the gods," and indeed Pindar obliquely recognizes her divine status by referring—perhaps metaphorically, perhaps not—to her "immortal mouth," ἀθανάτου στόματος (11). However, his prime concern is with masculine heroic or athletic *kleos*, and here Medeia's role in the Argonaut legend constitutes a distinct embarrassment.[69] Its hero not only succumbs to her womanly charms, which is bad enough, but, far worse, can only vanquish fire-breathing bulls and serpent, and thus win the Fleece, through her indispensable aid. There are two kinds of magic involved here, and neither is really compatible with Pindar's ideal.[70] What he celebrates is the age of the great *kouroi*, and as Beye remarks (1982, 48), his Jason, with that fine manly figure and flowing locks, courtly yet decisive, compared by wondering bystanders to Apollo or Ares, is very much in the *kouros* tradition. Hera engenders in him and his companions (*Pyth.* 4.184–87) an "all-persuasive sweet desire" (παμπειθῆ γλυκὺν πόθον) for the voyage, not to skulk at home in safety, but to pursue "the finest elixir (φάρμακον) of his excellence" with his coevals.

That word φάρμακον,[71] boldly transferred from Medeia to Jason himself, reveals a quite breathtakingly ingenious solution. If magic there must be, let the *kouros* have it first. But that is not all. In addition to cultivating his own heroic φάρμακον, as above, Jason also receives lessons in erotic magic, complete with a love charm, ἴυγξ, and incantations, from Aphrodite—the first of

---

much better, arguing that "what Pindar says makes little difference: he has achieved the absolute separation of form from content," a *reductio ad absurdum* of the apolitical literary attitude.

69. Segal 1986, 165: "To Pindar, as to other Greek poets from Homer to Euripides, female sexuality appears as a mode of treacherous craft (μῆτις), deceptive ornamentation, beguiling persuasion, and quasi-magical drugs, unguents, or enchantments."

70. On the other hand, Pindar is also already infected with fifth-century moral delicacy: he carefully ignores Medeia's murder of Apsyrtos, in the same spirit with which he shrinks from calling any god a cannibal for snacking off the shoulder of Pelops: see *Ol.* 1.51–52.

71. In an otherwise excellent note (1988, 271–72), Braswell misses the significance of φάρμακον in this context.

mankind to be so honored. The reversal of roles is complete: far from Medeia bewitching Jason, it is Jason himself who employs the devices of love-magic to dominate Medeia's heart, destroy her filial reverence, and fill her with a longing for Greece (213–19). His need for *her* φάρμακα (tactfully reduced here to mere "advice," ἐφετμαῖς, though she herself is παμφαρμάκου, "skilled in all drugs") has been anticipated and eclipsed by his own superior powers. Blending politeness and diplomacy with heroic magnificence (Segal 1986, 7), this Jason emerges as a born leader. Pindar's Medeia is left with the restricted and formal role, acceptable in a woman (Cassandra at once springs to mind, not to mention the Pythia), of prophetess.

For the two centuries between Pindar and Apollonius, evidence is sketchy and puzzles abound. The biggest single influence on the *Argonautika* is commonly said to be Euripides' *Medea* of 431; yet no one could guess this from the iconographic evidence, which largely ignores Medeia as *Kindermörderin* until the Roman period, when the motif suddenly acquires great popularity.[72] It would be useful if we had more of the *Lyde* of Antimachos (c. 400), which *inter alia* told the story of the expedition from the building of the *Argo* to the episode in Libya (frs. 56–65 Wyss)—especially since from fr. 64 (= schol. Ap. Rhod. 4.1153) we learn that Antimachos made Jason and Medeia ἐν Κόλχοις πλησίον τοῦ ποταμοῦ μιγῆναι, i.e., "have intercourse in the land of the Colchians, near the river." Hellanikos of Lesbos (late fifth century), the first Greek author to attempt to date myths (Dowden 1992, 44–45), was also in the business of "providing Athenian nobles with heroic pedigrees" (Forsdyke 1956, 143–46), and had a good deal of recondite knowledge about the Argonaut tradition (*FGrH* 4 F 122–33):[73] his attitude was probably not far removed from that of Isocrates, who used examples culled from before the Trojan War to demonstrate the character and power of Athens.[74]

Hints and guesses, as Eliot said: hints followed by guesses. As we move

72. *LIMC* s.v. "Medeia," 391–92, lists only three fourth-century South Italian vases (nos. 29–31) directly connected to the murders, plus five (35–37, 39–40) of Medeia in her *Schlangenwagen*, which are in all likelihood also inspired by Euripides' treatment.

73. See, e.g., 4 F 127 = schol. Ap. Rhod. 2.1144, where he informs us that Helle met her end off Paktye.

74. Isocr. 4 (*Panegyr.*) §§54–56. Invoking the case of the protection given to Heracles' sons fleeing from Eurystheus, Isocrates justifies his choice parenthetically: ἐκεῖθεν γὰρ δίκαιον τὰς πίστεις λαμβάνειν τοὺς ὑπὲρ τῶν πατρίων ἀμφισβητοῦντας. What he believed about the myths is open to doubt: when praising Athens in connection with Demeter and the Mysteries (ibid., §28), he argues καὶ γὰρ εἰ μυθώδης ὁ λόγος γέγονεν, ὅμως αὐτῷ καὶ νῦν ῥηθῆναι προσήκει, a calculated ambiguity, which could be taken to indicate either pious belief or a knowing accommodation with tradition.

into the fourth century, allegory and rationalizing meet us on every hand.[75] But here an odd fact strikes us. None of the allegorizing that has survived, except insofar as Heracles (allegorized ad nauseam) is involved, concerns the Argonaut myth. None of our ancient testimonia, including late collections such as that of Antoninus Liberalis, nor the most exhaustive modern survey, that by Félix Buffière, can produce a single instance of genuine Argonautic allegory. In a myth where the allegorizing imagination could surely have had ample scope (e.g., over the Fleece, or the Clashing Rocks, or the tests imposed by Aiëtes), history remains silent. Perhaps it was felt that this archaic tale of theft, seduction, and murder (including fratricide) was past rescuing in moral terms; more probably the answer lies in Homer's preeminence as a universal icon and educational tool,[76] which meant that would-be moral whitewashers concentrated on his *Iliad* and *Odyssey* to the exclusion of all else (Buffière 1956, passim). The Argonaut legend, on the other hand, tended to be tinkered with by rationalizing romantics anxious to preserve—at varying levels—their suspension of disbelief. That cheerful realist Diogenes of Sinope "used to say that Medeia was clever, but no magician."[77] Herodoros's most interesting reference to the Argonauts is the claim (shared by Sophocles and Euripides) that they simplified their return voyage—thus incidentally also saving the geographical appearances—by coming back the way they had gone.[78]

What even Plato and Aristotle both assume, and pursue, is that never-queried underlying kernel of historical truth in myth. For Plato, τὸ ψεῦδος is a φάρμακον: "Since we don't know the truth about the ancients, may it not be useful to approximate falsity to truth as closely as possible?" (*Rep.* 382C–D). He will impugn an aristocrat's moral character, but never question his pedigree (*Theaet.* 174E–175B). This lends extra edge to his attacks, following Xenophanes, on Homer, Hesiod, and other poets for immorally misrepresenting ancient mythic truths (*Rep.* 377D). Censorship was thus justified on didactic grounds (*Rep.* 378D), a view that left the field wide open for appearance-saving reinterpretations.[79] Aristotle, who sought to defend

75. Both are prominent in Herodoros (?430–?360 B.C.), who wrote not only an *Argonautika*, but also a 17-book work on Heracles: *FGrH* 31 F 5–10, 38–55 (*Argonautika*), 13–37 (*Heraklesgeschichte*). Cf. Nestle 1942, 146–48.

76. As Long (1992, 44) justly remarks, "All Greek literature and art, and just about all Greek philosophy, resonate against the background of Homer": a truth that the translator of Apollonius, to look no further, is never allowed to forget for long.

77. Cited by Stobaeus, 3.29.92: ὁ Διογένης ἔλεγε τὴν Μήδειαν σοφήν, ἀλλ' οὐ φαρμακίδα γενέσθαι.

78. Soph. fr. 547 Radt; Eur. *Med.* 432, 1263–64; Herodoros *FGrH* 31 F 10 = schol. Ap. Rhod. 4.259.

79. Cf. Thomas 1971, 174–75; Buffière 1956, 33–34, 230–31; Dowden 1992, 47–49; Buxton 1994, 20, 160; Heath 1987, 41–42; Feeney 1991, 25–26.

poetry against Plato's strictures,[80] had a low opinion of history, regarding it as a mess of particulars lacking universalism (*Poet.* 1451b5–11). Despite this, he had no time for allegory (*Metaph.* 1000a19), which for him was a mere decoration or sweetener that made truth more palatable (*Metaph.* 1074b1). Unable to credit nectar and ambrosia (*Metaph.* 1000a12), he still, like everyone else, accepted Theseus as a historical character, and seemingly the Minotaur, too (*ap.* Plut. *Thes.* 16.2). His attempt to bridge the gap between the heroic and the historical periods involved a curiously class-conscious compromise: "Only the leaders of the ancients were heroes—the people were merely men" (*Probl.* 922b).

Aristotle's distaste for allegory, however, was more than compensated for by the enthusiasm in this area that Stoics such as Apollonius's near-contemporary Chrysippos displayed. As Long says (1992, 64), "What passes under the name of Stoic allegorizing is the Stoic interpretation of myth." Veyne (1988, 65) puts it less politely, but with equal accuracy: "Since the Stoics are certain beforehand that myth and poetry speak the truth, they have only to put them to torture [i.e., on the Procrustean bed of allegory] to reconcile them with this truth." Chrysippos was at least capable of making the process enjoyable, and at the same time of deeply shocking all those who, with more than Victorian fervor, opposed anything even faintly redolent of αἰσχρολογία, obscenity: a certain notorious painting in Argos, of Hera fellating Zeus, he interpreted to mean "that Matter receives and holds within itself the spermatic λόγοι of the deity destined for the ordering of the Whole."[81] Mythic conservatism and moral prudery were between them in real danger, by the mid-third century, of creating a literary *reductio ad absurdum* for both rationalization and allegory.

In such a world, what kind of approach to the Argonautic myth should we expect? It so happens that for the mid-third century, the apogee of the Alexandrian Age, we possess, in addition to Apollonius's *Argonautika*, an extensive and fairly close summary (Diod. Sic. 4.40–56) of the prose *Argonautai* by Dionysios Skytobrachion ("Leather-Arm": perhaps an allusion to the quantity of his published work), a scholar from Mytilene.[82] To judge the current at-

---

80. Cf. Feeney 1991, 25–31; Heath 1987, 42–44 with further bibliography.

81. Cf. *SVF* 2:314, nos. 1071–75. The citation quoted in the text is from Origen (fr. 1074): ὅτι τοὺς σπερματικοὺς λόγους τοῦ θεοῦ ἡ ὕλη παραδεξαμένη ἔχει ἐν ἑαυτῇ εἰς κατακόσμησιν τῶν ὅλων. Diogenes Laertius (7.187 = no. 1071) coyly refrains from explaining what is going on, and insists that the interpretation (which he does not describe, merely referring to it as something ἃ μηδεὶς ἠτυχηκὼς μολύνειν τὸ στόμα εἴποι ἂν—I don't think this was meant to be funny) has to be Chrysippos's own invention. Other writers (Clement, Theophilos, Origen as above) are not so delicate: πρὸς τῷ τοῦ Διὸς αἰδοίῳ φύρων τῆς Ἥρας τὸ πρόσωπον (Clement, fr. 1072).

82. In what follows I am heavily indebted to Rusten's (1982) exemplary analysis, in particular

titude to myth (though it lacks a date for the expedition, such as Eusebius pro-vides), we also have the chronological list of the Parian Marble (264/3), which makes no distinction between mythical and historical events, attributing firm dates to both with equal confidence. When we compare these three very dif-ferent texts, what instantly strikes us, significantly enough, is the one central feature they all have in common: that unquestioning belief in the *historicity* of mythic tradition which this essay began by examining. Where they differ is in the means chosen—rationalization, chronological specificity, aetiologiz-ing traditionalism—to save the appearances in a new, cosmopolitan, and more skeptical age.

Skytobrachion's *Argonautai* is heavily rationalistic throughout, attempt-ing, as Rusten says (1982, 93–94), "to explain the fabulous stories connected with the heroes as misunderstandings of perfectly ordinary events, by putting forward a version which preserved τὸ εἰκός, i.e. something which could actu-ally have happened but was later 'mythologised' into an improbable fantasy." The Symplegades are simply ignored: Jason and his companions "set sail from Thrace and enter Pontos" (44.7).[83] To explain Aiëtes' fire-breathing bulls (ταῦροι), and the unsleeping serpent (δράκων) that guarded the Fleece, Sky-tobrachion falls back on that ever-popular device, the onomastic homonym: the ταῦροι were in fact fierce Taurian guards, while the sacred grove was watched over (simple error!) by a man named Drakon. Similarly with the magical flying ram (κριός): one of the two rationalizations here reported iden-tifies this Krios as Phrixos' *paidagogos*, who was sacrificed (no reason given) on arrival in Colchis. Since an oracle stated that Aiëtes would die should it be removed, the king had it gilded to convince the sentinels it was worth guarding [!] (47.2–3, 5).[84] The alternative explanation makes this κριός a ship with a ram as figurehead, from which Helle fell overboard in the throes of *mal de mer* (47.4).[85] It is surprising that Skytobrachion does not, like Strabo

---

1–21 and 93–101. In particular, I am convinced by his careful arguments leading to the conclusion that Skytobrachion's work can "be dated roughly to the period between 270 (the approximate date the θεοὶ ἀδελφοί were introduced) and 220 B.C. (P. Hibeh 2.186)," with a mid-century median, and by his comparison of Diodoros's summary with the citations of Dionysios in the scholia to Apollonius to demonstrate the generally close and faithful nature of that summary: see 13, 28, 93.

83. All references to Skytobrachion's *Argonautai* are to the relevant chapter and section in Book 4 of Diodorus. Since Rusten's monograph is not widely available, I have not used the numbers he assigns to this and other texts in his collection of the fragments.

84. One of the more pleasant paradoxes about Dionysios Skytobrachion is that his rationaliza-tions are not seldom at least as incredible as the mythical θαύματα they are designed to replace: why Pelias should have gone to the trouble of sending an expedition to fetch back a servant's flayed skin, gilded or not, is a question left unaddressed. At the same time, we should note that the names (Drakon, Krios) actually existed, and that the Ταῦροι were a real tribe (Rusten 1982, 94).

85. Though Skytobrachion's rational mind cannot accept a flying ram, he seemingly has no

(1.2.39, C.45) and others, rationalize the expedition as a colonizers' quest for gold.

There are several significant variations to the traditional narrative. To begin with, Jason himself is credited with the building of the *Argo* (41.1–2). This is a change that first appears in Herodotus (4.179.1), but may well have been introduced here to offset the fact that in the Skytobrachion version, it is Heracles who leads the expedition, and who remains with it throughout (41.3, 49.6: see below). The entire episode on Lemnos is omitted, perhaps as improper: one of Skytobrachion's more remarkable achievements is to eliminate throughout what had been the *Ur*-myth's strongest motivating factor, namely sex. The itinerary is also altered, not only, as we might expect, to get rid of the *Argo*'s more exotic return peregrinations (Italy, North Africa, the Danube, Po, and Rhône), but also to include two unforeseen landfalls, at Sigeion in the Troad and the Tauric Chersonese (42.1–7, 44.7, 47.2)—the latter probably for no better reason than to justify the existence of those "Taurian" guards (and to emphasize the barbarous habit of ξενοκτονία, the killing of strangers, well documented in the Chersonese). Skytobrachion, like Herodoros, Callimachus, and the dramatists,[86] sends the Argonauts home by their outward route, with stops at Byzantion and Samothrace then rather than earlier.

The most striking element in Skytobrachion's account, however, is something familiar to us from the political myth of Panhellenism, and recently the subject of several excellent studies:[87] the systematic effort at Hellenic self-definition by contrast with the Barbarian Other. From the very beginning of this narrative, it is emphasized that the inhabitants of the Black Sea region in those days were fierce, savage, and murderous, ξενοκτονούντων τῶν ἐγχωρίων τοὺς καταπλέοντας (40.4). Against them stands Heracles, Hellene par excellence, famous civilizer in distant lands, who deals appropriately with savagery wherever it may be found. At Sigeion he rescues Laomedon's daughter Hesione from a sea monster.[88] The Phineus episode, far from

---

trouble with a sea monster that picks off coastal victims (42.3). Similarly he has no hesitation in accepting oracles, the Samothracian mysteries, the miraculous calming of storms, or equally miraculous twin stars descending above the Dioscuri (Rusten 1982, 95 with nn. 9–10). Social pressures may well have applied here: even the most determined ancient rationalist is unlikely to have exposed himself to a public charge of atheism.

86. Soph. *Scyth.* fr. 547 Pearson; Eur. *Med.* 432, 1263; Herodoros *FGrH* 31 F 10; Callim. fr. 9 Pfeiffer.

87. See in particular E. Hall, *Inventing the Barbarian: Greek Self-Definition through Tragedy* (Oxford, 1989); P. Georges, *Barbarian Asia and the Greek Experience: From the Archaic Period to the Age of Xenophon* (Baltimore and London, 1994); and Cartledge 1993, ch. 3, "Alien Wisdom: Greek and Barbarian," 36–62. Cf. also below, chapter 5, passim.

88. Though the story of Laomedon's cheating Apollo and Poseidon (when they were doomed by Zeus to labor at building the walls of Troy for him) is as old as Homer (*Il.* 21.441–57), Skyto-

having the Boreads save a blinded Phineus from the Harpies, and Phineus reward them with a prophecy of their coming vicissitudes, ends with Heracles
and the Boreads killing Phineus for his treatment of his children.[89] The early
kleos that Heracles wins on the expedition, in fact, chiefly consists "in leading
the Argonauts against a variety of cruel barbarian kings" (Rusten 1982, 97).
The voyage once over, he founds the Olympic Games, proceeding thence to
further glory with a band of young followers—not alone: rationalism forbids
(53.4–7). It is hard not to see this treatment as in some sense propaganda for
Ptolemy II's vigorous program of colonial expansion.[90]

Of course, the acme of barbarian cruelty is encountered in Colchis; and
here we note another predictable revision of traditional legend. Medea—un-
canny virgin, enchantress, full of old divinity—is rationalized into a liberal
humanist's dream. Skytobrachion, like Diogenes before him, finds her σοφήν,
wise, but no φαρμακίδα—at least, not in any magical sense. Rather than a
witch, she is a skilled medical herbalist, who rapidly heals any Argonauts'
battle-wounds (48.5). At high risk to herself, she fights her father's policy of
ξενοκτονία, springing victims from prison and facilitating their escape. Arrested for these activities, she escapes at the time of the Argonauts' arrival
and seeks refuge with them. Her relationship with Jason is based on mutual
self-interest (46.4: τὸ κοινὸν συμφέρον) rather than passion: no arrows of
Eros here. Nor do we hear a word about the murder of Apsyrtos: only the
monstrous behavior of Pelias (50.1–2, cf. 6) can bring this Medea to kill after
years of selfless work for mankind's benefit.[91] Her one bravura act is her entry
into Iolkos (51.1–5), disguised as an old woman (the better to impress with her
ability to rejuvenate by secretly removing her make-up); and even then, after
persuading Pelias's daughters to cut their father up and boil him, she delicately avoids staying on to witness the butchery (52.1–4). It is not even a case
of all passion spent: in this Shavian world, reason is promoted as a desirable
substitute for all the passions, sex as well as ξενοκτονία.

---

brachion seems to have been the first to record the matter of Hesione's rescue by Heracles, with
its telltale resemblance to the episode of Perseus's rescue of Andromeda. See Apollod. 2.5.9, and
Frazer ad loc., 1921, 206–8 n. 2. All other surviving references are late.

89. See 43.3–44.7 passim, fleshed out by schol. Ap. Rhod. 2.206–8b = *FGrH* 31 F 19.

90. For lavish celebration of this policy, cf. Theocr. 17.85–94, and for the background, Green
1993, 146. In Skytobrachion, the familiar ploy of a Hellenic mission (whether of conquest, enlightenment, or one followed by the other) among the savage *barbaroi*, a theme exploited by orators and
politicians ever since the Persian Wars, comes across very clearly.

91. In the same way, years later in Corinth, it takes Jason's betrayal to evoke her innate barbarian
ὠμότης (54.7).

Where Skytobrachion reveals most of the intellectual trends of his age, Apollonius's *Argonautika* is, by contrast, quite astonishingly independent (to coin a paradox) in its traditionalism. The one basic quality both versions share is a sense of a Hellenic venture to the world's end, a confrontation between Greek civilization and barbarian savagery, deepened in Apollonius's case by the increasingly alien tribes encountered along the southern shore of the Black Sea during the *Argo*'s outward voyage. There may be a political element at work here—Ptolemy II not only nursed expansionist dreams, but liked to think of himself, *qua* Alexander's successor, as a protector of Greeks and Greek interests—but the underlying belief rested on that fundamental Hellenocentrism, or Panhellenism, which had been a constant factor in Greek affairs at least since the Persian Wars.[92] The geographical boundaries might have expanded —Alexander, of course, had opened up the οἰκουμένη in a wholly unprecedented fashion—but this had merely sharpened the Hellenic appetite for empire. The new world that emerged had also—and here we come back to the question posed at the beginning of this essay—produced a deep sense of deracination among emigrant Greeks, in particular the intellectuals of Alexandria. *Mutatis mutandis*, they faced the same agonizing dilemma as their ancestors in fifth-century Athens. Reason dictated a rejection of the heroic past; but emotion cried out for a return to one's ancient roots. The cry of μέγα βιβλίον μέγα κακόν ("Big book big bore") was matched by an ever-increasing addiction to aetiologizing. *Credo quia impossibile est:* what Apollonius attempted in the *Argonautika* was a reconciliation of opposites, an epic *geste* as experienced by heroic yet vulnerable human beings.

His decision to frame his narrative as an epic poem in itself represents a decision of great significance. The Callimachean rejection of this genre was due at least as much to social and historical realities as to literary theory. Hunter (1993, 154) sees the central issue very clearly:

> The decision to write *epic* in such a society, even (or particularly) an epic which constantly sets out to explore the cracks in what are set up as Homeric certainties, carried special weight. . . . The status of epic as embodiment and transmitter of traditional values is in constant tension with the novelty and literariness of Apollonius' project. . . . Apollonius must emphasise fracture and discontinuity both within the "heroic" age itself and between the past and the present, *as well as* the unbroken chain which bound his readers to the pre-Homeric heroes of his story.

92. Fusillo 1985, 162–67; Hunter 1993, 159–60, who also cites E. E. Rice, *The Grand Procession of Ptolemy Philadelphus* (Oxford, 1983), 106–7.

Skytobrachion, by rejecting both epic form (in favor of prose narrative: the E. V. Rieu of antiquity, I've always thought) and most aspects of the mythical that clashed with his circumscribed rationalism, refashioned the Argonaut legend as an unremarkable adventure novel, which not only lacked "the grandeur of epic or tragedy" (Rusten 1982, 101) but virtually wrote the Heroic Age out of existence. This was to ignore the problem rather than to grapple with it.

Apollonius, far bolder, sought no such easy and dishonest palliatives. The first, quite remarkable, thing that emerges from his narrative is that it never falls back on rationalism, and is also virtually free of allegory,[93] as though that particular intellectual tradition, of cosmetic patching for unwilling skeptics, had never existed. θαύματα of every sort—the Clashing Rocks, Aiëtes' fire-breathing bulls, the Spartoi, Talos, the Nereïds, Medeia's magic—are accepted without demur, as integral features of the heroic Unknown. There is no attempt, for instance, to *explain away* the Clashing Rocks, in the style of some modern scholars, for example as memories of encounters with icebergs in the Arctic;[94] nor to eliminate their awkward physicality by allegorizing them as some kind of moral hazard. Apollonius was, however, forced to accept one addition to the legend made necessary by exploration: the fusing of the rocks once they had been successfully navigated (2.604–6). Pindar (*Pyth.* 4.210–11) was right to describe this necessary end of an archaic belief as a τελευτάν, a kind of death (Braswell 1988, 293).

In sharp and deliberate contrast, the exploring Hellenes who penetrate this barbarous Bronze Age world of wonders and magic are drawn very much as Apollonius's contemporaries: enterprising yet vulnerable, wholly Hellenistic in their reactions, and human to a fault.[95] The confrontation of old and new, operating at social, mythical, and literary levels simultaneously, is what gives Apollonius's narrative its penetration and originality. The one great exception to this company of Hellenistic Candides, of course, is Heracles: a giant of gargantuan appetites, overwhelming strength, and unruly bi-

---

93. Hunter 1993, 80–83, 154, makes an attempt to find "near-allegories" in, e.g., the Harpies or Iris; but neither these examples, nor his suggestion that the Argonauts' adventures in Libya (Book 4) are "a kind of allegory of the Alexandrian Greeks lost in the cultural desert of North Africa," do I find really convincing.

94. See J. G. Frazer's edition of Apollodorus (1921, 2: app. 5, 355–85): he is probably right that the Clashing Rocks are an archetypal fairy-tale, with parallel versions recounted by (among others) Rumanians, Russians, and Eskimos.

95. We may note that the one supernatural item that actually accompanies them is the *Argo*'s "speaking beam," part of the tradition at least as early as Aeschylus's day (fr. 36 Mette), "carpentered into the forekeel" by Athena herself (1.524–27), and silent throughout the voyage until, with dramatic force all the greater for its rarity of utterance, it conveys Zeus's wrath at the murder of Apsyrtos (4.585–88).

sexual passions, who himself embodies the outsize virtues and vices of the Heroic Age. His mere presence threatens to destroy all proportion and harmony among Apollonius's latter-day Argonauts, whose understated virtues tend more toward the cooperative. Muscle-bound, ruled by his obsolete code, an embarrassing anachronism from a culture in which, "when the typical hero found his path to fame and glory blocked, his instinct was to batter his own or someone else's head against the obstacle until something broke,"[96] he serves briefly as object-lesson, and then is left behind—his absence unnoticed, for all his bulk, by the departing company.[97] It is doubly ironic that the uncontrolled violence that breaks his oar should lead, step by step, to his loss of Hylas and his severance from the expedition.

Apollonius's treatment of Heracles nicely symbolizes the ambiguous tensions in any attempt by men of the Hellenistic age to come to terms with their ancient heroic heritage. Recognition and acceptance of the past is essential, he is saying, but its reinstatement would be sheer disaster: a Heracles in Ptolemaic Alexandria would upset the boat in a more than literal sense. The Argonauts on several occasions (2.145-53, 2.774-95, 3.1232-34, 4.1436-82) lament his irreplaceable absence; but they have in fact managed quite well without him (e.g., in the matter of boxing, one of his specialties, successfully putting up Polydeuces against Amykos, 2.20-97), and, faced among the Hesperides with evidence of his destructive passage, they make it clear, despite their protestations (4.1458-60), that they are in fact much happier regretting Heracles' absence than dealing with his monstrous and unmanageable presence. On the other hand, he had to be handled delicately: he was claimed as an "ancestor" by the Ptolemies, and thus was much written about by Alexandrian court poets.[98] Dealing with his violent, emotional, and intermittently comic character thus presented a problem in the ethics of patronage in addition to everything else.[99]

---

96. W. B. Stanford, *The Ulysses Theme* (Oxford, 1954), 73.

97. See Ap. Rhod. 1.862-74, 992-1011, and especially 1153-1272. Apollonius is not above sly mischief at Heracles' expense: this hero did not get a rowing bench amidships simply as a mark of honor, but also (bearing in mind his enormous size) in order to preserve the *Argo*'s equilibrium: 1.399-400, 531-33. (There existed a tradition that the *Argo* herself rejected Heracles because of his weight: schol. 1.1289-91; Antimachos fr. 58 Wyss; Pherecydes *FGrH* 3 F 111a = Apollod. 1.9.19.) There is also high comedy in his determination, in a kind of strongman frenzy, to continue rowing when the winds are blowing again and everyone else has stopped (1.1161-71). The crew's failure to notice his absence [!] on leaving Mysia (1.1273-83) should thus be seen as witty paradox rather than a regrettable lapse from realism.

98. See J. Rostropowicz, "Das Heraklesbild in den Argonautika des Apollonios Rhodios," *Act. Class. Univ. Scient. Debreceniensis* 26 (1990): 31-34.

99. This, however, seems not to have proved too much of a deterrent: see, e.g., Callim. *H.* 3.145-

Heracles is indeed (Hunter 1993, 26) "anomalous among the Argonauts"; the longing for his superhuman aid, as Burkert sees (1985, 210), bears all the marks of a wish-fulfillment fantasy (perhaps not entirely surprising in those who habitually hired mercenaries to do their fighting for them). To interpret the traditional myth in terms of human psychology, even while accepting its magical elements, meant, first and foremost, dropping Heracles, "bestial and godlike" (Feeney 1991, 98), from the narrative, leaving him to slouch off through Mysia toward ultimate deification. Like the madman in drama, he would have made nonsense of moral issues, and indeed of personal relationships, continually acting as a lumbering *semideus ex machina:* what would have become of the dramatic tension, let alone Jason's complex relationship with Medeia, had Heracles been there at every turn to obliterate the opposition? [100]

This is clearly why most versions of the myth remove him from the narrative at an early stage.[101] Apollonius, however, keeps him long enough to get some fun out of making this polyphiloprogenitive stud upbraid his comrades (1.865–74) for dallying too long in the beds of the Lemnian women.[102] The paradoxes of Heracles' nature have led scholars both ancient and modern to extrapolate a moral, civilizing aspect of him to offset the guzzler, rapist, and murderer: Cynics and Stoics, indeed, turned him into a kind of muscular saint.[103] But this is surely no more than the attempt (with which we are now familiar) to clear up some of the hero's more embarrassing archaic features by means of allegory,[104] a pitfall that Apollonius carefully—and characteristically—avoids.

For some time now the *communis opinio* about the *Argonautika* has stressed its acute literary self-consciousness, and in particular the way in which it echoes, varies, or subverts Homer (we hardly need telling that as a scholar, Apollonius wrote on Homeric epic).[105] Though I am not primarily concerned

---

61 and Theocr. 17.26–33. More difficult was Hera's famous distaste for Heracles, since Hera figures throughout as the Argonauts' patron.

100. In fact, we get a fairly clear picture of the results from Skytobrachion's version of events: see Diod. Sic. 4.48–49.

101. Testimonia conveniently tabulated by Clauss (1993, 176 and n. 1): Herodoros even claims (*FGrH* 31 F 41) that Heracles never sailed with the expedition at all, being at the time enslaved to Omphale, thus reminding us of his internal antitheses: as Burkert says (1985, 210), "The glorious hero is also a slave, a woman, and a madman."

102. Hunter (1993, 33–34) is sensible on this point: whatever this speech may be, it is not, as has sometimes been suggested (Fränkel 1968, and Vian and Delage 1974, ad loc.), an old-fashioned declaration of misogyny by a high-minded heroic pederast.

103. Feeney 1991, 95–98 offers a good example of this.

104. As in the famous moral lesson, attributed to Prodikos by Xenophon (*Mem.* 2.1.21–33), of "Heracles at the crossroads."

105. See Pfeiffer 1968, 140–45. It is perhaps worth pointing out in this context that, for a scholar,

here with literary problems, this erudite awareness is important for evaluating the *perspective* (for want of a better term) that Apollonius gives to his quest into past time, his evocation of the Heroic Age, even his aetiologizing search for roots. In *creative* time, Apollonius wrote some four centuries after Homer, who becomes his legacy: as Eliot once remarked of past writers, "We know more than they did; and they are that which we know." But in *mythic* time, of course, the Argonauts' expedition to Colchis belongs to the generation *before* the Trojan War: Cheiron's wife cradles the baby Achilles as she waves them on their way (1.556–58). Thus, by a kind of mythic intertextuality, knowledge can jump forward as well as backward, offering to Apollonius an irresistible opening for deadpan narratological jokes, and to the modern historian enlightenment regarding ancient chronological awareness.

Both combine to solve one of the oddest problems in the *Argonautika* (4.784–90). Hera has requested that Thetis convoy the Argonauts past the dangers (well known to Homer's Odysseus) of Scylla and Charybdis and the Wandering Rocks (*Πλαγκταί*), all located in the Straits of Messina. But then she says: "You know how . . . I saved [Jason and his crew] as they threaded the Wandering / Rocks, with their fearfully roaring fiery tempests." Thetis is thus being asked to do again what Hera asserts she herself has once already done; but in fact this will be the *Argo*'s *first* passage through the strait. How are we to explain this contradiction? Was Hera really talking about the Clashing Rocks (*Συμπληγάδες*)? Hardly: Apollonius never confuses the two, and on that earlier occasion it was Athena, not Hera, who got the *Argo* through.[106] Textual emendation has proved equally inadequate.[107] As always with Apollonius, Homer helps. Describing the *Πλαγκταί* to Odysseus, Circe warns him (*Od.* 12.69–72, trans. Lattimore): "That way the only seagoing ship to get through was Argo, / who is in all men's minds (*πᾶσι μέλουσα*), on her way home from Aiëtes; / and even she would have been driven on the great rocks that time, / but *Hera saw her through*, out of her great love for Jason" (empha-

Apollonius evinces a striking practical knowledge and love of the sea and seafaring: cf. J. Rostropo-wicz, "The *Argonautica* by Apollonius of Rhodes as a Nautical Epos: Remarks on the Realities of Navigation," *Eos* 88 (1990): 107–17. The passage of the Symplegades (2.549–97) is a physically compelling hands-on description; and there is a similar precision and authenticity about the details of the *Argo*'s launching (1.363–93), probably picked up in the Rhodian shipyards. See F. Chamoux, "Le lancement du navire Argo," *Bulletin de la Société des Antiquités de France* (1983 [1985]): 45–49, and cf. 4.887–91.

106. Vian and Delage 1981, 41–43, demolishing earlier theories by E. Livrea, *Apollonii Rhodii Argonautikon Liber IV* (Florence, 1973), 234–36, and M. Campbell, "Further Notes on Apollonius Rhodius," *CQ* 21 (1976): 416, and pointing out, *inter alia*, that the "fearfully roaring fiery tempests" (*πυρὸς δειναὶ βρομέουσι θύελλαι*) could *only* refer to the volcanic *Πλαγκταί*.

107. See, e.g., Fränkel 1968, 534–36; G. Giangrande, *Zu Sprachgebrauch, Technik, und Text des Apollonios Rhodios* (Amsterdam, 1973), 37.

sis mine). These were famous lines, like the *Argo* herself "in all men's minds," certainly in those of Apollonius's audience. What Hera in effect says to Thetis is: "Well, I hardly need to repeat how I saved the Argonauts from the Wandering Rocks: you know your Homer as well as I do, and it's all in there." [108] The Homeric tag, suddenly shifted from its frame and thus relocated, is as arresting—and was meant to be—as another Hellenistic innovation, those looming high-relief fighters on the steps up to the Great Altar at Pergamon, which "set foot, hand and knee on the actual treads on which the worshipper mounted to the altar." [109]

Yet the most crucial element in the Argonauts' Unknown, as for the entire mythical era—above all by way of validation, belief, and instrument of cultural definition—had to be τὸ θεῖον, the divine, primarily as godhead, that is, major and minor deities, but also including θαύματα, magic, and the numinous in all its various manifestations. Like Athenians of the Periclean Age, torn between the Inherited Conglomerate and the sophistries of the New Rationalism, [110] Alexandrians in the mid-third century B.C. found their yearning for old roots and past certainties under constant assault by forces such as Euhemerism: no one, it is safe to say, had forgotten the hymn with which, in 291, Athenians greeted Demetrios Poliorcetes: [111] "The other gods are far away, / or cannot hear, / or are nonexistent, or care nothing for us; but *you* are here, and visible to us, / not carved in wood or stone, but real, / so to you we pray." But the other side of the case was equally strong, and is well exemplified, five or six years later, again in Athens, by the passionate outburst of a comic poet, Philippides, precisely *against* those blasphemous usurpations of godhead by Demetrios which, he asserts, have been directly responsible for Athens's misfortunes. [112] The split was not between two groups, but personal and internal. The resultant stresses are easily imagined.

It would be surprising had Apollonius *not* been affected by three centuries of rationalizing criticism in the area of religion: the remarkable thing is

---

108. Hunter (1993, 97) asks, casually, "Has Thetis read *Odyssey* 12 with its reference to Ἀργὼ πασιμέλουσα . . . or has she read the *Argonautica*?" but does not follow up the implications of his own question.

109. Martin Robertson, *A History of Greek Art* (Cambridge, 1975), 1:538.

110. Penetratingly analyzed by Dodds 1951, ch. 6, "Rationalism and Reaction in the Classical Age," 179-206.

111. Duris of Samos cited by Athen. 6.253e; cf. Green 1993, 55.

112. Philippides fr. 25 Kock. The blasphemies he catalogues—improper interference with the sacred calendar, using Athena's shrine on the Acropolis to house courtesans—as well as the signs of ill omen (frostbitten vines, a tear in the sail of the sacred ship during the Panathenaic procession) that were thought to have come about as a result, are also listed in Plut. *Demetr.* 10, 12, 23, 26, and 27.

how little impact it actually had on his work. Xenophanes' lethal dismissal of divine anthropomorphism (K-R-S frs. 167–69) has produced a certain awkwardness (perhaps calculated, sometimes witty) over the physical aspects of deity. Athena is weighty (cf. Hom. *Il.* 5.838–39) but can still travel by cloud (Ap. Rhod. *Arg.* 2.538–40), and at the Clashing Rocks thrusts the *Argo* through with one hand while bracing herself against a rock with the other (2.598–99). Are the Argonauts thought of as seeing her? Probably not (Feeney 1991, 74), any more than they see the Nereïds performing a similar function in the Straits of Messina (4.930–64). What is their relative size? We aren't told, but this passage makes us wonder. Hera, Athena, and Aphrodite, during their famous meeting at the beginning of Book 3, bear more resemblance (*pace* Feeney [1991, 78]) to the gossiping Alexandrian ladies of Theocritus (*Id.* 15) than to Homeric deities. In the delineation of Triton, as Feeney says (1991, 79), "the norms of anthropomorphism are adhered to in order to be destabilized." But such instances apart, what is striking is the all-pervasive degree of Apollonius's *anti*-rationalism, confronted with which (Feeney 1991, 67) "Xenophanes and Plato would have recoiled in disdain." Indeed, in many ways the *Argonautika* can be read as a subtle indictment of the whole Protagorean πάντων χρημάτων μέτρον ἄνθρωπος formulation ("Man the measure of all things"), the arrogance and inadequacy of which, after the events of the past two centuries, and despite Euhemerism, it was becoming increasingly hard to deny.

    This, surely, is the common factor linking a whole range of symptoms apparent throughout the poem: above all, that pervasive sense of human uncertainty, shiftlessness, and ignorance in the face of an Unknown that extends from the motives of the gods to the unpredictability of the future, from magic and other counter-natural powers to the cracks in the fabric of the heroic ethos. Judged by these criteria, Jason's much-debated ἀμηχανία, far from being a flaw, could be interpreted as a realistic recognition of man's limitations. Zeus is never seen, and recognition of his divine will (at least before the murder of Apsyrtos) remains fragmentary,[113] though at the same time his divine struggle for power may be quietly illuminating the all-too-similar deadly strife among Alexander's Successors.[114] Hera's revenge against Pelias is worked out by using Medeia as an unconscious agent; the emphasis in the *Argonautika* on human decision-making is balanced against the lack of knowledge on which such decisions are based, the arbitrary and unsus-

---

113. Feeney 1991, 58–62, 65–67; Hunter 1993, 79–80.

114. Feeney (1991, 68–69) perceives Apollonius's emphasis on struggle and usurpation in references to Zeus, but does not draw what seems to me the inevitable conclusion from it.

pected machinations of the gods: "For the most part, Apollonius' characters struggle in a cloud of ignorance and doubt" (Hunter 1993, 79). Phineus demonstrates the inadequacy of human prophecy, the ineluctable force of divine vengeance (2.250–51, 314–16). Deity no longer, as in Homer, consorts with mortals. These archaic gods are remote, unknowable, and in epiphany, as Apollo over Thynias, terrifying.[115]

We see then, in the end, that the fragments Apollonius has shored against his ruins are in essence not merely literary, or nostalgic, or indeed really fragments at all. What we rather find in the *Argonautika* is a remarkably consistent and thorough reversion to that archaic worldview consciously discarded by the intellectual pioneers of the Periclean Age—on the dead-end of which allegorists and rationalists were still hopefully battening. Like Euripides at the close of his life, when he wrote the *Bacchai*, Apollonius has seen, with deadly clarity, that reason alone is not enough, that the dimension of the Unknown formulated by myth has shrunk surprisingly little. There is no discussion here of the already old chestnut (Hunter 1993, 80) of whether Homer's gods "were 'real' or were 'metaphors' to be allegorized away": their power, tangible existence, and inscrutable control of mortal affairs permeate the entire narrative.

Perhaps most remarkably, the Fleece itself, the *raison d'être* of the entire epic *geste*, remains a complete (and highly numinous) mystery. The full reason for its Grail-like desirability, that can send a shipload of heroes to Colchis and back, is never explained. We are not even told what generates its unearthly magical glow (4.172–73, 177–78, 185). Apollonius, speaking of its "ruddy blush like a flame" (4.173), clearly is visualizing a deep metallic red-gold such as that of the royal *larnax* from Tomb II at Vergina: what substance are we looking at here? We can safely ignore (as does Apollonius) the numerous bathetic rationalizations (Braund 1994, 23–25). The Fleece was a magical symbol: of supernatural power, of entitlement, above all of kingship. The bravest thing Jason ever does in this poem is to consummate his marriage on it (4.1141–43), an act as potentially dangerous as laying impious hands on the Ark of the Covenant.

Apollonius was not, as we have seen, wholly immune to the pressures of his age; but these were restricted, in the first instance, to necessary changes

---

115. See 2.669–79. Many scholars have pointed out that Apollo's visitation here would inevitably evoke comparison with his murderous attack on the Greek camp in the *Iliad* (1.43–52): see, e.g., Feeney 1991, 50–51, 75. But the demonstration of power at Thynias, sometimes seen as a contrast to Homer's dark assault, is in fact at least as awe-inspiring. To rationalize this epiphany as no more than "a poetic version of sunrise" (Hunter 1989, 52–53, repeated 1993, 80) is to lapse into the kind of flaccid symbolism favored by Palaiphatos and Skytobrachion, not to mention the egregious Max Müller, who characterized Heracles' pyre on Oita as one more beautiful sunset.

imposed by the expansion of geographical knowledge—that is, by a genuine, *physical* diminution of the Unknown. He will not, for example, indulge arbitrarily in what came to be called ἐξωκεανισμός, that wandering off the known map which got so bad a mauling in his day (Romm 1992, 194-96). His journey home for the Argonauts, even though it works its way into Switzerland by way of the Po, returning to the Mediterranean (via a non-existent confluence) down the Rhône (4.552-651), never strays off into that Ocean so remorselessly deconstructed by Herodotus—indeed, at one point Hera in person turns the *Argo* back (4.637-44)—and carefully follows the track of Odysseus's Western wanderings as identified by earlier writers.[116]

Apollonius's literary concessions to Callimachean fashion—the self-conscious literary irony, the constant aetiologizing—do not for one moment affect his basic approach to the past. At heart, he embraces the ancient epic tradition with a courage that in the mid-third century can only astonish us (and is more than sufficient to explain the tradition, whether true or false, of his famous alleged quarrel with Callimachus): scorning to euhemerize the gods; not questioning the αἴτια, but accepting and going beyond them; not rationalizing or allegorizing clashing rocks or fiery bulls, but taking them in his stride as an integral part of those "high and far-off times" that exist no longer, yet must be preserved forever in men's memories, a guard against intellectual *hubris*, a reminder and validation of everything it meant to be a Greek.[117] That is why the intellectually fashionable Skytobrachion survives only in epitome, whereas Pindar and Apollonius have lived through the centuries to delight and inspire us still today.[118]

---

116. It is a nice point (setting mythical chronology—Argonauts before Odysseus—against writers' time—Apollonius after Homer) as to whether this "Western route" is to be thought of as having been laid out by Odysseus or by the Argonauts. The tendency in antiquity (when both were treated as historical) was to give preference to the Argonauts; the balance today (when both are regarded as "mythical" in the modern sense) is to opt for Odysseus: see, e.g., Beye 1982, ch. 4. Further bibliography in Romm 1992, 194 n. 51.

117. Cf. Green 1993, 206-15.

118. I would like to acknowledge here the very great help I have had from Erich Gruen and Paul Cartledge, whose ingenious suggestions for restructuring an originally unwieldy and ill-proportioned essay were only matched by the patience with which they waited for my revisions. It goes without saying that I remain responsible for the many defects that (I am uneasily aware) still remain, perhaps inevitably, in my treatment of a topic that is by its very nature of more than Protean elusiveness.

2

The Flight-Plan of Daedalus

THOUGH THE FLIGHT of Daedalus and his son Icarus from Crete is chiefly familiar to us in the two versions by Ovid,[1] it can be traced back in the literary tradition as far as the fifth century B.C.,[2] and iconographically considerably further. Icarus's fall is recorded on a black-figure hydria from the Acropolis dated before 500, while a red-figure Campanian kotyle of about 400 shows Daedalus helping his son to adjust his wings.[3] Kardara has plausibly identified both figures in a still earlier bronze relief from Afrati in Crete.[4]

Note: Originally published in *Echos du monde classique/Classical News and Views* 23 (1979): 30–35.

1. *AA* 2.19–98; *Met.* 8.183–235. For a comparison of the two versions, see R. Heinze, "Ovids elegische Erzählung," *Bericht über die Verhandlung der Sächsischen Akademie der Wissenschaften*, Phil.-hist. Klasse 71 (1919): 74–75; Renz 1935, 4–16; S. A. Schlueter, "Studies in Ovid's Ars Amatoria," diss., University of Texas at Austin (1975), 33–34.

2. Aesch. *Pers.* 890–91; Aristoph. *Peace* 140–41 with schol. ad loc., cf. *Frogs* 849–50; Xen. *Mem.* 4.2.33.

3. C. M. Dawson, *Romano-Campanian Mythological Landscape Painting*, Yale Classical Studies 9, ed. A. R. Bellinger (New Haven, 1944), 141; E. Pottier, Daremberg-Saglio II.1 4–9, with figs. 2278, 2281, and 2283 (a Lucanian vase-painting that closely matches Ovid's description). Sarah P. Morris, *Daidalos and the Origins of Greek Art* (Princeton, 1992), 193–96 and figs. 8a, 8b, 10d, and 12, lists an Etruscan gold bulla showing Daedalus and Icarus in flight, a black-figure skyphos of c. 540 B.C. with a winged figure that *may* be one of them, and an Apulian skyphos fragment (c. 420–400 B.C.) that depicts Daedalus fitting Icarus with his wings. For general consultation, see Jacob E. Nyenhuis's article "Daidalos and Ikaros," *LIMC* 3.1 (1986), 313–21, 3.2, 237–42 (figs. 1–57). Notable for early representation are no. 14, a fragment from an early sixth century hydria, showing the legs of a person labeled *ΙΚΑΡΟΣ*, who from his winged boots may be assumed to be thought of as flying (though he looks more as though he is running); and no. 31, an Italian neck-amphora of c. 550, that shows two male figures flying toward the right (the odd thing here is that *both* are bearded, whereas Icarus is generally represented as a beardless youth). There are no surviving representations of the Fall of Icarus until Roman times, and these may well have been inspired by Virgil's account, *Aen.* 6.9–44.

4. C. Kardara, "Some Remarks on Two Early Cretan Bronzes," *AAA* 2 (1969): 216–19: Haeg's

Most of our sources are comparatively late, but the details of the myth vary less than we might expect. Though different reasons are advanced for the imprisonment of Daedalus by Minos—his having supplied Pasiphaë with the wooden cow,[5] the part he played in the escape of Theseus and Ariadne, or simply a desire on Minos's part to exploit his inventive skills *sine die*[6]—his escape with Icarus follows a broadly identical tradition throughout,[7] broken only by some rationalists who, unable to swallow the idea of humans flying, rewrote the story with father and son making their getaway by ship.[8] One feature that recurs in almost every source, from Aeschylus to Arrian, is the identification of Icaria in the eastern Aegean as the island that took its name from Icarus's fall.[9] If ever proof were needed that rational motivation is entirely superfluous to mythography, the aetiology of the Icarian Sea surely provides it.

Daedalus was an Athenian: certainly an Erechtheïd, possibly a cousin of Theseus.[10] Exiled at some point for the murder of his nephew and pupil Talus,[11] he nevertheless cherished the desire, dear to the heart of every Greek then as now, to die on his native soil: that is, in Attica.[12] This formed the basis of his appeal to Minos. The wish was based on something stronger than mere ἐθνικισμός. To be buried—or, worse, *not* to be buried—in a foreign land was regarded as the worst fate that could befall a man.[13] When Minos proved obdurate, Daedalus, ingenious as ever, fabricated wings for himself and his son,[14] and they set off—either for Athens, as Cleidemus in fact tells us,[15] or perhaps, bearing Daedalus's ancient exile in mind, for some destination on, or just beyond, the frontiers of Attica.

The clearest, most connected version of their flight-plan is that given by

claim in PWK s.v. "Ikaros (2)," col. 986, that Icarus was originally unconnected with Daedalus, thus has little to recommend it. Cf. note 28 below.

5. Cleidemus *ap.* Plut. *Them.* 19.1; Diod. Sic. 4.77.5; schol. Eur. *Hipp.* 887 (p. 103 Schwartz).

6. Apollod. *Epit.* 1.8-12; schol. Hom. *Od.* 11.322, *Il.* 18.590, cf. Eustath. p. 1688 on *Od.* 11.320; Xen. *Mem.* 4.2.33; Diod. Sic. 4.61.4; Zenob. 4.92.

7. With Ovid's versions (note 1 above), compare, e.g., Hygin. *Fab.* 40; Strabo 14.1.19 (C.639); Apollod. *Epit.* 1.12-13.

8. E.g., Pausanias (9.11.4-5); cf. Diod. Sic. 4.77.5-6, and Cleidemus *ap.* Plut. *Them.* 19.1.

9. Aesch. *Pers.* 890-91; Apollod. *Epit.* 1.12; Diod. Sic. 4.77.5-6.9; Strabo 14.1.19 (c.639); Arrian 7.20.5; Paus. 9.11.5; Servius on Virg. *Aen.* 6.14; Ovid *AA* 2.79-82, 96, *Met.* 8.220ff.

10. Plut. *Thes.* 19; Paus. 7.4.5; Diod. Sic. 4.76.1.

11. Paus. 1.21.4; Apollod. 3.15.8; Diod. Sic. 4.76.4-7; schol. Eur. *Orest.* 1648.

12. Ovid (*AA* 2.25-28, *Met.* 8.184) is clearly drawing on ancient tradition here.

13. Soph. *El.* 1141; Virg. *Aen.* 5.871 (Palinurus); cf. Paul Brandt, *P. Ovidi Nasonis De Arte Amatoria Libri Tres* (Leipzig, 1902), 71.

14. The detailed description given by Ovid (*Met.* 8.189ff.) repays study.

15. *Ap.* Plut. *Thes.* 19.4.

Ovid. In it Daedalus tells his son not to navigate by the stars,[16] but simply to follow him. This, arguably, was a mistake. To begin with, however, all went well. From Knossos to Delos (*AA* 2.80), their route lay due north: Virgil (*Aen.* 6.16) confirms the direction. This, if not the most direct flight-path to Athens (which would have taken them northwest from Thera, now Santorini, by way of Siphnos, Seriphos, Kythnos, and Keos, the modern Kea), was—so far—a perfectly reasonable way of getting there. It used the major islands (Thera, Naxos, Paros) as landmarks, and from Delos onward could follow the long coastlines of Andros and southern Euboea. But at Delos, against all probability, Ovid makes Daedalus turn not northwest but *due east*. This is why, when the pair reached the island of Icaria, Samos lay ahead of them, a little to port, while the islands of Lebynthos, Calymne (now Kalymnos, renowned for its sponge-fishers), and Astypalaea were well away to the south, on their right hand, just as Ovid describes the scene:[17] a traveler on the Olympic Airways Athens-Samos flight gets a perfect bird's-eye gloss on this passage. Icarus now flew too near the sun, fell in the sea, and was drowned: the association of his name with Icaria in the eastern Aegean is vouched for by our earliest surviving literary source, Aeschylus, who in the *Persians* (890–91) writes of Λῆμνον Ἰκάρου θ' ἕδος καὶ Ῥόδον ἠδὲ Κνίδον, thus establishing the geographical context beyond any doubt.

What, at this point, does Daedalus do? A revision of itinerary is clearly called for; but in the event the new flight-plan proves as baffling as the old one. Instead of setting course for Athens, Daedalus, we are asked to believe, proceeded to fly nonstop for something like five hundred miles due west, finally touching down in either Sicily (Ovid *Met.* 8.260–61) or Campania (Virg. *Aen.* 6.14–17).[18] At this point Ovid describes him as "exhausted," and we may well believe it. Clearly, something is very badly amiss, not only with Ovid's account, but also with the whole popular tradition on which he drew. Strabo's explanation,[19] that father and son simply drifted off-course, must remain—

---

16. *AA* 2.55–58, *Met.* 8.206–8.
17. iam Samos a laeua (fuerant Naxosque relictae
    et Paros et Clario Delos amata deo)
    dextra Lebynthos erat siluisque umbrosa Calymne
    cinctaque piscosis Astypalaea uadis.

                    (*AA* 2.79–82)

          et iam Iunonia laeua
    parte Samos (fuerant Delosque Parosque relictae)
    dextra Lebynthos erat fecundaque melle Calymne.

                    (*Met.* 8.220–22)

18. Cf. Servius ad loc.; Juv. 3.25.
19. 14.1.19 (C.639): . . . μὴ κρατήσαντα τοῦ δρόμου. . . .

despite the notorious vagaries of Greek navigation from Odysseus's day onward—a mere counsel of despair. Questions crowd the mind. Why, after
reaching Delos, did Daedalus turn east instead of northwest? Further, if his
original route to Icaria and the eastern Aegean was planned, and not accidental, what was he meaning to do there in the first place, and why did he change
his mind? Why, after the death of Icarus, did he fly, not to Attica, but clear
out of the Aegean to Sicily or Campania?

The answer to all these questions is, as we shall see, both simple and obvious. What I find far more extraordinary (and deeply symptomatic of human
response to myth, in both antiquity and the modern world) is that virtually no one has ever been seriously put out by so glaring an inconsistency.
Only Strabo, in one casual phrase (see note 19) capable of more than one
interpretation, thinks any explanation is called for at all: our other ancient
sources—though occasionally, as we have seen, bothered by the idea of men
flying—accept Daedalus's geographically irrational flight-plan without a second thought. Even more significant is the fact that modern scholars, too, have
virtually ignored the problem. Korn's lackadaisical note, though recognizing
that a problem exists, makes no effort to solve it; Anderson is equally casual;
no one else even does as much.[20]

The psychology of rationalism is intriguingly selective: though the escap-
ers' mode of transport provoked some incredulity, where they went, or why,
remained a matter of benign indifference. To a Roman, or indeed to many
modern critics, *when dealing with myth*, the euphony of Aegean place-names
would take precedence over any functional significance they might possess
for an actual traveler. Like Chesterton's rolling English drunkard, Daedalus could go to Birmingham by way of Beachy Head (or the Mediterranean
equivalent) without anyone querying his motives for over two millennia—
even though the confusion was an elementary one, which three minutes'
thought could have cleared up. But (as Housman said in another context)
thought is irksome, and three minutes is a long time.[21] It would be pleasant to
assume that Ovid, at least, saw the contradictions very well, and set himself
to mock the whole literary tradition of Hellenistic historiography by leaving

---

20. O. Korn, R. Ehwald, and M. von Albrecht, eds., *P. Ovidius Naso: Metamorphosen VIII–XV*,
5th ed. (Zürich and Dublin, 1960), 17; William S. Anderson, *Ovid's Metamorphoses Books 6–10* (Norman, Okla., 1972), 353: "*For some reason* [italics mine], instead of heading back towards his beloved
Athens . . . Daedalus heads north*east*. . . ." There is no further comment; and why is east modified to northeast? To soften the paradox? Most surprisingly of all, Sarah Morris, the scholar who
has explored the Daedalus myth in all its multifarious ramifications, does not even allude to the
problem. It is as though myth (and she is far from alone in this) were allotted to a category, not so
much of a different mode of reason, as one where reason did not operate at all.

21. *D. Iunii Iuuenalis Saturae*, 2d ed. (Cambridge, 1931), xi.

them unresolved. The truth, however (I suspect), is that he was as blind, or indifferent, to matters of mythical geography as the next man, and was in any case prepared to let reason fly out of the window in pursuit of an impressive set-piece.

Yet he must surely have been well aware of the alternative tradition, according to which Daedalus *did* fly to Athens or Attica, just as we might expect.[22] Icarus's fall, indeed, is specifically located by the Euripidean scholiast in τὸ Παράλιον πέλαγος, "the sea by the Paralia," that is, the coastal waters of Attica. This valuable piece of information was willfully obscured by the modern editor of the scholia, Schwartz,[23] who, having read his Roscher, knew perfectly well that Icarus had drowned in the eastern Aegean, off Icaria, and therefore, with relentless Teutonic logic, helpfully emended Παράλιον to παρ' Ἀσίαν, a nice instance of apriorism messing up a perfectly sound text.

At this point a further question arises. If Daedalus's original flight-plan was rational, and in the Ur-version of the myth Attica was indeed his destination, then how did Icaria come to form so integral an element in the traditional account? The key to the whole story, in a vast preponderance of our sources, is, precisely, the eponymous association of Icaria, or the Icarian Sea (Ovid *AA* 2.96), or both, with the fall of Icarus.[24] Icarus gave Icaria its name. In the face of this consensus, it is not hard to see that tradition, very early on, settled for the wrong Icaria, picking on the best-known site so called with cavalier indifference to the requirements of the myth it was expounding. There is only one Icaria that offers a serious alternative to the eastern Aegean island of that name: the local Attic deme of Icaria or Icarion, which belonged to the Aegeid tribe.[25]

The site of the deme Icaria has been firmly established on archaeological grounds by the discovery, in 1888, of the sanctuary of Dionysus of Icaria, and later, of several deme-decrees.[26] It lay three or four miles southwest of Marathon, and east of the modern village of Ekali, as Leake had earlier deduced,[27] on an elevated plateau between the main massif of Pendéli and the smaller Dionysovouni, within easy reach of Marathon Bay (Σχοινιά). Its connection with Dionysus reminds us that one of its better-known demesmen was Thespis, the early exponent of Attic tragedy. If Daedalus was making for the

---

22. Schol. Eur. *Hipp.* 887; Cleidemus *ap.* Plut. *Thes.* 19.4.

23. E. Schwartz, *Scholia in Euripidem*, vol. 2 (Berlin, 1891), 103.

24. Apollod. *Epit.* 1.12–13; Strabo 4.1.19 (C.639); Arrian 7.20.5; Paus. 9.11.4–5; Servius on Virg. *Aen.* 6.14; Diod. Sic. 4.77.5–6, cf. *Aesch.* Pers. 890–91.

25. Steph. Byz. s.v. Ἰκαρία.

26. J. S. Traill, *The Political Organisation of Attica* (Princeton, 1975) 41.

27. W. M. Leake, *The Demi of Attica*, 2d ed. (London, 1841), 103–4.

Marathon region from Delos, his flight would take him directly over Andros and southern Euboea (the latter, as we shall see in a moment, may be significant). Icarus will then have perished between Marathon and Euboea, off the coast of Attica, in τὸ Παράλιον πέλαγος, just as the Euripidean scholiast asserted. We do not need to suggest a dubious identification between Icarus and Icarius, the local cult-hero and father of Erigone:[28] Icarius's death took place in very different circumstances.[29] It is worth noting, in this context, that the east coast of Attica (rather than Phaleron or Piraeus) seems to have formed the normal approach to Attica in prehistoric times.[30]

If Icarus, in the original version of the myth, was associated with Icaria-by-Marathon, where did Daedalus himself land? Can we explain or adjust the final stage of his paradoxical itinerary, that 500-mile swoop westward to Magna Graecia? Granted that he may well, in the course of time, have left Attica after these events to pursue his fortunes in the West, what was his immediate destination? Where did he turn after Icarus's death? The tradition followed by Virgil (*Aen.* 6.14ff.) is helpful here. The old Greek name for Cumae was Cyme; and we know two cities of that name in the Aegean world. One, the more familiar, lay on the coast of the mainland opposite Lesbos: it was from here that Hesiod's father sailed to Boeotia (cf. p. 55).[31] But the other lay on the Euboean coast, a high citadel looking out toward Scyros, a natural landfall for the aerial traveler,[32] and Daedalus could well have ended his journey there. From Cyme it would be a short and easy journey to Attica. Perhaps, in the original version of the legend, Daedalus found it prudent to remain in neutral Euboea until the matter of his exile and blood-guilt was finally settled. As Pottier says,[33] local patriotism must have played a large part in multiplying myths about him. If one strong tradition made him go to Sicily after Icarus's death, whether by air or sea,[34] it would be only too easy to claim him, as does Virgil, for Cumae—or, indeed, for the Icarian Sea.

Though Ovid does not mention Cumae, his entire sequence dealing with

28. As, e.g., does Hoeg, PWK s.v. "Ikarios (2)," cols. 987–88.

29. Apollod. 3.14.7; Hygin. *Fab.* 130.

30. See, e.g., Hom. *Od.* 7.80, where Athena's journey to Athens is by way of Marathon; and *HHDem* 123–26, where pirates from Crete land at Thorikon, a few miles north of Sounion (Sunium). I am grateful for discussion on this point to two now much-missed scholars: Professors W. B. Stanford and E. David Francis.

31. Hes. *WD* 633ff.; cf. Steph. Byz. s.v. Κύμη; also Strabo 9.2.25 (C.409), 12.3.21 (C.550), and especially 13.3.6 (C.623).

32. Steph. Byz. ibid.; cf. Geisan, PWK s.v. "Kyme (1)," cols. 2474–75.

33. Daremberg-Saglio, vol. ii.1, 6, s.v. "Daedalus."

34. Apollod. *Epit.* 1.12–13; Zenob. 4.92; Tzetzes, *Chil.* 1.506; Diod. Sic. 4.77.5, 9.

Daedalus could not fail to recall the dramatic opening of Book 6 of Virgil's
Aeneid (cf. lines 14 ff., and in particular 23 ff., where the whole myth of Pasiphaë,
the Minotaur, the Labyrinth, the ball of twine, and the death of Icarus is outlined). As Rutledge saw,[35] Daedalus, Aeneas, and Augustus are all symbolically
linked by Virgil. The great artificer is presented as "a mythological prototype
of the brilliant Augustus," to whose imperial achievements the latter part of
Book 6 looks forward. Just as Ovid had earlier mocked Virgil's pretensions
by applying the older poet's phraseology in a frivolous erotic context,[36] so
here Daedalus, as a symbol of creative achievement, is transferred from the
Virgilian context of Rome's future greatness to Ovid's equation with the *prae-*
ceptor amoris. Ovid claims (*AA* 2.19 ff.) that his task, as *praeceptor*, is to clip the
wings of a god[37] — a control that Minos could not even exercise over mortals.
His exploitation of the myth is by no means the mere virtuoso digression it
is so often held to be.[38] For Ovid, Icarus provides a horrific object-lesson of
what may happen when passion ignores the prudent guidance and restraint
of *ars*, relying on instinct alone:[39] the true culmination of Rome's destiny, he
says in effect, what the whole Daedalic myth led up to, was the art of picking up pretty girls in a sophisticated metropolis. With such weighty matters
to consider, perhaps it is not altogether to be wondered at that Ovid, like so
many of his predecessors, carelessly provided Daedalus with a wholly irrational flight-plan. Though *ars* was a *sine qua non* for Tiphys the helmsman (*AA*
1.6), it clearly did not extend to his aerial counterpart.

---

35. Harry C. Rutledge, "Vergil's Daedalus," *CJ* 62 (1967): 309-11, and "The Opening of Aeneid
6," *CJ* 67 (1971): 110-15.

36. *AA* 1.453: *hoc opus, his labor est,* directly quoted from *Aen.* 6.129. In the original context,
Aeneas has just made his heartfelt appeal to the Sibyl to show him the way to the underworld,
where, we remember, a climactic vision of Rome's future greatness awaits him (*Aen.* 6.756-853).
The way down, the Sibyl replies, is simple, but "to retrace your steps, and get out into the upper
air once more—this is the task, this the labor." For Ovid, of course, the task and the labor are to
get a girl into bed without laying out expensive gifts on her first. Why Kenney ("Nequitiae Poeta,"
in *Ovidiana* [Paris, 1958], 201, supported now by A. S. Hollis, *Ovid: Ars Amatoria Book I* [Oxford,
1977] 112) should suppose that Ovid is here "mocking not so much Virgil as his own pretensions," I
cannot understand. Once again Ovid has given a clear—and, this time, clearly labeled—indication
of his attitude to grandiloquent imperial propaganda: he prefers private life, poetry, and sex.

37. For the double sense of Amor, as emotion and personified deity, cf. *AA* 1.7.

38. See, e.g., R. M. Durling, "Ovid as Praeceptor Amoris," *CJ* 53 (1958): 160.

39. Cf. T. Greiner, "Beobachtungen zu zwei Stellen der 'Ars Amatoria' (in Stichworten)," in
Ovids Ars Amatoria und Remedia Amoris, Untersuchungen zum Aufbau, ed. E. Zinn (Stuttgart, 1990),
62-63; J. M. Fyler, "*Omnia Vincit Amor*: Incongruity and the Limitations of Structure in Ovid's
Elegiac Poetry," *CJ* 66 (1971): 203; Schlueter (as above, note 1), 27-33.

3

Works and Days 1–285:
Hesiod's Invisible Audience

THERE is a popular delusion that the personal family allusions scattered by Hesiod throughout the *Works and Days*, and at the beginning of the *Theogony*,[1] are straightforward and, for the most part, not in dispute. Careful attention to Hesiod's text should suffice to dispel the first impression, while a survey of modern scholarship in this area will very soon put paid to the second. As J. F. Latimer observed in 1930, "Hesiod's *Works and Days* is a veritable gold mine for those who would not inhibit their hermeneutical aspirations." It is indeed. The operation, however, entails considerable risk. Rival, and mutually contradictory, theories abound. Worse, as Latimer confessed, "often a reexamination of the author or of the passage in question completely upsets one's carefully formulated opinions."[2] Here I myself must plead as guilty as any. In 1960 I published[3] the following statement in the course of a discussion on Hesiod: "It seems clear that Perses not only disputed the terms of his father's will, but bribed local barons to give him the lion's share of the estate at arbitration." There is nothing in that sentence, apart from the first assertion (and I am not too sure about the idea of a will, either), that I would stand by today. Yet no new substantive discoveries have been made; the text, despite all West's efforts, is not all that far from where Rzach left it. True, a great deal of interpretative work has been published, some of it both innovative and meth-

---

Note: Original version published in *Mnemai: Classical Studies in Memory of Karl K. Hulley*, ed. Harold D. Evjen (Chico, Calif., 1984), 21–39: since then, it has been much modified and augmented.

1. See *WD* 9–10, 27–39, 190–94, 202–18, 225–27, 248–51, 260–64, 267–81, 298–301, 320–26, 340–41, 363–67, 371, 376–78, 394–404, 631–40, 646–47; Theog. 22–34, 79–97.

2. Latimer 1930, 70.

3. In *Essays in Antiquity* (London, 1960), 39, in an essay entitled "Hodge on Helicon: A Study of Hesiod and His Society."

odologically invaluable,[4] but the overall scene remains one of dogmatism and confusion.

Some scholars, from Gilbert Murray onward,[5] have argued that the entire quarrel between the brothers was a literary fiction, a view very much in accord with contemporary critical trends: Pietro Pucci's discussion, for instance, is conducted at so rarified a level of structural and semantic abstraction that the problem is simply ignored altogether.[6] Wilamowitz, while conceding the existence of Perses and the barons, claimed that they couldn't possibly be the real targets of Hesiod's dramatic attack, which has always struck me as having the worst of things both ways. There was no lawsuit, Krafft argues: "Er ist ein literarisches Motiv."[7] From the time of the early scholiasts, there have always been critics eager to theorize Perses himself out of existence, as a mere conventional addressee—in Dornseiff's case, with abundant parallel citations from Eastern wisdom literature. West declares: "Where the line between fact and fiction is to be drawn, I do not presume to know."[8] Yet no one supposes that Hesiod invented himself; and since his personal relationships stand at the heart of the *Works and Days*, it is hard to believe, from the circumstantial evidence he offers, that he has saddled himself with a fictitious father and brother for the occasion. (Nor, might I add, do I accept recent attempts to relegate Lycambes, Neobule, and the rest of Archilochus's personal circle to a mere property-closet for the conventions of iambic ψόγος.) As Walcot says, the *Works and Days* is an intensely personal poem: it is shot through with legal preoccupations, and these may reasonably be held to have stemmed from the long-simmering quarrel with Perses.[9] Indeed, many schol-

---

4. I would particularly single out three articles by Michael Gagarin: "Dikē in the *Works and Days*" (1973); "Hesiod's Dispute with Perses" (1974); and "The Ambiguity of *Eris* in the *Works and Days*" (1990).

5. Cf. *A History of Ancient Greek Literature* (London, 1897), 6–7, 53–55.

6. Pietro Pucci, *Hesiod and the Language of Poetry* (Baltimore, 1977), 45ff.

7. Wilamowitz 1928, passim. Krafft's comment is from *Vergleichende Untersuchungen zu Homer und Hesiod* (Göttingen, 1963), 90 n. 4, cited by Gagarin 1974, 104 n. 1. Cf. H. Munding, *Hesiods Erga in ihrem Verhältnis zur Ilias* (Frankfurt, 1959), 12ff.

8. See West 1978, 33–34, 40.

9. Walcot 1966, 104–6: his arguments are given added strength by Gagarin's contention (1973, 81ff.) that the fundamental meaning of δίκη in Hesiod is "'law,' in the sense of a process for the peaceful settlement of disputes." For the semantic flexibility of the term depending on context, cf. Van Groningen 1957, 159 n. 22. Similar arguments in favor of a biographical base for the quarrel are found in Sinclair 1932, xvi, and Puelma 1972, 92 n. 30. Cf. West 1978, 34–35. On Archilochus and iambic ψόγος, see G. Nagy, *The Best of the Achaeans* (Baltimore, 1980), 243–49, in contrast to the more judicious warnings of K. J. Dover, *Archiloque, Entretiens de la Fondation Hardt* 10 (Geneva, 1964). There is much of value in the long and detailed survey by Philippe Rousseau, "Un héritage disputé," in *La componente autobiografica nella poesia greca e latina fra realtà e artificio letterario*, Atti de

ars take it for granted that the dispute actually provided the original impulse (*Anstoss*) for the poem, however much Hesiod may afterward have added to the version that we possess.[10]

Yet even if we grant the historicity of Hesiod's family feud, and the interest it generated in his contemporaries, its details remain highly debatable. It is widely assumed, for instance, that there had been an earlier lawsuit, or arbitration, between the brothers,[11] even though opinions are divided as to whether Perses won[12] or lost[13] on that occasion. In fact, as we shall see, the very existence of such an event is, to say the least, highly problematical. Similarly, most scholars have, until very recently, taken it for granted that Perses bribed the βασιλῆες who presided over the case.[14] There is no hard evidence to support this allegation in the crude direct sense, and the whole concept of "gift-eating" in Hesiod needs to be modified in the light of modern anthropological parallels, mostly from Greece itself (see below, pp. 53–54). Can we even be sure, as Minna Jensen pertinently enquired,[15] which of the two brothers was the injured party, let alone which of them initiated litigation?[16] Walcot, in

---

Convegno, Pisa, 16–17 May 1991 (Pisa, 1993), 41–72; but his postulation (70–71) of "[l]'inscription de la prédication hésiodique dans le cadre fictif d'un *neikos* entre Hésiode et Persès" takes a fundamentally different approach from that pursued here. In the same volume, Glenn W. Most's article "Hesiod and the Textualization of Personal Temporality," 73–92, is mainly of value for its arguments establishing the *Works and Days* as later than the *Theogony*.

10. E.g., Rzach in PWK vol. 8, col. 1171; K. von Fritz, *Hésiode et son influence, Entretiens de la Fondation Hardt* 7 (Geneva, 1962), 29 ("Die Dichtung selbst sollte ihm die Waffen liefern, den Bruder und die Könige doch noch auf den Weg der Gerechtigkeit zu bringen"; Wade-Gery 1949, 90; contra, e.g., Østerud 1976, 17 n. 13.

11. E.g., by Mazon 1914, 45; Gagarin 1974, 106–7; Wilamowitz (1928) on *WD* 34 ("Einmal hat das νεῖκος des Perses gegenüber Hesiod Erfolg gehabt"); Van Groningen 1957, 155; other instances collected by Latimer 1930, 72–73 with n. 10; Latimer himself (76–77) is properly skeptical on the issue.

12. Mazon 1914 and Wilamowitz 1928, locc. citt.; Bonner and Smith 1939, 1:46; Sinclair 1932, (with some characteristic hedging); H. Diller, "Die dicterische Form von Hesiods Erga," *Akad. Wiss. u. Lit. Mainz* 2 (1962): 41–69, repr. *Hesiod Wege der Forschung*, vol. 44, (Darmstadt, 1966), 239–73; see esp. 247 n. 16. Cf. Van Groningen 1957, 153 n. 1.

13. Van Groningen 1957, 164–65 (though earlier, 155, he had written, "Comment le premier procès s'est-il terminé? Impossible d'en dire quoi que ce soit avec certitude"); followed by Gagarin 1974, 104, 106 n. 9 (with the same hedging as Van Groningen).

14. As Gagarin points out (1974, 109–10, with n. 19), he and Van Groningen (1957, 157–58) are the only scholars who have seriously challenged the notion that what Hesiod is describing is indictable corruption (rather than a legitimate, if excessive, passion for court fees). The common view is exemplified by Jula Kerschensteiner, "Zu Aufbau und Gedankenführung von Hesiods Erga," *Hermes* 79 (1944): 156: "Nicht zum *zweitenmal* darf er [Perses] hoffen, die *habgierigen* Könige so *bestechen*" (italics mine).

15. Jensen 1966 [1969], 10.

16. It is most often assumed that Perses originated the suit, but Latimer (1930, 77) and Forbes

Hesiod and the Near East (1966, 106), argues bleakly that "we do not know as yet, and probably never shall know, whether the pair of brothers quarrelled once or twice, or if their dispute ever reached a court of law." Both Jensen and Walcot seem to me a trifle over-pessimistic. I would like to approach the problem in two stages: first, by scrutinizing Hesiod's text, to determine what he actually does and does not say—as opposed to the statements more or less loosely attributed to him; and second, to consider the *dramatic setting* of *WD* 1–285, the context in which we, as readers or listeners, are to think of the poem as being delivered.

At the close of this initial appeal to Zeus (*WD* 1–10), Hesiod, with a certain imperative familiarity, delimits their respective spheres of activity. Zeus's job is to keep straight (ἴθυνε) the judgments (θέμιστας) handed down by the βασιλῆες,[17] to ensure that they are consonant with δίκη. The poet's own business is to expound home-truths to Perses (ἐτήτυμα μυθησαίμην). We are, it would seem, in for a λόγος παραινετικός, a hortatory argument, of the kind that Phoenix inflicted on Achilles.[18] Whether we read Πέρσῃ (dat.) or Πέρση (voc.) in line 10—and even that choice is not so clear-cut as, for example, West (1978, 142) would have us believe—Hesiod's addressee is introduced right at the beginning of the poem. On the other hand, he is not formally explained. We can infer (as no doubt the original audience did) that only relatives would quarrel over an inheritance (*WD* 37ff.); but it remains a fact that not until line 633 are we told, in so many words, that the two men are brothers.[19] The clear implication is that Hesiod's audience was assumed to be familiar with Perses and Hesiod and their differences already. On the other hand, to balance this withholding of background information, we observe that Perses himself, during the course of the poem, hears a good deal about his personal habits and family history, with which he must already be only too familiar.[20] Why is this? What assumptions led Hesiod to over-document his characters at one level, yet at another to fail to block in their most fundamental relationships?

We now come to the most crucial passage for any interpretation of the Hesiod-Perses debate: *WD* 27–39. It is not too much to say that the whole story of the quarrel, with its uncertain outcome and contested number of law-

---

(1950, 83) argue for Hesiod, who, Forbes observes, "corresponds most closely to the modern plaintiff." Cf. also Gagarin 1974, 111.

17. Though the βασιλῆες are not mentioned in this context, θέμιστες, like Anglo-Saxon "dooms," were essentially arbitrary, rulings that only they could pronounce: cf. Sinclair 1932, 2–3; West 1978, 141.

18. Cf. Østerud 1976, 16–17.

19. Well emphasized by Jensen 1966 [1969] 6.

20. As is correctly pointed out by West 1978, 33.

suits, rests fundamentally on these few lines. Hesiod urges Perses not to abandon work, spurred on by bad Eris, in favor of hanging about the agora for the purpose of watching, and listening to, νείκεα, litigation, disputes. A man in Perses' position, that is, a small farmer, would need to have a full year's supply of stores laid by (βίος . . . ἐπηετανός) to cover him through to the next harvest, before he could afford such self-indulgence.[21] It should be stressed that the kind of poverty envisaged throughout the *Works and Days* is always of this seasonal kind, the inability to survive between one harvest and the next: and though, as we know from the Solonian σεισάχθεια ("shaking off of burdens"), this misfortune could, ultimately, reduce the victim to serfdom, it is still thought of by Hesiod very much as a temporary fluctuating condition. Perses' poverty is never presented as absolute or irretrievable. More important, if the putative lawsuit has not yet taken place, charges of inconsistency in Perses' presentation—now rich, now poor—immediately vanish.[22]

"Only when you have your fill of βίος," Hesiod emphasizes, "can you promote disputes and conflict over other men's goods (κτήμασ᾽ ἐπ᾽ ἀλλοτρίοις)." The point he is making—no less familiar or applicable today than in antiquity—is that while litigation may be a source of profit to the wealthy, it costs the poor man, win or lose, time and money that he can ill afford.[23] Perses' role, as Hesiod presents it, is seen as more than that of a mere passive spectator: he is involved in the action (ὀφέλλοις), though to what extent is still uncertain. It could mean no more than the shouting of partisan comments or advice (see below, p. 61). There now follows (line 35) a surprising statement: "But you won't get a second chance to act thus" (σοὶ δ᾽ οὐκέτι δεύτερον ἔσται ὧδ᾽ ἔρδειν). To act how? And when are we to place the first action? One point is clear, and should not be fudged: δεύτερον can *only* mean "second," and not, in a loose sense, "further" or "later," a meaning badly needed by those who believe in an earlier trial: if the present altercation is the brothers' second, then Hesiod must be warning Perses that he will not get a *third* chance.[24] But

21. The situation is at once recognizable as that confronting many of the smallholders in Attica prior to Solon's reforms. See Arist. *Ath. Pol.* 2, 5–6; Plut. *Sol.* 13–14; and the excellent discussion in French 1967, ch. 2, "The Breakdown of the Old Order," esp. 12–13.

22. This at once answers some of the objections raised by West 1978, 35–40; cf. also E. A. Havelock, "Thoughtful Hesiod," *YClS* 20 (1966): 61–72.

23. Gagarin 1990, 176.

24. Gagarin 1974, 107 with n. 10, correctly opposing Krafft (89 n. 4, as in note 7 above), who argues for a meaning such as *weiterhin* or *später*. I do not, however, agree with Gagarin's attempt to reconcile this finding with the existence of an earlier trial by treating the present dispute "as part of one long dispute which includes the earlier one." Van Groningen claims (1957, 155) that Hesiod is telling Perses that the latter will not be able to bring *this second case*, a desperate resort at odds with all the known facts of the poem.

if Hesiod unequivocally says "second," and if ὦδ' ἔρδειν is taken as "bring suit against me," which Perses is in the process of doing, then the conclusion is inescapable: there was no prior litigation. As we shall see, such a hypothesis is perfectly consistent with Hesiod's text.

At first sight, it might be thought that the undesirable activity that Perses is admonished not to repeat is his time-wasting habit of watching, or taking part in, disputes in the agora, of encouraging strife over other (unnamed) men's goods. But a moment's thought shows that this is impossible. Such behavior is repetitive and habitual; what Hesiod objects to is something that has happened once only, and that (in his opinion) Perses will not be able to attempt *a second time*. It must, then, have a personal and specific application. In the lines that follow, the ongoing dispute between the brothers begins to emerge, and we see it is to this that ὦδ' ἔρδειν must refer.[25] Once again, Hesiod has assumed prior knowledge of the facts in his audience. The meaning is now clear. The present case coming up for arbitration is a kill-or-cure attempt, on Perses' part, to secure a greater share of his father's legacy. He has not hitherto resorted to the law — that Perses is the plaintiff emerges clearly from this passage: ἔρδειν implies positive action — and he will not, in his brother's opinion, get a second opportunity to do so. Once the case is decided, that is, he will not be able to repeat it. What basis could Hesiod have had for so confident an assertion? Gagarin has argued that the cost of bringing suit would effectively have ruined Perses, and this is possible; but surely a more immediate and obvious cause would have lain in the verdict itself. Since their θέμιστες were binding, any ruling handed down by the βασιλῆες would preclude further appeals on the same issue.[26]

Hesiod now invites Perses to come to a private agreement with him. "Let us settle our dispute for ourselves, here and now, with Zeus's straight judgments, the best." διακρινώμεθα, as Gagarin rightly saw,[27] must be taken in the reflexive sense; it is not a causative middle. This reading is confirmed by the sense of the passage as a whole. Hesiod prefers the sure workings of divine law (a point stressed throughout the *Works and Days*) to the fallible judgments of men.[28] αὖθι, as the majority of scholars are agreed,[29] must mean "here and

---

25. West (1978, 150) duly notes this inconsistency, but without drawing any significant conclusion from it.

26. Gagarin 1974, 111. On the principle of binding "obligatory arbitration," see Bonner and Smith 1939, 1:47–48; cf. West 1966, 184. On Perses as plaintiff, see Jensen 1966 [1969], 7–8; cf. A. Kirchhoff, *Hesiodos' Mahalieder an Perses* (Berlin, 1889), 40–41.

27. Gagarin 1974, 107.

28. A point well made by Van Groningen 1957, 156: "A l'appui de son point de vue Hésiode ne fait pas appel à la juridiction toujours faillible, telle qu'elle s'exerce dans les tribunaux, mais à la loi divine que même un auditoire non spécialisé comprend et accepte. Le poème tout entier est un

now." But even if we choose to take it in the (nonepic) sense of "again," that does not imply a previous lawsuit: in fact, quite the reverse. The estate, Hesiod reminds his brother, was divided between them the first time (ἤδη μὲν γὰρ κλῆρον ἐδασσάμεθ') without any hint of litigation. Why not repeat so eminently sensible a procedure?

We may assume that the original division was an equal one, at least as regards land, and perhaps was carried out by lot: ancient and modern customs in this respect seem to be very similar.[30] Even if Hesiod was the elder son, as has been ingeniously argued,[31] there was no right of primogeniture. What is more than likely is that the estate at issue was too small to be split in two and still allow each half to remain economically viable. Greek farms were, and are, minuscule, so that repeated divisions among heirs have always tended to reduce holdings to a size where they can no longer be worked: the problem confronting Hesiod—and Solon after him—remains endemic, even today. In the famous autobiographical passage describing their father's settling at Ascra (*WD* 631–40), Hesiod shows scant respect, and more than a little resentment, for his patrimony. His recommendation that there should be no more than one heir to a farm (376–78) is surely based on bitter personal experience. To be childless was, and is, an unmitigated disaster in Greece (e.g., Hom. *Il.* 9.453–56: *WD* 244, 284, 325–26); to have only one son was, for Homer, a curse rather than a blessing (*Il.* 24.538–40). (But then Homer was dealing with warriors, not farmers.) Equally reprehensible, on the other hand, is a failure to provide adequate living standards and material well-being for one's children after one. In straitened circumstances, the two principles will come into conflict, and the single male heir Hesiod recommends must be seen as the lesser of two evils for a struggling farmer. "That way wealth *piles up*," he says. "If you leave a second son, you need to die old," that is, it will take you proportionately longer to build up the capital, acquire the extra land, and establish the holdings necessary to provide for both of them.[32] It may also help to outlive any other relatives who might enter a claim on all or part of the estate.

exposé de ses dispositions de Zeus relative à l'existence humaine: il exige avant tout travail assidu et honnêteté scrupuleuse. Si Persès se soumet à ces règles et à tout ce qui en dérive, l'accord entre les deux frères sera retabli sans qu'un nouveau procès puisse encore être desiré par l'un des deux."

29. See, e.g., the conspectus in Latimer 1930, 72 n. 8; Sinclair 1932, 6; and (with some hedging) West 1978, 150. Paley (1883, 11) argued that "it is very doubtful if it can bear this sense."

30. Walcot 1970, 46–50, with further references. Contra, Gagarin 1974, 107 n. 12. For ancient instances of division by lot, see, e.g., Hom. *Od.* 14.199ff., 11.15.187–89; Dem. 48.12–13.

31. P. Walcot, "A Note on the Biography of Hesiod," *CPh* 55 (1960): 33–34, equates Hesiod with the "good Eris"; it would be improbable, he argues, "that Hesiod would claim priority of birth for the good Eris without being the older brother himself." Cf. Van Groningen 1957, 165.

32. On primogeniture, see Latimer 1930, 70–71; this is also the clear implication of *WD* 376–78. The largest Attic farm on record, even, in the classical period, is that of Alcibiades, about 70

It was, then, predictable that the division of their father's patrimony would lead to trouble between Hesiod and Perses. The most likely source of conflict, to judge from parallel cases, would be the house. Hesiod proceeds at once to tell his audience, while ostensibly addressing Perses, the background of their dispute. "For we'd already divided the estate"—no hint of litigation there, merely the implication that that should have settled the matter—"and [yet] many other things you kept trying to carry off by force, while greatly honoring [or perhaps 'giving great pleasure with your attentions to': see L-S-J s.v. κυδαίνω II] the gift-eating barons[33] who are ready to give judgment in this case." ἀλλά τε πολλά stands in sharp contrast to the κλῆρος: the phrase implies removable property such as tools, farm equipment, or household furniture.[34] Though Hesiod and Perses may have argued over the house and property boundaries (cf. the simile drawn by Homer, Il. 12.421-23), we should note that Hesiod does not say so. Indeed, the word ἐφόρεις is hardly one to use of such a disagreement. Houses and land stay where they are; only chattels are transportable. The force of κυδαίνων is temporal rather than causal, while the imperfect ἐφόρεις is surely conative:[35] Perses' attempts to remove disputed property take place concurrently with his careful cultivation of the barons, and the most we can infer about the latter is that it was designed to win their support or approval. We can only guess at what form it took. Van Groningen (1957, 157) argues that it was by assiduous attendance at meetings of the βασιλῆες, by loud approbation, by forming part of a voluntary claque. But the βασιλῆες are described as "gift-eating" (δωροφάγους). This need not per se imply gross corruption, since judges and arbitrators regularly took fees to settle disputes; nor is κυδαίνω ever found elsewhere in a pejorative context, meaning to bribe or flatter, but always in the sense of conferring honor or pleasure on the recipient.[36]

---

acres (French 1964, 181 n. 13), a size that still leaves little scope for further subdivision. On the size of farms in modern Greece, and their subdivision through inheritance, see A. N. Damaskenides, *Balkan Studies* 6 (1965): 25-28, and I. T. Sanders, *Rainbow in the Rock: The People of Rural Greece* (Cambridge, Mass., 1962), 60; cf. du Boulay 1974, 28, and esp. appendix 2, "Land Tenure," 265-73. For other recommendations in favor of leaving single heirs in ancient Greece, see West 1978, 251-52. I do not (as should be clear from my translation) subscribe to the theory (supported by West) that what Hesiod means by ἕτερον παῖδα is a grandchild. For the obligation to provide for one's heirs at all costs, see, e.g., Plato *Rep.* 2.372b; du Boulay 1974, 139-40; and E. Friedl, *Vasilika: A Village in Modern Greece* (New York, 1967), 18.

33. Not "kings" in our sense, but local landed aristocrats: "princes" or "barons" would be a very loose equivalent. Diodorus (4.9.24) tells us that Thespiae was governed by a group of seven δημοῦχοι who were, clearly, the later successors of these βασιλῆες.

34. Gagarin 1974, 107 n. 12 with ref.

35. Van Groningen 1957, 156; Gagarin 1974, 107-8.

36. Gagarin 1974, 109-10 with nn. 19 and 20; cf, Van Groningen 1957, 157.

Yet Hesiod is assuredly not being complimentary: the contrast with *Theogony* 84–92 alone would suffice to prove that. The βασιλῆες are, if not corrupt, at the very least rapacious. Even if they perform all the duties outlined in the *Theogony*, effecting restitution for the injured, resolving disputes, handing down straight judgments (all of which here is very much in question), they exact a stiff price for the privilege. We should also, of course, make allowance for the fact that, at all periods of Greek history, officials are invariably assumed (whether justifiably or not is another matter) to be corrupt by definition. The modern Sarakatsani refer to them as φαγάδες, "eaters," an epithet surprisingly close to Hesiod's δωροφάγοι, and gifts are regularly offered to them in the (often illusory) hope of favorable treatment. One gift or service is held to require another in return, a system that runs flatly counter to the nontribal concept of public administration. Like Hesiod, who elsewhere claimed that gifts persuade gods and kings alike (fr. 361 Merkelbach-West: the implication is that these two categories are harder to move than ordinary mortals), the modern Greek is convinced that his *douceurs* work: yet in fact Greek judges are no more bribable than those of other countries. It is the belief that counts.[37] If there is a causal sequence in lines 38–39, it is that the barons' *willingness* to give judgment in the present suit (τήνδε δίκην) may have been increased by Perses' previous cultivation of them. Yet this would scarcely be logical: to judge by *Theog.* 84ff., settling disputes was part of their accepted duty. Perhaps Hesiod is merely hinting, with the epithet δωροφάγους, that their appetite for the task has been whetted by the payment of substantial court fees.

Did Perses have any other kind of influence with the local aristocracy? We cannot be certain, but Hesiod's ironic description of his brother (*WD* 299) as δῖον γένος, "illustrious-born," in a context that suggests that Perses regarded status as an adequate substitute for hard work, at least gives one pause for thought. From the famous biographical passage concerning their father (631–40), it is clear that Perses' own pedigree was, at best, *déclassé*, and in all likelihood far from illustrious. (βίου κεχρημένος ἐσθλοῦ is a socially ambiguous phrase: "The life of a noble" or "good living"? Prestige or wealth? The dream of an ambitious outsider, or the nostalgia of a gentleman who'd been reduced to trade?) Could he have acquired status in his own eyes through marriage? There is something very personal about Hesiod's description of the γυνὴ πυγοστόλος, "prinking her butt," who is only out to get her hands on Perses' granary (373–74). We can trace a clear link between this woman and

---

37. For evidence of rapacity, cf. West 1978, 151; Jensen 1966 [1969], 9. For the widespread and perennial assumption of venality in public officials, see Walcot 1970, 102ff., cf. 80–81. The Sarakatsani on φαγάδες: Campbell 1964, 257.

the *Works and Days* version of Pandora, with her "bitch's mind and thievish nature" (κύνεόν τε νόον καὶ ἐπίκλοπον ἦθος, 78), who is fobbed off, in this version of the story (cf. *Theog.* 511–14), on the more foolish of two brothers, Epimetheus (83–89). It is hard not to infer that Hesiod's argument here must have been at least in part *ad hominem*, with himself in the admonitory Promethean role. Was it also *ad feminam?* At line 80 we find Pandora described, very oddly for narrative (so, rightly, West 1978, 164, on *WD* 80) as τήνδε γυναῖκα. The force is demonstrative, deictic; indeed, it is almost as though Hesiod were pointing at someone (I shall return to the significance of this phrase later). It is tempting, if wholly speculative, to argue that Perses had married an aristocratic lady from Thespiae with expensive tastes, a forerunner of Strepsiades' very similar *mésalliance* in *The Clouds* (41ff.). If this was how the now-impoverished Perses had wasted his time and substance, much of Hesiod's admonition (e.g., 27ff., 60–89, 94–95, 195–96, 235, 299–300, 356, 373–75, ?586, 695–705) acquires extra point and edge.

A great deal of inconclusive discussion has taken place over the precise meaning of the words οἳ τήνδε δίκην ἐθέλουσι δικάσσαι—mostly in *parti pris* attempts to make them fit a preconceived interpretation of what is going on. We sense, as so often, the ghost of that nonexistent first trial in the fact that so many scholars have, against the evident natural sense of the phrase in context, wanted τήνδε δίκην to mean "a suit *of this kind.*"[38] Schoemann, indeed, not only insisted that τήνδε δίκην referred to the first trial, but emended ἐθέλουσι δικάσσαι to ἐθέλοντι δίκασσαν in order to give his perverse reading a more plausible time-sequence.[39] Another line of approach is the assertion that τήνδε δικάσσαι can *only* mean "to pronounce a verdict," and that the phrase therefore means "who see fit to make this [but what?] their judgment." ἐθέλουσι thus has to lose all future sense and merely emphasize the "voluntary nature of their actions."[40] The trouble with this is that the βασιλῆες have not so far, except in the speculative minds of scholars, delivered a specific judgment of any sort apropos Perses' case: they are ready to (ἐθέλουσι), but that is all. Those commentators from Proclus to Wilamowitz (who, nevertheless, believed in a first trial), as well as Jensen, and now Gagarin,[41] who take τήνδε δίκην in its natural demonstrative sense and translate "are ready to give judg-

---

38. E.g., Paley 1883, 11; Sinclair 1932, 6; Mazon (Budé ed., 1928) translates "toujours prêts à juger suivant telle justice," and Evelyn-White (Loeb ed., 1914), "who love to judge such a cause as this."

39. Schoemann 1869, well disposed of by Mazon 1914, 47.

40. West 1978, 152.

41. West, ibid.; Wilamowitz 1928, 46; Jensen 1966 [1969], 7; Gagarin 1974, 107–8.

ment in this [present] case," have both common sense and syntax on their side. The semantic flexibility of the word δίκη in Hesiod has been well analyzed by both Van Groningen and Gagarin,[42] and their findings make the kind of straitjacketing that West proposes as unnecessary as it is inapposite.

Once we accept the fact that the whole notion of an earlier lawsuit is a mere scholarly chimaera, and that τήνδε δίκην, not merely in line 39, but also at 249 and 269, bears a specific reference to the case presented as pending,[43] two conclusions emerge. The first is that most of the supposed inconsistencies in Perses' actions (well summarized by West 1978, 33ff.) vanish into that limbo to which they should have been consigned long ago. In particular, we do not have to cope with the problem of a Perses who, at irregular and illogical intervals during the poem, is alternately rich and poor, but rather one who is poor, and feckless, throughout: what capital he had has already been either wasted or committed to litigation. Perses never got the lion's share of the estate at arbitration: that myth depends on Cuyet's emendation, at line 37, of ἄλλά τε πολλά to ἀλλὰ τὰ πολλά.[44] In fact, he never previously went to arbitration at all, and has so far got nothing out of the βασιλῆες: on the contrary, *he* seems to have invested quite a lot in *them*. Even his efforts to carry off bits of moveable property from his brother would seem to have been unsuccessful, or at best inconclusive: the imperfect ἐφόρεις is revealing. We are not even told, in so many words, whether he is disputing the division of the κλῆρος itself. Rather than the successful sharp crook of tradition, he begins to sound both pathetic and ineffectual, perhaps even a man with a genuine grievance.

What we *do* know is that, within the dramatic context of the poem, he is in the process of bringing suit against Hesiod, but that the case—his first and only one—has not yet been determined. Perses' financial status is shown to be precarious. He is certainly in debt (404, 647), and there may even be the possibility of someone buying his κλῆρος (341). He should stop going begging to neighbors—"as so recently you came to me," Hesiod says, adding that Perses

---

42. Van Groningen 1957, 159–60 n. 22; Gagarin 1973, passim, and 1990, 177, where he remarks: "Hesiod's *dikē* also exhibits a certain ambiguity. In the *Works and Days* he strongly supports justice and criticizes litigants and judges who corrupt it, but at the same time he recognizes that justice requires time and can thus be harmful to the interests of a poor man. He can also conceive of the possibility (270–73) that a just (*dikaios*) man may not benefit from justice (*dikē*): indeed, from his point of view this may have happened or be about to happen in his dispute with Perses."

43. Contra Van Groningen 1957, 162, who argues that here, "Hésiode parle non pas comme un homme qui pourrait être engagé, bon gré mal gré, dans un procès privé, mais en prophète, en moraliste, en défenseur des principes sur lesquels doit se baser la vie commune de la cité." I see no reason why Hesiod should not choose to make his general point through the specific instance.

44. Among modern editors and translators accepted only, to the best of my knowledge, by Evelyn-White, but still influential (I suspect) at a subliminal level.

can expect no further handouts, and should do an honest day's work instead if he wants to avoid starvation.[45] With regard to the suit itself, Perses is pointedly warned against perjury:[46] this must mean that at the hearing he would have an opportunity to testify on oath, presumably regarding his father's alleged (verbal?) disposition of family property, and this solemn oath might well be regarded as conclusive by his judges.[47] Goods, Hesiod reminds his brother, are not to be snatched (ἁρπακτά) or pirated by a clever tongue (ἀπὸ γλώσσης ληίσσεται, 320ff.). Similarly, the βασιλῆες themselves are urged to think over the case carefully (248–49) and avoid "crooked judgments" (250, cf. 225–26, 263–64), since these are not only observed by the gods (249–51, 267ff.), but also liable to possible retribution from the δῆμος (260–62).

The picture is now clear and consistent. Two brothers have, some while ago, divided an inheritance. One of them, Perses, impecunious and improvident (we should always remember, however, that it is Hesiod's account of events that we possess; Perses' side of the story might have been very different), regards this division as in some way unfair. After unsuccessful private attempts to alter the balance in his favor, and an investment of some sort in cultivating the βασιλῆες of Thespiae, who hold jurisdiction over property disputes, he has taken his case to arbitration. What we have in lines 1–285 of the *Works and Days* is a poetic evocation by his brother Hesiod of events either at the hearing itself, or immediately before it, or both: a dramatic reconstruction of a public difference that had deeply affected them, and still formed a talking-point long afterward. This is the second conclusion that emerges from, among other things, that telltale phrase τήνδε δίκην, and it suggests that we would do well to scrutinize not only the dramatic circumstances that Hesiod presupposes, but also the audience to whom he is addressing himself. For the purposes of this stage of our enquiry, the biographical truth of the subject-matter becomes irrelevant, and the entire story that Hesiod tells or implies can be treated as a fictional construct.

On account of the didactic or paraenetic label so regularly attached to the *Works and Days*,[48] its strikingly immediate *dramatic* qualities tend to be overlooked. Hesiod himself is too often treated as a mere quasi-autobiographical

---

45. *WD* 274–81, 298–301, cf. 397ff., 363–67, 404, 646–47; 394–97.

46. *WD* 219, 282–84, cf. 190–94, 803–4.

47. Forbes 1950, 85ff., citing the case of Antilochus (Hom. *Il.* 23.573ff.), who refused to take an oath rather than perjure himself in such a case; cf. Jensen 1966 [1969], 9–10.

48. See, e.g., Østerud 1976, 16–17; Puelma 1972, 88; F. Dornseiff, "Hesiods Werke und Tage und das alte Morgenland," *Philol.* 89 (1934): 397–415 (repr. *Wege der Forschung*, vol. 44 [Darmstadt, 1966], 131–50), and, most recently, West 1978, 3ff., who—developing Dornseiff's position—sets the poem in the comparative context of Near Eastern admonitory wisdom literature.

literary sage, handing out good advice from whatever the eighth-century equivalent of a study may have been. Yet a dramatic *persona* that we can similarly call "Hesiod" is very much present throughout the first 285 lines of the *Works and Days*—and indeed, with certain modifications, thereafter. The poem, in short, is not simply a παραινετικὸς λόγος; it is also a *dramatic monologue*, in the sense that Browning's "Fra Lippo Lippi" may be so described. Almost no one has appreciated this crucial point, let alone worked out its full implications. Wade-Gery took a step in the right direction: he observed, correctly, that in *WD* 1–285 the crisis (i.e., the lawsuit) is thought of as still being to come (though Hesiod must have gone on working at the poem long after the crisis itself had been resolved), and saw the origin of this section of the *Works and Days* in what he termed "agitation poems," recited while Hesiod was stumping the countryside to whip up support for his cause.[49] (It should, of course, be emphasized at this point that we do not know, and cannot tell, what Hesiod actually said *at the time:* how he went about defending his position, the actual language he employed before the βασιλῆες, and so on. All we have is his artistic reworking and dramatization of the event in retrospect, so that questions of literalism—for example, would a forensic speech, even c. 700 B.C., have been couched in dactylic hexameters?—become irrelevant. A more useful parallel, from a later period, is Thucydides' approach to his speeches: as there, we can only guess at the *degree* of verisimilitude, though it seems a fair assumption that *l'esprit de l'escalier* will have played its part in Hesiod's presentation.)

Only Forbes and Jensen come near the heart of the matter, by identifying both the dramatic nature and the dramatic setting of Hesiod's monologue;[50] and even they fail to pursue this striking insight to its logical conclusion, or to analyze Hesiod's text in the light of their findings to an adequate degree. Nor do they appear to have had any effect on subsequent scholarship. West, for example, completely ignores this line of approach, though in fact it could have solved several problems that baffle him in his commentary.[51] "The scene," Forbes states correctly, "is the crowded ἀγορά . . . with the magnates

---

49. Wade-Gery 1949, 81–93, esp. 88–90.

50. Forbes 1950, 83; Jensen 1966 [1969], 6–8. The same idea appears to have struck Havelock in passing in *The Greek Concept of Justice* (Cambridge, Mass., 1978), 212, where he writes: "Is this the scenario present before Hesiod's eyes when he asserts that Zeus is actually 'looking down at *these* things' and 'has not failed to notice what kind of justice *this* is, that is being confined within the city'? Are the demonstrative adjectives pointing to the scene?" He does not, however, follow this lead any further.

51. See, e.g., his notes on *WD* 35 and 80, and his whole introductory section on Perses, West 1978, 33ff.

in their places and Hesiod and Perses before them." He also describes *WD* 1–285 as "a complete rhetorical unit, a forensic speech, representing Hesiod's appeal to the conscience of the people, the princes and Perses" (83). Jensen follows Forbes in detail: for her, too, the scene is the *agora*, and the opening section of the *Works and Days* forms "the speech for the defence in an action brought against the poet by his brother Perses" (8). She also (6–7) isolates the force of αὖθι ("here and now") at line 35, and of the -δε demonstrative in such phrases as ὧδ᾽ ἔρδειν (35), τήνδε δίκην (39, 249, 269), or τάδε (268), the "goings-on"—actually in court, there in the speaker's presence—that the eye of Zeus, Διὸς ὀφθαλμός, observes. To these instances we can, of course, add many more. Demonstratives may suggest a dramatic pointing finger: τήνδε γυναῖκα at line 80 is said of the Pandora foisted off on poor gullible Epimetheus, but are we not also meant to imagine Hesiod looking hard at Perses' wife? Similarly with the appeal to Zeus at 9–10, the promise to tell Perses some home-truths, the direct apostrophes aimed at his opponent (e.g., 27–29, 213ff.), and, of course, those assumptions of knowledge on the part of his audience that I mentioned earlier—assumptions that have so unnecessarily bothered commentators. In a dramatic monologue, clearly, the audience must be well aware of the relationship between the two protagonists; no need to explain that Hesiod and Perses are brothers. At the same time, since what is being dramatized is a court case, a brief *résumé* of the facts, however familiar these may have been to the principals, becomes essential (37–39). Forbes and Jensen are, I think, over-strict in viewing the entire 285 lines simply as a forensic speech and nothing else; Hesiod is more flexible and digressive than that, and the poem as we have it has clearly been worked on and added to over a long period. But their central point is of fundamental importance.

I would, finally, like to develop further a point that Forbes only touches on in a phrase, and that is the identity of Hesiod's dramatic audience. The βασιλῆες and Perses, being apostrophized directly, are obvious components. But Forbes also mentions, in passing, "the conscience of the people," and here, it seems to me, he isolates a crucial dramatic element in the poem that has gone virtually unregarded. The spectators who, like Perses himself, made a habit of sitting in on these public hearings took a vigorous, and frequently vociferous, part in the proceedings. We at once recall the scene on the Shield of Achilles (*Il.* 18.487–508), where such a case draws a huge crowd (cf. *Theog.* 84–86), members of which yell advice and encouragement to whichever of the contestants they favor (ἀμφοτέροισιν ἐπήπυον, ἀμφὶς ἀρωγοί), and actually have to be held back by heralds (*Il.* 18.503) from physical intervention. The crowd is a key factor in any Greek lawsuit: its encouragement is worth getting, its censure is to be feared. When Hesiod dramatized the litigation in which he had been involved, I cannot believe that he ignored so integral a part of his experience, even if its remembered impact emerges only in a tone, an attitude, a series of appeals to shadowy and unspecified listeners.

This, then, is Hesiod's silent and invisible audience in the *Works and Days:* vocal enough in life, very much present at public hearings, a functional element taken for granted by Hesiod and those who listened to his poem at the time. Whenever Hesiod is not specifically addressing Perses or the barons, it is the crowd, the πληθύς in the agora, to whom his arguments are directed, and who—we need not doubt—could make their views on "crooked justice" uncomfortably clear. Thersites in the *Iliad* has the ring of contemporary truth about him; whether in Ionia or Boeotia, he is unlikely to have been an isolated phenomenon. Even passages such as 27–39 (to Perses) and 248ff. (to the βασιλῆες) are composed, dramatically speaking, with one eye to the effect that they will have on the bystanders. The repeated attacks on crooked judgments, gift-eating, or perjury, sometimes aimed directly at those sitting in judgment on the case (248–51, 262–64, 279–80, cf. 190–94, 225–27), make far more sense if they are seen as dramatic attempts to win the sympathy of the crown, the λαοὶ ἀθρώοι filling the agora. νέμεσις, public disapproval, was a force to be reckoned with in Homeric or Hesiodic society, as indeed in that of modern Greece.[52] If the wise man took care to get the crowd behind him, he also, whenever possible, exploited public feeling to discredit his opponents. Hesiod in the *Works and Days* does both. In his dramatization he was drawing upon a universally accepted, and familiar, tradition. This is nowhere more apparent than in his notorious, and puzzling, αἶνος addressed to the βασιλῆες, the fable of the Hawk and the Nightingale (202–12). Forbes's claim (1950, 84) that by lines 248–69 Hesiod "evidently feels the support of the crowd behind him" is correct: on the other hand, his assertion that until then Hesiod has handled the princes "rather lightly and circumspectly" cannot be sustained. The αἶνος itself forms its most telling refutation, and, properly interpreted, shows how the crowd's support was won.

Before embarking on his fable, Hesiod has expatiated at some length (174–201) on the almost unrelieved horrors of the present Iron Age in which men are living: an era of toil and stress, of collapsing social and familial values, of might-is-right ethics, perjury, blackmail, and "crooked accusations" (μύθοισι

---

52. Forbes 1950, 84: "We tend to underrate the power of opinion in early society." For νέμεσις, see, e.g., Hom. *Il.* 6.351, 13.121f., and Dodds 1951, ch. 1 ("Agamemnon's Apology"). For the force of public opinion in modern rural Greece, see Campbell 1964, 190, 197–98, 201–3, 307–10, 312–15; and du Boulay 1974, 73, 81–84, 108–9.

σκολιοῖς). The most he will concede is that "some good will yet be mixed with these evils" (179). He then narrates his fable, and when it is over, turns to Perses. "Perses," he exhorts him (213 f.), "*you* pay attention to δίκη, do not promote ὕβρις." The reason is clear: δίκη wins against ὕβρις in the end (ἐς τέλος ἐξελθοῦσα, 218). Those who act according to the dictates of δίκη lead happy lives (225–27), while divine retribution awaits the perverters of justice (248–51, 260–64, 267–75). Above all, Zeus has made the gift of δίκη that which distinguishes men from the jungle world of bird, beast, and fish (276–81): δίκη, in short, must be the good element that is mixed in with the bad for men of the Iron Age, the principle that can save them. Between these two striking passages—the jeremiad on current ills, and the isolation of δίκη as the one solution to such ills—Hesiod sets his short fable. It could scarcely be more prominent, and we can assume that this was no accident.

> Νῦν δ' αἶνον βασιλεῦσ' ἐρέω φρονέουσι καὶ αὐτοῖς·
> ὧδ' ἴρηξ προσέειπεν ἀηδόνα ποικιλόδειρον,
> ὕψι μαλ' ἐν νεφέεσσι φέρων, ὀνύχεσσι μεμάρπως·
> ἡ δ' ἐλεόν, γναμπτοῖσι πεπαρμένη ἀμφ' ὀνύχεσσιν,
> μύρετο· τὴν δ' ὅ γ' ἐπικράτεως πρὸς μῦθον ἔειπεν·
>   "δαιμονίη, τί λέληκας; ἔχει νύ σε πολλὸν ἀρείων·
> τῇ δ' εἶς ᾗ σ' ἂν ἐγώ περ ἄγω καὶ ἀοιδὸν ἐοῦσαν·
> δεῖπνον δ' αἴ κ' ἐθέλω ποιήσομαι ἠὲ μεθήσω.
> ἄφρων δ' ὅς κ' ἐθέλῃ πρὸς κρείσσονας ἀντιφερίζειν·
> νίκης τε στέρεται πρός τ' αἴσχεσιν ἄλγεα πάσχει."
>   (*WD* 202–11)

Now I'll tell you a tale for the princes: they understand it.
Thus spoke the hawk to the speckle-necked nightingale
as he carried her high in the clouds, firm-clipped in his talons,
while she, impaled on those hooked claws, kept wailing
pitiably, till he addressed her in his bullying manner:
"Wretched creature, why scream? One better by far has got you.
You'll go wherever I take you, songstress though you are.
The choice is mine: I can eat you for dinner, or free you.
Witless that man who goes head to head with the stronger:
He loses his fight, and is damaged as well as shamed."

The immediate message, considered *in vacuo*, is a morally depressing piece of cynical *Machtpolitik* that confirms all the worst of the Iron Age troubles, particularly those concerning χειροδίκαι, the might-is-right people, and the notion of δίκη subsisting merely "in [one's] hands," ἐν χερσί (190–94). The nightingale, though a singer (καὶ ἀοιδὸν ἐοῦσαν), is no match for the hawk: how, one wonders, could singing ever be presumed to arm one against a predator? (This, as we shall see, is to commit the cardinal error of thinking in hawk terms.) It is the hawk, in this fable, who bangs the moral home, with a brutal little speech on the realities of power (207-11) that puts one in mind of the Athenians on Melos or of Callicles in Plato's *Gorgias.*[53] This is in sharp contrast with a later fable in the *Aesopica* (Perry 1952, 567), where the hawk in turn falls victim to a fowler. As West says (1978, 205), "We find here what we miss in Hesiod, the subjection of the bad bird by another, higher power." Why should Hesiod introduce so bleakly pessimistic a motif at this point?

The situation is further confused by the fact that the nightingale *qua* singer, ἀοιδός, is naturally identified with Hesiod himself (so almost all commentators), and the hawk with the βασιλῆες.[54] Is Hesiod then representing himself as a helpless victim of the barons? Surely not:[55] the ἀοιδός of *Theog.* 79-97 stands equal in inspiration and authority to them, and Hesiod's tone here is one of grim self-assurance. Even so, at first sight it is hard to understand Wade-Gery's optimistic interpretation (1949, 91): "There have not been too many ages of the world when public opinion could really control governments. . . . From Hesiod through Solon to Aeschylus and Euripides, the Nightingale was a real power in Greek opinion and behaviour, and the Hawk had to listen." But, one protests, the hawk on this occasion does not listen at all; he has things very much his own way. It is only on further examination that we realize that Wade-Gery was, in fact, right, though perhaps not quite in the way he supposed.

The language, significantly, is that of a Homeric contest, ἀγών: as Puelma saw, Hesiod seems to be setting up the ἀοιδός as the proper source of true justice, in contradistinction to the false justice that he fears may be dispensed by the local βασιλῆες.[56] We have here a conflict of principle and of moral

---

53. See, e.g., Thuc. 5.105.2: ἡγούμεθα γὰρ τό τε θεῖον δόξῃ, τὸ ἀνθρώπειόν τε σαφῶς διὰ παντὸς ὑπὸ φύσεως ἀναγκαίας, οὗ ἂν κρατῇ, ἄρχειν; cf. Plat. *Gorg.* 890a, with Dodds's commentary ad loc.; also Thrasymachus in the *Republic*, 338b.

54. The most useful recent studies are those of L. W. Daly, "Hesiod's Fable," *TAPhA* 92 (1961): 45-51; Puelma 1972;, Østerud 1976, 21-23; Jensen 1966 [1969], 20-22 (though her identification of the hawk with Zeus—a view also advanced independently by C. B. Welles, *GRByS* 8 [1967]: 17-19—has, rightly, won few adherents), and Van Groningen 1957, 160-63.

55. So schol. 207-12 (Pertusi): τούτων δὲ τῶν στίχων ὁ Ἀρίσταρχος . . . ὀβελίζει τοὺς τελευταίους ὡς ἀλόγῳ γνωμολογεῖν οὐκ ἂν προσῆκον. Goettling (1843) and Rzach followed Aristarchus.

56. Puelma 1972, 97: "Der Sänger Hesiod als Volksredner des 'geraden Rechts' gegenüber den Richterkönigen als Sprechern der 'ungeraden Rechtssprüche'—diese Grundsituation des Gerechtigkeitsliedes der Erga (1-285) ist es offenbar, die sich in dem eigentümlich 'homerisch' obersteigerten Rivalitätsverhältnis von Habicht und Nachtigall der Fabel spiegelt."

authority. Yet we remember that in the *Theogony* (79–97), while ἀοιδοί may belong to the Muses and the βασιλῆες to Zeus, a good βασιλεύς is likewise inspired by the Muses (83, 93) to give "straight judgments" (86). He is, in short, the repository of oral tradition, of accumulated δίκαι. He remembers the oral laws. (Not for nothing were the Muses the daughters of Mnemosyne, Memory.) Hesiod's anxiety in the *Works and Days* seems to be that the βασιλῆες may abrogate their high responsibility—and who but the ἀοιδός can recall them to it? We should also remember that the *Theogony* was delivered before a predominantly noble audience (if, as seems very likely, it was the poem that won the prize at the funeral games of Amphidamas), whereas in the *Works and Days* it is the δῆμος that forms Hesiod's main audience; eulogy is thus predictable in the earlier work, but out of place here.[57]

The real stumbling-block for scholars has always been Hesiod's supposed endorsement of, or at least capitulation to, the hawk's attitude, in a poem that elsewhere consistently advocates the acceptance of Zeus's divine δίκη. It has even been suggested, as an awkward compromise, that Hesiod, while not positively condoning hawkishness, is simply pointing out the harsh facts of life.[58] But although such stoic resignation would be very much in line with archaic thought, Hesiod does not, in fact, endorse or condone the hawk's action at all: far from it.[59] The paradox, like the earlier court case, turns out to be a mere illusion. The hawk is the exemplar of an ideology diametrically opposed to that of the true ἀοιδός or βασιλεύς, an ideology that Hesiod is determined to pillory through exposure to public contempt. Once we accept the concept of the *Works and Days* as a dramatic monologue, not only does Hesiod's attitude become crystal clear, but the method he employs to drive it home likewise stares us in the face.

What in fact does he say? "Now I will tell you an αἶνος for the princes —*they* understand it (φρονέουσι καὶ αὐτοῖς)." Whom is Hesiod addressing here? Not, primarily, his readers, let alone modern critics. It is Hesiod's dramatic persona rather than Hesiod himself whom we now hear, making a bold bid for sympathy in the crowded agora. His words are aimed not so much at princes themselves as at the δῆμος, the crowd; he may be talking *about* those haughty aristocratic authoritarians, but not *to* them. Through his little fable he can show the hawkish βασιλῆες telling the unvarnished truth about the credo to which they privately subscribe, but prefer not to enunciate with quite such chilling clarity—just as modern political murderers are in the habit of talking

---

57. See Catharine P. Roth, "The Kings and the Muses in Hesiod's *Theogony*," *TAPhA* 106 (1976): 331–38; cf. West 1966, 44–45.
58. By V. A. Rodgers, "Some Thoughts on *ΔΙΚΗ*," *CQ* 21 (1971): 289–301, esp. 291.
59. So, rightly, Østerud 1976, 22.

about the "liquidation of undesirable elements." In symbolic yet transparent terms he is reminding the crowd (and, at one remove, all audiences whatsoever) of the attitude that such judges may be expected to take, of their moral assumptions about life and human relationships and the social order. "Witless that man," says the hawk, "who goes head to head with the stronger: he loses his fight, and is damaged as well as shamed." This is the very voice of the Penthelidae, the ruling aristocratic clan of Mytilene, whose idea of dealing with opponents was to club them into submission (Arist. *Pol.* 1311b25); it is Odysseus's instinctive response to a proletarian rabble-rouser like Thersites (Hom. *Il.* 2.243-77).[60]

But by Hesiod's day the tide was on the turn: the diffusion of a true, and easily mastered, alphabet, the increase of trade, the emergence of the hoplite phalanx, all tended to undercut privileged authority. The nightingale was finding a voice, and, more important, a power base; the recalcitrant hawk would indeed be forced to listen. Hesiod's audience has just heard this hawk tell his victim, the ἀηδών-ἀοιδός, the nightingale-singer, "You'll go wherever I take you, *songstress though you are*": the point is driven home past mistaking, what we are shown is violent ὕβρις committed against the sacrosanct mouthpiece of the Muses. Here, in person, are the χειροδίκαι, the privileged might-is-righters, against whom Hesiod had earlier delivered his general diatribe. The mass of the audience knows what it has to think.

It is at this precise point, with perfect dramatic control of the scene, that Hesiod turns to Perses (213)—we can almost see the theatrical gesture, the stabbing finger—and exclaims: ὦ Πέρση, σὺ δ' ἄκουε δίκης, "But Perses, *you* take heed of what's right." The emphasis, and its implications, are unmistakable. When, later (*WD* 248-64), he addresses the βασιλῆες directly, warning them of Zeus's "immortal guardians" (ἀθάνατοι . . . φύλακες) who observe mortal transgressions, exhorting them to abandon crooked judgments, to forego their diet of bribes, we know that they form a part, *but only a part*, of Hesiod's audience, and the force of his reproof becomes all the more effective through being delivered not only in public, but before a δῆμος, the larger part of which will have applauded such an attack. In this context the dramatic rhetoric becomes extraordinarily effective. The last thing Hesiod is doing is complaining alone, or in a literary void.

Thus what we have in *WD* 1-285 is the dramatic commemoration of a personal experience, important to Hesiod, and clearly of more than passing

---

60. *WD* 210-11: ἄφρων δ' ὅς κ' ἐθέλῃ πρὸς κρείσσονας ἀντιφερίζειν· | νίκης τε στέρεται πρός τ' αἴσχεσιν ἄλγεα πάσχει. For a very similar interpretation to that proposed here, see Marie-Christine Leclerc, "L'épervier et le rossignol d'Hésiode: Une fable à double sens," *REG* 105 (1992): 32-44.

interest to his local community. The poem, as he continued to work on it, acquired many other features, paraenetic or proverbial, and became, in the end, a holdall for various aspects of his philosophy of life. But the central impulse and core remain his conflict with Perses: that is fundamental. We are often reminded (to revert briefly to Walcot's objections, above, p. 50) that we do not know—which means that we are not specifically informed—whether Hesiod or Perses won the case, or indeed whether a trial was in fact held at all. From a dramatic viewpoint, as I have suggested, this makes little or no difference. At the same time, the whole tenor of the *Works and Days* supports a confident answer. That Hesiod based his poem on actual personal experience seems certain: the details are too circumstantial, too idiosyncratic, too *involved*, to suggest—especially c. 700 B.C.—a sophisticated fiction masquerading as truth. "We know how to tell many lies that resemble truth," the Muses indeed told Hesiod; but they also added, let us not forget, "but we also know how to utter truths when we so wish,"[61] and surely Hesiod's quarrel with his brother falls into the latter category. And if the case actually took place, that Hesiod won it can scarcely be open to doubt: as Jensen says, "If Hesiod's poem had not been successful we would hardly have had it today."[62] How far, if at all, parts of what we possess originally served—in whatever form—as a forensic plea before that tribunal in Thespiae we cannot tell, nor is it of great importance. What we do know, because we have the text before us, is how skillfully Hesiod recreated and dramatized this important event in his life—as important, in its own way, as his victory at the funeral games of Amphidamas—and how obstinately, for the most part, critics have refused to understand what he was about. I would like to think that in some small degree, after long sharing that blindness, I have helped to set the record straight: παθὼν δέ τε νήπιος ἔγνω.[63] Even a fool learns by experience.

---

61. *Theog.* 27-28: ἴδμεν ψεύδεα πολλὰ λέγειν ἐτύμοισιν ὁμοῖα, ǀ ἴδμεν δ' εὖτ' ἐθέλωμεν ἀληθέα γηρύσασθαι.

62. Jensen 1966 [1969], 10; cf. Forbes 1950, 85.

63. This essay has a long history. It was first delivered at a Classics Department colloquium in the University of Texas at Austin, and subsequently, in a revised and expanded version, before the Fellows of the Center for Hellenic Studies in Washington, D.C. An abbreviated summary of its conclusions was read in December 1980 at the annual meeting of the American Philological Association in New Orleans. The version published in 1984 benefited greatly from discussion and criticism on these various occasions. In the years that followed, I moved away from archaic poetry to other concerns. Retirement has given me the chance, now, to reconsider Hesiod. Though I have, I hope, taken adequate account of Hesiodic studies during the past decade, I find, rather to my surprise, that the argument made here still not only convinces me, but does not appear to have been superseded. That must be my excuse for republishing the piece, with revisions, in the present volume.

4

Athenian History and Historians in the Fifth Century B.C.

THE DIFFERENCES between the first and second editions of the *Cambridge Ancient History* symbolize a good deal more than half a century's accumulation of useful knowledge: they also testify eloquently to changing intellectual, social, and cultural assumptions, as much in the investigators as in the world under investigation. This was less immediately apparent in the earlier volumes, where new assumptions and approaches (though as evident in archaeology as anywhere else) tended to be swamped by the sheer massive accumulation of new data: no accident that volumes 1 and 2 underwent inflation to twice or three times their original size in the second edition. With the shift from prehistory to the era of written records, this trend has been sharply reversed: volumes 3 pt. 3, 4, and now 5 are roughly the same size as their predecessors (volume 5 runs to 603 pages today, as against 554 in the 1927 edition). Despite advances in epigraphy, numismatics, and archaeology, the actual body of new evidence added for the fifth century B.C. has been comparatively slight. What has changed most for this period is the way we look at what was there all the time, our unspoken priorities, the unquestioned (and often unexamined) beliefs we bring to the job.

This is especially true of the Periclean Age, not least because of its eponymous protagonist. I know at least one classical historian whose underlying motive, privately admitted, in attempting to downdate a whole group of openly imperialist decrees previously assigned to the 450s and 440s was his refusal to believe "that Pericles could have acted like that." Today I suspect we are all a little more politically realistic, if not plain cynical. At all events, the

---

Note: This essay embodies some material from reviews in the *Times Literary Supplement*, but in its present form is otherwise hitherto unpublished.

helmeted bust of the great man stamped in gold on the front cover of the first edition of volume 5 has been silently dropped from the second, and I doubt that this was done solely on grounds of economy.

Another revered figure whose infallibility is finally being challenged is Thucydides.[1] In a sensible, yet revealing, introductory statement on sources, chronology, and method, D. M. Lewis concedes that "this volume may sometimes be found surprisingly sceptical or critical of Thucydides" (that "surprisingly" speaks volumes), and the trend, one feels, is not to his taste. Thucydidean *suppressio veri*, yes, we all know about *that;* but "when he does report an event, it is only at our peril that we try to reinterpret it and it will seldom be good method to do so."

The Thucydides cult is one of the oddest phenomena known to me in all ancient historiography, and perhaps its most pernicious effect has been the systematic denigration, at every level, of Thucydides' great predecessor Herodotus. Significantly, Herodotus's most severe critics have almost always been classicists. Nonclassical historians, today as in previous generations, are quick to perceive the breadth and far-sightedness of his historiographical assumptions. Speaking in 1988, during a conference held at Scripps College with the provocative theme "History and . . ." (the blank to be variously filled by philosophy, anthropology, and other disciplines), the Princeton historian Carl E. Schorske, author of *Fin-de-Siècle Vienna: Politics and Culture* (New York, 1979), held Herodotus up for praise and emulation, "with his interactive dynamic between culture and politics, and between the diachronic and synchronic dimensions of history."[2] Having pointed out, correctly, that "while the narrative core of his work was the Persian Wars, [Herodotus] treated the conflict between Greeks and barbarians as a clash of cultural systems," he went on to remind us that "Herodotus's integrated historiography was unseated by the sharper but narrower political historiography of Thucydides."[3] It may be

---

1. See in particular E. Badian, *From Plataea to Potidaea* (Baltimore and London, 1993), chs. 4 and 6; and G. Cawkwell, *Thucydides and the Peloponnesian War* (1997). Badian writes, *inter alia:* "Thucydides has consistently tried to disguise [Athenian] *Realpolitik* by selective omission and disinformation, and by delivering his own interpretation of motives and intentions under the guise of facts" (184). Cawkwell is a good deal more cautious in his conclusions, as might be expected from someone who can claim (8) that Herodotus "had not shrunk from including a merry mix of nonsense in his account of the Persian Wars," and goes on: "In eschewing that, Thucydides manifested a new concern with the truth, a veritable passion." Jesting Pilate would have enjoyed that formulation.

2. Cited from Carl E. Schorske, *Thinking with History: Explorations in the Passage to Modernism* (Princeton, 1998), ch. 13, "History and the Study of Culture," 232.

3. Ibid., 221.

worthwhile to take another look at the causes of this change: not all of them are as solidly based in reason as Thucydideans like to believe.

In a very real sense, history as we know it begins with Herodotus. His predecessors—shadowy figures such as Hecataeus of Miletus, Hellanicus of Lesbos, or Charon of Lampsacus—traveled inquisitively, picked up oral traditions, retailed great-man anecdotes and genealogies, but never combined their enquiries (*historiai* in Greek) into one great Enquiry, the critical, discursive What and Why of the past. Other surrounding civilizations still hadn't advanced beyond priestly records, kinglists, celestial observations, or theological protocol: the *obiter dicta* of royal and religious authoritarianism, with no room for free rational debate. It is the singular inventive achievement of Herodotus to have taken the ethnic and geographical investigations of earlier Greek researchers and fused this material with the great epic tradition we know best from Homer to do, as he says, two things: save great past deeds from oblivion, and discover why Hellenes and *barbaroi* (foreigners who went *ba-ba-ba* instead of speaking Greek) came into conflict with each other. The What and the Why.

Interestingly, Herodotus's achievement was directly challenged in antiquity and has faced bitterly hostile criticism ever since. One major reason, emphasized again and again by Plutarch in his furious essay *On the Malice of Herodotus*, should really count in Herodotus's favor rather than against him: his broad-minded and cosmopolitan readiness to see both sides of an argument, to concede Persian virtue while admitting Greek faults. This quality arouses Plutarch's most splenetic attacks. For him Herodotus is, unpardonably, *philobarbaros*, what prior to P.C. enlightenment might have been termed a wog-lover: Plutarch's prime historiographical principle is clearly "my country right or wrong." Those who study contemporary modern Greek historians—on the Macedonian problem, say, or Greco-Turkish relationships—may reflect, ruefully, that Plutarch stands more in the Hellenic mainstream than did the Father of History; that the very virtues of Herodotus are, paradoxically, the chief reason why, almost as early, he was also pilloried as the Father of Lies, a lie being defined as what did not suit the ethnic group involved. Today this tactic has acquired an uncomfortably modern flavor.

Contemporary criticism, significantly, often attempts to prove not only errors—which certainly exist, and in such a work, with the resources available, it's surprising there aren't more of them—but *deliberate falsification* (one scholar's counterattacking book is bluntly titled *The Liar School of Herodotus*). The animus revealed by such a thesis, impossible to prove and inherently unlikely, suggests temperamental rather than rational hostility. It is Herodotus's *personality* that irritates a certain type of intellect: his sunny cosmopolitanism, his open-mindedness over questions of religion, his obvious enjoyment of women (and the large role allotted to them in the *Histories*), his addiction to anecdotes, his discursive digressions on anything from tribal *couvade* to the walls of Babylon, his refusal to take up any kind of ideological stance save in the pursuit of freedom (*eleutheria*), his preference for inductive as opposed to deductive reasoning—that is, amassing bits of evidence to see what, if any, pattern may emerge from them, rather than coming up with a theory first and trying to make the facts fit it. Not by accident, I feel, his severest critic in this field, the German scholar Detlev Fehling, is equally passionate in his wholehearted, uncritical endorsement of Herodotus's near-contemporary and historical successor, Thucydides. What can we deduce from this?

Thucydides is everything that Herodotus is not: obsessional, dogmatic, focused sharply on military and political affairs to the virtual exclusion of all else, a theorist trained by the Sophists, intellectually deductive by nature, and ready, as a result, to conceive universal generalizations that he proceeds to justify on the basis of a face-off between two local city-states (*poleis*) in mainland Greece. There are no women in his formalized world (Pericles' advice to them, in the famous Funeral Oration as Thucydides reports it, is simply not to get themselves talked about), and the humorless historian also excludes all private life and anecdotal material, explaining that his aim is instruction rather than entertainment. The enormous historiographical assumptions behind these statements—above all the jettisoning of Herodotus's cultural and anthropological methods *in toto*—are not examined as carefully or as often as they should be, especially since it has been Thucydides, not Herodotus, who bequeathed to future writers a method and a template for historical research that is still very much with us today.

One of the major (and most significant) differences between the two—a difference that tends to be disguised, if not obliterated, in the available English versions—lies in their sharply contrasting prose styles. Herodotus, as Aristotle informs us (and as even a cursory study of his Greek makes abundantly clear), wrote in what was termed the "old strung-along style." This meant a sentence-structure short on heavily subordinated clauses (i.e., avoiding constant value-judgments) that preferred brief main statements in sequence, with a corresponding narrative technique that strung episodes together like beads on a thread. There has also been a bizarre assumption among translators that Herodotus's Ionic Greek is both literary and archaic, and should be so represented. This equation of the Ionic dialect, through Homer (where a good deal else was mixed in), with old-fashioned literary trends, the kind of sub-Biblical pseudo-Tudor prose that Robert Louis Stevenson called "tushery" and W. E. Henley labeled "Wardour Street English,"[4] is particularly unfortunate, since the theory itself is nonsense. In fact, Ionic was, first and foremost, the language of scientific investigation, of Hippocratic medicine; and what Herodotus presents is, as he tells us (bk. 1, proem), the "exposition of his research." Far from being quaintly archaic, he was, as that overworked phrase goes, right on the cutting edge.

Thucydides, on the other hand, has a dense, thorny, and infinitely complex prose style, loaded with difficult abstractions, offering whole Chinese boxes of subordination in enormously protracted, often page-long sentences that are made to balance on subtly rhetorical nuances involving clause and counter-clause, and straining at the same time to avoid any hint of repetition, whether verbal or constructional, in either his narrative or, more particularly, those elaborately wrought speeches on matters of political debate that he puts at intervals into the mouths of his leading public figures, and that have always proved so mind-numbing a hazard to students hacking their way through his text, for the first time, in the original Greek.

Rather like that sentence, in fact.

Reading Burke, Hobbes, Clarendon, Gibbon, or Macaulay today, it is only too easy to see what classical influences have been at work on *their* styles: they are Thucydideans to a man. So have the vast majority of classical scholars been. But, just as in the great debate over Homer, between Unitarians and Separatists, it was the creative writers who saw unity, while the academic analysts isolated lays and layers into a congeries of *disiecta membra*, so today a very similar temperamental divide separates, and contrasts, those who enjoy the Father of History and the many more who identify intellectually with his great successor. It is only fair, at this point, to state openly (what should already have become clear) that, while trying to preserve an equable balance, I approach this subject as a convinced Herodotean—something, as far as professional academics are concerned, that at once puts me in a minority.[5] Ratio-

---

4. For a really horrible example of this, see J. Enoch Powell's version, *Herodotus*, 2 vols. (Oxford, 1949). The urge to treat Herodotus as an archaic simpleton springs, I have always suspected, from the intellectual contempt felt for him, his language, and his methodology by aprioristic rationalizers of the Thucydidean stamp. Powell went at him like a Victorian anthropologist anatomizing some exotic equatorial tribe, *de haut en bas;* no accident that it was Thucydides whose text (working from H. S. Jones's recension) he actually edited.

5. But in good company, too, e.g., that of Momigliano, who observed, in his seminal essay "The Place of Herodotus in the History of Historiography," in *Studies in Historiography* (London, 1966), 141, "the strange truth that Herodotus has really become the father of history only in modern times."

nal intellectual theorists love Thucydides. He is the darling of military and
political analysts, of think-tank gurus. He gets the modern English-language
commentaries (two big ones so far), whereas Herodotus still has nothing written later than 1928. It just goes to show what an effect you can have by *informing* your readers how objective you are, and writing in the third person to
reinforce the impression; because the evidence, when looked at impartially,
tells a very different story. Classicists in fact know very well, though they seldom mention the fact, that the more hard corroborative evidence shows up,
the better Herodotus looks, and the more shaky Thucydides' claims to objectivity become.

Thucydides' stance, in any case, was always debatable. Transpose the circumstances of his life and authorship into modern terms, and this at once
becomes glaringly apparent. If we were confronted with a history of World
War II written by a general dismissed for incompetence, who fled abroad
to escape a possibly fatal court-martial, and whose subsequent narrative of
events — never identifying its sources and omitting a clutch of key occurrences — crucified the politician responsible for his dismissal, while at the same
time drawing the enemy commander who had out-maneuvered him as a genius
so brilliant (and un-Spartan) that he was virtually undefeatable, what would
we think about such a work and such a man, however well he wrote? Not least
when his reiterated claims to objectivity were often contradicted by other testimony? Add the inadequate coverage of foreign, especially Persian, matters,
and the underplaying of dominant economic motives, and the response can
scarcely be in doubt.

Thucydides, make no mistake about it, is a great historian, and we're lucky
to have his unfinished work: but that work contains just as many personal flaws
and prejudices as the next man's, and to use him as a yardstick with which to
give Herodotus short measure does his pioneering predecessor a serious injustice. Cornford in 1907 made the point that what Thucydides created was
nearer to Aeschylean tragedy than to history in the modern sense, and the argument has never been adequately refuted. It is even possible (not least when
we recall his family connections with Cimon and the conservative opposition)
that what has been taken by the guileless as hero-worship of Pericles was in
fact mordant irony. Consider the macabre setting of the Funeral Oration in a
context of plague and military incompetence; consider the deadly epitaph on
Nicias, who offended Thucydides' two great gods, rationalism and the successful exercise of power.

The ancient sculptor who did a common bust of the two historians, leaving
them joined at the occiput like a pair of Siamese twins not on speaking terms,

facing in opposite directions yet inseparable, had a shrewder sense of their relationship than many historians have displayed. Between them they evolved all the fundamental principles of historiography—a preference for autopsy; close scrutiny, and comparison of sources; the use of ethnic and geographical evidence to create background perspective; the systematization of chronology, the delineation of character, the evaluation of reported speech. Unfortunately, since the Renaissance it has been the Thucydidean contributions to this legacy that have firmly established themselves. Only in recent times, with new emphasis on such elements as the sociology of environment, even on psychohistory, has Herodotus's original and far-sighted historiographical achievement begun to win the recognition it so strongly merits.

There is, inevitably, a good deal about Thucydides in this second edition of *CAH* vol. 5, most of it predictable; but nowhere do we find a really radical reassessment of his historiographical methods or motives. The most useful discussion is (not surprisingly) Martin Ostwald's, in a long and wide-ranging essay on "Athens as a Cultural Centre," where, as part of his analysis of Sophistic thought, he traces the impact of Protagoras (paired speeches or *antilogia*, arguments from probability, studied religious agnosticism), which "is more manifest in Thucydides than in any other fifth-century author." There is the usual bow to the *nomos-physis* controversy apropos the Melian Dialogue and the Mytilene debate, standard discussions of Thucydidean composition, chronology, and use of speeches, and very little else. David Lewis, who cheerfully admits in *CAH* that "to say that the Athenians built the Parthenon to worship themselves would be an exaggeration, but not a great one," is still capable of emotional fuzziness when it comes to the Funeral Oration.

The Athenian society depicted in the speech is inevitably an idealization that the Athenians did not achieve in practice, and there are aspects of the patriotism recommended in it that carry less conviction now than they did to the Edwardians, but Thucydides' attempt to reproduce Pericles' aspirations for Athens is a literary and political achievement that puts subject and author on a very high human plane. What doesn't get through here is the unpalatable truth that Pericles' chilly program of *de haut en bas* sociopolitical imperialism is simply another aspect of that Protagorean self-worship which he apparently takes in his stride. The Periclean myth, though dented, still persists.

Some parts of *CAH*[2] 5 are much better than others. The Athenocentric bias is, obviously, hard to avoid, and offers the advantage of structural cohesiveness. But in general the editors have been sensitive to new trends. The volume is now called "The Fifth Century" instead of "Athens" *tout court;* but since this is (we are told in the preface) "a period when, for the first and last

time before the Romans, great political and military power on the one hand
and cultural importance on the other, including the presence of historians to
describe that power, are located in the same place," Athens still holds pride of
place. Though Sallust's comment that "the actions of the Athenians were indeed vast and magnificent, but rather less substantial than report makes them"
(*Bellum Catilinae* 8.2) is duly quoted, one gets the feeling that for a good deal
of this book it is conveniently forgotten.

What is excellent about the editors' policy is a visible and for the most part
successful attempt at integrating areas previously treated separately, with all
the inevitable repetition and artificial pigeonholing that that entailed. *CAH*[1]
kicked off with a formal survey by M. N. Tod on "The Economic Background
of the Fifth Century," whereas *CAH*[2], more realistically, not only stresses the
social dimension of economics in both sections formally dealing with the topic
(J. K. Davies's essay on "Society and Economy" and Martin Ostwald's introduction to "Athens as a Cultural Centre," which, again, explores the economic
and social background), but also lets it be seen in the political chapters. Similarly, the essays on the visual arts, Athenian cults and festivals, and Athenian
religion and literature—by J. J. Pollitt, Walter Burkert, and Bernard Knox,
respectively—never lose sight of the social realities in which such phenomena
are grounded. At the same time, the old confident scholarly certainties have
been largely abandoned: as Davies admits (287), "The only statement which
can be made with security about Athenian society and economy in the Periclean period is that they were evolving rapidly but unsystematically," and that
"very much the same can be said of our scholarly understanding of those processes." Just so.

Thus *CAH*[2] 5 is in many ways offered as a provisional report, an update
both on academic progress in the field and on the various historical areas
where substantial change and, hopefully, progress have been made. Growing
criticism of M. I. Finley's economic assumptions is duly noted. The weaken-
ing of the *oikos* framework in the Periclean period is described (though not
adequately explained). Excellent detailed work on the demes of Attica (by
scholars such as Whitehead, Hansen, and Traill) is put to good use. Some
ideas have obviously germinated underground. In 1970 I argued at length a
case for Athenian expansion having been largely aimed at controlling imports
(grain, timber) at source, together with the routes by which those imports
could be secured, using the Sicilian Expedition as a test case. The theory was
universally ignored, so I was intrigued by Davies's unattributed characterization of it (300–301) as "the traditional view." This was all the more piquant
since the new edition's final chapters on the Peace of Nicias, the Sicilian Ex-

pedition, and the Ionian-Decelean War, by the late Antony Andrewes, don't mention it either, and indeed might just as well have been written for the original volume: they take no more than perfunctory account of recent work (e.g., that of Drögemüller on Sicilian topography), even to disagree with it, and give the impression of having been researched and composed in a kind of time-warp. What has happened? I suspect that the prejudice against economic explanations that modern scholars used to share with ancient historians has begun to dissipate, to the point where, at least to some, "If Thucydides doesn't mention it it probably never happened" has become a less compelling argument than it used to be. Or maybe, as I suggest elsewhere,[6] the activities of OPEC (not to mention the Gulf War) have given this perennial problem a modern, and highly relevant, twist capable of overriding ancient prejudices.

Unlike its predecessor, this is a thoroughly enjoyable volume to browse through. Indeed, it is likely to be read rather more than consulted, and that for one good reason and one bad. The contributors include a number of excellent prose stylists (Pollitt and Knox in particular), with original minds and a gift for lively discourse. But the editors have also, for some unfathomable reason, decided to drop the first edition's laudable practice of including lists of ancient sources with each chapter. These should have been not only retained, but developed. They filled a serious gap for students (and indeed for many professional scholars, especially in areas outside their own field): notoriously, the only critical source-book in existence for any period of Greek history, that of Hill (revised by Meiggs and Andrewes), merely covers the Pentekontaetia (the fifty-odd years between the Persian and Peloponnesian wars), and is in any case out of print and unobtainable. Needless duplication of research is the bane of any scholar's life, and the argument that what constitutes appropriate evidence remains a matter for debate (true enough) is no reason not to make a collection of basic texts and references (to inscriptions and coins as well as literary testimonia) easily and generally available. Some steps have been taken in this direction—exclusively in translation, which suggests, wrongly, that academics are thought to be above such aids—but much still remains to be done, and in the circumstances the decision to abolish them in *CAH*[2] 5 seems both inexplicable and unwarranted.

It is also true that the editors' integrationalist policy, admirable in itself, will make this volume harder to consult on specific points than its predecessor, which was firmly divided up under heads ("The Periclean Democracy," "Attic Drama in the Fifth Century," etc.) and devoted more space to straight

---

6. See below, pp. 94 ff.

political and military narrative. The tendency, a currently fashionable one, is for wide-ranging topics rather than cut-and-dried single themes. At the same time, while methodologically up-to-date, this remains in many ways a defiantly old-fashioned publication. Those in search of *parti pris* pronouncements on multiculturalism, political correctness, and feminist empowerment (or the absence of these) in fifth-century Athens will look in vain. Women rate only a tiny entry in the index (and then mostly with regard to cults, games, and festivals); homosexuality is restricted to a single passing reference, though pederasty, separately indexed (and thus perhaps held, arguably, to be a different phenomenon), also gets just one brief mention. Despite the excellent articles of Burkert, Knox, and Ostwald, there remains a certain almost Thucydidean selectivity of subject-matter, most noticeable in the political narrative. But within those limits we find some excellent work.

Davies, in his quick preliminary sketch "Greece after the Persian Wars," has some shrewd comments on the nature of Panhellenism and Athenian self-definition in relation to non-Greeks (clearly written before the appearance of Edith Hall's seminal monograph *Inventing the Barbarian*), and the economic consequences of a cultural preoccupation with self-sufficiency (autarky on the farm the microcosm, as it were, of *polis* separatism). He traces the gradually increasing encroachment of state on individual, with increased fiscal pressures, as well as the growing need for military cooperation under, variously, Athenian or Spartan hegemony. Such things, together with the development of chattel slavery, the increasingly secular world-outlook engendered by Sophistic thinking, and the erosion of the old aristocratic ethos, led to what he rightly sees as "not a conventional view of the early fifth century," but nevertheless a disturbingly cogent one: a picture of what was, at best, "uncomfortable transition in many fields of social activity at once," (33), and, possibly, acute crisis—to be compounded in the 450s by a vast population explosion.

The concept of crisis recurs in P. J. Rhodes's analysis of Athenian mid-century activities. He sees that grain may have been a motive behind the decision to help the Saïte Egyptian pretender Inaros in 460/59 with a massive invasion force, but doesn't relate this either to the high period of Athenian imperial aggression (459–454), when for once Athens had access to good cheap wheat in plenty during Inaros's period of independence from Persia, or to the telltale gift of grain to Athens by another hopeful Egyptian pretender, Amyrtaeus, in 445/4, when the supply had been cut off by Persian reconquest. Like Lewis, Rhodes is excellent, and mostly up-to-date, on the epigraphical material. I was, however, amused to see that the controversial dating of *IG* I³ 11 (the alliance with Egesta in Sicily), now confirmed, against traditionalists, as 418/7 through laser and infrared treatment of the stone by

Chambers, Gallucci, and Spanos (1990), has still only made it into a footnote, while Rhodes spends a paragraph of the text puzzling, understandably, over why Athens should have concerned itself with an alliance in western Sicily at the traditional date of 458/7. Well, he needn't have bothered. It now looks fairly certain that it didn't—as several of us argued long ago. It is hard not to suspect that the passionate opposition to the 418/7 date was generated by something more than the validity of the three-bar sigma as a dating criterion. As Cawkwell now openly concedes, if that date is right, Thucydides' account of Athens's dealings with Segesta will be seriously vitiated—a prospect that Thucydidean skeptics will contemplate, it's safe to say, with more equanimity than the faithful.[7]

Inevitably, not all the contributors speak with one voice. Lewis is inclined to sympathize with Pericles' appalling fish-and-fox strategy at the beginning of the Archidamian War; Davies, on the other hand, recognizes the brutal truth that "the Periclean strategy of retreat behind the Long Walls in 431 . . . placed in jeopardy that primary sector of the economy into which much effort, investment, and innovation had been committed in the previous fifty years" (301). No one, on the other hand, comments on Pericles' primitive notions of public hygiene, or the psychological impact on the Athenian hoplite force of being told that they were incompetent to meet Spartiates in the field in defense of Attica's farms and villages.[8]

There has also been a missed opportunity in the architectural section. It

---

7. See, e.g., H. Mattingly in *Historia* 12 (1963): 268–69, and *Chiron* 16 (1986): 167–70; T. Wick, *JHS* 95 (1975): 186–88, and *CPh* 76 (1981): 118–21 (with J. M. Balcer). I studied the stone in 1965 with Mattingly (see his remarks in the *Chiron* article above, 168–69) and reported my autopsy in *Armada from Athens* (London, 1970), x. Cawkwell's discussion (1997, 12–13: note that he still supports a date in the 450s!) is cast in emotionally apocalyptic terms: "Blackest of all is the mighty cloud that now hangs over [Thucydides], which if it bursts will deluge his reputation," etc. On the contrary: just one more instance of either slipshodness or *parti pris* historical slanting, take your choice. With any other witness, no critic would hesitate. Cawkwell in fact seems to feel (19) that despite the well-known cases of *suppressio veri* (e.g., over Persia), the pursuit of *Realpolitik* revealed in the speeches is what justifies Thucydides' text as a κτῆμα ἐς ἀεί.

8. Cawkwell's ch. 3, "Thucydides and the Strategy of the Peloponnesian War" (1997, 40–55), will disappoint those hoping for serious radical criticism. Cawkwell persists in finding justifications for Periclean policy, largely downplays the economic factor, and seems to think that Thucydides' most reprehensible error lay in underestimating Demosthenes as a general. But over Pylos and Sphacteria (Cawkwell's ch. 4, 56–74), the historian's errors were not those of a man lacking military judgment. Rather, here Thucydides reveals himself as activated by a blend of personal spite and politico-social prejudice. He hated Cleon, both as the instrument of his own downfall and as the embodiment of the banausic in power: if Cleon and Demosthenes not only collaborated to capture those Spartan hoplites, but (as seems almost certain: Thuc. 4.29–30.1–2, accident though he calls it) arranged to have the fire set that so conveniently smoked them out, this Thucydides would have regarded as a tradesman's trick unworthy of officers and gentlemen, and thus not fit for the permanent record. A chance conflagration was quite another matter.

is a notorious fact (much lamented by intelligent graduate students) that the only place they can find a full and detailed description, unless they happen to read modern Greek, of just *how* the Parthenon was built—the nuts and bolts, as it were, supporting the grand symbolism—is in the unpublished Ph.D. dissertation of T. Leslie Shear Jr. The new *CAH*[2] 5 would have been the ideal place for it. But the late R. E. Wycherley, who could have done the job brilliantly, restricts himself to the usual brief generalities. A pity.

Still, it would not be fair to end on a downbeat note. There are so many unexpected treats here—I am thinking in particular of N. J. Richardson's tautly sensitive discussion of the Panhellenic cults and the poets (Pindar above all) who celebrated them—that perhaps it is churlish to ask for more. One of the best things about Richardson and Knox is their ability to recognize the numinous element in Athenian religion and literature without abandoning rational criteria (E. R. Dodds was a pioneer in this, as in so many things). As Knox makes uncomfortably clear, in Athenian tragedy we are exposed to the terrifying force of the gods' arbitrary and absolute power, the force of curses, the dark generational stain of pollution (*miasma*). When in 1951 Dodds published *The Greeks and the Irrational*, he felt called upon to apologize for his borrowings from psychology and the anthropologists. One thing the present volume, old-fashioned or not, demonstrates with clarity is how far such borrowings have been absorbed into the mainstream of classical studies. It will be intriguing to see (for those still around when it happens) what changes the next half-century feeds into the third edition.

Thucydides began his history of the Peloponnesian War "in the belief that it was going to be a great war and more worth writing about than any of those which had taken place in the past" (1.1.1). He also set out to make his study "a possession for ever" (1.22.4). The first claim has always—not least in the view of Herodoteans—been debatable. No one would seriously contest the second, or the ambitious intellectual arrogance that fueled it. Whatever their ultimate status, that war, and its historian, remain as engrossingly enigmatic—and as relevant to the human condition—as they were two-and-a-half millennia ago. Thucydides tapped an archetypal vein in man's political psyche. That Thomas Hobbes chose to translate him need cause no surprise, nor indeed Hobbes's declared reason for doing so, as stated in his autobiography: "He made me realise how silly is democracy, and how much wiser a single man is than a multitude; I translated this author who would tell Englishmen to beware of trusting orators." Those for whom Greece (meaning, in effect, Athens) was the cradle of democracy would do well to recall that Thucydides, far from standing alone, belonged to a strong, persistent, and highly articulate anti-democratic (or antipopulist) movement that numbered among its adherents thinkers from Heracleitus to Plato.

By "orators" Hobbes clearly meant radical demagogues like Cleon, the particular object (and for good personal reasons) of Thucydides' disdain. Even so, his tribute to an author so imbued with the Sophists' rhetorical techniques looks, today, decidedly paradoxical. Yet paradox and change are fundamental to Thucydidean scholarship: only the passionate involvement remains constant. We need to remind ourselves at times of the great watershed dividing modern liberalism from the inbred oligarchical assumptions of the eighteenth century: that world in which Christianized authoritarianism regarded democratic aspirations with the same repugnance that filled sixteenth-century popes—or St. Thomas More—at the mere mention of Luther's name. We talk of historiographical change, its subtle mutability. Historiography in fact is the vehicle for metastasizing myth, and the myth itself takes substance from varieties of religious, political, and social conviction. Thucydides can embarrass us today with attitudes that Mitford—or Hobbes—enthusiastically endorsed. Even the changing structural fashions of historical writing betray their moral antecedents.

I have been stirred to these reflections by reading, and re-reading, Donald Kagan's *The Archidamian War,* the second installment of his magisterial four-volume general history of the long, grinding conflict (431–404) between Sparta, Athens, and their assorted allies. It has some liberal virtues that would have appealed to Grote and Busolt, others, in sharp contrast, that Hobbes, Mitford, Thirlwall, and probably Thucydides himself would have recognized. Kagan does not offer us the kind of general topical analyses that have emerged from an increasing historiographical (and philosophical) disbelief in the validity, or even the reality, of particularist "facts": instead we get an overall chronological narrative survey in the grand Victorian manner. Kagan does not tell us that he disbelieves the arguments against the so-called historicist position, the inductive accumulation of testimony, the approximation to truth in evidence: he doesn't need to. His approach clarifies his position *ab initio:* I find it (to put my own cards on the table) intellectually satisfying and emotionally congenial. Nor does he need to emphasize his natural sympathy with Thucydides' cast of mind: it shines through unmistakably in all his judgments, and here I cannot help but distance myself. Cleon may be a demagogic vulgarian; but I would rather have a dozen Cleons than Critias, Callicles, Plato's Nocturnal Council, or indeed any kind of intellectual control freak with an ideological agenda.

When Kagan says that "the subject has not been treated on a large scale since the turn of the century," what he really means is that it hasn't been treated in the way that a major nineteenth-century scholar would have handled it. As he readily concedes, the interim period has seen a mass of fundamental scholarship (mainly, but not exclusively, epigraphical) on the workings of the Athenian empire, and no falling-off of interest in the Peloponnesian War—quite the reverse, in fact (though the changing nature and emphasis of that interest is something into which he doesn't delve). An attempt at a new history, then, is, he argues, amply justified. It is indeed, and in more ways, perhaps, than he realizes. In fact, the work done in the last half-century on the Athenian tribute-lists would alone make some kind of revised general assessment inevitable. If the task has not hitherto been attempted in the form that Kagan now chooses, that, it seems clear, is because the contemporary historiographical *Zeitgeist* was, until very recently, altogether inimical to such an undertaking.

The analysts and structuralists have a lot of things going for them, but an evolutionary sense isn't one of them. Now and then they do need to be forcibly reminded of the danger of not seeing the wood for the trees, of the fact that linear time is, despite everything, a prime factor in history. The kind of *vue d'ensemble* that Kagan sets out to establish has a salutary, even a critical function to perform, and the fashion-conscious would do well to reflect on this before dismissing his work with an easy sneer about old-fashioned popularization. Like Thucydides himself, however, Kagan seems to have been beset by what German scholars like to call a *Kompositionsproblem*. When he wrote *The Outbreak of the Peloponnesian War* (Ithaca, N.Y., 1969), he gave no indication that this book was to form a prelude to larger matters. We must now, therefore, reconsider it as part of an ongoing *magnum opus* (I wrote this in 1974: the fourth and last volume did not appear until 1987). At the time of its original publication, Kagan's methods, theories, and general historiographical assumptions not surprisingly came in for some rough handling from one or two academic critics; and since then two major works in the same field, by Russell Meiggs and G.E.M. de Ste Croix, have provided it with heavy competition. How far—since the author states specifically that he did not change his basic working opinions or *idées reçues* between the first volume and the second—do those earlier criticisms also affect *The Archidamian War* and, a fortiori, the undertaking as a whole?

In the event, a good deal less than might at first sight have been expected. *Outbreak* (to borrow the author's own abbreviation), though an essential deck-clearing preliminary to Kagan's main task, was not, I suspect, the kind of book he felt altogether comfortable writing. Its theme required him to grapple with such elusive concepts as the principles of *Quellenforschung*. Worse, Thucydides' elusive philosophy of history lurked, uncomfortably, in the background, and for various reasons—some rational, some emotional—this struck me as a scholarly and psychological quagmire that Kagan was desperately trying to keep out of. Rightly or wrongly, I couldn't help feeling that what he really wanted to write (an impossibility, many will have assured him) was a straightforward narrative history of the Pentekontaetia, *les ans entre deux guerres* from 479 to 431, and that he kept being eternally frustrated in this purpose by the historiographical puzzles and lacunae that beset him at every turn, and that (being an intelligent professional scholar) he couldn't possibly ignore. I find it far from fortuitous that *Outbreak*'s most enjoyable sections are those with some sort of coherent story to tell (e.g., the interlude of the Samian Revolt, or the opening moves in the so-called First Peloponnesian War). Kagan carefully shuns abstractions, always preferring the concrete and specific. For him, ideas exist primarily as attributes of men in action. He loves the cut-and-thrust of political intrigue, but political theory bores him. A natural inductive thinker, if he sees no general conclusion, he has no interest in drawing one. In this, unlike Thucydides, he manifests no driving urge to view the world *sub specie aeternitatis*, an attitude I find unfashionable but refreshing.

This historiographical predilection not only explains Kagan's abiding sympathy with the massively expansive German ancient historians of an earlier era (Busolt, Beloch, and Meyer form his Trinity), it also sheds some light on his attitude toward historical evidence as such—an attitude that was sharply criticized by reviewers of *Outbreak*, and that (to judge from *The Archidamian War*), though modified in occasional instances, still upholds the same basic principles today. Kagan's feeling about testimonia is simple and straightforward: he wants to believe them. Literary sources, however late, derivative, or gossip-ridden, he will accept unless they are "demonstrably self-contradictory, absurd, or false." This is not quite so vulnerable a stance to adopt as some critics have suggested. The let-out clause, with its emphasis on rational scrutiny, will serve as a catch-all for most potential sources of confusion and error; while the skeptical excesses of those *parti pris* critics who regard incredulity per se as an intellectual virtue, and therefore look askance at *all* sources, good or bad (except, more often than not, Thucydides), have taken some bad knocks in recent years, as any student of Herodotus can testify.[9]

---

9. Cf. my further arguments in *The Greco-Persian Wars* (Berkeley, 1996), xxi–ii, especially regarding the basic fallacy of supposing that because a source can be shown to get facts wrong *some-*

However, Kagan was not only charged with overcredulity at the expense of critical judgment; he had also—as one well-known epigraphist soon pointed out—done a certain amount of tacit fleshing out and tidying up when presenting excerpts from various inscriptions and papyri as part of his historical exegesis. Let me quote from R. S. Stroud's review (*CJ* 67 [1971]: 87–89):

> Although pitifully few Attic inscriptions of the fifth century are intact and despite the fact that there are major disagreements about how they should be restored, Kagan presents the reader with translated "quotations" from these documents as if all the text were there in every case . . . and this is no mere quibble over epigraphic conventions since the restored contents of these texts play a substantial role in Kagan's interpretation of Athenian imperialism.

The process, in fact, was somewhat reminiscent of that adopted by certain modern translators of Sappho, who, finding the poet's surviving *ipsissima uerba* inadequate for their purposes, silently incorporated—as part of their text and without the saving grace of square brackets—large numbers of those speculative restorations *exempli gratia* which J. M. Edmonds ventured in *Lyra Graeca*. This somewhat specialized problem hardly arises in *The Archidamian War*, since (*pace* Harold Mattingly) there simply aren't the same type or number of key inscriptions for the period 431–421—and those that do show up are handled with careful circumspection. Kagan, to his credit, has always been ready to take sound critical advice.[10]

But what I find far more interesting than the mere fact of this methodological aberration is the implicit motive behind it. Kagan and Sappho's translators have at least one thing in common: they want to squeeze more out of the evidence that it can, on occasion, legitimately supply. This is also, I would guess, the main (if unacknowledged) reason why Kagan treats the speeches in Thucydides as substantially accurate reports of what was actually said at the time, almost like modern tape-transcripts. A certain type of historian, in pursuit of the truth, develops an uncontrollable *horror uacui* (epigraphists, too, are not always immune from this urge). It should, I think, be more widely recognized how great a part temperament plays in the scholar's treatment, no less than the selection, of his materials. A marked preference for synthesis over

---

times, it is safe, and logical, to assume from this that it *always* does. When the ancient world provides us with so little evidence, we can hardly afford to lose even part of that little through such false inferences.

10. A paperback reprint of *Outbreak* appeared in 1989, twenty years after the work's original publication.

analysis, for inductive rather than deductive reasoning (or vice versa), a natural tendency to reject (or to accept) evidence—such traits, however convincingly rationalized, hint at basic innate psychological patterns. Kagan clearly belongs, by temperament, among the narrators, the expositors, the synthesizers. Though well aware of the dangers involved (like Nietzsche, he knows how easily "monumental history" can degenerate into "mythical fiction"), he remains stubbornly loath to throw out ancient evidence without some truly compelling reason. And why not? History is littered with the discarded hypotheses of scholars who (wrongly, as things turned out) believed themselves superior to their sources.

In *Outbreak* (since the events of the Pentekontaetia depend almost entirely, Thucydides' skeletal outline apart, on late literary texts and fragmented inscriptions), such an approach could not but carry disproportionately high built-in risks. These Kagan did not entirely manage to avoid. In *The Archidamian War*, however, these risks, through the very scope and nature of the undertaking, are far lower. To begin with, we have a natural linear framework: the first ten (431–421) years of the war—named after the Spartan King Archidamus, who raided Attica almost annually except during the plague years—from its outbreak to the Peace of Nicias. Kagan's talent for well-organized descriptive narrative is here exercised on a sequence of inherently dramatic events: the early Spartan invasions of Attica, the onset and impact of the plague, Phormio's activities in the Corinthian Gulf, the revolt of Mytilene, *stasis* on Corcyra, Cleon's startling (and perhaps prearranged) coup at Pylos, the Delian debacle (like too many historians, Kagan overestimates Demosthenes as a general), the campaigns of Brasidas (so hyped up by Thucydides for his own purposes), the plodding negotiations that led at last to a settlement about as unsatisfactory as the Treaty of Versailles.

Whereas in *Outbreak* speed and mastery of narrative were often only achieved by excessive reliance on weak, ambiguous, or reconstructed evidence (including, of course, the Thucydidean "Archaeology" and "Pentekontaetia," which raise more problems than they solve), *The Archidamian War* enjoys the inestimable benefit throughout of Thucydides' own full account, and is, indeed, organized along the same annalistic lines. The problems, by and large, relate not to general principles but to specific actions, the thorniest concerning the viability of Periclean policy at the outbreak of war (more of that in a moment). The inscriptions are less crucial, the testimonia more trustworthy; once hostilities are actually declared, Kagan's debatable thesis of the war's noninevitability (does Thucydides in fact anywhere state that it *was* inevitable?) becomes, in every sense of the word, academic. Thus on several counts

The Archidamian War has a much better chance of success than its necessarily more controversial predecessor.

Other critical strictures appear to have been acted upon. The reproduction of Greek quotations has improved in accuracy (though occasional errors still creep in, and in general the number of typographical slips exceeds what one might reasonably expect from a respectable university press). Kagan is not so prone as once he was to invoke, by way of explanation for Sparta's foreign policy, a perennial opposition between war party and peace party. That some such split existed seems likely enough, and that King Archidamus belonged with the doves rather than the hawks is pretty certain; but I doubt whether the issues were ever so simple as the dichotomy Kagan presented in *Outbreak* would suggest. (The situation at Athens, for which we have rather better evidence, suggests a highly complex web of rival interests.) Though the author claims not to have changed his position on the non-Thucydidean literary sources, nevertheless they, as well as the epigraphical testimonia, are handled with noticeably more discretion. Kagan's bibliography is thorough, while his judgments tend toward unromantic common sense: where he can reconcile seemingly divergent witnesses, he does so.

Like all ancient historians, Kagan has his personal idiosyncrasies, the most obvious (and appropriate) being a distinctly Thucydidean indifference to anything outside the spheres of war or diplomacy. Later, as we shall see, this was to create a problem for him. Here it is merely irritating. Readers of *Outbreak* will recall the brisk relish with which he dismissed alternative theories of the war's "real causes," in particular those to do with economics (another un-Thucydidean topic, despite ingenious attempts to find it there). Anyone who opens *The Archidamian War* expecting to find the lessons of French and Finley (M. I., not J. H.) turned to good account is in for a disappointment.

Most surprisingly, despite his strong strategical interests, Kagan would seem, on the face of it, content to let other scholars do his traveling and topographizing for him. If he has gone over the ground at Sphacteria and Delium and Amphipolis, or tramped through Aetolia and Acarnania in the footsteps of Demosthenes and Nick Hammond, he modestly keeps such information to himself. I do not get that unmistakable taste of topographical autopsy from any part of his narrative: this comes across rather as the book of an armchair strategist. I get the impression that Kagan relies pretty heavily throughout on the reports of on-the-spot scholars such as Delbrück, Grundy, Pritchett, and Gomme (no mention, regrettably, of the still-valuable work done by Colonel Leake). Now, though Pritchett is pretty consistently reliable as a topographer, the same cannot always be said of the rest; and Gomme, whom Kagan uses throughout, was particularly erratic. Just as in *Outbreak* Kagan built overconfidently on epigraphists' reconstructions, so here he tends to take a site on trust from the handiest expert. Thus on topography he is (as critics are always saying of Diodorus Siculus in other contexts) as good as his current source.

But overall Kagan displays an enviable mastery of essentials—not to mention a cavalier indifference to nonessentials: he is the first student of this period I've come across who, quite justifiably on his own terms, doesn't seem to give a tinker's damn whether the Athenian plague was typhus, measles, bubonic, spotted fever, botulism, or collective D.T.'s. The character analyses are low-key, but within their political context effective. Kagan's determination *not* to be dazzled by the Periclean mystique is so intense that it occasionally leads him into surprising company. Following a lead of Geoffrey Woodhead's (whose politics he would seem to share[11]), he sets about rehabilitating, of all people, Cleon: not in social terms, to be sure, but as a preferable military commander to the Olympian (which arguably he was: see below).

Kagan's arguments, unfortunately, are not always of the best. "How accurate would our picture of Socrates be," he asks rhetorically, "if it depended on his portrayal in the *Clouds?* What would we think of Pericles if we believed Aristophanes, Eupolis, and the others?" (325). The alternative, of course, would be to rely on Thucydides, which (as Kagan doesn't seem to have noticed) would ruin his argument. In any case, it is too *faux-simpliste* by half. A partial, if distorted, element of truth surely runs through both portraits, and Kagan, clearly, is no more immune than the rest of us to that endemic historian's vice of citing the minor sources when they happen to support his argument, and turning up his nose at them when they don't. By and large, though, *The Archidamian War* remains sober, judicious, and comprehensive. There is nothing else like it available in English—certainly nothing that takes recent scholarship into account—and undergraduates, to look no further, should find it a godsend.

But for me Kagan's most valuable achievement in it is his carefully reasoned demolition of Thucydides' view—warmly embraced by too many scholars—that Pericles' war strategy was justifiable, made excellent sense, and only failed through circumstances entirely beyond his or anyone's control. (I can see why George Forrest once compared Thucydides to Malcolm Muggeridge, though this probably wasn't what he had in mind.) Since I have myself always found this policy both *fainéant* and crass, a ghastly blend of economic, mili-

---

11. See my *Shadow of the Parthenon* (London and Berkeley, 1972), 84–93.

tary, and psychological suicide, I was particularly fascinated by Kagan's analysis. He claims, with justice (against Delbrück, Westlake, and Wade-Gery[12]), that Pericles' aims were wholly defensive, that he "did not intend to exhaust the Peloponnesians physically but psychologically" (35), by convincing Sparta that it *could not* win a war against Athens. If the Athenians stayed behind their walls, Pericles argued, what could Sparta do? King Archidamus, similarly, believed Athens capable of holding out for an indefinite period. Yet the general opinion—with reason—was that Athens could stand no more than three years of this fish-and-fox stalemate. By that time its war chest would be empty (Kagan has an excellent excursus on Athenian financial reserves), Attica's agricultural economy in collapse, and the psychological damage to its adult males (told, officially, that they were no match, man to man, for Spartan hoplites in the field) more or less irreparable.

If Kagan is right, and I am convinced he is, then Pericles presents a quite appalling example of that intellectual hubris which destroys itself (and much more than itself) by planning exclusively in terms of its own limited rationalism. (Did Sophocles perhaps have him in mind when drawing Oedipus?) He would show the Spartans that their King Archidamus was right; and once they realized this, they would capitulate gracefully. A few minor naval raids would be conducted to make the point clear. With irritating lack of logic, the enemy dug in their heels and refused to see reason. This refusal was compounded by the onset of the plague—a not-so-random factor, due to Pericles' disregard for the known facts of elementary hygiene in cramming the area between the Long Walls with refugees from Attica. (To despise amulets was not good enough: a little Hippocratic or even Empedoclean common sense would have helped.) The whole object-lesson turned out an expensive failure. Had Pericles pursued an aggressive, flexible strategy—had he stationed a fleet at Naupactus on the first outbreak of hostilities, undertaken a serious blockade of the key Peloponnesian ports, persuaded the helots and Messenians to revolt, even led a task force up the Eurotas valley from Gytheion to unwalled Sparta while the Spartan army was away ravaging Attica—then the war, and Thucydides' *History*, might have taken a very different course. As it is, we are left with the paradox that, despite Thucydides' approval (which Hobbes surely understood all too well), the Periclean strategy was a failure *ab initio*, and Athens was saved, if only temporarily, by leaders like Cleon who stood that strategy on its head and went all out, with ruthless and ungentlemanly de-

---

12. H. Delbrück, *Geschichte der Kriegskunst*, vol. 1, *Das Altertum* (Berlin, 1920; reprinted 1964), 124–33; H. D. Westlake, *Essays on the Greek Historians and Greek History* (Manchester, 1969), 95–100; H. T. Wade-Gery, *Oxford Classical Dictionary*, 1st ed. (Oxford, 1949), 904.

termination, for unconditional surrender. If Kagan's study manages to drive this unpalatable fact home once and for all, it will have done the history of fifth-century Greece a very considerable service.

In March 421 B.C., after a decade of expensive and largely mismanaged fighting, Athens and Sparta cobbled up a precarious peace, largely in order to recuperate and rebuild. Aristophanes celebrated the occasion with a topical play lambasting Athenian arms-profiteers.[13] Its hero, Trygaios, flies up to heaven on a turd-fueled dung-beetle, thus making the perennial point, always welcome to Demos, that politicians are full of shit, a slur that subsequent events did little to refute. The so-called Archidamian War was now at last terminated by the so-called Peace of Nicias—Nicias, a cautious (not to say dithering) and somewhat old-maidish general, strongly pro-Spartan in outlook, being the chief Athenian negotiator. No one, not even, I am convinced, Thucydides—though here I have strong scholarly opposition—realized at the time that this cessation of hostilities ended nothing, that the larger part of what afterward was labeled the "Peloponnesian War" was still to come.[14]

However, they all learned soon enough. The treaty was supposed to last for fifty years: in fact, it held, precariously, for less than eight, with countless more or less serious prior infractions. As Donald Kagan says, toward the end of *The Peace of Nicias and the Sicilian Expedition* (Ithaca, N.Y., 1981—the third of his four-volume *magnum opus* on the Peloponnesian War), the Peace "had already become little more than a formality by the summer of 420, when Athens joined the Argive League" (354). Indeed, Sparta's allies were treated in so cavalier a fashion at the negotiating table that three of the most important, Corinth, Megara, and Boeotia, flatly refused to sign, then or later. Nicias and his opposite number from Sparta, King Pleistoanax, concentrated (to put it mildly) on their own special interests, to the point where Megara was left with an Athenian garrison still in its Saronic Gulf port of Nisaia, and Corinth

---

13. This was the *Peace*: it included a crack at Sophocles, whose father had owned a shield factory, and who was now supposed to be desperate for cash: so desperate, indeed, that he would, Trygaeus asserted (698–99), "go to sea on a sieve for profit" (κέρδος ἕκατι κἂν ἐπὶ ῥιπὸς πλέοι).

14. At 5.26.2 Thucydides observes that no one, considering the facts of the case, could fail to agree that a situation in which neither side gave back what had been stipulated was not, by any reasonable definition, a peace. But this remark comes during his so-called second introduction, which gives every sign of having been composed and inserted after the end of the war in 405/4. If so, it shows no more than revisionist hindsight wisdom after the event. It is noteworthy, too, that this insertion should have been made *before* the composition (never in fact completed) of the narrative covering the Ionian-Decelean War of 412–404. The later the event, the longer the historian, very wisely, waited to formulate his judgment on it. Omniscience can only be procured in retrospect.

got back none of its possessions in northwest Greece. The war had supposedly been fought, by the Peloponnesians and their allies, to "restore freedom to the Greeks"; yet the allies were now being sold short, while Athens still controlled Piraeus and the Long Walls, still maintained its powerful fleet, and, under the terms of the Peace, was actually to have Amphipolis restored to it (even if in the event this never happened). In the end Athens and Sparta, ignoring the rest, actually cobbled up an *alliance*. What kind of a peace was this?

Kagan sorts out the details of this fiasco with some percipience: dirty diplomacy always seems to bring out the best in him. At times, though, his Alcibiadean weakness for complex intrigue (and the more complex the better) leads him into what a modern Greek would call *koutoponería*, or silly-cleverness. He speculates that Nicias envisioned restoring Cimon's long-dead dream of a joint Spartan-Athenian hegemony over the rest of Greece: Nicias, whose natural cautiousness would make a snail look adventurous by comparison. He argues that the Boeotians rejected the Peace through fright that, now the Spartans were occupied with Argive ambitions in the Peloponnese, there would be nothing to stop Athenian aggression against Boeotia: except that, I'd have thought, the Athenians were exhausted, and Boeotia had nothing of real value to offer them anyway, except maybe the eels from Lake Copaïs. Neither of these scenarios is impossible: they just don't strike me as plausible. Like many other arguments of Kagan's, they depend on the unvoiced but ubiquitous assumption that all fifth-century Greek city-states were as naturally, and as permanently, inclined toward internecine warfare as Brooklyn street gangs or crabs in a bucket. This assumption relieves Kagan, much of the time, from hunting after underlying motives, a point to which I shall return later.

In many ways, nevertheless, *The Peace of Nicias and the Sicilian Expedition* is an admirable book. Kagan is the fortunate (and, among American historians, rare) possessor of a clean, crisp, elegant prose style: this—being blessedly free of trendy mayfly theories and the obfuscating jargon they generate—makes for reading as pleasurable as it is informative. He owes a considerable debt, acknowledged throughout, to the great German nineteenth-century historian Georg Busolt: this reveals itself in clarity, common sense, and a confident (yet never arrogant) handling of the evidence. He is solidly based—as all of us who explore this period must be—on the text of Thucydides, because Thucydides is by far the best surviving contemporary witness (if we had Ephoros and Philistos it might be a different story). At the same time, this neither leads him, as it has too many others, to credit that enigmatic historian (who could be as selective and prejudiced as the next man) with quasi-papal infallibility, nor to write off other lesser sources altogether, even when they diverge from the Thucydidean canon. As Housman emphasized apropos manuscripts, the best ones aren't immune from error, while the worst do actually sometimes get things right.

Andocides, for instance, may have been a shifty aristocratic blackguard with a knack of getting himself thrown into jail wherever he went; but he was also involved, up to the neck, in one of Athens's biggest scandals ever, and when he delivered his speech *On the Mysteries*, he was on trial for his life. We may not, indeed we obviously should not, believe everything this contemporary witness tells us: on the other hand, Kagan is dead right in assuming that we have to take his evidence very seriously indeed. Plutarch, too, though a *littérateur* who lived hundreds of years after the events he described, and had his own agenda when researching them, did, as Kagan reminds us, have access to "great stores of histories, chronicles, compendia, and poetry lost to the modern scholar." Even that late historical synthesist Diodorus Siculus has his moments.[15] He may be only as good as his source (something which scholars never weary of reminding us, and which looks increasingly dubious as time goes on), but one of those sources for the crucial events of 415–413 was Philistos, a Sicilian historian who actually lived in Syracuse throughout the Athenian siege, and from whose work Diodorus culled an insider's graphic eyewitness account[16] to offset or augment that of Thucydides.

Kagan's quality, too, it might be argued, varies with his source material. Book 5 of Thucydides, which covers the period 422–416, from the close of the Archidamian War to the Athenian reduction of the island of Melos (just a few months before the Sicilian Expedition), is notoriously complex and chaotic, besides probably, in part at least, unrevised. The reader suffers from too many unrelated facts and unsolved problems. Though Kagan determinedly airs the problems and sorts out the facts, often to excellent effect, nevertheless all but the most dedicated aficionados of political intrigue will find this first half of his study pretty hard going. Corinthian resentment, Athenian ambition, Spartan neuroses, and the power struggle between oligarchs and democrats in the key Peloponnesian state of Argos produced a series of labile alliances, diplomatic maneuvers, and military *démarches* that, it's safe to say, were not only more

---

15. See in particular K. S. Sacks, "Diodorus and His Sources: Conformity and Creativity," in *Greek Historiography*, ed. S. Hornblower (Oxford, 1994), 213–32, who emphasizes the individual stamp (as opposed to mere scissors-and-paste reproduction) that Diodorus puts on many passages of his *Bibliotheke*.

16. E.g., at Diod. Sic. 13.14.3–5, the reactions of Syracusans witnessing from the walls the battle in the Great Harbor; but Philistos's version can be detected at many other points.

exciting, but made a great deal more sense to the participants than they do (however skillfully glossed) to the modern reader.

Still, there are bright patches. One prominent public figure throughout the eight-year "phony peace" was Alcibiades, and though his somewhat fly-blown charms—not to mention his actual record of achievement, which during this period was nil—have been wildly exaggerated by sentimental Hellenists (among whom, I'm glad to note, Kagan is not included),[17] at least no one could call him *dull*. But for all his public and private exhibitionism, he lacked real substance, and most of his devious politicking behind the schemes, being too clever by half, came to nothing. In particular, his policy of a North Peloponnesian anti-Spartan alliance, based on Argos and backed by Athens, was blown to shreds in 418 by a crushing defeat at Mantinea.[18] Kagan, very much in control of the tactics and terrain, gives the most lucid account of this battle I have ever read. He is also excellent on the rigged ostracism (?416/5) of the Athenian radical demagogue Hyperbolus, who tried to get either Alcibiades or Nicias ostracized, only to have these political rivals get together (deep calling to gentlemanly deep in the emergency) and combine their support groups to ostracize *him*.[19] Most historians, following the ancient sources, treat this episode as a mere political joke, and assume that the device of ostracism was abandoned because Hyperbolus had irredeemably demeaned it. But this was an all-too-characteristic class-joke spread about "the lamp-maker" (probably in fact the owner of a lamp factory) by his aristocratic enemies; and Kagan is surely right when he argues that the real weakness of ostracism was that it could "confirm a leader or a policy supported by a clear majority, but . . . was useless where such clarity was lacking" (146)—as tended increasingly to be the case in the final decades of the fifth century. Better, in fact, if Nicias

---

17. See also the refreshingly acerbic monograph by Edmund Bloedow, *Alcibiades Reexamined, Historia* Einzelschriften Heft 21 (Wiesbaden, 1973).

18. Thucydides (6.16.6) reports Alcibiades as saying, in a speech before the Athenian Assembly three years later: "I made the Lacedaemonians stake everything on a single day's engagement at Mantinea: in consequence of which, *though they won the battle,* they have still not recovered their full confidence" (emphasis mine). This disingenuous attempt at damage control always got an unsolicited laugh from the students with whom I used to read Books 6–7.

19. If the Assembly so voted, an ostracism could be held at Athens in any year to decide which of two or more political rivals it would benefit the polis to exile for ten years, without loss of property or civic rights. The device was so named from the *ostraka,* or potsherds, on which voters scratched the name of their choice. A quorum of 6,000 was necessary to validate the proceedings. Its main object, clearly, was to resolve a political deadlock without bloodshed. Sources are divided as to whether the device was formulated by Cleisthenes as part of his reforms (Arist. *Ath. Pol.* 22), after 508/7, or, less probably, by Themistocles in 486/7, prior to the first known ostracism (Androtion, *FGrH* 324 F6).

and Alcibiades had refrained from collusion, since their act robbed Athens of clear leadership at a crucial point in its history.

This crucial point came in 415, with the final decision—taken after long discussion and against considerable reasoned opposition[20]—to launch a major assault upon Sicily. The narrative of Athens's grandiose, inept, and ultimately disastrous venture in the West takes up two complete books (6–7) of Thucydides, and evokes some of his most brilliant descriptive writing. Francis Cornford, in *Thucydides Mythistoricus* (1907), argued with some force that what these books contained was in fact tragedy masquerading as history (a view never effectively refuted). The spell is potent, and Kagan has, understandably, succumbed to it. "The historian," he proclaims, embarking on his own version of the Sicilian Expedition, "has the inescapable obligation to put questions even to the most authoritative interpretation, and Thucydides' account . . . clearly provokes such questions" (157). Fine words, and true enough; but in the event Kagan's questions tend to be sporadic and peripheral. As always, he prefers narrative to analysis, and here he has a gripping story to tell. He handles Thucydides (not to mention essentially conservative modern pundits like Dover) rather in the sedulous spirit of a government-sponsored journalist interviewing the prime minister. As a result, while he scores high on Ranke's dictum, getting the *wie*, the how, of events better than most, it's the why, the *warum*, that ultimately floors him.

Yet the events of the narrative are so extraordinary, so dramatic, that it is only too easy to overlook this serious omission. From the first fraught debating clash between Nicias and Alcibiades to the final death-march down the east coast of Sicily to the Assinaros River, the situation develops with a nightmarish inevitability. A good test case of Kagan's skills is provided by the mutilation of the Herms—those square-cut good-luck pillars that stood at most Athenian street corners and outside many town-houses, topped with the head of the god Hermes, and tailed (so to speak) with an erect phallus. In June 415, shortly before the expedition was due to sail, almost all of Athens's Herms were, in the course of one night, sacrilegiously defaced. This act of vandalism was, clearly, no casual prank, but most carefully planned. Its obvious apparent motive was to create a bad enough religious omen—Hermes being the god of

---

20. It is worth noting, especially when Euripides' *Trojan Women* (415) is so often cited as a great antiwar statement in the modern sense, that *not one* of those voting against the Sicilian Expedition (Socrates included) did so on moral grounds: every single argument hinged solely on the risk of failure, and that failure's inevitable unpleasant consequences. Yet eastern Sicily had been colonized, and was occupied, by fellow Greeks. See my article "War and Morality in Fifth-Century Athens: The Case of Euripides' *Trojan Women*," *AHB* 13.3 (1999): 97–110.

travelers—to stop the expedition from sailing. (This was the last thing Alcibiades wanted, and whoever else might have been guilty of the mutilation,
he almost certainly was not.) In the event, the gambit failed, though Alcibiades' radical enemies profited by the hysteria it created to confuse two quite
separate issues, and nail their *bête noire* on the alternative charge of blasphe-
mously parodying the Eleusinian Mysteries: that one stuck.[21] On this kind of
problem Kagan is at his best. He takes full advantage of new epigraphical and
prosopographical research. He analyzes the shifty and self-serving testimony
of Andocides (whose rural-conservative political club almost certainly organized the mutilation) with cool aplomb. Where ambiguities exist (e.g., over
the precise chronology), he faces them squarely.

The same well-informed common sense is in evidence throughout his narrative of the Sicilian campaign. We learn, with mounting horror and fascination, just how divisive and vacillating strategy in the field could be: Athens's
tripartite High Command (which recalls that old World War II definition of
a camel as a horse designed by a committee) was a sure democratic formula for
defeat. We see the advantage of surprise frittered away, applaud initial small
advantages that are then, mysteriously, never followed up. Alcibiades, recalled
to Athens for trial, defects to Sparta (small loss to the expedition, whatever
his more besotted admirers may say: his flashy hole-and-corner diplomatizing
was no substitute for sound aggressive tactics, such as those advocated by his
colleague Lamachos).[22] Walls and counterwalls rise and are destroyed during an abortive siege of Syracuse undertaken too late, and prosecuted with a
slackness that ought to have resulted in more than one scandal-ridden court-
martial. The Athenian Assembly, even in the face of cumulative and well-
documented failure, perversely refuses to cut its losses, or even to replace the
sick and lethargic Nicias—despite his own plea for recall—as commander-
in-chief of the task force. Instead, a relief expedition as large as the original
one is sent out, and at once calamitously defeated in a bungled night-assault
on the heights of Epipolae. After further crushing setbacks both on land and
at sea, when only immediate evacuation could save anything from the venture, there is a delay of almost a month, due to (of all things, among supposedly rational post-Periclean Athenians) the superstitious terror caused by
a lunar eclipse. Finally comes that annihilating blood-bath in the Assinaros
River.

---

21. The tactic is perennial. Its current version until 2000 seemed to be: "If finances won't wash,
try sex." Since then, finances have staged something of a comeback.

22. Cawkwell's best arguments (1997, ch. 5, 75–91, "Thucydides, Alcibiades and the West") deal
with Thucydides' omissions and changes of opinion concerning Alcibiades' role in Sicily and after
his condemnation.

All this Kagan narrates as well as I've seen it done, fleshing out Thucydides with judiciously deployed minor sources (Diodorus, Plutarch, Andocides, et al.) as well as the resources of modern scholarship, both exegetic and topographical. It ought to be enough, yet it isn't. Large questions pose themselves, to find no adequate response in Kagan's pages. Some may well be unanswerable: that is no reason not to ask them. For instance, it is possible to accumulate, mainly from Thucydides, a list of military aberrations so palpably gross as to suggest collective mental derangement. These constitute an important, if enigmatic, factor in the expedition, and should be stressed. Kagan, however, largely bypasses them.

This is odd, particularly since he has Nicias—despite occasional praise for his generalship in the field—cast as the inept villain of the piece, and such errors could, on the face of it, have strengthened his case. Even so, we have Nicias pushing Athens into committing a larger force than originally planned, pointing out the preponderance of Syracusan cavalry, yet not insisting on a strong cavalry brigade himself, finally mishandling his chances to the point of total destruction. Why, above all, did Nicias drag his feet so over the siege? What was he so hopefully waiting for that, in the event, never materialized? One obvious reason, noted by our sources, and indeed mentioned casually by Kagan (but never stressed or set in its proper context), is that, like almost every fifth-century commander, he was angling for collusion from an opposition group within the walls: the radical democrats hostile to Hermocrates and the old landowning class (Gamoroi) then in power. This radical group not only existed, but later in fact took over the government. At one point Syracuse did indeed come within a hair's breadth of betrayal and surrender, foiled only by the inopportune arrival of the Spartan general Gylippos.

Such fifth-column tactics were—as Polyaenus and, especially, Aeneas Tacticus's manual *Poliorketika*, on defense against sieges, continually remind us—the rule rather than the exception.[23] Capture by assault and battery was difficult, hazardous, seldom successful, and costly in lives. Reduction by famine required a more effective blockade than most armies could maintain, and could drag on for months or even years. Both methods were prohibitively expensive (the eight-month siege of Samos in 440/39 set Athens back over 1,400 talents).[24] It took much less cash (plus the prospect of power) to tempt

---

23. Both works, formerly elusive except for specialists, are now easily consultable in excellent and well-edited translations. Aineias the Tactician: *How to Survive under Siege*, trans. with introduction and commentary by David Whitehead (Oxford, 1990); Polyaenus: *Stratagems of War*, ed. and trans. by Peter Krentz and Everett L. Wheeler, 2 vols. (Chicago, 1994).

24. Nicias will not have forgotten the siege of Potidaea early on in the Peloponnesian War, which took two-and-a-half years and cost 2,000 talents (Thuc. 2.70.2).

a political group into collusion.[25] Philip of Macedon still remarked, a century later, when siege equipment and tactics had notably improved, that no
city was impregnable that had a postern-gate wide enough to admit a donkey
loaded with two panniers of gold.[26] Nicias had close and long-standing personal ties with Syracuse (a point that Kagan surprisingly doesn't mention):
he was, indeed, Syracusan *proxenos* (consular representative and commercial
counselor) in Athens. This office will have given him ample opportunity to
obtain or pass on information, particularly of a military or political nature. It
will also have facilitated his contacting the Syracusan opposition.[27]

He was, in addition, a wealthy man, whose superstitious piety did not stop
him making a tidy profit by leasing workers to the Laurium silver-mines. "It
is hard to imagine," Kagan says, "what business [Nicias] could have had in
Segesta [the Elymite city Athens had ostensibly invaded Sicily to help] other
than diplomacy" (226). Let me suggest the obvious answer. Not only was
Nicias in private life a slave-dealer; he had just, at Hyccara, taken numerous
prisoners. His business in Segesta was to turn a quick personal profit selling
off his surplus. At every level of the Sicilian Expedition we find public and private concerns very much intertwined. The fact of Nicias's *proxenia*, combined
with that striking, and uncharacteristic, reluctance in Athens to relieve him of
his command, strongly suggests some kind of commercial or economic motive behind the expedition. This suspicion is corroborated by the vast swarms
of merchants and speculators who accompanied the fleet (and whom, again,
Kagan plays down). There are also the lopsided logistics of the expedition
itself, so strong in ships, so deficient in hoplites and cavalry. All the evidence
suggests that what the Athenians were expecting was little fighting, easy exploitation, windfall profits: in fact, Eldorado. Betrayal from within by radical
sympathizers would fit into such a scenario quite naturally.

But what was the underlying reason—*aitia* rather than declared *prophasis*—
for so large-scale a venture, so soon after a protracted and exhausting war?
More than a quarter of a century ago, in the days before OPEC, Soviet grain
embargos, and, latterly, the Gulf War had revolutionized our economic thinking, I suggested, in *Armada from Athens*, that what drove Athens to embark on
its ill-fated Western grab-as-grab-can raid was, primarily, a desperate short-

---

25. A. L. Losada, *The Fifth Column in the Peloponnesian War* (Leiden, 1972), 24, lists no less than
twenty-seven occasions mentioned by Thucydides during that conflict when internal betrayal led
to the surrender of a city—an average of one per year!

26. Plut. *Mor.* 178B (= *Sayings of Kings and Commanders*, §14); cf. Cic. *Att.* 1.16.12; Diod. Sic.
16.54.3–4.

27. See A. Gerolymatos, *Espionage and Treason* (Amsterdam, 1986), 18, 64ff.

age of wheat and timber (the absence of the first signaled by intermittent famine, the latter a product of overcropping and soil erosion), coupled with its
dangerous inability to control the availability and supply of these two essential
imports *at source*, a notion now wearisomely familiar to all U.S. think-tanks,[28]
but at the time endowed with a certain novelty. My thesis, right or wrong (and
I have yet to see it adequately refuted),[29] was up against a persistent upper-
class and professional tradition, unbroken from Thucydides' day to Margaret
Thatcher's, that found economic causation demeaning because banausic, and
much preferred the Thucydidean formula (that might have been, and perhaps
was, designed to replace it) of self-generated power-politics operating in a
void.[30]

Kagan shows himself a devoted exponent of this method, which gives
Athens's costly and prolonged involvement in Sicily an air of lunatic inconse-
quentiality that I suspect to be undeserved. The tergiversations of the Athenian Assembly could, it's true, be pretty hair-raising; but more often than not,
especially when commercialists like Cleon or Hyperbolus had a hand in shaping policy, they were conducted, for all the fine rhetoric, with a beady eye on
the main chance. Not for nothing, as we learn from a casual remark in Aristotle's *Constitution of Athens* (43.4), did the grain supply figure as a standing
item on the Assembly's agenda in Athens; earlier, in Xenophon's *Memorabilia*
(3.6.13), we find Socrates quizzing a young would-be ruler on his ideas (nonexistent: his mind aspires to higher things) about monitoring and controlling
the existing stocks, calculating how long they will last, and planning for obtaining emergency supplies from abroad to avert famine.[31]

---

28. Mostly, it is true, apropos oil: but that grain can still play a major role in international
power-politics has been demonstrated, disturbingly, by Dan Morgan in his well-documented investigation *Merchants of Grain* (New York, 1979). He points out, *inter alia*, that those controlling
the great grain cartels have deliberately kept a very low profile by comparison with the oil barons.
Few have heard of Cargill, Inc., while for most the name Louis-Dreyfus suggests a member of the
Seinfeld cast rather than one of the most powerful grain dynasties in the world.

29. Certainly not Peter Garnsey, *Famine and Food Supply in the Graeco-Roman World: Responses to
Risk and Crisis* (Cambridge, 1988), 128–29, despite his very useful (if partial) assemblage of relevant
evidence.

30. Thucydides does, very briefly, state (3.86.4, 115.3–5) that one reason for the expedition was
to *stop* grain being imported to the *Peloponnese:* a curious claim (which Garnsey argues, implau-
sibly, to imply that "Athens did not need Sicilian grain as long as existing sources of supply were
maintained": the trouble was, they weren't). This odd negative sentence sounds rather to me like
the nearest Thucydides could bring himself to admit, in positive terms, that the grain was, rather,
needed for import by Athens.

31. Significantly, this upper-class youth, Glaucon son of Ariston, has never even thought of
turning his mind to so mundane a consideration; and when (3.6.5) Socrates asks him whether he
has analyzed the city's revenues or worked out ways of improving them, Glaucon's denial is angry

Yet to read Kagan, it's hard to believe that anyone in Athens ever thought about economics at all, let alone let policy be dictated by the nitty-gritty requirements of daily supply and demand. Even he has to admit that the continued loss to Athens of Amphipolis (one more good reason why the Peace of Nicias unraveled) was important because "the region was crucial to Athens as a source of money and timber," but he at once insists that "even more important was the need to recover lost territory, subjects, and prestige" (143). Glaucon would have heartily agreed. Politics first, every time. But trying to explain Athens's Western obsession in exclusively political terms (e.g., as a diversionary campaign), when the essence of Sicily, then as in Roman times, was its seemingly limitless wealth in timber, wheat, and cattle, leads Kagan into difficulties at all stages. "The Athenians, of course," he writes, apropos the original Egesta embassy that gave Athens its much-needed excuse to fish once more in Sicilian waters, "need not have involved themselves in the petty quarrels of these distant cities." Precisely: which suggests that we need to look for a more compelling reason why they did (and at such great cost) than any alleged by Kagan. The idea of Athens taking preemptive action against Syracuse for fear that Syracuse might join the Peloponnesian League against Athens was, and is, scraping the very bottom of the motivational barrel. Syracuse in 415 was so abysmally unprepared, so totally lacking in naval expertise, that nothing but inspired Athenian incompetence prevented its immediate defeat.

The truth is that no remotely adequate motive for an expedition on this scale, and conceived in such terms, can be adduced on political grounds alone. Nor will tragic overreaching hubris and plain imperial greed provide, by themselves, a credible impulse (though both were certainly there) for Athens's *degree* of commitment. Behavior of this sort is almost always fueled, at whatever remove, by those old familiar deities Fear and Necessity. When we ask ourselves—looking for a moment beyond the limiting Thucydidean round of interstate diplomacy and warfare, symptoms rather than cause—just what need, what anxieties were likely to pressure the Athenians in 415, we do not have far to look. If you draw two transparency-maps of the Mediterranean, filling in on the first the main sources of grain, timber, and precious metals, together with the routes connecting them to Athens's port of Piraeus, and on the second the most bitterly contested areas and linkage-points of the Peloponnesian War, and then superimpose the two, it will at once be apparent that

---

and emphatic: "By God, I most certainly have *not* given consideration to that!" (Ἀλλὰ μὰ Δι', ἔφη ὁ Γλαύκων, ταῦτά γε οὐκ ἐπέσκεμμαι.) To be even suspected of paying attention to financial matters he clearly regards as a class-based social insult. The entire interrogation seems designed to expose his dangerously antibanausic cast of mind. But Glaucon was a typical well-connected Athenian: the rule rather than the exception.

they coincide in almost every particular. Kagan is not unfamiliar with these and similar ideas, but he has gone out of his way to prevent any hint of them from contaminating his elegant exercise in post-Thucydidean historiography. To treat this ill-starred venture as a mere extension of that international gang-warfare—Athens's *West Side Story*, as it were—robs an otherwise admirable synthesis of the one major element essential for understanding what the Sicilian fiasco really meant.

The evolution of Athenian democracy, coupled with the rise and fall of that unique collective imperialism to which it, perhaps inadvertently, gave birth, remains a perennial obsession, and not only for classical scholars. After all, despite any adjustments of perspective that multiculturalism and its allied approaches may have brought, Greek (meaning first and foremost Athenian) culture is still fundamental to our inherited understanding of ourselves, certainly in Western Europe and North America, as rational, political, literate human beings. We have, in fact, an enormous investment in Athens and its cultural icons, from Pericles to Socrates, from the *Oresteia* to the *Republic*, from the Attic *kouroi* to the Parthenon, above all in the fiercely debated democratic ideal associated with Cleisthenes. This investment—something less often admitted than it should be—is at least as much emotional as intellectual, and thus generates a great deal of heat along with the sweetness and light. In addition, to a great extent, and until very recently, the custodians of the classical tradition were passionately committed to many of the social beliefs animating the authors they studied (another awkward fact seldom discussed). Prominent among these was, and to a surprising extent remains, that anti-banausic contempt for commerce, menial occupations, and the lower orders generally so central to figures as disparate in time and attitude as Theognis, Aristophanes, Plato, and Archimedes.

This is one of the factors that gives Athens's achievements so oddly paradoxical a flavor. Progress, like charity, began at home, and had unexpected limits. Cleisthenes enfranchised the garlicky multitude (*plēthos*); but exactly who benefited, and how the thing was done, our scanty evidence keeps just ambiguous enough to stave off unwelcome conclusions. Further, the common man might have the vote, but this did not mean that the wellborn were required to invite him to dinner, much less introduce him to their daughters. Whether by design or not, Cleisthenic legislation, while accommodating the (male, adult, ethnic) common man's political aspirations, left the old *de haut en bas* social structure virtually intact; and it was the *Oberschicht* (sometimes *geistige*, usually landed, always socially assured) that wrote the works that form the bulk of our surviving evidence. Class and occupational prejudice—mock-

ing, vicious, or plain hysterical—meets us at every turn in the surviving literature, and is, for whatever reason (embarrassment among modern egalitarian
romantics?), one of the least-discussed phenomena in Athenian culture.

From the Archaic age on, aristocratic poets lamented that money, and
nothing but money, now held all the power in the world. Thebes regarded
trade as so politically defiling that anyone who had spent time getting and
spending needed a ten-year cleansing intermission before he could run for
public office. When Cimon and his friends in the cavalry formally abandoned
their bridles and offered themselves for naval service during the crisis of the
Persian Wars, it was the socially demeaning aspect of their volunteerism that
earned them special praise. Plato's Athenian Stranger in the *Laws* (707B–C)
has nothing but contempt for the *nautikòs óchlos*, the "sailor rabble" that crewed
Athens's triremes, remarking tartly that whereas the city's land battles (fought
by agrarian hoplites and upper-class cavalry) brought Athenians not only
cachet but moral improvement, those fought at sea had precisely the opposite
effect. So much for Salamis. Aristophanes never misses a chance of sneering
at business entrepreneurs like Cleon, Hyperbolus, and Cleophon. Euripides'
mother selling vegetables in the market was always good for a laugh from an
Athenian audience. Whatever *isonomia*, "equality before the law," meant in
Athens, it had very little to do with social relationships. The fifth-century
upper crust despised and resented the politically dominant *plēthos*, reserving
special hatred for their wellborn leaders such as Pericles, whom they regarded
as traitors to their class. Each side also had a long memory for wrongs—that
mnēsikakia common to Greeks and Irishmen—with equally deplorable results
in both cases.

Athens's great thalassocracy, brought into being by a combination of disparate factors—the Cleisthenic extension of the franchise; the threat from
Persia that turned Athens into a naval power; the preference of its allies in the
Delian League for paying what was, in effect, protection money rather than
supplying ships for joint defense, thus facilitating Athens's road to empire—
also witnessed that great efflorescence of civic pride under Pericles that manifested itself in unsurpassed drama and public architecture. But two things
about this phenomenon cannot be sufficiently emphasized: it was politically
demotic, the offspring of naval domination and those who supported a naval
policy; and despite its cultural assertiveness it depended, as that sardonic critic
the Old Oligarch correctly noted, on economic exploitation of the subject-
allies, plus various *douceurs*, some financial, some political, handed out to the
common people who had the crucial votes.

On both counts this long-running regime appalled the old guard: the aristocrats, the landed gentry, those who, like Pindar, believed in inherited excel-

lence and tradition. Their opposition manifests itself throughout the century, with increasing violence and partisanship under pressure of war, defeat, and plague. When in the 440s Thucydides son of Melesias opposed Pericles' policies, he was ostracized for his pains. But (as Mark Munn reminds us in *The School of History: Athens in the Age of Socrates*) the long and agonizing showdown with Sparta produced disproportionately heavy casualties among the lower orders. This eroded their majority—though not to the radical extent that Munn theorizes: Cleophon's *appui* during the final years of the Peloponnesian War was still considerable—and thus opened the way for such violent reactionary movements as the revolution of the Four Hundred in 411 and, after Athens's final defeat, the ideologically driven totalitarian purges carried out, with Spartan backing, by the Thirty. In both cases it is significant that the first concern of the ultras after gaining power was to *disenfranchise* all Athenians except a limited body of property owners.

Looked at in such terms, it would be easy (and misleading) to see that quintessentially Periclean creation, "gleaming and violet-crowned and renowned in song, bulwark of Hellas, famous Athens, marvelous citadel," as no more than the precipitate thrown up by a run-of-the-mill power struggle between upper and lower classes, both equally greedy for the rich pickings of empire. At the same time, we cannot, and should not, ignore this factor altogether. There is still a notable tendency among ancient historians to view the Periclean dynamic as predominantly, if not exclusively, driven by intellect rather than by economics, a predilection Mark Munn shares, along with the extraordinary, indeed unparalleled, idolization of Thucydides, the historian's historian par excellence, "whose piercing eye," as Jenny Roberts observes in *Athens on Trial* (Princeton, 1994), "is still accorded a reverence long since withdrawn from his fellows" (296–97).

Munn grapples more boldly than most with the class conflicts and economic underpinnings of what Pericles himself saw as a demotic tyranny, but nevertheless still manages to imply that the polarized, and violent, social dissensions toward the end of the Peloponnesian War were created, rather than merely intensified, by that war's disasters. He also, emphatically, leaves Thucydides on his lonely intellectual pedestal: indeed, we are told that "by examining through a narrative of events the impact of experience on critical thought, I offer a new understanding of the conditions that gave birth to the luminary skills of both Plato and Thucydides" (9). The implied chronology is suggestive: as this quotation hints, Munn presents us, for good measure, with a dizzyingly improbable thesis regarding the date of the *History*, and Thucydides' primary motivation for writing it, which, luckily, does not affect the core of his book. I shall return to this later.

But first, credit where credit is due. Martin Ostwald, cited on the dust-jacket, describes Munn's massive study as "perhaps the fullest and most detailed cultural and intellectual history of the Athenian democracy that I have seen," a judgment with which I would enthusiastically concur. In particular, his narrative account of events between the Sicilian disaster of 413 and Socrates' trial and execution in 399 is unsurpassed in its richness of detail and superlatively thorough documentation. His treatment of Socrates struck me as refreshingly down-to-earth: politically realistic ("an incorrigible elitist" rather than, as I heard in Cambridge half a century ago, "Christ minus all the mumbo-jumbo"), with shrewd comments on the philosopher's strident self-righteousness in court, and that solipsistic direct line to heaven via his *daimonion* that so maddened pious civic convention. The charge of "introducing strange gods" makes a good deal more sense viewed in these terms, though the association with Critias, Alcibiades, and their friends must have weighed heavily too.

However, Ostwald's praise for Munn's "profound, comprehensive, and original insights" I found myself regarding, like Claudius in *Hamlet*, with one auspicious and one dropping eye. The profundity sometimes baffles, the originality on occasion can be plain wrongheaded, and one is aware throughout of Munn's tendency both to overpress good ideas and to see more in the evidence than is actually there. For instance, his emphasis on the increased addiction, from the end of the Peloponnesian War, to written sources of authority comes as a welcome corrective, and is well supported. But how much was more? How widespread was literacy? Reading Munn, you might sometime think late-fifth-century Athenian writers and politicians were as addicted to archival research as modern historians; but even Rosalind Thomas (whom he cites) stresses (1989, 90) that "they used documents infrequently, if at all," while W. V. Harris (whom he doesn't, and with good reason) puts the overall literacy rate in Attica (1989, 114) at somewhere between five and ten percent, which would make Munn's thesis, even if true, a symptom of elitism rather than of democracy. But then he is under the impression that in 415 (note the date!) Herodotus's work "was introduced as expert testimony to aid the deliberations of the Athenian *demos* and its Council" (116), while Thucydides, he claims, served a similar function at the time of the Corinthian War in 396/5, as though both had thoughtfully provided situation papers for a government of Gore-minded policy wonks. Though much of what Munn writes about *syngraphai*—sometimes, but not always, "commissioned reports," as he defines them—is both new and persuasive, this, surely, is to push what little evidence there is into the realm of anachronistic fantasy.

The central paradox of sovereign democracy is caught to perfection by Xenophon's anecdote of Alcibiades, as a precocious adolescent, tripping up his guardian Pericles in a discussion of the relationship between law and political power. What is law? Alcibiades asks, to get the unconsidered answer: What the *plēthos* approves in Assembly. Do they approve the good or the bad? The good, naturally. After forcing Pericles to retract an initial assertion that what minorities (oligarchs, despots) enact is also law, and to accept the proposition that to pass measures by virtue of authority rather than persuasion is compulsion rather than due process, the *enfant terrible* strikes home: "So whatever the whole *plēthos* enacts by its authority over property owners, rather than after persuading them, would be not law but force?" Munn is right to see the dilemma that confronted all thinking people at the opening of the fourth century as that "of finding reason within a community where all decisions are subject to the approval of a sovereign popular assembly" (6).

They had come to this point the hard way. As Thucydides and Xenophon imply, as Plato spells out with devastating clarity in his Seventh Letter, and as the activities of the Thirty confirm all too well, those who innocently supposed that a minority of intellectuals, if given a free hand, could deal more equitably with civic and political affairs than the *dēmos* had suffered a rude awakening. It turned out that clever ultras such as Critias were not only utterly ruthless, with even less regard for human life than the demagogues, but could, at the drop of a noose, produce convincing general theories in favor of executing their victims. Yet no one had forgotten the appalling abuse of power after the sea battle of Arginusae (406), when the *dēmos*, crying that "it was monstrous if anyone were to prevent the people from carrying out their will" (Munn 186, citing Xen. *Hell.* 1.7.12), gave a nice demonstration of the fallacy in Pericles' syllogism about law and authority by summarily executing half a dozen of the successful generals for failing to pick up survivors.

Munn points, correctly again, to the activities of the *nomothetai*, men entrusted with the revision and updating of the legal code, as evidence for the need to counterbalance such exercises of arbitrary will by the people with a body of incontrovertible written statutes. What he does not stress is how old this idea was. For almost three centuries, statute law had been welcomed precisely as a hedge against arbitrary authoritarianism, so that the democratic polis was now in the exact position of the Archaic Age *tyrannos*. But also, as young Alcibiades had seen (something his later career exemplified with embarrassing clarity), in the last resort those laws were no stronger than the men who made them: another well-known anecdote has him asking a clearly worried Pericles what was bothering him, and on hearing that his guardian was trying to find a way of rendering his accounts to the people, commented that what he really should be doing was figuring out a way *not* to. In that sense the polis as collective legislator in action bore an uncomfortable resemblance to a track-laying vehicle steered by its tracks.

After two-and-a-half millennia, Alcibiades continues, as in life, to cast his charismatic spell over people who ought to know better. For the Athenian *dēmos*, desperate to the point of hysteria as their empire unraveled, there may be some excuse. For the many modern historians who persist in being dazzled by this aging narcissistic *Wunderkind*, I can find none. Munn, so sensible over Socrates, is no more immune here than his predecessors. Indeed, he actually has Socrates fascinated by Alcibiades' political virtues (what, pray, may they have been?) rather than by his physical charms, and insists that Alcibiades didn't do anything so trivial as *parody* the Mysteries, oh no, he *enacted* them, as a symbolic politico-religious piece of self-identification with the polis. Worse, Munn misrepresents the evidence (as, I suspect, Alcibiades did himself) in order to depict him as the brilliant victor of the Ionian-Decelean naval campaign. The battles of Abydos, Cynossema, and Cyzicus were *not* fought with Alcibiades in command. Indeed, he was not even present at the first two, which were planned and won by Thrasybulus; and he only participated in the third as a deputy commander. (No wonder Byron once remarked that it was hard to remember what battles Alcibiades had won.) When he finally did assume overall command, after his emotional rehabilitation by Athens in 407, he promptly turned the fleet over (a fact Munn tactfully omits) to his steersman and drinking buddy Antiochus, who equally promptly got beaten up by Lysander, thus ending Alcibiades' career as admiral almost before it had begun.

This forcing of evidence is one among several symptoms of a larger problem. Like Thucydides, like Plato, Mark Munn is an intellectual horrified by Athens's self-willed descent into defeat and, worse, murderous civil war fueled by simmering class hatred. Most embarrassing of all—for him as for Plato— has to be the involvement of Athens's best minds and most distinguished families in an orgy of authoritarian purges. Plato abandoned both sides in despair; Thucydides was tempted by the moderate oligarchy of the Five Thousand; neither rated democracy highly. But Munn has to save the intellectual appearances: his thesis, remember, is how thinking men, Thucydides above all, dealt with the awful experiences of 413–403 within the framework of a sovereign *dēmos*. This, surely, is why he propounds the notion of Thucydides writing all that survives of his *History* in one sustained creative stretch between 397 and 396, for the guidance of the Athenian government, breaking off deliberately when the task became too politically fraught even for his insights. Munn even finds a symbolic reason for Thucydides stopping in the middle of a run-of-the-mill narrative paragraph. His final words in Book 8 are "to Artemis." His first words in Book 1 are "Thucydides the Athenian." *Voilà:* dedicator and dedicatee, and never mind that the actual dedicator is (of all people) the Persian Tissaphernes.

What drove so learned and otherwise admirable a historian to so bizarre a conclusion? I suspect it had to be the need to preserve Thucydides, at all costs, as an objective and infallible guide amid partisan chaos. The truth is that the evidence, internal and external, can be made to yield a very different picture. Here Thucydides, exiled for losing Amphipolis through his own dilatory incompetence, sets about his rehabilitation by writing an account of the Archidamian War that not only vilifies his accuser Cleon, but also describes Brasidas, the Spartan who defeated him, as too lightning-swift and brilliant a commander for anyone to match. He thinks, wrongly, that the war ended with the Peace of Nicias in 421, and has to revise to take account of later events (hence the "second preface" in Book 5). He sees the Sicilian Expedition, wrongly again, as an isolated incident, but later is forced to rethink this, too, with the development of the Ionian-Decelean War. He changes his mind about Alcibiades; he possibly decides to alter his technique by substituting analysis for reported speeches. He publishes much of this material during the course of the war, and is offered recall by Athens as a tribute to his historical acumen. However, like many others, he waits until well after the 404/3 amnesty before deciding to return home, correcting his manuscript in the light of current developments, and is then murdered en route by persons unknown, leaving the *History* incomplete in the form we have it today.

Every statement in this version (even the murder, vouched for in detail by both Pausanias and Didymus in the Marcellinus *Life*) has evidence to support it. Nevertheless, for obvious reasons, it is anathema to the bulk of ancient historians and classicists in general: just too much emotional capital has been invested in Thucydides' probity and objectivity. Paradoxically, Munn's *The School of History: Athens in the Age of Socrates*, despite its superficial oddities and confusions, is so thorough, exhaustive, and wide-ranging an investigation, and Munn, for all his obsessions, remains so excellent an investigator, that the attentive reader can still confront most of the enigmas and inconsistencies that bedevil this key period, and form his or her own theories from the ample materials provided. But the ancient testimony is too ambiguous, and modern convictions remain too passionate, for a final consensus ever to be likely.

5

The Metamorphosis of the Barbarian: Athenian Panhellenism in a Changing World

IN THE SPRING of 334 B.C., the young Alexander embarked on his campaign against the Achaemenid empire. The propaganda justifying this expedition was remarkable. If the king saw himself as a second Achilles, returning in triumph to Troy, he also was at great pains to present himself as the Captain-General of the Hellenes, whose mission it was to exact just, and long overdue, vengeance for Xerxes' invasion of Greece a century and a half earlier. "Xerxes made it clear that his expedition was the Trojan War in reverse; Alexander therefore in return reversed the details of this most famous of all oriental attacks."[1] Again and again he stressed, publicly, his role as *hegemon* of the united Greeks, his invasion as a vindication of the Hellenic ideal. Yet—as Ernst Badian has done more than most to demonstrate[2]—the facts of the case are in striking contradiction to Alexander's professed ideology. This champion of Hellenism destroyed Thebes before ever leaving Greek soil, left behind half his available troops under Antipater to hold down the resentful Greek states, distrusted his Greek fleet so profoundly that he took the enormous risk of dismissing it before he had full control of Asia Minor, never put Greek troops in the front line (and got rid of *them* as soon as he could afford to, at Ecbatana), and took a very tough line indeed with the Greek cities of Asia Minor he was supposedly liberating if they presumed to cross his will.[3] How are we to explain so fundamental a discrepancy?

Note: Originally published in *Transitions to Empire: Essays in Greco-Roman History, 360–146 B.C., in Honor of E. Badian*, ed. R. W. Wallace and E. M. Harris (Norman, Okla., 1996), 5–36. Copyright © 1996 by the University of Oklahoma Press, Norman, Publishing Division of the University.

1. Olmstead, 1948, 496.

2. See in particular "Alexander the Great and the Greeks of Asia," in *Ancient Society and Institutions*, ed. E. Badian (Oxford, 1966), 37–69.

3. See, besides Badian's article, Green 1991, 144–50, 156–59, 191–92, 322.

The answer lies in the concept of Panhellenism: an ideal policy of unity and collaboration between all Greek states, having as one of its major goals a retributive campaign against the Persian Empire. For decades that elderly but indefatigable Athenian pamphleteer Isocrates had been urging just such a Panhellenic anti-Persian crusade—since the Peace of Philocrates in 346 specifically under the leadership of Alexander's father Philip. The advantages of such a policy were obvious. Surely, Isocrates argued, it was better for the Greek states to challenge the Great King for his gold and lands rather than to fight each other for the hegemony? Besides, Persia offered (he emphasized) fabulous wealth for the taking, combined with the lure of a cowardly, effeminate, incompetent defense force.[4] Isocrates also carefully stressed Philip's Heraclid descent, while at the same time making it very clear that the Macedonian leader would be operating as the voluntary (i.e., unpaid) leader of a free Greek confederacy, his reward a reasonable amount of plunder and, more important, recognition by the Greek world at large.[5] Small wonder if historians have tended to dismiss Isocrates as a mere armchair pundit, and to see Philip, in this context, as a shrewd realist who knew just how to use the free propaganda thus offered him to his own best practical advantage. But the concept was, in fact, a great deal more ambiguous, influential, and emotionally complex than this black-and-white essay in *Realpolitik* might suggest; and its roots lie far back in the Greek past. On all counts it deserves re-examination—not least as a fertile source of fantasy and special pleading, an elusive cultural paradox.

Like the *patrios politeia* (or, indeed, *eunomia*), Panhellenism—a concept never defined, though much talked about, especially during the fourth century B.C.—meant, and still means, many things to many people. This, indeed, was one of its chief strengths, however much trouble it may have made for scholars trying to extrapolate a coherent system—political? cultural? both?—from our ancient sources, Demosthenes and Isocrates in particular.[6] However old the idea, the actual term seems only to have been coined by Grote;[7] and

---

4. Isocr. *Orat.* 5 passim.

5. Green 1991, 47–50.

6. For Demosthenes, see, e.g., Luccioni 1961, esp. chs. 2–4; Dunkel 1938, 291–305; P. Cloché, *Démosthènes et la fin de la démocratie athénienne* (Paris, 1957), esp. 312–29; for Isocrates, J. Kessler, *Isokrates und die panhellenische Idee* (Paderborn, 1911, reprinted Rome, 1965); Mathieu 1925, esp. chs. 3–5, 17; Sakellariou 1981, 128–45, 242–45; P. Cloché, *Isocrate et son temps* (Paris, 1963), esp. pt. 1, ch. 3, pt. 2, ch. 4.

7. J. P. Mahaffy, *Social Life in Greece from Homer to Menander*, 7th ed. (London, 1890), 342. Luccioni (1961, 1 n. 1), cites Littré as remarking in the 1873 edition of his *Dictionnaire* that the word had not yet reached the *Dictionnaire de l'Académie*.

though the word Πανέλληνες goes back—probably[8]—to Homer, Metternich still found himself unable, as late as 1815, to define the word "Greek" in any satisfactory sense.[9] For Beloch,[10] "*Partikularismus* was the abiding curse of the Greek people," and the tendency of nineteenth-century German historians—recently echoed by Arnold Toynbee[11]—to study the struggle between Philip II and Athens from what might be termed an 1848 viewpoint (pro-Macedonian, pro-Isocratean, the strong *Führer* bringing order to a collection of squabbling *Einzelstaaten*) is notorious.[12]

We need to start from the realization that general definitions, especially those of a consciously programmatic nature, are, in this context, not only misleading but meaningless. We should also beware of the contemporary tendency to assume that Panhellenism was *only* a cynical device employed by politicians to further their own polis-based ambitions, from Pericles' plans for Thurii to Alexander's representation of his assault on Achaemenid Persia as a Panhellenic crusade.[13] Academics and writers have always had a marked tendency to see all politicians as *consistently* mendacious and self-seeking Machiavellians, *tout court;* yet even a slight acquaintance with the actual world of politics should suffice to modify such a stereotype.[14] Emotional inconsistency is central to any profile of political idealism. Further, as a study of the fifth-century *asebeia* trials makes very plain,[15] it is quite impossible to manipulate

---

8. See Hom. *Il.* 2.530, a line, however, athetized by Aristarchus as an isolated anomaly, partly on the grounds that Πανέλληνες as a term must be a later interpolation (but cf. the equally suggestive term Παναχαιοί, which recurs frequently: *Il.* 2.404; 7.73, 159, 327, 385; 9.301; 10.1; 19.193; 23.236).

9. Cf. C. M. Woodhouse, *The Story of Modern Greece* (London, 1968), 132.

10. Beloch 1912-13, vol. 3, ch. 14, 515.

11. A. J. Toynbee, *The Greeks and Their Heritages* (Oxford, 1981), 65-70.

12. See Knipfing 1920-21, 657-71; Walbank 1951, 41-43 = 1985, 1-19 (esp. 1-3).

13. This assumption lurks behind even such otherwise excellent articles as S. Perlman 1976 or N. H. Baynes 1955 (in which Baynes makes unnecessarily heavy weather of Isocrates' many undoubted inconsistencies). See R. Wallace, *The Areopagus Council to 307 B.C.* (Baltimore, 1989), 158-73, for, *inter alia*, a good corrective analysis of Baynes's views.

14. In my own case, close friendship with two British parliamentarians (both now dead), C. P. Snow and Maurice Edelman, both of whom combined literary and political careers, made it abundantly clear that the Machiavellianism, though intermittently evident, was intermingled, exactly as one might expect, with idealism, ideological dreams, and bouts of plain silliness. The case of Themistocles suggests that things were not all that different in antiquity.

15. See in particular Eudore Derenne's *Les procès d'impiété intentés aux philosophes à Athènes au Vme et au IVme siècles avant J.-C.* (Liège, 1930, reprinted New York, 1976), not entirely superseded by Richard A. Bauman, *Political Trials in Ancient Greece* (London and New York, 1990), which seriously underestimates the groundswell of religious and superstitious passion generated by some of the incidents described. Both are complemented by Dover's excellent survey of the evidence, "The Freedom of the Intellectual in Greek Society," in *The Greeks and Their Legacy* (Oxford, 1988), 135-58.

religious or moral offenses for political ends unless the principles involved are seriously held and their violation results in genuine public outrage. Religious *indifference* offers no *point d'appui* for secular exploitation: mosques are not burned or *fatwas* issued for merely political ends. We have always to bear in mind that for many people, in all walks of life, Panhellenism *was* an ideal: elusive, perhaps unattainable—*aliudque cupido, / mens aliud suadet, uideo meliora proboque, / deteriora sequor:* "Desire urges me one way, reason another; I see the better course and approve it, but follow the worse"[16]—yet no less real than the equally passionate belief in *eleutheria* (another notoriously elusive concept), and far closer to the heart than the chilly authoritarianism of Plato's *Republic*.

The *locus classicus* both for the ideal and (less often recognized) for its endemic human weaknesses is the famous passage in Herodotus (8.144) where the Athenians speak of "the fact of Greek consanguinity and common language, the shrines of gods and the sacrifices that we share, our similar customs." We should remember the context in which this statement was made: reassurance to Spartan envoys that Athens could be trusted not to Medize. It follows a reminder of the burning by Persia of Greek temples, an act calling for revenge, and is concluded by the assertion that, should Athens betray such ties, "it would not be well." But of course, as Finley hardly needs to remind us, in such matters, "Indeed it was often not well with the Greeks": Medism was common, and interstate *stasis* even commoner. Nor, as Walbank emphasizes, can Herodotus's claim be easily reconciled with "an international community of completely independent national states" (11), much less with that endemic *Partikularismus* of which Beloch complained.[17]

Yet Panhellenism was not mere sociocultural aspiration; Hellas remained a *place*, the Balkan peninsula south of Thessaly,[18] and some statements exist[19] describing conflict between Greek cities as *stasis* rather than war. Isocrates in his *Panegyricus*, the Athenians who fought in the Lamian War, speak of Hellas as a κοινὴ πατρίς, a common fatherland.[20] The great Panhellenic Games not only reinforced the concept of Hellenic unity, but actively militated against conflict between Greek states, since a sacred truce was enforced for the duration of the festival, and firm exclusionary measures were taken against those (including, in 420, Sparta[21]) who were held to have ignored the ban.

---

16. Ovid *Met.* 7.20-21.

17. M. I. Finley, "The Ancient Greeks and Their Nation: The Sociological Problem," *British Journal of Sociology* 5 (1954): 253-64 (citation from 256); Walbank 1951, 11-13.

18. I. Weiler, "Greek and Non-Greek World in the Archaic Period," *GRByS* 9 (1968): 21-29, esp. 27-28.

19. Theognis 781; Hdt. 8.3; Plat. *Rep.* 5.470B-471B, cited by Walbank 1951, 11 n. 39.

20. Isocr. *Orat.* 4.81; Diod. Sic. 18.10.3.

21. Thuc. 5.49. In 412 the truce held (Thuc. 8.9-10): Athenians and Peloponnesians competed

Though the evidence from Homer is ambiguous (see note 8), Hesiod (*WD* 653) treats Hellas as mainland Greece, while both he and Archilochus[22] use the term Πανέλληνες. Aeschines' account of the oath taken by members of the Amphictyonic League (2.115, cf. 3.107–10, and Plat. *Rep.* 5.471B) refers to clauses forbidding the razing of member cities or the cutting off of their water supply (though just such actions could be taken against those who violated the oath, on a tit-for-tat basis). Walbank (above, note 12) notes the growth of conventions serving to humanize Greek warfare, what Euripides (*Suppl.* 311) described, c. 422 B.C., as νόμιμα πάσης Ἑλλάδος, "[customs] agreed on throughout Greece." Again, the widespread—and, from the Peloponnesian War onward, increasing—disregard of such νόμιμα is no proof of their non-existence. Who broke the rules? Equally important, who kept them? And how many fell into both categories, men who could say with St. Paul, "The good that I would I do not, and the evil which I would not, that I do"?[23]

The case of Pindar is of particular interest, since not only does he (almost alone among Greek writers) show an intermittent distaste for that prime Hellenic pursuit, war,[24] but he seems, despite the political cost to collaborationist Thebes imposed by the Greco-Persian conflict (490–479),[25] to have promoted throughout his career a Panhellenic ideal, based on what he saw as the universal values of creative art and aristocratic ἀρετή. He ignores Marathon; his main reference to Salamis (*Isthm.* 5.48–51) merely emphasizes bloody destruction, warns against boastful chauvinism; he is as ready to commemorate the dead who fought on the Persian side[26] as the "saviors of Hellas" glorified by Herodotus.[27] His relief at Greece having escaped "the stone of Tantalos

---

together, while Corinth scrupulously refrained from sending a squadron to aid the anti-Athenian faction on Chios until the truce was over.

22. Hes. fr. 130 = Strabo 8.6.6, C.370; Archilochus fr. 102 West.

23. Rom. 7.19; cf. Ovid *Met.* 7.20–21.

24. See in particular fr. 110 Snell: γλυκὺ δὲ πόλεμος ἀπειρά-/τοισιν, | ἐμπείρων δέ τις/ ταρβεῖ προσιόντα νιν | καρδίᾳ περισσῶς ("War is sweet to those without experience of it, but one who knows it fears its approach exceedingly in his heart")—a sentiment with which few veterans would disagree. The only other consistently antiwar Greek poet is Hesiod; Euripides' attitude (or to be more accurate, that of his characters) varies from militant jingoism to the agonies of defeat. Cf. Pind. *Isthm.* 5.48–51.

25. Cf. J. H. Finley, "Pindar and the Persian Invasion," *HSCP* 63 (1958): 121–32; C. M. Bowra, *Pindar* (Oxford, 1964), ch. 3 ("Echoes of Politics"), 99–158.

26. *Isthm.* 4.16–18: once again we observe the politically impartial note. War is seen not as a human, i.e., political, act, but rather as an impersonal force of nature.

27. Hdt. 7.139: νῦν δὲ Ἀθηναίους ἄν τις λέγων σωτῆρας γενέσθαι τῆς Ἑλλάδος οὐκ ἂν ἁμαρτάνοι τὸ ἀληθές, "But anyone now claiming that the Athenians were the saviors of Greece would not miss the truth." Cf. Pind. *Pyth.* 1.75–80 (praise for Athens over Salamis and Sparta because of Plataia, but no evidence for glory in military *kleos* as such).

hanging overhead," the freedom to which he looks forward, both imply (as he goes on to make clear) simply a return to the old Panhellenic (and fundamentally aristocratic) ideal, an end to partisan suspicion and hatred of pro-Persian Thebes among the Greek victors.[28] A true elite will survive even such indignities and vicissitudes: ἄτρωτοί γε μὰν παῖδες θεῶν (*Isthm.* 3.19). Pindar's devotion to *hēsychia* (quietude) is thus far more broadly based than, say, the Hellenistic pursuit of *ataraxia* (lack of disturbance). The exceptional nature of his vision becomes immediately apparent when we compare it with other manifestations of Panhellenism known to us, since virtually every one of these is specifically invoked as an instrument of either national crisis or national aggression.

This, surprisingly, is true even of Aristophanes, whose rural Panhellenism—above all in the *Acharnians* (425), the *Peace* (421), and the *Lysistrata* (411)—has long been taken for granted, and forms the subject of at least one passionately *parti pris* monograph.[29] Aristophanes in fact offers a good test case for examining a phenomenon central to my argument: the implementation (exploitation, certainly in this case, would be too strong a term), under strong military or political pressure, of what we have seen to be a genuine, if for the most part unformulated, longing, a *pothos*, for basic ethnic unity. Precisely because the ideal was never defined, let alone given a name, it proved infinitely adaptable to circumstance—though in fact there were no more than three main situations in which it was regularly invoked: collective aggression, collective defense, or, as in Aristophanes' case, their natural end-product, war-weariness, the simple craving for an end to hostilities, a return to normal country life and the disrupted agricultural year-cycle.

Dicaeopolis, in the *Acharnians*, makes a private peace for himself (130–279); warmongers (in the person of Lamachus) are satirized (1071–141, 1174–225). In the *Peace*, appeals by the Chorus to fellow Hellenes (292) and Panhellenes (302) soon give way to a more honest identification of the peace movement with *Athenian farmers* (508, 511).[30] Though the *Lysistrata* lays great stress on those Panhellenic fundamentals, common action, reconciliation, and compromise,[31] the entire thrust of the play is toward a normalization of wartime conditions, which bring about the deaths of sons, and by parting

---

28. *Isthm.* 8.10ff. It was not so long since Thebes' leading pro-Persian collaborators had been surrendered for execution to Pausanias (Hdt. 9.88), and Sparta had only been dissuaded by Themistocles (Plut. *Them.* 20) from expelling Thebes from the Amphictyonic Council.

29. Hugill 1936, passim.

30. Cf. Perlman 1976, 4 n. 9.

31. Hugill 1936, 15ff.

husbands and wives for long periods (a new development) create sexual frustration as well as play havoc with the farming year. More important for the
historian, Lysistrata's solution (1128–35 is the key passage[32]) envisages Athens
and Sparta, reconciled by memories of joint action at Artemisium and Thermopylae (1247–61), enjoying joint hegemony over Greece—an alliance ce-
mented by common hostility to the Persian, the Barbarian, their proper and
natural enemy rather than one another: the Barbarian, on whom they once
together inflicted a famous defeat, and whom they could, and should, defeat
again.[33]

Here we have, in the proverbial nutshell, what was to prove by far the most
influential manifestation of Panhellenism in all Greek history. The simple binary opposition of Self and Other that it presupposed; the identification of
that Other with "barbarism" (however defined), and Self with "civilization";
the division of the world, symbolically as well as geographically, into separate, delimiting, spheres of interest, to overstep which was to court *nemesis*
through *hubris*;[34] the subsequent justification of Hellenic (or more particularly Athenian) expansion into the barbarian sphere on grounds of racial, social, and cultural superiority—all this constitutes a key element in Athenian
fourth-century history, to which we must now turn.

From the aftermath of the Peloponnesian War to the rise of Philip of Macedon (and, for some, well beyond that), Athenian intellectuals promoted a
clear, seductive, and simple—indeed, politically artless—version of Panhellenism: let the quarreling Greek states unite against their true, natural, and
historical foe, the Achaemenid empire of Persia, now defined as the Barbarian
par excellence. In 392,[35] against a background of failed peace negotiations between Athens and Sparta (with renascent Athenian imperial ambitions holding out against Sparta's divide-and-rule proposals for general autonomy[36]),

---

32. Lysistrata chides both Athenians and Spartans, who "though barbarian enemies abound in
force / are still destroying Hellenic men and cities." On the passage in general, see J. Henderson,
Aristophanes' Lysistrata (Oxford, 1987), 199–200.

33. This is the second of the three "types" of Panhellenism analyzed by G. Dobesch, *Der panhellenische Gedanke im 4. Jahrhundert v. Chr. und der "Philippos" des Isokrates. Untersuchungen zum
Korinthischen Bund*, vol. 1 (Vienna, 1968), 4: "The one that regarded the interests of all Greeks as
best represented by a union of the leading powers of Hellas—which in practical terms primarily
meant Athens and Sparta."

34. Cf. Aesch. *Pers.* 721–26, 744–51.

35. A. Momigliano, *Filippo il Macedone: Saggio sulla storia greca del IV secolo a.C.* (Florence, 1934,
reprinted Milan, 1987), 184.

36. Hamilton 1979, 233–59, esp. 258–59. Andocides' *On the Peace* stresses the (comparatively
new) notion (3.17) of a κοινὴ εἰρήνη, common peace, between the Greek states; though his mo-

Gorgias delivered an oration,[37] appropriately enough at the Olympic festival, calling on Greece's bitterly divided *poleis* to forego their endless *stasis* in favor of treating "the land of the barbarians," rather than one another's cities, as the "prize to be won"—not so far from the concept, later popularized by Alexander and his successors, of γῆ δορίκτητος, "spear-won territory."

That it was Persia Gorgias had in mind is made clear from Philostratus's account[38] of the funeral oration he delivered in Athens: the same text reveals, with striking force, Athenian ambivalence toward the whole notion of Panhellenism, whether as a "common peace," κοινὴ εἰρήνη, or mere vague *homonoia*, since Gorgias (we are told) kept off the latter topic altogether, the Athenians having a "passion for empire" (ἀρχῆς ἐρῶντας) with which, he felt, it would not sit well. Instead, he dwelt on their victories in the Persian Wars, which he compared favorably with those over fellow Greeks, the latter being a fitter subject for dirges than for paeans.

Four years later (388)[39] Lysias, again at Olympia, delivered another very similar exhortation. The full speech does not survive, but its opening has been preserved by Dionysius of Halicarnassus.[40] Lysias, like Gorgias, attacks *stasis* and rivalry among the Greek states, arguing that the Great King is both a fitter target and a more serious danger. Unlike Gorgias, however, he brackets the Achaemenid monarch with Dionysius I of Syracuse, the barbarian with the tyrant. This is interesting, not only because of the *tyrannos-barbaros* equation, or even because Dionysius, a Greek, was himself engaged in fighting *barbaroi* in the shape of the Carthaginians,[41] but for the politically labile concept of the Barbarian Other that it reveals: Demosthenes, for instance, had no hesitation in casting Philip of Macedon in the role. Many Greeks, Lysias argues, exist "under barbarian rule," many cities have been "rendered desolate by tyrants." He then appeals to the Spartans—with ill-disguised impatience—on the basis of their military reputation and historical record, to take the lead against both. The implementation of the King's Peace a year later, *inter*

---

tives in this Spartan political scheme are suspect, Hamilton is wrong in asserting (259) that "the idea of common peace did not prevail because the concept of a common good, to which it might have corresponded, did not exist."

37. Cited by Philostr., *Vit. Soph.* 1.9 (§§493–94). Cf. Arist. *Rhet.* 3.14 (1414b30ff.).

38. Philostr. *Vit. Soph.* 1.9 (§§493–94).

39. Diod. Sic. 14.109.1–4. I see no reason, with Perlman (1976, 20 n. 64) and others, to ignore this chronologically explicit and circumstantial testimony, and redate the occasion to the next Olympiad (384). The crux of the matter is whether Lysias delivered his oration before or after the King's Peace; to me his words only make sense in a context where Sparta's decision is still uncertain (and thus possibly amenable to rhetorical persuasion).

40. Dion. Hal. *Lys.* §§29–30.

41. Perlman 1976, 20 and n. 68.

alia ceding the Greeks of Asia Minor to Persian rule, rendered that appeal
moot—which, predictably, did not stop various politicians and pamphleteers,
above all Isocrates in the *Panegyricus* of 380, from promoting the idea of a campaign against the Great King led jointly by a reconciled Athens and Sparta.[42]

Historically, this appeal had good precedent, in the by now thoroughly
mythicized episode of the Persian Wars, which must bear considerable responsibility both for the final shaping of the Hellene/Barbarian dichotomy,
and for the firm identification of the latter with the Achaemenid empire. As
Edith Hall rightly stresses, "The idea of the barbarian as the generic opponent to Greek civilisation was a result of this heightening in Hellenic self-
consciousness caused by the rise of Persia."[43] It is significant that the one well-
known earlier collective effort by the Greek states—equally mythicized, if not
actually mythical; equally only brought about by war—had nothing to do with
Persia, and (if we can trust Homer) was also carried out in total ignorance
of that privileged Hellenic status which fourth-century politicians and pamphleteers took for granted. Both sides in the Trojan War are treated by Homer
on an equal basis; they are ethnically indistinguishable; and some of the worst
atrocities are committed by Greeks.[44]

Until Aeschylus's patriotic play *The Persians* (472), the term βάρβαρος is
seldom found. Homer's Carians are βαρβαρόφωνοι (*Il.* 2.867), "barbarian in
speech," which may indicate a *Distanzgefühl*[45] but has no culturally pejorative
sense, any more than does the parallel term ἀλλόθροος in the *Odyssey* (1.183,
3.302, 15.453, etc.). By the sixth century, we can detect a slight change: Anacreon (fr. S 313 Page *SLG*) can say "[I fear] you may use barbarian terms," μή
πως βάρβαρα βάξῃς—the emphasis is still on language, but the tone is contemptuous—while that class-conscious elitist Heraclitus is reported[46] to have

---

42. Isocr. *Orat.* 4.15-17. Justification for the crusade was easy: despoil those with excessive
wealth, humble the arrogant, preempt the danger of an attack (rumors of Persian plans to invade
Greece were current between 356 and 354), visit revenge on those who are Greece's hereditary
enemies and natural slaves. See, e.g., 4.181, 183-84; 5.124-25; *Ep.* 9.19.

43. Hall 1989, 9.

44. Ibid., 22-31, 40ff. Cf. also the comment of Jüthner 1923, 2: "The inhabitants of the besieged
city speak the same language, have the same customs, clothes, and weapons, and worship the same
gods as the Greeks. Of barbarism in its later sense there is as yet no trace."

45. Weiler 1968, 22, citing H. Herter, *Gnomon* 38 (1966): 577-87. Thucydides (1.3.3) denies the
existence of the term βάρβαρος in Homer's day (for which he was later taken to task by Strabo,
14.2.28, C.661); this *may* indicate that the βαρβαρόφωνοι were a later interpolation, but does not
constitute proof.

46. 22 B 107 D-K, cited by Sext. Emp. *Math.* 7.126. On the argument over the implications of
this fragment, see Hall 1989, 10 with n. 31 and references there cited; Weiler 1968, 24-25; H. C.
Baldry, *The Unity of Mankind in Greek Thought* (Cambridge, 1965), 27-28.

declared, c. 500 B.C., that κακοὶ μάρτυρες ἀνθρώποισιν ὀφθαλμοὶ καὶ ὦτα βαρβάρους ψυχὰς ἐχόντων, "Eyes and ears are bad witnesses for men with barbarian souls": a difficult fragment (is he referring merely, as some suppose, to language difficulties, or more generally to intelligence and education?), but clearly pejorative in its implications.

Colonization also played a part in the development of the *Distanzgefühl*. To Greeks of the early Archaic Age, *autrui* still lay outside the human dimension, in the world of mythical monsters, Titans, Gorgons, Cyclopes, Amazons, Centaurs, what Hall labels "supernatural barbarians." These gradually merged with the (scarcely less mythical) oddities—Skiapods, Manticores— produced by travelers' garbled tales as exploration pushed back the frontiers of the unknown.[47] The spread of knowledge, intelligent research of the kind carried out by the Milesian physicists, inevitably carried with it potential contempt for those outside the magic circle of Hellenic ἱστορίη. Thus it comes about that by the time of *The Persians*, we are already confronted, in detail, with "the absolute polarisation in Greek thought of Hellene and barbarian."[48] The concept was strengthened by Hippocratic notions of geographic influence on character (Asiatics are sluggish, effeminate, unwarlike[49]) and formulated as a rule of nature in two famous passages of Aristotle.[50]

Thus despite the visible, if slow, development among the Greeks of a sense of conscious ethnic (and to some extent cultural and intellectual) distinction from, and superiority to, the surrounding world, Schwabel is surely right in his assertion[51] that the fundamental Greek/barbarian, freedom/tyranny dichotomy was only precipitated by the violent crisis of the Persian Wars. There is nothing like a dangerous enemy in view (as we know too well today) to encourage stereotyped racism and emotional hyperbole—not to mention the arguments (more often than not, like those in *Airs Waters Places*, pseudo-scientific) regularly adduced to justify both. In other words, one of the fifth and fourth centuries' most dynamic and influential concepts was based on

---

47. O. Reverdin, "Crise spirituelle et évasion," in *Grecs et barbares*, Fond. Hardt 8 (Geneva, 1962), 100–103; cf. Hall 1989, 51–55, 68.

48. Hall 1989, 57.

49. Hippocr. *Aër* 16.

50. *Pol.* 1.1252b7–9, citing Eur. *IA* 1400; fr. 658 Rose, citing Aristotle's advice to Alexander on dealing with men, "to show himself a leader to the Greeks, but a master to the barbarians, caring for the former as friends and family, but treating the latter like animals or plants."

51. H. Schwabel, "Das Bild der fremden Welt bei den frühen Griechen," in *Grecs et barbares* (above, note 47), 23. The criticisms of Weiler (1968, 21ff.) and others do not damage his fundamental position.

mere historical contingency. The Persian threat made self-definition easy. It also meant that the formulation was framed in binary terms, a classic μὲν-δέ structure, since the self can only be defined in contrast to what it is not.

The dichotomy was—had to be—political.[52] Nascent Athenian democracy emerged, from the late sixth century onward, in sharp contradistinction (as Herodotus later emphasized) to the theocratic, authoritarian monarchies of the Near East. The customary law (νόμος) of free men was opposed, in a dramatic and emotionally evocative comparison, to despotism and the compulsion of the lash, nowhere more consistently and strikingly than in the *Histories* of Herodotus.[53] This formed the core of the fourth-century rhetorical argument calling for a united Hellenic crusade against the Barbarian.

Yet the argument, especially insofar as it invoked the notion of Panhellenism, remained riddled with contradictions. What an Athenian, a Spartan, a Corinthian, an Argive fought for, in the last resort, was his polis. If he joined a συμμαχία, alliance, it was for short-term, primarily military, purposes.[54] As Finley says,[55] "Demosthenes gave his life in the attempt to organise common resistance against Philip and Alexander; but he fought for federation against a potential conqueror, so that the Greek communities might be able to continue their independent existence, not for the creation of a single Greek state." The ethnic, religious, and cultural unity that inspired Pindar made no sense at all in political terms except as a call to arms in times of crisis or expansionism. It took five hundred years of the Turkish occupation to bring Greece, stubbornly particularist still, to the threshold of national sovereignty.

Nor did the concept of "the Barbarian," not least in its political application, rest on anything more solid than a diffuse xenophobia compounded of linguistic ignorance, parochial ethnocentricity, and, in Athens's case, defensive arrogance sharpened, from the beginning of the fourth century, by a humiliating military defeat. Indeed, one traditional myth made the Achaemenid royal line Greek by descent, from Perseus and Danaë.[56] So much for the im-

---

52. See Hall 1989, 13–19, for a thorough discussion of the problem.

53. See in particular Demaratus's exposition to Xerxes of the forces sustaining Spartan valor (7.104).

54. Walbank 1951, 50–51 (= 1985, 9–10).

55. Finley 1954, 262.

56. Hdt. 7.61, 150–51. There was also a Trojan stemma for the Persians through Memnon: see P. Georges, "The Persians in the Greek Imagination, 550–480 B.C.," diss., University of California, Berkeley (1981), 196–97 and 234–35 (nn. 9–11a). This association had the result that "the Trojans were henceforth definitively barbarized in Greek thought and literature" (Georges, 210), rather than the Persians being Hellenized by their association with Troy. Cf. Jean M. Davison, "Myth and the Periphery," in *Myth and the Polis*, ed. D. C. Pozzi and J. M. Wickersham (Ithaca and London, 1991), 61–63, for the legitimizing function of Io's wanderings: "To the extent that itinerary

mutable Other: the vagueness of the formulation is well illustrated by the fact that the Barbarian could, under pressure of changing circumstances, be variously identified with the Achaemenids, the Argeads, and, finally, the Romans.

The political and the cultural concepts, furthermore, were, not surprisingly, at odds with one another, particularism against *homonoia;* and nowhere is this clearer, again, than in Herodotus. Though he remains, with Aeschylus's *Persae,* the fundamental source for that Hellene/Barbarian, freedom/tyranny dichotomy so well analyzed by Schwabel, nevertheless his work abounds in generous and approving descriptions of individual Persian *mores,* while his initial account (1.4) of Io's role in the supposed eternal enmity between Greece and Persia reads suspiciously like a good-natured parody of the *ad hominem* (or in this case *ad feminam*) excesses engendered by strident nationalism. From the beginning of the Peloponnesian War, both sides angled briskly for Persian support and Persian gold.[57] Xenophon, whose *Anabasis* did so much to encourage the feasibility of an anti-Barbarian crusade,[58] also composed, in the *Cyropaedia,* a highly romanticized tribute to the ἀρετή of a Persian prince.

It was the Peloponnesian War that perhaps did more than any other single factor to reemphasize the artificial dichotomy between Europe and Asia, liberty and tyranny, Hellene and Persian.[59] It became easy to exploit, on the one hand, the common man's war-exhaustion and yearning for peace; on the other, ethnic shame at defeat and the determination to recover imperial power.[60] A weak, wealthy, militarily incompetent and morally contemptible enemy offered a splendid field for united Hellenic action: hence the *political* attraction of Panhellenism, in itself the polar antithesis of polis ideology.

The ambiguity of the literary evidence reflects a corresponding dualism in Athenian society. Isocrates and Demosthenes, each in his own way, exemplify this. Neither (it is crucial to recognize) was a cynical manipulator; each preached what he passionately believed. The dualism, moreover, was one that they had inherited from the fifth century. Nowhere is this clearer than in the plays of Euripides. These frequently emphasize both the Panhellenic motif

---

and genealogy formed the basis of the Greek view of their own prehistory, the myth of Io was central to this comprehension. . . . The peculiarity and exotic nature of other areas, combined with an internal cohesion provided by extended genealogies, made the Greeks conscious of their own singularities."

57. Aristoph. *Ach.* 99-115; D. M. Lewis, *Sparta and Persia* (Leiden, 1977), 61-65.

58. Cf. J. Morr, "Xenophon und der Gedanke eines allgriechischen Eroberungszuges gegen Persien," *Wiener Studien* 45 (1926-27): 186-201. Isocr. *Orat.* 4.145-49 is clearly based on a close reading of Xenophon.

59. See, e.g., Thuc. 4.50.2-3 (a reference called to my attention by Prof. E. Harris).

60. Aristoph. *Ach.* 130-625, *Peace* 551-1016; Isocr. *Orat.* 4.110-22.

and the Hellene/Barbarian dichotomy, variously expressed in terms of language, costume, social taboos, religious practice (including human sacrifice),
intelligence, moral imperatives, and innate character (barbarians, as Iphigenia stresses, are slavish by nature, Hellenes free: τὸ μὲν γὰρ δοῦλον, οἱ δ'
ἐλεύθεροι—even the shift of gender is judgmental).[61] This emphasis on Athenian freedom, frequently expressed,[62] could not but encourage, as an ingre-
dient of self-definition by contrast, barbarian servitude. The same is true of
Euripides' preoccupation with a common law or custom binding on all Greeks
(*Orest.* 495):[63] another distinguishing mark, since barbarians were held to be
subject, not to law, but to autocratic tyranny.[64]

   Yet at the same time, as Hall well demonstrates,[65] Euripides on numerous
occasions deconstructs "the orthodox polarization of Hellene and barbarian"
(211) by offering mythical examples both of Greeks who behave uncommonly
like barbarians (e.g., Agamemnon sacrificing Iphigenia in the *IT*, where the
imagery is linked to that of human sacrifice among the Taurians) and of barbarians—mostly, it is interesting to note, Trojans, such as Polyxena or Cassandra—who display Greek standards of fortitude and restraint in sharp contrast
to the conduct of actual Greeks with whom they have to deal. The concept of
the Noble Savage, later to be given such memorable expression by the Attalids'
Pergamene sculptors, can here be glimpsed in embryo. Furthermore, Euripides' Panhellenism is constantly undercut, especially in the Archidamian War
plays, by his sometimes jingoistic polis patriotism: "What is dearer to a man
than his native land?" one fragment asks.[66] The rhetorical question carries implications that extend far beyond Athens: indeed, Euripides takes it as axiom-
atic that every πατρίς, every polis, however small, has sovereign rights over
its citizens' hearts and emotions,[67] indeed their lives.[68] This agrees very well

61. *IA* 1400-1401; see also *Orest.* 574; *IA* 350, 1274-75, 1375-83. Cf. J. H. Sussmann, *Die Grund-
züge der panhellenischen Idee im 5. und 4. Jahrhundert v. Chr.* (Zürich, 1921), 31ff.; Hettich 1933, ch. 3;
Hall 1989, 47, 73-74, 118-19, 136-37, 150-51, 178, 185-90.
   62. *Heraclid.* 62, 111, 189-203, 284-87; *Suppl.* 403-8, 426-56; cf. Hettich 1933, 29-32.
   63. Cf. also *Hel.* 1241, *Suppl.* 311, *Heraclid.* 1010, *Alc.* 683-84, *Orest.* 485-87.
   64. *Hel.* 276, *Orest.* 1167-71, *Med.* 536-40.
   65. Hall 1989, 21-23.
   66. Hettich 1933, chs. 1-2, with an exhaustive conspectus of passages: see, e.g., fr. 6 Nauck (cited
in the text), *Phoen.* 991-1018, and for specific references to Athens, *Elect.* 1289, *IT* 1088, *Suppl.* 387,
Med. 824-32, *Hipp.* 1094-95.
   67. Hettich 1933, 17-25, collects a striking array of examples: see, e.g., *Phoen.* 358-60, *Hel.* 460-
63 (any slur is quickly resented), *Andr.* 454-55 (destruction of one's city can be equated with one's
own death), *Med.* 650-51 (to be cut off from one's homeland is the worst of fates). Exile (Hettich
1933, 21-23) is the ultimate horror.
   68. *Phoen.* 991-1018, 1054-60, 1313-14.

with what history tells us, but is hard to reconcile, in any political sense, with the Panhellenic ideal—a fact that, not surprisingly, seems to have bothered no one in antiquity.[69]

Athens, to complicate matters further, had been, until the close of the fifth century, a great imperial power, by no means lacking in those qualities—arrogance, civic self-aggrandizement, exclusivity—which tend to be the natural concomitants of empire, and which Athenians were far from shy about proclaiming.[70] Euripides was no exception.[71] He also did not hesitate, in wartime, to saddle the Spartans, undoubted fellow Hellenes, with characteristics more appropriate to barbarians;[72] on one occasion, indeed, in the *Andromache* (?426), he makes the same character, Hermione, deliver scathing attacks, successively, on both "the barbarian race" (168–75: incest, murder, lawlessness) and the Spartans (445–53: treachery, intrigue, murder, αἰσχροκερδία [shameful greed]). The Spartans are πᾶσιν ἀνθρώποισιν ἔχθιστοι βροτῶν . . . ψευδῶν ἄνακτες, "the most hateful of mortals to all mankind . . . lords of deceit," with twisted, diseased minds. As Hall says,[73] "In this play the Spartans have gravitated to the conceptual space elsewhere occupied by non-Greeks, for the vices imputed to them . . . are familiar themes from rhetoric against the barbarian."[74]

---

69. Some modern scholars, on the other hand (e.g., Prof. Harris *per litt.*) find the antithesis between polis ideology (i.e., strictly local political loyalties) and the loosely ethnic notion of Panhellenism exaggerated, or even nonexistent. "Why," Harris asks, "should love of community be incompatible with some larger ethnic loyalty?" In many ways, of course—linguistic, social, religious—as we know from that famous passage in Herodotus (8.144), it was not: politics, as so often among the incurably particularist Greek states, was what marked the real polarity. Though Greeks were also capable (as my anonymous referee rightly reminds me) of sharing "the common human propensity to engage in what George Orwell so appropriately called 'double-think'," I most certainly do not share his—and others'—belief in the existence of a general assumption that (to paraphrase a former czar of the automobile industry) what was good for Sparta/Athens/Corinth etc. was good for Greece, or vice versa. The "ability of many Greek thinkers to propound apparently antithetical policies of local patriotism and panhellenism at the same time," so often remarked on, is no more than the perennial politician's urge to sound altruistic while pushing essentially selfish goals.

70. See, e.g., Thuc. 1.73–78, and cf. R. Meiggs, *The Athenian Empire* (Oxford, 1972), ch. 21 ("Fifth Century Judgements"), 375–403.

71. As may be seen from the *Ion:* see 671–75, 719–24, 1058–60.

72. A catalogue (including lies, murder, treachery, militarism, arrogance, hypocrisy, and the masculinization of women) in Hettich 1933, 40–43. See, for example, *Suppl.* 184–89, *Tro.* 208–9, 953–57.

73. Hall 1989, 214.

74. Prof. E. Harris makes an interesting comment: "I think we have a rhetorical strategy here. To justify attacks on fellow Greeks, one had first to deprive them of their credentials for Greekness. This was similar to justifying attacks on the constitutional rights of American leftists during the 1950s by first labelling them 'Unamerican'."

The categories, then, were far from sharply defined: the Persians had no inherent monopoly on the role of *barbaros*, which could be stretched (with greater or lesser emphasis) to include not only Thracians, Phrygians, or other obvious non-Hellenes, not only such borderline cases as the Macedonians (a boon for Demosthenes and Theopompus in the fourth century), but even, under stress of military confrontation, the Spartans. Similarly, a yearning for Hellenic *homonoia* could, without any apparent sense of contradiction, be held at the same time—indeed, by the same person—as the most chauvinist local patriotism. The logic may have been faulty, but the passions were genuine.

Aristophanes offers an excellent instance of this. That rural nostalgia for peace, good farming, and ancient tradition, so prominent in the plays written before 421, is predicated on something more than simple war exhaustion. Zimmern hit the mark when he criticized Thucydides—and, by implication, the whole Sophist-inspired *Realpolitik* of the later fifth century—for not caring "about all that the brutal heel of war trampled down—the quiet homely country life in the smaller Greek states, the old-world sentiment of the Panhellenic gatherings, the memories of the days before power became a passion and empire a calculation."[75] Those days, when Cimon could talk (and even at the time the remark betrayed a curious insulation from political reality) about going to Sparta's aid, "begging them not to let Hellas go lame, nor their city to lose its yoke-fellow,"[76] were long past. In any case, ironically enough, Sparta's Messenian enemies were not only downtrodden serfs, but fellow Greeks now fighting for their freedom: so much for the community of blood, speech, and cult.

Athens's imperial attitude is summed up in one telltale word: its fiscal officers, responsible for collecting tribute from the subject-allies, were known as

75. A. E. Zimmern, *Solon and Croesus, and Other Greek essays* (Oxford, 1928), 103. It has been put to me that this represents, at best, "the views of a small privileged elite in ancient Greece," and that Zimmern himself, when he wrote the passage, was in fact influenced by "the idealized view of pre–World War I Europe found among many representatives of the European propertied class who had lived through the war." But this is to stand the situation on its head: it was, precisely, the powerful and well-connected minority that nursed imperialist ambitions, and backed them with might-as-right theories, while small farmers and ordinary country folk (as opposed to the urban populace) recalled Attica's slow recovery from Persian devastation, only to watch new inroads being made by Sparta's (unopposed) hoplites.

76. Plut. *Cim.* 16. Plutarch comments on the political climate of the period (ibid., 17): "Men's differences then were political, while personal passions were kept within bounds, and could easily be subsumed to the common good; even ambition, though dominant over all the emotions, acknowledged the supremacy of the state's needs in a crisis." I am sure Plutarch believed this; more to the point, I am sure that Cimon and many of his contemporaries did, too. Not surprisingly, it was Ephialtes (ibid.) who had argued in favor of letting Sparta's pride "lie low and be trampled." But that is another story.

Ἑλληνοταμίαι, "comptrollers *of Greece*." If this was Panhellenism, it was of the sort questionably identified by Dobesch as "that which wished to see Hellas led by a supreme power, free from all *Egoismus* [*sic*], and wholly devoted to the united states of Greece."[77] This, as the Congress Decree clearly indicates,[78] was indeed how Athens saw itself; but, fortunately or not (depending on one's attitude), *Egoismus* in others obstinately blocked the way. After defeat and a scarring civil war, the Athenians entered the fourth century humiliated, temporarily impoverished, bitterly resentful, but in essence unchanged, least of all in their political ambitions. Their one overriding thought was to recover Athens's lost glory and prestige in the only way they understood (thus, too, third-century Sparta under Cleomenes III); and for such a purpose, a crusade against the Barbarian, linked to the emotionally potent appeal of Panhellenism, struck a more than responsive chord.

Such was the legacy that Isocrates drew on in his public political statements, from the *Panegyricus* (380) to the *Philippus* (346). Born in 436/5,[79] he could have seen Pericles as a child, and his most impressionable years coincided with the first decade of the Peloponnesian War. Yet he also lived long enough to hear the news of Philip II's victory over the Greek alliance at Chaeronea in 338.[80] He thus can serve as a valuable witness—more valuable, perhaps, than has sometimes been realized—for the evolution of social and political beliefs during that momentous era. He has been criticized for inconsistency,[81] opportunism,[82] and authoritarian, pro-monarchic leanings.[83] There is some truth in all these charges, and they are precisely what gives his evidence its unique value.

From the Corinthian War through the King's Peace to the final, fatal con-

---

77. Dobesch 1968, 4.

78. Donald Kagan, *The Outbreak of the Peloponnesian War* (Ithaca and London, 1969), 110–13.

79. [Plut.] *Mor.* 836F; cf. Dion. Hal. *Isocr.* 1.

80. [Plut.] *Mor.* 837E; Dion. Hal. *Isocr.* 1. The report that he starved himself to death (at the age of ninety-eight) is not necessarily incompatible with the genuineness of *Ep.* 3 to Philip, composed shortly after the battle; Dionysius reports that he ended his life (with symbolic appropriateness) at the time of the burial of Athens's war-dead, "it still being unclear how Philip would use his good fortune when he took over the government of the Greek states." Cf. G. C. Chilver, in *OCD*², 554–55.

81. See Baynes 1955, passim.

82. Kennedy 1963, 174–203.

83. M. M. Markle, "Support of Athenian Intellectuals for Philip: A Study of Isocrates' Philippus and Speusippus' Letter to Philip," *JHS* 96 (1976): 80–99; G.E.M. de Ste Croix, *The Class Struggle in the Ancient Greek World* (London, 1981), 295–301. Many may feel, as I do, that anyone capable of provoking Ste Croix to such spluttering vituperation ("the odious Isocrates," 301) must have some good in him somewhere.

frontation with Philip, Isocrates is a sounding-board for the changing views of Athens's wealthy, conservative, rhetorically articulate intellectuals.[84] His allegiance to the democracy depended—certainly after 358—on the existence of an active imperialist policy: his *Panegyricus* may not (as has sometimes been thought) have led to the formation of the Second Athenian Confederacy,[85] but it was certainly the existence of the Confederacy that kept his hankering after a strong *Führer* under reasonable control. At first he seems to have fancied his friend and ex-student Timotheus, Conon's son and the Confederacy's commander, for such a role: Timotheus was rich, aristocratic, antidemotic, and imperialist in his views.[86] But very soon he gave up Timotheus and began shopping around for his anti-Persian leader elsewhere, not only outside Athens, but among the Greek world's more notorious autocrats: first Alexander of Pherae, then Dionysius of Syracuse (367: so much for Lysias's dismissal of this *tyrannos* in the same breath as the Barbarian!), later, possibly, King Archidamus of Sparta (356), and, finally, in 346, Philip of Macedon.[87] The reversion to authoritarianism so characteristic of fourth-century intellectuals (Speusippus is only the most extreme example) finds clear expression here: once again we see Isocrates faithfully reflecting a trend.

It is also, surely, significant that, as Jebb saw long ago,[88] Isocrates "lives and thinks and feels almost exclusively in the years 380–338 B.C." He tells us virtually nothing of his early life—the family fortune made by the manufacture of pipes,[89] which drew gibes from the comedians, but was lost by the end of the Peloponnesian War, or of the school on Chios.[90] He goes out of his way to deny, by implication,[91] his early career as a forensic speechwriter (his adopted son Aphareus openly stated that his father had never composed such

---

84. Cf. Dobesch 1968, 14. Obviously not all intellectuals fell into this limited category; but it existed, made itself felt, and consolidated its position with time.

85. Baynes 1955, 144. I should perhaps say here that though I have found Jack Cargill's *The Second Athenian League* extremely useful in its detailed treatment, I find myself flatly opposed to his conclusion that "there is no reason to believe that the Second Athenian League ever became—or tried to become—another Athenian Empire" (196). That particular leopard did not change its spots so easily.

86. See the remarkable tribute Isocrates pays Timotheus in 354/3 (after the general's death in exile) in *Orat.* 15.107–29; and cf. Mathieu 1925, 96–98.

87. Sakellariou 1981, 132.

88. R. C. Jebb, *The Attic Orators from Antiphon to Isaeos* [*sic*] (London, 1876), 2:1–2.

89. The proper nomenclature of *auloi* has caused a certain amount of scholarly puzzlement. The latest, and most thorough, examination of the problem, by M. L. West (*Ancient Greek Music* [Oxford, 1992]), wavers (82–85) between "pipe," "shawm," and "oboe" (or possibly "clarinet"). The one fact on which everyone agrees (ibid., 1–2) is that "flute" is wrong.

90. [Plut.] *Mor.* 836E–837B; Dion. Hal. *Isocr.* 1.

91. See, e.g., *Orat.* 15.36–39, 49.

speeches, though several survive).[92] Nor does he care to recall his attempted defense of Theramenes at the time of the latter's arrest, to his credit though that was.[93] What Isocrates in fact is at pains to suppress is the no longer fashionable pro-democratic sentiment that permeates early speeches such as the *De Bigis* and the *In Lochitem* and made the episode with Theramenes an embarrassing memory.

While he also, as has been suggested,[94] may well have wanted to bury the early speeches because "they were written for hire and are essentially mundane"—the antibanausic prejudice ran deep—the fact that "he never says anything about his first forty years except that he had a good education and lost his property" surely goes deeper. Isocrates seems to have been one of those literary figures (Paul de Man, I suspect, was another[95]) whose intellectual narcissism is such that they adapt themselves, chameleonlike,[96] to any social or political circumstances that will further their scholarly or artistic obsessions. If ever a man was (as Disraeli said of Gladstone) "a sophisticated rhetorician inebriated with the exuberance of his own verbosity," it was Isocrates: even the *Philippus* is, in the last resort, more concerned with rhetorical niceties and his own literary standing than with the major political issue it sets out to treat.[97]

How will such a man make his case? In particular, how will he formulate the dichotomy between Hellenism and Barbarism, on which that case is built? By defining his version of the Barbarian Other (which was immensely influential), what can he tell us about the fourth-century Athenian concept of Greekness? When, after a decade of tinkering, Isocrates finally published the *Panegyricus* in 380, the prevailing mood among Athenian *literati* was one of bitter and festering humiliation. Lysander's occupation, the savage reign of the Thirty, the scars left by civil war, Sparta's iron-fisted ineptitudes, and the final outrage (as they saw it) of the King's Peace, which ratified topsy-

---

92. Dion. Hal. *Isocr.* 18. Cf. Kennedy 1963, 176–77.

93. [Plut.] *Mor.* 836F–837A. There is a double twist here, since Theramenes was the victim of his own former associates, the Thirty: cf. Baynes 1955, 164.

94. Kennedy 1963, 177.

95. Unlike many liberals, I do not believe that Paul de Man was basically anti-Semitic: anti-Semitism simply happened to be in favor with the authorities at the time, and he went along to facilitate his career—just as in America he embraced a new and different set of principles for the same ultimate purpose. It is significant that his alleged anti-Semitism came as a total surprise to his Jewish friends in the United States. The outdated past was buried, no longer applicable. Cf. D. Lehman, *Signs of the Times: Deconstruction and the Fall of Paul de Man* (New York, 1991), 182–83.

96. The case of Alcibiades presents interesting parallels: Plutarch (*Alcib.* 23) credits him with the power "of assuming, and adapting his character to, other people's interests and lifestyles, changing his own habits more swiftly than a chameleon."

97. So, rightly, Kennedy 1963, 199–202.

turvydom by reversing the symbolic roles of Hellene and Barbarian,[98] and was handed down by Achaemenid royal fiat,[99] with the active cooperation of the Spartans[100]—all this could not fail to leave its mark on Isocrates' outlook and propaganda. No Greek, ancient or modern, has ever been expected to adhere strictly to truth in a panegyric, where "to emphasize . . . virtues rather than unfortunate errors" is normal procedure;[101] Isocrates is no exception to the rule. Baynes[102] regards his ingenious rewriting and distortion of history as deliberate sophistic practice; I suspect that in fact, much of it may have rested on passionate wishful thinking, which at the time he may even have convinced himself was actually true.

The *Panegyricus*, as Sakellariou says,[103] "exudes Isocrates' indignation over the undignified position of the Greeks" vis-à-vis the Great King. Artaxerxes, with good reason, holds the Greeks in absolute contempt.[104] Athenians and Spartans alike have ceded Asia, Greek *poleis* included, to his rule. *Yet these are the Barbarians:* our natural and hereditary enemies (Isocrates asserts), cowardly, effeminate, unwarlike, corrupted by luxury, possessed of vast wealth that they deserve less than does the poorest Greek (a telltale argument to which I shall return in a moment), incapable of withstanding a Greek invasion (remember the march of the Ten Thousand!), surly minions bred to slavery, an ill-disciplined mob, physically pampered, arrogant when not servile, and cringing in abject terror before their overlord, to whom they prostrate themselves as to a god.[105] What distinguishes this kind of tirade from the portrait drawn by Aeschylus, Herodotus, or the Hippocratic author of *Airs Waters Places*—and a fortiori from the good-humored mockery of foreign jabber exercised by Aristophanes at the expense of such figures as Pseudartabas, a Scythian archer-policeman, or the uncouth Triballian deity in the *Birds*[106]—

---

98. I would like, in this context, to pay tribute to Ernst Badian's lapidary (and characteristically hard-headed) article "The King's Peace," in *Georgica: Greek Studies in Honour of George Cawkwell*, *BICS*, suppl. 58 (1991): 25–48, which, among many other virtues, has spared me the necessity of discussing the negotiations of 392/1! See, for present purposes, pt. 3, 35–48.

99. Xen. *Hell.* 5.1.31.

100. Badian (as in note 98), and "The Peace of Callias," *JHS* 107 (1987): 27–30.

101. Dion. Hal. *Ep. ad Pomp.* 1 (p. 354 Usher), cited by Baynes 1955, 166. Similarly Cicero, writing to the historian L. Lucceius in April 56 B.C. (*Fam.* 5.12.3–5), openly urges him, in writing up the events of Cicero's consulship and its aftermath: "ut et ornes ea uehementius etiam quam fortasse sentis, et in eo leges historiae neglegas, gratiamque illam . . . ne aspernere amorique nostro plusculum etiam, quam concedat ueritas, largiare."

102. Baynes 1955, 165–66.

103. Sakellariou 1981, 130.

104. Isocr. *Orat.* 4.136.

105. Isocr. *Orat.* 4.138–49 (examples of military incompetence: for the Ten Thousand, see §§145–49), 150–52, 184; 5.124, 137.

106. Aristoph. *Ach.* 91–125; *Thesm.* 1001–1225; *Birds* 1572–1679.

is its tone, which comes across (perhaps not surprisingly) as both hyperbolic and hysterical. Educated Athenians did not take well to political humiliation (cf. Isocr. *Orat.* 5.132).

How, one wonders, can this parodic picture of Persian degenerate *faiblesse* be reconciled with the picture of aggression drawn earlier in the *Panegyricus* (§67), where the Persians are bracketed with Thracians and Scythians—but not yet, in 380, with the Macedonians—as dangerous aggressors, indeed as "the most dominating and powerfully aggressive . . . of all races"? Perlman[107] argues that there is no inconsistency, that they are seen as both aggressive *and* weak; Isocrates himself (*Orat.* 4.137-38) gets around the difficulty by arguing that the Great King's power "accrued through our folly, certainly not through his strength." More significant is the determination (which, even if not original to Isocrates, does not gain currency until *after* Athens's defeat by Sparta) to find, in the Persian-as-Barbarian, an ugly scapegoat for ruined imperial dreams, a legitimate target for compensatory violence by the vanquished, an easy mark for the restoration, not only of wealth and power, but also of self-respect, of *kleos*, and—through a collective venture that would, it was hoped, involve all major Greek states—a means of recovering Athens's old position of leadership in the Greek world. Hence (among other reasons) the careful emphasis on Panhellenism.

At first sight this Panhellenism might seem genuine enough, at least in its essentials. Its most famous formulation (Isocr. *Panegyr.* §§49-50) recalls the equally famous statement of Herodotus (8.144). Yet they reveal fundamental differences. What Herodotus emphasizes are the ties of kinship: common speech, common blood, shared religion and social customs (ἤθεα). Isocrates, in contrast, is promoting the value of *verbal skills*, τῶν . . . λόγων τῶν καλῶς καὶ τεχνικῶς ἐχόντων, "words well and artfully arranged," which are οὐ μετὸν τοῖς φαύλοις "not something possessed by the lower orders": the possessor of such skills, he insists, wins power at home and honor abroad. This should be borne in mind when we consider the passage most generally quoted:

> So far has our polis outstripped mankind at large in reasoning and speaking that her students have become the teachers of the rest, and she has brought it about that the title "Hellenes" is thought of no longer as one of race but of intelligence, and that they are termed Hellenes who partake of our education rather than our common stock.[108]

---

107. S. Perlman, "Isokrates' Advice on Philip's Attitude towards Barbarians (V, 154)," *Historia* 16 (1967): 338-43, esp. 342.

108. Isocr. *Orat.* 4.50.

In other words, even if Isocrates is (as Baynes argues[109]) making a covert jibe at the boorishness of the Spartans, even if *paideusis* is advocated as a weapon against the Barbarian,[110] what this passage really amounts to is an advertisement for Isocrates' own school, for his successful and profitable educational system.

Thus, though, as should by now be clear, Isocrates had a natural instinct for picking up, and capitalizing on, trends that were in the air—war-weariness and the resentment of defeat hardly needed to be invented by the rhetoricians—it is also important to consider what other personal motives he may have had, aside from professional self-enhancement, for so persistently advocating redemption through a joint anti-Persian crusade. Here his preoccupation with peace, security, and, to a lesser extent, *hēsychia* is significant.[111] As we know from a much-cited line in Aristophanes, and as Isocrates emphasizes himself (though he puts the assertion into the mouth of Archidamus), war in the early fourth century was a source of income to the penurious, but liable to prove disastrous for the well-off, landowners in particular.[112] The complaint was very much ad hominem. Though, as we have seen, he lost his patrimony during the Peloponnesian War (*Orat.* 15.161), Isocrates afterward became enormously wealthy—his course fee was 1000 drachmas, and Nicocles paid him no less than 20 talents for the oration written in his honor—and thus not only was liable to the *eisphora*, but was challenged three times to undertake the trierarchy (which he twice evaded by pleading illness).[113]

In his arguments for a Panhellenic, anti-Persian crusade, Isocrates stresses, again and again, the fractious animosity between the Greek states—and also, internally, between rich and poor.[114] It becomes apparent that one of his major reasons for an invasion of Asia is to facilitate a large-scale colonization

---

109. Baynes 1955, 152–53.

110. Isocr. *Orat.* 12.219–20. I am also reminded of Klaus Bringmann's comment, in *Studien zu den politischen Ideen des Isokrates* (Göttingen, 1965), 109, that "Isocrates treated myth and history as a fund of παραδείγματα [precedents], which he subordinated to the immediate political requirements of any speech."

111. εἰρήνη and compounds: 58 occurrences (see, e.g., *Orat.* 4.106, 115, 116, 121, 126, 172, 173, 175, 177, 182; 5.7, 8, 39, 50, 51, 56, 73, 87; 6.11, 13, 29, 33, 34, 39, 49, 50, 55, 75, 87, 104). ἀσφαλής, ἀσφάλεια: 49 occurrences (see, e.g., *Orat.* 4.41, 53, 76, 149, 166, 173; 10.18, 19, 20, 21, 23, 34, 51, 119). ἡσυχία, ἡσυχάζω, 10 occurrences.

112. Aristoph. *Eccles.* 197–98.

113. [Plut.] *Mor.* 837D–E, 838A; Dion. Hal. *Isocr.* 1, where it is claimed that he made "more money than anyone whose income was derived from *philosophia*"; Isocr. *Orat.* 15.145. As Raphael Sealey correctly notes (1993, 115), for Isocrates *philosophia* is "the rhetorical education he provided in his school."

114. See, e.g., *Orat.* 4.136, 167, 174, 189; 5.121–23.

scheme, designed to rid the Greek mainland in general, and Attica in particular, of homeless exiles, wandering mercenaries, subversive demagogues, and riff-raff (φαῦλοι) who might threaten stability and the political order, might even (as Baynes points out in the course of a shrewd analysis[115]) demand that recurrent bugbear of the landed classes, a γῆς ἀναδασμός, "redistribution of land."[116] Here we are suddenly on familiar ground: more than one fifth-century cleruchy seems to have been designed for precisely the same purpose,[117] and indeed, cleruchs were still being sent out during the Second Athenian Confederacy.[118]

What Isocrates really wants, in short, is ἀσφάλεια (security) *for property-owners:* pack the trouble-makers off overseas to fight as a "volunteer" army, with land as the bait, and security for *bien-pensants* at home as the real goal.[119] Or, even better, get some outsider, a Jason, a Philip—who will be only too glad of the honor—to undertake the task on your behalf.[120] That way, at very little expense, you can achieve *homonoia*, remove a domestic threat to the established order, *and* open up Asia for profitable exploitation. As should be at once apparent, not the least striking element of this scheme is the vein of pure self-complacent fantasy running through it: for example, Isocrates clearly assumes that Philip (to Demosthenes, himself the Barbarian Other!) would be only too happy—and privileged—to oblige as crusade leader, with no thought of recompense other than the *kleos* that would accrue to him for retrieving the honor of the Hellenes.[121] "It is fitting for you," Isocrates told the Macedonian king,[122] "to consider all Hellas your fatherland"—rhetorical hyperbole meant to reassure the rough northerner whose claim to Hellenism was regarded as dubious, but in the event taken all too literally by its recipient.

We see, then, that Isocrates inherited two traditions from Athens's past: a concept of the Barbarian defined by the Persian Wars, and a sense of Hellenic

---

115. Baynes 1955, 154-55.

116. Cf. *Orat.* 4.34-37; 12.14, 165-66; 5.122-23.

117. See, e.g., Meiggs-Lewis no. 49, B 40-42, for the decree that the colony to Brea should be drawn ἐχ θετῶον καὶ ζε[υ]γιτῶν; or, for the settlement at Amisos known as "Piraeus," Theopompus fr. 389 Meyer.

118. See Cargill 1981, ch. 9, "Kleruchies, Garrisons, and Governors," 148-50.

119. Isocr. *Orat.* 4.173-74, 182, 185; 5.96; cf. Baynes 1955, 155-56.

120. Baynes, ibid. Cf. Isocr. *Orat.* 5.95.

121. Isocr. *Orat.* 5.16, 30-36 (where Philip is not only advised to reconcile the four leading Greek states, Athens, Sparta, Thebes, and Argos, but given various specious mythical reasons why he owes them *a debt of gratitude!*), 68-71 (the *locus classicus:* we may note that none of the rewards Philip is promised are tangible), 95, 140, 154; *Ep.* 2.3. Nowhere is there any hint of financial support (to take an obvious point) for Philip's army.

122. Isocr. *Orat.* 5.127.

community, primarily religious and cultural, that had been intensified, again, by the conflict with Persia, but only took on political dimensions (and even then on a strictly temporary and emergency basis) under stress of a threatened invasion or in furtherance of imperial conquest—the tradition, that is, of Panhellenism as the binding element in an ad hoc military συμμαχία. Insofar as he looked beyond his own career and the autonomous power of rhetorical discourse, his allegiance was to the power and interests of Athens: for all his talk of Hellas as κοινὴ πατρίς, he remained a polis man, with an attitude, paradoxically, not so very different from that of Demosthenes.

He could even, if the situation called for it, drop his anti-Persian propaganda: at the end of the Social War he favored reconciliation with the allies, a renewal of the King's Peace, and avoidance of a rash war against the Barbarian. Athens, in the last resort, came first.[123] This is true even when he sought a crusade leader elsewhere: as we have seen, men like Dionysius, Jason, even Philip, were regarded, despite specious references to the saving of "all Greece," as no more than the servants through whom Athens would regain its rightful hegemony in Hellas.[124] It seems not to have occurred to Isocrates and those who thought as he did (any more than it did to the Tarentines in their dealings with Pyrrhus[125]) that Philip might not be satisfied—to put it mildly—with the role of unpaid generalissimo so patronizingly assigned to him.

As for the Barbarian Other, and the part played by this phenomenon in defining the identity of a proud but defeated imperial power seeking recovery, nothing could be more revealing than the ease with which the face of barbarism could change according to circumstance. Philip, hopefully described by Isocrates, as late as 346, as the man future generations would eulogize as "the statesman preeminent among the Hellenes for his benefactions, and the soldier who by his generalship overthrew the barbarians,"[126] was at the same time being pilloried by Athens's most famous orator as the Barbarian himself.[127]

Was Demosthenes a Panhellenist? Grote certainly thought so: "But what invests the purpose and policy of Demosthenes with peculiar grandeur, is

123. Cf. Perlman 1976, 26–27, citing Isocr. *Orat.* 8.16, 20, cf. 68. Note that in §142, while stating the need "to hate . . . all tyrannical rule and imperial powers," Isocrates also (and almost in the same breath) exhorts Athens, by abandoning its ruinous internecine wars, "to win . . . for our city supreme power for all time."

124. Isocr. *Ep.* 1.7–9; *Orat.* 5.95, 119, cf. *Ep.* 6.1, 3; *Orat.* 5.2–9, 36, 115, 154; and cf. note 121 above.

125. Green 1993, 230–31.

126. Isocr. *Orat.* 5.140.

127. See, e.g., Dem. 3.17; 20; 9.31.

that they were not simply Athenian, but in an eminent degree Panhellenic also." [128] That view was predictable—no less predictable than the contrary opinion of various German historians, from Droysen to Kaerst and Beloch, [129] who (strongly influenced by "the amalgamation of the small warring German states under the Prussian Empire" [130]) praised Philip—and Isocrates— while attacking Demosthenes' regrettable *Lokalpatriotismus*. [131] There is, as I hope this study has made clear, a certain element of unreality in the ascription of such ideological attitudes. Whatever philosophers might argue— I am thinking of such *obiter dicta* as Plato's on the distinction between *polemos* (war involving Greeks against barbarians) and *stasis* (war between Greek and Greek) [132]—bore very little relation to what actually went on. The ravaging of land, the destruction of homes, the victimization of the civilian population (all things that Plato's Guardians were to outlaw, and that for Isocrates had been added incentives to an anti-Persian crusade) were universal facts of Greek life, not some purely barbarian aberration. They were also (as we saw when examining Aristophanes) what kept the paradoxical ideal of Panhellenism, of *homonoia* between fundamentally separatist Greek states, very much alive. *Video meliora proboque, deteriora sequor.*

It is, at the same time, hardly surprising that we find a blurring of categories, so that even Isocrates can speak of qualities that place the Spartans below barbarians, [133] while Demosthenes, in the Fourth *Philippic*, actually advocates an alliance with the Great King against Philip, calling on the Athenians "to drop the foolish prejudice that has so often brought about your discomfiture—'the barbarian,' 'the common foe of us all,' and all such phrases." [134] It is hard to escape the conclusion that both *homonoia* and the "common foe" were variously invoked in the fourth century according to the ideological convictions of each advocate, reacting as he saw best to the immediate demands of Athenian polis patriotism; [135] nor, indeed, that the targeting by Isocrates of the Persians, and by Demosthenes of Macedon, as the

---

128. G. Grote, *A History of Greece* (London, 1888), 10:264.

129. See Knipfing 1920–21, 659ff.; Dunkel 1938, 291–92; Perlman 1976, 23ff.

130. Dunkel 1938, 292.

131. Beloch 1912–13, vol. 3, ch. 13, 507. It is much to the credit of Arnold Schaefer, whose *Demosthenes und seine Zeit* (2d ed., 3 vols. [Leipzig, 1885–87]) is still in many ways the most valuable study of its subject, that he should be largely free from such distorting preconceptions.

132. Plato *Rep.* 470B–471B.

133. Isocr. *Orat.* 12.209.

134. Dem. 10.31–34 (trans. J. H. Vince).

135. This is, essentially, the position of Dunkel (1938, 305) and (with reservations) of Perlman (1976, 24–25). What both seem to me to ignore is the strong element of genuine (if at times self-deluding) Panhellenic belief that motivated even polis patriots to act as they did.

universal enemy, the Barbarian Other, the scapegoat for Athens's imperial devaluation, reveals a progressive, and inevitable, shift of power in the Hellenic
world. The Second Athenian Confederacy, with all its nervous concessions,
bears eloquent witness to Athenian efforts to reverse this trend. With its failure, the symptoms of frustration and despair grew ever more acute.

It was now that Isocrates began seeking a leader for his crusade elsewhere
than in Athens, even though Athens and the other Hellenic states were still
envisaged as the crusade's rightful beneficiaries. It was now, too, after the rise
of Philip and the disaster, for Athens, of the Social War, that Demosthenes
began to attack the Macedonian king as "the implacable enemy . . . of civic
government and democracy,"[136] that is, as the Other, the polar opposite of the
Hellenic ideal. This change of enemy is interesting inasmuch as its basis remained the same: that is, barbarism was not identified with a specific race (as
Isocrates conceived it) but could be ascribed freely wherever conduct seemed
to warrant. Thus formulated, it could be seen as an ethical analogue to Isocrates' own claim (*Panegyr.* §50) that Athens "has ensured that the name of the
Hellenes no longer suggests a race but rather a quality of intelligence." This
explains why Demosthenes, without any sense of inconsistency, can and does
invoke Athens's glorious past role in the Persian Wars as "common champion of the freedom of all"[137]—can, indeed, on an appropriate occasion, and
despite the sentiments cited above, himself refer to Persia as the common
enemy.[138]

Two points should be noted here. First—again unlike Isocrates—Demosthenes never advocates the anti-Persian crusade as a solution to the ills of
Hellas. Indeed, he advises Athens *not* to go to war with Persia. The nearest he
comes to Isocrates' position is in 354, when rumors of a Persian invasion by
Artaxerxes II were rife: then, drawing the obvious parallel with the events of
480, he argues (and who would contradict him?) that such an attack must inevitably unite Greece against the Barbarian.[139] His policy in this case is strictly
defensive. Second, he makes it very clear[140]—and here he had a century of
self-assertion on which to draw—that Athens's record in combating the Barbarian validated its hegemony in the Greek world, and it is this hegemony
that he constantly defends. Philip's territorial gains are seen as theft of Athenian property;[141] as Perlman says, "The *Panhellenic* war against Philip is not

136. Dem. 8.43.
137. Dem. 15.30; cf. 14.6; 9.19-20, 45, 70-74; 19.64, 271-72, 312-13; 18.64, 71-72.
138. Dem. 14.36.
139. Dem. 14.31-34.
140. Dem. 14.40, cf. 35-36.
141. Dem. 3.20; 4.4-6; 6.7-10; 8.6; 19.22; cf. Dunkel 1938, 297-99; Perlman 1976, 24-25.

only conformable with Athenian aspirations to hegemony, but they supplement each other." [142]

Yet Demosthenes was also acutely aware of a gap—social and moral no less than historical—between past and present, of the loss of some impalpable quality that had fired the Persian War generation to embrace *eleutheria*, an animating spirit that had triumphed over the vast resources of the Achaemenid empire to keep Hellas free, a quality "the loss of which has spoiled everything and left all our affairs in confusion." [143] He may have been naive to identify and delimit the destructive canker as bribery (though bribery—that constant in Greek political history—there undoubtedly was [144]); but at a deep level he was right. It was his personal tragedy that he pursued a policy of intransigent resistance to Macedonia that terminated in the disaster of Chaeronea, as Polybius, with the benefit of hindsight, saw so clearly. [145] Yet, as Cawkwell says, "A defence might be made in these terms. It is better to die in liberty than live without it." [146] *Give me liberty or give me death.* "It was the failure not only of the statesman but of his city," Sealey declares: [147] a failure on which he deliberately refrains from passing judgment. To us, as to Polybius, the ineluctable shift of power—so clearly symbolized by the desperate demonization first of Persia, then of Macedon, the vaunting of Hellenic values against the barbarian ethos of Philip or the Great King—must make that failure look a foregone conclusion. It did not seem so at the time.

For a century and a half, the Hellenic world had been to a great extent defined by its ethnic and cultural distinction from the Persian Empire, which (as we have seen) the Greeks, by historical accident, were enabled to identify with their own arbitrary and ethnocentric concepts of barbarism. But the rise of Philip created an alternative—and more nearly Hellenic—Barbarian Other: just how far Macedonian non-Greekness was a figment of Demosthenic propaganda remains a touchy question even today. [148] Alexander's conquest of Asia at one stroke rendered an ancient demon obsolete (the collapse of the Soviet empire presents interesting parallels). From now on Macedonia, in Athenian eyes, was the enemy; and during the years that followed, both

---

142. Perlman 1976, 25.

143. Dem. 9.36.

144. Jack Cargill, in "Demosthenes, Aischines, and the Crop of Traitors," *AncW* 11 (1985): 75–85, argues convincingly for the systematic corruption of Athenian officials by Philip.

145. Polyb. 18.13–14.

146. G. Cawkwell, *Philip of Macedon* (London, 1978), 130–31.

147. Sealey 1993, 219.

148. As Ernst Badian is well aware: see his article "Greeks and Macedonians," in *Studies in the History of Art*, vol. 10, Symposium Series 1, *Macedonia and Greece in Late Classical and Early Hellenistic Times*, ed. B. Barr-Sharrar and E. N. Borza (Washington, D.C., 1982), 33–51, esp. 33–34.

the Hellene/Barbarian dichotomy[149] and the Panhellenism that had been so closely associated with it lost their original power and urgency. I suspect there were not a few Athenians in the late fourth century who would have endorsed Cavafy's words: "And now what is to become of us without barbarians? These people were at least some kind of solution."[150]

The spirit of Panhellenism was nowhere to be seen in the revolts of Thebes (335) and Sparta (331), which both failed through complete lack of support from other Greek states.[151] It revived briefly in the campaign against Antipater (323/2), when Athens led a coalition of states in what was called the "Hellenic War," modeled its Council on the Greek League of 480, and consciously identified the Macedonians as the successors of the Persians;[152] yet even here Athens was very much the dominant force, using (as so often when Panhellenism was invoked) alliances in an emergency for its own ends. Similar propaganda underwrote the Chremonidean war against Antigonid Macedonia, portrayed as "a Panhellenic venture aimed at liberating Greece from outside intervention,"[153] but still very much, in essence, an Athenian undertaking. The later futile alliance with Mithridates VI that led Sulla to sack Piraeus and Athens[154] was a mere desperate gesture in pursuit of lost *eleutheria:* Panhellenic unity played no part in it, any more than it did in the strictly pragmatic activities of the Achaean and Aetolian Leagues. Indeed, the "freedom of the Greeks," as Flamininus well knew,[155] could be used, via the insistence on autonomy, as a convenient device for breaking up dangerous federations. Athens's obsession with Macedonia had led it to underestimate the new barbarians of the West; too late it became clear that the frontier between Hellenes and a deadlier Other than they had ever known was now formed by the Tiber.[156]

---

149. The judgment of H. Dörrie, "Die Wertung der Barbaren im Urteil der Griechen. Knechtsnaturen? Oder Bewahrer und Künder heilbringender Weisheit," in *Antike und Universalgeschichte (Festschrift Hans Erich Stier)*, ed. R. Stiehl and G. A. Lehmann (Münster, 1972), 173, that "the hitherto dominant attitude of belief in Greek superiority is latterly [after Alexander] no longer defended by anyone," despite exaggeration, contains more than a grain of truth.

150. C. P. Cavafy, *Collected Poems*, trans. E. Keeley and P. Sherrard, ed. G. Savidis (Princeton, 1975), 32.

151. Cf. Cawkwell (as above, note 146), 131.

152. Diod. Sic. 18.10.2; *IG* II² 1.249; N.G.L. Hammond and F. W. Walbank, *A History of Macedonia*, vol. 3, *336–167 B.C.* (Oxford, 1988), 110; N. G. Ashton, "The Lamian War—*stat magni nominis umbra*," *JHS* 104 (1984): 152–57.

153. I owe this formulation to the percipience of my anonymous referee. For a general account of the Chremonidean War, cf. Green 1993, 146–47.

154. Ibid., 562–63.

155. Ibid., 414–15.

156. J. J. Pollitt, "What Is 'Hellenistic' about Hellenistic Art?" in *Hellenistic History and Culture*, ed. P. Green (Berkeley and London, 1993), 105.

As for the demon of barbarism, that too lost its pristine power. It is symptomatic of the Hellenistic era that when a new potential Barbarian appeared, in the shape of the Gauls who invaded Greece between 279 and 277, the geographic and ethnic cosmopolitanism brought about by Alexander's conquests should have subtly modified the alien sense of otherness that had hitherto defined such phenomena. These Gauls, in the eyes of latter-day Greeks—urbanized intellectuals and businessmen who hired mercenaries to do their fighting for them—displayed many of the old Homeric virtues: bravery, heroic ἀρετή, a warrior code of honor. Thus the splendid Pergamene sculptures that commemorated Attalus I's victory over them (238/7?) nevertheless also ask two clear unspoken questions: who is truly civilized? Where does honor lie? We have come very close here to that other, equally potent myth: the cult of the Noble Savage.[157]

As Athens settled into its new, politically impotent role of "mere university city,"[158] its opposition to barbarism, with all-too-symbolic aptness, reverted to the original distinction, that of language: a finicking contempt for dialects, an insistence on "pure" Attic.[159] The third-century comic playwright Posidippus[160] presented a Thessalian criticizing an Athenian for "atticizing" while "we Hellenes hellenize," with the reminder that Ἑλλὰς μέν ἐστι μία, πόλεις δὲ πλείονες, "there are many cities, but one Hellas." The claim was not true then; it was not fulfilled until the establishment (under an externally imposed Bavarian monarch!) of the Kingdom of Greece in the nineteenth century.

Today, when Macedonia and Alexander III no longer represent the Barbarian Other but have long figured as cherished "North Greek" icons in a nationalist quarrel, when the Turks are cast in the role once reserved for the Persians, and when the Balkans have lately run red with the blood of ethnic and religious "cleansing," we may legitimately wonder how much real progress has been made since that "great shout" at Salamis—the *Urgeschrei*, as it were, of the Panhellenic tradition—called on the sons of Greece to free fatherland, children, wives, shrines of the gods, ancestral tombs.[161] The cry then was νῦν ὑπὲρ πάντων ἀγών, "Now the struggle is on behalf of all": today, for good or ill, it still is. The appeal to a common heritage, the demonization of the enemy, are instincts that reach deep into the human psyche. What happened in the fourth century could, and did, happen again. Like Thucydides, I have

---

157. Green 1993, 133–34, 150–51, 339–40.
158. Louis MacNeice, "Autumn Journal," in *Collected Poems* (London, 1966), 118.
159. Jüthner 1923, 38–43.
160. Fr. 28 Kock (vol. 3, 345).
161. Aesch. *Pers.* 401–5.

written this study for people who are concerned τῶν τε γενομένων τὸ σαφὲς σκοπεῖν καὶ τῶν μελλόντων ποτὲ αὖθις κατὰ τὸ ἀνθρώπινον τοιούτων καὶ παραπλησίων ἔσεσθαι—"to have clear insight into both past events, and those which, human nature being what it is, are likely to recur in the same, or very nearly the same, manner."[162]

---

162. Thuc. 1.22.4.

6

Text and Context in the Matter
of Xenophon's Exile

LIKE THUCYDIDES, like Polybius, Xenophon spent a substantial portion of his life in exile. But there is one great difference between them. In the cases of Thucydides and Polybius we know, precisely, when, why, and for how long they were cut off from their homeland. With Xenophon, all three questions remain a subject for debate. Was he exiled in 399, in 394/3 (the two most popular dates, being the *termini post* and *ante quem* respectively), or at some intermediate point?[1] And what was the charge against him? Presumably some form of treason, προδοσία; but its nature, as we shall see, remains unclear. Various theories—association with Cyrus, fighting against a force that included his own countrymen at Coronea, an attempt by the Athenians to curry favor with Artaxerxes II, or mere general Laconism—have each had their ancient and modern supporters. The most recent scholarship (Rahn, Tuplin) favors a late date, and interprets what evidence there is in the light of Athens's post-395 *rapprochement* with Persia and renewed hostility against Sparta. It is my belief, however, that the evidence points incontestably to 399 as the date of Xenophon's exile, and also provides a motive for it so large that it has, paradoxically, hitherto escaped our notice.

Note: Originally published in *Ventures into Greek History*, ed. I. Worthington (Oxford, 1994), 215-27. Reprinted by permission of Oxford University Press.

1. 399: Delbrück 1829, 51ff.; Klett 1900, 25ff.; Delebecque 1957, 117-23; Erbse 1966, 490ff.; Anderson 1974, 148ff.; Higgins 1977, 22-24; K. W. Krüger, *Historische-philologische Studien* 1 (Berlin, 1836), 244-52; H. Baden, *Untersuchungen zur Einheit der Hellenika Xenophons* (Hamburg, 1966), 43-46. 394/3 (either before or after the battle of Coronea): Roquette 1883, 18-23; Schwartz 1889, 163ff.; Wilamowitz 1884, 330ff.; Breitenbach 1967, cols. 1570-75; Rahn 1981, 103-19; Tuplin 1987, 59-68; B. G. Niebuhr, *Kleine historische und philologische Schriften* (Bonn, 1828), 467; G. Grote, *History of Greece*, vol. 7 (London, 1872), 343-45; A. Croiset, *Xénophon: Son caractère et son talent* (Paris, 1873), 259ff. For supporters of intermediate dates (advancing no new arguments but merely varying the chronology), see Tuplin 1987, 59 nn. 4-5.

Let us begin with the ancient testimonia. These are scanty and for the most part late, which at once suggests that, as in the case of Ovid's *relegatio*, the true cause may soon have been forgotten—if, indeed, it was ever published, a point we should bear in mind. Xenophon himself, by no accident, is less than helpful. In all his writings he gives no hint as to the reason (whether declared or covert) for his exile. Indeed, he only makes specific reference to it twice, both times in a studiedly vague chronological context; and of these two references, one is ambiguous in expression and may not in fact be talking about exile at all.[2] Thus we see, *ab initio*, that over both date and cause the exile himself did little to clear the record, and quite possibly hoped to obscure it. We may legitimately ask ourselves why.

In February or March of 399, Xenophon notes that at this point the vote exiling him had not yet been passed: οὔ . . . πω ψῆφος αὐτῷ ἐπῆκτο Ἀθήνῃσι περὶ φυγῆς. He was in fact making preparations to return home to Athens. What he does *not* tell us is how soon afterward the vote actually took place, much less its actual terms. Hence the present debate. Our next clue comes five years later. In spring 394, when about to accompany Agesilaus from Asia back to Greece, on the campaign that culminated in the battle of Coronea— the "march against the Boeotians," as he carefully calls it, τὴν εἰς Βοιωτοὺς ὁδόν—he left a sum he planned to dedicate to Ephesian Artemis in the care of the temple warden (νεωκόρος) Megabyzus. The expedition, he explained, would be hazardous. If he himself came through unscathed (ἤν μὲν αὐτὸς σωθῇ), the money was to be returned to him. If not, Megabyzus was to make a suitable dedication in his name.

Xenophon, as we know, did survive; and, he goes on, when he was living at Skillous, near Olympia, Megabyzus visited him there and returned his deposit. He prefaces this statement (*Anab.* 5.3.7) with a short clause that is, frustratingly, in textual dispute.[3] The phrase ἐπεὶ (or ἐπειδὴ) δ' ἔφυγεν (or ἔφευγεν, or, just possibly, πέφευγεν, though this reading is generally discounted) ὁ Ξενοφῶν can be variously translated: (1) "After Xenophon was exiled," (2) "While [or, since] Xenophon was in exile," or (3) "After [or, since] Xenophon [had] survived," that is, after Coronea.[4] All we know for sure from

---

2. *Anab.* 5.3.5–7; 7.7.57.

3. See Tuplin 1987, 60–65, for a detailed discussion of the variant readings.

4. Delbrück 1829, 55f., Erbse 1966, 491f., and Higgins 1977, 150 n. 15 all explain Xenophon's use of φεύγειν here according to (3), i.e., as "escape" or "survive." They are challenged by Tuplin (1987, 63–64), who asserts that "the suggested use of φεύγειν without an expressed object as a synonym for σώζεσθαι is most unnatural." A computer scan of -φευγ- and -φυγ- in Xenophon's works suggests otherwise: see, e.g., *Hell.* 1.6.16, 23; 3.4.24.

this passage is that Megabyzus visited Xenophon at Skillous in 392.[5] We cannot use it to date, or even certainly to establish, the Athenian's exile. He himself makes no other direct reference to it, though in a passage of the *Anabasis* (3.1.5) he hints fairly broadly at association with Cyrus as being the antecedent cause. This, though it may agree with the public record, is, as we shall see, πρόφασις (excuse) rather than αἰτία (reason), and so regarded by all those directly involved.

The external evidence is late, hardly more informative, and in one important respect, as we shall see, difficult to accept at face value. Pausanias, Dio Chrysostom of Prusa, and an epigram cited by Diogenes Laertius all agree that Xenophon was exiled on account of his friendship with, and service under, Cyrus.[6] Pausanias adds that at the time the Great King was friendly toward Athens (σφισιν εὔνουν ὄντα), while Cyrus was the Athenian people's worst enemy (πολεμιωτάτῳ τοῦ δήμου). This is puzzling, since the Great King's benevolence toward Athens (see below) did not predate 395, while the only time at which Cyrus seriously threatened the Athenian people was after his appointment as commander-in-chief (κάρανος) in Asia Minor toward the end of the Peloponnesian War (408/7).[7] Whether Xenophon's service was held to include his subsequent command of the Ten Thousand is a moot point, but is worth serious consideration.

Diogenes Laertius, in his brief *Life* (2.51), tells us that, immediately after the misfortunes of the Cyrean troops with the Thracian king Seuthes, Xenophon enlisted them, again as mercenaries, in the service of Sparta, and then returned to Asia (early 399). Unfortunately, Diogenes states that he enlisted them *under Agesilaus*, who did not appear in Asia until 396: the commander to whom he actually turned over his men in 399 was Thibron.[8] Even if we assume (as I do) that here "Diogenes has foreshadowed events by jumping straight to Xenophon's association with Agesilaus,"[9] the text still creates a doubt regarding the chronology: 399 or 396? And the doubt is important, because Diogenes goes on: "*About this time* (παρ' ὃν χρόνον) he [Xenophon] was condemned to exile by the Athenians for Laconism" (ἐπὶ Λακωνισμῷ φυγὴν ὑπ' Ἀθηναίων κατεγνώσθη).

---

5. The date is certified by the fact that Megabyzus was in Olympia θεωρήσων, i.e., to attend the Games: the first Olympiad after the year 394 was the 97th, which fell in 392.

6. Paus. 5.6.5; Dio Chrys. 8.1; *AP* 7.9.8 = Diog. Laert. 2.58.

7. Xen. *Hell.* 1.4.1–3; Diog. Laert. 14.12.8, 19.2; Plut. *Artax.* 2; cf. Xen. *Anab.* 1.1.1–2, 9.7. See G. Cousin, *Kyros le Jeune en Asie Mineure* (Paris, 1905), 14ff.

8. *Anab.* 7.8.24; *Hell.* 3.1.4–5.

9. Tuplin 1987, 66–67.

There is, lastly, the statement by Istros[10] that Xenophon was both exiled and restored by decrees of Euboulos. We do not know if this reference is to the Athenian statesman, who in any case, having been born c. 405, would have been six years old in 399 and eleven in 394, and thus far too young to have moved the decree of exile. Either this Euboulos was another man altogether, or else two men of identical or similar name (one of whom *may* have been the statesman) have been confused by Istros or his source. In either case, this snippet of information is virtually useless. The attempt to peg Xenophon's exile to 394 by assuming that the man responsible was Euboulides, the archon for 394/3, and emending the text to reflect this, has been properly dismissed as "un chapelet d'hypothèses."[11] It is quite plausible that the statesman Euboulos should have been responsible for Xenophon's recall—late works, the *Poroi* in particular, with its concern for Athenian economics, would tend to support this—but since the date of that recall, and indeed its legal basis, remain quite uncertain, this floating piece of ambiguous evidence contributes little, if anything, to our problem.[12]

This is all the substantial ancient evidence on the matter that we possess, and its validity is, at the very least, seriously undermined by an *argumentum ex silentio* brought to my attention by Professor Joseph Roisman, who "cannot recall any example of a judgment given against an absent person for an act done outside Attica and not against Athenians, which ended in his banishment."[13] If that is true (and my own impression coincides with Professor Roisman's), then we are forced to one of several conclusions: either (1) the evidence was invented, in ignorance of Athenian usage, by writers long after the event, faced with a lacuna regarding the cause for Xenophon's exile; or (2) such explanations were manufactured at the time, in an attempt to cover up the real ones, which (for whatever reason) it was thought essential to keep secret; or (3) the explanations given were the true ones, and this was (again for whatever reason) an exceptional, indeed a unique, $\psi \acute{\eta} \phi \iota \sigma \mu \alpha$ on the part of an Assembly notorious, in the half-century following the Peloponnesian War, for whimsical or arbitrary decisions that paid scant regard to legal precedent.

So much for the direct texts: clearly, if any progress is to be made, it must be through careful scrutiny of context and background. The preference of recent scholarship (e.g., Tuplin and Rahn) for a late date has been largely dictated by the search for a set of historical circumstances in which association

10. *FGrH* 334 F 32 = Diog. Laert. 2.59: Ἴστρος φησὶν αὐτὸν φυγεῖν κατὰ ψήφισμα Εὐβούλου, καὶ κατελθεῖν κατὰ τοῦ αὐτοῦ.

11. Delebecque 1957, 117; cf. the comments of Tuplin 1987, 67–68 and Rahn 1981, 117.

12. Cf. G. L. Cawkwell, "Eubulus," *JHS* 83 (1963): 47–67.

13. Personal communication, 17 January 1992.

with Cyrus and/or Laconism *could*, in fact, be treated as indictable offenses. Briefly put, the argument—which in effect assumes scenario 3 above, though without showing awareness of the difficulties involved—runs as follows. In 399 Athens was officially allied with Sparta and still on terms of unresolved hostility with Persia, so that Xenophon could not then be exiled for Laconism—nor, indeed, for supporting Cyrus, since Sparta had covertly supported him as well.[14] Nor, as we have seen, was the motive of seeking favor with Artaxerxes, to which Pausanias refers (5.6.5), applicable at this time. The diplomatic turning-point only came after the outbreak of the Corinthian War in 395, which renewed Athens's old conflict with Sparta, while at the same time creating, through the mediation of Conon, a *rapprochement* between Athens and Persia. It is now that we are asked to place the decree exiling Xenophon, when Laconism was once more frowned upon, and Athens had good reason to make conciliatory gestures to the Great King.

Quite apart from the legal unlikelihood of a ψήφισμα based on such vague and dated charges, there is something inherently implausible about this scenario. Why should Artaxerxes be bothered, five or six years after the event, by the successful efforts of a Greek mercenary captain (as he would see it) to get his men to safety after defeat in the Babylonian heartland? If anything, he would have been more inclined to admire Xenophon's skill and recruit his services for Persia (a regular Achaemenid practice). In any case, the supposed gesture of conciliation was nothing of the sort. Exiling Xenophon *from Athens* still left him free to make a pest of himself, along with his Spartan friends, in the Great King's territory of Asia Minor, which was, indeed, precisely what he then did. All such a "friendly gesture" would have achieved at Susa was a reminder of the proverbial untrustworthiness of Greek gifts.

Further, why should Xenophon, more than any other soldier of fortune, have incurred the Athenians' displeasure in 394? (As far as we know, he had not so much as set foot on Attic soil since 401, when he left to join his friend Proxenos under Cyrus.[15]) Because, it has often been asserted, he accompanied Agesilaus to Coronea, and very probably fought in the battle, thus laying himself open to a charge of treason, προδοσία, since Athenians were engaged on the other side.[16] Hence his exile: this penalty seems to have been employed

---

14. Paul Cartledge, *Agesilaos and the Crisis of Sparta* (Baltimore 1987), ch. 11, pp. 180ff., esp. 190–91.

15. Xen. *Anab.* 3.1.5–7; Diog. Laert. 2.49–50, 55.

16. Xen. *Hell.* 4.3.15–23; Plut. *Ages.* 17–18; Diog. Laert. 2.51; *IG* II² 5222 = *GHI* 104, pp. 18–20 (for the presence of Athenian cavalry). Breitenbach (1967, col. 1575) is typical: "Diese Teilnahme [not certain!] an der Schlacht bei Koroneia ist selbst verständlich der Grund seiner Verbannung": cf. Wilamowitz 1884, 333.

only in cases of treason and unintentional homicide,[17] and no one has tried to accuse Xenophon of the latter.[18] Indeed, one of the few aspects of this problem on which everyone seems reasonably in agreement is that the charge against Xenophon was, in some way or another, that of προδοσία.

But this confronts us with another basic improbability. Despite his admiration of Spartan *mores*, Xenophon all his life remained an Athenian through and through. He served with the Athenian cavalry; his son Gryllos died bravely, also as an Athenian cavalryman, during a skirmish before the battle of Mantinea in 362.[19] Polis patriotism was central to Xenophon's character. His first thought after surviving his Asiatic *anabasis*, reiterated again and again, was to *return home*.[20] Is it conceivable that, had he been a free agent, he would have accompanied Agesilaus to Coronea, let alone have fought there, in full knowledge of what the inevitable consequence must be? The only logical explanation for his presence on that occasion (his personal participation in the battle cannot be proved) is that he was *already an exile*, so that he stood to lose nothing that he had not lost already.

But this, it will be objected, does not exclude the various attempts to place his exile in 394 *before* Coronea (thus Croiset and Tuplin), or even earlier.[21] We must now shift our ground and consider the positive factors that point to a date not later than the spring of 399, as well as the true motives—αἰτία rather than πρόφασις—that lay behind the decree of banishment, and are compatible both with Xenophon's own deep sense of patriotic loyalty and with his palpable embarrassment over the whole episode.

Xenophon was a cavalryman, a member of the elite and largely aristocratic corps of knights (ἱππεῖς).[22] This body had always been conspicuous for its vigorous, highly publicized oligarchic sympathies. It actively supported the revolution of 411, and its members afterward, as a result, suffered severe civic penalties, being, until 405/4, banned from speaking in the Assembly or

---

17. D. M. MacDowell, *The Law in Classical Athens* (London, 1978), 255.

18. But see Tuplin 1987, 59 n. 3, who cites Kahrstedt and Canfora for the bizarre and wholly unsubstantiated theory that the charge was attempted murder.

19. Ephorus *ap.* Diog. Laert. 2.54; Xen. *Hell.* 7.5.15–16; cf. Paus. 1.3.4; 8.9.5, 10; 9.15.5.

20. Xen. *Anab.* 6.2.13; 7.1.4, 6, 8, 30, 38–40; 7.2.8, 27; 7.6.ll, 33; 7.7.57; cf. Delebecque 1957, 115ff.; also J. Roisman, "Anaxibios and Xenophon's Anabasis," *AHB* 2.4 (1988): 80–87, esp. 83 and n. 13.

21. See, e.g., G. L. Cawkwell's introduction (p. 14 n. 2) to Rex Warner's Penguin Classic translation of the *Anabasis* (there entitled *The Persian Expedition*, 2d ed., 1972). Cawkwell suggests, without explanation, that attempts to win the Great King's favor may have begun as early as 397 or 398.

22. See Bugh 1988, ch. 4, pp. 120ff. Cf. also Rahn 1981, 103–4, Breitenbach 1967, col. 1573, and (for the possibility of Xenophon's participation in various military actions during the Ionian-Decelean War) 1900, Klett 6–7.

serving on the Council of Five Hundred.[23] Worse, there is abundant evidence that the cavalry supported the Thirty, fighting against the "men of Piraeus" at Phyle and Munychia, as well as participating in the capture of Eleusis.[24] It is clear from the way Xenophon describes these events that he was an eye-witness—his description of the noise the grooms made as they curried their horses is particularly revealing—and probably an active participant.[25] In re-action against the increasing violence and disregard for property shown by the Thirty,[26] he, like many others, probably aligned himself with the moder-ate Theramenes, and it seems likely that after Theramenes' death his property was confiscated: in 399 he had to sell his horse (a truly desperate resort for a ἱππεύς) to pay for his planned return home, and clearly had no home funds on which to draw,[27] a fact that should be borne in mind when considering his subsequent actions.

But as far as his reputation was concerned, the damage had been done, and he was hardly helped by the conduct of his more extreme colleagues. Many of the cavalry continued to back the Thirty; some actually joined the Spartan Pausanias in his attack on Piraeus.[28] They "were thought to be more deeply implicated in the oligarchy than the remainder of the Three Thousand,"[29] and with good reason: not only had they supported the oligarchy, but they "actu-ally joined ranks with the enemy which had crushed their empire and robbed them of their freedom a scant year before."[30] At the same time, it is important to remember that their oligarchic activities, even those involving Spartan col-laboration, were directed exclusively against their *internal* political enemies (a not uncommon feature of polis life). It comes as no surprise, then, to find members of the Athenian cavalry in 394 distinguishing themselves, under a democratic regime, in actions at Corinth and Coronea.[31] Patriotism of this sort is no guide to political beliefs.

---

23. Andoc. 1.73, 77–79, cf. Bugh 1988, 114–19.

24. Xen. *Hell.* 2.4.2–10, 15, 24, 26, 31; cf. Diod. Sic. 14.32.2, 4; 33.1.5; Arist. *Ath. Pol.* 38.2; and in general, Bugh 1988, 122–29, with further references.

25. See, e.g., *Hell.* 2.4.2–7 (the remark about the grooms who ψήχοντες τοὺς ἵππους ψόφον ἐποίουν is at §6), 10–12, 18–19, 23–27.

26. For Xenophon's criticisms of the Thirty, in particular of their rapacity, see *Hell.* 2.3.14, 17, 21; 2.4.1, 10.

27. Xen. *Anab.* 7.8.1, 2, 6. Rahn (1981, 104 n. 9) suggests convincingly that loss of property ex-plains his otherwise curious refusal to borrow against the tithe for the gods entrusted to him (*Anab.* 5.3.4–5): he saw no way of repaying the debt.

28. *Hell.* 2.4.26–27, 31–32; Arist. *Ath. Pol.* 38.2, with Rhodes' *Commentary* (1981), 458.

29. Rhodes, ibid.

30. Bugh 1988, 128.

31. See *GHI* 104 (casualties at Corinth and Coronea) and 105 (the memorial of Dexileos, who also fell at Corinth, summer 394), pp. 18–21.

Scholars tend to overestimate the impact of the official amnesty between factions orchestrated by Pausanias in 403.[32] Wars, and civil wars above all, are not so easily written off. Greeks and Irishmen have always had a special talent for μνησικακία, the nursing of ancient wrongs. Cavalry service under the Thirty continued to be brought up against public figures as late as 382.[33] When in 399 the Spartan commander Thibron requested three hundred cavalrymen from Athens, offering to pay for their services himself, the Athenians (Xenophon writes) "sent some of those who had served as ἱππεῖς under the Thirty, thinking it would be a gain to the δῆμος if they went overseas and died there."[34]

So we come back to Xenophon, who of course was with Thibron at the time. Obviously Athens, even after the amnesty, was no comfortable place for a man with his political record: his decision to join Proxenos in Asia in 401[35] is more than understandable. So is his careful assertion that he went as neither general nor captain nor soldier, but as a private individual, who was, moreover, enticed under false pretenses (ἐξαπατηθείς),[36] a claim made in a long passage of self-justification.[37] When he consulted Socrates about his proposed venture, he tells us, Socrates "suspected that his becoming a friend of Cyrus might lay him open to a charge from the polis, since Cyrus was held to have actively supported the Spartans against Athens."[38] This prediction agrees with some of the later evidence[39] in seeing association with Cyrus as the cause of Xenophon's exile, but (in sharp contrast to that evidence) is looking at the Cyrus of 408–405, Sparta's ally in the final phases of the Peloponnesian War, rather than the would-be Achaemenid usurper of 401, whose army Xenophon accompanied to Cunaxa.

The curious thing is that in neither case could Xenophon have been *legally* charged with προδοσία. His involvement with Cyrus came more than three years after the war was over, at a time when Athens was technically Sparta's ally, and Sparta was in any case secretly aiding Cyrus against Artaxerxes (see above). We are therefore dealing with an excuse, a πρόφασις—one, moreover,

---

32. For the amnesty, see Xen. *Hell.* 2.4.38, 42–43; Arist. *Ath. Pol.* 39.6–40.4; cf. Bugh 1988, 128 with nn. 19–20; Krentz 1982, 102–8.

33. Lys. 26.10, cf. Bugh 1988, 141.

34. *Hell.* 3.1.4.

35. *Anab.* 3.1.4–7; Diog. Laert. 2.49.

36. *Anab.* 3.1.10.

37. *Anab.* 3.1.7–47.

38. *Anab.* 3.1.5: ... ὑποπτεύσας μή τι πρὸς τῆς πόλεως ὑπαίτιον εἴη Κύρῳ φίλον γενέσθαι, ὅτι ἐδόκει ὁ Κῦρος προθύμως τοῖς Λακεδαιμονίοις ἐπὶ τοὺς Ἀθηναίους συμπολεμῆσαι.

39. Paus. 5.6.5; Dio Chrys. 8.1; *AP* 7.9.8 = Diog. Laert. 2.58.

that seems to have been embraced both by the Athenian authorities and by their victim, who went out of his way to validate it by invoking Socrates (of all people!) as a witness to its feasibility. We therefore have to ask ourselves what motive there could be for both the Athenian *dēmos* and the man they charged to agree on this seemingly impossible explanation for his exile. That it *was* the public charge brought seems certain; the proceedings could not have been kept secret, and to lie about their nature would have been pointless. Scenario 2 (above, p. 136) must therefore be accepted.

Official reconciliations notwithstanding, the three-cornered civil war and the factional enmities it inspired still cast a baleful shadow over Athens. In 401/0, the diehard oligarchs at Eleusis, desperate to regain power and excluded from the original Spartan-backed settlement, launched a fresh campaign against the City.[40] To do this they were reported to be hiring mercenaries, and it would be interesting to know where they looked for them. In the face of this threat, the *dēmos* took ruthless action. The commanders in Eleusis were lured out to a meeting under promise of safe conduct, and then seized and executed. The separatist movement collapsed. Oaths were taken to forget past wrongs.[41] But as subsequent events were to prove—a melancholy truth of which we have evidence in plenty today—μνησικακία is not eradicated by legislation. Indeed, the suppression of the Eleusis faction seems to have encouraged the democrats to take further covert action against their opponents: it is in this atmosphere that the different yet related trials of Andocides and Socrates—both early in 399, each in its own way politics masquerading as religion—should be evaluated.[42] It would indeed be surprising if the extremists were not still desperate to salvage their position through the recruiting of mercenaries. Nor is it hard to see where they might seek salvation. In Thrace, and available, were at least 6,000 seasoned veterans, led by an Athenian cavalry officer, one of their own, who through an extraordinary feat of arms (which, as we know, like the exploits of T. E. Lawrence, lost nothing in the telling) had become the most successful Greek general in decades. It would be extraordinary if an approach was *not* made to Xenophon at this point. It would be extraordinary if he was not, at the very least, tempted by it. It would be equally extraordinary if the *dēmos* had not heard about or, more probably, anticipated such a move, and taken emergency steps to forestall it.

Was Xenophon guilty (in fact rather than in the eyes of the *dēmos*) of

---

40. Xen. *Hell.* 2.4.43; Just. 5.10.8–11; Krentz 1982, 120–24.

41. Xen. ibid.: . . . ὁμόσαντες ὅρκους ἦ μὴν μὴ μνησικακήσειν; Just. §11: . . . omnes iure iurando obstringuntur, discordiarum oblivionem fore.

42. Cf. Rahn 1981, 115.

treasonable actions? Impossible to tell, but it seems unlikely. Briefly considered treasonable *intentions* (though not in his own mind regarded as such), a willingness to confabulate with representatives of the Eleusis rump, may well be another matter—and quite enough, when reported, to cause panic in Athens. In that city's fraught internal history, factionalism and στάσις never impugned a man's polis patriotism in his own eyes; and Xenophon in 399 would have been all too conscious of the treachery by which the *dēmos* had killed his good friends a year before. Yet the caginess in his own writings suggests, at the very least, embarrassment: for the *dēmos*, an oligarch's patriotism bore an uglier name. Xenophon could, too, show prejudice and vicious bias against individuals on occasion—though, interestingly, the two most flagrant instances both involved Spartans, Thibron and Anaxibios.[43] Unless he is more subtly disingenuous in his writing than anyone has given him credit for being, I would argue that, leaving intention aside, he was probably innocent of treasonable or stasiotic action—the move against him (unprecedented in this, too) being preemptive, to ensure that, were he to lead troops into Attica, he could at once be branded as a mere criminal. What argues against his involvement (again, characteristic of his kind of moral conservatism) is the obviously genuine disgust (above, note 26) that he displays at the excesses of the Thirty and their adherents.

Xenophon was eager, after his long campaign, above all to *go home*, and indeed was making preparations to do so.[44] His men, not surprisingly, felt the same inclination.[45] All this is repeatedly emphasized. No adequate explanation has ever been given for his abrupt change of mind.[46] The obvious answer is that his mind did not change, that the decision was forced on him. A preemptive ψήφισμα of exile would at one stroke have cancelled all his plans. Since it could hardly be stated in public that the object of the decree was to discourage the appearance in Attica of several thousand mercenaries under a general bent on restoring the oligarchy, some vaguely satisfying and innocuous excuse had to be found, and at short notice. The answer—just as Socrates had foreseen, or at least as Xenophon claimed he foresaw—lay in the holdall charge of association with Cyrus, a harmless fiction that both sides had good reason to go along with, and to which the even more generalized taint of Laconism would naturally attach itself.

---

43. P. Krentz, "Thibron and the Thirty," *AncW* 15 (1987): 75–79; J. Roisman, "Anaxibios and Xenophon's Anabasis," *AHB* 2.4 (1988): 80–87.

44. *Anab.* 7.6.11, 33; 7.7.57.

45. *Anab.* 5.1.1–4; 6.6.14, 23, 24.

46. See, e.g., Roisman (as above, note 43), 87.

Xenophon's exile thus falls into the same general category as the exactly contemporaneous trials of Andocides and Socrates, as part of a vengeful anti-oligarchical backlash that sought to circumvent the terms of the amnesty, and was fueled by a very real fear (whether justified or not) of a military-backed counter-revolution. In one sense, too, the charge of association with Cyrus was emotionally, if not legally, damaging, since Cyrus, together with Lysander, had done more than most to ensure Athens's final defeat in the Peloponnesian War. Thus one way and another, the stigma of προδοσία hung over Xenophon—that passionately loyal Athenian—for a great deal of his life. When he accompanied Agesilaus to Coronea in 394, he must have despaired of ever rehabilitating himself (though this did not stop him, like Ovid, from putting the best possible face on all his actions in order to secure a reprieve). Even when, at long last, that reprieve had been granted,[47] he still preferred, despite visits to Athens, to domicile himself in Corinth,[48] away from the ever-present reminders of Athenian μνησικακία: a morally decent country gentleman who had had the bad luck to be in the wrong place at the wrong time, a classic early victim of political correctness.[49]

---

47. His son Gryllos's service in the Athenian cavalry would have been conditional upon the removal of Xenophon's ἀτιμία: cf. Bugh 1988, 148ff.

48. Diog. Laert. 2.53, 56.

49. An earlier version of this paper was given at the A.P.A. convention in Chicago, December 1991. I am grateful to all those who discussed it with me then or later, and offered helpful criticism, in particular Professors Joseph Roisman and C.M.C. Green. Neither they nor any other commentator should be held responsible for the blemishes that remain.

7

Rebooking the Flute-Girls: A Fresh Look at the Chronological Evidence for the Fall of Athens and the Eight-Month Rule of the Thirty

ONE OF THE best-known and most dramatic moments in Greek history is when, on 16 Mounychion in the year 405/4, after the formal surrender of the Athenian government, "Lysander sailed into Piraeus, the exiles came home, and they began to demolish the walls, with great enthusiasm, to the music of flute-girls, thinking that this day marked the beginning of freedom for Greece." As a set-piece it ranks with the description, also by Xenophon, of how the news of the defeat at Aegospotami was brought to Athens by the state trireme *Paralos*, "and wailing ran from Piraeus up the Long Walls to the city."[1] It is followed by the establishment of the Thirty, and an eight-month reign of terror: the death of Theramenes, the persecution of the metics, the installation of a Spartan garrison on the Acropolis, the successful counter-revolution by Thrasybulus. The story is familiar: perhaps too familiar. Yet the evidence bristles with problems (and, as we shall see, pseudo-problems); scholarly unanimity has by no means been achieved; and the improper manipulation of evidence to *parti pris* ends is not unknown. On all counts, then, further analysis of this crucial episode may be useful.

There are no fewer than three main dates advanced for the establishment of the Thirty in the year 404: April, June–July, and September. Each has had fairly recent supporters.[2] Their arguments are not of equal merit. Advocates of April point to the fact that Plutarch, Lysias, Andocides, and Xenophon

---

Note: Originally published in *Ancient History Bulletin* 5 (1991): 1–16: the version here presented has modifications and additions.

1. Xen. *Hell.* 2.2.3–4, 23; Plut. *Lys.* 15.1–4.

2. April: Lotze 1964, 96–97, cf. *Philol.* 18 (1974): 215–17; Bommelaer 1981, 134–41. June–July: Hignett 1952, 378–83; Hamilton 1979, 63. September: Adelaye 1971, 194–205; Colin 1933, 31–34; Hackl 1960, 81–95; Krenz 1982, 147–52 (who also discusses earlier theories).

(in two difficult passages) all seem to place the Thirty at a point immediately following the destruction of the walls, loosely equated with the surrender of the city;[3] and 16 Mounychion is generally calculated to have fallen on or about 22–23 April in that year.[4] But the massive fortifications of Piraeus and the Long Walls could not—as common sense suggests and the evidence confirms—be demolished overnight, not least when there was deliberate stalling on the part of the Athenians (below, p. 154). In the event, the process took over four months, and may well not have been completed even then.

Bommelaer (1981, 139) confirms the April date by placing the fall of the Thirty in December–January 404/3 (since it is known that their period of rule lasted eight months[5]), his argument being that the Thirty were deposed after a snowstorm, which surprised them in fine weather during their attack on Phyle.[6] There is in fact no clear statement as to the period of time that elapsed between the debacle at Phyle and the fall of the Thirty (it could have been several months), and, more to the point, as I have witnessed and Hignett (1952, 386) confirms, snow can fall in Attica as late as the end of March. To maintain an April date also involves rejecting the evidence of Aristotle,[7] who specifically dates the establishment of the Thirty in the archonship of Pythodorus (404/3).[8] Since the evidence cited to associate this event with Lysander's first entry into Piraeus does not in fact say what is claimed for it (besides contradicting other testimony), the April date can be confidently rejected.[9]

There remain the possibilities of June–July or September. In Krentz's view (1982, 149), "To reach an undisputed decision between the middle and the

---

3. Plut. *Lys.* 15.5–6; Lys. 13.34; Andoc. 1.80; Xen. *Hell.* 2.3.3, 11.

4. Lotze, seizing on the fact (undoubtedly true) that the Athenian calendar was irregular, argued that 405/4 could have begun as far back as 18 June, so that 16 Mounychion would then have fallen toward the end of March 404: see his article "Der Munichion 404 v. Chr. und das Problem der Schaltfolge in Athenischen Kalendar," *Philol.* 111 (1967): 34–46. He had, however, a good reason for wanting this date (see p. 144 n.2), and thus his pursuit of an irregularity becomes per se suspect.

5. Xen. *Hell.* 2.4.21.

6. Xen. *Hell.* 2.4.3.

7. *Ath. Pol.* 35.1; cf. Xen. *Hell.* 2.2.4 (καὶ ὁ ἐνιαυτὸς ἔληγεν), 2.3.1 (τῷ δ᾽ ἐπιόντι ἔτει . . . ἐγένετο . . . αὕτη ἡ ὀλιγαρχία). On the possibility of interpolation, see my remarks, p. 146.

8. Though Pythodorus was appointed, as Xenophon says (*Hell.* 2.3.1.), ἐν ὀλιγαρχίᾳ (i.e., probably after the installation of the Thirty), his name was subsequently used to denote the entire archon-year: cf. Krentz, 149. The year was not intercalary, and ended on 2 July: Meritt 1928, ch. 9, 88, 107–11.

9. Munro, in his article "The Constitution of Dracontides," *CQ* 32 (1938): 133–35, tries to reconcile the apparent inconsistencies by having the Thirty appointed as commissioners to establish the πάτριος πολιτεία in April, and in the fall (late October, Munro argues, but his reasons are inadmissible, cf. pp. 154–58) as a ruling government. This is ingenious but unconvincing, and even if true would not affect the main course of my argument.

end of the summer is not possible." I hope to demonstrate that a date at the very end of September or beginning of October is not only possible, but virtually certain, and in the process to clear away a certain amount of confusion over the evidence and how it should be handled. To take the most obvious examples: it has been a near-unanimous article of faith, at least since Beloch's day,[10] that Xen. *Hell.* 2.3.1–2 is an interpolated passage. The main reason for this belief is that the text as it stands appears to contradict a tradition, supported by Lysias and Diodorus (Ephorus),[11] that Lysander came over to Athens, at the invitation of the oligarchs, *after* his reduction of Samos; whereas Xenophon (it is claimed) places this visit, and the establishment of the Thirty with which it is associated, *before* Samos fell: τούτων [i.e., the events surrounding the vote in the Assembly] πραχθέντων ἀπέπλει Λύσανδρος πρὸς Σάμον (*Hell.* 2.3.3). Agis's evacuation of Decelea is placed at the same time: there are strong reasons, as we shall see, for dating this event in the fall. With the excision of 2.3.1–2, the argument runs, τούτων πραχθέντων will refer to Lysander's entry into Piraeus and the demolition of the walls, and the first reference to the Thirty will come at 2.3.11, thus removing the supposed inconsistency with Lysias and Diodorus.

This cavalier treatment of unwelcome evidence is, to put it mildly, disturbing, though almost no scholars, to my knowledge, have shown signs of being disturbed by it.[12] It is, moreover, by no means unique. Another instance at once comes to mind. Attempts (none of them viable) have been made to date the inception of the Thirty's rule by working backward from the date of their fall. Not more than two days after the battle of Munychia, in which Critias lost his life and the Thirty their power, some of the "men of Piraeus" went out foraging for ξύλα καὶ ὀπώραν (Xen. *Hell.* 2.4.25). At what season of the year could this be done? At any time that happens to suit a theory, it would seem: *quot capita, tot sententiae.* Late autumn to December (apples and olives), Beloch asserted; March to April (stored in cellars through the winter!), says Lehmann; May or June, argue Colin and Krentz, erroneously relying on a reference in Polybius that does not, in fact, support their claim.[13] But it was left

---

10. Beloch 1912–13, iii², 2:204–7; Hignett 1952, 379–80; O. Blank, "Die Einsetzung der Dreissig zu Athen im Jahre 404 v. Chr.," diss., Freiburg (1911), 2–15; Rhodes 1981, 436f.

11. Lys. 12.71; Diod. Sic. 14.3.4–5.

12. Colin (1933, 111) is a rare and welcome exception: after listing most of the questionable devices mentioned here, he declares, with justice, "Je me suis efforcé d'éviter toujours ces subterfuges désespérés." (It is a symptom of the sad state of Xenophon studies that this brilliant monograph, published as long ago as 1933, should have reached me via Interlibrary Loan *with its pages still uncut.*)

13. Beloch 1912–13, iii², 2:209; Lehmann 1972, 219 n. 47; Colin 1933, 66; Krentz 1982, 150. Polyb. 4.66.7, read in the context of Philip V's seasonal campaigning, in fact refers to August or Sep-

to Busolt, who saw well enough that the Thirty fell from power in spring 403, to suggest emending ὀπώραν to ὄσπρια (pulse), presumably because he, like most scholars, was under the impression that the former could be harvested only in the fall.[14] In fact, different kinds of ὀπώρα could be gathered (then as now) at different times of year. Alciphron[15] refers to an alfresco picnic enriched with every kind of *spring* ὀπώρα, which will have included vegetables, salad, and green figs. Thus the evidence is in fact almost useless for chronological purposes: there is only one season of the year, winter, where it could show an inconsistency with other testimony, and it most certainly cannot be used to refine it. My point here, however, is that Busolt thought it could, and was quite ready to emend a text arbitrarily because it clashed with his conclusions. Let us see what can be made of the evidence as it stands before resorting to such desperate (and, I fear, dishonest) remedies, which can only be entertained as a last resort when all attempts to reconcile, or logically explain, seeming inconsistencies have failed.

Thucydides (5.26.3) tells us that the Peloponnesian War, which began early in March 431, lasted twenty-seven years and "a few days in addition," ἡμέρας οὐ πολλὰς παρενεγκούσας. How many is οὐ πολλάς, a few? Counting from Anthesterion 27 (= c. 3 March?), we would come to a point about mid-March 404. But Plutarch, as we have seen (*Lys.* 15.1), dates Lysander's entry into Piraeus on 16 Mounychion, that is, about 22–23 April. Forty-eight days, a good month and a half, is not, by any argument, "a few." Andrewes[16] finds the figure, with good reason, "disquietingly high." Other evidence also points to mid-March. According to Diodorus (13.108.1), Darius II died "shortly after the peace," μικρὸν τῆς εἰρήνης ὕστερον; we know from the Persian archives[17] that Artaxerxes was acknowledged king by 1 Nisan = 10 April. The sequence of events from Aegospotami in September 405—two months for food supplies to run short in Athens, the initial peace feeler to Agis about mid-November (Xen. *Hell.* 2.2.1), Theramenes' three-month mission to Ly-

tember: see F. W. Walbank's *Commentary on Polybius*, vol. 1 (corr. ed., Oxford, 1970), 521; vol. 2 (Oxford, 1967), 640–41.

14. G. Busolt, rev. H. Swoboda, *Griechische Staatskunde* (Munich, 1926), 2:912–13 n. 7: "Sie endigte also im Frühjahr 403. Dazu passen alle übrigen Angaben . . . ausser II.4.25 . . . Wahrscheinlich liegt hier aber eine Verschreibung aus ὄσπρια vor."

15. Alciphr. *Ep. Amat.* 4.13.10 (= fr. 6.10): ὅσα . . . ἀγρὸς ἡμῖν ἐαρινῆς ὀπώρας ἐπεδαψιλεύετο.

16. A. W. Gomme, A. Andrewes, and K. J. Dover, *A Historical Commentary on Thucydides*, vol. 4 (Oxford, 1970), 12. Andrewes does not appear to have read Munro 1937: see below.

17. R. A. Parker, W. H. Dubberstein, *Babylonian Chronology, 626 B.C.–A.D. 45* (2d ed., Chicago, 1946), 16, 32, cited by Krentz 1982, 32 n. 8.

sander begun not later than the first week in December[18]—is consistent with this date of mid-March.

Munro's convincing solution[19] was to place Athens's formal acceptance of the Spartan terms (Xen. *Hell.* 2.2.21-22, Diod. Sic. 14.3.2) in March, to be followed, on 16 Mounychion, by Lysander's formal entry into Piraeus, a ceremonial occasion that, as Munro correctly observes, needed much preparation—the removal of harbor dams (Xen. *Hell.* 2.2.4), the hiring of musicians and organization of parades and *corvées*, the assembly of exiles. Above all, there had to be time for diplomatic negotiations over the final terms of the peace. Both historiographically and in terms of practical realities, this is far more plausible than Detlef Lotze's attempt (see note 4) to manipulate 16 Mounychion back into March, a gambit on a par with Busolt's hankering after ὄσπρια.[20]

Plutarch (*Lys.* 14.8) cites directly, in Laconian dialect, the conditions presented to Athens by the Spartan ephors: the Long Walls and Piraeus fortifications to be pulled down, the exiles to be restored, all the cities of the empire to be evacuated (so that Athens's authority was restricted to Attica). One last clause provides for the number of ships that Athens could keep to be decided on the spot. As we know from other sources, and as common practice would presume, several further points were thus determined. The ephors' terms simply represented a firm base for negotiation. The absence of any clause from the original συνθήκη is no proof, as has sometimes been supposed, that it was not genuine: (7) below, for example, is clearly a concession to the Athenians.

The final instrument (presumably agreed upon before Lysander's arrival) consisted, then, of the following terms:

(1) The Piraeus fortifications and at least 10 stades (Xen. *Hell.* 2.2.15) of the Long Walls (Lys. 13.14 says ὅλα τὰ μακρὰ τείχη, all of them, but Xenophon's testimony is preferable) to be destroyed: Xen. *Hell.* 2.2.20; Plut. *Lys.* 14.8, 15.1, 5; Andoc. 1.80, 3.11-12 (autopsy of stele); Lys. 13.14, 34; Diod. Sic. 13.107.4, 14.3.2; Just. 5.8.5.

(2) The Athenian fleet to be surrendered, except for twelve vessels: Andoc. 3.12 (autopsy of stele); Xen. *Hell.* 2.2.20; Diod. Sic. 13.107.4 (rounds

---

18. Cf. Krentz, ibid.

19. Munro 1937, 32-38.

20. It also leaves time for the opposition bid by Strombichides, Dionysodorus, and their democratic supporters (Lys. 13.13ff., 30.14), which took place between Theramenes' return to Athens and Lysander's entry, events requiring "the lapse of several weeks, a month rather than a day" (Munro 1937, 34).

this figure to ten); cf. also Lys. 13.14, 34; Andoc. 3.11; Plut. *Lys.* 14.8, 15.1, 5; Just. 5.8.5.

(3) Athens's exiles to return home: Plut. *Lys.* 14.8; Xen. *Hell.* 2.2.20; Andoc. 1.80, 3.11 and 12 (the latter with autopsy of stele, and the comment ἐξ ὧν ὁ δῆμος κατελύθη, "with the result that the democracy fell"): cf. below, p. 156 with note 59.

(4) Athens to be the subordinate partner in an alliance with Sparta: Xen. *Hell.* 2.2.20; Diod. Sic. 13.107.4.

(5) The cities of the Athenian empire to be evacuated: Plut. *Lys.* 14.8; Diod. Sic. 13.107.4.

(6) A deadline to be met for the destruction of Athens's fortifications: Plut. *Lys.* 15.2.

(7) Government to be according to "ancestral custom," the πάτριος πολιτεία: Arist. *Ath. Pol.* 34.1; Diod. Sic. 14.3.2.[21]

(8) The islands of Lemnos, Imbros, and Scyros to be retained by their present occupants (ἔχειν τοὺς ἔχοντας): Andoc. 3.12 (autopsy of stele).[22]

All this should be borne in mind when we consider the events of 16 Mounychion and what followed.

Lysander's activities between October 405 and April 404 are not, in general, our present concern; but there is one important exception: the siege and eventual reduction of Samos. This is crucial both chronologically and as a guide to Lysander's priorities. It was his one serious setback during this period: a problem still unresolved, and very much on his mind, at the time of his formal entry into Piraeus. Immediately after Aegospotami, the Samians, declaring their continued allegiance to Athens, σφαγὰς τῶν γνωρίμων ποιήσαντες κατεῖχον τὴν πόλιν, "massacred the upper classes and took over the city," and were rewarded by the Athenians with ἰσοπολιτεία for so doing.[23] A major naval base, Samos could not be ignored. After other essential mopping-up operations,[24] Lysander sailed east. Lesbos and Chios presented no prob-

---

21. I am not primarily concerned here with the precise meaning of this provision; but my basic belief is that it simply allowed the Athenians to retain control over their own political institutions (rather than being subjected to the imposition of a decarchy and a harmost), and that the political strife recorded by both sources as ensuing (which exactly matches the situation in 510–508, after another Spartan intervention) amply confirms this. Cf. Andoc. 3.12 and note 20 above.

22. Justin's assertion (5.8.5) that the imposition of the Thirty was a condition of the peace contradicts all other testimony and seems to derive from a simple, and characteristic, telescoping of events.

23. Xen. *Hell.* 2.2.6–7; *IG* II² 1 = Meiggs-Lewis no. 94.

24. Xen. *Hell.* 2.2.1–2; Plut. *Lys.* 13.5–9, 14.3; Diod. Sic. 14.3.4, 10.1–2.

lems.[25] He then (mid-October) moved on to Samos and began the siege of the city himself.[26] When he moved on to his rendezvous with Agis outside Athens,[27] he probably left a holding force of forty vessels behind.[28] The Athenians proved equally obdurate, and with good reason: many states, just as they feared (Xen. *Hell.* 2.2.3), were pressing for their total destruction,[29] and it was probably now (October) that Agis and Lysander, frustrated by this unexpected resistance, made a similar proposal.[30] Their violence is understandable. They found themselves with two major sieges on their hands, one of which at least was against a city, Athens, that boasted virtually impregnable defenses. Siege warfare was expensive,[31] time-consuming, and required equipment and skills that the Spartans, notoriously, did not possess.[32]

The only solution, certainly in Athens's case, was to establish a tight naval blockade and do the job by slow attrition. Pausanias took his army home, Agis returned to Decelea, and Lysander (after decreeing the death penalty for blockade runners,[33] an act that suggests that his siege techniques were proving less than successful) sailed back to Asia Minor,[34] having presumably decided that Samos would be an easier nut to crack. He was wrong. When Theramenes

---

25. Xen. *Hell.* 2.2.5; cf. Hamilton 1979, 44.

26. Diod. Sic. 13.106.8. Diodorus correlates this action with the dispatch of Gylippus to Sparta, as escort for the booty of Aegospotami and 1,500 talents in silver. This is surely correct, and would not require comment were it not for the fact that Plutarch (*Lys.* 16.1) places Gylippus's escort duties a year later, after the establishment of the Thirty. However, Xenophon (*Hell.* 2.3.8-9) makes it clear that this was a different occasion: the cash (the balance of Cyrus's tribute) only amounts to 470 talents, representing what Lysander retained to finance the remainder of his campaign, above all the siege of Samos. Hamilton (1979, 55 with n. 121) dates Gylippus's return to Sparta as late as May 404: that Lysander would have delayed eight months before sending home the spoils of Aegospotami is — even allowing for his arrogant high-handedness — totally incredible.

27. Xen. *Hell.* 2.2.7-9; Plut. *Lys.* 14.1; Diod. Sic. 13.107.2; cf. Just. 5.8.1-2.

28. Lysander sailed to Lesbos with a fleet of 200 (Xen. *Hell.* 2.2.5), of which ten vessels were detached to Thrace under Eteonicus; when he reached Piraeus he had 150 (Xen. *Hell.* 2.2.9). Lotze (1964, 40-41) argues persuasively that the missing forty were left behind to blockade Samos.

29. Xen. *Hell.* 2.2.10-11; Diod. Sic. 13.107.2; cf. Krentz 1982, 30 and n. 6.

30. Paus. 3.8.6; cf. Hamilton 1979, 51-52.

31. The most notable recent instance had been Pericles' siege, again, of Samos (440-439), which cost Athens between 1,404 and 1,410 talents, a precedent that Lysander will undoubtedly have had very much in mind. Cf. G. Shipley, *A History of Samos, 800-188 B.C.* (Oxford, 1987), 116-19, with references there cited.

32. Yves Garlan, *Recherches de poliorcétique grecque* (Paris, 1974), 128-31, 147; Bommelaer 1981, 140.

33. Isocr. *Orat.* 18.61.

34. Diod. Sic. 13.107.3; Plut. *Lys.* 14.2. Diodorus says that the Peloponnesians decided τὰς ... δυνάμεις ἀπαγαγεῖν ἐκ τῆς Ἀττικῆς, but this cannot include Agis's force at Decelea, which Xenophon (*Hell.* 2.3.3) retains *in situ*, just as we might expect, until after the installation of the Thirty — or at least, even accepting 2.3.1-2 as an interpolation, until after the fall of Athens. It is hard to imagine any sane commander removing it sooner.

was sent out to negotiate with him, about the beginning of December,[35] he was still besieging the island.[36] He had had, and would continue to have, other calls on his time and energy in the north Aegean;[37] but Samos remained, apart from Athens, by far his biggest problem.

Initial peace feelers to Agis in November 405, and the negotiations that followed, had shown one thing very clearly: the Athenians were determined to keep their walls—and, thus, their autonomy—intact, even though the blockade was already beginning to cause considerable privation. A proposal to concede the ten-stade demolition clause resulted in jail for the proposer and a ψήφισμα making it illegal even to entertain such a notion. This gesture of defiance was orchestrated by Cleophon and the democratic ultras.[38]

Now Theramenes had come, with powers to negotiate (cf. note 36), though just what his brief from Athens was remains uncertain. Xenophon (*Hell.* 2.2.16) represents him as undertaking simply to find out why the Spartans insisted on the demolition of the walls: πότερον ἐξανδραποδίσασθαι τὴν βουλόμενοι . . . ἢ πίστεως ἕνεκα, "whether in order to enslave the city . . . or as a guarantee of good faith," the clear implication being that in the latter case, despite Cleophon's threats (Aeschin. 2.76; Xen. *Hell.* 2.2.15), the terms would be accepted. Lysias, in two separate speeches (12.68, 13.9), claims that Theramenes promised to negotiate a peace that would keep the walls intact, avoid the surrender of the fleet, and involve no giving of hostages. The two versions are not necessarily incompatible: perhaps Theramenes hoped to establish an alternative basis for guarantees of good faith.

The crux of the matter, however, is that he remained with Lysander for

---

35. Xen. *Hell.* 2.2.16; Lys. 13.9.11, cf. 12.68-69.

36. P. Mich. inv. 5982, lines 35-43, ed. R. Merkelbach and H. C. Youtie, *ZPE* 2 (1968): 161-69; cf. the further comments by A. Henrichs, *ZPE* 3 (1968): 101-8, and A. Andrewes, *ZPE* 6 (1970): 35-38; also Lys. 12.71.

37. The bulk of his activities took place, as we might expect, in the weeks immediately following Aegospotami. His first thought was to cut off the Black Sea grain supply to Athens by securing Sestos (Diod. Sic. 13.106.8), Byzantium, and Chalcedon (Xen. *Hell.* 2.2.1), just as Agis had planned in 401 (Xen. *Hell.* 1.1.35). His expedition to the East Greek islands (Xen. *Hell.* 2.2.5; Diod. Sic. 13.106.8) and his descent on Piraeus (Xen. *Hell.* 2.2.7-9; Plut. *Lys.* 14.4; Diod. Sic. 13.107.2; Just. 5.8.1-2) can both be placed in October 405. Several sources describe, without specific detail, a general cruise around the Aegean, imposing harmosts and decarchies, and dismantling or reversing Athenian institutions: Plut. *Lys.* 13.5-9; Diod. Sic. 14.3.4, 10.1-2; Nep. *Lys.* 1.5-2.1; Just. 5.7.3. We can assume that Lysander continued to supervise this procedure into the spring of 404. After that, Athens and Samos occupied him until his final victorious return to Sparta in October of that year. Andrewes (as above, note 36), 35 n. 1, and Lotze 1964, 51-52, assume, improbably, that all such testimonia can be referred to one single, tidy voyage. There is no more reason to believe this than that Lysander made one trip only to Samos, an assumption that has generated a crop of imagined inconsistencies where none in fact exist.

38. Xen. *Hell.* 2.2.10-11, 15; Lys. 13.8; Aeschin. 2.76.

not fewer than three months, and at the end of this period (late February or early March 404) was dismissed with the assertion that only the ephors at Sparta had the authority to answer his questions. Theramenes' explanation of this delay before the Athenian Assembly was that Lysander had forcibly detained him. The reason given, we may note, seemingly satisfied his hearers (a notoriously captious body), since they promptly appointed him head of a ten-man mission to negotiate with the Spartan government (Xen. *Hell.* 2.2.17). But both Xenophon and Lysias (13.11) explain it as deliberate delaying tactics on Theramenes' part, designed to reduce Athens's resistance to a point where it would accept even the harshest terms. This fantasy, clearly aimed at providing a convenient scapegoat for a humiliating situation, has taken in a surprising number of modern scholars.[39] Krentz (1982, 36–41) offers a different but even less plausible solution: Theramenes was hoping, by this prolongation of his absence, to *prevent* Athens from surrendering.

Neither of these scenarios makes any practical sense, since Theramenes, *qua* petitioner, was in no position to procrastinate, let alone to dictate the course of events (cf. Harding, *EMC/CV* n.s. 3 [1984]: 100–101). In what circumstances can we imagine him hanging around Lysander's headquarters, day after day, on his own initiative, especially if the Spartan, an impatient man at the best of times, wanted to get the matter settled? (And if he moved elsewhere, the story would very soon get back to Athens.) No: it was Lysander alone who could dictate matters in this way, putting off the Athenian with one excuse after another, if not actually keeping him under house arrest, and finally creating yet further delay (what he could have made clear, had he so wished, right from the beginning) that he lacked authority to treat. It was Lysander, rather than Theramenes, who needed to have the Athenian *dēmos* reduced to the point where it would give in and break down its own defenses rather than challenge a Spartan army to do what twenty-seven years of warfare had so signally failed to achieve. Theramenes, in fact, had spoken no more than the plain truth.[40] Lysander had had no luck so far with Samos, a far less impreg-

---

39. A convenient conspectus in Krentz 1982, 35–36 with n. 31.

40. Bernadotte Perrin, the Loeb translator of Plutarch, realized this: see "The Rehabilitation of Theramenes," *AHR* 9 (1903/4): 667, cited by Krentz 1982, 35 n. 20; and Detlef Lotze (1964, 43) at least conceded the possibility that Theramenes *was* detained by Lysander, "der erkannte, wie unklug Theramenes' Ruckkehr zu diesem Zeitpunkt gewesen wäre, wo die Athener noch nicht genügend zermürbt waren." Krentz is quite wrong in claiming that "Lysander had nothing to gain by holding Theramenes"—he had a very great deal—and correspondingly underrates the desperate resistance the Athenians put up. Blockades were seldom one hundred percent efficient in the ancient world, and it probably took a long time for Agis and Lysander to find, and plug, all the gaps.

nably defended city; against the great bastions of Piraeus and the Long Walls, nothing but starvation would prevail. Theramenes knew this as well as Lysander. Clearly he had hoped for a quick settlement, and had instead come up against Lysander's stalling tactics. His enemies would not be slow to blame their emissary for the resultant crisis.

Lysander had judged his moment well. The food situation had by now become really desperate,[41] and the Spartan was kept informed both of this (Plut. *Lys.* 14.5) and of other developments, including the hardening of opposition against the (largely democratic) no-surrender group. Cleophon was impeached and executed,[42] the anti-oligarchical coup by Strombichides, Dionysodorus, and others was detected and put down.[43] A humbled Athenian embassy took home the terms of surrender (see above) from Sparta. A date for their ceremonial implementation was set a month or so ahead,[44] and on 16 Mounychion Lysander made his triumphal entry into Piraeus. It is from this moment that our real problems begin.

The occasion, clearly, was symbolic. We do not know how, where, or indeed (as we shall see) exactly when the Athenian fleet—or what remained of it—was handed over to Lysander, or what proportion of it was burned, though we can make an intelligent guess.[45] A formal surrender offered small scope for such activities. Even more problematical is the matter of the demolition of the walls. We know from Thucydides (1.93.5) that the Themistoclean circuit-wall of Piraeus was built with iron-clamped ashlar blocks, and was wide enough for two carts to pass on its upper level. Archaeological evidence for this, the Cononian wall that succeeded it, and the Long Walls confirms the formidable nature of these fortifications.[46] The beginning of the demolition work, with its flute accompaniment, meant no more, in concrete terms, than the formal laying of a foundation-stone, or the turning of a sod with a golden spade. Lysander, who, better than most men, knew the value of good publicity, made sure the flute-girls were Athenian (Plut. *Lys.* 15.5), and in all likelihood the laborers, too.[47]

---

41. E.g., Xen. *Hell.* 2.2.11; Diod. Sic. 13.107.4.
42. Xen. *Hell.* 1.7.35; Lys. 13.12, 30.10–14.
43. Lys. 13.13 ff.; cf. Hamilton 1979, 54.
44. Cf. Munro 1937, 34–37.
45. Plut. *Lys.* 15.5, cf. 1; Lys. 13.4.
46. R. Garland, *The* [sic] *Piraeus from the Fifth to the First Century B.C.* (Ithaca, N.Y., 1987), 163ff.
47. Another question no one has ever bothered to ask. Plutarch's κατέσκαπτε merely indicates Lysander's authority in the matter. Diodorus (Ephorus) 14.3.1 says that the Athenians did the job, but gives no details. Xenophon (*Hell.* 2.2.23) and Lysias (13.34) are discreetly vague: Lysias (like some modern politicians) takes refuge in a passive (κατεσκάφθη), while Xenophon has an

Most ceremonies mark either a beginning or an end, and this one was no exception; yet a superficial consideration of the evidence might lead—has, indeed, in some cases, led—to the conclusion that Lysander's visit celebrated both at once, something that should instantly arouse our suspicion. The terms of a surrender had been agreed upon, but were not susceptible to instant implementation: this applied in particular to the breaching of the fortifications, for which, as we have seen, a time limit was set. No source specifies the deadline, but circumstantial evidence (see below) makes the end of Alexias's archonship (June/July 404) a tempting *terminus ante quem*. The demolition was merely *begun* (κατέσκαπτον, an inceptive imperfect), after which, says Xenophon, ὁ ἐνιαυτὸς κατέληγεν, "the year ended," and whether we take this as the archontic or the Thucydidean year, there is ample evidence to show that the dismantling operation dragged on. Lysander complained of missed deadlines and unfulfilled specifications.[48]

At this point we can profitably turn our attention to the latter end of the summer. The establishment of the Thirty, dated by both Aristotle and Xenophon to the archonship of Pythodorus (404/3),[49] is also placed immediately (εὐθύς, ἐπεὶ τάχιστα) after the demolition of the walls.[50] Can we date it more precisely? Xenophon refers (2.3.4) to an eclipse of the sun that can confidently be identified as that of 3 September 404. "About this time," he reports (κατὰ ... τοῦτον χρόνον), *inter alia* the Thirty took power, after which (τούτων ... πραχθέντων) Lysander sailed from Samos and Agis withdrew his army from Decelea.[51] How near is "about"? In my opinion, such a time indicator, to have any real meaning, covers a span of two months at the outside, and more probably one—in this case August–September (or the beginning of October), with a strong presumption in favor of September.

---

unattached active (κατέσκαπτον). The Loeb translator, quite gratuitously, identifies the laborers as the Peloponnesians, an assumption followed by D. M. Lewis, *Sparta and Persia* (Leiden, 1977), 67, with n. 109; Hatzfeld, in the Budé version, tactfully hedges his bets: "*L'on* commença à démolir les murailles. . . ." The Peloponnesians were there to gloat over Athenian discomfiture, not to act as pick-and-shovel men; not even the Athenian exiles, who might just offer a subject for Plutarch's verb (καὶ οἱ φυγάδες κατῆσαν καὶ τὰ τείχη κατέσκαπτον), were going to do so πολλῇ προθυμίᾳ, which has to be a dative of accompanying circumstance (not unlike the flute music), and experienced not by the defeated, but by Lysander and his party. No wonder Xenophon and Lysias, from opposite ends of the political spectrum, both glossed over this detail: Athens was forced to provide the *corvée* itself, to do the unthinkable thing that it had made it illegal even to discuss (Xen. *Hell.* 2.2.15).

48. Diod. Sic. 14.3.6; Plut. *Lys.* 15.2.5; cf. Lys. 12.74.

49. Arist. *Ath. Pol.* 35.1; Xen. *Hell.* 2.3.1-2.

50. Xen. *Hell.* 2.3.11; Plut. *Lys.* 15.1.6.

51. I do not propose to waste space discussing the alleged inconsistencies discovered in these statements by ingenious critics; the evidence is *prima facie* plausible, and, as I hope by the end to have shown, true.

Is there any further evidence pointing to a September date? I think so. When informing us that Lysander entered Piraeus on 16 Mounychion, Plutarch (*Lys.* 15.1) adds that this was "the same day on which they defeated the barbarian in the naval battle at Salamis," a claim that has, understandably, worried scholars, who failed to see what valuable implications the error had. As Plutarch himself elsewhere (*Camillus* 19.6) makes very clear, with a reference to his own lost monograph Περὶ Ἡμερῶν, the actual date of Salamis was c. 20 Boedromion, that is, about 28–29 September.[52] The mistake is Plutarch's only one of the sort,[53] and is repeated in his essay on the Athenians (*Mor.* 349F), where he further identifies Salamis as a battle in which Athens was aided by the full moon (πανσέληνος), which was not the case. Both this latter passage and that in the *Life* of Camillus consists of lists of famous dates; and a comparison of these at once makes it clear that Plutarch, probably citing from memory, confused Chabrias's victory off Naxos (which *was* fought at the full moon, and in Boedromion) with that of Salamis. But how, it will be asked, did the date of 16 Mounychion then attach itself to this error, since everyone knew that Salamis had been fought in autumn? It has even been suggested[54] that what Plutarch really had in mind was the mid-fifth century sea-battle off Salamis *in Cyprus* that came to be associated with Cimon; but ingenious though this solution is, the mention of Salamis *tout court* can only, in default of specific indication to the contrary, refer to the most famous naval battle in all Greek history.

The answer, surely, is much simpler. Chapter 15 of Plutarch's *Life* of Lysander is, as has often been pointed out,[55] chronologically compressed, in a way highly characteristic of Greek thought. Plutarch remembered two traditional dates associated with Lysander's entering Athens: 16 Mounychion, and the anniversary of Salamis. The mistake he made was in referring them carelessly

---

52. Despite all the work done in this field by scholars such as Pritchett and Meritt, it remains true, as Bickerman conceded (*Chronology of the Ancient World* [London, 1968], 36), that "the proposed schemes of the Athenian civil year can only be tentative." An approximation is often the best we can hope for.

53. E. Badian and J. Buckler, "The Wrong Salamis?" *RhM* 118 (1975): 226–39, esp. 228.

54. Ibid. Professor W. Heckel suggests to me that another possible source of confusion over the date may be the second, later, battle of Salamis-on-Cyprus in spring 306, in which Demetrius Poliorcetes defeated Ptolemy I (Diod. Sic. 20.49–52; Plut. *Demetr.* 16; Paus. 1.6.6), and in which thirty Athenian vessels took part; but as he says, this can have nothing to do with Plutarch's error.

55. E.g., by Krentz 1982, 148. An exactly parallel compression can be observed in Plutarch's version of the dispatch of a Spartan garrison to Athens under Callibius as harmost. Xenophon (*Hell.* 2.3.13–14) makes it clear that they were sent some time *after* Sept./Oct. 404, and at the request of the Thirty themselves; Plutarch (*Lys.* 15.6) runs the two events together in a way that implies Lysander was solely responsible, and has sometimes been taken (wrongly, I think) to imply their installation before Lysander left for Samos.

to the same occasion, rather than to the beginning and conclusion of a sequence of events that began in April 404 (16 Mounychion) and only ran its
course in late September (20 Boedromion). It is my belief that Lysander *held
a second formal ceremony*, very like the first, to celebrate the final implementation of the terms of surrender, and that, with characteristically cruel irony, he
chose a day for it that would underscore Athens's humiliation by subverting
its traditional claim to glory. Plut. *Lys.* 14.5, then, like Xen. *Hell.* 2.2.23, will
refer to April, while 15.5 describes the second ceremony at the end of September, and 15.1 is a confusion of both. Other sources[56] simply confirm the
relative order of events without suggesting any absolute date for them. That
Plutarch, in the circumstances, mixed up the two occasions need surprise no
one.

Let us accept this time scheme as a working model and see how the rest of
our evidence fits it. The advocates of interpolation at Xen. *Hell.* 2.3.1–2 (and
Raubitschek without benefit of interpolation[57]) will have Lysander returning
to Samos and Agis withdrawing his whole force from Decelea in April (Xen.
Hell. 2.3.3). This is appropriate enough for Lysander, whose first thought undoubtedly was to return to a difficult siege; but it is quite incredible that, at a
time when Athens's walls were still largely intact, and its fleet in all likelihood
not yet fully dispersed, the Spartans would have removed all occupational control from Attica. Agis's force will have been withdrawn only in September or
early October, after the installation of the Thirty. This factor offers another
powerful argument against interpolation.

We do not know precisely when the exiles returned: our evidence, such
as it is,[58] suggests, as we might expect, that they continued to come in during
the early summer. They clearly played an active role in the ongoing dissension over the form the government should take, for which we have the evidence of Aristotle and Diodorus,[59] and which pitted democrats against both
moderate and extreme oligarchs.[60] Nor do we know exactly when Lysander

---

56. Andoc. 1.80; Lys. 13.34.

57. A. E. Raubitschek, "Die sogenannten beiden Büchern von Xenophons 'Griechische Geschichte'," in *Akten des VI Internationalen Kongresses für Griechische und Lateinische Epigraphik* (Munich, 1973), 315–25, appositely cited by Krentz 1982, 148–49 and n. 40.

58. Xen. *Hell.* 2.2.3; Andoc. 1.80.

59. Arist. *Ath. Pol.* 34.3; Diod. Sic. 14.3.2–3; Andoc. 3.12. Note also the establishment of five
Spartan-style "ephors," δημοκρατίας ἔτι οὔσης (*Lys.* 12.43–45), which confirms strong oligarchic
activity before Lysander's intervention.

60. I am not immediately concerned here with the historiographical and political problems involved in this episode, especially as regards the "ancestral constitution" (πάτριος πολιτεία). On
this, see Rhodes 1981, 427ff.; Fuks 1953, ch. 3, 52ff.; M. I. Finley, "The Ancestral Constitution,"

returned to Samos—Hamilton suggests mid-May,[61] as good a guess as any— or, indeed, when he secured its surrender,[62] except (a crucial point) that this happened shortly (προσφάτως) before the arrival of an oligarchic delegation from Athens, asking for his intervention on their behalf in the political squab- bling going on there. What we *do* know, now, is that this delegation must have reached Samos in early or mid-September, since the result of their appeal was Lysander's second formal descent on Piraeus; so if we place the surrender of Samos at the end of August, we will probably not be far out. As we shall see, Lysander left unfinished business behind him, and returned to complete it.

Lysander, then, sailed for Athens[63] about mid-September. It was on ar- rival that he complained (presumably after personal inspection) that the Long Walls and the fortifications of Piraeus had not been breached by the deadline, or according to specification.[64] Both Xenophon and Plutarch emphasize[65] that the great debate in which Lysander played a prominent part, and which re- sulted in the establishment of the Thirty,[66] took place immediately after the demolition work had been properly completed.

But as we have seen, and as Plutarch confirms,[67] on 20 Boedromion, *be- fore the debate*, there took place a second public ceremony emphasizing the final execution of the terms of surrender. The flute-girls had been rebooked, a last symbolic block would be removed from the breached walls. On the anni- versary of Salamis, with grim irony, there would be a ceremonial burning of triremes.[68] There is no hint elsewhere of the wholesale destruction of the fleet, an act that seems in any case improbable, and is directly contradicted by Xeno- phon (2.3.8), who claims, just as we might expect, that Lysander took τὰς ἐκ Πειραιῶς τριήρεις πλὴν δώδεκα, "all but twelve of the triremes in Piraeus," with him as prizes of war when he made his triumphal return to Sparta. The

---

The Use and Abuse of History (London, 1975), 34–59; K. R. Walters, "The 'Ancestral Constitution' and Fourth-Century Historiography in Athens," *AJAH* 1.3 (1976) 129–44.

61. Hamilton 1979, 55 with n. 121. He also, less plausibly, dates Gylippus's return to Sparta with the Aegospotami booty now, an unbelievable delay: cf. above, note 26.

62. Xen. *Hell.* 2.3.6; Plut. *Lys.* 14.2; Diod. Sic. 14.3.4. Xenophon makes it clear that, after months of inconclusive siege, Lysander was now ready to risk a direct assault, and that this was the decisive factor in the Samian decision to surrender. It seems likely that after the submission of Athens, he had received reinforcements from Sparta.

63. Diod. Sic. 14.3.5; Lys. 12.71; cf. Xen. *Hell.* 2.3.8.

64. Diod. Sic. 14.3.6; Plut. *Lys.* 15.2, 5; cf. Lys. 12.74.

65. Xen. *Hell.* 2.3.11; Plut. *Lys.* 15.1, 6.

66. Xen. *Hell.* 2.3.1–2; Lys. 12.71–77; Diod. Sic. 14.3.5–7; Plut. *Lys.* 15.1–3; Arist. *Ath. Pol.* 34.1–3. Again, for my present purposes I do not need to discuss this crucial episode in detail.

67. Plut. *Lys.* 15.5.

68. Ibid., καὶ τὰς τριήρεις κατέφλεγε πρὸς τὸν αὐλόν.

burning of, probably, not more than one or two triremes was ceremonial, an object-lesson, a deliberate humiliation of pride. Lysander, who had already given ample proof of his ruthlessness,[69] now showed himself equally adept at political propaganda.

Having settled matters in Athens, Lysander sailed back to Samos, where he turned over power τοῖς ἀρχαίοις πολίταις (i.e., to the unrestored oligarchs) under a ten-man junta[70]—an arrangement that virtually duplicated his dispositions for the Athenians. The grateful Samian oligarchs responded by renaming the Heraea, the great festival of Hera, the Lysandreia, and honoring Lysander himself as though he were a god: the first Greek, so far as we know, to receive such an accolade during his lifetime.[71] It seems more than likely that he himself requested it; the extensive record of his honors and dedications[72] reveals a man by no means averse to the cult of personality. He now at last, as summer was ending, τελευτῶντος τοῦ θέρους, made arrangements for his triumphal return to Sparta.[73] Agis, too, was on his way home, having evacuated Decelea and dismissed his allied contingents.[74]

Lysander's progress was leisurely: he still, as always, saw his role as the enforcer of discipline and good (i.e., oligarchic, pro-Spartan) government. It will have been now, after the decommissioning of much of the Spartan fleet, that he turned Sestos over to his pilots and boatswains.[75] He exhibited his savagery once more at Thasos, tricking the pro-Athenian faction with sworn guarantees and then slaughtering them.[76] From Piraeus he collected the surrendered triremes of the fleet, if he had not already removed them (with mercenary crews?). Then he made for home, taking with him the prows of captured enemy ships, an assortment of gold crowns offered him by various cities, 470 talents (representing the surplus of Cyrus's funding for the prosecution of the war), and much miscellaneous booty.[77] En route, never at a loss for a symbolically effective gesture, he "restored" the Melians to their island.[78] *Athenian* atrocities were not to be forgotten.

---

69. Diod. Sic. 13.104.7, 106.8; Xen. *Hell.* 2.1.31-32; Plut. *Lys.* 13.1-2, and in general 19.1-4.

70. Xen. *Hell.* 2.3.3, 7.

71. Duris *FGrH* 76 F 71; Hesych. s.v. Λυσάνδρεια; cf. Hamilton 1979, 70-71 with nn. 4-6 for earlier scholarship on this phenomenon.

72. Exhaustively surveyed by Bommelaer 1981, ch. 1, 7-23; cf. Meiggs-Lewis nos. 94-95; Paus. 10.9.7-10; Plut. *Lys.* 18.

73. Xen. *Hell.* 2.3.8-9; cf. Plut. *Lys.* 16.1.

74. Xen. *Hell.* 2.3.3.

75. Plut. *Lys.* 14.3.

76. Nep. *Lys.* 2.1-3; Polyaen. 1.45.4. During this voyage he probably also visited Thrace: Plut. *Lys.* 16.1, cf. 20.7.

77. Xen. *Hell.* 2.3.8-9.

78. Plut. *Lys.* 14.14.

This interpretation of the course of events between April and October 404 requires neither textual emendation nor wholesale excisions. It assumes that, more often than not, our sources are trying to get at the truth; that any assumption to the contrary is not to be lightly undertaken, and puts the onus of disproof squarely on the challenger; and that theories involving forgery, manipulation, hostile propaganda, chronic stupidity, interpolation—those regular standby panaceas of the lazy or arrogant—need to have a far more thorough demonstration both of motive and of opportunity than they usually get. Seeming discrepancies, as I hope to have demonstrated in the present instance, often turn out to be more apparent than real; and those which incontrovertibly do occur need, above all, to be *explained*. It is not enough (as, *mutatis mutandis*, textual critics are well aware) simply to weigh authorities one against the other, or to claim that the evidence has, for whatever reason, been tampered with. Ancient historians too often show themselves overready to second-guess and improve on the available, and generally inadequate, testimonia: skepticism tends to attract more intellectual cachet *per se* than the painstaking reconciliation of witnesses. Sometimes (though not nearly so often as is commonly believed) the skeptics are right. But in a very real sense, the testimonia are all we have, and we need to treat them with far greater circumspection.

A demonstration that (*pace* Krentz 1982, 409) the Thirty were undoubtedly installed at the end of September 404[79] may seem a *ridiculus mus* to emerge from so much argument, even though much other evidence falls into place as a result. But the realization that many of the problems at which historians have gnawed for years are purely illusory, and that the *only* true inconsistency of evidence in this episode is furnished by Plutarch's well-known habit of telescoping events—this, I think, represents a historiographical conclusion of some importance, which invites both wider application and further critical discussion. The ancient mythopoeia that we study is liable to infect our own thinking without our knowing it.

---

79. Colin (1933, 33–34), working from different premises, reaches an identical conclusion: he correlates the ephorate of Endius with the autumn solstice (Xen. *Hell.* 2.3.9–10).

8

A Variety of Greek Appetites

OUR VIEW OF, and attitude toward, the ancient world are in perpetual flux: a Heracleitan assertion itself liable to be dismissed—on impeccably rational grounds, *ça va sans dire*—by a new generation of critics. We look in the mirror and see ourselves: the age and style of the mirror make little difference, even, or perhaps especially, when (as in Andrew Stewart's *Art Desire and the Body in Ancient Greece*) it's adorned with explicit erotica, and was the cherished possession of a woman who *may* have been Leaina ("The Lioness"), a Corinthian beauty (c. 320–300 B.C.) whose skill at "riding" her sexual partners, jockey-style, won an enthusiastic tribute from that noted gynophile Demetrius the Besieger. Both Stewart and James Davidson in *Courtesans and Fishcakes* stress, rightly, the variant idiosyncrasies in perception (erotic or other) of different ages, as well as their obstinate insistence on judging the alien from their own local and temporal viewpoints. Both also become involved with current trends and theories in the process. Davidson takes these on and dismantles them; Stewart at first pays them lip service, but later, for long stretches, to the reader's considerable benefit, forgets about them. Both, to a quite unusual extent, are quirky, idiosyncratic, and brimming over with original insights.

What goes for sex also applies to culture in the widest sense. One age's trash is the next one's treasure. The enthusiastic stripping of the Acropolis in the early nineteenth century consigned tons of priceless neolithic sherds to the rail-bed of the Athens-Piraeus Metro: passengers today who fancy they're riding on history are in fact, in a far more literal sense, riding roughshod over prehistory. (The recent extension-tunnelling under central Athens has

Note: Originally published in the *Times Literary Supplement*, no. 4950, 13 Feb. 1998, 8–10.

widened the image in a highly dramatic manner: the Syntagma subway station now has its own archaeology, very strikingly, on permanent display.) Many early archaeologists, obsessed with palaces and precious artifacts, strike us today as barely distinguishable from the crassest kind of treasure-hunter; but if they could witness our own contemporary sifting of daily detritus, they would, in their turn, dismiss us contemptuously as mad proletarian scavengers. That upper-class disdain for the banausic that formed so crucial an element in the Athenian character, and was adopted with enthusiasm by earlier generations of classicists, isn't wholly dead even today. James Davidson lays out the ample evidence for Athenians' obsession with fish, and gets a protest (admittedly only a mild one) in a review by the Regius Professor of Greek at Oxford, arguing that since a large chunk of the evidence comes from Athenaeus, that lip-licking picker-up of ancient gourmet allusions, the problem is still to a great degree literary, that is, unreal. But then, fish are about as banausic as you can get.

As Davidson pointed out in a spirited rebuttal, both Athenaeus and he himself are interested in a good many other things besides fish (notably wine and sex, the second of which has only fairly recently established itself as a main-line, indeed hot, topic for analysis by up-and-coming classicists), and anyway the fish obsession was social, based on class-conscious snobbery and wealth, and even used to attack one's political enemies. Here, of course, Davidson was being cleverly disingenuous, having no illusions (as *Courtesans and Fishcakes* makes abundantly clear) about the traditional conservative attitude toward any kind of radicalism as applied to Athenian democracy. (This being academe, of course, maverick Marxists, the exceptions that prove the rule, have always been encouraged to muddy the waters. Indeed, Geoffrey de Ste Croix, by stressing its populist element, contrived, *mirabile dictu*, to put a kind of *cordon sanitaire* round Periclean imperialism.) To acknowledge, for example, that Cleisthenes—by an act of political legerdemain that would be hard to beat even today—gave the landless proles the franchise while leaving Athens's old social hierarchy largely intact remains highly repugnant to neo-romantics (of whom the profession has quite a few, some in high places). Those who doubt this should try to find any remotely realistic account, in political terms, of just what Cleisthenes *really* was up to in 508/7, and just why, after a string of rebuffs at the polls, he suddenly managed a successful (and arguably illegal) end-run around a duly elected Archon.

In one sense, *Courtesans and Fishcakes*, even down to its title, is very much a product of its age. A quasi-Platonic frowning on appetites as such long prevailed in the classical field, encouraged and nurtured by those anxious to

reconcile their endeavors with the public requirements of Christianity. The
same instinct for moral authoritarianism all but sanctified Pericles, and saw
his (Thucydidean) Funeral Oration as an embodiment of Greek idealism at
its loftiest. But during the last thirty years or so things have changed out of all
recognition. Self-restraint came to be viewed with great suspicion as a symptom of some deep psychological hang-up. Truth, as a viable moral or philosophical commodity, came to be treated, along with the author, as virtually
nonexistent by those who fancied themselves on the cutting edge of scholarship. Post-colonialism joined forces with post-modernism, so that Pericles
was reduced to the role of colonial imperialist, and damned as a chilly prig
into the bargain, while the Funeral Oration was seen as the acme of elitist arrogance. Athens the "educator of Hellas" indeed: who did these cultural over-
achievers think they were? Scholars who objected—not only conservatives—
found themselves stuck with most of the same labels.

Anthony Burgess once drew a picture of Western society veering endlessly between the polarities of Augustinian denial and Pelagian permissive-
ness, what he termed Pelphase and Gusphase. "Sexual intercourse began," as
Larkin put it, "in 1963," which was late for a whole lot of people besides him,
including a surprising number of classicists. Pelphase swept in with a bang.
The appetites, long reined in, made up for lost time. Everything hung out.
Gusphase countered with the AIDS epidemic, thus creating cynicism rather
than monasticism. The targets multiplied as feminists, egalitarians, minorities, and those just freed from (or still struggling against) colonial rule raised
their voices, the love that once dared not speak its name shouting louder than
most. The collapse of Soviet communism left a lot of intellectual ideologues
without a drum to beat, and only too glad to enroll in one of these new movements. Professors of English rapidly picked up the dogma, and jargon, of
French gurus from Foucault to Lacan, without (except for a few hardy logi-
cians like John Searle or Raymond Tallis) bothering to analyze their headily
nihilistic *obiter dicta* too closely. The "old in-out, in-out" (Burgess again) suffered further reductionism by being enrolled in alterity, the Us vs. Them syn-
drome, as a stark Foucault-inspired equation of phallic plus-signs (power)
over against anal—and occasionally vaginal—minus-signs (victimization), a
world of Penetrators and Penetrated.

The persuasive force of this movement overall has been quite extraordinary, infiltrating not only sex and gender, but social and even political life
in the widest sense. (Just how persuasive can be judged from the review of
Davidson I mentioned earlier, which offers us the arresting spectacle of a
Regius Professor rather nervously trotting along, like Teiresias or Cadmus in

Euripides' *Bacchae*, after things with which one feels he doesn't in his heart of hearts agree: texts simply as evidence of attitude, really poisonous class-enmities in Athens.) Davidson is, in one sense, necessarily the product of this movement. Had it never existed, he might well never have written a book about (to quote his subtitle) "the consuming passions of classical Athens" at all; even had he done so, it would, almost certainly, have lacked its present sharply combative approach. But there's an ironic twist here. What, in addition to its subject-matter, gives *Courtesans and Fishcakes* its compulsive readability is the realization, very early on, that Davidson is at least one jump ahead of the field (to Terry Eagleton's two?). An ultra-radical himself in his approach, he's nevertheless gleefully deconstructing the deconstructionists throughout, in the name of revisionist logic. Whenever he sees that the Emperor of Theory has no clothes, he says so: loudly, cogently, and with irreverent relish.

We catch the temper of his mind on the very first page. He takes as his text the mosaic by Sosos of Pergamon known as "The Unswept Floor," familiar to all ancient art-historians, and here well described: "Across a white background is an even scattering of debris: a wish-bone, a claw, some fruit, various discarded limbs of sea-creatures, the remains of a fish." Illusionistic expressionism? Not a bit of it: this detritus is deliberately nonrepetitive and well-ordered. Yes, we have a floor that depicts a floor, but thus one impossible to clean: what about that closure between art and life now? Anyway—quick corollary—it isn't the floor itself that's the real subject, but rather the unseen banquet, which, as Davidson notes, *is still going on:* between eating and the drinking that followed, the floor would be swept clean. More disconcerting still, considering how familiar that mosaic is, he alleges that "some of the debris casts rather strange shadows as if it is hovering half a millimetre above the ground, as if it has a little way still to fall"—and he's unmistakably right: the fowl's claw clinches it. Mosaic as instant photo. It's an arresting initial demonstration of expertise. The message is clear: Davidson can see what we can't, and he'd now be obliged if we'd stop fussing and pay attention.

He's also watching out for our natural laziness. We're supposed to pay attention, but not to let our critical faculties fall asleep. Was it by accident that while the excellent reproduction of "The Unswept Floor" I consulted shows those shadows clearly, on Davidson's own dust-jacket they are almost lost? Or that in his introduction he then produces no less than three judgments in a row that run flat counter to common sense? I doubt it. Was there in fact a law at Athens banning fishmongers from drenching their fish with water to make them look fresh? Davidson says no, what we have here is mere

Aristophanic fancy. But knowledge of Athenian markets and market inspectors (*agoranomoi*), then or now (which Davidson later shows that he possesses
in full measure), makes that law a virtual certainty. Also, what makes him so
certain, not only that Athenian women never contemplated revolution, but
that they never talked to their lamps? Hasn't he seen *Shirley Valentine?* Even
so, the point we *know* he's making to test our alertness is when he blandly asserts that we don't believe estates or fortunes could be lost as the result of
lavish parties, rapacious women, or affairs with boys. In Athens, London, or
New York, they could be, they were, they are; and once again, in a subsequent
chapter, Davidson proves that he knows this as well as we do.

Ah, but you see, the point of this last example is that it's what the Athenians
believed: attitudes again. "Ultimately," Davidson says, "the subject of this book
is not so much the pleasures of the flesh themselves, but what the Greeks, and
especially the Athenians, said about them, the way they represented them, the
consequences they ascribed to them, the way they thought they worked. Instead of looking at the ancient sources as windows on a world, we can see them
as artefacts of that world in their own right" (xxi). This isn't just a sideswipe at
Andrew Dalby's *Siren Feasts.* Davidson is harking back to Foucault again, this
time apropos the so-called study of discourse. But—as that disclaimer about
"windows on a world" makes plain—the Master is about to get his comeup-
pance. Prescriptive and philosophical texts, Davidson shrewdly observes, are
things to be suspicious of: almost invariably they have an agenda. Thus a direct approach often turns out to be the least reliable. The gratuitous definition of a gourmand, the careful distinction drawn between wives, *hetairai*, and
tarts—these we should regard with deep suspicion. Foucault, Davidson argues, did not: was, indeed, in his work on Greek eroticism, largely dependent
on such *parti pris* sources. (Davidson is referring, not, as we might expect, to
Foucault's *Histoire de la sexualité* [Paris, 1976], but to the English translation
of *L'Usage des plaisirs* [trans. R. Hurley, New York, 1985], though, again, it's
only later we discover this.) The result—reinforced, though Davidson is too
polite to say so, by Foucault's own *parti pris* homoerotic attitude—has hardly
anything on women, and "gives the impression the Greeks were much more
interested in boys."

The systematic demolition of this widely held view is among the most
original and intellectually challenging features of a book that never for one
moment allows the reader's concentration to slacken, and has a very short way
with treasured academic *idées reçues.* Davidson's immediate response is brisk:
"Any examination of comic fragments, vase-paintings and Attic oratory . . .
shows this impression is quite false, a Platonic mirage" (xxiii–xxiv). The les-

sons of Dover's *Greek Popular Morality* (Oxford and Berkeley, 1974) have not been lost on him. On the other hand, some of the fundamental conclusions he reaches in regard to sex are as dismissive of Dover's views elsewhere as they are of Foucault's. Good though his generic hits are (Foucault writes "as if the Greeks walked around in a virtual reality they had constructed for themselves from discourse," xxv), it's Davidson's concentration on the nitty-gritty specifics that carries most weight.

Foucault's application to Greek sexuality of the Them-and-Us bipolarity ("this Manichaean view") popularized by the Hellene-Barbarian opposition, with Us (adult male citizen text-writers) as Penetrators, and Them (slaves, women, barbarians, etc.) as the Penetrated, Davidson skewers as an "absurd oversimplification" that "predictably produces very banal self-fulfilling results" (xxv). The ample evidence supporting this conclusion, deployed in illustrations, many of which are hilariously funny, takes up much of the rest of the book. Davidson moves easily from the bedroom to the public world of power politics, never forgetting (as many do) the all-important economic factor in sex: "It seems very obvious and it is amazing that so many have overlooked it, but the crucial point about prostitutes is not what they get up to in bed, for ultimately that is mere speculation; it is that they are for sale" (277). This downgrading of the importance to be attached to sexual preferences, as opposed to the degree of subjection to sexual activity in general, becomes a key element in Davidson's revisionist (or, more accurately, counter-revisionist) take on classical Greek eroticism in general.

Slaves, he muses, are not always like women, or vice versa; nor have they magically lost their phalluses, even if only in a metaphorical sense. Yes, the Greeks were very fond of bipolarities and binary terms; but this was primarily a mode of discussion (as every student knows, μέν and δέ, "on the one hand" and "on the other," are about the most common words in the Greek language), and anyway the poles were always shifting: Greeks vs. Persians, Persians vs. Scythians, and so on. The modern instinct of scholars (that view in the mirror again), feminist scholars in particular, anxious to deromanticize male fantasies, has been to divide Greek women into two simple groups: Wives (Respectable Women might be a more accurate definition) and The Rest. This kind of black-and-white binary categorization, as Davidson sees, obliterates, on irrelevant moral grounds, important distinctions between *hetairai* (high-class courtesans, nicknamed "the heifer infantry": no wonder pimps were known as *pornoboskoi*, "whoreherders"), *pallakai* (concubines), and *pornai* (common prostitutes). Worse, the word *gynē* could mean both "woman" and "wife," prompting significant circumlocutions concerning marriage and mistresses. Nor were women the only sexual commodities: on a smaller scale, male prostitution (as we know from Aeschines' speech *Against Timarchus*) was equally well established.

What will undoubtedly trigger most argument, however, is Davidson's direct and specific assault on the popular view (popular in part precisely because of its oversimplified reductionism, its starkly dualistic terms) of sex in Athens as a matter of Penetrators and Penetrated, a power scenario with its main emphasis on anal sodomy. This concept has always bothered me. Why, if it were true, was the masculine ideal, enunciated by Right Logic in Aristophanes' *Clouds*, and visible in innumerable vase-paintings, a well-developed body but a discreetly small penis? Why were satyrs and silens, so hugely and permanently erect, not only not favored, but (as Stewart well notes) "increasingly unwelcome in the civilized society of the classical *polis*' (191), which found their nonstop power trip, their manic and solipsistic urge to fuck or bugger every divinity, man, woman, or animal in sight, so acutely embarrassing that by the end of the century they'd saddled them with domesticity and detumescence? Surely here, if anywhere, is where we should seek that elusive Snark-like concept, the "Reign of the Phallus"? But not a bit of it. There's always been a contradiction lurking here, and Davidson brings it right out in the open.

The key to the problem is what the Greeks called *enkrateia*, self-control, together with its opposite, *akolasia*, licentious excess, the balance between them being nicely summed up by the Delphic aphorism "Nothing too much" (μηδὲν ἄγαν). A Greek abhorred extremes in either direction. No monasteries, no total abstention; but, on the same principle, no socially disruptive bingeing, whether with liquor, weapons, or what Robert Graves euphemized as "great yards." Oddly, Foucault emphasized *enkrateia* without ever seeing what it was really about in erotic terms: for him it had to be a function of sexual control in a dominant or manipulative sense, and so he came up with what Davidson rightly characterizes as "the bizarre notion of ethical passivity" (175). On the one hand, phallic penetrators, patriarchal, legislative, and in control; on the other, those penetrated—either victims or, if they admitted liking it, objects of patriarchal contempt as womanish, slavish, weak. This binary proposition was not only easy to grasp, but offered a wonderful handle to ideologues, feminists in particular. Further, since in just about any society (as Dover's work shows: after all, men have always been in control) you can find a fair number of would-be phallocrats eager to sexually dominate—or, in pathological cases, rape—as the favorite mode of expressing their male power, it is all too easy to promote the concept as a socially, indeed anthropologically, valid general principle for Greece or anywhere else.

In a recent *Times Literary Supplement* review, Alastair Fowler observed, "In the Renaissance, people were categorized less by the deviation than by the elevation of their sexuality." *Mutatis mutandis*, Davidson is making precisely the same point about Athenians in the fifth century B.C. It wasn't the specific mechanics of what they fancied (which in any case "was a subtle and complex relationship, an intricate nexus of exchanged values involving love, gifts, desirability and favours, not a rigid 'zero-sum game' that the penetrator always won" [169]) so much as the degree and intensity of their passion, coupled with the widely varying mental and emotional attitudes they brought to it. Davidson's arguments are cumulative, but his most compelling point emerges from a close study of two extreme categories, the *katapugones* (καταπύγονες) and *kinaidoi* (κίναιδοι), regularly used by the penetrationists to vindicate their own contentions. For them, who typecast Athenians, as Davidson reminds us, "not according to the gender of the persons to whom they were attracted but by the role they assumed in the act of intercourse" (168), *kinaidoi* and *katapugones* were simply those with a yen for being sodomized: the submissive, the womanish, the losers, whose servile natures naturally craved what Foucault described as "the passive, dominated, and inferior position" (cited by Davidson, 169).

This scenario of phallocratic aggression matched with submission sounds fine, but for something allegedly ubiquitous proves hard to run down when we start looking for hard evidence. Further, specific instances of *katapugosyne*— what I suppose Foucault's epigoni might think of as "penetrateeishness"— quickly reveal that the urge to be screwed, though occurring on occasion, is very far from defining this particular beast. Over-spiced dishes earn a reputation for *katapugosyne* in comparison with plain meat. The phrase is used of women in contexts that suggest, not so much a taste for being buggered (though of course that existed), but rather high general lasciviousness. Lysistrata, faced with sisters who'd rather go through fire than do without prick (τοῦ πέους), castigates the race of womankind as *pankatapugon*, that is, sexmad. Other *katapugones* include mice and the sea-wrasse, creatures noted not for their erotic passivity, but rather for unrestrained and promiscuous lust. The Persians may regard gorgers and swillers as the only real men; but for Dicaeopolis in Aristophanes' *Acharnians*, such creatures are mere *katapugones* (Davidson's neat correction of previous mistranslations).

In short, the *katapugon* is defined by excess, *akolasia*, lack of control, primarily (but not always) as regards sexual activity. Similarly with *kinaidos*, which finds its best definition as a not-so-metaphorical leaky vessel, an incurable itch, "the paradigm of insatiability, of desire never-to-be-fulfilled"

(174). Far from being victimized or subject to humiliating domination, the "*kinaidos/katapugon* . . . is a nymphomaniac, full of womanish desire, who dresses up to attract men and has sex at the drop of a hat" (179). Looked at this way, labels such as *lakkoproktos* or *euryproktos* ("cistern-arse," "wide-arse") take on rather different implications.

Just how misleading Foucault's theory can be is strikingly demonstrated by Dover's interpretation of a curious red-figure wine-pourer (c. 450?). One male figure, Scythian-bearded, semi-erection in hand, clad only in a cloak, moves purposefully around the vase toward a second Scythian in a body-suit, half bent over, bearded face toward the viewer, and hands raised in a gesture that has, I think, been universally misunderstood. One thumb touches each temple; fingers are spread out. This is not acquiescence, and certainly not terrified surrender: the Scythian's expression is cheeky, indeed mischievous. Waggle the fingers a little, and any schoolboy will tell you what the message is: *Yah boo, sucks to you.* All that's missing is the slightly protruding tongue. The vase carries a message: I AM EURYMEDON I STAND BENT OVER. There is some uncertainty as to how these words are distributed between the two figures.

It may come as a surprise to the uninitiated to learn that for Dover and many others this is a clear symbolic portrayal of Cimon's amphibious victory over Achaemenid forces at the Eurymedon River (466?), and what the scene is saying is, *We've buggered the Persians.* Never mind that this modern meta-phorical sense of penetration (like the Italian *inculato*) is virtually unknown in classical Athens; or that these figures are not an Athenian and a Persian soldier but two Scythians, probably master and squire; or that the buggering has not yet taken place; or that the identification of the Eurymedon River with either figure makes no sense, either politically or symbolically; or that the gestures and expressions are hopelessly wrong; or that all these problems were pointed out as early as 1984 (*JHS* 104: 181–83) by G. F. Pinney, whose division of the message between the two figures is also convincing. Never mind, finally, about logic or common sense: politicized penetrators, even prior to consummation, must have their way.

In fact, "Eurymedon" was not only or even primarily a river, but a common male name (interestingly, that of both Nestor's and Agamemnon's squires in Homer), meaning "Wide-Ruler." In a sexual context the association with *euryproktos*, "wide-arsed," is inevitable. "I'm Wide-Ruler," says the master, im-plying, "And you're —" "I'm Bent-Over," replies his squire, with a gesture that says *Catch me if you can.* Davidson (who, less convincingly, attributes the whole inscription to the second figure) conjures up a witty scenario involving an in-cautious symposiast who follows the scene around the vase and realizes, too late, amid cat-calls, what he's just read out aloud. "*He's* Eurymedon and he's been had." This example demonstrates, in no uncertain fashion, just how radically Foucault's theory can skew straightforward evidence, and how easy it is for normally intelligent scholars to succumb to its findings. (Andrew Stewart, in the ordinary way the most robust and pragmatic of critics, swallows it whole without a qualm.) Davidson is not trying to deny that the evidence contains quite a few instances of phallocratic penetration and humiliation: it would be surprising if it didn't. What he *is* arguing against, and I think with great cogency, is the crass reductionism implied in the theory as a whole. What *Courtesans and Fishcakes* celebrates is the richness and complexity (in Athens as it happens, but it could be anywhere) not just of sex but of all the appetites, indeed of life as a whole: what MacNeice in his poem "Snow" called "the drunkenness of things being various."

Stewart's *Art Desire and the Body in Ancient Greece* inevitably covers a lot of the same ground as Davidson's more general survey, but always from a sharply visual viewpoint: the two books complement one another in a continually stimulating manner. Seldom have two works of ancient scholarship come my way that are so continually full of rich new meat, so devoid of otiose fat. What, for me, makes Andrew Stewart a truly great art-historian is that, unlike too many in his field, he can and does write as a historian *tout court*, always alert to the politics, economics, and civic nuances that form the supporting (or occasionally destructive) matrix for art, and much of the time using visual evidence just as he might use texts or inscriptions: to plot social change. Like Davidson, he covers much more than can be adequately described in even a long review: almost every *aperçu* (again, like Davidson's) deserves detailed explication and discussion. I emphasize all this since between his classic study of Alexander, *Faces of Power* (1993), and his present undertaking, Stewart seems, at first rather disconcertingly, to have gone overboard, not only for the penetrationists, but also for that bizarre theory of gaze-and-glance ("visuality" for short) dreamed up by Sartre, elaborated (with Freudian frills) by Lacan, and now gaining ground among sociologists, filmbuffs, and communication experts.

For the uninitiated, there are two "scopic polarities" [*sic*] here: in Stewart's words (13–14), "the *glance*, which emanates from the self, and the *gaze*, which issues from the Other." These are in constant conflict. Self, feeling stared at, glances, freezes, and looks away, but at the same time adapts to the Other. The gaze thus limits freedom, induces feelings of shame "at being caught naked," makes Self's body a mere "object of the Other's scrutiny." This (Sartre again) applies even to lovers, each determined "to possess the other's freedom." The result? "A sadomasochistic contest of glance and gaze," with no escape and no closure. What sounds remarkably like the reactions of a shy, neurotic, intellectual male adolescent at his first high-school dance has been elevated into a general principle, the dogmatic reductionism of which almost takes one's breath away. As a theory, it affects me much as the poems of Robert Montgomery affected Macaulay: why, for example, can Self only glance, the Other only gaze? What would happen if they reversed roles? And how on earth did Stewart, the most down-to-earth of scholars (one of the best things in his book is a superbly told and illustrated account of hollow-cast bronzemaking) ever get involved with this kind of thing?

Behind all the pontificating, of course, as usual, lie a few unremarkable social commonplaces, easily adaptable to the visual arts, where how you look at objects has a certain importance. Stewart (whether tongue in cheek or not I'm uncertain) exploits the theory to determine how such objects (the Aphrodite of Cnidos, a Gorgon-head, a Minoan snake-goddess, a caryatid mirror) look at *you*, and, a fortiori, what effect they had on contemporary viewers. His questing eye probes, debates, puzzles. Why the absence of true linear perspective? Perhaps because Helen's famous view-from-the-wall, her *teichoscopia*, offered the chance for panoramic surveillance, rather like a wide-angle camera lens, zooming in occasionally to pick out individual features? Why did the Greeks, for one century, choose to see their young males as tall, dazzlingly proportioned *kouroi*, when in fact they were stocky, lumpish, and undersized?

Page after page throws up new questions. Why did red-figure pornography emphasize the features it did, and decline with the emergence of the polis triumphant? Why a sudden fascination with Amazons about the time of Pericles' citizenship law? What lay behind the Hellenistic Age's increasing preoccupation with portraits? Why did Praxiteles choose to portray the Aphrodite of Cnidos as a true woman, rather than as the mutated male that had been *de rigueur* hitherto? Why were such a disproportionate number of the male figures on the Parthenon frieze meltingly beautiful adolescents, and thus "potentially junior partners in a homoerotic relationship" (7, cf. 82)? And why, in the last resort, were warriors, in the face of all reality, portrayed as naked anyway? We may not agree with all of Stewart's answers; we may even challenge some of his questions; but no art-historian in recent years has forced us to re-examine so many of our basic assumptions.

He also must be about the only scholar who can find a reason to *welcome* the growing public ignorance of, and indifference to, Greek art. The too-familiar, he argues, becomes boring, it needs the restoration of *strangeness* to let us see these artifacts anew. "For the familiar is only what we choose to see;

what has been preselected for us; or what we have appropriated for our own ends" (3). Common sense, so sure of its own rightness, and convinced, despite everything, that the sun really moves around the earth (which of course, from the visual artist's point of view, it does), is what breeds this familiarity. Whether it's familiarity and common sense that lie at the root of greater evils, as Stewart implies, is another matter. The cynical might argue, indeed, that common sense was what, in the last resort, protected us against penetrationism or the gaze-and-glance theory. Still, Stewart is honest enough to see that the mirror mentioned at the beginning of this discussion, with its clear implication of sexual equality in pleasure, triumphantly refutes the penetrationist reductionism that he began by accepting, and that Davidson spends so much of his time cutting up.

Stewart's flirtation with post-Sartreanism is not all that surprising. Since the late 1980s, as he well knows, the Greek body and its nakedness have formed a minor growth industry for *nouvelle vague* classicists, many of whom have been busily mining ancient science, literature, and art to support their new theoretical notions (not so new, some of them) on sexuality, gender roles, or erotic practices and fantasies. But despite manifestations of alterity and the impact of artistic *facture*, Stewart remains in essence very much his own man. As he himself admits, "At heart I am probably more of an empiricist and an opportunist than a theorist" (xiii): one determined, moreover, to use theory rather than let theory use him. In this endeavor he has been more successful than he might at first sight appear. Significantly, his prose style, always one of his great virtues, has avoided infection, remaining terse, clear, logical, and refreshingly jargon-free. (One wonders, though, how he reacted to a blurb that, with phallocratic fervor, describes his book as a "penetrating study" of a "seminal topic"?)

I do not think it over-imaginative to see in these innovative and original studies the development of a seismic shift (first heralded by Eagleton's 1996 *Illusions of Postmodernism*) in the Anglo-American attitude to French-inspired literary and artistic theorizing. Neither Stewart nor Davidson is against theorizing as such: Stewart cites with evident approval Keynes's famous *mot* about those who claim to get along better without new theories simply being in thrall to an old one. What he and Davidson do, each in his own way, is to skim off whatever good they can get out of hit-and-miss dogmatists such as Sartre or Derrida or Lacan, leaving the stripped carcasses to be disposed of by professional philosophers. The result has been two pioneering explorations of the ancient world that should, with luck, get rid of more than one worn-out intellectual shibboleth, and stimulate fresh debate for many years to come.

9

Alexander's Alexandria

A RECENT Italian article[1] asked, in its title, the (not entirely rhetorical) question, "Egyptian Alexandria—a myth?" Wisely, the writer omitted a main verb. If *is* evokes memories of Forster, Cavafy, and Durrell,[2] *was* takes us back to the Alexander Romance, to the grandiose dreams and processions of Ptolemy Philadelphos, to Cleopatra's suicide after Actium, to the Arian and Monophysite heresies.[3] Alexandria has always had a mythic quality about it. Cavafy, the poet of homosexual nostalgia ("Days of 1896 . . ."), reached back into the city's Hellenistic and Byzantine past for imagery and examples: sophists and soldiers, political lies, dynastic fantasies, moments of memorable defeat,[4] and always, unchanging down the ages, ephemeral yet eternal in their agonizing beauty, the young men for whom his heart and body hungered. Though Alexandria had had a reputation for good-looking and available boys almost since its foundation—Herodas in the early third century B.C. mentions them in the same breath as gaudies, philosophers, and gold[5]—it remains true

Note: Originally delivered in April 1993 as the keynote lecture of a symposium on "Alexandria and Alexandrianism," at the J. Paul Getty Museum, Malibu, California, and subsequently published in *Alexandria and Alexandrianism: Papers Delivered at a Symposium Organized by the J. Paul Getty Museum and the Getty Center for the History of Art and the Humanities and Held at the Museum, April 22–25, 1993*, ed. K. Hamma (Malibu, Calif., 1996), 3–25.

1. S. Daris, "Alessandria d'Egitto: Un mito?," *Paideia* 45 (1990): 103–20.

2. Cf. J. L. Pinchin, *Alexandria Still: Forster, Durrell and Cavafy* (Princeton, 1977).

3. Expounded with clarity and wit by E. M. Forster in what Bonamy Dobrée once described as "surely the best guide-book ever written": *Alexandria: A History and a Guide* (rev. ed., London, 1982), introd. by L. Durrell, afterword and notes by M. Haag, 79–82.

4. I am thinking particularly of the strange poem "Ἀπολείπειν ὁ θεὸς Ἀντώνιον," "The God Abandons Anthony," its title and theme taken from Plutarch's *Life* of Antony (ch. 75), in which the defeated Roman hears ἀόρατος θίασος νὰ περνᾷ μὲ μουσικὲς ἐξαίσιες, μὲ φωνές ("an unseen troupe pass by, with wonderful music, with voices")—a sign that the god "to whom he most likened and attached himself" was abandoning him.

5. Herod. *Mim.* 1.29: cf. Green 1993, 245.

that Cavafy (like Durrell after him, like André Gide in Algeria) was in effect shamelessly using another country as a name for his own obsessions.[6] This habit has not been restricted to poets and novelists.

Another factor encouraging mythicization has always been Alexandria's more-than-symbolic separation from Egypt. Both in the Hellenistic and in the Roman periods it was officially known as "Alexandria *by* Egypt," seldom as "Alexandria *in* Egypt."[7] This was appropriate in more than one sense. It distinguished the royal foundation of the Greco-Macedonian ruling elite from the old Pharaonic capital of Memphis. It enshrined the concept of a government that regarded Egypt as alien "spear-won territory," fit for economic exploitation. It rubbed in the fact that no Ptolemy until the last representative of the dynasty, Cleopatra VII, ever bothered to learn Egyptian, preferring to operate through a corps of Greek-speaking Egyptian interpreters. Seers at its foundation had prophesied, accurately, that the city would be a melting-pot of all nations[8]—perhaps what Durrell's Nessim meant when he characterized Alexandria as "the great wine-press of love"[9]—and this was to remain true throughout Alexandria's long and colorful history, except that the nations never, in any important sense, included Egypt itself until after the 1956 Suez War. Mohammed Ali was a nineteenth-century Turkish adventurer who operated much in the spirit of the Ptolemies or Alexander's governor Cleomenes (of whom more later): "He exploited the fellahin by buying grain from them at his own price: the whole of Egypt became his private farm."[10] Neither Cavafy nor Durrell, we may note, cultivated Egyptian friends or made any serious attempt to integrate Egyptian realities into their Alexandrian myth.[11] In this they were simply adhering to an age-old tradition.

The magic of Alexandria, in fact, can be seen from start to finish as the

6. The idea is Ernest Gellner's: see his review-article "The Mightier Pen? Edward Said and the Double Standards of Inside-Out Colonialism," *Times Literary Supplement*, no. 4690 (19 Feb. 1993), 3–4. Gellner continues: "No doubt it was easier to find attractive homosexual partners in Biskra than among the *haute bourgeoisie protestante*, but this does not mean that the Algerian oasis was a residue of ancient Mediterranean sensuous harmony, liberty and fulfilment." Nor, he might have added, was the ancient Mediterranean. *Mutatis mutandis*, the same criticism can be leveled at both Cavafy and Durrell.

7. Fraser 1972, 1:107, 2:196–97, nn. 110–18. The Roman prefect's title was *Praefectus Alexandreae et Aegypti*, and Romans in Alexandria write of traveling *to* Egypt (much as a modern Greek will speak of going *to* Europe).

8. Plut. *Alex.* 26.10; Steph. Byz. s.v. Ἀλεξάνδρειαι. The seers told Alexander to be of good cheer, πολυαρκεστάτην γὰρ οἰκίζεσθαι πόλιν ὑπ' αὐτοῦ, καὶ παντοδαπῶν ἀνθρώπων ἐσομένην τροφόν.

9. L. Durrell, *Justine* (London, 1957, reprinted 1985), 14.

10. Forster 1982, 95–96.

11. Cf. Mahmoud Manzalaoui, "Curate's Egg: An Alexandrian Opinion of Durrell's *Quartet*," *Études Anglaises* 15.3 (1962): 248–60.

powerful by-product of a cosmopolitan and (in Graham Greene's sense) seedy colonialism, at once rootless and exploitative, of which the casual pick-ups of Herodas and Cavafy—not to mention Durrell's grisly child-prostitutes—can serve as an eloquent symbol. Alexandria became the embodiment of Hellenistic culture precisely because it had no national basis. The Cynic philosopher who proclaimed himself a *kosmopolitēs,* a "citizen of the world," might well have had the Ptolemaic capital in mind. The scholarship and the editing in the Mouseion, the obsessional search for past literature that characterized the Library (and at least one monarch, Ptolemy III Euergetes I, who forfeited his fifteen-talent deposit so as to keep the official Athenian copies of Aeschylus, Sophocles, and Euripides[12]); the scientific expertise that went into the construction of the Pharos, the great lighthouse that guided night-travelers through the shoals and reefs outside Alexandria's main harbor; the medical pioneering work of an Erasistratos or a Herophilos, that depended on royal protection against current religious prejudice to allow human dissection and vivisection;[13] the literary activities of a Callimachus or a Theocritus, blissfully innocent of any influence from native Egyptian literature—all these things were imported, imposed, alien. Hybridization, when it came, began in the lower strata of society, a fertile seed-bed for exotic superstition and religious syncretism.

Thus the regret sometimes expressed by romantic Hellenists for the post-1956 demise of the "old Alexandria" has an ironic twist to it: the nostalgia might well be regarded as akin to that of displaced French *pieds noirs* for the opium dens of the Casbah, and Islam's wary suspicion of the city from the time of its conquest by Amr (A.D. 640) was no less national than religious in nature. The silting up of harbors and canals can perhaps be ascribed in part to ingrained Arab distrust of the sea and of naval warfare;[14] but Forster was surely right in essence when he wrote that "Amr and his Arabs . . . instinctively shrank from Alexandria; she seemed to them idolatrous and foolish . . . though they had no intention of destroying her, they destroyed her, as a child might a watch."[15] But it was not until the regime of Gamal Abdel Nasser, the first truly Egyptian ruler of Egypt in two-and-a-half millennia, that Alexandria was finally integrated into the body politic on which for so long it had existed as an alien and exotic growth. Readers of Cavafy and Durrell may per-

---

12. Galen *Comm. in Hipp. Epidem.* 3 (cited at length by Fraser 1972, 2:480).

13. Von Staden 1989, ch. 6, pp. 138–53; Green 1993, 859–60 with further references there cited.

14. A. L. Udovitch, "L'énigme d'Alexandrie: Sa position au moyen âge d'après les documents de la Geniza du Caire," *Revue de l'Occident Musulman et de la Mediterranée* 46 (1987): 71–79.

15. Forster 1982, 84, 62.

haps reflect that this change was, on balance, no bad thing: that exoticism can be bought at too high a price.

Those researchers who, like myself, normally react to a myth by wanting to get behind it have a more than usually tough problem on their hands with Alexandria—not least if they hope, as I do, to clarify the circumstances of the city's original foundation. When we look at our literary evidence, it at once becomes clear that mythification began very early. The Alexander Romance— despite a stratum of valuable early Hellenistic evidence—ascribes Alexander's begetting to the last independent Pharaoh, Nectanebo II, cites his correspondence with the Amazons, has him arrive in Egypt after a *razzia* through Sicily, Italy, and Africa, and describes his exploration of the sea-bottom in a magical diving-bell.[16] The historian Ammianus Marcellinus, writing in the fourth century A.D., has Cleopatra VII responsible for building both the Pharos and the Heptastadion (the seven-furlong causeway linking the island of Pharos and the mainland), though both in fact antedated her by almost three centuries.[17] The earliest detailed description of the city to survive is that by the geographer Strabo,[18] who was in Alexandria from 24 to (probably) 20 B.C.,[19] and is thus, similarly, three hundred years out of date—the difference, to take a modern parallel, between the London of Samuel Pepys and the city I know today. By the date of Strabo's visit, the original foundation had already been transformed almost beyond recognition, since Diodorus Siculus (who was there only a few years before Strabo) writes[20] that "all subsequent kings of Egypt vied in the city's development. Some adorned it with splendid palaces, some with dockyards and harbor works, others again with various further notable dedications and works of art, to the point where most people reckon it the first or second city of the inhabited world."

The normal recourse in such circumstances would be to the so-called "hard" evidence of papyrology, epigraphy, numismatics, and the archaeological record. But here Alexandria presents an unusual and frustrating case.

16. Ps.-Call. 1.4–12, 3.25–26, 1.29–30, 2.38 (ed. H. Van Thiel). The best available translation in English is that by Ken Dowden, *Collected Ancient Greek Novels*, ed. B. P. Reardon (Berkeley, 1989), 650–735.

17. Amm. Marc. 22.16.9–11.

18. Strabo 17.1.6–10 (C.791–95).

19. Fraser 1972, 1:7; 2:12–13 n. 29.

20. Diod. Sic. 1.50.6–7: οἱ κατὰ τὸ ἑξῆς βασιλεύσαντες τῆς Αἰγύπτου πάντες ἐφιλοτι-μήθησαν εἰς τὴν ταύτης αὔξησιν. οἱ μὲν γὰρ βασιλείοις μεγαλοπρεπέσιν, οἱ δὲ νεωρίοις καὶ λιμέσιν οἱ δ᾽ ἑτέροις ἀναθήμασι καὶ κατασκευάσμασιν ἀξιολόγοις ἐπὶ τοσοῦτον ἐκόσμησαν αὐτὴν ὥστε παρὰ τοῖς πλείστοις πρώτην ἢ δευτέραν ἀριθμεῖσθαι τῶν κατὰ τὴν οἰκουμένην πόλεων.

Though the city has survived without interruption from antiquity, neverthe-less, from the Middle Ages until the advent of Mohammed Ali in 1805, only the western part, in particular the silted-up neck of the former Heptastadion, remained under continuous occupation. As Fraser says,[21] "Even within living memory much of the area east of the Great Harbour consisted of sand-dunes." Since this was precisely where the interior of the Ptolemaic city was located, it might have been thought that the opportunities for excavation were excel-lent. Two factors—one man-made, one natural—combined to render such a project all but impossible. The rapid expansion of Alexandria as a port during the nineteenth century, in particular under Khedive Ismail, not only effec-tively buried the ancient strata under new buildings, but also, in the construc-tion of the Corniche (1906), created an artificial coastline up to 300 meters in depth.[22] To make things even worse, in many districts ancient sherds were redeposited, in complete confusion, on top of later strata.

But such frustrating human activities were eclipsed by those of nature. Over the centuries there has taken place—partly through seismic disturbance, partly through the weight of silt washed down by the Nile—a general sub-sidence of up to four meters. As a result, much of the coastal section of the Ptolemaic city (which, as we know, included at least some of the royal palaces) now lies under the waters of the Mediterranean, and the on-site papyrological evidence that could have told us so much about the capital's functioning has been totally destroyed.[23] Thus if we want to understand the circumstances of Alexandria's foundation, we find ourselves compelled to re-examine the lit-erary evidence within the framework of various historical factors: strategic, economic, commercial, cultural, even religious. Some of these are perennial, so that, surprisingly, we find modern Alexandria shedding light on its ancient counterpart.[24]

---

21. Fraser 1972, 1:8–9.

22. Fraser, ibid., cf. also M. Rodziewicz, "Le débat sur la topographie de la ville antique," *Revue de l'Occident Musulman et de la Mediterranée* 46 (1987): 39–48.

23. How much would have come down to us, even granted optimum physical conditions for survival, remains a matter for debate. It is a curious fact that documents referring to Alexandria from elsewhere in Egypt only begin about the middle of the reign of Ptolemy Philadelphos (283–246), i.e. in the mid-third century (Fraser, 1972, 1:6; 2:9–10 n. 23); whether this is evidence for the slow bureaucratic growth of the capital, or (more likely) for the gradual extension of Alexandrian control over the *chora*, remains uncertain.

24. Of especial value in this context is Peter M. Fraser's illuminating article "Alexandria from Mohammed Ali to Gamal Abdel Nasser," in *Alexandrien: Kulturbegegnungen dreier Jahrtausende im Schmelztiegel einer mediterraneen Großstadt*, ed. N. Hinske (Mainz am Rhein, 1981), 63–74. For the general reader interested in surviving antiquities, a good starting-point is *Alexandria: The Site and the History* (New York, 1993), which not only offers really excellent photographic reproductions

Let us begin, then, with the enigmatic founder himself. Alexander III of Macedon from adolescence on made a habit of creating or taking over cities and naming them after himself. His first recorded venture of the sort was at the tender age of sixteen. Appointed regent while Philip was campaigning against Byzantium and Perinthos, he dislodged a group of rebellious Thracian tribesmen and established a military outpost, Alexandropolis, to match the Philippopolis his father had set up two years previously.[25] Alexander never lacked the competitive spirit. Plutarch (*Mor.* 328E) credits him with no less than seventy foundations in all: each named Alexandria, and many of them no more than frontier fortresses. Alexandria-by-Egypt proved by far the most successful. It was also the one in which he seems to have taken the most personal interest.[26] We may legitimately ask ourselves why.

This question forms part of a larger problem: why did Alexander choose to go to Egypt at all? After the battle of Issus (Sept. 333), why did he not at once pursue the defeated and disorganized forces of Darius eastward to Babylon? Why, instead, did he march over three hundred miles out of his way down the coast of the Mediterranean, spend seven months besieging Tyre and a long winter in and around the Nile Valley, and not resume his career of conquest until late April of 331? To understand this we must appreciate (as Alexander himself undoubtedly did) the dangerous and fluid situation that had developed behind his advance, in Asia Minor and the Aegean, and that now seriously threatened his ever-lengthening lines of communication.

Since his siege and capture of Miletus in 334, Alexander had operated, except for one small transport squadron, without a fleet. There have been various reasons suggested for this; but the truth of the matter seems to have been that the bulk of the navy was supplied by his reluctant Greek allies, whom he distrusted so deeply that he actually preferred the risk of rebellion in his rear—not to mention the challenge of neutralizing every key port from the landward side—to their continued presence.[27] Worse, the Persians had also decided to carry out an aggressive, and highly successful, naval campaign in the Aegean, for which they mainly employed the large Phoenician fleet. After Issus, Darius gave this campaign top priority: Miletus and Halicarnassus were

---

of tomb-chambers, coins, statues, mosaics, and other artifacts (including some unfamiliar items: a gilded silver goblet with vintage motifs in high *repoussé* technique, a huge marble arm gripping a baseball-sized sphere), but also contains several elegant and informative essays by leading Egyptian scholars.

25. Plut. *Alex.* 9.1; Steph. Byz. s.v. Ἀλεξάνδρειαι (no. 3); Theopompus fr. 110.

26. Arrian 7.23.7; cf. Bosworth 1988, 246–47.

27. E. Badian, "Alexander the Great and the Greeks of Asia," *Ancient Societies and Institutions: Studies Presented to Victor Ehrenberg on His 75th Birthday* (Oxford, 1966), 37–69, esp. 48.

recaptured, while King Agis III of Sparta, already planning a nationalist rebellion, was furnished with gold and no less than 8,000 mercenaries, and the
Persian cavalry commander Nabarzanes, campaigning in Anatolia, threatened
to sever Alexander's landward lines of communication.[28]

In the circumstances, the sea lanes and ports of the eastern Mediterranean assumed enormous strategic importance. Alexander had done what he
could to secure them as far as Cilicia. What remained now were Phoenicia and Egypt,[29] on both of which Persia — being itself a nonmaritime inland
country — habitually drew for its fleet. It should now be immediately apparent
why Alexander spent seven months besieging the great offshore stronghold of
Tyre. Tyre's neighbor and rival Sidon, having been reduced savagely by Artaxerxes Ochus in 345 after an attempted rebellion,[30] welcomed the Macedonians with open arms. But Gaza also gave Alexander trouble, and another two
months were spent in reducing it. Besides being a spice entrepôt at the head
of the eastern caravan routes, it could serve as a military fortress guarding the
land approaches to Egypt.[31]

From Gaza, Alexander made the 130 miles to the frontier stronghold of
Pelusium, at the mouth of the Nile, in just under a week. The small fleet he
had retained got there before him, and he found it at anchor in harbor.[32] Since
Artaxerxes Ochus had earlier (343) dealt with Egypt just as bloodily as he
did with Sidon,[33] Alexander met with no opposition at Pelusium, was indeed
welcomed as a liberator.[34] Both Phoenicia and Egypt were now safely under
Macedonian control.

Alexander's strategy at this point is clear enough. It would take Darius at
least a year to recruit, train, and deploy a new army. Since there was nothing Alexander wanted more than another full-scale — and, with luck, decisive — engagement, he was well content to let Darius prepare for this, while
he himself dealt with other pressing problems. So far he had secured Cilicia
and the Phoenician coast (thus safeguarding much of the East Mediterranean
sea-route), but there still remained North Africa. To the west of Cyrene lay

28. Green 1991, 211–12, 216–18, 242–43; A. R. Burn, "Notes on Alexander's Campaigns, 332–
330 B.C.," *JHS* 72 (1952): 81–91.

29. Hogarth 1915, 53–60.

30. Olmstead 1948, 436–37.

31. Bosworth 1988, 68.

32. Arrian 3.1.1; Curt. 4.7.2.

33. Olmstead 1948, 437–40. In addition to looting the temples and committing other outrages,
Ochus drove into exile the last native Pharaoh, Nectanebo (Nekht-har-hebi) II — later touted in
myth as the father of Alexander.

34. Diod. Sic. 17.49.1–2; Curt. 4.7.1; P. A. Brunt, *Arrian* (Cambridge, Mass. and London, 1976),
1:223 n. 3.

"barbarism and Carthage,"[35] about which not much could be done as yet. But Cyrene itself, and a fortiori the Nile Delta, had to be made safe. Whatever other considerations Alexander had in mind as he marched through the desert to Heliopolis,[36] this one was surely prominent.

Mazaces, the Persian satrap, whose garrison had been taken from him to fight at Issus, and who was thus virtually defenseless, crossed the river from Memphis and surrendered the city to the Macedonians, together with 800 talents and the royal furniture.[37] In Memphis, according to the Romance,[38] Alexander was not only enthroned as Pharaoh, but also, on being shown a statue of Nectanebo II, the last Egyptian Pharaoh, inscribed with a prophecy that he would come again to rid Egypt of the Persians, declared himself Nectanebo's son: perhaps, if there is any truth in the story, to strengthen his own claim as Egypt's new ruler. At the same time, while duly sacrificing to the Egyptian gods, he also held lavish Greek-style games, both musical and athletic, with top-level competitors imported from the Greek mainland:[39] a nice example of his increasing need, as his career of conquest advanced, to be all things to all men. While in Memphis (perhaps after a tour of inspection through the nearby countryside), he settled the future administration of Egypt in his usual manner, that is, by changing nothing apart from those in charge at the top.[40]

What he did next has been the subject of considerable disagreement among historians, ancient and modern alike. Both Quintus Curtius Rufus and Diodorus (note 40) clearly state that his next act was to pay a visit to the oracular shrine of Ammon in the Siwah Oasis. In particular they, like Justin,[41] place the foundation of Alexandria *after* this visit—though it is only the Alexander Romance that develops the *post hoc, propter hoc* argument that Alexander's purpose in visiting the shrine was to discover what site the god favored for his new city, and that Ammon duly responded with an oracle instructing the king to "found his famous city across from Proteus's isle."[42] On the other hand, both Arrian and Plutarch[43] appear to place the foundation of Alexandria *be-*

---

35. Hogarth 1915, 54.
36. Arrian 3.1.1–3.
37. Curt. 4.7.4–5; Arrian 3.1.2.
38. Ps.-Call. 1.34: ἐνεθρονίασαν αὐτὸν οἱ Αἰγύπτιοι . . . ὡς Αἰγύπτιον βασιλέα.
39. Arrian 3.1.4.
40. Curt. 4.7.5: a Memphi eodem flumine uectus, ad interiora Aegypti penetrat, compositisque rebus ita ut nihil ex patrio Aegyptiorum more mutaret adire Iouis Hammonis oraculum statuit; Diod. Sic. 17.49.2: καταστήσας δὲ τὰ κατὰ τὴν Αἴγυπτον προῆλθεν εἰς Ἄμμωνος.
41. Just. 11.11.1–2, 13: reuersus ab Hammone, Alexandream condidit et coloniam Macedonum caput esse Aegypti iubet.
42. Ps.-Call. 1.30–31, esp. 1.30.5: κτίζε πόλιν περίφημον ὑπὲρ Πρωτηίδα νῆσον.
43. Arrian 3.1.5–2.2, 3.3.1ff.; Plut. *Alex.* 26, passim.

fore the visit to Siwah. We have here what has more often than not been taken
(mistakenly, I think) as a fundamental conflict of primary sources.

Bradford Welles, in an influential article,[44] argued that the Alexander
Romance was right: that no Greek city could be founded without divine
approval, and that the evidence of Arrian and Plutarch must therefore be
rejected. Previously "Alexander historians [had] unhesitatingly accepted the
Ptolemaic version" of Arrian.[45] Now, for a while, Welles's thesis gave rise
to a *simpliste* and misdirected debate between the advocates of "before" and
"after."[46] It was Brian Bosworth who looked in the right direction for a solution to this problem. There was no reason, he argued, why Alexander should
not have first picked a site, then obtained divine approval for it at Siwah, and
finally established an official "foundation day" on his return. One might also
stress the fact that oracular consultants, including would-be colonists, habitually framed their questions in such a way as to solicit approval for a choice
already made.[47] With these considerations in mind, we can make our sources
yield a fairly consistent and plausible account of what actually happened.

From Memphis, Alexander sailed down the Canopic branch of the Nile.[48]
He already had in mind the determination to found a new city in the area. It
was to be large, well-populated, prosperous, with a good safe harbor.[49] Arrian
on several occasions[50] mentions Alexander's motives in founding cities. While
he had an eye for a strategically or otherwise advantageous site, his main
concern always seems to have been to leave a large and famous memorial of
himself, an extension of his quest for glory (*kleos*). This was why every such
foundation bore his name, to shed a natural luster on it. His other recipe for
success was a large population, so that we regularly find him not only directing
Greek and Macedonian colonists into his new cities, but forcibly relocating
indigenous inhabitants from surrounding areas. It is also clear that his motivation was very often, in part at least, commercial. This being so, during
his voyage he must at the very least have seriously considered the claims of a

---

44. See Welles 1962, 271–98. Though I regard his fundamental premise as misconceived, I
would emphasize that there is a great deal of original and valuable scholarship in Welles's article
on points of detail.

45. A. B. Bosworth, "Errors in Arrian," *CQ* 26 (1976): 136 n. 102.

46. See, e.g., E. N. Borza, *Historia* 16 (1967): 369; P. M. Fraser, *Opuscula Atheniensia* 7 (1967):
30 n. 27.

47. Bosworth (as in note 45), 136–39. Cf. H. W. Parke, *Greek Oracles* (London, 1967), ch. 5,
"Oracles and Colonisation," pp. 44ff., esp. 45.

48. Arrian 3.1.4.

49. Arrian 3.1.5, εὐδαίμονα; Plut. *Alex.* 26.4, μεγάλην καὶ πολυάνθρωπον; Diod. Sic. 17.52.1,
μεγάλην; Curt. 4.8.2, magnae sedis; Vitruv. II *praef.* 1.4, portum naturaliter tutum.

50. Arrian 4.1.3–4, 24.7; 6.15.2, 22.3; 7.31.

famous Greek emporium already long established on the Canopic branch of the Nile: Naucratis.[51] Naucratis had been a privileged commercial entrepôt for the Greeks at least since the early sixth century, and it is hard to believe that the rich businessmen who surely went out of their way to entertain the Macedonian conqueror when he reached Naucratis during his tour of inspection did not try also to sell him the idea of turning Naucratis into the city of his dreams. It is even possible that they for a brief while succeeded. Plutarch, in a passage that has elicited surprisingly little comment, records that on the advice of his technical consultants, he had already selected a site — was, indeed, on the point of measuring it off and enclosing it — when a prophetic dream turned his attention to the off-shore island of Pharos.[52] That this was Naucratis is made even more probable by the fact that one of his advisers, Cleomenes, was himself a native of the city, and almost certainly (as his subsequent career suggests) one of its leading financiers.[53]

During the night, according to Plutarch, Alexander dreamed that a white-haired and venerable old man stood beside him and declaimed two lines from Homer's *Odyssey* (4.354–55): "There is an island in the ever-surging main, / offshore from Egypt: Pharos is what men call it." The king's religiosity was one of his strongest characteristics.[54] Struck by this vision, he sailed on to the coast, explored Lake Mareotis, and examined Pharos itself. His first instinct seems to have been to follow his dream to the letter and build a city actually on the island, only being dissuaded from this plan by the realization that Pharos was not big enough for what he had in mind.[55] But then, surveying the long limestone ridge between lake and sea, noting the natural deep-water harbor, the protection afforded by Pharos, and the lack of comparable facilities elsewhere along the coast, he decided, Plutarch says, that Homer "was not only extraordinary in other respects but also a very clever town-planner."[56]

---

51. For a useful survey of Naucratis, see John Boardman, *The Greeks Overseas: Their Early Colonies and Trade*, 3d ed. (London and New York, 1980), 117–34, with further bibliography. For a description of the emporium in the Archaic period, cf. Hdt. 2.178–79, with the commentary of A. B. Lloyd, *Herodotus Book II: Commentary, 99–182* (Leiden, 1988), 222–31.

52. Plut. *Alex.* 26.4: λέγουσι γὰρ ὅτι ... τινα τόπον γνώμῃ τῶν ἀρχιτεκτόνων ὅσον οὐδέπω διεμετρεῖτο καὶ περιέβαλλεν.

53. H. Berve, *Das Alexanderreich auf prosopographischer Grundlage* (Munich, 1926), 2:210, no. 431, asserts that Cleomenes "vermutlich der höchsten Finanzaristokratie von Naukratis angehört haben."

54. Berve (ibid., 1:85–100), assembles the evidence.

55. Curt. 4.8.1–2: contemplatus loci naturam, primum in ipsa insula statuerat urbem nouam condere; inde ut apparuit magnae sedis insulam haud capacem esse, elegit urbi locum, ubi nunc est Alexandrea.

56. Plut. *Alex.* 26.7: εἰπὼν ὡς Ὅμηρος ἦν ἄρα τά τ' ἄλλα θαυμαστὸς καὶ σοφώτατος ἀρχιτέκτων.

At this point, says Arrian (3.1.5), "a longing (*pothos*) for the work took hold of him," and in his usual impulsive, enthusiastic manner, he began marking out the future city's main features: the site of the agora, the number and location of temples—mostly to Greek gods, but also to Egyptian Isis and Sarapis (the Homeric dream may even have taken place during an incubation in the existing shrine of Sarapis at Rhacotis[57])—the streets, laid out in a right-angled grid pattern and so placed as to catch the cool prevailing breeze,[58] hugely strong ramparts, a massive great royal palace.[59] These features are all specifically attributed to Alexander rather than to his successors. One further feature for which he can safely be given the credit is Alexandria's remarkable system of underground drains, conduits, cisterns, and sewers.[60] This clearly had to be in place *ab initio.* It is referred to by the author of the *Alexandrine War*,[61] and (according to the Alexander Romance) was actually recommended to Alexander by one of his technical advisers.[62]

One factor that undoubtedly influenced Alexander as strategist in favor of the site was its striking resemblance to that of Tyre.[63] Again, he found an offshore island capable of controlling access to the mainland, and his original notion of establishing Alexandria on Pharos itself confirms the comparison. That the island was too small to contain the kind of city he had in mind was not the only argument, however, in favor of preferring a site centered on the limestone ridge known as Rhacotis. What Alexander had done at Tyre by driving a great causeway from shore to island[64] others might yet achieve here. Better to anticipate them. What was more, Alexander at once perceived that the existence of such a causeway, quite apart from its strategic advantages, would greatly improve the docking facilities.[65] From an open roadstead

---

57. On Alexander's relations with Sarapis, see Welles 1962, 283ff.

58. Diod. Sic. 17.52.2. Cf. R. Martin, *L'Urbanisme dans la Grèce antique* (Paris, 1956), 42–43. I am no more convinced than was Martin that the orientation of Alexandria's street plan had a religious or ritual significance.

59. Diod. Sic. 17.52.3, 4: τὸν μὲν περίβολον αὐτῆς ὑπεστήσατο τῷ τε μεγέθει διαφέροντα καὶ κατὰ τὴν ὀχυρότητα θαυμάσιον . . . προσέταξεν δ' ὁ Ἀλέξανδρος καὶ βασίλεια κατασκευάσαι θαυμαστὰ κατὰ τὸ μέγεθος καὶ βάρος τῶν ἔργων.

60. Mahmoud Bey 1872, 29–32.

61. [Caes.] *Bell. Alex.* 5.1: Alexandrea est fere tota suffossa specusque habet a Nilo pertinentis, quibus aqua in priuatas domus inducitur.

62. Ps.-Call. 1.31: The adviser's name is given as Hyponomos (though this may be no more than the excuse for an aetiological pun): οὗτος συνεβούλευσεν τῷ Ἀλεξάνδρῳ τὴν πόλιν ἐκ θεμελίων κτίσαι, ἐν αὐτῇ δὲ καὶ ὑδρηγοὺς πόρους καὶ ὀχετηγοὺς ἐπιρρέοντας εἰς τὴν θάλασσαν. καλεῖται δὲ ὑπονόμος διὰ τὸ ὑποδεῖξαι <αὐτὸν> ταῦτα.

63. Cavenaile 1972, 94–112.

64. For the siege of Tyre in general, see Green 1991, 247–63, with testimonia there cited.

65. Strabo 17.1.6, C.792, who in his discussion of the Heptastadion informs us that originally it also served as an aqueduct to Pharos.

merely sheltered by Pharos, the port of Alexandria would at one stroke acquire major eastern and western harbors, each easily protected against both violent storms (from whatever quarter) and attack from the sea. For these reasons I am inclined to believe that the Heptastadion formed part of Alexander's original plan, and was implemented during his lifetime. In a passage much contaminated with later myth, Ammianus picks up one tradition that has the ring of truth about it: the Heptastadion, he reports, was remarkable not only for its size (it was nearly a mile in length), but also for the "scarcely credible speed" with which it was built.[66] The kind of speed that amazed those who saw it (and a fortiori those who became its victims) was, of course, one of Alexander's best-known characteristics.

That Alexander's purpose in founding Alexandria was at least as much strategic as commercial seems certain.[67] Egypt's remarkable ability, even under the most inept of the Ptolemies, to resist successful invasion by land or sea testifies in retrospect to his foresight. His acquisition of the Nile Valley guaranteed him almost inexhaustible supplies of grain and other produce. Memphis gave him control of the Delta. Pelusium had only limited facilities for the maintenance of a fleet; but with the establishment of a deep-water port in Alexandria (at the one point on the Egyptian littoral where this was possible), Alexander clinched his domination over the eastern Mediterranean. Two world wars have amply confirmed the port's crucial importance as a naval base. Alexander's emphasis on the size and strength of the city walls suggests a determination to make his foundation equally invulnerable from the landward side.

The site of Rhacotis had been used as a defense post in earlier periods. Strabo[68] describes how the Pharaohs established a garrison there, to keep out foreigners, primarily Greeks (on economic grounds, it is alleged, which sounds like an anachronism from Ptolemaic times), and "gave them as a dwelling-place the area known as Rhacotis, now that part of the Alexandrians' city situated above the dockyards, which was then a village; and the land around the village they gave to herdsmen, who also were able to prevent incursions by outsiders." Strabo's evidence is confirmed in some detail by the Alexander Romance, where, in a difficult and in places corrupt passage,[69] we

66. Amm. Marc. 22.16.10: heptastadium sicut uix credenda celeritate, ita magnitudine mira construxit.

67. Cf. Cavenaile 1972, 103ff.

68. Strabo 17.1.6 (C.792): κατοικίαν δ' αὐτοῖς ἔδοσαν τὴν προσαγορευομένην Ῥακῶτιν, ἣ νῦν μὲν τῆς Ἀλεξανδρέων πόλεώς ἐστι μέρος τὸ ὑπερκείμενον τῶν νεωρίων, τότε δὲ κώμη ὑπῆρχε· τὰ δὲ κύκλῳ τῆς κώμης βουκόλοις παρέδοσαν, δυναμένοις καὶ αὐτοῖς κωλύειν τοὺς ἔξωθεν ἐπίοντας.

69. Ps.-Call. 1.31.2, best studied in the text and commentary provided by A. Ausfeld, "Zur

hear of a dozen small villages surrounding Rhacotis itself, which served as their administrative center. Even more intriguing, though extremely hard to evaluate, are the extensive underwater ruins of a huge harbor complex lying to the north and west of Pharos: they could be a millennium older than the foundation of Alexandria, and the most plausible theory identifies them as part of the Minoan thalassocracy centered on Knossos.[70] Pottery deposits suggest, as we might expect, a Greek presence in the area at least since the mid-seventh century.[71] Herodotus and Thucydides both refer to garrison posts in the area, the one in the sixth century, the other in the fifth, in each case as part of a description of Egypt's general defense-system.[72] There is no reason to suppose that Alexander, who had all Homer and a good deal of Euripides by heart, would not also be familiar with the two great exponents of his own themes of conquest and empire.

The shape of the original city wall is likened by several of our sources to a chlamys, a Macedonian military cloak,[73] which was formed from a rectangular piece of cloth shaped somewhat like the segment of a circle: a convex lower edge subtended to two straight sides converging on a much narrower top edge, the latter straight or slightly curved.[74] The city's dimensions are also variously reported, Strabo's figures — 30 stades from east to west, but no more than 7–8 stades north to south, between Lake Mareotis and the sea[75] — being probably the most accurate. Strabo also makes it clear that the city boundary stopped short, in the west, of the suburb known as Necropolis, "in which are many graves and gardens and embalmers' parlors."[76] A similar *terminus ad quem* is provided in the east by the cemetery of Chatby.[77] Insofar as the chlamys image bore any relation to reality, it seems to have envisaged an area

---

Topographie von Alexandria und Pseudokallisthenes I 31–33," *RhM* 55 (1900): 348–84, esp. 350–53. Cf. also Fraser 1972, 1:5–6, 2:2, p. 7 n. 18.

70. See Fraser 1972, 2:8–9 n. 21, for a good bibliographical survey of the scholarship on these tantalizing underwater ruins. The Cretan connection was first advanced by R. Weill, "Les ports antéhelléniques de la côte d'Alexandrie et l'empire crétois," *Bulletin de l'Institut Français d'Archéologie Orientale* 16 (1919): 1–37.

71. See in particular M. S. Venit, "Two Early Corinthian Alabastra in Alexandria," *JEA* 61 (1985): 183–89; earlier bibliography in Fraser 1972, 2:6 n. 16.

72. Hdt. 2.30; Thuc. 1.104.1, with the analysis of Cavenaile 1972, 103–5.

73. See, e.g., Diod. Sic. 17.52.3; Plut. *Alex.* 26.8; Strabo 17.1.8, C.793; Plin. *NH* 5.62.

74. F. B. Tarbell, "The Form of the Chlamys," *CPh* 1 (1906): 283–89, esp. 284–85.

75. Strabo 17.1.8, C.793; Steph. Byz. s.v. Ἀλεξάνδρειαι (34 × 8 stades); Diod. Sic. 17.52.3 (40 stades × 1 plethron); Joseph. *BJ* 2.16.4 (30 × 10 stades); Plin. *NH* 5.10 (15 miles circumference). Cf. Fraser 1972, 2:26–27, n. 64.

76. Strabo 17.1.10, C.795: ἐν ᾧ κῆποί τε πολλοὶ καὶ ταφαὶ καὶ καταγωγαὶ πρὸς τὰς ταριχείας τῶν νεκρῶν ἐπιτήδειαι.

77. Fraser 1972, 1:13.

roughly rectangular, but narrowing northward as it approached the harbor area.

If Alexander wished to obtain divine approval for his foundation, it had first to be defined. This is the true *raison d'être* behind the most famous anecdote concerning his activities at the site: most of our sources record it,[78] but none perceives its relevance. When Alexander had fixed on the site at Rhacotis, he strode around, Arrian says, marking out (we are not told how) various features of his new city. But the chalk or lime used for marking ran out, and was replaced, in this emergency, by the barley meal or polenta that formed the troops' and workmen's rations (what they had to say about losing their lunch is not recorded). A vast swarm of seagulls and marsh birds appeared, and devoured the barley meal. Alexander, superstitious to a degree, was concerned as to what this might portend, but got welcome reassurance from Aristander and his other seers, who declared that the city would abound in wealth and provide sustenance for men of every nation.[79]

What has escaped notice about the barley-meal anecdote is that in every version of it what Alexander is marking out is, specifically, the city's perimeter, its fortifications, its defining boundary walls.[80] This lends some credibility to the generally disregarded comment of Quintus Curtius, who informs us that the use of barley meal to establish the outer circuit, what a Roman would call the *pomerium*, of a new city was "a custom of the Macedonians."[81] In any case, what Alexander was doing was making a ritual declaration of intent, at least as much for divine as for human notification. He then "offered sacrifice for these actions, and the sacrifice appeared favorable."[82]

At this point,[83] Alexander's lieutenant Hegelochus arrived by sea with welcome news from the Aegean, where the naval campaign was everywhere turning in the Macedonians' favor. It was now that, once again, Alexander was seized by a sudden urge, a *pothos*, to visit the shrine of Zeus Ammon in the

---

78. Arrian 3.2.1-2; Plut. *Alex.* 26.8-10; Curt. 4.8.6; Strabo 17.1.6, C.792 ad fin.; Ps.-Call. 1.32; cf. Amm. Marc. 22.16.7; Steph. Byz. s.v. Ἀλεξάνδρειαι.

79. If this is an example of Alexander's alleged policy of racial fusion, we should bear in mind that the fusion was to be carried out under strict Greco-Macedonian overlordship: as Justin 11.11.1-2, 13 reports, Alexandria—by Egypt, but not of it—was to be not only the capital, but "a Macedonian colony."

80. Strabo: τὴν τοῦ περιβόλου γραμμήν; Plut.: κυκλοτερῆ κόλπον; Arrian: τὸν κύκλον . . . τοῦ περιτειχισμοῦ; Curt.: orbem futuri muri; Ps.-Call.: τὸ περίμετρον τῆς πόλεως; Amm. Marc.: ambitus lineales; Steph. Byz.: τὸ σχῆμα.

81. Curt. 4.8.6: "Ut Macedonum mos est." The fact that this custom is not reported elsewhere does not offer *prima facie* grounds for rejecting it.

82. Arrian 3.1.5: καὶ ἐπὶ τούτοις ἐθύετο, καὶ τὰ ἱερὰ καλὰ ἐφαίνετο.

83. Arrian 3.2.3-7.

Libyan desert.[84] This *pothos* may not have been exclusively religious in nature. Alexander still needed to secure Cyrene. Here luck was on his side. Before he reached Paraetonium (Mersa Matruh), envoys met him from Cyrene bearing rich gifts and soliciting a treaty of alliance, which he was only too glad to grant them.[85] Hogarth argued that Alexander only went to Siwah at all because he now had no need to proceed to Cyrene, and felt he might as well make the long march worthwhile.[86] Alexander's religious nature suggests otherwise; but Hogarth is undoubtedly right in his contention that the journey was also strategically motivated.

We are only concerned here with two facets of this much-discussed episode: the possibility that one reason for Alexander's foray into the desert was to secure Ammon's blessing on the proposed new city, and a search for evidence establishing the chronology of both the pilgrimage itself and the city's foundation. The only source claiming that Alexander consulted the oracle regarding his proposed foundation is provided by the Alexander Romance.[87] Though as an unsupported witness this text does not inspire confidence, Bradford Welles has offered convincing reasons why in this case we should believe what it tells us. As he says,[88] "Did any Greek individual or community ever found a new city without first consulting an oracle? . . . Anyone in antiquity knew that Alexander must have had divine guidance in founding his name city." The oracle, according to the Romance, instructed the king to do so "opposite the isle of Proteus," just as he had hoped, "over which Aion Ploutonios himself presides, / turning the boundless world on its five-hilled ridges."[89] This deity, the Romance duly informs us,[90] was none other than Sarapis. Though the degree of Alexander's personal involvement in the Sarapis cult is much debated,[91] the existence of a Sarapeium in Rhacotis seems certain, and it clearly occupied the same site as the later temple, that is, in the southwestern part of the city, on the little hill where "Pompey's Column" (actually part of the temple itself) still stands.[92] That Alexander received ap-

---

84. For this episode, see Arrian 3.3.1–4.5; Curt. 4.7.6–32; Plut. *Alex.* 26.6–27; Diod. Sic. 17.49.2–51.4; Just. 11.11.2–12.

85. Diod. Sic. 17.49.2–3; Curt. 4.7.9.

86. Hogarth 1915, 57–58.

87. Ps.-Call. 1.31–33 passim.

88. Welles 1962, 275–76.

89. Ps.-Call. 1.30.5–7: ὑπὲρ Πρωτηίδα νῆσον | ἧς προκάθητ' Αἰὼν Πλουτώνιος αὐτὸς ἀνάσσων | πενταλόφοις κορυφαῖσιν ἀτέρμονα κόσμον ἑλίσσων.

90. Ps.-Call. 1.33.1–4, 8.

91. See, e.g., Welles 1962, 282ff.; Fraser 1972, 1:248ff.

92. Strabo 17.1.10, C.795; cf. Mahmoud Bey 1872, 53–56; Fraser 1972, 1:268–70, 2:84ff. n. 190.

proval for his foundation from Ammon, and that this approval was in some way linked to the cult of Sarapis, seems highly probable.

The journey to Siwah was marked by two phenomena that enable us to date it with reasonable precision: heavy rain,[93] and a sand-storm,[94] produced by the southwest khamsin winds. Both of these are restricted to the winter months.[95] Alexander had arrived in Egypt during November 332: he probably consulted the oracle in late December or early January. The Alexander Romance offers an Egyptian date, 25 Tybi, for the foundation of Alexandria.[96] Conversion to a Julian date depends on whether the writer of the Romance was calculating from the Ptolemaic calendar, which gives us 7 April, or from Augustus's Roman calendar, which works out at 20 January.[97] Since a few lines earlier he equates Tybi with January, the latter seems more probable, and fits very well with the climatic evidence. In any case, Alexander left Memphis for Phoenicia "at the very first sign of spring,"[98] and this will certainly have been before the second week in April. The one true inconsistency in our testimonia (which also baffled Arrian, who reports it) concerns his route back. Did he return by the same route (thus Aristobulus, followed by Quintus Curtius), or make the shorter, but far more dangerous, trek across the desert through the Qattara Depression, directly to Memphis?[99] The only reason he would have chosen to do the latter would be if he were pressed for time. With a January rather than an April date, he had no such urgency. He was also, undoubtedly, eager to see his now divinely sanctioned project under way. I therefore believe

---

93. Diod. Sic. 17.49.3–5; Curt. 4.7.14; Plut. *Alex.* 27.1; Arrian 3.3.4.

94. Diod. Sic. 17.49.5; Plut. *Alex.* 27.3; cf. Curt. 4.7.11–12.

95. Welles 1962, 278–79 with n. 36.

96. Ps.-Call. 1.32.6.

97. See Fraser 1972, 2:3 n. 9, with bibliography.

98. Arrian 3.6.1: ἅμα τῷ ἦρι ὑποφαίνοντι. R. S. Bagnall, "The Date of the Foundation of Alexandria," *AJAH* 4 (1979): 46–49, argues for 7 April on the grounds that no Alexandrian would receive a traditional date in January that he then converted to Tybi. Perhaps not; but this assumption underrates both the cosmopolitanism of Roman Alexandria, and the fact that the city's foundation date must have been common knowledge, and indeed a public holiday, in either (adjusted) calendar. The meteorological evidence also gives us a *terminus ante quem* (February at the latest, I would judge): I am not convinced that Arrian's phrase cited above is as vaguely flexible as Bagnall would like it to be. The fact that Alexander *could*, in theory, have left Memphis as late as April and still have kept his date with destiny at Gaugamela is no proof that in fact he *did*; and the other evidence is all against it.

99. Arrian 3.4.4, cf. Curt. 4.8.1. A. B. Bosworth, *A Historical Commentary on Arrian's History of Alexander* (Oxford, 1982), 1:274, has a brief but sensible discussion of the problem, suggesting, plausibly, that Arrian may well have misinterpreted his sources: "If Aristobulus had a detailed statement that Alexander returned via Paraetonium to Egypt while Ptolemy said baldly that Alexander returned to Memphis, it would have been possible for him to draw a mistaken inference from Ptolemy's brevity and assume that two routes were at issue."

that Aristobulus was right, and that he traveled back via Paraetonium and the coast road to Rhacotis.

In a brief notice, Diodorus[100] records the sequence of his actions at this point: "King Alexander charged certain of his Friends with the building of Alexandria, made all arrangements in Egypt, and set out back for Syria with his army." Who were these Friends, and what, precisely, were the instructions they received? There was the dubiously named Hyponomos, who (according to the Alexander Romance[101]) advised Alexander on the installation of a sophisticated underground system of water supply and sewers, the existence of which is confirmed both by later literary evidence and by archaeology.[102] With him are also named Numenius, a stonemason, Craterus of Olynthus (not the Macedonian general), and Cleomenes of Naucratis, described as an engineer ($\mu\eta\chi\alpha\nu\iota\kappa\acute{o}s$). The first two are otherwise unknown. Cleomenes, on the other hand, together with the architect Deinocrates (whom the Romance also mentions[103]), was directly responsible for the implementation and initial development of Alexander's dream city. Justin bluntly states that Cleomenes "built Alexandria."[104] If he built it, Deinocrates was responsible for its unusual design.[105] Both of these larger-than-life men are worth a closer look. Alexandria would not have been Alexandria, perhaps might not even have survived, without them.

Vitruvius, the Roman architectural writer, describes in detail[106] how Deinocrates, armed with letters of introduction, sought Alexander's patronage. Impatient at the delay in obtaining an introduction to the king, Deinocrates hit on a decidedly theatrical scheme. Being a tall, handsome, well-built man, he stripped off at his lodging house, oiled himself, put on a wreath of poplar leaves, draped a lion skin over his left shoulder, and marched out, grasping a club, to the tribunal where Alexander was giving judgment. The appearance of this deutero-Heracles caused a sensation. Alexander, curious, summoned him. The sales pitch was ready. Deinocrates, who had a taste for the kind of public gigantism that afterward distinguished the Ptolemies,[107] and who

100. Diod. Sic. 17.52.6. More detailed accounts in Arrian 3.5.2–7; Curt. 4.8.4–9.

101. Ps.-Call. 1.31.9–10.

102. [Caes.] *Bell. Alex.* 5.1; Mahmoud Bey 1872, 29ff.

103. Ps.-Call. 1.30.6.

104. Just. 13.4.11: Cleomenes, qui Alexandriam aedificauerat. . . .

105. Vitruv. 2 *praef.* 4; Plin. *NH* 5.62; Val. Max. 1.4.7, ext. l; Amm. Marc. 22.16.7.

106. Vitruv. 2 *praef.* 1–4.

107. Among other things, he had a hand in designing the vast new temple of Artemis at Ephesus: Strabo 14.1.22–23, C.640–41, cf. W. B. Dinsmoor, *The Architecture of Ancient Greece*, 3d rev. ed. (London, 1950), 224.

clearly shared Disraeli's belief that when flattering royalty you should lay it on with the proverbial trowel, announced a plan to carve Mt. Athos into the likeness of Alexander himself, with one hand holding a basin to collect the flow of water, and the other supporting a city of 10,000 inhabitants.[108] Alexander announced himself pleased with this monstrous piece of vulgarity, but, with his usual practical eye for logistics, asked whether the city had an adequate local grain supply. When he heard that all grain would have to be imported, he killed the plan—but at the same time expressed approval of the concept,[109] and enrolled Deinocrates as a member of his staff, intending to make use of his services.

This revealing anecdote tells us a lot, not only about Alexander's architect, but also about Alexander himself and his grandiose plans. Deinocrates went to Egypt in the king's train, and was there commissioned with the planning of Alexandria[110]—in the king's name, which suggests that he was given a free hand to improvise during Alexander's absence in the East. Nevertheless, it seems likely that much of the essential planning was done with Alexander's prior approval, and that some of it may be attributable to the king himself. Blanche Brown reminds us[111] of Alexander's interest in siegecraft, harbor-dredging, and drainage schemes. As we have seen, he was probably responsible for the underground water-supply system. We may also detect his hand in the creation of vital canals: one linking the Western Harbor with Lake Mareotis, another, some miles in length, between Lake Mareotis and the Nile, thus connecting the country's internal and external transport systems.[112] Deinocrates was responsible for the chlamys-like shape of the city perimeter,[113] and for the orthogonal street system, though it may have been Alexander who insisted that at least the two main axis streets should be (like those of Brigham Young's Salt Lake City) a *plethron*, that is, no less than a hundred feet, in breadth—a most unusual stipulation for that day and age.[114] The Alexander Romance, on the other hand,[115] represents both Deinocrates and Cleomenes as dissuad-

---

108. Vitruv. 2 *praef.* 1–3; Plut. *Alex.* 72.3–7; Strabo 14.1.23, C.641.

109. Vitruv. 2 *praef.* 3: ". . . formationem puto probandam. . . ."

110. Vitruv. 2 *praef.* 4: ibi Alexander [after noting the advantages of the site] . . . iussit eum suo nomine ciuitatem Alexandriam constituere.

111. Blanche R. Brown, "Deinokrates and Alexandria," *Bulletin of the American Society of Papyrology* 15 (1978): 39–42, esp. 41–42.

112. Strabo 17.1.4, C.789.

113. Plin. *NH* 5.62: metatus est eam [Alexandriam] Deinocrates . . . ad effigiem Macedonicae chlamydis.

114. Diod. Sic. 17.52.3; Strabo 17.1.8, C.793.

115. Ps.-Call. 1.31 passim.

ing Alexander from creating an over-large territory ($\chi\acute{\omega}\rho\alpha$) for Alexandria, arguing that he would never be able to find enough people to fill it; the king seems to have taken their advice, since the actual territory the Romance tells us he agreed on more or less coincides with historical fact. The same source states (§8) that he ordered anyone living in this area within thirty miles of the city boundary to move into the city itself, at the same time granting them land and Alexandrian citizenship. Curtius adds that he evacuated some other local towns and "filled the new city with a vast population." [116]

Cleomenes of Naucratis is an altogether more formidable figure. It may have been his engineering skills that first led Alexander to enlist his services for the building of Alexandria; but it very soon became apparent that this ambitious Greek's chief qualification was as a tough, and highly unscrupulous, financier and administrator.[117] His first official appointment was as tax collector for the region east of the Delta, and subsequently for all Egypt and the adjacent part of North Africa.[118] His instructions were to let the nomarchs continue to rule their districts in accordance with long-established tradition, but to extract tribute from them, which they for their part were ordered to pay. So successful was he that Alexander soon established him as governor of Egypt, the equivalent of a Persian satrap.[119] In that capacity he ruled Egypt from Alexandria until 323/2. After Alexander's death, however, when Ptolemy got Egypt as his own satrapy, Cleomenes was demoted to deputy governor.[120] In fact, Ptolemy had no intention of retaining so ambitious and unscrupulous an administrator, whose reduced position was an open invitation to conspiracy: indeed, rumor had it that Cleomenes was already in secret communication with Ptolemy's *bête noire*, Perdiccas. It is, then, not surprising that almost as soon as Ptolemy arrived in Egypt, he had Cleomenes arrested and executed.[121] Inspection of the treasury revealed that his prede-

---

116. Curt. 4.8.5: ex finitimis urbibus commigrare Alexandream iussis nouam urbem magna multitudine impleuit. How quickly was this relocation carried out? Even if the new Alexandrians were summoned to build their new homes from scratch on the land allotted them—private enterprise at the service of public works—a considerable period must have elapsed before the new city was ready for occupation.

117. For a thorough, if over-kind, study of Cleomenes (represented as the victim of Ptolemaic propaganda, see Fraser 1972, 1:7), cf. also J. Seibert, *Untersuchungen zur Geschichte Ptolemaios I* (Munich, 1969), 39–51.

118. Arrian 3.5.4 specifies the more limited area of "Arabia toward Heroönpolis"; Curt. 4.8.5 refers to "eiusdem [i.e., 'quae Aegypto iuncta est'] Africae Aegyptique." The natural inference is that his authority was extended as time went on.

119. [Arist.] *Oecon.* 1352a17; Arrian τὰ μετ' Ἀλεξ. 1.5ᵃ, 2ᵇ Roos; [Dem.] 56.7; Paus. 1.6.3.

120. Arrian, ibid.; Just. 13.4.11.

121. Paus. 1.6.3.

cessor had managed to amass no less than 8,000 talents during his years of office.[122]

A great deal of this money had been acquired by manipulating the grain market. Demosthenes (or whoever wrote the speech against Dionysodorus) draws a graphic picture of price-fixing and resale deals by a cartel consisting of men who were all "subordinates and confederates" of Cleomenes.[123] Further details are provided by the pseudo-Aristotelian *Oeconomica*,[124] which not only confirms the price-fixing charges, but gives us a glimpse of Cleomenes' other activities. In particular, he was responsible for implementing Alexander's relocation policy, which included the area of Canopus, together with its public market. His dealings with the priests and property owners are instructive. First he announced he would transfer them. They then bribed him to leave the market where it was. He accepted—until the building material was ready. Then he returned and demanded a vast sum "which he said represented the difference to him between having the mart near the Pharos and at Canopus." When they told him this was impossible, he transferred them anyway. Readers of *The Alexandria Quartet* will at once recognize a spiritual ancestor of Memlik Pasha. All the anecdotes concerning him exemplify his ingenious ways of extracting money from the unwilling and the unwary.

None of this, clearly, bothered Alexander, who was quite happy as long as Cleomenes did his job efficiently and remained loyal. The governor, for his part, made sure that Alexander got the lion's share of any profits (one extract from a letter he wrote the king lists smoked quail and thrushes by the thousand[125]). Toward the end of his life, Alexander wrote to Cleomenes, instructing him to erect a shrine to Hephaestion—"of vast size and unparalleled magnificence"—on the island of Pharos, name it after Hephaestion, and issue a decree obliging business contracts to have Hephaestion's name written into them. Do this, Alexander concluded, "and any wrong you have done in the past, I will pardon, and in future, however you may err, you will suffer no harm from me."[126] This attitude profoundly shocked the respectable Arrian,

---

122. Diod. Sic. 18.14.1.

123. [Dem.] 56.7ff. Demosthenes is appealed to as a witness at the close of this speech (§50); but it has been argued that his name was inserted by a later scribe when the speech had found a place in the Demosthenic corpus. In any case, since Cleomenes' tenure of office is spoken of as over (§7 refers to the ὑπηρέται καὶ συνεργοὶ . . . Κλεομένους τοῦ ἐν τῇ Αἰγύπτῳ ἄρξαντος), the speech must have been delivered, at earliest, only a month or two before Demosthenes' flight and death in 322.

124. [Arist.] *Oecon.* 2.2.33a-f, 1352a17-1352b25, passim; 2.2.39, 1353b1-7.

125. Cited by Athenaeus, *Deipnos.* 9.393c.

126. Arrian 7.23.6-8: εἴ τέ τι πρότερον ἡμάρτηκας, ἀφήσω σε τούτου, καὶ τὸ λοιπόν, ὁπηλίκον ἂν ἁμάρτῃς, οὐδὲν πείσῃ ἐξ ἐμοῦ ἄχαρι.

who characterizes Cleomenes (quite justifiably) as "a bad man who had perpe-
trated many injustices in Egypt," and cannot bring himself "to approve such
a mandate from a great king to a person ruling over so wide an area and so
many people."[127]

Yet this, like him or not, was the man who guided and formed Alexandria
through the first crucial decade of the city's existence, and we can be certain
that he left his own idiosyncratic stamp on Alexander's original plans. It seems
clear that one of the first things Cleomenes established in Alexandria — just
as we might expect, considering his commercial instincts — was a functioning
mint.[128] His dealings in grain show that right from the start, the new foundation formed a natural entrepôt for East-West trade. Mercantile requirements
suggest that the harbors and docks — and, naturally, the Heptastadion — had
priority when it came to construction work, along with the city walls. Alexander's palace and the shrine of Sarapis were, similarly, features that no prudent
governor would neglect. Nevertheless, it is worth emphasizing that at the time
of Cleomenes' death, none of the major features we associate with Alexandria — the Pharos, the Museum, the Library, the royal mausoleum (Sema), the
more extravagant palaces — had even been started. The cross formed by the
two great central thoroughfares must have been in place, but many smaller
streets and alleys were left to evolve at random, with little regard for the orthogonal grid.[129]

This natural deviation from rectilinear consistency may have been responsible in part for the persistent denigration of Mahmoud Bey's pioneer work in
plotting the remains of the ancient city. He, like almost every scholar since, assumed that the street plan was absolutely regular throughout. The most tren-
chant criticism came from D. G. Hogarth, who, with E. F. Benson, excavated
briefly in Alexandria in 1895.[130] His chief complaint (apart from generalized
sneers at Mahmoud Bey's amateur status, incompetence, and lack of experience) was that the orientation of streets on Mahmoud Bey's map could not
be reconciled with that of walls and pavement found by Hogarth himself.[131]
Since both men believed in a strict axial grid, it is easy to see how this mis-

---

127. Arrian 7.23.8, 6: Κλεομένει, ἀνδρὶ κακῷ καὶ πολλὰ ἀδικήματα ἀδικήσαντι ἐν Αἰγύπτῳ. . . . τοῦτο ἀνδρὶ ἄρχοντι πολλῆς μὲν χώρας, πολλῶν δὲ ἀνθρώπων ἐκ βασιλέω
μεγάλου ἐπεσταλμένον, ἄλλως τε καὶ κακῷ ἀνδρί, οὐκ ἔχω ἐπαινέσαι.

128. Fraser 1972, 1:13, 2:10 n. 25.

129. Rodziewicz 1987, 45–46.

130. D. G. Hogarth and E. F. Benson, "Report of Prospects of Research in Alexandria, with
Note on Excavations in Alexandrian Cemeteries," *Egypt Exploration Fund 1895*, (London and Boston), 1–33.

131. *Ibid.*, 17, where Hogarth writes: "For instance, his Canopic Street (on which all his *grille* of

understanding came about; but it was doubly unfortunate in that Hogarth's strictures meant that Mahmoud Bey's work was almost wholly neglected until very recent times. Recent excavation has, to a surprising degree, vindicated his original plan.[132] We still know very little about early Alexandria in archaeological terms; but what we do know (e.g., that the Canopic Way followed the line of the modern Rue Rosette, today the Sharia Horreya[133]) we largely owe to Mahmoud Bey.

If we have succeeded to any degree in rescuing Alexander's Alexandria from myth, this is scarcely due to the eponymous founder himself, whose main contribution was to add some highly potent myths of his own. As Hogarth pithily reminds us,[134] Alexander "stayed in the Nile Valley just about the time that an ordinary tourist spends on a single visit, and he never returned to it except as an embalmed corpse." In death he ceased to be a tourist, and became a tourist attraction. Ptolemy Soter diverted the funeral procession and in effect hijacked Alexander's remains to Egypt, where they remained on permanent display (rather like Lenin in Red Square), first in a gold coffin, and then (when a later Ptolemy sold that for cash to pay mercenaries) in a replacement of glass or alabaster. Julius Caesar meditated over him. Augustus accidentally broke off a bit of his nose. Caligula stole his breastplate for personal use. Septimius Severus restricted access to the tomb. Caracalla, in an unwontedly generous gesture, took off his own purple toga, his rings and jewels, and placed them on the bier (A.D. 215). After that, oblivion. The tomb, its occupant, and the palace area generally were probably destroyed c. A.D. 273, during the disturbances of Aurelian's reign. A century later John Chrysostom is asking, rhetorically: "Tell me, where is Alexander's tomb? Show me, tell me the day on which it ceased to exist!"[135]

Despite this, from antiquity to the present day, hopeful fantasists have continued to search for the Macedonian conqueror's last resting-place: Alexander's posthumous charisma (which so inhibited his Successors that they

---

streets depends) lies at an angle which fits very ill with the direction of the walls found by me to the south of it."

132. Rodziewicz 1987, 44–47: "Des fouilles récentes de plus en plus nombre uses ont montré que ce plan était juste et que nous avons là le seul plan fiable des rues principales" (47).

133. Mahmoud Bey 1872, 18ff.; cf. Delia 1992, 1456 with n. 26.

134. Hogarth 1915, 53.

135. Diod. Sic. 18.26.3, 28.2–4; Paus. 1.6.3; Strabo 17.1.8, C.794; Ael. *VH* 12.64; Curt. 4.6.29, cf. Lucan *BC* 10.16–52 (Caesar); Suet. *Div. Aug.* 18.1, Dio Cass. 51.16.3–5 (Augustus); Suet. *Cal.* 52 (Caligula); Dio Cass. 70.13 (Septimius Severus); Herodian 4.8.9 (Caracalla); John Chrysost. 26.12: ποῦ γάρ, εἰπέ μοι, τὸ σῆμα Ἀλεξάνδρου; δεῖξόν μοι, καὶ εἰπὲ τὴν ἡμέραν καθ᾽ ἣν ἐτελεύτησε.

held council meetings in the presence of his empty throne and regalia[136]) still retains all its old magnetism.[137] The quest has mostly concentrated on the mosque of the prophet Daniel on Nabi Daniel Street, the presumptive site of the Sema. Despite the archaeologists' flatly negative findings,[138] optimists, mostly amateurs, continue undeterred.[139] My own favorite "sighting" is one that Forster records,[140] by a dragoman of the Russian Consulate ("probably a liar," Forster mildly comments) who, in 1850, claimed to have seen through a hole in a wooden door "a human body in a sort of glass cage with a diadem on its head and half bowed on a sort of elevation or throne. A quantity of books or papyrus were scattered around." Wishful thinking is a great promoter of visions.

We know a little of Alexander's plans for Alexandria; we know virtually nothing of its ultimate importance in his scheme of things had he lived, much less how close a resemblance (if any) the shape that the city finally assumed bore to the vision he had in mind as he strode about the site at Rhacotis, architects and aides scrambling behind him, dribbling trails of barley meal over dark soil and limestone outcroppings. Victor Ehrenberg's romantic assumption[141] that Alexander planned to make Alexandria-by-Egypt the capital of his empire is wholly unsupported by evidence and unlikely in the extreme: the capital, as has often been said, was wherever Alexander happened to be, his notion of imperial rule being (to put it kindly) dynamic rather than static. Even Fraser's claim that he "continued to take an interest in the city until he died"[142] rests on nothing more than the king's request for an outsize monument to Hephaestion and his awareness of Cleomenes' financial peccadilloes. Alexander never saw Alexandria in his lifetime, even though he became the city's resident *daimōn* once he was dead. Could he have miraculously come back to see what had been done in his name, would he have approved what he saw?

The city indeed became large and populous, though with a ribald cosmopolitanism that might have disconcerted him, since his notions of fusion

---

136. Curt. 10.6.4; Diod. Sic. 18.60 passim, 19.15.3–4; Plut. *Eum.* 13; Nep. *Eum.* 7.2–3; Polyaen. 4.8.2.

137. For a comprehensive (though unevenly documented) survey, see Fawzi el Fakharani, "An Investigation into the Views Concerning the Location of the Tomb of Alexander the Great," *Bulletin of the Faculty of Arts, Alexandria University* 18 (1964): 169–99, with figs. 1–11.

138. See Fraser 1972, 1:15–17, 2:34–41 nn. 82–90; Delia 1992, 1456 n. 27.

139. The most recent attempt I have seen is that of Thomas Stelios (described as an international executive and a Fellow of the AIA[?]) in *The Mediterranean* 1.2 (1985): 26–33.

140. Forster 1982, 112–13.

141. V. Ehrenberg, *Alexander und Ägypten*, Beitr. z. Alten Orient VII (Leipzig, 1926), 28.

142. Fraser 1972, 1:7; 2:10 n. 24.

always left Macedonians firmly in charge. On that score, the Ptolemaic court and the Alexandrian bureaucracy, while allaying his fears, would also have aroused his puritan antipathy to luxury and self-indulgence. The harbors, docks, canals, and city walls probably turned out much as he had envisaged them. The Pharos would have pleased his taste for practical science while also appealing to his sense of gigantism. Aristotle's pupil, who had taken endless geographers, botanists, and historians with him on his conquest of the East, can hardly have failed to approve of the Museum and Library, though the backbiting antics of its resident faculty would no more have appealed to him than they did to Timon of Phlius when he wrote: "In the polyglot land of Egypt many now find pasturage as endowed scribblers, endlessly quarrelling in the Muses' birdcage."[143]

Where I suspect he would have felt most alien from the Alexandria of later myth is in the solipsistic sexual phantasmagoria that proved so potent a stimulus to Forster, Cavafy, and Durrell (or, for that matter, to Callimachus). Despite Hephaestion (whom Cavafy, for one, would have dismissed as the most stunning of square bores), despite the Persian eunuch Bagoas, so tantalizingly romanticized by Mary Renault, Alexander would surely have found the "great wine-press of love," not least its too-seductive dregs, both repellent and terrifying. In a moment of unguarded candor, he once declared that he was never so conscious of his own mortality as when asleep or in the act of sex.[144] Offered two beautiful boys, he asked the donor what shameful quality he had perceived in his king that he should make such foul proposals. Soldiers guilty of rape he ordered put to death "as wild beasts born for the destruction of mankind." Persian women he described as "irritants to the eyes."[145] So much for Justine, Durrell's child prostitutes, and the seedier denizens of the Rue Lepsius. Perhaps, had Alexander lived, the city he founded at the crossroads of East and West might have assumed a different character. Perhaps: but at heart I doubt it. The melting pot of all nations proved as mythically durable as its founder, even throwing up, in Cleopatra VII, a figure whose brilliance and charisma matched Alexander's own. Only by turning back to Egypt could the multiracial spell be broken: and for that the city had to wait over two millennia.[146]

---

143. Timon of Phlius fr. 60 Wachsmuth, cited by Athen. *Deipnos.* 1.22d: πολλοὶ μὲν βόσκονται ἐν Αἰγύπτῳ πολυφύλῳ | βιβλιακοὶ χαρακῖται ἀπείριτα δηριόωντες | Μουσέων ἐν ταλάρῳ.

144. Plut. *Alex.* 22.6: ἔλεγε δὲ μάλιστα συνιέναι θνητὸς ὢν ἐκ τοῦ καθεύδειν καὶ συνουσιάζειν. Cf. *Mor.* 65F, 717F.

145. Plut. *Alex.* 22.1, 4; 21.10: ἀλγηδόνες ὀμμάτων αἱ Περσίδες.

146. I record with grateful thanks the generous help I have had in the preparation of this paper from my friend Professor Diana Delia, who put her great knowledge of Alexandria—and her re-

Afterword (2002)

Since this essay was written (early 1993), there have been extensive, and much-publicized, underwater excavations in and around the Great Harbor of Alexandria. These have not to date (2001) added all that much to our knowledge of the city; but they have confirmed, in the most striking fashion, the Ptolemaic passion for gigantism. The best-known find has been a colossal royal torso (11.4 tons in weight), probably of Ptolemy I or II, to which the head has since been added. Other retrievals have included a female statue and several sphinxes, all on a huge scale, as well as giant blocks from the Pharos lighthouse. An excellent illustrated record of these discoveries is available in *Alexandria: The Sunken City* (written by William La Riche, photographs by Stephane Compoint/Sygma [London, 1996]): the photographs make up for a quite stupefyingly cute text. The more recent hoopla about "Cleopatra's palace" scarcely merits discussion. There is one reference only in ancient literature to the tiny island of Antirrhodos recently excavated by Franck Goddio: Strabo 17.1.9, which merely credits it with "a palace and small harbor," βασίλειον ἅμα καὶ λιμένιον, but makes no mention whatsoever of Cleopatra. It is also made clear in context that the main palace complex was elsewhere, on the mainland behind the Lochias promontory. But Goddio (who must know this perfectly well) has to keep up public interest for funding purposes: hence the hoopla, as well as his popular book *À la recherche de Cléo* (Paris, 1996) and Laura Foreman's *Cleopatra's Palace* (Del Mar, Calif., 1999), to which he contributed the foreword, and which in 2000 appeared in a French translation.

---

markable collection of rare or inaccessible Alexandrian scholarship—freely at my disposal. Naturally she is not to be held responsible for any of my errors or wilder flights of fancy.

10

The Muses' Birdcage, Then and Now

IN 1980, Mary Lefkowitz contributed to *ZPE* a paper entitled "The Quarrel between Callimachus and Apollonius," of which the main thrust was that the quarrel, like snakes in Iceland, was a latter-day fiction.[1] The following year she published a volume on the *Lives of the Greek Poets*, from which it became clear that, in her opinion, virtually all the surviving biographical material about these Hellenic literary figures was invented, for want of genuine information, by Hellenistic critics, working primarily from the poets' own texts.[2] The climate of opinion was exactly right for such a thesis. The "biographical fallacy" had been trashed by a nucleus of influential scholars, and others, spotting a trend, were quick to sign on. The age of the persona had come, bringing with it license to discount authorial intention in any shape or form—and, as an extra benefit, freedom to float the most bizarre critical fantasies without fear of contradiction. More insidiously, those who preferred to position themselves immediately behind the cutting edge of research (rather than leading it) were presented with that most precious of gifts for the intellectually lazy—a rule of thumb well-suited to general application. Lefkowitz's findings about the lives of Greek poets gave them a dogma that required no serious critical sifting of evidence, but rather a presupposition of nonsense. Even better, its deconstructive, negative nature offered the unearned intellectual cachet that too often attends skepticism of any sort. In short, it was irresistible.

Note: Originally composed as a contribution to a formal discussion of Alan Cameron's *Callimachus and His Critics,* under the auspices of the Classical Association of the Midwest and South, Boulder, Colorado, March 1997, and subsequently published, with modifications, in *Arion* 6.2 (1998): 57–70.

1. M. R. Lefkowitz, "The Quarrel between Callimachus and Apollonius," *ZPE* 40 (1980): 1–19.
2. M. R. Lefkowitz, *The Lives of the Greek Poets* (London, 1981).

Obviously, the older the poet, the easier the thesis is to maintain. Homer, Hesiod, and most of the lyric poets are pushovers. But as time goes on, and record-keeping improves, the axiom behind Lefkowitz's argument—that no one at the time cared about poet X or Y's life, thus forcing a later generation of the curious to raid the persona or invent blatant fairy-tales—becomes harder to sustain. Did these people never learn? Was there not even enough local, civic, or familial interest to provide material for an obituary? What became of all the funeral encomia? When Herodotus claimed to have written so that the great deeds of men should not become ἐξίτηλα, pass from knowledge, were poets excluded from the canon? Surely not. Indeed, in one case we can see the process of commemoration at work. The so-called Archilocheion, the shrine on Paros dedicated to Archilochos, contained a long inscription concerning the poet's life and work, which (just as we might expect) offers a nice blend of fantasy and fact.[3]

Further, as time went on, and better records were kept, and widespread interest began to develop in αἴτια—origins as well as causes—it would seem reasonable to assume that more reliable evidence began to be collected. After all, if earlier generations of poets had frustrated latter-day knowledge-seekers, would the latter not be doubly careful to document their own contemporaries, and save scholars still unborn from such desperate measures as they had sometimes been forced to take themselves? It was Hellenistic Alexandria that spearheaded the movement to retrieve the Greek past: how odd if it had displayed no interest in its own present! Thus Lefkowitz, and now Cameron,[4] have had to face a decidedly tricky challenge when they set out to discredit, not only the supposed facts of Apollonius's life, but every detail of his alleged literary quarrel with Callimachus. For a period where unshakable evidence is hard to come by, skeptics can without trouble cast doubt on most specifics: their real difficulty comes when they try to discount general patterns or trends. To take the most obvious example: μέγα βιβλίον, μέγα κακόν. It needs (and, I may say, it gets) some remarkably disingenuous casuistry to eliminate the obvious conclusion that, whatever else he might also have had in mind, Callimachus was targeting contemporary epic.

When we look at Cameron's *Callimachus and His Critics*, it becomes apparent that a large part of this immensely erudite book is devoted to countering objections to Lefkowitz's thesis. No one could accuse Cameron of pulling his punches, or holding back from outsize radical solutions. To take one obvious

3. F. Lasserre, *Archiloque: Fragments* (Paris, 1958), cv–cvii.
4. A. Cameron, *Callimachus and His Critics* (Princeton, 1995).

example: his answer to μέγα βιβλίον, μέγα κακόν—apart from assuring us (ix-x) that Callimachus's "tongue was firmly in his cheek" when he wrote it— is simply, as far as he can, to expunge epic altogether from the high Hellenistic period: if it didn't exist, Callimachus couldn't possibly have been attacking it. *Jam yesterday, jam tomorrow, but never jam today:* epic was there from Homer to Antimachos; it was there again in the Greco-Roman period—indeed, *ad nauseam*, as Juvenal (among others) reminds us, in the opening lines of his first Satire—but somehow, so conveniently for Cameron's argument, under the early Ptolemies it went into near-total temporary eclipse. Why then, we may wonder, did the Romans, in their eager (not to say slavish) pursuit of Greek literary models, pick up and develop such an unfashionable non-starter? What, indeed, did Apollonius imagine he was at when he wrote the *Argonautika?* If this epic poem was an anomaly, a reversion to the past (and in fact, despite its Callimachizing attempts at modernism, it may well have been), then it was all the *more* likely to be savaged by hostile critics. What Cameron in fact has provided here is an extra argument (even though a false one) *in favor of* the quarrel in which he so firmly refuses to believe.

Epic poetry (considered for a moment in social rather than literary terms) lay at the very heart of the ongoing debate between *mythos* and *logos*. It is sometimes assumed by intellectuals that the arrival of *logos* will always be welcome, that *mythos* is simply awaiting enlightenment. Nothing could be further from the truth. Heart long remained in stubborn resistance against head: *mythos* persisted against all odds. The archaic worldview it represented was dangerous, baffling, and wholly unpredictable; it stressed—perhaps more realistically than Anaxagorean confidence in man-the-measure-of-all-things —human helplessness, ἀμηχανία, against nature and divinity. That ἀμηχανία formed so prominent a feature of Jason's make-up in the *Argonautika* was no accident. Meanwhile poets, historians, and mythographers anxious to "save the appearances" were forced either to explain away or to reinterpret those elements of each *mythos* which seemed incompatible with the demands of sophisticated *logos*. The two ways they found of doing this were rationalization and allegory: the first dealt with physical or historical impossibilities, the second with matters morally repugnant or embarrassing to the new urban middle classes.

Epic, Homer above all, was vulnerable here. It preserved the great mythic cycles. It made no distinction whatsoever between the mythical and the historical, treating both as unquestioned fact, the cumulative legacy of the past (something that renders Cameron's distinction between historical and mythical epic otiose). It thus catered not only to antiquarians but also to the great mass of thinking (and in Alexandria, expatriate) Greeks who sought validation for their culture. Since the mythic tradition formed the prime source for that validation, not least through systematic aetiological enquiry, an open avenue existed by which scholars as well as poets (many, of course, were both) could explore and develop the genre in literary terms. Yet there were serious objections. The acknowledged supremacy of Homer meant that any modern epic would be relentlessly measured against the *Iliad* and the *Odyssey*. At the same time, as was all too clear, the heroic world, with its values, had gone forever. Besides, the current taste for epigrammatic concision was sure to discourage would-be Homeric epigonoi. Quasi-secular rationalism could not but find the whole divine apparatus of epic—those disconcertingly anthropomorphic Olympians, paranormal phenomena like the Clashing Rocks, the Cyclops, or Aiëtes' fire-breathing brazen bulls—both artificial and embarrassing. Even were there no evidence whatsoever for a fundamental conflict between the Callimachean school and the author of the *Argonautika*, it would still be necessary to postulate its existence.

It is true, and a fact that Cameron exploits to its full extent, that our evidence for the existence of other Hellenistic epic poets than Apollonius, let alone for their texts, is woefully inadequate. Yet that does not, of course, mean per se that such poets never existed, and about some of them we do have a little evidence. Antimachos of Colophon, an earlier poet who flourished about 400, seems in many ways (glosses, neologisms, *variatio*, obscure allusions, erotic elegy) to have anticipated the scholar-poets of the mid-third century. He wrote an epic *Thebaïd*, and his two-book elegy *Lydē*, composed in memory of his mistress, and dealing with unhappy love-stories, contained in Book 1 an account of Medeia and the Argonauts' expedition that surely influenced Apollonius's portrayal of Medeia in *Arg.* 3.[5]

Apropos the *Lydē*, and Callimachus's undoubted dismissal of it as "fat," we have an excellent example of Cameron's favorite forensic device: the confident assertion that readers are left to digest without further argument (337): "So there was no great dispute about different types of poetry; no battle between traditional epic and modern poetry; between bad, boring long poems and elegant, witty brief ones. Just a few contemporaries who disagreed about one particular poem. Epic had nothing to do with it. The debate about Antimachus centered on his elegy the *Lydē*. There is no reason to suppose that even Callimachus disapproved of his epic *Thebaïd*." There isn't? Presumably

---

5. R. Wyss, ed., *Antimachi Colophonii Reliquiae* (Berlin, 1936), frs. 56–65. See now the new edition of V. J. Matthews, *Antimachus of Colophon: Text and Commentary* (Leiden, 1996).

this is why Cameron so casually dismisses, unquoted, a key article by Vessey,[6] who argues that if Callimachus disliked the *Lydē*, a fortiori "he is likely to have had an even lower opinion of the *Thebaïs*, which he must have regarded as an example of that hated genre τὸ ποίμα τὸ κυκλικόν." There is no reason to think that he would have thought otherwise about contemporary writers of epic.

Here, as I say, the trouble is lack of evidence, though perhaps the lacuna isn't quite as great as Cameron would like us to think. Of Rhianos of Crete's *Herakleias*, or a *Thebaïd* by Antagoras of Rhodes, it is true, we know only enough to whet our curiosity for more. Rhianos wrote local quasi-historical epics, such as his *Messeniakà*: both he and Antagoras, interestingly, produced erotic verse as well as epic, a versatility that must weaken Cameron's claim that the debate was exclusively over elegy.[7] Even more interestingly, Dionysios Skytobrachion, an exact contemporary of Apollonius[8] — but, except for three brief casual references, ignored by Cameron — produced an *Argonautika* (summarized at length by Diodorus, 4.40–56) that ruthlessly rationalizes the myth throughout, and is, in fact, just what we would expect a Callimachean intellectual to approve. The contrast with Apollonius is immediate and striking. Ziegler, indeed, argued that the Callimachean movement, far from being representative of mainstream thinking (the average reader preferred epic anyway), was a mandarin aberration, and only much later, under Neoteric influence, actually achieved the position of authority to which, in the mid-third century, it had briefly aspired.[9] No wonder Cameron trashes him.[10]

Cameron asserts flatly (264) that "both quarrel and controversy are entirely modern inventions." This is not the only claim in his book that fails to match up to the evidence. Though the *Suda* is regularly trawled for useful (i.e., supportive) evidence, but briskly dismissed as late and untrustworthy when it records evidence at odds with the theory *du jour*, the entry on Callimachus (its format suggesting derivation from Hesychius of Miletus) contains the following comment on one title in a list of Callimachus's works: "*Ibis*, a poem of deliberate obscurity and abusiveness, directed against a certain Ibis, who had become Callimachus's enemy: this person was Apollonius, the author

---

6. D.W.T.W. Vessey, "The Reputation of Antimachus of Colophon," *Hermes* 99 (1971): 1–10; quotation from p. 3.

7. Green 1997, 19.

8. J. S. Rusten, *Dionysius Scytobrachion*, Papyrologica Coloniensia, 10 (Opladen, 1982), 93–101.

9. K. Ziegler, *Das hellenistich Epos: Ein vergessenes Kapital griechischer Dichtung*, 2d ed. (Leipzig, 1966), 13.

10. See, e.g., Cameron 1995, 264 with n. 10.

of the *Argonautika*."[11] A specific enough assertion, this, to require the usual last-ditch refutation: that the words constitute a parenthetical interpolation (along with forgery, the favorite recourse of a classical theorist in trouble). Sure enough, Cameron, following Hutchinson,[12] makes the predictable claim. It does not carry conviction.

As we have seen, there is every a priori reason for assuming (at the very least) a fundamental difference of opinion here. The reason for the hostility is not stated, but there is a strong chance of it having been literary. That such feuds were common in the Museum we might have guessed, and Timon's famous squib confirms it (even if we accept Cameron's mildly *outré* suggestion that what τάλαρος really means isn't a wicker cage but a bird's nest): "In the polyglot land of Egypt many now find pasturage as endowed scribblers, endlessly quarrelling in the Muses' birdcage."[13] Callimachus himself, imitating Hipponax (and, like him, presumably on the principle of "Don't do as I do, do as I say"), urged scholars to eschew mutual jealousy.[14] But, as Pfeiffer observes, what with "free meals, high salaries, no taxes to pay, very pleasant surroundings, good lodgings and servants," there was "plenty of opportunity for quarrelling with one another."[15] Leisure, combined with the arbitrary uncertainties of royal patronage, must have made backbiting and paranoia endemic.

Despite the vast amount of scholarship generated by this topic, direct testimony for what Callimachus actually *disliked* in Hellenistic literature is limited. There are three main items of evidence that, taken together, offer a fairly consistent picture: lines 105–14 of the *Hymn to Apollo;* the partly fragmentary preface (1–38) of the *Aitia,* attacking the "Telchines" (malevolent mythical dwarves here representing literary opponents); and a much-discussed six-line epigram (28 [30] Pfeiffer) on the theme of distaste for what is "base, common, or popular."[16] There are a few other hints—for example, the last

11. Suda s.v. Καλλίμαχος (no. 227 Adler): Ἶβις (ἔστι δὲ ποίημα ἐπιτετηδευμένον εἰς ἀσάφειαν καὶ λοιδορίαν, εἰς τίνα Ἶβιν, γενόμενον ἐχθρὸν τοῦ Καλλιμάχου· ἦν δὲ οὗτος Ἀπολλώνιος, ὁ γράψας τὰ Ἀργοναυτικά).

12. G. O. Hutchinson, *Hellenistic Poetry* (Oxford, 1988), 86–87.

13. *Ap.* Athen. 1.22d: πολλοὶ μὲν βόσκονται ἐν Αἰγύπτῳ πολυφύλῳ | βιβλιακοὶ χαρακῖται ἀπείριτα δηριόωντες | Μουσέων ἐν ταλάρῳ. Athenaeus specifically identifies the target of Timon's satirical comments as the Museum intellectuals.

14. Fr. 191 Pfeiffer, *dieg.* 6.2ff.

15. Pfeiffer 1968, 97.

16. 28 [30] Pfeiffer = *AP* 12.43. Since Cameron (1995, 387) makes much of the supposed scholarly preference for simply citing the first five words of this epigram, I append it here in its entirety:

ἐχθαίρω τὸ ποίημα τὸ κυκλικὸν, οὐδὲ κελεύθῳ
　χαίρω τίς πολλοὺς ὧδε καὶ ὧδε φέρει·
μισέω καὶ περίφοιτον ἐρώμενον, οὐδ᾽ ἀπὸ κρήνης

line of one epigram (8 [10] Pfeiffer) wittily closes with a six-syllable word, βραχυσυλλαβίη, meaning "brevity"—but these three texts form the basis for all argument.

"All that's commonplace makes me sick" (σικχαίνω πάντα τὰ δημόσια) is the epigram's central message: the targets include—fact merging into literary metaphor—not just indiscriminate lovers, as Cameron suggests, but also public fountains, over-populated highways, and "cyclic" poetry. Popularity, in short (a perennial academic tenet, this), is suspect. The avoidance of well-trodden roads is a theme that recurs in the preface to the *Aitia* (25–28), as advice from Apollo. Also, a poet should chirp like the cicada, not bray like the ass (29–32); poems should not be measured by their length or loudness (15–18). The "Telchines" mutter (ἐπιτρύζουσιν) against Callimachus because he has not written one sustained epic, many thousands of lines in length, about kings or heroes (3–5), but instead turns out short poems, like a child (5–6), and is a man of few lines (ὀλιγόστιχος, 9). The cryptic postscript (105–14) to *Hymn 2* has Envy (Φθόνος) whispering to Apollo (106): "I do not admire that poet whose utterance lacks the sweep and range of the sea"—to which Apollo replies, with a contemptuous kick (ποδί τ' ἤλασεν), that a river such as the Euphrates may have a vast current (μέγας ῥόος), but it also carries down a mass of silt and refuse; whereas Demeter's priestesses bring her, not just any water, but only (111–12) that "thin trickle, the ultimate distillation (ἄκρον ἄωτον), pure and undefiled, that rises from the sacred spring."

The general message is clear. Callimachus is advocating three fundamental qualities in poetry: brevity, originality, and refinement, whether of style, language, or form. He is criticized for not having produced a "major" or "substantial" work (not the same as an accumulation of αἴτια). Bulk, he replies, means dross and (the donkey's bray applies here) vulgarity of utterance. How far can this be taken as directed against epic in general, Apollonius in particular? The "cyclic poem" (τὸ ποίημα τὸ κυκλικόν) might be thought specific enough; but critics have not been slow to remind us that κυκλικόν also carries the secondary meaning of "commonplace," "conventional," even "platitudinous."

On the other hand, Callimachus (as the same critics emphasize) had an exquisite ear for the *mot juste*, and cannot have set up so striking a verbal ambiguity by accident. The message, conveyed with pregnant brevity, is: epic = cliché. Theocritus (7.45–48) scorns those who try to rival Homer. It is epic,

---

πίνω· σικχαίνω πάντα τὰ δημόσια.
Λυσανίη, σὺ δὲ ναίχι καλὸς καλός· ἀλλὰ πρὶν εἰπεῖν
τοῦτο σαφῶς, ἠχώ φησί τις "ἄλλος ἔχει."

too, thousands of lines long (5,835 to the *Argonautika*), that at *Aitia* 3-5 Callimachus is reproached by the "Telchines" for not writing.

This judgment would have remained comparatively simple were it not for the existence of the Florentine scholia (Pfeiffer vol. 1:1-3), where several of the "Telchines" are identified, and a little fitful light is shed on the kind of critical debate, if not literary in-fighting, that went on between members of the Alexandrian intellectual coterie. The problem, of course, is that nowhere in the Florentine scholia or related material is there any specific mention of Hellenistic epic, let alone of Apollonius. The genres discussed are elegy and epigram. Cameron makes the most of this *argumentum ex silentio:* far more, in fact, than it deserves. If Callimachus thought it preferable, as clearly he did, to write short rather than long poems (not excepting the *Aitia*, which is simply a string of short poems masquerading as a long one), it is not only in the field of elegy that this preference will apply—even though he may well have picked that genre when defending himself against the specific charges brought by "Telchines" such as Asklepiades and his friends. It is also worth recalling that, according to one scholiast,[17] Callimachus wrote the *Hekale* in response to those who derided his inability to compose a lengthy work. There seems no compelling reason to doubt this. From the numerous surviving fragments it becomes apparent that to attain even this length (no more than one book of the *Argonautika*), Callimachus resorted to a whole series of individual anecdotes and *aitia* concerning both protagonists, and indeed other mythical figures (e.g., Erichthonios and the daughters of Cecrops, fr. 70 Hollis = 260 Pfeiffer).

The evidence, then, suggests that the tradition of literary dissension between short poems (personal, aetiological) and long ones (heroic, mythical) was in fact genuine. If Callimachus included epic (the "cyclic poem" in its basic sense) among the types of long poem to which he objected, then Apollonius, as by far the most distinguished living exponent of the genre, must have figured as one of his targets for scorn. If Callimachus approved of a contemporary *Argonautika*, the odds are very long that it will have been the trendily rationalizing version by Dionysios Skytobrachion. The tradition of Callimachus having composed a derisive poem attacking Apollonius under the name of Ibis thus makes perfectly good sense. Did his victim strike back? It would seem so. We have an epigram ascribed to Apollonius,[18] composed in the form of two mock encyclopedia entries: "*Callimachus:* Trash, cheap joke, block-

---

17. Schol. Callim. *H.* 2.106.

18. *AP* 11.275 = Callim. *test.* Pfeiffer 25: Καλλίμαχος· τὸ κάθαρμα, τὸ παίγνιον, ὁ ξύλινος νοῦς· | Αἴτιος· ὁ γράψας Αἴτια Καλλιμάχου.

head. *Original Sin:* Writing Callimachus's *Origins.*" Despite Cameron's argument that "this crude and feeble piece" (his words, 227) is irrelevant, doesn't fit the situation, turns on a mere pun, and (last-ditch argument again) must be the work of some other Apollonius, I see no reason not to treat it as genuine. That the two men would be at odds over the viability of epic poetry is certain.

Finally, the matter of Apollonius's life.[19] It is my contention that the evidence, scanty though it is, enables us to construct a reasonable and consistent *vita* for Apollonius, which neither Lefkowitz nor Cameron has succeeded in disproving. Using this evidence, I maintain that Apollonius, son of Silleus and Rhodē, was an Alexandrian by birth, of the Ptolemaïs tribe, and thus probably the first native-born Alexandrian poet (though his family may have moved to Alexandria from Naukratis). Since he flourished under Ptolemy II Philadelphos—a point to which I shall return—and had Callimachus as a teacher, perhaps when the latter was still a *grammatikós* in the Alexandrian suburb of Eleusis (i.e., before 285), he will have been born c. 305. Thus his precocious, and unfortunate, public reading of what ended as Book 1 of the *Argonautika* will have taken place—if the term "youth" (ἔφηβον) be strictly interpreted— when he was between eighteen and twenty, that is, at some point between 285 and 280, while he was still attached, as student or assistant, to Callimachus. It was after this, late in the day (that ὀψέ, in context, is highly ironic), that he decided, for now, to concentrate on poetry rather than scholarship, and removed himself to Rhodes for that purpose.

Rhodes left its mark on the *Argonautika*. Rostropowicz[20] has shown how much knowledge Apollonius's epic reveals of navigation, maritime life, shipbuilding, and nautical expertise in general. The Rhodian shipyards were the most famous in the Mediterranean, their fleets kept the seas safe, and their famous maritime laws were passed on to Rome and the Venetian Republic. On Rhodes, Apollonius completed his *Argonautika*, after carefully revising Book 1 (fragments of the prior draft of which survive embedded in the scholia), pursued a distinguished teaching career, took part in public life, and achieved a position of some literary eminence. All this took time. The *terminus ante quem* for his return to Alexandria had to be the inception of his tutorial duties with the future Ptolemy III Euergetes. The boy was born between 288 (the year of his father's marriage to Arsinoë I) and 275. He cannot have been less than twelve or more than fifteen when assigned his tutor. Thus we are looking

---

19. Green 1997, 1–8.

20. Joanna Rostropowicz, "The *Argonautica* by Apollonios of Rhodes as a Nautical Epos: Remarks on the Realities of Navigation," *Eos* 88 (1990): 107–17.

at a date not earlier than 273 and possibly as late as 260, with the earlier period a great deal more likely. If Apollonius emigrated to Rhodes in the period 285–280, he will have spent at least thirteen, and more probably up to twenty, years on the island. He could easily have turned forty—a more than acceptable age for such honors—when he made his triumphant return, to be appointed by Ptolemy II both royal tutor and director of the Library. I would suggest a date c. 265.

There followed a long period of uneventful success and productiveness. It will have been during these years that Apollonius wrote foundation poems on the origins of Alexandria and Naukratis, and an aetiological poem entitled *Kanobos*, just as during his Rhodian residence he had similarly composed works about Caunos, Cnidos, and Rhodes itself. He was equally busy in his capacity as a Museum scholar, with critical works on Homer (including a monograph attacking Zenodotos, the Library's first director), Hesiod, and Archilochos. This career was only ended in 246, when on his accession Ptolemy III summoned Eratosthenes from Athens to take over the directorship. There was no question of his old tutor being dismissed, let alone exiled. Apollonius had served with distinction for twenty years, was now in his sixties, and had earned an honorable retirement. If there is any truth in the tradition that after he died (probably in the 230s) he was buried beside Callimachus, that suggests not—as has been romantically inferred—a reconciliation between the two men, but rather the existence of a private cemetery for the directors and other distinguished members of the Museum and Library community.

There are undoubted difficulties and contradictions in our testimonia, but these tend not to be as impossible as they are generally made out. Take the matter of Apollonius's *floruit*. Most manuscripts of *Life* A state that he lived "during the reign of the Ptolemies," ἐπὶ τῶν Πτολεμαίων. This is generally rejected as being, in Hunter's words, "too obvious to need saying."[21] If so, why was it said? In fact "the Ptolemies," plural, are, and can only be, Ptolemy II Philadelphos and his sister-wife Arsinoë, the "Sibling Gods" (Θεοὶ Ἀδελφοί), the first and by far the most famous of the dynasty's incestuous royal couples, regularly portrayed together on both gold and silver coinage. Wendel, however, emended the text to read ἐπὶ τοῦ τρίτου Πτολεμαίου, thus bringing it into agreement with the *Souda* article,[22] which makes Apollonius a coeval of Ptolemy III, and the successor, rather than the predecessor, of Eratosthenes as director. The obvious explanation of this discrepancy (apparent

21. R. L. Hunter, *Apollonius of Rhodes: "Argonautica" Book III* (Cambridge, 1989), 1 n. 3.
22. *Souda* s.v. Ἀπολλώνιος, no. 3149 Adler [1:307].

from a comparison with P. Oxy. 1241[23]) is that the writer of the *Souda* article confused our Apollonius with Apollonius the Classifier (εἰδογράφος), also an Alexandrian, but of a later generation. Yet Cameron and others regard not only P. Oxy. 1241 as more reliable evidence than the rest, which is reasonable, but also the *Souda* article, which most certainly isn't. Why should they do this? I rather suspect it may have something to do with the long, acrimonious, and largely pointless debate about the relative originality of Callimachus, Apollonius, and Theocritus. A late date for Apollonius would be a godsend for scholars specializing in this kind of *Quellenforschung*. Set him in the 270s and, as the record makes all too plain, it is impossible to prove which of these poets influenced the others. Shift him down into the 230s, and a large part of the problem vanishes. It is striking, but perhaps not surprising, how many of the arguments about Apollonius's life are susceptible to this kind of *parti pris* interpretation. It is, after all, one of the few ways available to discredit the existing evidence.

What *is* surprising is how often Cameron's flat assertions turn out to be not quite right. He stresses (217) that both *Lives* place the composition of the whole *Argonautika* in Alexandria: in fact, both state that the poem's final completion was accomplished on Rhodes. He also tells us that "the Lives do not bring Apollonius back to Alexandria: he leaves Alexandria as a youth and spends the rest of his life in Rhodes." In fact, *Life* B records the tradition of his return and subsequent elevation. Endeavoring to muddy the waters by claiming that this Rhodian Apollonius was in fact a later (120 B.C.) sophist from Alabanda, Cameron supports his claim by insisting that *Life* B's statement about Apollonius being "active in public affairs" and lecturing on rhetoric would be "absurd for the poet."

But Alexandria virtually invented the scholar-poet, and since when have poets been debarred by definition from politics or civic activism? This kind of argument, I'm happy to report, sometimes backfires. Though he goes to ingenious (if unconvincing) lengths to deny that Callimachus started life as a suburban schoolmaster, casts literary doubts (in sharp contrast to Wilamowitz) on his putative homosexuality, and makes him out to have been, *qua* general's grandson, a Royal Page at court during his adolescence, Cameron doesn't join Rudolf Blum in claiming that he held the directorship of the Library. Why not? Because, he tells us, "the Oxyrhynchus list [P. Oxy. 1241]

---

23. P. Oxy. 1241, col. ii (published as *The Oxyrhynchus Papyri*, edited by Grenfell and Hunt, pt. 10 [London, 1914], 99ff.) is a fragmentary text containing part of a *catalogue raisonné* of successive directors of the Alexandria Library. The first name here (preceded by a half-column lacuna) is that of our Apollonius; the last is that of Aristarchus. The names are, clearly, listed in chronological order. See Green 1997, 4–5 for a translation and discussion.

has proved that [Callimachus] was never chief librarian" (11). But in fact, as even a photograph makes clear, it does nothing of the sort. At least half a column is missing before the crucial passage, and anything could have been in the lacuna.

Other arguments smell unmistakably of the bottom of the barrel. The statement in *Life* B that Apollonius "was found worthy (ἀξιωθῆναι) of the Museum's Libraries," clearly refers to his appointment as Librarian (it had earlier been used of his enrollment as a Rhodian citizen); yet Cameron prefers Pfeiffer's uncharacteristically weak (and weakly supported) claim that it meant the admission of his works to the Library's holdings—something for which inclusiveness, not merit, was the criterion.[24] Sometimes he bites his own tail: "The series of Egyptian poems," he informs us (215), "lends no support to the claim of an early departure from Alexandria." Indeed they do not, being written, as we have seen, after his return; and since Apollonius very probably never left Alexandria again, this is not too surprising. Sometimes evidence is abandoned altogether, and dismissive derision has to do the work of reasoned argument: the notion of Rhodian influence on the *Argonautika*, for example, is simply brushed aside (263) as the acme of extravagance.

What comes over most clearly in all this is that the negative thesis comes first, and the evidence is either slanted, trimmed, or, if necessary, ignored in order to advance it. Texts are credible or rejected primarily depending on whether they support or contradict it. The trouble with theories in a case like this is that they are never fully demonstrable. There is always the temptation to appeal to common sense, or rely on dogmatic assertion, when the evidence runs out. Cameron is no more immune to this temptation than the rest of us. I lost count of the times when he comes up with phrases like "obviously," "undoubtedly," "unlikely," "it would not be surprising if," "easy to see why," "something approaching certainty," "it can hardly be coincidence," "we may reasonably assume," "must surely have been," etc., etc.—all the familiar labels of persuasive rhetoric. We are both of us arguing, in the last resort, like good Greek orators, on the basis of probability, ἀπὸ τοῦ εἰκότος. I cannot prove my thesis beyond doubt; but then, Cameron cannot disprove it either, only *say* he has, in the hope—not always vain in this world—that his readers (like those of F. R. Leavis) will be alternately charmed and bullied into mistaking mere assertion for proof.

He enjoys, of course, the double advantage of putting a case that not only is negative (thus earning him automatic credit for skepticism), but that also

---

24. Pfeiffer 1968, 141–42, 284–85.

surfs, as I suggested in my opening remarks, on the wave of a contagious new academic theory. In exactly the same way, a surprising number of anthropologists have, in the last few years, bought into the notion, against a mass of evidence, that cannibalism is, and was, a nonexistent fantasy of the colonial mind:[25] as an intellectual concept, not quite up to Holocaust-denial standards, but well on the way. The lies-not-lives epidemic currently spread through the study of Greek poets is small beer by comparison, but the psychological pattern is identical.

---

25. See *Lingua Franca* 7.4 (1997): 28–38.

II

How Political Was the Stoa?

THE EFFECTIVE relationship between philosophy and politics, between social theory and social practice, between ideology and action, has always been one of the most fiercely debated topics in the history of ideas (or, for that matter, in our ideas of history). Are poets and thinkers, as Dr. Johnson and Shelley argued, the world's true (if unacknowledged) legislators, the force shaping human conduct and conflicts? Or are they product rather than cause, rationalizing the phenomena of a world over which they have no control: at best, diagnosing its symptoms, at worst, providing intellectual justification for political cynics anxious to cut a good figure in the court of public opinion? How far, in other words, is the development of philosophical thought (in the broadest sense) autonomous, and how far the by-product of a historical process largely immune to conscious control by planners, sages, philosopher-kings, revolutionaries, poets, *et hoc genus omne?* The question obviously transcends academic considerations, yet at the same time is rooted in them, since academics themselves tend (not surprisingly) to be *parti pris* in their answers: philosophers assume autonomy as an article of faith, while historians are far more likely, as T. W. Africa puts it, to regard "the notion that ideas are efficacious in politics" as "a comforting illusion in a world of self-interest and endemic folly."[1]

Thus the appearance of a book, *The Hellenistic Stoa: Political Thought and Action* (1990), by Andrew Erskine, that sets out to examine the political thought of the Stoics "from Zeno, its founder, through to its emergence in Rome," and to do so, moreover, "in its historical context and so explore the

Note: Originally published in *Ancient Philosophy* 14 (1994): 147–56.
1. In his review of Erskine 1990, *AHR* (1991): 1514.

interaction between thought and events," is both rare and extremely welcome. So is its author's determination "to trace how what began as a radical doctrine came to be so closely identified with the Roman establishment" (1–2), one of the more tantalizing paradoxes of Hellenistic history. Philosophers, trained to examine problems *sub specie aeternitatis*, in terms of timeless logic, tend to be natural anti-Heracleitans when it comes to history, insensitive to, and often impatient with, those temporal perspectives silently conditioning everything from war to lovemaking, from the most abstract concepts to the very language in which those concepts are expressed.

Andrew Erskine has the training and background to avoid such pitfalls. *The Hellenistic Stoa* is a revised version of the Oxford D.Phil. thesis he wrote under George Forrest and P. S. Derow, and he himself is a former Lecturer in Ancient History at the University of Birmingham, currently [1994] teaching in University College, Dublin. But in the event a very odd thing has happened. After bringing his philosophers into the historical marketplace, Erskine proceeds to let them take it over. For him, whether in the Chremonidean War, the Spartan reforms of Cleomenes III, or even the agrarian program sponsored by Tiberius Gracchus, it is, each time, some back-room Stoic *éminence grise*— a Sphaerus, a Blossius—who emerges as the true broker of events, the agent of historical change. Philosophers, therefore, especially those with a weakness for the kind of romantic radicalism so popular in *les ans entre deux guerres*, are likely to be predisposed in favor of this book, and their chief complaint will probably be the one already voiced by Stephen A. White,[2] that Erskine "tends to exaggerate the influence of political and economic pressures and to underestimate the importance of philosophical argument." On the contrary: if we really want to know what inspired Zeno's radicalism, and—equally important—what made the Middle Stoa increasingly back off from such views in the direction of authoritarian conformism, then we need not less about the "political and economic pressures," but a good deal more.

Some of the major factors Erskine does acknowledge. In a preliminary section on "The Political Background" (33–42), subsumed to his analysis of Zeno's *Politeia*, he mentions, *inter alia*, the impact of Alexander of Macedon and the Diadochi, which left Athens "redundant as an independent political force" (34); the instability and class polarization of the city-states, leading to social unrest and calls for redistribution of land and the cancellation of debts; and the corresponding fear, among the propertied classes, of revolution from below—circumstances exacerbated by rising prices and static, or

2. *Journal of the History of Philosophy* 30 (1992): 296.

even falling, wages. But he only remembers these facts when it suits him, and never examines them, as we shall see, against the longer perspective of Greek history. His emphasis throughout is on the reconstruction of Stoic political thought (from late, tendentious, and, too often, scanty sources) as a consistent, rational, *democratic* instrument of policy and advice, crucially influential on the direction that, at various critical junctures, events in the Hellenistic world were to take.

There is something *déjà vu*, indeed decidedly old-fashioned, about such an approach: we are back in the innocent meliorist world of the Conflict of Ideas, the world of G. B. Shaw and the Webbs, of utopian fable. One is also put in mind of the romantic Marxism fed by this tradition, which flourished in the 1920s, and saw Cleomenes III as a revolutionary idealist (a fiction memorably enshrined by Naomi Mitchison in her haunting novel *The Corn King and the Spring Queen*). Erskine's treatment of the third-century "Spartan revolution" in fact offers an excellent test case for studying his methodology in general. His thesis (123) is "that it was Stoicism which gave the Spartan revolution its coherency and potency." To maintain this, he must counter the more generally accepted view (with which I am in substantial agreement) "that the Spartan revolution can be explained in terms of Spartan tradition and consequently there is no need to introduce philosophy" (131). The way he goes about proving his case is instructive.

To begin with, he argues that Plutarch's account of Agis IV's revolutionary career in fact draws on the later program of Cleomenes, retrojecting the latter in order to fill out the inadequate record presented by earlier sources. This at one stroke throws doubt on the nature of Agis's activities, and provides the "Cleomenean revolution" with extra ideological back-up. Now, it is quite true that Plutarch shows the two kings behaving in a very similar way (though the natural conclusion from this, surely, is that both were pursuing the same goal, rather than that one account is a doublet of the other). Both claim the quasi-mythical Lycurgus as their model,[3] with a wealth of traditional lore; critics also—significantly, as we shall see—are cited as faulting Cleomenes for his imitation of Solon in the matter of debt cancellation.[4] Both (again with Lycurgus as justification) argue for the authority of the kings over the ephors—hardly, one would have thought, a democratic attitude.[5] Both, above all, repeatedly stress what Erskine sees as social *égalité* in the full revolutionary sense.[6] I shall return to this in a moment.

---

3. Plut. *Ag.* 10, 19; *Cleom.* 10, 16, 18; *Comp.* 2.
4. Plut. *Cleom.* 18.
5. Plut. *Ag.* 12; *Cleom.* 10.
6. Plut. *Ag.* 6, 7, 9; *Cleom.* 2, 7, 8.

Now taken at its face value, Plutarch's *Life* of Agis IV shows a leader utiliz-
ing the abolition of debts, the reestablishment of a landed fighting elite, and
aggressive military action,[7] in order to restore Sparta's lost glories. Erskine's
source analysis is calculated to discredit this evidence: he even suggests that
Agis's telltale promise of land allotments to his soldiers "seems to owe more
to a Roman tradition than a Greek one," and that even if he did cancel debts,
this "may be derived from the Spartan custom of cancelling debts to the king
and treasury on the accession of a new king" (130, 131 n. 25, citing Hdt. 6.59).

What is the point of so systematic an attack? Obviously, to discount a
perfectly clear and coherent tradition, in which only by thoroughgoing historiographical casuistry can the goal of militaristic revival be ignored, and the
dream of high-minded Stoic-inspired egalitarianism promoted. To observe
this process in action we need look no further than the passages of Plutarch
adduced in support of "equality." We should never forget (though Erskine
does so to the best of his ability) that the basis of Sparta's original military reforms lay in the establishment of an elite body of privileged warrior-
citizens (Spartiates)—equals (ὅμοιοι) only in a limited, and decidedly Orwellian, sense—who had passed through the rigorous training-program known
as the ἀγωγή, were supported by the produce of their estates or allotments
(κλᾶροι), and served the state all their adult lives as a uniquely constituted
professional fighting force.

After the terrible defeat at Leuctra (371 B.C.) and the consequent loss
of Messenia as a free granary worked by serf labor, Sparta fell to the level
of a second-class Peloponnesian power: the ὅμοιοι (whether forfeiting their
κλᾶροι, and status, through poverty, or because of a general decline in the
birth-rate) steadily dwindled, the ἀγωγή was discontinued, and the bulk of
Spartan territory, κλᾶροι included, fell into fewer and fewer hands (including
those of women), until perhaps not more than a hundred families virtually
divided all Lacedaemon between them. To remedy this appalling state of affairs, to restore Sparta's lost glories—not least through redistribution of the
land to a new, debt-free, body of ὅμοιοι—became a national obsession that
existed long before Agis's attempt to realize it, and was continued after the
death of Cleomenes: for example, by Nabis, on whose activities Erskine (using
tainted sources, once again, as the excuse for *recusatio*) is somewhat less than
forthcoming.

All this should be borne in mind when we examine the claims made here
for Cleomenes, in particular, having carried the banner of social *égalité* in (and
indeed beyond) Sparta, since ἰσότης forms the linchpin of Erskine's argu-

7. Plut. *Ag.* 14.

ment. Agis's aim (Plut. *Ag.* 6) was ἐξισῶσαι καὶ ἀναπληρῶσαι τὴν πόλιν, that is, to restore the citizen-body to its old strength and equality.[8] This clearly means the restoration of the ὅμοιοι and the ἀγωγή, and is confirmed, in the same passage, by the military-athletic enthusiasm of the young men, who συναπεδύσαντο πρὸς τὴν ἀρετήν, "stripped off together in pursuit of glory." The oracle that ordained this equality, on the basis of Lycurgus's original law (Plut. *Ag.* 9), was directed, specifically and exclusively, τοῖς Σπαρτιά-ταις. At *Cleom.* 2, ἰσότης is once more mentioned as part and parcel of ἀσκή-σεως . . . καὶ σωφροσύνης νέων καὶ καρτερίας, that is, life as organized for the old-style Spartan warrior. At *Cleom.* 7 and 18, equality, both of the person and of property (τῇ τῶν κτημάτων ἐξισώσει), is directly linked to "the recovery of Sparta's national *mores*" (πατρίων ἐθῶν) and educational system, its ultimate objective being to win back the leadership of Hellas (ἐπὶ τὴν Ἑλλάδος ἡγεμονίαν) and regain control of the Peloponnese. In other words, what both Agis and Cleomenes sought was national regeneration through a return to Sparta's ancient warrior code. The abolition of debts, the redistribution of land, the slogan of ἰσότης—all this was aimed at the reestablishment of the ὅμοιοι as a crack fighting force that would win back Sparta's old dominant role in Greece. Idealistic notions of general equality played no part in it whatsoever. Such a thesis is no more tenable than Erskine's confident assertion (145) that "the idea of equality . . . had no basis in earlier concepts of old Sparta." What sort of equality, and for whom?

This still leaves the question of whether Agis and Cleomenes availed themselves, even incidentally, of Stoic ideas, whether for their dream of national resurgence or for any other purpose. We know from Plutarch (*Cleom.* 2) that as a young man (μειράκιον) Cleomenes studied philosophy with Sphaerus, who had come to Sparta—because of its tradition of anti-Macedonian activity, Erskine tendentiously suggests (99)—for the purpose of teaching "the young men and ephebes," τοὺς νέους καὶ τοὺς ἐφήβους. But what did he teach them? Not, almost certainly, politics, least of all egalitarian socialism (which would have gotten him deported in short order by the Spartan authorities), but more probably general moral principles: "preaching against fear, anger and cupidity, in favour of self-control and philanthropy,"[9] subjects compatible with his treatises on Duty and Kingship.[10]

But he also wrote on Lysander and Socrates, and the history of the Spartan constitution, which at once suggests why[11] Cleomenes solicited his help in the

---

8. Plut. *Ag.* 8.
9. F. H. Sandbach, *The Stoics* (London, 1975), 141.
10. Diog. Laert. 7.178.
11. Plut. *Cleom.* 11.

restoration of the ἀγωγή: Erskine is almost certainly right in his suggestion (137) that Sphaerus served the king as an antiquarian expert on Sparta, supplying him with ancient traditions based on historical research. It is far from clear what else he could have done, and the fragments about him collected by von Arnim[12] offer little scope for speculation. Plutarch (*Cleom.* 2) very plausibly suggests that Sphaerus—like Tyrtaeus before him—aimed to encourage Cleomenes and the youth of Sparta in manliness (τὸ ἀνδρῶδες) and noble ambition (φιλοτιμίαν). They would be filled (as their ancestors had been by Tyrtaeus's martial poems) with enthusiasm for battle, and be made reckless of their lives in a great cause. Such evidence fits excellently into a military scheme for national regeneration, but is somewhat lacking in the doctrines of idealistic socialism.

At one level, I suspect, Erskine (perhaps subconsciously) knows this very well. It is surprising how often, in mid-argument, he will make a crucial admission out of the corner of his mouth, so to speak, and then hurry on as though nothing has happened: for example, that the reforms "emphasised and strove for absolute equality, *albeit of a limited number*" (132, emphasis mine), or that the weight attached to youth and physical strength in the admission of citizens was because these men "were to make up the Spartan army" (141). In the same spirit, while, in pursuit of his elusive social ideal, he must needs have Cleomenes at least attempt to export ἰσότης beyond the confines of Sparta (no revolution without proselytization!), he has to admit, "There is no statement in the sources that Cleomenes did intend to introduce social and economic reforms outside Sparta, only that people thought he would" (148). Argos, for example,[13] reversed its allegiance to Cleomenes when the populace (τὸ πλῆθος) found that the Spartan was not carrying out the cancellation of debts (χρεῶν ἀποκοπάς) that they had hoped for. Obviously a case of wishful thinking. But for Erskine, far from showing that Cleomenes had no *intention* of spreading ideological revolution through the Peloponnese at large, this episode merely proves that in the event he was *unable* to. You can't keep a good idealist down.

At this point it may be desirable to take some of the phenomena specifically associated by Erskine with the influence of Hellenistic Stoicism, and restore them to that wider historical context where they more properly belong. In the case of the Spartan reforms, what is not traceable to Lycurgan tradition seems to derive from Solon: the emphasis on equality harks back to the famous apothegm (Plut. *Sol.* 14) that "equality breeds no war," τὸ ἴσον πόλεμον οὐ

---

12. *SVF* 1:139–42, nos. 620–30.
13. Plut. *Cleom.* 20.

ποιεῖ (as indeed also to Cleisthenic ἰσονομία), while the cancellation of debts and redistribution of land (χρεῶν ἀποκοπὴ καὶ γῆς ἀναδασμός) formed the slogan not only of Solon's dispossessed, but of every other Greek populist movement thereafter. Nor was the fear that Cleomenes' activities engendered throughout the Peloponnese—among property-owners and *bien-pensants* generally—anything new. Indeed, the League of Corinth in Philip II's day stipulated ([Dem.] 17.15), among other things, that there should be "neither reallotments of land, nor cancellations of debts, nor the freeing of slaves for the purpose of revolution," μηδὲ γῆς ἀναδασμοί, μηδὲ χρεῶν ἀποκοπαί, μηδὲ δούλων ἀπελευθερώσεις ἐπὶ νεωτερισμῷ,[14] and a similar provision forms part of the treaty (302 B.C.) between Demetrius Poliorcetes and the Hellenic League.[15]

Thus Erskine's conclusion (149)—despite these references, which he knows—that second-century Stoics went conservative in reaction against Cleomenes' ideological fervor falls to the ground: they were, rather, part of a widespread sociopolitical trend that had begun much earlier, and on which the influence of the Stoa was minimal if not nonexistent. If Sphaerus used Stoic notions of concord (ὁμόνοια) to justify what Agis or Cleomenes were doing, it was not in a mood of general egalitarianism: ὁμόνοια was strictly for the ὅμοιοι. Similarly, what fueled the Chremonidean War was not so much Zeno's putative ideas about freedom and concord as entrenched anti-Macedonian prejudice and the well-worn inflammatory rhetoric of Panhellenism. Indeed, Stoicism got more from Sparta than it gave: Spartan *mores* had always heavily influenced the Stoa's concept of the ideal state.[16]

This tendency to exaggerate possible Stoic influence while ignoring or downplaying other far more obvious ideological sources is most striking when Erskine comes to discuss arguments justifying the Roman empire. Stoic theories of subordination (ὑπόταξις) can only be pressed so far. When Dionysius of Halicarnassus advises the Greeks to resign themselves to Roman domination, "since it is a law of nature common to all . . . that the stronger always rules the weaker" (φύσεως γὰρ νόμος ἅπασι κοινός . . . ἄρχειν ἀεὶ τῶν ἡττόνων τοὺς κρείττονας),[17] it is not, I would submit, Stoic ὑπόταξις that first comes to mind (even if Dionysius "had some familiarity with Stoic concepts," 202), but the Melian Dialogue. Thucydides was an author whom we know Dionysius read with the closest attention, as his long critical essay on that historian

---

14. [Dem.] 17.15.

15. L. Moretti, *Iscrizioni storiche ellenistiche*, vol. 1 (Florence, 1967), 107, no. 44, fr. ii, lines 44–45.

16. See, e.g., Plut. *Lycurg.* 31; cf. Diog. Laert. 7.172, Athen. 16.681c.

17. Dion. Hal. *Ant. Rom.* 1.5.2.

demonstrates. What we have here is a direct and conscious echo, not of some Stoic theory, but of the Athenians' famous argument that "the powerful exact what they can, and the weak yield what they must."[18] Similarly, P. Rutilius Rufus had no need of "the Stoic theory of empire" (203) to enlighten him on Rome's moral obligations to its subject allies: for this the *mos maiorum* was perfectly adequate.

What, we have to ask ourselves, is going on here? Erskine is a highly intelligent and well-read scholar, with a sharp talent for source analysis (even if the talent is too often employed in the systematic discrediting of those testimonia which cannot be forced into conformity with his arguments). But like any right-thinking liberal anxious to make a political case for the Stoa, he has to deal with several awkward, and at times embarrassing, factors. (1) Greek intellectuals as a whole, Stoics included, tended to stay out of practical politics; and when they did become involved (Critias in Athens, Plato in Sicily, Demetrius of Phaleron in Athens, Cercidas in the Peloponnese), they showed themselves either inept, or dictatorial, or both. (2) Stoics in particular seem to have had a marked weakness for royal patrons: Aratus and Persaeus served Antigonus Gonatas, Sphaerus in turn Ptolemy III, Cleomenes, and Ptolemy IV; even Blossius's patron, the rebel Aristonicus, called himself Eumenes III and was arguably a legitimate pretender to the Attalid throne. Chrysippus listed kings as a proper source of income (*SVF* 3:693). (3) Zeno's *Politeia*, that sustained exercise in utopian polis-trashing (abolition of law-courts, temples, religious statues, marriage, private property, gymnasia, and coinage; group sharing of women; sanctioning in certain circumstances of incest and cannibalism), took, and takes, almost as much explaining away as the moral hypocrisies of Seneca. A tradition that begins, on the face of it, in disruptive anarchism and ends as the quasi-official, indeed the divinely sanctioned, instrument of Roman imperial *auctoritas* presents a stiff challenge to any radical sympathizer.

Erskine's solution is to assert, with what one can only describe as breathtaking insouciance, that "the whole tenor of Stoic thought inclined towards democracy" (72). Says *what*? To compound the paradox further, he apparently identifies "democracy" with the kind of anarchic utopianism preached by Zeno in the *Politeia*. Far from discounting this work, as was done even in antiquity,[19] as a mere youthful aberration, Erskine spends much time and ingenuity arguing that, on the contrary, the *Politeia* represents Zeno's mature thinking (the early date being asserted later as a sop to Middle Stoa embarrass-

---

18. Thuc. 5.89: δυνατὰ δὲ οἱ προύχοντες πράσσουσι καὶ οἱ ἀσθενεῖς ξυγχωροῦσι. Similar sentiments appear at 105.2 and 111.4.

19. Philod. 9.1–6; Diog. Laert. 7.4.

ment), and continued to influence his successors, Cleanthes and Chrysippus included, for longer than is usually assumed.

If he is right, if Zeno did indeed continue to promote this anti-polis utopia throughout his adult career, then we have a new problem on our hands. Why should the Athenians, whose obsession with polis government was still intense, who were civic-minded and litigious to a fault, have taken Zeno so completely to their hearts? They entrusted him—quite exceptionally for a foreigner—with the keys of the city. They voted him a statue and a gold crown. They built him a tomb at public expense in the Kerameikos (as they did later for Chrysippus, but then Chrysippus had acquired citizenship). The text of the decree authorizing these expenditures survives, and cites his moral influence on the youth of Athens "toward virtue and moderation" (ἐπ' ἀρετὴν καὶ σωφροσύνην).[20] This does not (to put it mildly) suggest teaching based on the *Politeia*. Erskine, rightly, rejects the story that the Athenians were strongarmed into honoring Zeno by Antigonus Gonatas;[21] but then he is skeptical of *any* evidence linking Zeno to the Macedonian court, preferring to treat him as a source of Athenian democratic inspiration, for which the evidence is equally shaky. Not all the circumstantial anecdotes about Zeno and Antigonus can be dismissed out of hand: Antigonus was, after all, the nearest thing to a genuine Stoic ruler around, and it would be surprising, in the circumstances, if the two men had *not* been on friendly terms. Zeno may have refused, in the interests of peace and quiet, ἡσυχία, to join the Macedonian court; but he had no hesitation about sending Persaeus in his place.[22]

The political and ideological history of the Hellenistic Stoa that Erskine draws for us is thus consistently slanted: *all, all of a piece throughout.* What we are presented with is a radical utopian movement, firmly grounded in rational theory, and influencing the course of events on that basis. If these thinkers associate with kings, it is to bring them, by precept and advice, to wisdom. The program is seen as egalitarian and democratic, with true ἰσότης as its goal, and best exemplified in the revolutionary aims of Cleomenes, formed under the guidance of Sphaerus. Even the fundamental shift in outlook, toward property-conscious conservatism, legal rather than moral justice, exhibited by the Middle Stoa, is made, we are told, on the basis of "arguments which had developed as a reaction to the Spartan revolution" and "were adopted in Rome to counteract the Gracchan propaganda" (161), itself (of course) Stoic in origin. The vulgar thought that Greek philosophers might simply be trim-

---

20. See Diog. Laert. 7: §6 (keys of the city), §1 (statue and crown), §182 (public tomb, cf. Paus. 1.29.15), §§11–12, 15 (decree).

21. Diog. Laert. 1.15.

22. Diog. Laert. 7.6.

ming their sails to suit the new dominant wind of Roman law and Roman officialdom does not find mention.

In this tidy intellectual world, despite Erskine's concession (2) that "the philosopher is engaged in constant interaction with the society in which he lives," society loses every round. Herbert Spencer's famous apothegm, that "opinion is ultimately determined by the feelings, and not by the intellect,"[23] keeps coming to mind. Furthermore, when the Stoa really *did* begin to have an impact on public conduct, under the Romans, it offered, at best, a panacea for those suffering permanent ὑπόταξις, and at worst, a handy anodyne to the conscience of the rich and powerful, anxious for guilt-free moral uplift while also reaping the rich practical rewards of ambition. It was, unfortunately, not the last time that philosophy was thus to prostitute itself in the political arena (the present century can offer some particularly odious examples), and Erskine, not surprisingly, ends his study with a survey of early justifications for empire, before things got really out of hand.

One of the most intriguing things about *The Hellenistic Stoa* is the way in which Erskine, at bottom a most thorough and systematic researcher, continually supplies the evidence with which to refute his own theories. Throughout these pages, the political and social upheavals of the Successor kingdoms and the residual city-states again and again cast their silent shadow over the narrative, making nonsense of the well-articulated rational *Begriffsgeschichte* in which we are asked to believe. Behind the move away from the polis toward some kind of ideal society grounded in universal law and "natural concord," ὁμόνοια κατὰ φύσιν (22), we glimpse the despair engendered by anarchy and defeat. At a theoretical level Erskine knows this: "Political thought is surely susceptible to influence from the political conditions of the time" (33). But, one imagines him adding to himself, not all *that* susceptible. Very plausibly, he argues (38) that "what prompted Zeno to highlight *eleutheria* [freedom] in his treatment of the ideal society was its emergence as a major policy issue at the close of the fourth century." Just so; but *why* did it become an issue? Surely by being lost. You don't miss it until it's gone. We should remember, too, that though Zeno posited a classless society as his ideal, it remained true that, for Stoics, "freedom is only freedom if it is correctly used and this requires wise men" (39). Small wonder that from the Peloponnesian War onward, ἐλευθερία was "considered as desirable only for the upper classes." The link between this kind of thing and the Stoa's later comfortable adaptation to Roman rule seems not to have struck Erskine at all.

His historiographical principles, though, are impeccable. I am sure he

---

23. H. Spencer, *Social Statics* (London, 1850), pt. 4, ch. 30, §8.

really believes (2) that "philosophers are not separate from society but part of it and consequently, whether they are analysing or rejecting contemporary society, the nature of their analysis or rejection is conditioned by the form of that society, its values and its beliefs." *Fabula de te narratur,* the cynic might mutter: is it entirely coincidental that books like this and Doyne Dawson's recent *Cities of the Gods: Communist Utopias in Greek Thought* (1992), with their safe emphasis on theoretical models, have begun to appear at exactly the same time as the final discrediting of communism as actually practiced in the former Soviet empire and Eastern Europe? In any case, Erskine's conclusions too often stand the theory on its head. Both the *simplisme* and the lurking social danger of some Stoic thinking seem to elude him. In ways, Zeno sounds like a child playing "Let's pretend." The world is full of knaves and fools? Then create a society restricted to σοφοί. Class conflicts are tearing society apart? Abolish classes! What about debt cancellation and land redistribution? Simple: ban coinage and private property. And so on. As for the danger, a world where the wise man's λόγος was in harmony with that of the universe, microcosm with macrocosm, comforting though such a concept was, opened the way for that fixed hierarchy of rule which afterward proved so useful in buttressing the eternal authority of Rome (Erskine does not explore the political ramifications of Stoic cosmology). Worse, if slavery "is a result of the moral badness of men" (55), then it is no surprise to find the later Stoa evolving comfortable maxims about being kind to your slaves, and a "hierarchy of subordination" did not come amiss when justification of the social status quo was called for.

On the details of specific argument, often skillfully extrapolated from a variety of opaque, recalcitrant, or misleading late sources, Erskine is at his best—the discussion of Stoic ideas about property and justice (103–22) offers an excellent example of this—and perhaps the most lasting value of *The Hellenistic Stoa* will be as an exhaustive critical survey of testimonia. But in its historical analysis, it remains compromised by its political and social idealism (which consistently misreads the testimony so painstakingly gathered), and its constant over-valuation of the effective force exerted by philosophical ideas on the rough-and-tumble world at large—a world that obstinately remains so messy, so unpredictable, so regrettably in thrall to violent prejudice and irrational inconsistency, so oblivious to the dictates of sweet reason.

Perhaps, though, it is just as well that politicians in real life take so little notice of abstract ideas, and tend to get them wrong when they do, since the results are as often as not both authoritarian and unpleasant (e.g., Nazi borrowings from Plato's educational system), and worse still when intellectuals themselves are in the driver's seat. Clever brains are far from indifferent to the lust for power: they enjoy bossing the world for its own good, and have no shortage of blueprints from which to work. Further, the habit of thinking exclusively in abstract terms (as revolutionaries and authoritarians throughout history have demonstrated in horrifying detail) anesthetizes one's mind against the raw realities of life and death. No accident that both Robespierre and Lenin killed human beings like flies in pursuit of theoretical ideals. George Orwell, who understood this kind of thing very well, stingingly rebuked Auden for writing, in his famous poem "Spain," apropos the life of a Party member, about "the conscious acceptance of guilt in the necessary murder," remarking that the line could only have been written by someone to whom murder was just a *word*. That comment (which, incidentally, drove Auden to emasculate the line in subsequent editions) passed through my mind more than once when studying Erskine's book, into which it is tempting to read, as subtext, a political cautionary tale—though not, I would guess, one that the author intended.

12

Ancient Ethics, Modern Therapy

MY OLD FRIEND Anthony Burgess, canny Catholic and one of the sharpest moral dialecticians ever to grace a saloon bar, used to argue that the Western world moved in recurrent twin cycles, liberal and puritan, which he
labeled Pelphase and Gusphase, after their respective theological patrons,
Pelagius and Augustine. It has seemed to me for some while now that the
United States is well into a new round of Gusphase, something not fully appreciated by the perennially Pelagian media. The political successes of the
religious right, including such sleaze-factors as the Falwell tapes and Ollie
North's Senatorial candidacy, didn't happen in a vacuum. The broth is cooking nicely. In particular, the country is waking up to a still rather dozy and
elementary interest in moral ethics. Michael Faye gets his buttocks opened
up by four slashes from a wet rattan cane, and property owners everywhere
howl approval. Bill Bennett puts together an anthology of Victorian copy-
book maxims and just-so snippets, calls it *The Book of Virtues: A Treasury of
Great Moral Stories*, sells about a million copies, and hits *The New York Times*
best-seller list for five months.[1] It seems a fair assumption that if this move-

---

Note: Originally published in the *New Republic*, 5 Sept. 1994, 38–42.

1. *2002 postscript:* Only eight years on, but already in another world, where Falwell, North and
Co. look quaintly old-fashioned by comparison with what's been going on lately. The Bill-and-
Monica imbroglio offered us, for the price of a single spectator seat, (1) a President of the United
States whose compulsive urge to get himself blown on a regular basis outstripped even the most
elementary rules of self-protection; (2) a special prosecutor, with unlimited funds and powers,
whose zeal to upset (1) was so powerful that, frustrated on the financial front, he pursued a non-
criminal act between consenting adults to the point where the domestic white lies associated with
such behavior were elevated to the status of perjury and obstruction of justice; and (3) a media-
cum-political elite apparently incapable of distinguishing this sordid but hyped-up peccadillo from
those "high crimes and misdemeanors" required to justify presidential impeachment. Meanwhile
the American public at large, schoolchildren included, retained a reassuring sense of proportion

ment has already acquired *nouvelle vague* status, somewhere or other there's going to be an intellectual surfer riding the wave and hoping to look like a trendsetter.

I was therefore more than a little intrigued when first confronted with Martha Nussbaum's book, *The Therapy of Desire: Theory and Practice in Hellenistic Ethics*, since the title, ambiguous though it was (desire *as* therapy? therapy *for* desire?), looked as though she might be opening up an area of investigation that—as I'd found during my own researches—bore a decidedly unsettling resemblance to our own problems, weaknesses, and preoccupations today. In particular, the popularity of Stoicism struck me then, and still does, like all really popular philosophies, as decidedly suspect. Too much of it, in ethical terms, seemed to consist, if you were a have-not, of reconciling your lot with the idea of a benign but immutable authority, and if you were a have, of formulating moral principles that would let you enjoy power and wealth while paying lip-service to virtue. It thus proved a godsend to ambitious Roman politicians (Seneca being a particularly egregious example), who had their political cake and ate the moral icing, too: in the end, the unchanging Stoic cosmos became, to all intents and purposes, identified with the Roman empire.

In a rather different way, Epicureanism was, is, equally unsettling. What we see here is an early version of the ideological-cum-religious commune, a group that simultaneously rejects, while still depending on and battening off, society at large. Like so much in the Hellenistic Age, this phenomenon has worrisome parallels in the modern world, from uncontrolled financial scams (the Bhagwan's Rolls Royces, Jim Bakker's misapplied millions) to pathological authoritarianism (Jonestown, Waco). "Act always," Epicurus instructed his followers, "as though Epicurus is watching": there is a Big Brotherish flavor about Epicureanism. It has been described as "the only missionary philosophy produced by the Greeks" (De Witt 1954, 26), and with its rules, its dogma, its Forty Principal Doctrines, its Pauline-style letters, its feasts in memory of

---

over the whole affair. If they're the gallery these exhibitionists were playing to, they were (to put it mildly) not impressed. What we are confronted with here is a historical myth of hurricane strength in the making, and as such it more than merits a place in these pages.

Of course, since then we have moved worlds yet again. 11 September 2001 was a true, and horrific, landmark in historical awareness, dividing past from present as surely as C.E. from B.C.E. Whether it was fortunate that it coincided with a Gusphase-prone, at times indeed Armageddon-minded, government will long be debated. There have been few sources of real unintentional amusement in officialdom since (by its very nature relentless gung-ho dead-or-alive patriotism is short on humor), but the figleaf-minded John Ashcroft's decision, as Attorney General, to spend $8,000 of public funds in draping a large partially nude statue that hardly anyone had even noticed before came, to my mind, as a most welcome diversion from more serious matters.

the Savior-Founder, one can see why. "Live unnoticed" (λάθε βιώσας) was the key slogan, and with the ample contributions of well-heeled supporters, this was not too difficult: there is no record of anyone in the community actually working, and theories about the Garden being a retreat for have-nots are seriously misleading.

One thing, however, that Stoicism and Epicureanism—indeed, just about all Hellenistic philosophies—had in common was their prime declared goal: the abolition of pain, worry, or, as we would tend to say, stress. This emerged in negative form: the key word was *ataraxia, absence* of worry, the initial *a*-being a privative particle, which attached itself to various other subsidiary ideals, such as *aponia,* absence of toil, and *alypia,* absence of grief. Politically and socially, this is revealing to a degree. What does it say to us? The world is a horrible place. Public involvement is useless. Turn inward—if you have the income—and cultivate your soul or your garden. You cannot change this post-Alexander mess of impotent city-states, giant bureaucratic kingdoms, and the inroads of early Megalopolis. So learn to adapt, work at microcosmic level, study to heal your soul. The malaise seems to have been ubiquitous. Epicurus's obsession with the idea of pleasure as relief from pain may have been dictated in part by his own chronic gastroenteric disorders, but it was also symptomatic of his age: like most philosophies, Epicureanism was in the first instance a by-product of social forces rather than itself a force for change.

It is this therapeutic aim of Hellenistic ethics, this desire to relieve humanity's ingrained suffering, that Nussbaum sets out to analyze. At first sight her book conveys some worrisome symptoms. To begin with, there is the dust-jacket. The front consists of a fine photograph of boulders and trees—the latter both living (richly green) and dead (bare-bones white)—against a blue sky. Very nice, but what's the relevance? "A depiction," we're told, "of some of the Senecan imagery of the Stoic world and Medea's 'countercosmos'." Excuse me? In her acknowledgments, Nussbaum glosses this as

> the contrast between a pure white that is linked with death and a green that grows up darkly indefatigably behind it; between clean straight lines and messier shapes of life; between the unsullied blue sky and the strange hot light that cuts straight through both sky and tree, a light coming, as it were, from Medea's countercosmos, set over against the world of Stoic virtue.

Such posturing imagism is neither philosophically sound nor poetically valid: the only proper place for it is Pseuds' Corner in *Private Eye.* Further investigation leads us to an overheated meditation on Seneca's *Medea* entitled "Serpents in the Soul" (*sic:* one begins to think of *The Devil and Miss Jones*), at the climax (oh yes) of which

> the serpent Jason, twining in ecstasy around his partner, moves him-
> self, winged, reborn, beyond the gods, beyond the Stoic universe in
> which gods dwell everywhere. Deep in the cosmos . . . there now ap-
> pears a flickering hot light, an irregular, snaking motion. We are wit-
> nessing a triumph. It is the triumph of love.

It is? Even Seneca, whose perfervid imagination fueled some of the most lurid Jacobean fantasies, might have gagged on this essay in cosmic erotica; and the picture of Jason as pious moralist (*sic*, again) that introduces it can only con-firm all our worst fears about Seneca's Stoic hypocrisy. Add to this a chorus of rave blurbs from distinguished philosophers (who, let's face it, are not quite like the rest of us); epigraphs from Karl Marx telling us that "this world is the world of the head" and from Wallace Stevens philosophizing that "not to have is the beginning of desire" (*reculer pour mieux sauter?*); plus a note that the royalties are going to Amnesty International (clearly not even Camille Paglia's fulminations dented that particular fashion for moral self-advertisement)— and the temptation, as Dorothy Parker said, not to lay this book aside but to throw it with considerable force becomes almost irresistible.

It should, nevertheless, be resisted. Despite her prolixity and occasional preciousness, despite the sense that she's basically writing for an in-group of high-minded admirers (are there such creatures as philosophical groupies? if so, Nussbaum's more likely than any philosopher I can think of to have them), nevertheless this long and complex book sets out to ask fundamental questions, and on that account alone demands our serious attention. I'm not too happy about the (all-too-familiar) declared motive—there turn out to be others, too—for undertaking it: Nussbaum wants to assuage her intellectual guilt at enjoying the leisured life not only by contributing to approved causes (e.g., AIDS action committees or Amnesty International), but also by using philosophy to ameliorate the lot of those less fortunate than herself. Since that was exactly what a number of Stoic thinkers were after (though some might call it an exercise in quietening the conscience in order to maintain an enjoyable status quo), one can see the attraction of such a topic.

It also may partly explain why Nussbaum stretches the definition of "Hel-lenistic" to include the Romans Cicero, Lucretius, and Seneca, as well as the medical theorist Sextus Empiricus (second century A.D.). The standard argu-ment (employed in this book) is that these late or non-Greek authors form a crucial source for working out the thought of lost earlier thinkers, both Stoic and Epicurean. True enough; but the Greco-Roman era also happens to be much richer in persuasive reasons for not meddling with the divinely established order of things. We hear a lot about the proper definition of slavery, for instance, and the humane treatment of slaves, but virtually no argument in favor of abolition, least of all on moral grounds: Aristotle put the hard truth in a nutshell when he argued that if tools could perform their own work, then (and only then) would there be no need of slaves.[2] In other words, it wasn't ethics (Stoic, Christian, or other) that led to abolition but, quite simply, the development by the Industrial Revolution of efficient servo-mechanisms, which then allowed thinkers the luxury of a conscience.

Nussbaum, a realist at heart despite herself, is well aware of such problems:

> Even among the Stoics, whose commitment to the intrinsic value of justice is plain, we hear less about how to alter the political fact of slavery than about how to be truly free within, even though one may be (politically) a slave; less about strategies for the removal of hunger and thirst than about the unimportance of these bodily goods in a wise life; less about how to modify existing class structures and the economic relations that (as Aristotle argued) explain them, than about the wise person's indifference to such worldly distinctions.

She is also worried by the antisocial implications of *ataraxia*, by arguments that "do not so much show ways of removing injustice as teach the pupil to be indifferent to the injustice she suffers," by the soft-pedaling of material conditions and political change, by the lack of genuine social commitment. Perhaps because of this she tends, I think, to over-estimate such social ideas as Hellenistic thinkers did in fact promote; and this is doubly unfortunate, because most of them enjoyed a decidedly checkered afterlife, being implemented, with singular lack of imagination or humanity, by communist ideologues. No accident that Karl Marx's doctoral dissertation was on Epicurus.

Nussbaum is a passionate idealist. What she cherishes is "the idea of universal respect for the dignity of humanity in each and every person, regardless

---

2. Arist. *Pol.* 1253b33f.: καὶ ὥσπερ ὄργανον πρὸ ὀργάνων πᾶς ὑπηρέτης· εἰ γὰρ ἠδύνατο ἕκαστον τῶν ὀργάνων κελευσθὲν ἢ προαισθόμενον ἀποτελεῖν τὸ αὑτοῦ ἔργον, ὥσπερ τὰ Δαιδάλου φασὶν ἢ τοὺς τοῦ Ἡφαίστου τρίποδας, οὕς φησιν ὁ ποιητὴς αὐτομάτους θεῖον δύεσθαι ἀγῶνα, οὕτως αἱ κερκίδες ἐκέρκιζον αὐταὶ καὶ τὰ πλῆκτρα ἐκιθάριζον, οὐδὲν ἂν ἔδει οὔτε τοῖς ἀρχιτέκτοσιν ὑπηρέτων οὔτε τοῖς δεσπόταις δούλων.

"And every servant is as it were a tool replacing tools; for if each tool could carry out its work when ordered, or by prior perception (as the tale is told of Daedalus's creations [mobile robots: see Plato *Meno* 97D] or the tripods of Hephaestus, which the poet [Hom. *Il.* 18.369] says 'enter the gods' assembly self-propelled'); if thus shuttles were to weave and plectra play the lyre unaided, then works-directors would have no need of assistants, nor masters of slaves."

of class, gender, race, and nation." Whether that is also "an idea that has ever since been at the heart of all distinguished political thought in the Western tradition" remains debatable—depending, I suppose, on what you mean by "distinguished." She claims, correctly, that it's Stoic in origin. The trouble is the company it has kept from Zeno's day onward, including the theoretical abolition (fortunately not put into practice until after 1917) of just about everything that sustains Western society as we know it, from private property to the nuclear family, from religious faith to the currency. An authoritarian society run from scratch on the basis of intellectual abstractions is going to be not merely inefficient but also frigid; and since planners can deal more easily with paper concepts such as the elimination of undesirable elements than with organized genocide (though some manage that, too), it follows that revolutionary theorists, from Robespierre to Lenin and Pol Pot, can murder thousands without turning a hair. I doubt if Zeno or Chrysippus or Epicurus ever dreamed of the holocaust that twentieth-century activists would make of their theories; but that dark shadow lies across all their utterances for the modern reader, and no one—least of all Nussbaum, whose aims are educational as well as therapeutic—can afford to ignore it.

To sweeten the pill of philosophical exposition, she has had the attractive idea of picking a known member of Epicurus's circle as her student for instruction, thus infusing a dialectical quality into each debatable proposition. No one, though, could say that her choice was not *parti pris*. We know about this student, Nikidion ("Little Victory" or "Victorietta"), from an anti-Epicurean anecdote by a disgruntled ex-member of the commune, who alleged, *inter alia*, that Epicurus "consorted with" courtesans, and cites their nicknames (e.g., Mammarion, "Big Tits"). Nikidion is in this list. Nussbaum thus has it both ways: the lady is real (the anecdote comes from clearly authentic material preserved by Diogenes Laertius in his *Lives of the Philosophers*), while her alleged status can be dismissed as male slander ("We can see . . . that the beginnings of female philosophizing went hand in hand with the beginning of sexist 'humor' about the character of the women concerned," 45 n. 38).[3] I wouldn't for one moment deny that some women philosophers have had a tough time of it—think of Hypatia, torn limb from limb by a pack of hysterical monks—but somehow I scent a faint whiff of excessive *ad feminam* protest here.

---

3. Diog. Laert. 10.7. The defector's name was Timokrates. Among other charges, he asserts that "among other courtesans who kept company with him and Metrodorus were Mammarion ['Big Tits'], Hedeia ['Sweetie'], Erotion ['Lovey'], and Nikidion ['Victorietta']": συνεῖναι τε αὐτῷ τε καὶ Μητροδώρῳ ἑταίρας καὶ ἄλλας, Μαμμάριον καὶ Ἡδεῖαν καὶ Ἐρώτιον καὶ Νικίδιον.

On the other hand, the moment Nussbaum really gets down to arguing her case, all such complaints vanish. Intellectual penetration is matched by orderly deployment of ideas, crystalline clarity of thought, and a style that— *Deo gratias*—remains uncontaminated by modern philosophical jargon. Better still, she has latched on to an extraordinarily pervasive idea. Epicurus is the star witness: "Just as there is no use in a medical art that does not cast out the sickness of bodies, so too there is no use in philosophy, unless it casts out the suffering of the soul" (Usener 221). (Nussbaum does all her own translations: they're both accurate and non-tendentious, quite an achievement in this area.) But a Stoic like Chrysippus is equally emphatic: yes, there is a therapeutic for soul as well as body, and by no means inferior to medicine. This (as Cicero spelled out) is philosophy. Even the Skeptics hoped to "heal by argument." The metaphor had already been used by Socrates, who thought of himself as a midwife to the soul, and Plato, who similarly nursed hopes of healing the sick body politic (a notion with which Col. Papadopoulos made great play during the Junta years in Greece): something in it for everybody. About the only people not to get in on the act were the Cynics, a counter-culture group hooked on anarchic exhibitionism and panhandling: Nussbaum gives up on them, and small wonder.

For every philosophical sect, as Nussbaum emphasizes, "the medical analogy is not simply a decorative metaphor; it is an important tool both of discovery and of justification" (14). Rival theorists competed for attention in just the same way as their medical exemplars; and anyone who has studied the extraordinary history of the ancient medical schools—Dogmatists, Empiricists, Methodists, and Pneumatists, corresponding roughly in theory to Stoics, Epicureans, Skeptics, and Eclectics—will know just how tangled and complex a skein Nussbaum has set out to unravel. Since all medical practice had a sizable psychosomatic component (witness the ex-voto inscriptions at healing centers such as Epidauros), it is often hard to tell where metaphor ends and medical research begins. A surprising amount of Nussbaum's ancient philosophical evidence reads like modern psychiatry.[4] Now, like then, the driving motive is the urgency of human suffering, and the goal *eudaimonia*, which Nussbaum translates as "human flourishing" rather than "happiness."

That, at least, all could (and, one hopes, still can) agree on. There was also a fair consensus that logically tough reasoning minus human compassion, academic yet nonaffective, was inadequate for the job. Cicero, criticizing the

---

4. The complex competing theories cannot but remind a contemporary reader of the exactly analogous debates in the early 1990s over President Clinton's proposed health plan; if Hillary Clinton really wanted to find out just how deep she'd gotten herself in, this book would be no bad place to start.

Stoa for this (though a better target would have been Plato and his followers), wrote in the *De Finibus* that such "narrow little syllogistic arguments prick their hearers like pins. Even if they assent intellectually, they are in no way changed in their hearts."[5] The problem is fundamental, and still haunts us today.

What we may call the Platonic vision sees ethical norms as absolute— "quite independently of human beings, human ways of life, human desires" (17), simply *there*, perfect and unattainable. Nussbaum reminds us that two versions of this model are still in vogue: one scientific, one religious. Popular belief (undermined to some extent, as she concedes, by recent philosophers of science) sees the scientific study of nature as objective and "pure," uncontaminated by background interests or cultural prejudice. More pervasive is the Augustinian version of Christian ethics (Gusphase again!), according to which God has established absolute moral values independent of the human ability to live up to them. "Truth and God's grace are out there; but the ability to see ethical truth or to reach for grace is not something we can control" (18). It is the despair engendered by such absolutism that, as Nussbaum sees it, therapeutic thinking, armed with the medical analogy, set out to subvert. *The Therapy of Desire* examines the philosophical underpinning of this endeavor, charts the various, and sometimes conflicting, courses it took, and tries to assess their value. She scores a really remarkable success with the first two of these aims; I'm by no means so sure about the third. As a philosopher she'd dearly love the therapeutic to work: but did it?

Here, ironically, it's the medical analogy itself that offers warning signals. To begin with, a great deal of the theory on which it was based was elaborate nonsense, and we have to ask ourselves whether the psychological patterns that Nussbaum extrapolates do much better. The rationalists who exploded superstitious beliefs concerning the so-called Sacred Disease (epilepsy) then rather spoiled the effect by explaining it as the descent of phlegm from the brain.[6] The influential but entirely imaginary doctrine of the Four Humors (not in Nussbaum's index) postulated four cardinal fluids, based on the four elements of matter, as constituents of the human body: blood, phlegm, yellow bile, black bile, one's health depending on their correct proportional balance. Since each represented a psychological type (sanguine, phlegmatic, bilious, melancholic), such considerations were also bound to influence the "therapeutic of the soul."

Further, since many Hellenistic philosophers, Stoics in particular, saw a di-

---

5. Cic. *De Fin.* 4.7: pungunt quasi aculeis interrogatiunculis angustis, quibus etiam qui assentiuntur animo et iidem abeunt, qui uenerant.

6. Hippocr. *Morb. Sacr.* 2, 8–10.

rect and immutable link between the movement of the heavens and all human activity, between macrocosm and microcosm, the regularity of the first was held to imply equal regularity in the second. Hence fatalism, a flourishing trade in astrology, and a tendency to regard existing political institutions (at the time more often than not monarchic, oligarchic, or subject to these) as permanent and unchangeable. Hence, too, of course, that preoccupation with the status quo which so bothers Nussbaum. If you can't change society, then you have to learn to live with it, cultivating your inner resources. Too much therapeutic advice from the major Hellenistic schools is of this nature. Possessions, wealth, status, ambition are unimportant: in his (even in her) soul, the slave can be free. It seems safe to say that such a doctrine would do more for the slave-owner's peace of mind than for that of the slave. Just how ingrained such an attitude was can be gauged from the terms, in both Greek and Latin, for making a revolution (νεωτερίζειν, *res nouare*): both carry the simple literal sense of doing something new, *making a change*.

Thus behind Nussbaum's elaborate, learned, and brilliant exegesis there lurks a socially uncomfortable shadow, which, despite her acknowledgment of the importance of historical context, she never quite succeeds in eliminating. Is it unduly cynical to point out that in 70 b.c., at a time when both Cicero and Lucretius (two of Nussbaum's star witnesses) were toying with the idea of "the creation of a therapeutic community, *a society set over against the existing society* [emphasis mine], with different norms and different priorities," Crassus was busy crucifying some 20,000 rebel slaves along the highway between Capua and Rome, for the heinous crime of having tried to implement just such an alternative society in sober practical fact? Yes, these thinkers have a normative sense of health. Yes, they aim at individual amelioration. Yes, they rigorously scrutinize emotions. Yes, in a sense they show commitment to action—though too often, as Nussbaum knows, this manifests itself in a concern with "correct beliefs and desires," something we are experiencing once more today, and finding a mixed blessing. Yes, they seem to be probing the notion of the unconscious. But—a problem, not surprisingly, much discussed—it often happened that the philosopher worked out a nice general theory of human spiritual ailments, yet somehow failed to cure most of the individuals on whom he'd based it. This (as Nussbaum, again, concedes) was regularly blamed on obstinate patients failing to see the error of their ways.

The at times uncomfortable similarities between the Hellenistic world and our own should not blind us to their even more profound differences, especially since the latter to a very great extent dictated the form that philosophical therapy took. From Plato's Athens to the final convulsive decades of the Roman Republic, civil and interstate warfare—with their antisocial concomitants, brigandage and piracy—had increasingly become the norm rather than the exception. Cicero wrote his philosophical works in retreat from that endemic conflict, and lost his life when he returned to it. Lucretius's great poem reveals the traumatized psyche of one who had witnessed the ravages of too many murderous private armies at close quarters. Even Plato's Theory of Ideas (if we can trust the famous Seventh Letter) seems to have developed as a desperate response to the horrors of democrats and oligarchs at each others' throats.

> Both the letter and the spirit of the laws were being destroyed, and this process was accelerating at an extraordinary rate. . . . [I concluded that] the ills of mankind would never cease until either a race of truly upright philosophers achieved political power, or else, by some divine quirk of fate, our present rulers genuinely embraced philosophy.[7]

Somewhere above the diurnal struggle, absolute truth and goodness had to reside.

Yet at the same time, for the modern student, a distasteful thread of ubiquitous and ingrained class prejudice runs through all the surviving literature. The indifference to, and contempt for, the lower orders is all-pervasive, and is summed up in the dismissive epithet "banausic": descriptive of anything to do with artisans' work or manual labor, hence base, common, vulgar. Thinking was hierarchical to such a degree that Archimedes even found applied science below his dignity. That stony callousness which is the one real perception in Flaubert's otherwise appalling historical novel *Salammbô* derives from the fact that a Greco-Roman minority elite in effect treated the rest of society as nonexistent, or at best on the level of beasts of burden. The ideal was an inherited or otherwise unearned fortune. Work, above all for others, was a social disgrace. Therapy was primarily for one's equals, for those with the leisure, and income, to write, read, or otherwise improve their minds. Insofar as thinkers took cognizance of "the masses" at all, it was, as Plato (that quintessential aristocrat) demonstrated in *The Republic*, to legislate for them *de haut en bas*, or, as too many Hellenistic therapists hoped, to reconcile them to their lot by promoting the inner life. Peace of mind was for one's own class, and was cer-

---

7. Plat. *Epp.* 7.324B–326B, esp. 325D, 326A-B: τά τε τῶν νόμων γράμματα καὶ ἔθη διεφθείρετο καὶ ἐπεδίδου θαυμαστὸν ὅσον . . . κακῶν οὖν οὐ λήξειν τὰ ἀνθρώπινα γένη, πρὶν ἂν ἢ τὸ τῶν φιλοσοφούντων ὀρθῶς γε καὶ ἀληθῶς γένος εἰς ἀρχὰς ἔλθῃ τὰς πολιτικὰς ἢ τὸ τῶν δυναστευόντων ἐν ταῖς πόλεσιν ἔκ τινος μοίρας θείας ὄντως φιλοσοφήσῃ.

tainly not to be gotten by disturbing the status quo. Even the economic ideal was stability rather than growth.

There is also the problem—with which, I don't doubt, a real philosopher would have begun—of whether, even in ethics, philosophy has any business being in the therapy game at all; whether its object, far from understanding and ameliorating human desires or fears, should not rather be to pursue truth, not least in an age when deconstructionists and others are assuring us that truth doesn't exist. Back to Plato again. But then, a good deal of this century's philosophizing has been in pursuit of correct definitions, a theme that Hellenistic thinkers, too, especially Stoics, attacked with some assiduity (e.g., in the matter of slavery). Here the best thing about Nussbaum is her unusual blend of passionate attachment and obstinately open-minded skepticism. Her assessment of Stoic political thought is balanced and shrewd: she gives all credit to its far-reaching *humanitas*, but raps it severely for its dogmatic claim that inner well-being remains independent of material status, so that it ultimately makes no difference whether you're a slave or not. When analyzing Lucretius, she strikingly isolates the value of *narrative* (as opposed to mere abstract propositions) for enriching the emotional understanding of human relationships. That doesn't stop her slyly subverting his pathological notion (not unknown today) of the ideal marriage as something minus the passions (anger and jealousy above all): a rational friendship with occasional sex thrown in.

Despite its great learning, *The Therapy of Desire* remains (like most of Nussbaum's work) an intensely personal book. While reading it I had come to the conclusion that the problem of anger was her prime topic and motivation in investigating Hellenistic ethics long before I found (on p. 508!) a specific statement to that effect. In an earlier study, *The Fragility of Goodness*, she had (as she says here) "portrayed the best human life as one that takes on the risk of loss and grief." She hadn't, she confesses—a most suggestive admission—yet gotten around to the idea "that the best life runs the risk of corrosive anger." Aeschylean πάθει μάθος, wisdom through suffering, seems to have been at work in the interval. Extirpation of the passions, anger included, was a cardinal proposition for Hellenistic thinkers. "A motivation for me in writing about them was to discover whether it was possible to accept their arguments about the elimination of anger, while still rejecting their more general attack on passions such as love, fear, and grief."

As things turned out, it wasn't. But if ever the old adage about asking the right questions rather than finding the right answers was justified, it is in this personal search. By turns wise and witty, silly and Socratic, critical and compassionate, Nussbaum proves herself an extraordinarily addictive literary companion. She has illuminated my thinking on death; she has reminded me (perhaps not by intention) of how much I detest both Seneca and the Plato who in old age wrote *The Laws;* she has, unexpectedly, provided perceptive glosses on one of my favorite modern poets, Wallace Stevens; and she has triumphantly proved, if proof were needed, that the life of the mind— and never mind about elitism—can be one of the highest and most rewarding pursuits known to man, including woman. If Nikidion got one-tenth of the educational pummelling, excitement, and stimulus (both intellectual and emotional) in the Garden of Epicurus as Nussbaum provides in this densely argued volume, I should be very much surprised. When I closed the last page, my immediate impulse (in an already overloaded working schedule) was to start all over again from the beginning. Her faults, however irritating, are superficial. This is a book to live with.

13

Getting to Be a Star:
The Politics of Catasterism

DURING THE LAST year of his life, Julius Caesar became increasingly preoccupied with the notion of establishing a divine monarchy—one, moreover, that was solidly rooted in Roman and even Etruscan rather than Greek tradition.[1] After the Ides of March, one of the chief preoccupations of the young Octavian, as Caesar's heir, was to secure posthumous divine honors for him. Antony, on the other hand, though in his funeral speech he "lauded Caesar as a god in heaven,"[2] changed his tack very fast once the will was read and Octavian's position became clear. A god's will overrode ordinary laws, and the god's son—adopted or not—would be in an unassailable position.[3] The maneuvering between them from March to July of 44 B.C. over the matter of divine honors was intense. Brutus, organizing the *Ludi Apollinares* (6–13 July) as praetor *in absentia*, was faced with a double embarrassment: of doing so in a month now named after the dead dictator, and worse, of the final day of the festivities (13 July) being Caesar's birthday. He did what he could by insisting that the ancient name for the month, Quinctilis, be used instead.[4]

Note: Originally published in *Fenway Court* (Boston, 1994), 52–71, as part of the proceedings of a symposium on *Myth and Allusion: Meanings and Uses of Myth in Ancient Greek and Roman Society.* The text here presented contains some important modifications.

1. See in particular Ross Taylor 1931, 58–77; Cerfaux and Tondriau 1957, 286–90; P. Green, *Classical Bearings* (London, 1989), ch. 12 ("Caesar and Alexander: *Aemulatio, Imitatio, Comparatio*"), 193–209, 289–96. Caesar affected, *inter alia,* the high red boots associated with the kings who reigned in Alba Longa: Dio Cass. 43.2.

2. App. *B.C.* 2.143: ὡς θεὸν οὐράνιον ὕμνει. See a longer version of the speech in Dio Cass. 44.36–49.

3. Ross Taylor 1931, 82.

4. Cicero has some half-amused, half-shocked comments on this (and on the nervous cancelling of a performance of the tragedy *Brutus*): *Att.* 16.1.1, 4.1, 5.1. Further details given by Ross Taylor 1931, 83–90.

However, at Caesar's own posthumous games, the *ludi Victoriae Caesaris*, formerly *Veneris Genetricis* (20–30 July), Octavian, who gave them, was presented with a heavenly sign, traditionally baleful, which he managed to utilize as a "powerful symbol of his adopted father's divinity."[5] Antony, obstructionist as always, banned the exhibition in the theater of Caesar's gilded chair and jeweled crown, even though this had been sanctioned by decree;[6] he may well have remembered the divine implications lurking behind the similar use, by the Successors, of dead Alexander's empty throne, robe, and diadem.[7] It was at this point that the heavens took a hand in the matter. We possess a fragment of Augustus's own *Memoirs*, transcribed by the elder Pliny, describing what happened:[8]

> During the very days of my Games a comet was seen for seven days in the northern quarter of the sky. It would rise about the eleventh hour of the day [i.e., between 5:00 and 6:15 P.M., or about an hour before sunset], and shone brightly, being visible from all regions. This star was popularly believed to signify that Caesar's soul had been received into the divine company of the immortal gods, for which reason that emblem [a star: this comet, like many, seems at first to have been mistakenly so identified] was added to the portrait-bust of him that we shortly thereafter dedicated in the Forum.

Other sources confirm and amplify this remarkable statement. Dio Cassius and Suetonius both agree with Augustus that the *belief* in Caesar's apotheosis, and the interpretation of the comet that went with it, stemmed from the common people (rather than, it is implied, being an official pronouncement of the College of Augurs). Both claim that the comet (which shone con-

---

5. Dio Cass. 45.6.4; Suet. *Div. Jul.* 88. The date is now confirmed, with meticulous arguments, by Ramsey and Licht 1997, 19–57; citation from their discussion of ancient accounts of the comet, 65. Octavian's real luck over the interpretation of the comet seems to have been that Capricorn (rightly or wrongly) he regarded as his natal sign (Suet. *Div. Aug.* 94), and that on 23 July 44 Capricorn was in the ascendant (147–53).

6. Dio Cass. 45.6.5; App. *B.C.* 3.4.28; Nic. Damasc. *Vit. Caes. Aug.* fr. 130, 28.108.

7. Plut. *Eum.* 13; Diod. Sic. 18.60–61.

8. Plin. *NH* 2.94: iis ipsis ludorum meorum diebus sidus crinitum per septem dies in regione caeli quae sub septentrionibus est conspectum ⟨est⟩. id oriebatur circa undecimam horam diei clarumque et omnibus e terris conspicuum fuit. eo sidere significari uolgus credidit Caesaris animam inter deorum immortalium numina receptam, quo nomine id insigne simulacro capitis eius, quod mox in foro consecrauimus, adiectum est. For text and commentary, see now Ramsey and Licht 1997, 71ff., 135ff., 158–59. Despite problems with our testimonia, it seems very probable that the comet seen in July of 44 (the identification of which is not a major concern here, though its reality is) was that also recorded, and thus guaranteed, by Chinese observers (details in Ramsey and Licht 1997, 65ff.).

tinually for a week) was Caesar's soul being taken up into heaven, and that this was the reason why a star was subsequently placed on his image (and indeed, as we know, also on some coins).[9] Dio, however, gives a significant variation on the terms of this apotheosis. According to him, the common belief was that "Caesar had been made immortal and *admitted into the number of the stars*."[10] Octavian himself took the comet seriously, but for a different astral reason: he privately believed it to be the sign of a new age dawning, the inception of a Great Year (*magnus annus*), which—since it was associated with the coming of a child—portended his own symbolic rebirth.[11]

It was left to Ovid (of all people) to spell out the details of Caesar's apotheosis in the greatest detail, with his (posthumous) metamorphosis into "a new star and comet."[12] In his narrative, Jupiter instructs Venus, Caesar's putative ancestor, to "snatch his soul from its slain body, so that from his high temple Julius the God (*diuus Iulius*) may ever look down on our Capitol and Forum."[13] Venus, nothing loath, instantly swoops down, invisible, catches Caesar's soul, and flies up with it toward the stars. It begins to blaze and burn in her bosom, so she releases it: up it arches, over the moon, leaving a fiery trail behind it, to gleam, finally, as a star in the firmament.[14] Though Ovid may be

---

9. Ross Taylor 1931, 91 n. 21, citing a sestertius of L. Aemilius Buca, dated to late 44 B.C. Cf. also Serv. *ad* Virg. *Ecl.* 9.47.

10. Dio Cass. 45.7.1: ἐπεὶ μέντοι ἄστρον τι παρὰ πάσας τὰς ἡμέρας ἐκείνας ἐκ τῆς ἄρκτου πρὸς ἑσπέραν ἐξεφάνη, καὶ αὐτὸ κομήτην τέ τινων καλούντων καὶ προσημαίνειν οἷά που εἴωθε λεγόντων, οἱ πολλοὶ τοῦτο μὲν οὐκ ἐπίστευον, τῷ δὲ δὴ Καίσαρι αὐτὸ ὡς καὶ ἀπηθανατισμένῳ καὶ ἐς τὸν τῶν ἄστρων ἀριθμὸν ἐγκατειλεγμένῳ ἀνετίθεσαν, θαρσήσας χαλκοῦν αὐτὸν ἐς τὸ Ἀφροδίσιον, ἀστέρα ὑπὲρ τῆς κεφαλῆς ἔχοντα, ἔστησεν.
Suet. *Div. Jul.* 88: in deorum numerum relatus est, non ore modo sed et persuasione decernentium sed et persuasione uolgi. siquidem ludis, quos primos consecrato ei heres Augustus edebat, stella crinita per septem continuos dies fulsit exoriens circa undecimam horam, creditumque est animam esse Caesaris in caelum recepti; et hac de causa simulacro eius in uertice additur stella.
Cf. also Sen. *NQ* 7.17.2; Zonar. *Epit.* 10.13; Jul. Obs. 68; Servius on Virg. *Aen.* 1.287, 8.681, *Ecl.* 9.47; Plut. *Caes.* 69.3; other testimonia collected by Ramsey and Licht 1997, app. 1, 155–81.

11. Plin. *NH* 2.94: haec [the quotation from the *Memoirs*, above, note 8] ille in publicum: interiore gaudio sibi illum natum seque in eo nasci interpretatus est. Ross Taylor (1931, 91) reminds us that a Great Year was at hand "when sun, moon, and planets return to the same relative position from which they had set forth at the beginning of the cycle," and that Octavian thus "turned it as he did the other signs of Caesar's godhead to his own glory." On this *magnus annus*, see Cic. *De Rep.* 6.24.

12. Sidus . . . nouum stellamque comantem (*Met.* 15.749). Ovid's hyperbole is apposite in a way he could not have foreseen, since the kind of astral sighting involved might be either a nova or a comet, but not both in one!

13. Ovid *Met.* 15.840–42: 'hanc animam interea caeso de corpore raptam / fac iubar, ut semper Capitolia nostra forumque / diuus ab excelsa prospectet Iulius aede.

14. Ibid., 843–50: uix ea fatus erat, medii cum sede senatus / constitit alma Venus nulli cernenda suique / Caesaris eripuit membris nec in aera solui / passa recentem animam caelestibus intulit

having some sly fun here (e.g., with the notion of Caesar's *anima* as a firework suddenly igniting in Venus's cleavage), we have no reason to suppose that he was not retailing the approved version of events. No one was laughing; or if they were, they had the good sense to keep their amusement to themselves.

What is more, despite the disclaimers about popular superstition, this nexus of beliefs concerning Caesar's apotheosis proved remarkably durable. The elder Pliny, an erudite polymath of good family with nothing popular about him, could argue that no praise was high enough for the astronomer Hipparchus (fl. second century B.C.), on the grounds that "no one had done more to prove the stars' kinship with mankind, and that our souls form a part of heaven."[15] Augustus himself might officially discourage attempts to deify him during his own lifetime (no temples to be dedicated to him unless he shared them with the goddess Roma[16]), but once he was dead, "returning his heavenly spirit to heaven," as Velleius, that pious conformist, put it,[17] he got the full works. His catafalque in the Campus Martius was topped by a wax portrait-image of him. As this was consumed in the flames, it released an eagle, which "flew aloft, supposedly bearing his spirit heavenward."[18] This symbolic device subsequently became standard practice at an emperor's funeral. The importance attached to it is revealed by the fact that Augustus's widow Livia is said to have paid a quarter of a million sesterces to one Numerius Atticus, an ex-praetor who testified on oath that he had seen Augustus ascending to heaven in the traditional manner associated with Romulus.[19] On 17 September A.D. 14,[20] the Senate declared Augustus immortal, voted him a shrine, and appointed Livia his priestess.

I have chosen this phenomenon to discuss for several reasons: primarily because it highlights the question of just what needs such mythic modes of

---

astris / dumque tulit, lumen capere atque ignescere sensit / emisitque sinu: luna uolat altius illa / flammiferumque trahens spatioso limite crinem / stella micat.

15. Plin. *NH* 2.95: idem Hipparchus numquam satis laudatus, ut quo nemo magis adprobauerit cognationem cum homine siderum animasque nostras partem esse caeli.

16. Suet. *Div. Aug.* 52. There was, of course, an extensive borderline area where literary metaphor could do what was forbidden to official decrees: when Virgil wrote (*Ecl.* 1.6–8) that "deus nobis haec otia fecit," and his character vowed to sacrifice on the altar of the (unnamed) *deus* in question, or Horace, more specific, described Augustus (*Odes* 3.5.1–4) as a *praesens diuus*, they were treating him (as the Greeks had long done their outstanding figures) as ἰσόθεος, godlike, rather than claiming actual godhead on his behalf. Cf. Dio Cass. 51.20.

17. Vell. Pat. 2.123.2: animam caelestem caelo reddidit.

18. Dio Cass. 56.42.3: ἀετὸς δέ τις ... ἀνίπτατο ὡς καὶ δὴ τὴν ψυχὴν αὐτοῦ ἐς τὸν οὐρανὸν ἀναφέρων. For the catafalque, see 34.1.

19. Ibid., 46.2.

20. *CIL* I² p. 244 [Fasti Amiternini]: Divo Augusto honores caelestes a senatu decreti. Cf. Dio Cass. 56.46.1–2.

perception may have satisfied in the Greek and Roman world, and—a far trickier point—to what extent, and in what sense, they were actually believed, or generated faith (not always the same thing). It is clear[21] that throughout ancient history, even—or perhaps especially—during those periods (e.g., the age of the Sophists in Periclean Athens) when rationalism seemed most predominant, the vast majority of the population clung stubbornly to their age-old, often highly irrational, beliefs.[22] The contrast drawn by contemporary witnesses, when discussing Caesar's apotheosis in particular, between informed opinion and that of "the majority" suggests strongly that such was the case with regard to imperial deification.

Yet even so, the distinction was far from clear-cut, and it would, I think, be a mistake to suppose that what we have here is a simple case of rationalist cynics consciously manipulating the masses for political ends. Politics, of course, entered into it, as so often in religious matters; but when the sedulous Velleius wrote of Tiberius that he "deified his father [stepfather in fact] not by imperial fiat but through genuine belief: he did not merely call him a god, but made him one,"[23] the insight, despite Velleius's known partisanship, rings true. The elder Pliny, as we have seen, believed in a living, sentient cosmos. There would always be the intellectual scoffers: Seneca, when he wrote the *Apocolocyntosis*, portraying the reception in heaven of a shambling, drooling Claudius; Lucian, in the *Icaromenippos;* and as time went by, the emperors themselves, who sometimes took their elevation less than seriously (Vespasian during his last illness remarked: "Oh dear, I think I'm turning into a god"[24]). Yet the practice of deification by assumption was retained for centuries: it even survived the change from paganism to Christianity. Constantine accepted the dedication of a temple, on condition that his name was not "soiled by the reprehensible practices of dangerous superstition." The first emperor actually to refuse the honor seems to have been Gratian, toward the close of the fourth century A.D.[25] Whatever we may feel about this formalized process of apotheosis, there can be no doubt that it was regarded seriously.

Its constituent features include some of the fundamental building-blocks of the mythic worldview, not least its physical ordering. Heaven is in the sky,

---

21. For a more detailed treatment of this point, see chapter 1 above, pp. 6ff.

22. See in particular on this topic Dodds 1951, ch. 6, 179–206, "Rationalism and Reaction in the Classical Age."

23. Vell. Pat. 2.126.1: sacrauit parentem suum Caesar non imperio, sed religione, non appellauit eum, sed fecit deum.

24. Suet. *Div. Vesp.* 23.4: ac ne in metu quidem ac periculo mortis extremo abstinuit iocis . . . prima quoque morbi accessione, "vae," inquit, "puto deus fio."

25. See G. Boissier, "Apotheosis," in Daremberg-Saglio 1:323–27, esp. 326.

just as Hades or Tartaros lies beneath it, and the same word, *caelum*, οὐρανός, does duty for both. Perception is balanced between animism and anthropomorphism, with the unknown and formless terrors of the first slowly being conquered by the emergent Promethean insights of the second: to reason is human, apparent purpose implies reason, and thus evident patterns (e.g., in the movement of the stars) must needs imply the presence of some guiding mind. It follows that divine power both is rooted in the unknown and presents curiously human features. Thus it is not at all surprising to find that the god-king, the mediator between heaven and earth, is, as Frankfort remarks,[26] at the very heart of the oldest civilized societies, where "the purely secular—in so far as it could be granted to exist at all—was the purely trivial. Whatever was significant was imbedded in the life of the cosmos, and it was precisely the king's function to maintain the harmony of that integration."

The key to mythic function in highly evolved societies such as those of Greece and Rome is the remarkable, and often unacknowledged, ability of such archetypal perceptions, not only to survive in a rational climate, but still to shape the beliefs and attitudes of people who, on the face of it, we might expect to react very differently. To take an obvious example: the sphericity of the world was known as a possibility before Herodotus, argued for by Aristotle in the *De Caelo*, and by Strabo's day taken for granted.[27] Yet throughout the Greco-Roman period, and indeed for much longer, all poetic and theological cosmic imagery obstinately remained based on the kind of archetypal flat-earth, heaven-above-and-hell-below concept that had survived in early thinkers such as Anaximenes or Democritus.[28] The nature of eclipses was quite clear to thinkers by the late fifth century B.C.: that did not stop an intelligent and educated Athenian, Nicias, from losing an entire expeditionary force in Sicily (Sept. 413) by refusing to move for almost a month after an eclipse of the moon.[29]

Examples could be multiplied. In particular, that stubborn anthropomorphism so characteristic of the Greco-Roman world both formed the basis for Protagorean secular humanism—"Man the Measure of all things"[30]—and, for

26. Henri Frankfort, *Kingship and the Gods: A Study of Ancient Near East Religion as the Integration of Society and Nature* (Chicago, 1948), vii, 3.

27. Arist. *De Caelo* 2.13–14, 293a15–298a20; Strabo 2.5.10, C.116; cf. O.A.W. Dilke, *Greek and Roman Maps* (Ithaca, N.Y. and London, 1985), 24–38.

28. Arist. *De Caelo* 2.13–14, 294b14–22; cf. Anaximander frs. 122–34 K-R-S (pp. 133–4), and (on Democritus) W.K.C. Guthrie, *A History of Greek Philosophy*, vol. 2 (Cambridge, 1965), 422.

29. Thuc. 7.50.44 (with Gomme-Andrewes-Dover's note, 428–29); Diod. Sic. 13.12.6; Plut. *Nic.* 23.

30. D-K 80 fr. B.1 = Diog. Laert. 9.51: πάντων χρημάτων μέτρον [ἐστιν] ἄνθρωπος.

the many, helped to break down the barriers between men and gods. After the Olympians failed Athens at Syracuse and Aegospotami, at Chaeronea and Crannon, it is not hard to see how attractive a mortal Savior and Benefactor, Σωτὴρ καὶ Εὐεργέτης, might look. In September 290 B.C. the Athenians welcomed Demetrius the Besieger as a god.[31] Alexander's conquests, it was argued, had outdone those of Heracles and Dionysus. Euhemerus of Messene was popularizing the view that the Olympian deities "were terrestrial beings who became gods, acquiring immortal honor and fame through their benefactions to men."[32] The Roman poet Ennius translated Euhemerus into Latin. The background is becoming clearer. If Alexander, let alone Demetrius, could legitimately aspire to divine status, then why not Caesar? Besides, Romans who so obstinately gagged on the title of *rex* might—indeed, did—find that of *diuus* less objectionable, even though this was an idea that, like so much else, they had borrowed from Greece.[33]

A *praesens diuus*, then, to borrow Horace's phrase describing Augustus.[34] But the Ides of March confronted Octavian with a new problem. Euhemerus, to Cicero's outrage,[35] described cases in which gods died and were buried, the clear implication being that here, too, their mere mortality was made manifest. Apotheosis, then, was essential. This, like divine descent, was not something natural to the Roman mind;[36] but there was one famous and highly suitable precedent: Romulus.

Traditionally,[37] Romulus vanished from the Campus Martius during a sudden storm, amid peals of thunder, enveloped in a dark cloud.[38] Cicero, our

---

31. The ithyphallic paean, recorded by Duris of Samos in Book 22 of his *Histories*, and preserved by Athenaeus *Deipnos.* 6.253d-f, is a remarkable document: for a recent discussion, see A. Henrichs in *From Myth to Reason? Studies in the Development of Greek Thought*, ed. R. Buxton (Oxford, 1999), 223-48.

32. Diod. Sic. 6.1.1-2 (*ap.* Euseb. *Praep. Ev.* 2.2.52-53) = Euhemerus of Messene fr. III.25 Winiarczyk; cf. Cic. *ND* 1.42.119.

33. See W. Warde Fowler, *Roman Ideas of Deity in the Last Century before the Christian Era* (London, 1914), ch. 4, 81-106, esp. 90ff.

34. See above, note 16.

35. Cic. *ND* 1.42.119: ab Euhemero autem et mortes et sepulturae demonstrantur deorum; utrum igitur hic confirmasse uidetur religionem an penitus totam sustulisse?

36. Warde Fowler (as above, note 33) 96. St. Augustine quotes (*Civ. Dei* 3.4) a characteristic opinion expressed by Varro on the subject: utile esse ciuitatibus dicit [Varro], ut se uiri fortes, *etiamsi falsum sit* [emphasis mine], diis genitos esse credant, ut eo modo animus humanus uelut diuinae stirpis fiduciam gerens res magnas adgrediendas praesumat audacius, agat uehementius et ob hoc impleat ipsa securitate felicius.

37. Our main sources are Cic. *De Rep.* 1.16.25, 2.9.17-19; Livy 1.16 passim; Plut. *Rom.* 27-28; Ovid *Fast.* 2.491-509, *Met.* 14.806-27; Dion. Hal. *Ant. Rom.* 2.56.1-7.

38. Livy 1.16.1; Plut. *Rom.* 27.6-7; Dion. Hal. *Ant. Rom.* 2.56.2; Ovid *Met.* 14.816-17, *Fast.* 2.493-94.

earliest witness, has the great merit of stating his case *before* Caesar's supposed apotheosis, and thus escapes the obvious suspicion of contamination by propaganda that can be brought against our other sources, whether pro or con. He also speaks of an eclipse of the sun.[39] Our other sources leave it uncertain as to whether the sun's darkening was caused by eclipse or storm; but Ovid makes it clear[40] that in either case, these celestial phenomena were regarded as the sign of apotheosis. Romulus's soul, freed of its mortal integument,[41] had been taken up to heaven and admitted to the company of the gods.[42] Most curious of all, one Procul[ei]us Julius, described by Plutarch as a high-born patrician, and by Cicero as a country bumpkin,[43] swore to the Senate that Romulus had descended from heaven before him in a divine epiphany as the Roman deity Quirinus, with instructions to announce Rome's future as the capital of the world, and had then "departed on high once more."[44] This highly promising charter myth was certainly preferable to the alternative version (indignantly denied by Ovid[45]), which had Romulus murdered by a mob of senators, and his dismembered body smuggled out piecemeal and secretly buried,[46] with the supposed apotheosis as a cover story.[47]

Dionysius of Halicarnassus, who came to Rome in 30 B.C., the year after Actium, and lived there for a quarter of a century, was a fluent Latin speaker and an expert on Roman antiquities.[48] His verdict on the traditional account

---

39. Cic. *De Rep.* 1.16.25 (he dates it to 5 July, 714 B.C.!), cf. 2.9.17.

40. *Met.* 14.805–28.

41. Ovid expresses this in a striking image (*Met.* 14.824–26): corpus mortale per auras / dilapsum tenues, ceu lata plumbea funda / missa solet medio glans intabescere caelo.

42. Cic. *De Rep.* 2.10.17: deorum in numero conlocatus; Livy 1.16.6; Plut. *Rom.* 27.7: ἀνηρπασμένον εἰς θεοὺς καὶ θεὸν εὐμενῆ γενησόμενον αὐτοῖς ἐκ χρηστοῦ βασιλέως; Dion. Hal. 2.56.2 (skeptical): οἱ μὲν οὖν μυθωδέστερα τὰ περὶ αὐτοῦ ποιοῦντες ... φασιν αὐτὸν ... ἀφανῆ γενέσθαι καὶ πεπιστεύκασιν ὑπὸ τοῦ πατρὸς Ἄρεος τὸν ἄνδρα ἀνηρπάσθαὶ; Ovid *Met.* 14.824–26.

43. Plut. *Rom.* 28.1: ἄνδρα τῶν πατρικίων γένει πρῶτον, ἤθει τε δοκιμώτατον; Cic. *De Rep.* 2.10.20: Procul[ei]us, homini agresti.

44. Livy 1.16.5–7: "haec," inquit, "locutus sublimis abiit"; Cic. *De Rep.* 2.10.20; Plut. *Rom.* 28 passim; Ovid *Fast.* 2.499–509.

45. *Fast.* 2.497–98: luctus erat falsaeque patres in crimine caedis.

46. Dion. Hal. *Ant. Rom.* 2.56.3–5; Plut. *Rom.* 27.5–6.

47. Cic. *De Rep.* 2.10.20 describes Proculeius as being primed by the senators "quo illi a se inuidiam interitus Romuli pellerent"; cf. Plut. *Rom.* 27.7. Cicero is at some pains to support the concept of apotheosis (as a validation for the SPQR), arguing that Romulus's death occurred at a time when Greece was already civilized, "minorque fabulis nisi de ueteribus rebus haberetur fides."

48. Dion. Hal. *Ant. Rom.* 1.7.2: ἐγὼ καταπλεύσας εἰς Ἰταλίαν ἅμα τῷ καταλυθῆναι τὸν ἐμφύλιον πόλεμον ὑπὸ τοῦ Σεβαστοῦ Καίσαρος ἑβδόμης καὶ ὀγδοηκοστῆς ὀλυμπιάδος [32–29 B.C.] μεσούσης, καὶ τὸν ἐξ ἐκείνου χρόνον ἐτῶν δύο καὶ εἴκοσι μέχρι τοῦ παρόντος γενόμενον ἐν Ῥώμῃ διατρίψας, διάλεκτόν τε τὴν Ῥωμαϊκὴν ἐκμαθὼν καὶ γραμμάτων τῶν

of Romulus's apotheosis therefore carries some weight: the deification of Caesar had taken place only fourteen years before his arrival, and we know that, as well as studying written histories, he made a habit of interviewing erudite witnesses.[49] What he says is: "It is apparent that the divinely occasioned events linked with this man's conception and dissolution offer no small support to those who divinize mortals and elevate the souls of the illustrious to heaven."[50] A very Roman argument: no reader of Livy or Julius Obsequens can fail to be struck by the Roman obsession with heavenly portents—*ostenta, monstra, prodigia*, widely regarded as "precursors of social, political, or dynastic changes."[51] Among these portents, stars, comets, and eclipses figured prominently. At both the conception and the death of Romulus, Dionysius writes, tradition recorded "a total eclipse of the sun and darkness like night covering the earth."[52]

Clearly, then, if portents had any validity, Caesar's death, too, must be marked by an eclipse. The comet, normally presaging disaster, could be adapted as a sign of apotheosis (and, as luck would have it, the year of Caesar's birth, 100 B.C., was similarly marked by the fall of a blazing meteor[53]); but for a truly convincing sign, an eclipse was what was needed, and our sources duly record a most striking one.[54] Unfortunately, astronomical records show no eclipse whatsoever as visible in Italy during 44 B.C.[55] What actually happened? The evidence is suggestive. First, the "obscuring of the sun's rays"[56] lasted a long time, almost a year, blocking off warmth as well as light, so that

---

ἐπιχωρίων λαβὼν ἐπιστήμην, ἐν πάντι τούτῳ τῷ χρόνῳ τὰ συντείνοντα πρὸς τὴν ὑπόθεσιν ταύτην διετέλουν πραγματευόμενος.

49. Ibid. §3: καὶ τὰ μὲν παρὰ τῶν λογιωτάτων ἀνδρῶν, οἷς εἰς ὁμιλίαν ἦλθον, διδαχῇ παραλαβών, τὰ δ' ἐκ τῶν ἱστοριῶν ἀλεξάμενος.

50. *Ant. Rom.* 2.56.6: ἔοικε δ' οὐ μικρὰν ἀφορμὴν παρέχειν τοῖς θεοποιοῦσι τὰ θνῆτα καὶ εἰς οὐρανὸν ἀναβιβάζουσι τὰς ψυχὰς τῶν ἐπιφανῶν τὰ συμβάντα ἐκ τοῦ θεοῦ περὶ τὴν σύγκρισιν τοῦ ἀνδρὸς ἐκείνου καὶ τὴν διάκρισιν.

51. "Divination," *OCD*², 357.

52. *Ant. Rom.* 2.56.6: ἔν τε γὰρ τῷ βιασμῷ τῆς μητρὸς αὐτοῦ . . . τὸν ἥλιον ἐκλιπεῖν φασιν ὅλον καὶ σκότος παντελῶς ὥσπερ ἐν νυκτὶ τὴν γῆν κατασχεῖν ἔν τε τῇ τελευτῇ αὐτοῦ ταὐτὸ συμβῆναι λέγουσι πάθος.

53. Jul. Obs. §45: fax ardens Tarquiniis late uisa subito lapsa cadens.

54. Virg. *Georg.* 1.463ff., and Servius ad loc.; schol. Lucan 1.541; Tibullus 2.5.75; Ovid *Met.* 15.785ff.; Plut. *Caes.* 69; Plin. *NH* 2.98; M. Antonius *ap.* Joseph. *AJ* 14.309.

55. Oppolzer's *Canon of Eclipses* (New York, 1962, translation of the *Canon der Finsternisse*, 1887) lists two solar eclipses for 44 B.C.: one on 18 April, total in the northern Pacific Ocean and Mexico, but invisible in Europe, since there it took place at night; and a second, annular eclipse on 11 October, over South America, also invisible in Europe. Cf. F. Boll, "Finsternisse," *PWK* 6.2355. Despite the false information perpetuated in various classical commentaries (Ramsey and Licht 1997, 194), there was no eclipse visible in Italy in November (or any other month) of 44.

56. Plut. *Caes.* 69.3: τὸ περὶ τὸν ἥλιον ἀμαύρωμα τῆς αὐγῆς.

fruit shrivelled while still half-ripe.[57] Second, unusual visual phenomena were recorded in the sky: a rainbow-like halo round the sun,[58] and, most strikingly, the illusion of three solar orbs appearing together.[59] Such effects are produced partly by upper-level ice crystals, partly by the presence in the atmosphere of large quantities of volcanic dust, and partly by the resultant atmospheric warming.[60] Now from Virgil's *Georgics*, together with Servius's note citing a lost passage of Livy, we know that the spring of 44 B.C. did, in fact, see a particularly violent eruption of Mt. Etna, the effects of which were felt over a widespread area, and almost certainly produced the conditions described.[61] It was not an eclipse; but it was near enough to do duty for one in the minds of pious believers (or ambitious cynics), and very quickly found its way as such into the literature. It may also explain the failure of our Italian sources to note the "Caesar comet" in May, at a time when Chinese records show it to have been visible.

Augustus's demise was not so lucky: the dearth of portents meant that

---

57. Ibid., §4: ὅλον γὰρ ἐκεῖνον τὸν ἐνιαυτὸν ὠχρὸς μὲν ὁ κύκλος καὶ μαρμαρυγὰς οὐκ ἔχων ἀνέτελλεν, ἀδρανὰς δὲ καὶ λεπτὸν ἀπ' αὐτοῦ κατῄει τὸ θερμόν, ὥστε τὸν μὲν ἀέρα δνοφερὸν καὶ βαρὺν ἀσθενείᾳ τῆς διακρινούσης αὐτὸν ἀλέας ἐπιφέρεσθαι, τοὺς δὲ καρποὺς ἡμιπέπτους καὶ ἀτελεῖς ἀπανθῆσαι καὶ παρακμάσαι διὰ τὴν ψυχρότητα τοῦ περιέχοντος. Cf. Plin. *NH* 2.98: fiunt prodigiosi et longiores solis defectus, qualis occiso dictatore Caesare et Antoniano bello totius paene anni pallore continuo; Jul. Obs. §68: multis mensibus languida lux fuit.

58. Dio Cass. 45.4.4: ἶρις πάντα τὸν ἥλιον πολλὴ καὶ ποικίλη περιέσχεν; cf. Suet. *Div. Aug.* 95; Jul. Obs. §68; Plin. *NH* 2.98: circa solis orbem ceu spiceae coronae et uersicolores circuli, qualiter Augusto Caesare in prima iuuenta urbem intrante post obitum patris.

59. Plin. *NH* 2.99: soles plures simul cernuntur, nec supra ipsum nec infra sed ex obliquo, numquam iuxta nec contra terram, nec noctu sed aut oriente aut occidente . . . trinos soles antiqui saepe uidere, sicut . . . M. Antonio P. Dolabella . . . coss. [44 B.C.]; Jul. Obs. §68: soles tres fulserunt, circaque solem imum corona spiceae similis in orbem emicuit. Cf. Dio Cass. 45.17.5, 47.40.2.

60. See Robert Greenler, *Rainbows, Halos, and Glories* (Cambridge, 1980), 142–43 (corona around the sun, known as "Bishop's Ring"), citing D. E. Archibald, "The Large Corona Round the Sun and Moon in 1883–4–5, generally known as 'Bishop's Ring'," in pt. 4§ 1(E) of the Royal Society's report, *The Eruption of Krakatoa and Subsequent Phenomena* (London, 1888); 176 (the "*spicea* effect" described by Pliny, above, note 59); 26–28 (false suns, "sun dogs").

61. Virg. *Georg.* 1.471–73: quotiens Cyclopum efferuere in agros / uidimus undantem ruptis fornacibus Aetnam, / flammarumque globos liquefactaque uoluere saxa.

Servius ad *Georg.* 1.472: malum omen est quotiens Aetna, mons Siciliae, non fumum sed flammarum egerit globos; et, ut dicit Liuuius, tanta flamma ante mortem Caesaris ex Aetna monte defluxit ut non tantum uicinae urbes, sed etiam Regina ciuitas, quae multo spatio ab ea distat, adflaretur.

2002 note: I arrived at my conclusion (regarding Etna's role in these episodes of pseudo-eclipse) independently, and published it in my original 1994 article. I was therefore delighted to read Ramsey and Licht's detailed section (1997, 99–107) setting out an identical explanation, and backing it with detailed evidence, *inter alia* from Chinese records and glacier-coring, that I had not known when I wrote.

those concerned had to manufacture their own. Hence the release of an eagle from the pyre; hence the testimony of Numerius Atticus, so clearly modeled on that of Proculeius Julius, that he had seen the emperor's soul ascending to heaven.[62] The best that heaven could manage in return was an eclipse of the moon on 27 September, ten days after Augustus's official deification;[63] and even this seems not to have been connected, then or later, to the presumed apotheosis.[64]

We see, then (to recapitulate), that those seeking apotheosis for Caesar and Augustus used the case of Romulus as an empowering precedent. This was inevitable. Romulus, whatever his royal or divine status, had been Rome's founder: no claimant to second-founder status could possibly ignore him. Besides, there was no one else. Rome, like the Greek states, had experienced a long period of what might be termed egalitarian rationalism, when archaic superstitions and personal self-aggrandizement were equally suspect. That deep-rooted anthropomorphism that was at once the curse and the glory of both peoples had (as we are always being told) fostered the spirit of secular invention and research, scorning superstition, mocking—paradoxically—anthropomorphism itself when it appeared, as it was bound to, in religion: as early as the sixth century B.C., Xenophanes pointed out that Thracian gods had blue eyes and red hair, and that if horses could draw or sculpt, their icons would come out equine.[65]

It is less well understood that the same instinct underlay that reversion to authoritarianism which marked the fourth century B.C. and the Hellenistic era. Euhemerism and its natural concomitant, ruler worship, might, as we have seen, resuscitate and exploit certain archetypal instincts of the human psyche, not least for a god-king who enjoyed assumption to heaven; but they did so at the expense of the Olympian pantheon, while still remaining obstinately anthropomorphic. Since the non-Olympian cosmology on which they drew—primarily that derived from the Pythagoreans—lacked an anthropomorphic dimension altogether, the result was a most curious intellectual and symbolic impasse. Nothing demonstrates this more strikingly than the starry apotheosis decreed for Caesar and Augustus, deriving as it does from an improbable marriage between simple popular beliefs and a complex, intellectually rarified tradition to which thinkers from Alcmaeon to Plato, from Aristotle to Chrysippus, all contributed.

---

62. See above, p. 237, with notes 19 and 20.

63. F. Boll, "Finsternisse," PWK 6.2360.

64. What it *was* related to was the mutiny of the Pannonian legions: see Tac. *Ann.* 1.28; Dio Cass. 57.4.4.

65. Xenophanes frs. 168–69 K-R-S.

The night sky was comfortingly familiar, and a reassuring help in need to sailors and farmers, as both Hesiod and Aratus remind us. Here, too, anthropomorphism and theriomorphism had been at work, reducing planets, constellations, the zodiac[66] to familiar entities: Jupiter, Mars, Venus, Perseus, the Charioteer, Andromeda, Orion the Hunter, and various swans, bears, dogs, serpents, fishes, sea monsters, water carriers, rams, and so on. But how did an ancient viewer conceive these phenomena? What, above all, did catasterism, the translation to heaven of mythical figures—heroes, or later, human aspirants—actually *mean?* Where, and what, was the "heaven of Zeus" that, in Aratus's poem, the Horse forever circles?[67] The moment we pose questions like this, we realize that there is no answer in visual terms. Olympus is a *place*, even in its mythic formulation, and we can imagine both pantheon and palace. So are Hades or the Elysian Fields. It is no accident that when Seneca wanted to satirize the apotheosis of Claudius, he firmly placed the scene in Olympus, with Jupiter and Mercury, Hercules and Janus, as characters. A clutch of sentient stars would hardly have served his purpose. A similar consideration was in Lucan's mind when apostrophizing Nero: let the weighty god-emperor after death settle in mid-firmament, not destroy the balance of heaven by landing off-center![68] The Greco-Roman tradition of apotheosis, unable to assimilate what Judeo-Christian apocalyptics took in their stride,[69] had wound up somewhere between poetic metaphor and a philosophical abstraction: anthropomorphism, after boldly enlisting the support of the mystical Higher Nonsense, had then been totally defeated by it.

It is a curious logical trail, but its central tenet is absolutely clear: the stars are living bodies, with soul and intellect.[70] In ancient Greece and Rome, they had virtually no formal cult (which seems to have been dismissed as either foreign or archaic[71]), and it is not hard to see why: the Milesians and their successors explained them in material terms, while the religious found them lacking in anthropomorphic personality. It was the Pythagoreans of Magna Graecia who were sufficiently imbued with mysticism both to regard them

---

66. I am inclined to accept the thesis propounded by E. J. Webb, *The Names of the Stars* (London, 1952), ch. 10, 157–75, that the zodiacal scheme was formulated *in Greece*, shortly before 500 B.C., by Cleostratus: cf. Plin. *NH* 2.31.

67. Arat. *Phaen.* 223–24: . . . αὐτὰρ ὁ Ἵππος | ἐν Διὸς εἰλεῖται καί τοι πάρα θηήσασθαι.

68. Lucan *B.C.* 1.45–60. See esp. 53–58: sed neque in arctoö sedem tibi legeris orbe, / nec polus aversi calidus qua uergitur austri, / unde tuam uideas obliquo sidere Romam. / aetheris inmensi partem si presseris unam, / sentiet axis onus. librati pondera caeli / orbe tene medio.

69. See M. Himmelfarb, *Ascent to Heaven in Jewish and Christian Apocalypses* (New York, 1993).

70. The most thorough analysis of this belief known to me is Alan Scott's *Origen and the Life of the Stars: A History of an Idea* (1991), to which this essay is heavily indebted. I do not think it accidental that Scott, a theologian, has investigated it with more attention than any classicist.

71. See, e.g., Aristoph. *Peace* 406; Plat. *Crat.* 397 c8–d2; Arist. *Met.* 1074a39–b8.

as gods and to believe "that the human soul comes from heaven and returns there at death."[72] In the Periclean Age, such views provoked widespread intellectual skepticism, but also continued to attract those who, as the Athenian Stranger observes in Plato's *Laws*,[73] regarded astronomy as the high road to atheism.

Plato himself played with the idea, to which he grew more attracted as he grew older. Since he believed that intelligence (νοῦς) and soul (ψυχή) were necessarily coexistent,[74] the regularity of movement in the cosmos led him to credit it, too, with both.[75] As Scott observes,[76] "Increasingly Plato wrote as if the direction to which the soul pointed was upward," so that in the *Phaedrus* the Olympians are described in quasi-astral terms. He never really came to terms with this problem; but (to quote Scott again) "it is surprising how physically located higher religious realities are: the higher one goes physically, the nearer (it would seem) one is to God."[77] This mixture of abstraction and specificity is not made easier by the astral soul being invisible.[78] In the Academy, too, Xenocrates argued that the stars and planets were gods, as did Heraclides Ponticus.[79] The pseudo-Platonic dialogue *Epinomis* virtually assumes a religion of the heavenly bodies: the stars are not only gods but overseers of mankind, living and provident.[80] For the Stoics, the regular motion of the heavenly bodies offered proof of their divinity, and indeed of divine providence.[81] Cicero in the *Somnium Scipionis* offers a glimpse of the planetary deities, complete with the music of the spheres;[82] but he also describes this half-abstract, half-astronomical scene as "the place where great and outstanding men find their full reward," with "a path to heaven existing for those who have deserved well of their country,"[83] and alludes to the moment "when the spirit of Romulus penetrated this very shrine."[84]

What he meant by this is singularly hard to determine. When the pious

---

72. Scott 1991, 4, citing D-K 58 B 1, 23 B 8; Aristoph. *Peace* 832–34; and Louis Rougier, *L'Origine astronomique de la croyance pythagoricienne en l'immortalité céleste des âmes* (Cairo, 1933), 80–82 and passim.

73. Plat. *Laws* 967a1–5.

74. Plat. *Soph.* 249a4, *Phileb.* 30c9–10, *Tim.* 30b2, 46d4–6.

75. Plat. *Phil.* 30a5–8, *Tim.* 36d8–e5.

76. Scott 1991, 9.

77. Scott 1991, 13.

78. Plat. *Laws* 898d9–e3.

79. Xenocrates frs. 15, 17 Heinze; Heraclides Ponticus fr. 111 Wehrli.

80. [Plat.] *Epin.* 982e1–4, 985e3, 986e6.

81. Cic. *ND* 2.16, 54, *Pro Milone* 83; Sen. *De Prov.* 1.2; Scott 1991, 48–49 with further references.

82. Cic. *De Rep.* 6.16–19.

83. Ibid. 6.25, 26: hunc locum . . . in quo omnia sunt magnis et praestantibus uiris . . . siquidem bene meritis de patria quasi limes ad caeli aditum patet.

84. Ibid. 6.24: cum Romuli animus haec ipsa in templa penetrauit.

followed the course of the comet that they held to be Caesar's immortal soul, or watched the ascent of the eagle that symbolized an identical progress for Augustus, how did they envisage the heavenly regime to which these deified spirits were supposedly admitted? Not, it seems safe to say, as a kind of mathematically precise, and probably invisible, celestial planetarium. It seems far more likely that historical necessity, sharpened by a whole sequence of contingencies—Alexander's conquests, the devaluation of the Olympian gods, the rise of Euhemerism, the convulsive civil conflict that devastated the late Roman Republic—created an atmosphere in which an escalating archetypal hunger for σωτηρία and divine redemption overrode all rational considerations in the many, a tendency duly noted and exploited by the few. The translation of heroes to heaven was an age-old belief.[85] As Pascal said, "Le coeur a ses raisons que la raison ne connaît point": the heart has reasons of which reason knows nothing. This is a dictum that must always have applied to catasterism and apotheosis, both of them processes heavily dependent on symbolism (What did a catasterized person *look* like? Where in the *caelum* or οὐρανός was his dwelling?) and worse, on nonpredictable heavenly signs.[86]

This last consideration is probably the main reason why, despite the increasingly frequent deification of monarchs during the Hellenistic period, catasterism remained rare, only becoming a viable option when the spread of Stoic cosmology established a close interconnection (συμπάθεια) between microcosm and macrocosm, so that a ruler's progress was held to be dictated by, and in step with, the movements of the heavenly bodies.[87] Full catasterism demanded, ideally, the appearance of a "new" star, which in that age of naked-eye astronomy[88] meant either a comet or a nova; and the disadvantage of both of these was that they rapidly vanished again. (A cynic, surveying the course of Hellenistic history, might decide that this was all too appropriate; but a court astronomer who valued his life would hardly have agreed.)

Alternatively, the person deified and catasterized could be assigned to an existing but appropriate star. Such was the case with Arsinoë II, sister and wife of Ptolemy Philadelphos, who in 270 was (according to Callimachus[89])

---

85. F. Cumont, *After Life in Roman Paganism* (New Haven, 1923), 153–64.

86. Cf. Edwyn Bevan, "Deification (Greek and Roman)," in J. Hastings' *Encyclopedia of Religion and Ethics*, 12 vols. (Edinburgh and New York, 1908–26), 525–33, esp. 530, discussing Augustus's obsequies: "As the timely appearance of a comet could not be counted upon, an eagle was liberated at the funeral, to represent visibly the soul of the Emperor flying to heaven."

87. Cf. Green 1993, 454–55, 595–97.

88. The telescope was only invented c. 1608, probably by Hans Lippershey, and developed by Galileo and Kepler: *Encyclopedia Brittanica*, 12th ed., vol. 21, cols. 903–4.

89. Callim. dieg. 10.10 (= Pfeiffer *Callim.* fr. 228): Ἐκθέωσις Ἀρσινόης· φησὶν δ' αὐτὴν ἀνηρπάσθαι ὑπὸ τῶν Διοσκούρων. The surviving papyrus fragment of the poem contains an

elevated to the constellation of Ursa Minor: from other sources[90] we know
that she became a protector of sailors, and thus that her catasterism was to the
Pole Star. In this capacity she was an avatar of Isis,[91] who in her turn was as-
similated, *inter alia* as navigational guide, by the Virgin Mary. It seems highly
probable, then, that the title Star of the Sea (*Stella Maris*), associated with the
Virgin from an early period,[92] applied equally to star and to catasterized goddess, and was the attribute not only of Isis but also of Arsinoë. Here, then, we
find a *function* that could compensate for the lack of embodied reality. The
most famous catasterism, however, was a mere literary *jeu d'esprit*. Berenice,
wife of Ptolemy III, dedicated a tress of her hair in thanks for her husband's
safe return from the Third Syrian War (247–246 B.C.). The tress was stolen,
and Conon, Ptolemy's court astronomer, identified it as a faint star-cluster
between Leo and Virgo. Callimachus wrote a poem on the subject, closely
imitated by Catullus.[93] At most, this episode testifies to the increasing erosion
of barriers between earth and heaven.

The paradoxical conclusion facing us, then, is that Rome, at the death of
Caesar and for long thereafter, felt a greater need—whether religious or political—for the mysteries of divinization and apotheosis than had ever been
experienced in the great Hellenistic kingdoms. Early on, even Alexander had
been forced to solicit deification for himself, and had provoked some fairly
abrasive comments when he did so (e.g., from Demosthenes: "Son of Zeus?
Sure: of Poseidon, too, if he fancies it").[94] Catasterism, which to begin with
had survived as a popular superstition,[95] was, in the late first century B.C.,
given a tremendous boost by the growth of astrology, itself largely due to

---

intriguing reference to the queen's apotheosis: νύμφα, σὺ μὲν ἀστερίαν ὑπ' ἄμαξαν ἤδη |
[Ἀνάκων ὑπὸ κλεπτομέν]α παρέθει<ς> σελάνᾳ. Further, if Barber's emendation is good, Arsinoë had been regarded, with remarkable implications, as a (metaphorical?) star *during her lifetime*, so that catasterism simply relit a stellar light that had been quenched: [ἀστὴρ . . . τ]ί παθὼν
ἀπέσβη.

90. See G. Macurdy, *Hellenistic Queens* (Baltimore, 1933), 126–28; Fraser 1972, 1:239ff., 2:668–
69; R. E. Witt, *Isis in the Graeco-Roman World* (Ithaca, N.Y. and London, 1971), 126 and n. 301.

91. Witt, ibid., 48, 214.

92. R. H. Allen, *Star Names: Their Lore and Meaning* (1899, reprinted New York, 1963), 454.
On the numerous connections between Isis and Christianity (the Virgin Mary in particular), see
Witt (as above, note 90), 267, 272ff.

93. See Hygin. *Astron.* 2.24 Le Boeuffle; Callim. fr. 110 Pfeiffer; Catull. 66 with Fordyce's commentary, 328–41; and in general Fraser 1972, 1:239, 729–30, 2b:1021–26; Cerfaux and Tondriau 1957,
199–200.

94. Hyp. *c. Dem.* 31.15; cf. Plut. *Mor.* 219E; Diog. Laert. 6.63.

95. See, e.g., Aristoph. *Peace* 832ff.: οὐκ ἦν ἄρ' οὐδ' ἃ λέγουσι κατὰ τὸν ἀέρα, | ὡς ἀστέρες
γιγνόμεθ', ὅταν τις ἀποθάνῃ. It is interesting that Ion of Chios, referred to at 835–37, is described
in this context, not entirely by way of jest, as ἀστὴρ νῦν ἐκεῖ.

the Stoic cosmological theory of συμπάθεια between microcosm and macrocosm.[96] Its combination with that other characteristic symptom of the age,
the deification of kings, was probably inevitable. The deep need for σωτηρία,
salvation, which now manifested itself throughout the eastern Mediterranean,
found its answer—between the apotheoses of Caesar and Augustus—in the
witness of a man who was also a king, also God, and whose story likewise
involves both a symbolic star and direct assumption into Heaven.[97]

---

96. This is an enormous subject, which I can only touch on here. For a useful introduction, see
M. Nilsson, *Geschichte der griechischen Religion*, vol. 2, *Die hellenistische und römische Zeit*, 3d ed. (Munich, 1974), 216–81, 486–519; F. Cumont, *Astrology and Religion among the Greeks and Romans* (1912,
reprinted New York, 1960); F. H. Cramer, *Astrology in Roman Law and Politics*, vol. 1 (Philadelphia,
1954: vol. 37 of the *Memoirs* of the American Philosophical Society).

97. I am deeply grateful to Professor Kate Bracher of Whitman College for so generously
giving of her time and expert knowledge to help me understand the astronomical implications and
possibilities of the celestial phenomena discussed in this essay. Professor Robert Greenler of the
Physics Department, University of Wisconsin, Milwaukee, and Professor Emeritus David Evans
of the Department of Astronomy, University of Texas at Austin, have also greatly clarified my
thinking on comets, novas, and meteorologically occasioned optical effects such as "sun dogs."
They should not be held responsible for any scientific *cocasseries* that survive in my text.

14

The Innocence of Procris:
Ovid *AA* 3.687–746

ONE OF THE more notable features of Ovid's *Ars Amatoria* is the group of extended narrative *mythoi* with which the poet, at certain points, breaks up and enlivens his didactic precepts. Though mythical parallels are invoked throughout the *Ars*, these set-piece narratives clearly have a more important function. There are not all that many of them. In Book 1 we find two dealing with Roman history, one ancient, the other contemporary: the Rape of the Sabine Women (1.101–34), and Caius's Eastern Expedition (1.177–228). The latter is not, clearly, a narrative *mythos* in the strict sense, that is, as either the Rape of the Sabines or Ovid's more conventional retelling of myth might be regarded; its substance falls rather into the subdivision of grandiloquent imperial prophecy, a type of utterance familiar to us from Virgil and Lucan. Yet its Ovidian function as illustrative parable justifies its assimilation here to the narrative *mythos* category.

These two are balanced[1] against three drawn from Greek myth: Pasiphae's

Note: Original version published in *Classical Journal* 75 (1979): 15–24, and reprinted here by permission of *CJ* and the Classical Association of the Midwest and South.

1. I am not directly concerned in this essay with the structural patterns apparent in the *Ars Amatoria*, a problem that I touch on briefly in *Ovid: The Erotic Poems* (1982), 14–20. Some useful, but not definitive, work in this area has been done by the contributors to the little monograph *Ovids Ars Amatoria und Remedia Amoris: Untersuchungen zum Aufbau*, ed. B. Zinn (Stuttgart, 1970): for Book 3, see, in particular, Alf Hermann's "Versuch einer Aufbauanalyse des 3. Buches der 'Ars amatoria'," pp. 29–34 (though I do not accept all his conclusions). I agree with W. Port, "Die Anordnung in Gedichtbüchern augusteischer Zeit," *Philol.* 81 (1926): 281, and C. Lörcher, *Der Aufbau der drei Bücher von Ovids Amores* (Amsterdam, 1975), 3, that Ovid never employed (as Lörcher says) "a rigid, numerically determined symmetry," but created his structural patterns thematically and rhetorically, by the grouping of topics and images. Book 3, I would argue, is divided into three main parts: (1) Proem and Captatio (1–100); (2) Elementary Precepts (101–498); and (3) Advanced Precepts (499–808), each part containing twelve sections, with balanced internal groupings, in which the narrative *mythoi* have an important role to fulfill.

passion for the bull (289–328), the rescue of Ariadne by Bacchus (525–64), and the seduction of Deidameia by Achilles (681–704). Book 2, in contrast, has one narrative *mythos* only, that of Daedalus and Icarus (2.21–96), which gains in significance both from its prominent position near the beginning, and because of its solitary status.[2] Book 3, like Book 2, offers one narrative *mythos* only, this time near the end: the story of Cephalus and Procris (3.687–746). The *Remedia Amoris* contains no narrative *mythoi* at all.[3] It seems reasonable to assume that Ovid used these set-pieces deliberately, and found less occasion for them as he proceeded. Various other explanations have been found for them, some more frivolous than Ovid's own *praecepta*. They were trial runs for the stories in the *Metamorphoses*. They simply betray Ovid's harmless pleasure in over-icing the cake, his liking for digressions with a neoteric, Alexandrian flavor. They suggest exercises in *ekphrasis*, based on his obsession with the visual arts.[4]

Such suggestions may have considerable incidental value—Ovid always enjoyed multilevel imagery and complex double meanings—but they remain peripheral. In the last resort, the *mythoi* are there to point a moral rather than adorn a tale; they form a functional element in his didactic method, occupying a position roughly akin to that of the parable in an old-fashioned sermon. Thus the way Ovid positions and handles them is worth careful scrutiny: it is unlikely that they will differ significantly in attitude from the more explicitly didactic passages of the *Ars*. The latter consistently reveal their author as a sophisticated, urbane ironist, a shrewd deflater of stuffy officialdom—his anti-Augustan stance is only political in the Orwellian sense that *every* position taken up vis-à-vis society and authority has, like it or not, a political basis, something Ovid the political butterfly learned too late, the hard way—and a sexual realist with a paradoxical relish for elaborate games-playing, a man whose social conscience might best be qualified as vestigial. We should expect his *mythoi*, his parables, to underscore or illustrate the general message he is propounding: this, I submit, is precisely what they do.

Throughout Book 3 we are conscious of a certain sly ambivalence in the narrator's attitude. On the face of it, his aim is to arm both sides for the battle

---

2. The passages involving Ulysses and Calypso (123–42) and Mars and Venus (561–92) are not narrative *mythoi* proper but merely extended *exempla*.

3. Again, the *exempla* involving Circe and Ulysses (263–88) or Phyllis and Demophon (591–608) are simply illustrations to a didactic point—don't trust magic, avoid solitude when you're in love.

4. On this fascinating topic, see H. Bartholomé, *Ovid und die antike Kunst* (Leipzig, 1935), esp. ch. 4, "Die ovidische ἔκφρασις," 74–90; cf. L. P. Wilkinson, *Ovid Recalled* (Cambridge, 1955), 172ff.

of the sexes, and thus to set up an evenly matched encounter (3.1ff.): *ite in bella pares*. But while ostensibly showing the girls, with caustic concision,[5] just how to manipulate male stupidity and male egotism, Ovid is in fact quietly programming them to do just what will suit men best: this becomes clear during his advice on sexual techniques (769–808). His pose (667ff.) that he has betrayed his own sex turns out, on scrutiny, to be a pose and nothing else. (Yet Cephalus, as we shall see, is hardly an admirable character.) While the women are busily working (673–74) to make their men feel loved, the men can sit back and enjoy the attention they are getting. The myth of Procris is a cautionary tale designed (683–86) to curb over-suspiciousness in girls regarding the fidelity of their husbands or lovers: no good, it is argued, will come of such investigative practices. But the clear implication of all that has gone before (in particular, Books 1 and 2) is that the girls indeed have something to be suspicious about. *Ars*, in this case, is indeed *celare artem*. We would therefore expect Ovid to choose an *exemplum* in which the mythical lover had been — and *was traditionally known to have been* — guilty of infidelity, but to manipulate its presentation in such a way that the faithless protagonist should, for once, appear convincingly innocent. (Those sophisticated readers, male or female, who were well up in the by-ways of mythology, and knew by heart, like Tiberius's professors,[6] just what songs the Sirens sang, could draw their own private conclusions.) An analysis of the Procris legend's treatment makes it only too clear that this is precisely what Ovid has done.[7] Let us consider the evidence.

At first sight this story, at least as narrated in the *Ars*, has a tragic innocence and pathos: as romantic scholars have not been slow to suggest, it can be construed as a celebration of true conjugal love, an interpretation applicable a fortiori to the reworked version that Ovid published in the *Metamorphoses* (7.672–862).[8] Yet the only other ancient sources that seem aware of this notion are Servius (on *Aen.* 6.445) and Hyginus (*Fab.* 189.1), who both clearly got it from Ovid. More important, why such love should have a place in the *Ars* at

---

5. H. Fraenkel, *Ovid: A Poet between Two Worlds* (Berkeley and Los Angeles, 1945), 204 n. 3.

6. Suet. *Tib.* 70.3. Lenz (1962, 178 = 299, cf. below, note 7) hits on this point, though without apparently realizing its significance, when he observes that the Procris of the *Remedia* (453) "in wenigen Wörten, aber für den Leser, *der den Mythos kennt* [my italics], deutlich genug mit Absicht ganz anders [from the version in the *AA*] dargestellt ist."

7. No scholar who has discussed the episode seems to have grasped this simple fact. See, e.g., Rohde 1929, 40–51; Renz 1935, 22–35; Pöschl 1959, 328–43; Lenz 1962, 177–86 (= *Opusc. Select.* 298–307); Brooks Otis 1966, 381–84; Galinsky 1975, 150ff.

8. E.g., Pöschl 1959, 332ff.; Otis 1966, 176, 268, 383–84; Lenz 1962, 178 (= 299), 186 (= 307); Galinsky 1975, 150–51 (but note his uneasy, and well-justified, proviso, 152: "We are also kept aware of Ovid's manipulation of the story and have to be careful with interpreting it as a heartfelt manifesto").

all is a question seldom asked, and never adequately answered. Lenz merely asserts that for Ovid, "these two [Cephalus and Procris] are simply a man and his wife living in a marriage based upon love, who become involved in a tragic and utterly irreparable event."[9] This begs the question. If Ovid wanted mythic *exempla* of star-crossed marital fidelity, there were many far more suitable ones readily available. Why pick on so unsavory and scandalous a tale in the first place, and, having done so, why keep reminding the reader, with pointed allusions,[10] of just what was being left out? Ovid, of all poets, who not only placed numerous echoes, both mythological and literary, in his work as an integral part of the creative process,[11] but also expected any cultivated reader to recognize them, and to appreciate the resonances they set up, was the last man on earth to pick myths, much less drop hints, by accident or at random. He was a master of intertextuality *avant la lettre* (see below, p. 262).

The apparent gross incongruity between material and treatment has not been wholly lost on scholars,[12] but they seem reluctant to face its full implications. Pöschl, for instance, like Lenz, stresses that for Ovid, "everything derives from one single motive: the great and extraordinary love that animates and fulfils them both" (1959, 332); for him, Ovid's nudging hints about Aurora (see below) are merely "a mark of sensitive discretion and artistic superiority" ("ein Zeichen vornehmer Diskretion und künstlerischer Überlegenheit") (p. 336 n. 3). Rohde (1929, 41–42) theorizes that the embarrassing details were omitted because they were (shades of Richard Heinze!) unsuitable for epic; and that Cephalus appears as narrator in the *Metamorphoses* version of the story to make the omissions more plausible, which is true, but not quite in the way Rohde thought. Yet he is clearly worried by the sly allusions to unspoken scandal; and even the modern reader who comes to this passage without the background knowledge that Ovid assumes—and exploits—will find several points to make him a trifle uneasy. Why was Procris so quick to scent infidelity (699ff.), especially since "Aura" ("Breeze") could hardly be

9. Lenz 1962, 178 (= 299): ". . . Sind die beiden nichts als ein Mann und eine Frau, die in einer auf Liebe begründeten Ehe leben und zwischen denen sich ein tragisches Geschehen abspielt, das durch nichts wiedergutgemacht kann."

10. *AA* 3.684, 701, 741; *Met.* 7.687–88, 748–51 (noticed as long ago as 1883 by Wilamowitz, *Hermes* 18, 425 n. 2; cf. Rohde 1929, 41–42, 44).

11. See Kathleen Morgan, *Ovid's Art of Imitation: Propertius in the Amores* (Leiden, 1977), developing the earlier investigations of scholars such as A. Zingerle, *Ovidius und sein Verhältnis zu den Vorgängern und gleichzeitigen Römischen Dichtern* (Innsbruck, 1869–71), and C. Ganzenmüller, "Aus Ovids Werkstatt," *Philol.* 70 (1911): 274–311. As she says, until recent times "analysis and interpretation of how and why Ovid imitated as he did was generally secondary."

12. See, e.g., Otis 1966, 381–84; cf. W. S. Anderson, *Ovid's Metamorphoses, Books 6–10* (Norman, Okla., 1972), 313–14.

called a common girl's name? Why (733–34) was Cephalus so uncommonly quick off the mark with his javelin (cf. Renz 1935, 30–31)? Why, if it comes to that, did he spend so much time on Hymettus apostrophizing the spring breezes out loud (697–98, 728), a habit, one might have thought, liable to scare off prospective game, at any rate of the four-footed variety?

Ovid's presentation does undoubtedly epitomize, with many vivid touches, that perennial topos, the Jealous Misunderstanding Leading To Fatal Results, a horrid example of *quantum cito credere laedat* (685: i.e., the damage that can be done by jumping to conclusions). It performs its job with admirable effectiveness—until, that is, we consider it in terms of the traditional myth on which it was based, and which it is at such oblique pains to have the reader keep in mind. We do not even need, initially, to consult Ovid's extended treatment of the same theme in the *Metamorphoses*, where the same points are made with even greater emphasis. Cephalus has already been introduced twice in the amatory poems (*Am.* 1.13.39–40; *AA* 3.84), on each occasion as the lover of Aurora, the Dawn, a role that he filled as early as Hesiod's day,[13] siring on this exotic mistress the ill-fated Phaethon.[14] The verbal similarity Aura-Aurora is obvious, and Servius[15] duly notes it: he suggests that Cephalus constantly sighing about "Aura" on Hymettus attracted the attention of the goddess, who presumably misheard him, and was then aroused to passion by his remarkable beauty (cf. Hygin. *Fab.* 270). This *malentendu*, again, is traditional: it can be traced back to Pherecydes.[16] In his apostrophe (as reported by the scholiast who cites Pherecydes as his source), Cephalus exclaims: ὦ νεφέλη παραγενοῦ ("Come, Nephele [Cloud]!"). "Nephele" is no odder a female name than "Aura" (in fact, rather more common), and a heat-exhausted hunter in Attica would be just as likely to pray for cloud cover as for a cooling breeze. But the apostrophe, of course, is not (as the informed reader well knows) as innocent as it seems: behind it lies a lurid saga of adultery, corruption, bribery, transvestism, possible sodomy, and (in at least one early version of the myth) deliberate murder. As a basis for the celebration of true conjugal love, this appears a trifle *outré*. Let us examine the *testimonia* in detail.

Since, as we have seen, the central core of the myth was known to Pherecydes (fl. c. 550 B.C.), and at least one key element in it, the seduction of Cephalus

---

13. *Theog.* 986–87; cf. Paus. 1.3.1.

14. Cf. Wilamowitz, "Phaethon," *Hermes* 18 (1883): 396–434, esp. 422–25.

15. *Ad* Virg. *Aen.* 6.445: "[Cephalus] labore fessus ad locum quendam in silvis ire consueverat et illic ad se recreandum aurum vocare. quod cum saepe faceret, amorem in se movit Aurorae," etc.

16. Pherecydes *ap.* schol. Hom. *Od.* 11.321, Dindorf 2:505 (= Jacoby *FGrH* 3 F 34).

by Eos/Aurora, the Dawn, goes back to Hesiod, there is no possibility of the Cephalus-Procris story being a mere Hellenistic confection, however much later writers (e.g., Nicander) may have modified or romanticized it,[17] supplying material and attitudes that were subsequently picked up by Ovid himself and many later mythographers, such as Antoninus Liberalis.[18] The earlier the details, the less romantic they tend to be.

Procris was the daughter of Erechtheus, king of Athens. (Her sister was Orithyia, who acquired notoriety through getting herself raped by Boreas:[19] winds with sexual characteristics seem endemic to this story.) She married Cephalus, the son of Deion, or Deioneus, from Thorikon in southern Attica.[20] According to Pherecydes (ibid.), Cephalus abandoned his bride ἔτι νύμφην οὖσαν ("while still a bride/marriageable girl")—an ambiguous phrase, which I suspect here means before consummation of the marriage[21]—and went abroad for no less than eight years. He then returned, in disguise, and proceeded to test Procris's fidelity by offering her rich presents if she would sleep with him. Other sources modify, but do not essentially change, this intriguing scenario: they dispense with the eight years' foreign residence, and merely have Cephalus absent himself on a hunting trip, while a servant, acting as go-between, offers the bribes—which, after an initial show of resistance, followed by a raising of the stakes, Procris demurely accepts.[22] Apollodorus knows an alternative (or perhaps a supplementary) version according to which Procris was seduced by one Pteleon in return for a gold crown.[23] In either case the message is clear: Procris came expensive, but her favors—like those of other famous mythological ladies, such as Alcmena or Eriphyle—could ultimately be bought. As a model of conjugal devotion, she is something less than convincing.

In the circumstances it might be thought that Cephalus's elaborate test of his wife's virtue was based on nothing more significant than a shrewd estimate of her character; but once again things are not quite what they seem. The test, we find, was a direct outcome of Cephalus's own prior seduction by Aurora,

---

17. On this point, see, e.g., Pöschl 1959, 330; Otis 1966, 381–82. The work of Nicander most often postulated as a contributory source for Ovid's version is the *Heteroioumena*.

18. Pöschl (1959, 332) speaks of "the cheerfully frivolous novelettes by unknown Hellenistic story-tellers"; on sources used (and cited) by Antoninus Liberalis, see the excellent Budé edition (Paris, 1968) of Manolis Papathomopoulos, esp. pp. xi–xxiii. All citations are taken from Papathomopoulos's text.

19. Plato *Phaedr.* 229B–C; Paus. 1.19.5; Ap. Rhod. 1.212ff. with schol. on 212 (citing Pherecydes and Simonides); Ovid *Met.* 7.694–95, 796–803; Apollod. 3.15.2.

20. Apollod. 1.9.4, 3.15.1; Hygin. *Fab.* 189.1; Ant. Lib. 41.1.

21. For νύμφη in this sense, see, e.g., Hom. *Il.* 9.560; Hes. *Theog.* 298.

22. Ant. Lib. 41.2–3; cf. Hygin. *Fab.* 189.3.

23. Apollod. 3.15.1, followed by Tzetzes, *Chil.* 1.542ff.

which took place a month or two after his marriage to Procris, while he was out hunting on Mt. Hymettus.[24] Ovid used this episode in the *Metamorphoses*, and clearly had it at the back of his mind when composing the descriptive set-piece that opens his version of Procris's death in the *Ars* (3.687ff.): the latter now takes on (to put it mildly) suggestive associations. Hymettus is not merely Cephalus's favorite hunting-ground, but Aurora's, too; and though Cephalus, in Ovid's later version, claims to have been so besotted by his loyal devotion to Procris that he was no more than an unwilling victim of the goddess's advances,[25] it is interesting how regularly thereafter he goes back, unaccompanied and apostrophic, to the scene of his supposed discomfiture.

What is more, according to the tradition that Ovid adapted—or invented —in the *Metamorphoses* (7.71ff.), the notion of testing Procris was put into Cephalus's head by Aurora herself. Servius and Hyginus[26] develop this motif further by having Cephalus initially repulse the goddess's advances; at which, gaily exclaiming, "I wouldn't have you unfaithful unless she's been so first" (*nolo ut fallas fidem nisi illa prior fefellerit*), she either disguises him, or has him disguise himself, as a merchant, and sends him off to nullify Procris's moral advantage in this early version of *La Ronde* by demonstrating that Little Miss Virtue is as seducible as the next woman. "Wie spiessbürgerlich!" ("How bourgeois!") Pöschl exclaims (1959, 337).

Aurora in the mythic tradition was a notorious man-eater[27] whose other victims included Ares, Orion, and Tithonus;[28] but Wilamowitz was surely right, in his commonsensical way, to stress the fact that in the *Metamorphoses*, Cephalus is narrating his own apologia, and therefore "Ovid has to suppress the worst bits" ("das argste muss Ovid verschweigen!").[29] Cephalus got Aurora with child (Hes. *Theog.* 986-87), and to judge by his subsequent behavior on Hymettus would seem to have found her advances more attractive than his protestations of monogamous devotion suggest. Procris, no innocent herself, was not deceived. When she fell into the trap that Cephalus had set for her, and the *soi-disant* merchant—either before[30] or after[31] completing

---

24. Apollod. 1.9.4; Paus. 1.3.1; Hes. *Theog.* 986-87; Ant. Lib. 41.1; Ovid *Met.* 7.700-713 (cf. 813-20, 835-37), the most detailed and specific account; Servius (as in note 15); Hygin. *Fab.* 189.2-3.

25. Ovid *Met.* 7.705-10, cf. Hygin. *Fab.* 189.1-2.

26. Servius loc. cit; Hygin. *Fab.* 189.2-3.

27. Apollodorus (1.4.4) explains that because Eos (Aurora) had slept with Ares, Aphrodite by way of punishment ἐποίει . . . αὐτὴν . . . συνεχῶς ἐρᾶν.

28. Ibid.; cf. 3.12.4; also *HHAphr.* 218ff.

29. Wilamowitz (as above, note 14), 425 n. 2.

30. Ant. Lib. 41.3; Ovid *Met.* 7.740-42. Rohde's comment (1929, 43) is: "Apud Ovidium, qui lascivum narrationis χαρακτῆρα tollere studet, res non eo venit."

31. Hygin. *Fab.* 189.3; Servius, loc. cit.; Pherecydes, loc. cit.

her seduction—revealed his true identity, "she realized she had been tricked by Aurora."[32] When, later, Cephalus returned to his practice of hunting on Hymettus, it is hardly to be wondered at that Procris first had him tailed,[33] and subsequently spied on his activities herself,[34] having meanwhile, very resourcefully, paid him out for his entrapment with an even more ingenious masquerade of her own,[35] to which I shall return in a moment.

But this is to anticipate. After her exposure by Cephalus, Procris fled to Crete, to the court of King Minos,[36] with whom she shared a common passion for, *inter alia*, hunting.[37] However, when not roaming the Cretan hills under the protection of Diana (Artemis),[38] she devoted herself to sport of a more *recherché* nature. Because of his chronic promiscuity, Minos had been bewitched by Pasiphaë, so that when he had intercourse with any other women, "he would ejaculate snakes and scorpions and millipedes [*sic*], and the women with whom he had intercourse would die": this not only rendered him childless but also, not unnaturally, proved a severe deterrent to any prospective mistress. Pasiphaë herself, being immortal, was immune.[39]

Procris, ever resourceful, devised a form of contraception for Minos involving a goat's bladder (Ant. Lib. 41.5) and eventually cured his childlessness. She then, after cautiously giving him a prophylactic decoction of the "Circaean root," (i.e., moly), consented to sleep with him herself: true to form, Minos had been hot to seduce her from the start.[40] In gratitude for these assorted favors, he presented Procris with a javelin that never missed its mark, and a hunting dog that caught whatever it pursued.[41] In the *Metamorphoses* (7.754–56) Cephalus concedes that these telltale gifts were bestowed on Procris in Crete, but tactfully identifies the giver as her fellow-huntress there, the goddess Artemis (cf. Paus. 9.19.1). Hyginus agrees, but feels com-

---

32. Hygin. *Fab.* 189.4, cf. 9: sensit se ab Aurora deceptam.
33. Pherecydes, loc. cit.; cf. Ovid *AA* 3.699–700, *Met.* 7.821ff.
34. Pherecydes, loc. cit.; Apollod. 3.15.1; Hygin. *Fab.* 189.9; Ovid *AA* 3.709ff., *Met.* 7.833ff.
35. Ant. Lib. 41.6–7; Hygin. *Fab.* 189.6–8.
36. Apollod. 3.15.1; Ant. Lib. 41.4; cf. Hygin. *Fab.* 189.4.
37. Hygin. *Astron.* 2.35.
38. Hygin. *Fab.* 189.4–5, cf. Ovid *Met.* 7.745–46.
39. Apollod. 3.15.1; Ant. Lib. 41.4: οὔρεσκεν ὄφεις καὶ σκορπίους καὶ σκολοπένδρας καὶ ἀπέθνῃσκον αἱ γυναῖκες ὅσαις ἐμίγνυτο. It seems clear that Minos's symptoms, here presented in quasi-mythic form, actually describe some form of venereal disease, perhaps an acute gonococcal infection, which would be liable to produce the *sensation* of what Apollodorus so graphically conveys: during World War II, I more than once heard fellow servicemen describe the symptoms of a dose of clap as being "like pissing broken bottles."
40. Apollod. 3.15.1; cf. Hom. *Od.* 11.321; Ovid *RA* 453; Lenz 1962, 180.
41. Apollod. 3.15.1, cf. 2.4.7; Ant. Lib. 41.5. Minos himself had these gifts from his mother Europa, who had them from Zeus; the javelin had been made by Hephaestus (Nicand. fr. 97 Schneider = Pollux *Onom.* 5.38).

pelled (189.5) to explain the presents as a token of Artemis's chaste sympathy for Procris's deception by Aurora[!]. This piece of whitewashing was almost certainly invented by Ovid, as appropriate to Cephalus's self-exculpatory narrative.

The Ur-plot of the myth continues to thicken. Justifiably alarmed by Minos's divine wife Pasiphaë, who clearly viewed these goings-on with something less than enthusiasm,[42] Procris now went home to Thorikos in Attica, taking Minos's gifts with her: an ingenious lady, she put them to good use. She cut off her hair, put on masculine attire, and proceeded to pass herself off as a boy, "and no one who saw her recognized her" (Ant. Lib. 41.6). Thus disguised, she became Cephalus's hunting-companion, and very soon, because of the magical properties invested in dog and javelin, aroused his jealous envy. Seeing that the javelin always hit its mark, and the dog never failed to run down its quarry, Cephalus asked her to sell them. She refused. He then offered her the proverbial half of his kingdom in exchange, still without success.

Procris, having baited the trap, now made her own offer:[43] "If that's what you've absolutely set your heart on," she told him, "give me what boys are wont to give" (Hygin. Fab. 189.7). Giving her "what boys are wont to give" can only mean that she was requiring him to submit to anal or intercrural intercourse. Cephalus, hot with concupiscence, agreed. When they were in bed, Procris revealed just what, and who, she was, upbraiding Cephalus for "having committed a far more shameful act than she did": justifiably, since those who allowed themselves to be buggered for profit were universally despised in the ancient world.[44] However, since a bargain is a bargain, and Cephalus is recorded as having obtained both dog and javelin, even after Procris's revelation, it seems legitimate to deduce that originally she was supposed to have had her will of him, presumably with a dildo ($\ὄλισβος$), before he learned either her sex or her identity. When Ovid's Cephalus, describing their supposedly romantic reunion (Met. 7.747–56), refers to the dog and javelin that Procris so sweetly brought him as homecoming presents, we know what we have to think. A mercenary adulterer-turned-pathic has been neatly checkmated by his whorish wife: clearly these two deserve each other.

At all events, Procris and Cephalus, our sources are agreed, now achieved

---

42. Apollod. 3.15.1.

43. Ant. Lib. 41.6–7; Hygin. Fab. 189.6–8: si utique . . . perstas id possidere, da mihi id quod pueri solent dare.' (Hyginus also, §5, attributes the instigation of this tit-for-tat trick to Artemis, who gave Procris the javelin and dog, with instructions to go and compete with Cephalus, "et iubet eam ire et cum Cephalo contendere.")

44. Cf. K. J. Dover, Greek Homosexuality (London, 1978), 99–109, 140–47.

(in whatever circumstances) an uneasy reconciliation.[45] Procris, however, being all too well aware of her husband's habits, "suspected ... that he was having sex with another woman" (Pherecydes loc. cit.), and sent a servant to spy on him while he was out hunting.[46] The servant duly reported on his master's extravagant appeals to "Aura,"[47] which Ovid describes in significant detail, Cephalus's first-person version being the most revealing.[48] *Vocibus ambiguis* is his phrase for the apostrophe, and the ambiguity was clearly double-edged. "Fearing Aurora" (Hygin. *Fab.* 189.9), Procris decided to observe matters for herself. She secretly followed her husband on his next hunting expedition, hid in a well-placed thicket, and "concealed herself in order to catch her husband with his mistress."[49]

Cephalus began his usual flirtatious address, whether to breeze or divine lover; Procris, suspecting the worst, jumped up and came crashing through the undergrowth to confront him. Pherecydes (loc.cit.) claims that Cephalus saw her, "instantly became beside himself" (αἰφνιδίως ἔξω ἑαυτοὺς γίνεται), and while thus transported with mad rage deliberately ran her through. Our other later sources make the death accidental: Cephalus took the commotion in the bushes for some wild animal, threw the unerring javelin, and only then found that he had killed his wife.[50] In consequence of her death he was tried by the Areopagus, sentenced to banishment for life, and retired to Thebes.[51] The sentence suggests that Pherecydes' version of events may have had more substance to it than later mythographers chose to remember.

Such is the traditional structure of the myth—well known to any educated Greek or Roman audience—against which we must estimate Ovid's intentions when he used Cephalus and Procris as an admonitory just-so story in the *Ars Amatoria*, or, later, made Cephalus produce his elaborate *apologia pro vita sua*

---

45. Apollod. 3.15.1; Pherecydes loc. cit; Hygin. *Fab.* 189.8.

46. Pherecydes loc. cit.

47. Ovid *AA* 3.699–700; *Met.* 7.821–23.

48. Ovid *Met.* 7.808–20, cf. *AA* 3.697–98. The apostrophe in the *Metamorphoses* is far more explicitly erotic. Perhaps this is what led Servius (loc. cit.) to assume that it was *Aurora* who gave Cephalus the dog and javelin—a piece of dramatic economy for which our other sources provide no support, and which is contradicted by the firm linking of the javelin's genesis to Minos and his family (above, note 1).

49. Servius loc. cit., cf. Pherecydes loc. cit.; Hygin. *Fab.* 189.9; Ovid *AA* 3.709ff. The fact that she knew where to go—something of which scholars have made heavy weather: see, e.g., Lenz 1962, 181–82 (= 302–3)—can be explained by the fact that she herself regularly went hunting with Cephalus (Apollod. 3.15.1) and therefore knew his favorite haunts; Apollodorus in fact claims that her death occurred during such a joint expedition, but this, when we recall the part that Aurora played in the earliest versions of the myth, seems unlikely.

50. Apollod. 3.15.1; Hygin. *Fab.* 189.9; Servius loc. cit.; Ovid *AA* 3.731–46, *Met.* 7.840–62.

51. Apollod. 3.15.1, cf. Tzetzes, *Chil.* 1.552; Paus. 1.37.6.

to round off Book 7 of the *Metamorphoses*. As should by now be abundantly clear, he would have been hard put to find a more squalid legend in the entire mythical corpus when putatively searching for innocence, pathos, and marital fidelity. This should come as a surprise only to those romantic scholars who see Ovid as pioneering a "new conception of love" (Brooks Otis 1966, 384), or can believe, with Pöschl (1959, 332), that Cephalus's story is "a poem that comes close to tragedy." Ovid might have declaimed on the overriding claims of marital passion as an adolescent,[52] but since then he had learned, the hard way, to conceal his emotions behind a mask of fashionable cynicism. The *praeceptor amoris* and cuckolds' scourge who narrates the *Ars* is plainly hell-bent on assaulting and demeaning marital fidelity wherever it may be found;[53] in this respect he comes far closer to Pöschl's characterization (1959, 332) of Antonius Liberalis, whose version of the myth he sees as an Ionian-style novella with elements reminiscent of Attic comedy, and looking forward to Boccaccio. Ovid does not need to make explicit mention of the seamier episodes we have discussed, though he is only too well aware of them: a series of discreet hints does his business to perfection.

The moment he begins to describe Hymettus (*AA* 3.686ff.), the reader's mind picks up the allusion to Cephalus's notorious intrigue with Aurora (openly described in *Met.* 7.76off.). As a result, the first thought we have—an effect that Ovid doubtless planned with great care—is that his supposed address to the personified breeze (*aura*) was in fact a hopeful early morning appeal to his divine ex-mistress. And where better to seek her than on Hymettus, the scene of their original encounter, above whose summit—as I can testify from personal experience—she rises each morning in unforgettable splendor?[54] Through the mutual protestations of devotion that Ovid sets forth, there runs, like a silent counterpoint, that earlier, grimmer tale that we have just examined, and with every detail of which Ovid shows himself familiar. When Cephalus is asked about his magical javelin, "but one blushes to tell / the price he paid for it" (*Met.* 7.687–88), the point is nudged home in a way no one could miss, and not all Cephalus's fulsome protestations of monogamous devotion let us forget it. When he refers so obliquely to Procris's activities in Crete, and confesses, with disingenuous candor, "that I too might have been

---

52. Sen. *Controv.* 2.2.9ff., a fascinating and seldom-cited passage.

53. I argue this point at length (and suggest a possible reason for it) in §§2–3 of the introduction to my translation of Ovid's erotic corpus: *Ovid: The Erotic Poems* (1982), 17–25.

54. This statement is rapidly now (2002) becoming an anachronism: recent photographs show Hymettus almost invisible behind a thick haze of industrial smog that would not disgrace Los Angeles or Mexico City.

bribed into such wrongdoing, had so great a bribe been offered me" (*Met.* 7.743–50), what at once comes to mind is that lurid scene of transvestism and gift-acquisition through homosexual favors. The teasing verbal ambiguities of *Met.* 7.835ff. even suggest that Cephalus, on the very morning of Procris's death, may have been making yet another attempt to get in touch with Aurora. "All, all of a piece throughout," as Dryden wrote; "thy chase had a beast in view"—but not, I think, the ostensible quarry, a judgment applicable equally to Cephalus and to Ovid.

And what, in the *Ars*, was the message to be driven home by this ambiguous example? *Nec cito credideris* (685): "Don't jump to conclusions." Silly girls were expected to take their cue from this silly Procris (a far less sophisticated figure than Pherecydes knew), and swallow any latter-day Cephalus's ad hoc excuses whole, without question. Though allowance should be made for possible Hellenistic romanticizing, the evidence at our disposal strongly suggests that it was Ovid himself who first introduced the concept of marital devotion into the myth, and for far-from-romantic purposes. The concept was carefully set up in order to be ridiculed by discreet allusions emphasizing the eternal gap, in husband-and-wife relationships, between appearance and reality—with appearance always favoring the (far from virtuous) husband. Ovid's literate male audience would enjoy every word of it with particular relish.

It was for them that the exquisite irony of Procris's dying words—"Now my spirit goes out on the breeze whose name I suspected" (*nomine suspectas iam spiritus exit in auras, AA* 3.741)—was primarily intended; they would read the whole episode (in either version) with sharply malicious literary pleasure, and their faith in male double standards comfortably reinforced. *They* knew that Procris was a loose and greedy little trollop who deserved all she got; they also believed, as Juvenal said in another context,[55] that a husband should be allowed his solecisms in peace. When Lenz[56] referred to "the denunciation of a disastrous zealot, involving himself in matters that are none of his business," he spoke truer than he knew. For sheer deadpan allusiveness, Ovid's little *mythos* would be hard to beat; and when we reflect on the prominent position it occupies in Book 3 of the *Ars*, it surely tells us a great deal (though, I would submit, nothing surprising) about the tone and temper of the poem as a whole.[57] Ovid in his own way found women highly enjoyable; but no one who

---

55. Juv. *Sat.* 6.456: "soloecismum liceat fecisse marito," a plea to stop the bluestocking wives bent on correcting their husbands' grammar and literary style.

56. Lenz 1962, 181 (= 302): ". . . die Angeberei eines verhängnisvoll Eifrigen, der sich in Dinge mischt, die ihn nichts angehen."

57. The catalogue of qualities that Galinsky lists (1975, 153) for the *Metamorphoses*—"amused

so consistently likened them to crops, cows, and other natural phenomena really, *au fond*, can have believed (as he affected to for the occasion) in the equality of the sexes.[58] Women, to be sure, needed *cultus;* so did a well-run farm; but *ars* (and possibly *ingenium* too) remained, in the last resort, a male prerogative.

Afterword (2002)

The writing of this essay was in part a by-product of my work for *Ovid: The Erotic Poems* (1982), but also in response to Charles Segal's long article "Ovid's Cephalus and Procris: Myth and Tragedy," *Grazer Beiträge* 7 (1978): 175–205, which seemed to me to be conducted in the kind of rarefied literary terms that would have provoked Ovid to sly derision, and, worse, to seriously misread his intentions. "What in the Greek sources," Segal asserted, "is a lascivious interplay of carefully balanced and symmetrical seductions becomes in Ovid . . . a tale of high pathos and tragic misunderstanding" (175). This, quite apart from falling (as Ovid intended his women readers to do) for the romantic version he served up, completely ignores his bookish, Tiberian, and extremely modern passion for mythic intertextuality. Segal, and others, go on the assumption that variant versions of a myth could function each in its own literary vacuum, without reference to the tradition as a whole. Dubious in principle, this notion becomes the merest paradox when applied to Ovid, who carried a vast, rich, and various mythic store in his head, and, equally important, *expected his readers to do the same.*

Nor was this mischievous and mocking subverter of public virtue and private stuffiness given to serving up romance because he believed in it: the kind of marital tragic pathos that Segal so enjoys formed a natural target for him, and I hope that I have demonstrated just how he went about deconstructing it. In fact, this afterword would not have been necessary had it not been for Joseph Fontenrose's attack on my original article, "Ovid's Procris," *CJ* 75 (1980): 289–94, accusing me of falling into the so-called documentary fallacy, a charge echoed, without further comment, by W. S. Anderson in "The Example of Procris in the *Ars Amatoria*," in *Cabinet of the Muses*, ed. M. Griffith and D. J. Mastronarde (Atlanta, 1990), 131–45 (at p. 145 n. 15). In fact, Fontenrose, who was also pursuing his own agenda (cf. my *Classical Bearings* [1989],

detachment, irony, parody, travesty, grotesque exaggeration, over-explicit visual detail, literary wit and allusiveness, incongruities jarring and subtle, bathos and burlesque"—surely applies here also.

58. On this point, see the penetrating analysis by E. W. Leach, "Georgic Imagery in the *Ars Amatoria*," *TAPhA* (1964): 142–54.

106-9), made the elementary mistake of assuming Ovid to be the narrator rather than Cephalus; but quite apart from this, the essence of the "documentary fallacy," for the most part a modern invention, is precisely that each narration of fictional myth has its own isolated self-sufficiency and can, should, be treated without reference to any other version. The only trouble with this arbitrary fiat in the present instance is that Ovid had never heard of it, took no interest in it, and indeed habitually used the rich variety of Greco-Roman myth as a background or baseline against which, with the cooperation of a knowledgable audience, to counterpoint his own deconstructive, and most often subversive, comments on tradition. Morally or socially embarrassing archaisms were meat and drink to him. In this he formed an exact parallel to the earlier dramatic usages of Euripides.

15

Magic and the Principle of Apparent Causality in Pliny's *Natural History*

LIKE MANY POLYMATHS, the Elder Pliny was a man of uncertain beliefs. This nowhere emerges more clearly than in his pronouncements on magic and superstition.[1] He devotes considerable space at the beginning (§§1–18) of Book 30 of the *Natural History* to a refutation of what he describes as *fraudulentissima artium*, arguing that such "shadows of truth" (*ueritatis umbras*) as it may possess owe their power to the poisoner's rather than the magician's art (§17). He shows particular hostility to the various spells or remedies associated—whether correctly or not—with the Persian Magi,[2] and is contemptuous of deified diseases and plagues.[3]

Yet a little earlier (28.19) he had admitted that "no one is not afraid of being hexed by spells" (defigi quidem diris deprecationibus nemo non metuit), and elsewhere (28.85) he shows himself ambivalent to the point of blind credulity about various aspects of magic; at one point, indeed, he quotes, with evident approval, a spell to counter the quackery of the Magi ("those utter

---

Note: An early version of this article was given as a paper at the 1986 meeting of the A.P.A. in San Antonio. I have since brought my original text up to date and, in response to detailed criticism, have rethought, partially rewritten, and greatly expanded it.

1. See E. Riess, "Pliny and Magic," *AJPh* 17 (1896): 77–83; P. M. Green, "Prolegomena to the Study of Magic and Superstition in the *Natural History* of Pliny the Elder," Ph.D. diss., Cambridge University, 1954; Ernout 1964, 190–95; Martini 1977, 133–64; Luck 1985, 37–39; Nutton 1986, ch. 4, 30–58; Addabbo 1991, 11–27; Hahn 1991, 209–39; Beagon 1992, chs. 1–3 (26–123); Jordan, Montgomery, and Thomassen 1999, 293–94, Dickie 2001, 118–21, 123–26, 135–36 and elsewhere.

2. In *NH* 30.1–18 he outlines the origins and development of the Magi and "Magian" magic. References to specific "Magian" formulas abound throughout his work, particularly in Books 20–32 on medical topics: some are given without comment, but very often he is condemnatory. See, e.g., 24.156–57; 25.106; 28.85–86, 228–29; 29.68; 30.18. Cf. Beagon 1992, 105–6 with n. 29.

3. *NH* 2.15–16, apropos the temples of Febris on the Palatine and Mala Fortuna on the Esquiline.

impostors"): smearing doorposts with menstrual blood![4] Despite his skepticism, *Roman* superstitions force him, however reluctantly, to a dangerous concession. Discussing the belief that the Vestal Virgins know a *precatio* capable of rooting runaway slaves to the spot (provided they are still within the city limits), he writes: "If this claim be once accepted, that the gods listen to certain prayers, or can be swayed by any form of words, then we have to credit the entire hypothesis."[5]

This kind of thing should not surprise us. No ancient rationalist exposed to the Stoic belief in universal συμπάθεια — that system of natural or magic influential affinities which Pliny knew and discussed[6] — could fail to have a certain weakness for the doctrines of *similia similibus* and *pars pro toto* that underpin so much magical reasoning. Most of the great pharmacologists and physicians in antiquity, from Dioscorides to Galen, however scornful they might be of "magic," nevertheless believed in sympathetic remedies,[7] for which, indeed, they had good literary precedent.[8] Further, it has been demonstrated[9] that Pliny had considerable faith, *malgré lui*, in the power and efficacy of the written or spoken word ("die Macht des Wortes"), and thus in the validity of *carmina* or φάρμακα. The metaphorical nexus between magic and persuasive rhetoric had been a commonplace long before Gorgias's *Helen*,[10] and was still being reworked in the Augustan Age by a poet such as Ovid, who extolled the magic of poetry while specifically rejecting just the kind of superstitious clap-trap that Pliny and others chose to retail.[11]

Such literary or symbolic solutions, however, were not for Pliny. His φάρ-

---

4. id quoque conuenit, quo nihil equidem libentius crediderim, tactis omnino menstruo postibus inritas fieri Magorum artes, generis uanissimi, ut aestimare licet. Cf. Luck 1985, 39.

5. *NH* 28.13: si semel recipiatur ea ratio et deos preces aliquas exaudire aut ullis moueri uerbis, confitendum sit de tota coniectatione. Cf. Addabbo 1991, 11ff. For Pliny's ambivalence, see also Ernout 1964, 190–95; Martini 1977, 160ff.; and Parry 1992, 40 n. 34.

6. See, e.g., *NH* 1.20, and cf. Luck 1985, 38.

7. Cf. Edelstein 1937, 201–46, esp. 230ff.; Ankarloo and Clark 1999, 184–85, 229, 235–36; Faraone and Obbink 1991, 148–51.

8. See, e.g., Soph. *Ajax* 581-82: οὐ πρὸς ἰατροῦ σοφοῦ | θρηνεῖν ἐπῳδὰς πρὸς τομῶντι πήματι.

9. By Bäumer 1984, 84–99, esp. 97ff. See also Entralgo 1970, a work apparently unknown to Bäumer.

10. See the *Helen*, §§10 and 14, for the use of such terms as ἔθελξε, γοητείᾳ, μαγείας, and ἐφαρμάκευσαν; and for a full discussion of the magical power of poetry from Homer onward, De Romilly 1973, 155–62; De Romilly 1975, esp. ch. 1, "Gorgias and Magic," 1–22; and—a particularly full and illuminating discussion—Parry 1992, pts. 1.4 (63ff.), 1.6 (105ff.), and 2.10 (197ff.).

11. See Ovid *Am.* 1.6, 2.1.21–28 (with play on *carmen*), *AA* 2.99–106 (philtra nocent animis), and above all *RA* 249–70, esp. 251–52: ista ueneficii uetus est uia; noster Apollo / innocuam sacro carmine monstrat opem. Cf. Green 1982, 75, 366–67.

μακα remain firmly in the realm of hocus-pocus. Yet he admits that the "best brains" reject such "uerba et incantamenta carminum,"[12] and gives his catalogue of superstitions with a kind of angry impatience,[13] observing, apropos magical graffiti on walls (*NH* 28.19–20): "It is not easy to say whether our faith is more violently shaken by the foreign, unpronounceable words, or by the unexpected Latin ones, which our mind forces us to consider absurd, being always on the look-out for something big, something adequate to move a god, or rather to impose its will on his divinity."[14]

Immo uero quod numini imperet: Pliny knows very well that the essence of magical operations is *control*, whether over human beings, divinities, or the otherwise immune natural processes of the cosmos. His awareness of the *uis naturae*, his sense of nature as providential, divine, and the central creative force in the world,[15] was matched by an awareness of magic as the effort made by individuals to manipulate this *uis* for their own advantage.[16] Of Nero's interest in magic he observes, with psychological acumen, that the emperor's overriding desire was to force the gods to do his will.[17] Power, in this world, is the name of the game. Magic, in fact, to borrow a modern analogy, is the precise equivalent of a private hacker obtaining illegal access to, and mastery over, an official computer system. This is truer of the Greek than of the (pre-Ptolemaic) Egyptian *mise-en-scène*, where, as David Martinez reminds me, "magic is a gift of the gods and part of the official cult"; but the late Greco-Egyptian magical papyri reveal, nevertheless, a world immeasurably remote — after centuries of Lagid and Roman overlordship — from the ancient Pharaonic system: a world of petty outsiders, obsessed with winning the key to private control, and nursing fantasies of power and revenge.[18]

I am only too well aware that nowadays this is regarded as an outmoded attitude in magical studies, where the old perception of magic as an *effective*

---

12. At *NH* 28.10, in answer to the rhetorical question "polleantne aliquid uerba et incantamenta carminum," he concedes that "uiritim sapientissimi cuiusque respuit fides," but reminds us (a) that there is world-wide, sometimes unconscious, belief in such recourse; and (b) that "si uerum est, homini acceptum fieri oportere conueniat."

13. See in particular *NH* 28.22ff.

14. Neque est facile dictu externa uerba atque ineffabilia abrogent fidem ualidius an Latina inopinata et quae inridicula uideri cogit animus semper, aliquid inmensum exspectans ac dignum deo mouendo, immo uero quod numini imperet. The translation is that by W.H.S. Jones, *Pliny: Natural History VIII, Libri XXVIII–XXXII* (London and Cambridge, Mass., 1963), 15.

15. Beagon 1992, passim, esp. 26–54, 65–66, 84–86, 92–102, 189–90.

16. Ibid., 106–7: For Pliny, "the magicians' claim to master *uis naturae* violates the whole basis of the man-nature relationship in the *HN*."

17. *NH* 30.14: . . . primumque imperare dis concupivit. . . .

18. Personal communication, Prof. D. Martinez. On the "world of petty outsiders," cf. Green 1993, 598–601.

(or not-so-effective) instrument of would-be self-empowerment has been re-placed by a view of it as "affective, expressive or symbolic," to be judged on the basis of *appropriate performance*, as felicitous rather than practically suc-cessful.[19] I remain deeply suspicious both of the new concept as such, and in particular of its multicultural, let alone its universal, validity. General defini-tions of magic, whether anthropological, sociological, or historicist, continu-ally fall short through an inability to fit the almost infinite variety of cultural patterns in those societies (the large majority) in which "magic," however con-ceived, can be shown to play some part. Pliny's Rome has already moved away, even if only minimally, from Hellenistic Alexandria: the terms of power, and hence the attitudes, are subtly different. To lump either or both in with Bush-men or Trobrianders to promote a general theory is absurd.

What Pliny and his contemporaries saw in magic (and in a good deal else beside) was indeed the individual pursuit of effective power, not least when that power seemed unobtainable by other means or denied by the *uis natu-rae*. What Lloyd refers to as the "performative or illocutionary" quality of the transaction was undoubtedly important, indeed crucial—but, specifically, only insofar as it was an article of faith that prescriptions had to be accu-rate in every detail, and incantations correctly pronounced, to the last letter, if successful results were to be obtained. It should not, then, surprise us to find (*NH* 30.2) Pliny declaring of magic: "It is generally agreed that it first came into existence through medicine."[20] This is shrewd: it was also a widely held belief.[21] If magic is the professed art of acquiring mastery over natural or divine functions for one's own private benefit, then medicine will always have formed one of its two prime targets, the other being sex.[22] Both, in an-tiquity—and still, it might be argued, today—had, have, a dangerously large area of the unknown about them; both were, and remain, vital to human well-being. Both demand transformations far beyond the reach of human reason or of the rational medical pharmacopoeia. Indeed, since erotic passion was commonly regarded in antiquity as a species of sickness, their identities some-

---

19. Lloyd 1979, 2–3, citing Tambiah 1973, 199–229, esp. 220ff.; though at 227–29, as Lloyd points out, Tambiah (quite rightly, in my opinion) "expresses reservations concerning the applicability of this point to the whole of magic." Tambiah 1990 is largely analytical of various anthropologi-cal traditions, and does not formally reconsider the question. Cf. also the cautionary remarks of Riddle 1985, 82–83, and for a recent survey, Richard Gordon in Ankarloo and Clark 1999, 161–265.

20. Natam primum e medicina nemo dubitabit. Pliny goes on to suggest that it then added, first, "uires religionis," and next, "artes mathematicas," because the public was in the dark about the first, while believing that the second offered the surest route to their prime desire, "futura de sese sciendi." A modern advertising agent would approve his reasoning. Cf. Nutton 1986, 44.

21. Edelstein 1937, 238.

22. Cf. Winkler 1991, 214–43.

times merge, so that the only distinction is that between the malicious and the apotropaic, between curing a disease and inflicting it. Thus the erotic binding-spell (κατάδεσμός, *defixio*) is designed to make "the beloved suffer the symptoms of love-sickness for the spell-operator."[23]

A third area of the unknown, the future, also had its professional adepts, who, like other types of magician, were ready to usurp (and very often win over) reason with pseudo-reason. Astrologers, known with good cause as *mathematici*, utilized the movements of the heavenly bodies to predict and diagnose individual human expectations. Most Stoics believed their inge-niously computed fictions; even for Galen—despite his vast medical expertise —astrology was not only rational (once granted its premises, an understand-able assumption), but empirically demonstrable.[24] As Riddle points out,[25] "Magic adopted the vigorous logical organization and systematization of sci-ence and formed systems and disciplines of its own, for example, astrology, alchemy, necromancy, and divination." The attraction for intellectuals was considerable, and Pliny (*NH* 2.94, 97) does no more than discredit the more vulgar manifestations of an immensely popular creed.

He was not unconscious of this dilemma. He saw that there were diseases (in particular what we would describe, but he could not, as complaints occa-sioned by viral or bacterial infections) that defied the medical expertise of his day. Heating a dysentery patient's drinking-water with red-hot irons (*NH* 34.151) was a step in the right direction, but nobody knew why it worked: would he, should we, call this medicine or magic? Pliny also realized, human nature being what it is, just where this was liable to lead. "In quartan fevers," he remarks, "clinical medicine is virtually useless. I shall *therefore* [empha-sis mine] set down several of the magicians' remedies. . . ."[26] There follows a stomach-turning list of ingredients for amulets and similar remedies: this *materia medica* includes the longest tooth of a black dog, the dust in which a

---

23. Personal communication, Prof. D. Martinez; cf. also Martinez 1991, 59–60. On κατάδεσμοί and *defixiones*, in addition to the standard collections of Audollent (1967) and Wünsch (1912), see now Gager 1992, and Daniel Ogden in Ankarloo and Clark 1999, 1–90.

24. Galen 9.913 Kühn: καὶ τοῦτο πρὸς τῷ τοῖς ἀστρονόμοις ὁμολογεῖσθαι πάρεστιν, εἰ βούλει, καί σοι παραφυλάξασθαι. εἰ δὲ μὴτ᾽ αὐτὸς παρατηρεῖν ἐθέλεις τὰ τοιαῦτα μήτε τοῖς τηρήσασι πιστεύεις, τῶν νῦν ἐπιπολαζόντων τις εἰ σοφιστῶν· οἳ λόγῳ κατασκευάζειν ἡμᾶς ἀξιοῦσι τὰ σαφῶς φαινόμενα, δέον αὐτὸ τοὐναντίον ἐκ τῶν ἐναργῶς φαινομένων ὁρμωμένους ὑπὲρ τῶν ἀδήλων συλλογίζεσθαι. See also Ptol. *Tetrab.* 1, proem 1; cf. Thomas 1971, 337; Beagon 1992, 102–4; Faraone and Obbink 1991, 154–56, 177–79.

25. Riddle 1985, 83.

26. *HN* 30.98: in quartanis medicina clinice propemodum nihil pollet. quamobrem plura eorum [Magorum conj. Warmington] remedia ponemus. Cf. 29.95, where he comments, shrewdly, that "it is especially in fevers that true medicine is opposed to the doctrines of these quacks [i.e., magi-cians]" (praecipueque febrium medicina placitis eorum renuntiat).

hawk has rolled, the heart of a live viper (some problems there!), a mouse's muzzle and ear-tips, and the right eye gouged out of a living lizard.[27]

It is important to realize that what causes Pliny's incredulity and anger in such cases is the *lack of any apparent or rational connection* between complaint and prescription, coupled with natural distaste for the bizarre and frequently disgusting nature of the recipes recommended. One Magian remedy for a quartan fever he records consists of an amulet containing feline excrement and a screech-owl's claw. "Who, I ask you, could have discovered such a thing?" he exclaims. "What sort of a recipe is this? Why specially pick on an owl's claw?"[28] At the same time, his incredulity remains marginal: while inveighing against mouse brain, weasel ash, or dried hedgehog's flesh as a cure for delirious fever, he makes it clear that his objection stems from natural revulsion, "even if the treatment works,"[29] and is perfectly happy, it would seem, with "a warm sheep's lung tied round the head."[30]

The magical papyri similarly more or less give up on medical remedies for fevers, however *outré* (to be distinguished from purely magical cures), and, like Pliny, offer a selection of amulets: inscribed olive-leaves, reductive *Ephesia Grammata* on papyrus (as these lines shrink, so may the fever), an unwinding helical appeal (combined with reduction) to Athena as Gorgon-slayer.[31] In an era that had not yet even discovered the therapeutic value of quinine,[32] supernatural control of otherwise intractable and incomprehensible phenomena seemed the only answer. This attitude was, predictably enough, something of a commonplace: when the physician failed, it was frequently said, men turned to incantations and amulets.[33]

---

27. *HN* §§98–99; cf. also 28, 46, 107, 228–29; 30.100–102; 32.113–16.

28. *NH* 28.228–29: quartanis Magi excrementa felis cum digito bubonis adalligari iubent . . . quis hoc, quaeso, inuenire potuit? quae est ista mixtura? cur digitus potissimum bubonis electus est? The reader must decide whether Pliny exempted the cat-shit from his commination out of delicacy or from genuine belief in its therapeutic properties. For other examples, see, e.g., 30.95–96, and cf. Beagon 1992, 107.

29. *NH* 30.95: Who, he asks, could administer such filthy stuff to a patient, "etiamsi certa sit medicina"?

30. Ibid.: pulmo pecudum calidus circa caput alligatus.

31. *PGM* 7.213–14, cf. 119b1–5, and *GMPT* 315; *PGM* 7.218–21, 33.1–25 = *Suppl. Mag.* 1.9 (pp. 24–25), cf. *GMPT* 91.1–14; *Suppl. Mag.* 1.3 (pp. 10–13), cf. *GMPT* 130.1–13; *PGM* 18b.1–7.

32. See H.-J. Horn, "Fieber," in *Reallexikon für Antike und Christentum*, vol. 7 (Stuttgart, 1968), cols. 877–909, esp. 881: "Die Ohnmacht einer medizinischen Wissenschaft, die noch nicht über das rettende Chinin im Kampf gegen die Malaria verfügt, ist wohl dafür mitverantwortlich, daß die rationale Medizin im ausgehenden Altertum durch magische Wundermittel überwuchert wird." Cf. Jones 1909, 137.

33. See Diod. Sic. 31.43: ὅταν ταῖς παρὰ τῶν ἰατρῶν θεραπείας ὑπακούσαντες μηδὲν βέλτιον ἀπαλλάττωσι, καταφεύγουσιν ἐπὶ τὰς θύτας καὶ μάντεις, ἔνιοι δὲ προσδέχονται τὰς ἐπῳδὰς καὶ παντοδαπὰ γένη περίαπτων . . .; Plut. *Mor.* 920B: οἱ ἐν νοσήμασι χρονίοις πρὸς

It is therefore only logical that the ratio of magical or scientifically non-demonstrable cures—those, that is, with no sign of a modern cause-and-effect basis in actual medical experience—should be in inverse proportion to the degree of knowledge available concerning any specific disease. Analysis of the remedies to be found in the *Natural History* and the Greco-Roman papyri tends to confirm this diagnosis. Obviously, nothing would stop many people from using magical remedies for anything, often in tandem with rational prescriptions, just to be on the safe side. The Hippocratic author of *Regimen IV* offered this pithy advice: "Prayer is good, but while calling on the gods a man needs to lend a hand himself, too."[34] In dealing with powers natural and supernatural, the average petitioner, especially in a baffling crisis, would all too often reverse these laudable priorities. But among the writings of educated skeptics (or even ambivalent skeptics, like Pliny), we can see a clear effort to stand by reason. It was not always successful: superstition, like cheerfulness, would keep breaking in, often when least suspected. Like Ovid's Medeia (another notable dealer in exotic drugs), the author of the *Natural History*, if pressed, would too often be forced to confess failure despite good intentions: "video meliora proboque, deteriora sequor."[35] Nevertheless, the will to reason is clearly articulated in Pliny's work, and can help to clarify much of that grey area where ancient medicine and magic intersect.

We can establish a very clear line beyond which rational research could not advance in antiquity, and which, indeed, hardly shifted its position until the mid-nineteenth century. The key concept here is what, somewhat hesitantly, I term the "principle of apparent causality": limitations, that is, imposed on scientific investigation by a crippling lack of accurate mensuration and, worse, of observational instruments that could offer better results than those obtainable by the unaided human hand and eye, or, failing these, by hopeful theorizing. Such handicaps were further compounded by powerful taboos, in most areas and periods, against the dissection of the dead or, a fortiori, of the living, human body.[36] Thus the clearer the connection, in everyday observational terms or by logical analogy, between cause and effect in disease,

---

τὰ κοινὰ βοηθήματα καὶ τὰς συνήθεις διαίτας ἀπειπόντες ἐπὶ καθαρμοὺς καὶ περίαπτα καὶ ὀνείρους τρέπονται. Edelstein 1937, 244 with n. 139, cites instances involving Pericles (Plut. *Per.* 38), Bion (Diog. Laert. 4.54), and Cleomenes (Plut. *Mor.* 223E).

34. Hippocr. *Reg.* 4.87 = Littré 6.643, Jones 1931, 4:423: καὶ τὸ μὲν εὔχεσθαι ἀγαθόν· δεῖ δὲ καὶ αὐτὸν συλλαμβάνοντα τοὺς θεοὺς ἐπικαλεῖσθαι.

35. Ovid *Met.* 7.20–21, cf. 192–209.

36. For a thorough discussion, see von Staden 1989, ch. 6, 138–53. The extra-, indeed anti-, social nature of witches such as Horace's Canidia (*Epode* 5.37–38) or Lucan's Erictho (*BC* 6.667ff.) is emphasized by their indifference to this particular taboo.

the better the chances of applying rational criteria to its diagnosis, and the smaller the need for recourse to magic—which tended to operate most exclusively where science, or even rational guesswork, was at a loss, or in areas treated as taboo by medicine or religion, including not only the interior of the human body, but also, curiously, the underworld.[37] Reason might not always find the answers even if it asked the right questions; but to understand, however imperfectly, the seeming cause of a complaint was at least a stimulus to the search for a rational solution. Logic might sometimes fail, the nervous would always hedge their bets (as both Pliny and the magical papyri make very clear); but at the very least, favorable circumstances for trying to solve the problem existed. It was not a case (like that of infection) where total ignorance bred mere desperate fantasies. Applying the principle, we can soon argue with some confidence as to which areas of ancient medicine did or did not operate at any level, partially at least—though never, to the best of my knowledge, entirely—on a true rational basis, and why.

Orthopedic surgery, the treatment of fractures or dislocations, offers an excellent example. Read the Hippocratic treatises on these topics, and you at once recognize the voice of practical experience.[38] The author may on occasion be wrong (e.g., on the time necessary to consolidate a broken collarbone),[39] but he is never fantastic. On the rare occasions when he does mention hearsay, such as the Amazons' supposed habit of dislocating the knee-joints of their male children in early infancy to prevent sexist plotting against their feminine regime,[40] he issues careful disclaimers. This clarity should not surprise us. If a man falls down and breaks his leg, it is apparent how the trouble came about, and easy enough, by analogy, to suggest a cure. A broken spear can be splinted[41] and bound; fruit trees are grafted, and the graft takes. Experience shows that a leg can be dealt with in the same way: the principle of συμπάθεια has always encouraged such homely analogies. Complaint and treatment, from start to finish, are both comprehensible. We find ourselves in the area par excellence where eye and hand can do a very good job unaided. There were, of course, exceptions. Consider that notoriously difficult,[42] often

---

37. See, e.g., Lucan *BC* 6.730ff., with Martinez 1991, 73–74.

38. Περὶ Ἀγμῶν and Περὶ Ἄρθρων, both excellently edited by Dr. E. T. Witherspoon, *Hippocrates*, vol. 3 (1928), 94ff.

39. For this and other examples, see Witherspoon 1928, 89.

40. Περὶ Ἄρθρων 53 (Witherspoon 1928, 320–21).

41. On ancient surgical splints, see Witherspoon 1928, xxi–xxii.

42. Περὶ Ἄρθρων 51–61 passim, 70; for the pessimism frequently engendered by such malfunctions see esp. 58.56–59 Witherspoon: φαίη μὲν οὖν ἄν τις, ἔξω ἰητρικῆς τὰ τοιαῦτα εἶναι· τί γὰρ δῆθεν δεῖ περὶ τῶν ἤδη ἀνηκέστων γεγονότων ἔτι προσσυνιέναι; (Emphasis mine.).

despaired-of problem, the dislocated hip. If Cato, a not excessively superstitious man, regarded the recital of the formula "huat huat ista sistas sistar-
dannabon dannaustra" daily as essential to the healing process,[43] we can be
tolerably certain that cures were hard to come by. Nor is the principle disturbed by the fact that fantastic remedies still abound in an area where reason, even plain common sense, had full play. Pliny himself offers numerous
exotic prescriptions (including dog brain and ash of fieldmice or earthworms)
for dealing with fractures.[44] Similarly, with the extraction of darts or arrow-
heads—common and obvious surgery that must have accumulated a mass of
good practical techniques down the centuries—Pliny still recommends poul-
ticing the wound with anything from a lizard's head to a split mouse.[45] But
there may be a practical problem here: that of infection (see below), the cause
of which was anything but apparent.

Practical experience kept theoretical fantasy at least at arm's length. Men
who spent a significant part of their lives fighting with sword and spear had
a precise knowledge of just what effects wounds in various parts of the body
were liable to produce. In the Hippocratic treatise *The Physician*, we find
would-be surgeons advised to follow mercenary armies to gain experience.[46]
As early as Homer's day, observation is clinically accurate. A spear driven into
the buttock (*Il.* 5.65) pierces the bladder and emerges under the pubic bone.
An epigastric wound exposes the pericardium (*Il.* 16.41). When Ajax hurls a
rock that crushes Hector's breastbone, the victim becomes faint and dizzy,
gasps for breath, and coughs up blood (*Il.* 14.437). Here the easy deduction
of internal hemorrhaging came up against a profound ignorance of internal
anatomy. Similarly, the Hippocratic treatise *On Wounds in the Head*[47] knows
exactly what type of weapon or blow will produce what kind of fracture or
contusion (chs. 11–22).[48] Once again, the cause of damage is known, even if
the precise nature of that damage remains elusive, and the cure suggests itself.

But with wounds, a crucial unknown element also enters to complicate the
picture: sepsis. *On Wounds in the Head*, besides offering an (in every sense)

---

43. Cato *De Agr.* §160.

44. *NH* 30.119.

45. *NH* 30.122, cf. *PGM* 13.247.

46. *Περὶ Ἰητροῦ* 14 Littré. Discussing the surgery of wounds, particularly those περὶ τὴν
ἐξαίρεσιν τῶν βελέων, Hippocrates recommends that τὸν . . . μέλλοντα χειρουργεῖν στρα-
τεύεσθαι δεῖ καὶ παρηκολουθηκέναι στρατεύμασι ξενικοῖς· οὕτω γὰρ ἂν εἴη γεγυμνασμένος
πρὸς ταύτην τὴν χρείαν.

47. *Περὶ τῶν ἐν κεφάλῃ τρωμάτων*, edited and translated in Witherspoon 1928, 2–51.

48. See, e.g., 11.36–41 Witherspoon: τῶν δὲ βελέων ῥήγνυσι μάλιστα τὸ ὀστέον τάς τε
φανερὰς καὶ τὰς ἀφανέας καὶ φλᾷ τε καὶ ἐσφλᾷ ἔσω ἐκ τῆς φύσιος τῆς ἑαυτοῦ τὸ ὀστέον
τὰ στρογγύλα τε καὶ περιφερέα καὶ ἀρτίστομα, ἀμβλέα τε ἐόντα καὶ βαρέα καὶ σκληρά.

scalp-raising guide to trephining (ch. 21), also gives a graphic description (chs. 19–20) of the gangrene and bone necrosis that killed so many patients. Appallingly, the same word, ἕλκος, means both "wound" and "purulent ulcer": the two things almost invariably went together.[49] Indeed, the erroneous notion of "laudable pus"—in fact no more than one symptom of a comparatively mild infection—persisted until Lister's day in the nineteenth century. However much they might stress the need for precise clinical observation, however vigorously they attacked false philosophical apriorisms in the practice of medicine (as the Hippocratic pamphlet *On Ancient Medicine* does with some vigor[50]), the fact remains that Greek doctors were condemned, like it or not, to generalize, always, from hopelessly inadequate evidence.

Without clinical thermometers, stethoscopes (though doctors did practice a crude form of auscultation), and, above all, microscopes, research was limited (I repeat) to what could be seen, and interpreted, by the naked eye. Furthermore, in addition to being thus debarred from any understanding of bacterial or viral infection,[51] ancient physicians also suffered untold disadvantages from not being allowed, for most of antiquity, to explore the interior of the human body. They could describe Hector's hemorrhage, but had no real idea either of its cause or of how to stop it. When Odysseus suffered that gash to his thigh, the sons of Autolycus staunched the flow with skillful bandaging, but, significantly, also used a magic ἐπαοιδή as back-up.[52] Until Ptolemy II Philadelphos licensed Herophilus and Erasistratus to dissect,[53] knowledge of human anatomy was not only sketchy (even with animal analogies easily avail-

---

49. See Majno 1975, 183.

50. *VM* 1-2, 13-15, 17, 20.

51. Even had microscopes been available, there is no guarantee that the correct conclusions would have been drawn from them, or that religious and other prejudices might not have hampered their full use: Kipling treated this theme with remarkable insight in his medieval tale "The Eye of Allah," *Debits and Credits* (London, 1926), 365–94. Such considerations must be borne in mind when assessing Varro's claim that marshy areas should be avoided "quod crescunt animalia quaedam minuta, quae non possunt oculi consequi, et per aera intus in corpus per os ac nares perueniunt atque efficiunt difficilis morbos" (*RR* 1.12.2 Heurgon). Heurgon (1978, 134 n. 4) confidently identifies this as an allusion to malaria. Even if true, that does not mean that Varro understood the true cause of the disease. At best it was a lucky guess, on a par with the Democritean atomic theory; more probably Varro was thinking of tiny insects, by analogy with the mosquito. I owe this intriguing reference to my former colleague Lesley Dean-Jones.

52. Hom. *Od.* 19.457, cf. Plin. *NH* 28.21. See now R. Renehan, "The Staunching of Odysseus' Blood: The Healing Power of Magic," *AJPh* 113 (1992): 1–4, esp. 2: "Since most wounds, if properly bandaged, stop bleeding soon enough, it is easy enough, by a natural mental confusion, to attribute a curative efficacy to the incantation which regularly accompanied the bandaging on the principle of *post hoc, ergo propter hoc*." The practice also, of course, betrays a fundamental lack of scientific knowledge.

53. Cels. *De Med.* proem. §23, cf. Tert. *De Anim.* 10.4, 15.3.5. See von Staden 1975, 178–99.

able), but too often liable to suffer, like so much in the ancient world, from inappropriate moralizing.

In this connection, Plato's description of the digestive and respiratory system[54] as a structure resembling a wicker lobster-pot, equipped with pipes circulating fiery πνεῦμα, at once comes to mind. And what about his belief[55] that the head controls the body because of its *roundness*, that is, as a microcosmic equivalent of the spherical universe? Or the notion that the mind projects visible images on the liver, which itself serves to control the lower appetites, with the spleen serving as a kind of duster to polish up the mirror-surface of the liver and keep it clean and bright?[56] Even if Plato is writing tongue-in-cheek here, this characteristic urge to moralize bodily functions is not only a sure mark of the philosophical domination over anatomy, but a reminder of just how little was really known, before the great Alexandrian researchers, about the inner workings of the human body. Observation, lacking depth or precision, was always outstripped by theory, however exotic, from the Four Humors to arterial πνεῦμα or a monadic system such as Methodism, which attributed all diseases to improper constriction or relaxation of the pores. The author of the Hippocratic treatise generally translated as "The Art" (Περὶ Τέχνης) knew this. He was confident that medicine could cope with the visible diseases (τὰ φανερὰ τῶν νοσημάτων), and felt that it should not be at a loss regarding the less visible ones (τὰ ἧσσον φανερά), either. After a rather tortured paragraph attempting to describe parts of the internal system and the musculature, he admits: "Without doubt no man who sees only with his eyes can know anything of what has been here described . . . for what escapes the eyesight is mastered by the eye of the mind." When perception fails, reasoning (λογισμός) takes over.[57]

Thus we see that a crucial area of medical research in antiquity was de-

---

54. Plat. *Tim.* 78A–79A.

55. Ibid., 44D. Even if this is a joke (by no means certain), the form it takes is significant.

56. Ibid., 69E–73A. Some of these fantasies are extraordinarily long-lived. At *Tim.* 91C–D we read of the supposed peripatetic nature of the womb when frustrated by nonfertilization: according to Plato, it *wanders through the body* in a kind of biological snit, blocking up air passages and inducing diseases (τὰς τοῦ πνεύματος διεξόδους ἀποφράττον, ἀποπνεῖν οὐκ ἐῶν, εἰς ἀπορίας τὰς ἐσχάτας ἐμβάλλει καὶ νόσους παντοδαπὰς ἄλλας παρέχει). This phenomenon was frequently represented on magical amulets: C. Bonner, *Studies in Magical Amulets, Chiefly Graeco-Egyptian* (Ann Arbor, 1950), 79–94. More striking still, it survived into modern times, distorted but still recognizable, as the "wandering navel" or "waist out of place" of Greek folk-medicine: see R. and E. Blum, *Health and Healing in Rural Greece* (Stanford, 1965), 53, 69, 91, 166–73, 189–92.

57. Hippocr. *Art.* 11: Οὐ γὰρ δὴ ὀφθαλμοῖσί γε ἰδόντι τούτων τῶν εἰρημένων οὐδενὶ ἔστί εἰδέναι . . . ὅσα γὰρ τὴν τῶν ὀμμάτων ὄψιν ἐκφεύγει, ταῦτα τῇ τῆς γνώμης ὄψει κεκράτηται.

pendent, literally, upon nothing but the more or less intelligent imagination of the researcher: "Hints and guesses, hints followed by guesses." We are accustomed, when judging between such theories, to praise apparent rationalism while dismissing superstition. This is not always quite fair. For one thing, cures that are categorized as superstition may nevertheless have therapeutic value: letting a demon out of the skull by trephining must have sometimes relieved a depressed fracture, while Asclepiad ἐγκοίμησις, or *incubatio*, has left far too solid a record of *ex voto* offerings from grateful patients[58] for us to ignore its obvious success, however we may choose to explain the phenomenon. Geoffrey Lloyd reminds us that "a very considerable body of evidence can be assembled to show how much of Greek science consists in the rationalisation of popular belief."[59] Also, with the death rates recorded—of the forty-two cases described in *Epidemics* 1 and 3, no less than twenty-five, or almost 60 percent, terminated fatally[60]—Hippocratic physicians will have been only too happy to turn over cases to the god that lay beyond their own merely human competence.[61] Self-help and prayer were mutually interdependent.[62]

The moral of that, of course, is that a secular false hypothesis, however much we may prefer it *en principe*, will not on that account necessarily give better results than a religious or magical one. We are often reminded that the author of the famous Hippocratic treatise *On the Sacred Disease*[63] had very little time for magicians or quacks: such persons, he records, "being at a loss, and having no treatment that would help . . . concealed and sheltered themselves behind superstition, and called this illness sacred, in order that their utter ignorance might not be manifest."[64] His introductory assertion[65] has become a kind of humanist watchword: "It [i.e., epilepsy] is not, in my opinion, any more divine or more sacred than other diseases, but has a natural

58. Aristoph. *Plut.* 400–414, 633–747; *IG* iv² (1) 121–22; Edelstein and Edelstein 1945, 1:221 ff., esp. no. 423, passim; C. A. Meier, *Ancient Incubation and Modern Psychotherapy*, trans. M. Curtis (Evanston, Ill., 1967).

59. G.E.R. Lloyd, *Science, Folklore and Ideology: Studies in the Life Sciences in Ancient Greece* (Cambridge, 1983), 202.

60. Jones 1923, 1:144; 2:ix–xiii.

61. Edelstein and Edelstein 1945, 2:169.

62. Hippocr. *Reg.* 4.87 = Littré 6.643 (Jones 1931, 4:423]: καὶ τὸ μὲν εὔχεσθαι ἀγαθόν· δεῖ δὲ καὶ αὐτὸν συλλαμβάνοντα τοὺς θεοὺς ἐπικαλεῖσθαι.

63. *Morb. Sacr.* (Περὶ ἱερῆς νούσου), Jones 1923, 2:138–83.

64. *Morb. Sacr.* 2.6–10: οὗτοι τοίνυν παραμπεχόμενοι καὶ προβαλλόμενοι τὸ θεῖον τῆς ἀμηχανίης τοῦ μὴ ἔχειν ὅ τι προσενέγκαντες ὠφελήσουσι, καὶ ὡς μὴ κατάδηλοι ἔωσιν οὐδὲν ἐπιστάμενοι, ἱερὸν ἐνόμισαν τοῦτο τὸ πάθος εἶναι.

65. Ibid. 1.1: οὐδέν τι μοι δοκεῖ τῶν ἄλλων θειοτέρη εἶναι νούσων οὐδὲ ἱερωτέρη, ἀλλὰ φύσιν μὲν ἔχει καὶ πρόφασιν.

cause." This heartening broadside in favor of scientific rationalism is much better known—and with good reason—than the "natural cause" that follows, since the writer goes on to assure us, with a plethora of fanciful detail, that what in fact causes the disease is the melting and dispersal of phlegm from the brain.[66] There could be no better demonstration of the glories and short-comings of Greek medicine. A lapidary scientific principle is undercut and nullified by a false theory based on inadequate evidence and what can only be described as poetic speculation (e.g., that phlegm reaching the heart will make you hump backed[67]).

In a world where speculation, unsupported for the most part by experimental observation,[68] and often suspicious of it on intellectual or social grounds,[69] played, of necessity, so dominating a role, the prevalence of medical magic should not really surprise us. Visible causality could go only so far. The Four Humors themselves depended largely on casual external observation of bodily fluids (e.g., the fact that phlegm tends to increase in winter), plus borrowed theorizing (a revamping of the Empedoclean doctrine of the Four Elements), while metaphors derived from mixing ($\kappa\rho\hat{\alpha}\sigma\iota\varsigma$) and cooking ($\pi\acute{\epsilon}\psi\iota\varsigma$), applied in particular to the digestive process, suggest domestic analogies between a full stomach and a stewpot bubbling on the kitchen range.[70] On this reach-

---

66. Ibid. 6–10 passim (Jones 2:152ff.).

67. Ibid. 9.1–4 Jones: ἢν δὲ ἐπὶ τὴν καρδίην ποιήσηται ὁ κατάροος τὴν πορείην . . . ἔνιοι δὲ καὶ κυφοὶ γίνονται.

68. This is not to claim—as has been too often alleged—that experiment played virtually no part at all in ancient medicine or science: for convincing evidence to the contrary, see von Staden 1975, 179ff.

69. The intellectual's contempt for what he regards as mere vulgar application seems to be perennial. Socrates expressed disdain (Xen. *Mem.* 3.7.6, cf. 1.2.9) for the craftsmen and artisans in the Assembly. Plato and Euclid both despised the notion of putting mathematics to practical use (Stob. *Flor.* 4.205; Plut. *Mor.* 718F), an attitude shared by Aristotle (*Pol.* 1258b33ff.) and, notoriously, Archimedes, who (Plut. *Marcellus* 17) "regarded the business of mechanics and every skill that grapples with men's daily needs as ignoble and vulgar." Seneca (*Ep. Mor.* 90) regarded practical inventions as beneath the contempt of thinking men, and in 1825 David Hume (*Essays and Treatises on Several Subjects* [London, 1788], 195) confidently proclaimed that banausic or mechanical occupations "debase the minds of the common people, and render them unfit for any science or ingenious profession." The same belief animated the great Cambridge mathematicians and physicists as recently as the interwar years of the twentieth century. G. H. Hardy (*A Mathematician's Apology*, rev. ed. [Cambridge, 1980], 34) dismissed industrial work as dull and "only fit for second rate minds." Cavendish stars such as Gowland Hopkins and Rutherford "had no interest whatsoever in technical problems or in technology" and indeed "seemed to nurse prejudices against them" (John de la Mothe, *C. P. Snow and the Struggle of Modernity* [Austin, 1992], 36).

70. The key role of metaphor in ancient medicine is something that calls for closer study than it has hitherto received. Perhaps the greatest medical metaphorist of the ancient world was Herophilus, whose work on the pulse elicited a whole slew of metaphors, many borrowed from Aristoxenus

me-down basis, the theory—worthless, but infinitely adaptable—went on as the fundamental prop of European medicine for over two millennia.[71] Why should people *not* have believed it—or, for that matter, the principle of συμπάθεια, which had a great deal more going for it, and has recently made something of a comeback among cosmologists? The influence of the moon on tides was manifest: the Stoic worldview took for granted a universal system of correspondences between microcosm and macrocosm.[72]

Only connect, then, is a prescription with a venerable history; and the elder Pliny, to look no further, offers innumerable examples of allegedly curative properties dependent either upon a physical resemblance between the prescriptive item and the part to be cured or, even more commonly, upon a verbal similarity of nomenclature: another potent instance of "die Macht des Wortes" ("the power of the word"). In the first category we may consider a group of plants, the best-known today being the orchid, credited with aphrodisiac powers through a supposed resemblance of their seeds or root-tubers to testicles.[73] In the second, we find a whole range of *nomina-numina:* the dog's bite that is cured by the dog-rose; the *serpyllum* (thyme) supposedly cognate with the verb *serpere*, and thus deemed efficacious against snakes (*serpentes*); the ashes of a sea-crab (καρκίνου, *cancri marini*) that are used to check carcinoma/cancer.[74] The principle of *similia similibus* was capable of almost infinite

of Taras. Some of his physiological coinages are still in use today: the "tunics" (membranes) of the outer eye, the "ravine" of the portal hepatic fissure, the *calamus scriptorius*, the *torcular Herophili.* Herophilus likened the posterior surface of the iris to a grapeskin and the *os uteri* after parturition to the head of a cuttlefish. He described the pulse as bounding like a gazelle (δορκαδίζων) or fluttering like a trail of ants (μυρμηκίζων) beneath the physician's finger. See J. Longrigg, "Superlative Achievement and Comparative Neglect: Alexandrian Medical Science and Modern Historical Research," *History of Science* 19 (1981): 155–200, esp. 166, 174, 176–77; Fraser 1972, 1:354–55.

71. See Majno 1975, 178.

72. Cf., e.g., S. Sambursky, *The Physical World of the Greeks* (London, 1956), ch. 4, 81ff. T. Hopfner, *Griechisch-Ägyptischer Offenbarungszauber, Studien zur Palaeographie und Papyruskunde* 21, ed. C. Wessely (Leipzig, 1921, reprinted Amsterdam, 1974), §§619–42 (pp. 368–87) deals with the magical aspects of this συμπάθεια, primarily on the basis of late zodiacal evidence.

73. Plin. *NH* 26.95–99: gemina radice testiculis simili, ita ut maior . . . excitet libidinem (§95); . . . radice gemina ad formam hominis testium alternis armis intumescente ac residente . . . (§96) . . . thelygonon et arrenogonon, quarum semen testium simile est, etc. Regrettably, neither Theophrastus himself (*HP* 9.18.9) nor Pliny, citing him (*NH* 26.99), identifies the aphrodisiac that allegedly stimulated *septuageno* [*sic!*] *coitu durasse libidinem.* Cf. *NH* 26.162; 27.65; 28.99, 106, 248; 30.41, 123. For a cure (on the *similia similibus* principle) for swollen testicles, see *PGM* 7.209ff.

74. Plin. *NH* 8.152–53; 20.245 (serpyllum a serpendo putant dictum . . . aduersus serpentes efficax); 32.126, cf. 30.134 (cancri marini cinis usti cum plumbo carcinomata compescit). Cf. also, e.g., 8.98, 25.89 (*hirundo*, i.e., χελιδών = *chelidonia*); 27.113 (the plant *sanguinaria* checks a hemorrhage). See also Ernout 1964, 194–95. *Similia similibus* had an extensive application through color: see *NH* 30.94, 37.169 (*icterus* cures jaundice, hematite restores a healthy, i.e., sanguine, complexion) 37.162 (*galactites* induces lactation).

extension.[75] So, with even greater plausibility, was the concept of the part for the whole (*pars pro toto*), a species of magical synecdoche. If Mithridates VI of Pontus could immunize himself by taking poison in graduated doses[76] (the perfectly sound principle behind all inoculation), was it not equally plausible to believe that menstrual headaches could be cured by smearing the forehead with ashes of menses, that snakebite could be neutralized by the application of a snake's entrails, or that diseases of the genitals could be arrested by the use of urine, preferably the patient's own?[77]

Having mapped the areas where such theories are most likely to prolifer-ate unchecked, namely viral illnesses such as fevers, internal complaints, and bacterial infections generally, we can then test the thesis of visible causality against our available evidence: in the present instance, that of the magical papyri and the *Natural History*. To a striking degree, the thesis is confirmed. Four groups of illness in particular evoke magical cures of a more or less fan-tastic nature:

1. *Fevers and agues:*[78] cures include amulets, nail-parings, reductive formu-lae, and the invocation of various daemons and deities.
2. *Ophthalmia and related eye diseases:*[79] cures include saliva, ligation of two fingers, snake's-eye amulets, and she-goat's dung swallowed in wax at the new moon.
3. *Headaches and migraines:*[80] cures include a suicide's rope or a fox's penis tied round the temples.

---

75. Cf. Audollent 1967, 491-92; C. A. Faraone, "Hermes but No Marrow: Another Look at a Puzzling Magical Spell," *ZPE* 72 (1988): 279-86, esp. 280-82 with nn. 6-10; Martinez 1991, 4 with n. 17.

76. App. *Mithr.* 97-105; Dio Cass. 36.45-54; 37.1-5, 7a, 11-14; Plut. *Pomp.* 30-35; Joseph. *BJ* 1.138, *AJ* 14.53.

77. Plin. *NH* 28.67, 85; 29.71. Cf. also the remedy for being bitten by a mad dog: the application to the wound of ash from a burnt dog's head (29.98).

78. Plin. *NH* 28.46, 86, 107, 228-29; 30.85, 98-99, 102; 32.113-16; *PGM* 7.211-14, 218-21; *PDM* 14.1219-27 [= *GMPT* pp. 250-51]; *PGM* 18b.1-7, 33.1.25, 43.1-27, 44.1-18, 47.1-17, 87.1-11 [= *GMPT* pp. 301-2], 88.1-19 [= *GMPT* p. 302], 89.1-27 [= *GMPT* p. 302], 90.14-18 [= *GMPT* pp. 302-3], 104.1-8 [= *GMPT* p. 310], 106.1-10 [= *GMPT* pp. 310-11], 115.1-7 [= *GMPT* p. 314], 119b.4-5 [= *GMPT* p. 315], 121:1a.56-68 [= *GMPT* p. 316], 128.1-11 [= *GMPT* p. 323], 130.1-13 [= *GMPT* p. 323]. (N.B.: Here and below I cross-reference to *GMPT* for items in *PGM* vol. 3, since this volume was destroyed by enemy action in World War II while in the process of publication, and though xerox copies of the proofs have been obtained by some scholars, the text is not readily available.)

79. Plin. *NH* 28.38, 42, 44, 170; 29.131-32 (and cf. 117-30); 32.74; *PGM* 7.197-98; *PDM* 14.1097-1109 [= *GMPT* p. 247]; *PGM* 94.22-26 [= *GMPT* pp. 304-5].

80. Plin. *HN* 28.49, 76, 166; 29.112-14; *PGM* 7.199-202, 18a.1-4, 20.1-4, 13-19, 65.4-7, 94.39-60 [= *GMPT* p. 305], 122.51-55 [= *GMPT* p. 317].

4. *Antidotes for poison:*[81] cures include binding spells, intercourse, or the brains and blood of a wild boar.

In all four categories, the principle of visible causality applies; epilepsy, too, as we might expect, evoked some remedies of last resort, including children's bone marrow and the blood of gladiators. The papyri suggest that *le grand mal* was regarded as a daemonic visitation, a thesis that the modern psychiatrist might find more fruitful than that of phlegm descending from the brain.[82] Other maladies dealt with include boils and abscesses, eczema, warts, dysentery, toothache, gout, insomnias, bad breath, sore throat, and sciatica.

Two points at once strike us on surveying this material, and should form a starting-point for future research. First, no writer in antiquity ever seems to have subjected such prescriptions to systematic proof,[83] even when this would have been comparatively simple: was the educated antipathy to simple experiment (despite known exceptions) really so all-pervasive? Researchers, it is true, might think twice about waving the plant *adamantis* in front of lions to see if they really would "sprawl out on their backs with a lazy yawn" when so confronted;[84] but why should anyone assume for one moment that goat's blood would dissolve a diamond,[85] much less that toothache would stop if the sufferer applied to the tooth a piece bitten off from lightning-struck timber by someone with his hands clasped behind his back?[86] In such cases desperate belief (or literary tradition) was obviously far more important than knowledge, let alone an effective cure. Pliny in his more realistic moments knew this: discussing (*NH* 30.104) a peculiarly *outré* cure for tertian fever, he remarks that it may just be worth trying "since suffering enjoys hoping against hope." Certainly anyone who believed a fever could be cured by attaching crabs' eyes as an amulet to themselves before sunset, after releasing the blinded crabs back into the water (*NH* 32.115), had to be absolutely desperate.

81. These are predominantly occasioned by the bites of snakes or scorpions, as we might expect in the Mediterranean: Plin. *NH* 28.36, 40, 44, 52, 121, 149–55 (snakes), 156 (mad dogs), 158–62 (poisons); 29.90; 37.139; *PGM* 7.193–96; *PDM* 14.554–62, 585–93 (dog bite: = *GMPT* pp. 226–27); *PGM* 28a–c passim and 112.1–15, 113.1–4 (scorpions: = *GMPT* p. 313).

82. Plin. *NH* 28.4, 8, 34, 36, 43, 63 (drive an iron nail into the place where a victim fell), 224ff.; 30.91; 37.157; *PGM* 104.1–14 (= *GMPT* p. 313).

83. At *NH* 30.31 Pliny tells us: "I find (*inuenio*) that a heavy cold clears up if the sufferer kisses a mule's muzzle." Though the vision of a sneezing and phlegm-ridden Pliny pottering out to the mules' stable for a miraculous dose of Contact has undeniable appeal, I regretfully suspect that the discovery was, as usual, made in a book, and not the result of personal experiment.

84. Plin. *NH* 24.162: hac [adamantide] admota leones resupinari cum hiatu lasso.

85. Plin. *NH* 37.59.

86. Plin. *NH* 28.45: et ligno fulgure icto reiectis post terga manibus demorderi aliquid et ad dentem qui doleat admoueri remedio esse produnt.

Second, and of greater significance, is the fact that though the pattern of these "remedies" confirms the principle of visible causality, it also reveals some striking, and no less significant, omissions. Fundamentally these are all *minor* complaints: the remedies occupy more or less the same place that home medical encyclopedias do today. No doctor, however fanciful a theorist, is in sight: not even a barber-surgeon. The closest we come to a life-threatening illness (apart from the mixed bag of "fevers," which covers a multitude of troubles, ranging from influenza to chronic malaria) is renal or prostatic calculus; and such internal stones, then as now, there was always the hope of dissolving and passing,[87] however improbable the prescription recommended.[88]

That terrible range of killing diseases we know from Galen, Celsus, or the Hippocratic Corpus is almost wholly absent. There is no attempt to deal with the prime killer, purulent sepsis,[89] nor indeed any suggestion that sufferers stood in risk of death. Though clearly concentrated, as we have seen, in those areas that lay beyond the reach of human investigation, the tradition carefully stopped short of tangling with hopeless cases. That dubious privilege was left to the professional physicians, who, to their credit, made no attempt to palliate the bleak facts, and as a result were continually lampooned by satirists for killing more than the plagues they failed to halt. The concluding *obiter dictum* of *Aphorisms*[90] says it all: "Those diseases which medicine cannot cure, the knife cures; those which the knife does not cure, [cautery by] fire cures. Those that fire does not cure you must consider incurable." By then the patient would be far beyond the reach of spells, amulets, or the ingredients—quaint when not actively emetic—of the *materia magica*.

---

87. E.g., by spontaneous ejaculation during sleep: see Edelstein and Edelstein 1945, 1:224, no. 423 (xiv).

88. Plin. *NH* 28.42 (attach a voided stone above the pubis), 102 (take hyena's liver in drink), 212 (relieve pain by consuming urine and bladder of a wild boar); 30.65 (rub mouse-dung on the belly).

89. See, e.g., the Hippocratic treatise *On Wounds in the Head* (Περὶ τῶν ἐν κεφάλῃ τρω-μάτων) 19-20. The nearest Pliny and the magical papyri come to this is the treatment (with horse's blood, cow-dung, *vel sim.*) of boils and ulcers: *NH* 22.135; 26.93; 28.52, 147, 241-43; 30.108, 113-18.

90. *Aph.* 7.87: Ὁκόσα φάρμακα οὐκ ἰῆται, σίδηρος ἰῆται· ὅσα σίδηρος οὐκ ἰῆται, πῦρ ἰῆται· ὅσα δὲ πῦρ οὐκ ἰῆται, ταῦτα χρὴ νομίζειν ἀνίατα.

APPENDIX A

Tanglewood Tales for the Yuppies

The suburbanization of Hellenic myth has a long and depressing history. Already by the sixth century B.C. Xenophanes of Colophon was complaining about the improprieties that Homer and Hesiod attributed to the Olympian gods, and taking rationalist sideswipes at divine anthropomorphism, pointing out that Thracian gods had red hair and blue eyes, while the black gods of the Nubians had snub noses and woolly hair—and if oxen could draw, he added, guess what *their* gods would look like. Attacked on one flank by developing sexual *pudeur*, and on the other by Sophistic reason, the old myths suffered serious censorship and secularization even before they got clear of antiquity and into the tender allegorizing hands of medieval Christianity. Roberto Calasso's *The Marriage of Cadmus and Harmony*, a pretentious rehashing of the seedier and steamier legends (originally, I suspect, as a joke for Rome's smart set, but now in translation aimed at the *New Yorker* crowd and the more literate denizens of Marin County) proves, if proof were needed, that this process is still going strong.

Emergent middle-class mores found the miscegenetic habits of Zeus (or, worse, Pasiphaë) acutely embarrassing, the muscle-bound swillings, murders, and multiple cherry-poppings of Heracles worse than vulgar, and the ecstatic rending and devouring of raw flesh (ὠμοφαγία, σπαραγμός) practiced by Dionysiac devotees plain scary. Euripides took the whole archaic smorgasbord of divine cannibalism, rape, incest, and absolute amoral power, and turned it into a deadly theatrical device with which to shock bourgeois sensibilities by serving up raw primitive myth as a framework for contemporary social realism. The sophist Protagoras, as is well known, made man the measure of all things, and the Hellenistic Age took the process one step further by bringing the gods down into the marketplace and making them behave uncommonly like market shoppers. Thus the goddesses in Apollonius Rhodius's *Argonautika*, for all their immortality and omnipotence, soothe middle-class sensibilities by aping the speech and manners of the Alexandrian *lumpenbourgeoisie*.

Note: Originally published in *New Republic*, 10 May 1993, pp. 50–52.

In the political arena, Protagoreanism was neatly adapted to the huge ambitions of Alexander's heirs and successors by the fabulist Euhemerus, who opened up the field of dynastic self-invention by proclaiming that the Olympian gods had started life as great kings or generals whose noble deeds had won them deification: a new kind of enskyment through merit. Alexander's eastern exploits, after all, had arguably eclipsed those of Heracles and Dionysus both, and Heracles (as everyone knew) had, *through merit*, bridged the gap between earth and heaven. Besides, there were distinct advantages to be had from this kind of God Manifest (*Epiphanes*), the main one being proximity. A here-and-now deity was a good deal more accessible to petitions than the Olympians. This was precisely the point emphasized in the famous paean with which in 290 the Athenians greeted Demetrius Poliorcetes. The other gods might be deaf or absent, as unresponsive as their images, "but *you* are here, and visible to us, not carved in wood or stone, but real: so to you we pray." No wonder the Epicureans sidelined the Olympian pantheon into a remote and ineffectual Elysium.

This erosion of faith in the intangible, if anthropomorphic, Olympians—with a corresponding upsurge of interest in foreign cults, preferably violent and visceral, that promised a great deal more emotional bang for the drachma—was bound to have an impact on the attitude to Greek myth, since the genesis of the latter had been intimately bound up with the Bronze Age development of the old Indo-European pantheon, not least in its uneasy assimilation to indigenous Mediterranean cults such as the Mistress of Beasts (πότνια θηρῶν) or the Mother Goddess (Ma or Cybele). As the numinous quality drained out of mythic narrative, as urbanism began to defuse the old life-and-death cycle of the year, as meteorology and astronomy cut into the privileges of weather-gods such as Zeus (no divine bolts, no angry thunder), what remained came to be more and more seen as a series of often indecent *contes drôlatiques*, as anachronistic material suitable for literary exploitation or philosophical allegorizing. Escapism, too: all those Euripidean choruses wishing they were far away and quite different, preferably changed into birds, had their logical cumulation in Ovid's *Metamorphoses*, where the random urges (more often than not sexual) of Zeus or Apollo could at least be thwarted by the dissolution and reconstitution of the object as tree or river, while those with divine aspirations could envisage a splendid starry future in the sky, revamped as a constellation.

What got left out as the polis developed (we can see the process clearly in the visual arts) was the archaic sense of terror and helplessness in the face of the unknown, a world in which deities behaved uncommonly like outsize versions of the tribal patriarchs and viragoes on whom they had been unconsciously modeled: powers of nature endowed (because one begins from what one knows, first and foremost oneself) with a human face and human attributes, yet immortal, ageless, untrammelled by even rudimentary morality in the human sense, and as touchy, spiteful, and self-absorbed as the small children whom in so many ways they resembled. To cross them was rather like touching a high-voltage cable: you fried, and no canting nonsense about virtue or good intentions could save you.

Science and sophistry got the intellectuals of the Hellenistic (and, later, the Greco-Roman) world away from this primal terror, but left them with a psychological problem that proved remarkably persistent: is, indeed, still with us today. Their brains might be amenable to sweet reason, but their inherited archetypal beliefs most certainly weren't. Thus their heads told them one thing, their hearts another. A third-century epigram by Callimachus (*AP* 7.524) debriefs a dead man. Pluto is a fable, he tells his questioner, there's nothing but darkness here, it's all lies about resurrection (ἄνοδοι). The questioner cries out in horror, "We are undone!" (ἀπωλόμεθα). These people desperately needed the myths in which they could no longer rationally believe—not only for psychological comfort, but as a source of moral and social validation. It is extraordinary how often even a skeptical, ironic intellectual like Ovid will appeal to myth for what today would probably be called empowering precedent. That old platitude about Homer being the Bible of the Greeks is more precisely true than is generally realized.

What is even more surprising is the magnetic pull that ancient myth still retains today. Freud, Jung, and his epigonos Joseph Campbell, Cassirer, Lévi-Strauss: all have dug deeply into various aspects of the mythic tradition (incest seems to be a constant), and each has his devoted followers. The stories that evolved (partly aided—as new research is constantly making clearer—by Near Eastern borrowings) among the warring baronies of Mycenaean Greece display universal elements: they have a kind of epidemic appeal, even (perhaps especially) to folk with only the haziest, if any, notion of the Bronze Age itself. They are, as Jung said, archetypal. And where there's a market, there's money to be made. Roberto Calasso is only the most recent fisher to throw a baited hook to this myth-hungry audience. To judge by the hype since his book's original publication in Italy (1988), the hook is well and truly in.

So how does he go about it? What are his assumptions, what ingredients has he put together to form his bait, and what kind of person does he have in mind as his ideal captive listener? A well-heeled, semi-educated, culturally pretentious yuppie, is my guess: with minor variations, this animal shows up at every chic watering-hole from Paris to San Francisco. Not someone like me, that's for sure: above all, *not* a reader who actually knows something about classical history and classical myth, in whom Calasso is likely to generate by turn irritation, torpor, and irreverent fits of the giggles. By the time I'd slogged my way through nearly 400 pages, I felt like the wedding guest pinned down by an unstoppable and archly loquacious Ancient Mariner.

Calasso has two styles: jocose but leaden narrative fiction (seemingly with one eye on the kiddies) when retailing the myths themselves, and explicatory discourse heavy with assertive aphorisms. The opening words alone almost stopped me, there and then: "On a beach in Sidon a bull was aping a lover's coo. It was Zeus." We get the Aeschylean version, the Herodotean version, the Apollodoran version, and (God help us) the Nonnian version, all refracted through Calasso's suburban eye and platitudinously condescending manner. Once or twice I began to hope that he was putting us on, as with the *Ariadne auf Naxos* myth: "Ariadne has been left behind. The clothes fall from her body one by one." (They do? How?) But alas, no. What she's in for, in her unclothed state, is Dionysus, "bursting with youth, his Bacchants buzzing all around him."

As for the aphorisms, I began to collect them in a kind of bemused incredulity: "Dionysus's phallus is more hallucinogenic than coercive." "Heracles is contaminated by the sacred, it persecutes him his whole life." "Every notion of progress is refuted by the existence of the *Iliad*." "Since Olympia is the image of happiness, it could only have appeared in the Golden Age." "The dense green in the Peloponnese has a hallucinatory glow to it." "The crown was a mobile *templum*, bringing together election and danger." "What we call Homeric theology was a reckless interval in the lives of the gods." "In Greece, myth escapes from ritual like a genie from a bottle." Despite the high percentage of pure nonsense, there's a kind of perception at work here. But (like the ancient deities themselves) it's random, arbitrary, and self-indulgent.

At the same time, Calasso knows his subject backward. On internal evidence he's read all the ancient sources, even (perhaps particularly) the latest and most *recherché*, not to mention a great deal of the modern scholarship. Most nonspecialist critics, even if they disliked what he did, realized this. They had neither the knowledge nor the moxie to tangle with him, so wisely played it safe; and quite a few of them, being unable to distinguish good taste from the latest smart trend if their life depended on it, actually bought into his new *Tanglewood Tales* with gushing enthusiasm. In fact, Calasso's expertise makes what he actually *does* with his research even more of an anticlimax: all we get is his playful reworking of various well-known myths as pseudo-fiction, interspersed with *obiter dicta* on the human condition. Thus, paradoxically, the usual complaint about works of this sort, that they're academically uninformed, doesn't apply. The trouble with *The Marriage of Cadmus and Harmony* is something quite different: an all-pervasive lack of creative imagination, though creative imagination is precisely the quality for which critics who ought to know better have been praising Calasso to the skies.

To take the measure of Calasso's inadequacy, one need only compare his mythic insights with those demonstrated by Michael Ayrton in *The Maze Maker* (1967), that triumphant tribute by one daimon-driven craftsman, sculptor, metallurgist, and creative artist to another. It is the testament of Daedalus, narrated in the first person, and there are passages in it that still make me shiver every time I read them, with their unique mixture of numinous awe and maker's knowledge. They include the fall of Icarus, and the great white bull's possession of Pasiphaë in the wooden cow that Daedalus had made for the queen: Ayrton doesn't shy away from the challenging set-pieces. His understanding of the Minotaur (perhaps in part inspired by G. F. Watts's famous painting) goes straight to the heart of the matter, the terrible cloudy inner tension in the Minotaur's mind between beast and man: "Cud gags, cud gags, mounts in his mouth, gags speech, man's speech, cud, cud, no man makes cud, no man near man no man, no man. . . ." So what is Calasso's take on all this? "Asterius has a bull's head," he announces brightly, "because his father was the big white bull Pasiphaë fell in love with." Well, kiddies, now you know.

Calasso takes as the epigraph to his book a quotation, slightly mistranslated, that he gives as "These things never happened but always are," and that presumably serves as his excuse for treating all his sources, from Homer to Lucian, from Hesiod to Nonnus and the Byzantine mythographers, as though they were contemporary with one another. The quotation is ascribed to "Sallust, *Of Gods and the World*," an author whom the unwary may identify with the Roman historian best known for his monographs on Catiline and Jugurtha. In fact, this Sallust—more correctly, Saloustios (*Σαλούστιος*)—was a Greek Neoplatonist of the fourth century A.D., a friend of the emperor Julian; and I cannot help wondering whether Calasso took to heart also the opening words of Saloustios's treatise: "Those who would learn about the gods need to have been well educated from childhood and must not be bred up among foolish ideas; they must also be good and intelligent by nature, in order that they may have something in common with the subject." It's somehow of a piece with the rest of his book that he should try and argue for the universalism of his theme from an essay that is a string of Neoplatonic platitudes. Perhaps he was even encouraged by the thought that Saloustios, like Julian, was trying to rehabilitate the old gods in the face of Christianity.

As the comparison with Ayrton shows, there is a fundamental superficiality about Calasso's approach to his subject that can only be partly explained by his specious hankering after universality. It is true that he did not set out to write a work of history; and yet his technique robs his presentation of a complicating historical perspective. It also prevents him from remarking upon his own position, which is a little like that of the Hellenistic *littérateurs*, who were full of nostalgia for past tradition, hell-bent on retrieving primal innocence, busy trawling among ancient testimonia for some key to the human condition: etiologizing magpies whose academic taste for obscurity was only equaled by their determination to explain every odd myth and ritual in sight. *These fragments have I shored against my ruins:* Pound and Eliot, too, have contributed to what in many ways presents an uncomfortably similar *mise-en-scène* to that of the Hellenistic Age. Calasso is riding a trend.

Which brings me back to his potential audience. Here we have these artfully selected retellings of myth, mainly concerned with sexual goings-on, the gods in human, nonthreatening, hot-tubbish mode, with the additional advantages of magical stamina and transformation scenes, Everyman and Superman in one, plus a few pseudo-profundities for cultural uplift that (as Mary Lefkowitz recently observed, with great politeness) "do not so much challenge [Calasso's] readers to think hard about what they have been reading as reassure them that they have without real effort experienced something deeply significant." That shot hits the gold. Insofar as Calasso's book is premised on just such passively credulous and sensation-hungry readers, and satisfies them that it has done all their work for them, it's an exercise in classicizing kitsch. Those who swallow this synthetic pabulum will be, I suspect, much the same sort of people as the well-heeled Hellenistic middle classes (with a smattering of intellectual pretensions) who watched the plays of Menander. Calasso has indeed produced a *Tanglewood Tales* for our times, something to please (and make a good profit off) the cultural yuppies of Europe and, now, America.

Worse, the book gets one thoroughly depressed, after a while, with Greek myth as such. This may well be primarily due to Calasso's emphasis on tabloid sex ("With a little girl's infatuation, she described Cadmus's body, fantasized his hand boldly touching her round breasts," and so on) and resolute avoidance of the numinous or truly terrifying (Dionysus becomes a comic stud, Prometheus and his eagle are wisely ignored). Still, it remains true that the ubiquity of rape as a motif ("the sign of the overwhelming power of the divine," Calasso pontificates: feminists have unkinder explanations), the self-absorbed narcissism of these deities, the endless incidents of cannibalism, incest, murder, and betrayal do not exactly enhance the bright dawn of Western civilization. It is not the duty of a mythographer, of course, to make the gods look good, or to cheerlead for their culture (though quite a few writers have tried both); Calasso, unfortunately, while cheerleading with the best of them, still somehow manages to turn his Olympians into comic cut-outs.

The Marriage of Cadmus and Harmony leaves us on the verge of literate history ("No one could erase those small letters, those fly's feet that Cadmus the Phoenician had scattered across Greece"). However, when forced to face the various nastinesses of Tantalus, Pelops, Thyestes, and the rest, Calasso can only argue that "to invite the gods ruins our relationship with them but sets history in motion. A life in which the gods are not invited isn't worth living. It will be quieter, but there won't be any stories"—a conclusion that, by now, some may well welcome. *Parturient montes, nascetur ridiculus mus.* The mountainous parturition of Calasso's illustrated aphorisms has finally come out with this risible mouse. Then, as though to disprove his own findings, he throws in long anecdotal digressions on Athens and Sparta in historical times, again chiefly predicated on sex (Athenian pederasty, the sodomization of Spartan brides before marriage). At one point he picks up on the idea of reasoned thought, the *logos* of Heracleitus or Anaximander or Parmenides, overriding the paratactic particularities of myth ("Like the cipher, like the arrow of Abaris, the *lógos* transfixes in the merest atom of time what the rhapsodes had strung together and repeated over and over for night after smoky night . . . the resulting thrill was without precedent"). But thrill or no thrill, we end with the comforting thought that the gods are really only outsize funny human beings and that it's sex-and-symbolism that makes the world go round. Baby boomers—not least the pols and media gurus inhabiting the Beltway, who appear on current form to understand little else—will buy this book in droves. Fair enough. Seldom can author and audience have deserved each other more.

APPENDIX B

Homer for the Kiddies

Like Camille Paglia and quite a few other classics buffs, curious but apprehensive—justifiably, as things turned out—I recently spent two evenings watching the nearest thing to an animated comic strip that you can do with live actors: NBC's expensive and much ballyhooed *Odyssey*. I wish I'd known then some of the ripe titbits about the making of this extravaganza with which Paglia had earlier regaled us so enjoyably—not least the prospect of the executive producer lining up *Crime and Punishment* and Dante's *Inferno* for similar future treatment. (Schwarzenegger as Raskolnikov? Flashback from the seventh *bolgia* to Julia Roberts on Cloud Nine singing "Somewhere in Heaven"?) Paglia's theory was that Halmi and Konchalovsky were "bringing the classics to a mass audience." This is to insult the masses. What we saw was prepubertal pap geared to illiterate ten-year-olds whose minds, if one may so describe them, had been addled by TV-watching from the egg, reinforced by that vague yet revolting have-a-nice-day togetherness too often whimsically confused, by theorists who ought to know better, with primary education. The version that *was* for the masses, the Italian *Ulysses* starring Kirk Douglas (1954), did infinitely better on a fraction of the budget: I was delighted to find Paglia giving it its due, and for all the right reasons, in particular "its lean narrative and psychological astuteness" (e.g., doubling the parts of Penelope and Circe). The thing could be done; has, after a fashion, been done. But not this time.

Credit, to begin with, where one can give it. There were, intermittently, things to admire. Aegean coastal landscape, of which we got quite a lot, is always stunning, and only those really far gone in Greek *ethnikismós* have been heard to complain about most of it being located in Turkey. Someone had done quite a bit of visual homework, if not always appropriately. There were genuine Mycenaean decorations (though the Ithaca palace was a blue-painted mini-Knossos), and a nice Bronze Age apotropaic sphinx on the sail of Odysseus's ship. The approach to Hades borrowed, briefly but unmistak-

Note: Originally published in *Arion* 5.3 (1998): 145–54.

ably, from one of the famous *Odyssey* paintings rescued in 1848 from a house on the Esquiline, and now in the Vatican Library. The archery challenge (to shoot "through" those axes) was convincingly staged, and in accordance with the theory currently favored, that is, through the hanging-rings on the up-ended axes' butts. In other words, like Homer's memories of the Bronze Age, this television production was best on artifacts. When it tried, nervously, to deal with any kind of human relationship, it foundered in a sea of deadening cliché. The titles announced it as based on Homer's poem, but this you would never have guessed from the script, of which more in a moment.

This *Odyssey* left me with a lot of small questions, and one big one: the niggling incidents were legion, and not all due to my being a classicist. Some of them were duly picked up by Paglia, who added a rich crop of her own. Full marks for her on-target shot at the PC rewrite of the opening to the birth of Telemachus, with Odysseus galloping through woodlands to be there among the midwives, "the great Greek warrior introduced as Mr. Mom, Lamaze graduate." Vintage Paglia, that. And incidentally, if you're going to spend all that time on Telemachus's birth, why then pass up the chance to show the proud father (who traditionally feigned madness to dodge the draft) plough-ing the beach and sowing it with salt to show how dotty he is, but swerving aside at the last moment when the baby is set down in line with the plough-share? Very dramatic, very photogenic.

Why was Achilles (as both Paglia and I noted) made to prance around in battle naked to the waist? Especially, it occurs to me, after Hephaestus had gone to all that trouble to forge him splendid new armor? Obligatory beef-cake? Vague gladiatorial memories? Worse, why, both during the scenes at Troy (put in, reasonably, to provide background for nonclassicists) and later, *chez* Menelaus in Sparta, did we neither see, nor hear one word about, the true cause of the whole mess, namely Helen? Why make the entire Greek fleet, plus Agamemnon, sail right out of its way up to northwest Greece to collect Odysseus? (Oh, come on, any teacher could answer that one: it makes an im-pressive display, and how many fifth-graders know northwest Greece from Tasmania?) All right then, why force Odysseus to climb a sheer rock-face to get to Circe's palace (which Paglia compared to an Egyptian temple, but for my money more resembled Grand Central Station)? Easy: in order to stage the weird scene halfway up in which the campiest pretty-boy Hermes I've ever seen floats round our hero like an outsize horizontal butterfly, and stuffs his mouth with alleged moly, which actually more resembles—in either sense— a handful of grass. (White flower, black root, Homer specified: what did *he* know?)

This list could go on forever. Like Paglia, I wondered why so few of these Aegean wanderers, Odysseus included, seem to have acquired beards, tans, or, in some rather egregious cases, muscle. And when is it, I asked myself (having done time on Aegean fishing-boats and small caïques) that they manage, or even want, to *shave* on shipboard? Why does Telemachus have different accents as kid and adult? Maybe because Mom and Dad have different accents too, and he got confused? Why is Hades done up to resemble a Karnak temple or the Baths of Constantine? Why are there great globs of liquid fire permanently dropping from the roof? Who got the bright idea of having poor Irene Papas, as Odysseus's mother Anticleia, commit suicide by marching out into the sea? In this last case I suspect the allusion of being cinematic rather than Homeric: the scene had *déjà vu* written all over it. A generation that seldom reads books has developed a habit of quoting famous early movies, much in the same spirit as Eliot embodied snippets of prior literature in *The Waste Land.*

Even the special effects—so popular in Hollywood and Cinecittà (swooping Harpies, Moses parting the Red Sea, etc.), and, as a notoriously inflated line-item in production budgets (Paglia got that one right), a good indication of where priorities lie—tended in this *Odyssey* to be overdone when not botched. The one really original and effective touch was computer-generating Poseidon's sea-face out of a gigantic cresting wave, and even there the effect was spoiled for me by the knowledge that you just don't get waves like that in the Aegean (and Paglia can't get around this by invoking the tsunami that followed the eruption of Thera, which happened at least two centuries earlier than the Trojan War). Laocoön (here pronounced "Lah-koon," to rhyme, sort of, with "raccoon": why do these ventures always mispronounce ancient names so bizarrely?), while helpless with laughter (justified, I thought), found himself entangled by the cutest little loop of pink rubber out of the sea you ever saw. Presumably this gadget wasn't capable of handling his sons as well, since the latter never showed. Scylla, who's reaped some tributes from the unwary (dig those tentacles: there's a sucker born every moment), instead of posing a problem to traffic in the Straits of Messina, here lurks in the roof of a huge water-cavern, presumably to camouflage her operative mechanisms. No reason was given, and I doubt whether one existed, for Odysseus and his crew to venture in there. Bunches of what looked like dispirited squids dangled out of darkness, occasionally lunging down at lightning speed (*"Gotcha!"*) to knock off a sitting-duck rower.

Whoever organized these stunts clearly believed the old movie adage that nothing succeeds like excess. Paglia found the episode involving Aeolus and

the winds "a spectacular success." Spectacular *excess* is more like it. The release of the winds from Aeolus's bag blasts crew members sky-high into the
empyrean, just as the whirlpool of Charybdis sucks them dizzyingly down into
a deep vortex that closes, finally, like the mouth of a bit. The trick photogra-
phy in the Cyclops's cave fails to keep the relative sizes of giant and humans
steady, and despite a nice crunchy sound-effect as the monster snacked on his
first sailor (I *knew* Paglia would go for that bit), Polyphemus himself looked
fundamentally ridiculous, a cross between Quasimodo and Humpty Dumpty.
(In fact, when you come to think of it, a sumo wrestler wearing a large latex
headpiece is pretty comic by definition.) This is interesting, and maybe significant. The late Jim Henson's team did that head. They also manufactured
Scylla and Laocoön's serpent. Nothing there to scare anyone. But those boys
can turn out really terrifying stuff when asked to. No one who saw that wonderful film *Dreamchild*, about Lewis Carroll and Alice, is ever going to forget
their huge, predatory Gryphon, their malevolent (and seemingly syphilitic)
Mad Hatter. Once again it becomes clear that the target being aimed at is not
"the masses," who can't get enough blood, horror, violence, and (if it comes
to that) sex, but those beavis-and-butthead kiddies who haunt TV marketers'
minds.

Proof of this hits us at every turn in NBC's *Odyssey*. Those responsible
carefully avoid any incidents that suggest the conniving side of Odysseus, or
the more brutal habits of the age, or indeed anything liable to set up uncomfortable reflections (indeed, thought of any kind, not that they need have worried) in their juvenile audience. Grown-up viewers waited in vain for any hint
of adult interplay between the characters. Whatever Homer may have supplied to this version, it certainly wasn't the dialogue. Characters speak for the
most part in the kind of comic-strip cliché that would have gotten a sitcom
scriptwriter fired on the spot. All the most subtle scenes are either omitted
or reduced to nullity. I've already mentioned the elimination of Helen: a real
femme fatale, as opposed to a fairy-tale one, was clearly seen as unacceptable
in a production set on plugging family values. But where does that leave the
larger part of the original plot-line? In the case of Helen, it knocks out one
of the greatest comic scenes in world literature: with young Telemachus as
spectator, she plays the smart society hostess in postwar Sparta, abetted by
a complacent Menelaus, handing out nepenthe like high-class hash, and re-
galing guests with anecdotes of her own wicked earlier incarnation (or *was* it
an *eidōlon?*) among all those big handsome muscular Trojans. MacNeice got
those two right: "The whore and the buffoon will come off best." Helen, who
saved her skin at Troy's capture by bobbing her tits to an angry husband, and

then got herself "reinstated in the new regime," wasn't, clearly, an acceptable role-model in this brave new Disneyfied world.

Worse still, but equally symptomatic, we got not a word of the wonderful exchanges between Odysseus and Nausicaä. Their first encounter on the beach—virgin princess and shipwrecked hero delicately seeking the proper protocol—was silent and brief, and (in defiance of Nausicaä's concern for social proprieties) the Wanderer came into town along with her and the laundry. What was the trouble here? American squeamishness over the age difference? After all, nothing could be more respectable (or, for me, moving) than Odysseus's marvelous vindication to this nice young girl, her head buzzing with romantic dreams, of the marital condition: "For there is nothing greater or better than this: when in common accord man and wife make their home together, much grief to their foes, much joy to their well-wishers, but their own hearts know it the best" (*Od.* 6.182–85). And why, when we (all too briefly) meet her father, King Alcinoös, is he made up like a transvestite drag queen? As for Queen Arete, Paglia must have sharper eyes than I do: a ripe and fleshy look-alike for Egyptian Rahotep's wife Nofret should have been guaranteed to catch my attention, but clearly came and went so fast I missed her.

But the worst and least forgivable loss is the whole long and brilliant psychological by-play between Odysseus and Penelope after the Wanderer's return. The symbolic dreams, the nervous testing, the who-recognizes-who gambits—all are gone without trace. A waxy, periwinkle-eyed Athena—Isabella Rossellini, and I won't even try to match Paglia's well-merited hatchet-job on this spectacular piece of miscasting—ages Odysseus in a flash (he not having aged noticeably otherwise throughout) into a fair imitation of the Leonardo da Vinci self-portrait: senile grunge while you wait. She then restores him to his handsome youthful self—*zap!*—the moment he's won the bow test, thus at one stroke eliminating the ruthless ravages of time and lifting the difficult reunion of husband and wife after twenty years into the realm of fairy-tale fantasy—not quite what Homer had in mind. What follows is all of a piece. Penelope, on seeing her magically rejuvenated *Mensch* (no makeover for *her*, alas), faints like any Victorian heroine. Embrace. Finis. If you were expecting any of the *real* problems liable to come up between husband and wife reunited after a long war (be it Troy or Viet Nam)—in other words, if you were naive enough to think you were going to get Homer—forget it.

What seems to me important is to establish the rationale, if any, behind all these choices. Too easy to say stupidity and Goldwynism and let it go at that. Censorship, it seems clear, has been at work: but what sort of censorship, and to what end? First, we don't see the really grim side of Homer's world: the cruelty, callousness, sadism, blood, and ruthless violence. Why not? At its worst, that world, so far as I can see, wasn't anything like as revolting as *Straw Dogs* or a dozen other movies we all could name. And the nastier bits of Homer's *Odyssey* are carefully omitted, too. For instance, we're spared the vengeful hanging of Melantho (why change her name to Melante? in case anyone thought a name ending in -o had to be masculine?) and the other promiscuous maids when the slaughter's over. In this version, Melantho and Eurymachus are skewered with one arrow, the nearest we get to a comment on their relationship: Paglia mentions the change, but seems to have disdained comment on such crummy symbolism. The final butchery and sulphurous clean-up of the resultant mess are both very carefully sanitized. Again, one wonders why: as I pointed out earlier, today's mass audiences are no more averse to gore and slaughter than Roman arena-addicts. Targeting the kids seems the only possible answer.

But what really drives this argument home beyond a doubt is the fact that nothing seems to have given the makers of NBC's *Odyssey* bigger prime-time jitters than Homer's whole attitude to women and sex. In an age when movies have, with increasing explicitness, covered the entire erotic spectrum from homosexuality to incest and, now, necrophilia, such nervous-nelly prissiness invites speculation. The hope of high-exposure adult television marketing, including all that pious cant about "family values," can only explain so much. When we've made every allowance for that deep native streak of puritanism which would recoil by instinct from Homer's open, guiltless, passionate, and happy appreciation of sexual enjoyment (even, let's face it, in marriage), the cautious pussy-footing that's gone on in order to rewrite Homer's plot with so marked a reduction of sexual content still amazes. Haven't these people seen *Caught*, never mind about something really kinky like *Crash?* Or have they deluded themselves into supposing that what they're serving up is actually educational?

One of the first hints you get of what's afoot is the way in which the sexual high-jinks are modified by altering Homer's chronology. There's now an extended five-year communal stay with Circe (safety in numbers?), during which time Odysseus's crewmen seemingly spend all their time lolling about in baths, perhaps as a tactful alternative to bed: they must have got as wrinkled as prunes. The main reason for this seems to be to cut down Odysseus's solo dalliance with Calypso from seven years to two, presumably on the grounds that the shorter time illicit sex goes on, the less reprehensible it is. (This reminds me of the Victorian housemaid whose apology to her mis-

tress for having an illegitimate baby was that it had been *a very small one.*)
Indeed, the whole business of Odysseus's carnal interludes with these quasi-
deities seems to have caused acute embarrassment. Circe, as Victorian artists
well knew, was a dark and powerful sexual magician: Homer makes it all too
clear that while Odysseus and his oh-so-symbolic sword may have begun by
mastering her, *she* ends by mistressing *him:* indeed, his long-suffering crew
have to drag him away by main force. Calypso's case is even worse: the only
reason Odysseus finally decides he wants to leave *her,* as Homer reveals in one
deadly little phrase, is because he's got sexually bored with her, ἐπεὶ οὐκέτι
ἥνδανε νύμφη. He may have escaped physical metamorphosis, but he's a sexist
pig just the same, afflicted with a classic seven-year itch.

What are our producers to do about this? In Circe's case the difficulty is
circumvented in two ways. First, the transformation into animals becomes a
harmless campy romp: aficionados will relish the scene in which hungry sailors
chase a squealing porker all round the beach only to find out at the very last
minute that it's one of their chums. Second, and most effectively for antaphro-
disiac purposes, the role of the Lady of Beasts has been allotted to Bernadette
Peters. No dark tall powerful magician this, but a small plump doll, all giggles
and bubble-curls, with a voice like a mid-West corncrake that's been noshing
on hemp-seed. Even when she leads off Odysseus (Armand Assante) to her
boudoir, you get the impression that the most exciting thing they're going to
do is leaf through her high-school yearbook together. Miz Peters was about
as appropriate a choice for Circe as picking Dolly Parton to play Antigone;
but I don't think there's much doubt as to what factors influenced the casting
director.

Calypso, on the other hand, presented a different problem. Hermes, in
Homer's version, swoops down on her paradisal island of Ogygia to find her
singing at the loom, in a country scene of birdsong and greenery: she's the
quintessential complaisant nymph, offering the perfect male fantasy of endless sex and nurturing with no responsibilities: "The world forgetting, by the
world forgot." Since it's a fair bet that no one involved in the making of this
TV *Odyssey* would turn down an offer like that, out it had to go. Instead, their
Calypso (Vanessa Williams) is so comic-stripped and formalized—her island
is treeless, her attire seems to consist chiefly of bits of metal, and her giggling
gaggle of watchful maidservants would send Casanova running for the nearest monastery—that few are likely to see any problem about Odysseus turning
down her offer of immortality, unfading youth, and an eternal island womb-
with-a-view in favor of wife, home, and the looming prospect of old age and
death. She's *kinky,* see: of course any decent man would try to get away from
her. (I can see her attraction for Paglia, though: not that Paglia was the kind of

viewer Halmi had in mind.) No adult hard choices there. And come to think of it, no Sirens in this version either (though just think what Henson's boys could have done with *them* if given a free hand!): knowledge was obviously as big a no-no as sex, something that will come as no surprise to the author of *The Dumbing Down of America.*

Trivialization, then, certainly: the retrojection into Homer's world of pop psychology and PC, the notion that prickly self-esteem and personal feelings somehow have value simply by existing. Against such well-fed warm complacencies, the great basic themes of hunger (who was it called the *Odyssey* the "eatingest epic"?), terror, desire, battle, survival, return—the bloody rawness of man against nature, the unknown, his fellow-men—don't really stand a chance. Epic is for adults. This *Odyssey* isn't. Odysseus is, or should be, the embodiment of that wonderful line thrown off by Polly Garter in *Under Milk Wood:* "Isn't life a terrible thing, thank God?" The big problem I mentioned at the beginning, and have been prowling round ever since, should now be tolerably clear. This NBC *Odyssey,* like so many dramatic shots at the ancient world and its classical authors, seems designed, with its sappy dialogue, its avoidance of adult relationships, and its emphasis on the Homeric equivalent of Dungeons and Dragons, to cater to the Star Wars generation of children and young adolescents, and one has to ask oneself why. What is more (as I know from a heated internet debate), plenty of adults, teachers included, think this is a thoroughly good thing.

The feeling seems to be that you can trivialize, eviscerate, change, simplify, and rewrite all you've a mind to *as long as it gets the kids interested.* The question is, interested in what? Not Homer, that's for sure: anyone who opens the *Odyssey* (even Rieu's ghastly prose version, so inexplicably preferred by Paglia as a teaching tool) in the fond belief that it's remotely like what they've seen on the screen is in for a massive disappointment. In the real world, this would be categorized as false advertising and render the promoters liable to prosecution. And why target this audience anyway? What I find even more puzzling is that the phenomenon is *not* universal, but seemingly restricted to the ancient world. Thus it can't be argued (as some have tried to do) that what we have here is simply consideration for the great semi-educated masses who watch TV, an assumption that—like too many politicians—badly underestimates the overall intelligence of the viewing public. The contrast between this *Odyssey* and the high-level adaptations of Jane Austen and Henry James that have been such successes on the box is too striking to ignore. No comic-strip dialogue or dumbed-down mentality there. Why is it Greece and Rome that always get the short end of the stick?

I'm not sure I know the answer to this one, but I suspect it may have something to do with a tradition going back to Bulwer-Lytton, *Cabiria*, and D. W. Griffith's *Intolerance:* the notion of the ancient world as a totally unreal fancy-dress party, taking place in large buildings composed mainly of columns or pillars, and as devoid of remotely realistic day-to-day life (a shortage of essential domestic furniture seems *de rigueur*) as of believable, let alone adult, dialogue. Why, someone once plaintively asked, do characters in ancient-world fiction or movies always talk like characters in ancient-world fiction or movies? To put it another way: the *Odyssey* has been *wrongly categorized:* it belongs with Shakespeare, Austen, and James, and should get the same adult treatment. Back in the early sixties—probably inspired by *The Seventh Seal* and *The Virgin Spring*—I had a dream of seeing Ingmar Bergman make the *Odyssey*, in black and white, on a shoestring, shooting it round the Scandinavian fjords, using his regular actors (Max von Sydow as Odysseus, Gunnel Lindblom as Circe: the movie cast itself), with all the emphasis, as was Homer's, on personal relationships and character under stress, and no rubbishy special effects. Too late for that now; but I still hope that someone, some day, will give us a real *Odyssey*, an *Odyssey* for grown-ups. God knows the material is rich enough, and there waiting for someone wise enough to know, as the old Alexandrian wrote, that "Ithaca gave you the wonderful journey, that without her you would not have set out."

BIBLIOGRAPHY

Addabbo, A. M. 1991. "Carmen magico e carmen religioso," *CCC* 12: 11–27.

Adeleye, G. 1971. "Studies in the Oligarchy of the Thirty." Diss., Princeton, 1971.

Anderson, J. K. 1974. *Xenophon.* London.

Ankarloo, B., and S. Clark, eds. 1999. *Witchcraft and Magic in Europe: Ancient Greece and Rome.* Philadelphia.

Audollent, A. 1967. *Defixionum Tabellae.* Reprint. Frankfurt. (Originally published Paris 1904.)

Bäumer, Ä. 1984. "Die Macht des Wortes in Religion und Magie (Plinius, *Nat. Hist.* 28.4–29)." *Hermes* 112: 84–99.

Baynes, N. H. 1955. "Isocrates." In *Byzantine Studies and Other Essays,* ch. 8, 144–67. London.

Beagon, M. 1992. *Roman Nature: The Thought of Pliny the Elder.* Oxford.

Beloch, K. J. 1912–13. *Griechische Geschichte.* 2d ed. 4 vols. Leipzig and Berlin.

Betz, H. D. 1992. *The Greek Magical Papyri in Translation, Including the Demotic Spells.* Vol. 1: *Texts.* 2d ed. Chicago. (Abbreviated *GMPT.*)

Bevan, E. R. 1901. "The Deification of Kings in the Greek Cities." *English Historical Review* 16: 625–39.

Beye, C. R. 1982. *Epic and Romance in the Argonautica of Apollonius.* Carbondale and Edwardsville.

Boardman, J. 1974. *Athenian Black Figure Vases.* London.

———. 1975. *Athenian Red Figure Vases: The Archaic Period.* London.

———. 1980. *The Greeks Overseas: Their Early Colonies and Trade.* 3d enlarged ed. London and New York.

———. 1989. *Athenian Red Figure Vases: The Classical Period.* London.

Bommelaer, J.-F. 1981. *Lysandre de Sparte: Histoire et Traditions.* Athens and Paris.

Bonner, R. J., and G. Smith. 1939. *The Administration of Justice from Homer to Aristotle.* 2 vols. Chicago.

Bosworth, A. B. 1988. *Conquest and Empire: The Reign of Alexander the Great.* Cambridge.

Braswell, B. K. 1988. *A Commentary on the Fourth Pythian Ode of Pindar.* Berlin and New York.

Braund, D. 1994. *Georgia in Antiquity: A History of Colchis and Transcaucasian Iberia, 550 B.C.–A.D. 562.* Oxford.

Breitenbach, H. R. 1967. "Xenophon (6)." PWK vol. ix A2, cols. 1570–2052. Stuttgart.

Brillante, C. "Myth and History: History and the Historical Interpretation of Myth." In Edmunds 1990, 91–140.

Buffière, F. 1956. *Les Mythes d'Homère et la Pensée Grecque.* Paris.

———, ed. 1962. *Héraclite: Allégories d'Homère.* Paris.

Bugh, G. R. 1988. *The Horsemen of Athens.* Princeton.

Burkert, W. 1985. *Greek Religion.* Trans. J. Raffan. Cambridge.

Buxton, R. 1994. *Imaginary Greece: The Contexts of Mythology.* Cambridge.

The Cambridge Ancient History. 1992. Vol. 5: *The Fifth Century B.C.* 2d ed. Edited by D. M. Lewis, John Boardman, J. K. Davies, and M. Ostwald. Cambridge.

Cameron, A. 1995. *Callimachus and His Critics.* Princeton.

Campbell, J. F. 1964. *Honour Family and Patronage.* Oxford.

Cargill, J. 1981. *The Second Athenian Sea-League.* Berkeley and Los Angeles.

Carlier, P. 1984. *La Royauté en Grèce avant Alexandre.* Strasbourg.

Cartledge, P. 1993. *The Greeks: A Portrait of Self and Others.* Oxford.

Cavenaile, R. 1972. "Pour une histoire politique et sociale d'Alexandrie: Les origins." *Ant. Class.* 41: 94–112.

Cawkwell, G. 1997. *Thucydides and the Peloponnesian War.* London and New York.

Cerfaux, L., and J. Tondriau. 1957. *Le culte des souverains dans la civilization gréco-romaine.* Tournai.

Chambers, M. H., R. Gallucci, and P. Spanos. 1990. "Athens' Alliance with Egesta in the Year of Antiphon." *ZPE* 83: 38–63.

Charlesworth, M. P. 1935. "Some Observations on Ruler-cult, Especially in Rome." *HThR* 28: 5–44.

Clauss, J. J. 1993. *The Best of the Argonauts: The Redefinition of the Epic Hero in Book One of Apollonius' Argonautica.* Berkeley, Los Angeles, and Oxford.

Colin, G. 1933. *Xénophon historien d'après le livre II des Helléniques (hiver 406/5 à 401/0).* Paris.

Cornford, F. M. 1907. *Thucydides Mythistoricus.* London.

Daremberg, C., and E. Saglio. 1877–1919. *Dictionnaire des antiquités grecques et romaines.* Paris. (Abbreviated Daremberg-Saglio.)

Davidson, J. 1997. *Courtesans and Fishcakes.* London.

Delbrück, F. 1829. *Xenophon.* Bonn.

Delebecque, E. 1957. *Essai sur la Vie de Xénophon.* Paris.

Delia, D. 1992. "From Romance to Rhetoric: The Alexandrian Library in Classical and Islamic Traditions." *AHR* 97: 1449–67.

De Romilly, J. 1973. "Gorgias et le pouvoir de la poésie." *JHS* 93: 155–62.

———. 1975. *Magic and Rhetoric in Ancient Greece.* Cambridge, Mass.

De Witt, N. W. 1954. *Epicurus and His Philosophy.* Minneapolis.

Dickie, M. W. 2001. *Magic and Magicians in the Greco-Roman World.* London.

Diels, H., and W. Kranz. 1966. *Die Fragmente der Vorsokratiker.* 12th ed. 3 vols. Dublin and Zürich. (Abbreviated D-K.)

Dittenberger, W. 1903–5. *Orientis Graecae Inscriptiones Selectae*. 2 vols. Leipzig. (Abbreviated *OGIS*.)

Dobesch, G. 1968. *Der panhellenische Gedanke im 4. Jh. v. Chr. und der "Philippos" des Isokrates. Untersuchungen zum Korinthischen Bund*. Vol. 1. Vienna.

Dodds, E. R. 1951. *The Greeks and the Irrational*. Berkeley and Los Angeles.

Dowden, K. 1992. *The Uses of Greek Mythology*. London and New York.

Dräger, P. 1993. *Argo Pasimelousa: Der Argonautenmythos in der griechischen und römischen Literatur*. Vol. 1: *Theos Aitios* (*Palingenesia* 43). Stuttgart.

du Boulay, J. 1974. *Portrait of a Greek Mountain Village*. Oxford.

Dunkel, H. B. 1938. "Was Demosthenes a Panhellenist?" *CPh* 33: 291–305.

Edelstein, L. 1937. "Greek Medicine in Its Relation to Religion and Magic." *BHM* 5: 201–46.

Edelstein, E. J., and L. Edelstein. 1945. *Asclepius: A Collection and Interpretation of the Testimonia*. 2 vols. Baltimore.

Edmunds, L., ed. 1990. *Approaches to Greek Myth*. Baltimore.

Ehrenberg, V. 1946. "The Athenian Hymn to Demetrius Poliorcetes." *Aspects of the Ancient World*. Oxford. Ch. 12, 179–98.

Entralgo, P. 1970. *The Therapy of the Word in Classical Antiquity*. Trans. and ed. by L. J. Rather and J. M. Sharp. New Haven.

Erbse, H. 1966. "Xenophons Anabasis." *Gymnasium* 73: 485–505.

Ernout, A. 1964. "La magie chez Pline l'Ancien." In *Hommages à J. Bayet*, ed. M. Renard and R. Schilling, 190–95. Brussels.

Erskine, A. 1990. *The Hellenistic Stoa: Political Thought and Action*. Ithaca, N.Y., and London.

Faraone, C. A. 1999. *Ancient Greek Love Magic*. Cambridge, Mass.

Faraone, C. A., and D. Obbink, eds. 1991. *Magika Hiera: Ancient Greek Magic and Religion*. Oxford.

Feeney, D. C. 1991. *The Gods in Epic: Poets and Critics of the Classical Tradition*. Oxford.

Ferguson, W. S. 1911. *Hellenistic Athens: An Historical Essay*. New York.

Festa, N., ed. 1902. *Mythographi Graeci, III.2: Palaephatus περὶ ἀπίστων*. Leipzig.

Finley, M. I. 1954. "The Ancient Greeks and Their Nation: The Sociological Problem." *Brit. Journ. Soc.* 5: 253–64.

Forbes, P.B.R. 1950. "Hesiod versus Perses." *CR* 64: 82–87.

Forsdyke, J. 1956. *Greece before Homer: Ancient Chronology and Mythology*. London.

Forster, E. M. 1982. *Alexandria: A History and a Guide*. Rev. ed. New York.

Fränkel, H. 1968. *Noten zu den Argonautika des Apollonios*. Munich.

Fraser, P. M. 1972. *Ptolemaic Alexandria*. 3 vols. Oxford.

Frazer, J. G. 1921. *Apollodoros*. 2 vols. London.

Fredricksmeyer, E. A. 1981. "On the Background of the Ruler Cult." *Ancient Macedonian Studies in Honor of Charles F. Edson*, ed. by H. Dell, 145–56. Thessaloniki [Institute of Balkan Studies].

French, A. 1964. *The Growth of the Athenian Economy*. London.

Friedländer, P. 1914. "Kritische Untersuchungen zur Geschichte der Heldensage: I, Argonautensage." *RhM* 69: 299–317.

Fuks, A. 1953. *The Ancestral Constitution: Four Studies in Athenian Party Politics at the End of the Fifth Century B.C.* London.

Fusillo, M. 1985. *Il Tempo delle Argonautiche: Un' analisi del racconto in Apollonio Rodio.* Filologia & Critica, vol. 49. Rome.

Gagarin, M. 1973. "Dikê in the *Works and Days.*" *CPh* 68: 81–94.

————. 1974. "Hesiod's Dispute with Perses." *TAPhA* 104: 103–11.

————. 1990. "The Ambiguity of *Eris* in the *Works and Days.*" In *Cabinet of the Muses,* ed. M. Griffith and D. J. Mastronarde, 173–83. Atlanta.

Gager, J. G. 1992. *Curse Tablets and Binding Spells from the Ancient World.* Oxford.

Galinsky, G. K. 1975. *Ovid's Metamorphoses: An Introduction to the Basic Aspects.* Berkeley and Los Angeles.

Gantz, T. 1993. "Iason and the Argo." *Early Greek Myth: A Guide to Literary and Artistic Sources,* ch. 12. Baltimore.

Goettling, C. 1843. *Hesiod: Carmina.* 2d ed. Leipzig.

Gomme, A. W., A. Andrewes, and K. J. Dover. 1970. *A Historical Commentary on Thucydides.* Vol. 4. Oxford. (Abbreviated Gomme-Andrewes-Dover.)

Gould, J. 1985. "On Making Sense of Greek Religion." In *Greek Religion and Society,* ed. P. E. Easterling and J. V. Muir, 1–33. Cambridge.

Green, P. M. 1954. "Prolegomena to the Study of Magic and Superstition in the *Natural History* of Pliny the Elder." Ph.D. diss., Cambridge University.

————. 1982. *Ovid: The Erotic Poems.* Harmondsworth.

————. 1991. *Alexander of Macedon, 356–323 B.C.: A Historical Biography.* Repr. Berkeley and Los Angeles. (Originally published Harmondsworth 1974.)

————. 1993. *Alexander to Actium: The Historical Evolution of the Hellenistic Age.* 2d corr. printing. Berkeley and Los Angeles.

————. 1997. *Apollonios Rhodios: The Argonautika.* Berkeley and Los Angeles.

Hackl, U. 1960. "Die oligarchische Bewegung in Athen am Ausgang des 5. Jahrhunderts v. Chr." Diss., Munich.

Hahn, J. 1991. "Plinius und die griechischen Ärzte in Rom: Naturkonzeption und Medizinkritik in der Naturalis Historia." *Sudhoffs Archiv. Zeitschr. f. Wiss.* 675: 209–39.

Hall, E. 1989. *Inventing the Barbarian: Greek Self-Definition through Tragedy.* Oxford.

Hamilton, C. D. 1979. *Sparta's Bitter Victories: Politics and Diplomacy in the Corinthian War.* Ithaca, N.Y.

Harris, W. V. 1989. *Ancient Literacy.* Princeton.

Heath, M. 1987. "Meaning and Emotion." In *The Poetics of Greek Tragedy,* 37–89. London.

Henrichs, A. 1975. "Two Doxographical Notes: Democritus and Prodicus on Religion." *HSCPh* 79: 93–123.

————. 1976. "The Atheism of Prodicus." *Bollettino del Centro Internazionale per lo studio dei Papyri Ercolanesi [Chronache Ercolanesi]* 6: 15–21.

———. 1984. "The Sophists and Hellenistic Religion: Prodicus as the Spiritual Father of the Isis Aretalogies." In *Actes du VIIe Congrès de la Fédération Internationale d'Études Classiques*, ed. J. Hannatta, 2: 339–53. Budapest.

Hettich, E. L. 1933. *A Study in Ancient Nationalism: The Testimony of Euripides.* Williamsport.

Heurgon, J. 1978. *Marcus Terentius Varro: Économie Rurale.* Paris.

Higgins, W. E. 1977. *Xenophon the Athenian.* Albany.

Hignett, C. 1952. *A History of the Athenian Constitution to the End of the Fifth Century B.C.* Oxford.

Hogarth, D. G. 1915. "Alexander in Egypt and Some Consequences." *JEA* 2: 53–60.

Hugill, W. M. 1936. *Panhellenism in Aristophanes.* Chicago.

Hunter, R. L. 1989. *Apollonius of Rhodes: Argonautica Book III.* Cambridge.

———. 1993. *The Argonautica of Apollonius: Literary Studies.* Cambridge.

Huxley, G. L. 1969. *Epic Poetry from Eumelos to Panyassis.* London.

Jacoby, F. 1923–58. *Fragmente der griechischen Historiker.* Berlin and Leiden. (Abbreviated *FGrH*.)

Jensen, M. S. 1966 [1969]. "Tradition and Individuality in Hesiod's *Works and Days. Class. et Med.* 27: 1–27.

Jessen, O. 1896. "Argonautai." *PWK* ii, cols. 743–87. Stuttgart.

Jones, W.H.S. 1909. *Malaria and Greek History.* Manchester.

———. 1923–31. *Hippocrates.* 4 vols. Cambridge, Mass. and London.

———. 1963. *Pliny: Natural History VIII, Libri XXVII–XXXII.* London.

Jordan, D. R., H. Montgomery, and E. Thomassen, eds. 1999. *The World of Ancient Magic.* Papers from the first International Samson Eitrem Seminar at the Norwegian Institute at Athens, 4–8 May 1997. Bergen.

Jüthner, J. 1923. *Hellenen und Barbaren: Aus der Geschichte des* Nationalbewußtseins [= *Das Erbe der Alten*, ser. 2.viii]. Leipzig.

Kagan, D. 1974. *The Archidamian War.* Ithaca, N.Y.

Kennedy, G. 1963. *The Art of Persuasion in Greece.* London.

Kirk, G. S., J. E. Raven, and M. Schofield. 1983. *The Presocratic Philosophers: A Critical History with a Selection of Texts.* 2d ed. Cambridge. (Abbreviated K-R-S.)

Klett, F. 1900. "Zu Xenophons Leben." *Programm des Grossherzoglichen Friedericianum Schwerin.* Schwerin i.M.

Knipfing, J. R. 1920–21. "German Historians and Macedonian Imperialism." *AHR* 26: 657–71.

Krentz, P. 1982. *The Thirty at Athens.* Ithaca and London.

Latimer, J. F. 1930. "Perses versus Hesiod." *TAPhA* 61: 70–79.

Lehmann, G. A. 1972. "Die revolutionäre Machtergreifung der 'Dreissig' und die staatliche Teilung Attikas (404–401/0 v.Chr.)." In *Antike und Universalgeschichte*, Festschrift Stier, 201–33. Munich.

Lenz, F. W. 1962. "Kephalos und Procris in Ovids *Ars Amatoria.*" *Maia* 14: 177–86. (= *Opuscula Selecta* 298–307.)

Lesky, A. 1932. "Medeia." *PWK* xv, cols. 29–65. Stuttgart.

Lloyd, G.E.R. 1979. *Magic Reason and Experience.* Cambridge.

Lobel, E., and D. L. Page. 1955. *Poetarum Lesbiorum Fragmenta.* Oxford. (Abbreviated L-P.)

Long, A. A. 1992. "Stoic Readings of Homer." In *Homer's Ancient Readers,* ed. R. Lamberton and J. J. Keaney, 41–66. Princeton.

Lotze, D. 1964. *Lysander und der Peloponnesische Krieg.* Abhandlung der Sächsischen Akademie der Wissenschaften zu Leipzig, Phil.-hist. Klasse, 57. Berlin.

Luccioni, J. 1961. *Démosthène et le Panhellénisme.* Paris.

Luck, G. 1985. *Arcana Mundi: Magic and the Occult in the Greek and Roman Worlds.* Baltimore and London.

Mahmoud Bey. 1872. *Mémoire sur l'antique Alexandrie.* Copenhagen.

Majno, G. 1975. *The Healing Hand: Man and Wound in the Ancient World.* Cambridge, Mass.

Martinez, D. 1991. *P. Michigan XVI: A Greek Love Charm from Egypt (P. Mich. 757).* American Studies in Papyrology 30. Atlanta.

Martini, M. C. 1977. *Piante medicamentose e rituali magico-religiosi in Plinio.* Rome.

Mathieu, G. 1925. *Les idées politiques d'Isocrate.* Paris.

Mazon, P. 1914. *Hésiode: Les Travaux et les Jours.* Paris.

———. 1928. *Hésiode: Théogonie, Les Travaux et les Jours, Le Bondieu.* Budé edition. Paris.

Meiggs, R., and D. M. Lewis. 1969. *Greek Historical Inscriptions to the End of the Fifth Century B.C.* Oxford. (Abbreviated Meiggs-Lewis.)

Meritt, B. D. 1928. *Athenian Calendar in the Fifth Century.* Cambridge, Mass.

Meuli, K. 1921. *Odyssee und Argonautika: Untersuchungen zur griechischen Sagengeschichte und zum Epos.* Berlin.

Müller, K., and Th. Müller. 1841–85. *Fragmenter Historicorum Graecorum.* Paris. (Abbreviated *FHG.*)

Munn, M. 2000. *The School of History: Athens in the Age of Socrates.* Berkeley.

Munro, J.A.R. 1937. "The End of the Peloponnesian War." *CQ* 31: 32–38.

Nestle, W. 1942. *Vom Mythos zum Logos: Die Selbstentfaltung des griechischen Denkens von Homer bis auf die Sophistik und Sokrates.* 2d ed. Stuttgart. (Reprinted Aalen 1966.)

Nilsson, M. P. 1972. *The Mycenaean Origin of Greek Mythology.* Reprint, with introduction and bibliography by E. Vermeule. Berkeley and London. (Originally published 1932.)

Nussbaum, M. 1994. *The Therapy of Desire: Theory and Practice in Hellenistic Ethics.* Princeton.

Nutton, V. 1986. "The Perils of Patriotism: Pliny and Roman Medicine." In *Science in the Early Empire: Pliny the Elder, His Sources and Influence,* ed. R. French and F. Greenaway, 30–58. London.

Olmstead, A. T. 1948. *A History of the Persian Empire.* Chicago.

Østerud, S. 1976. "The Individuality of Hesiod." *Hermes* 104: 12–29.

Otis, B. 1966. *Ovid as an Epic Poet.* Cambridge.

Page, D. L. 1962. *Poetae Melici Graeci.* Oxford. (Abbreviated *PMG.*)

———. 1974. *Supplementum Lyricis Graecis.* Oxford. (Abbreviated *SLG.*)

Paley, F. 1883. *The Epics of Hesiod.* London.

Parry, H. 1992. *Thelxis: Magic and Imagination in Greek Myth and Poetry.* Lanham, Md. and London.

Pauly, A., G. Wissowa, W. Kroll, and K. Ziegler. 1894–1980. *Real-Encyclopädie der classischen Altertumswissenschaft.* 83 vols. Stuttgart. (Abbreviated PWK.)

Perlman, S. 1976. "Panhellenism, the Polis, and Imperialism." *Historia* 25: 1–30.

Perry, B. E. 1952. *Aesopica: A Series of Texts Relating to Aesop.* Urbana, Ill.

Pfeiffer, R. 1968. *A History of Classical Scholarship from the Beginnings to the Hellenistic Age.* Oxford.

Pöschl, V. 1959. "Kephalos und Procris in Ovids Metamorphosen." *Hermes* 87: 328–43.

Preisendanz, K. 1973–74. *Papyri Graecae Magicae: Die griechischen Zauberpapyri.* 2 vols. 2d ed. Stuttgart. (Abbreviated *PGM.*)

Puelma, M. 1972. "Sänger und König: Zum Verständnis von Hesiods Tierfabel." *Mus. Helv.* 29: 86–109.

Radermacher, L. 1943. *Mythos und Saga bei den Griechen.* 2d ed. Munich and Vienna. (Reprinted Darmstadt 1968.)

Rahn, P. J. 1981. *"Xenophon's Exile," Classical Contributions: Studies in Honor of M. F. McGregor.* Locust Valley, N.Y.

Ramsey, J. T., and A. Lewis Licht. 1997. *The Comet of 44 B.C. and Caesar's Funeral Games. APA* American Classical Studies no. 39. Atlanta.

Renz, H. 1935. *Mythologische Beispiele in Ovids erotischer Elegie.* Würzburg.

Rhodes, P. J. 1981. *A Commentary on the Aristotelian Athenaion Politeia.* Oxford.

Riddle, J. M. 1985. *Dioscorides on Pharmacy and Medicine.* Austin.

Robert, C. 1921. *Die Griechische Heldensage.* (= L. Preller, *Griech. Myth.* pt. ii, vol. 3.1.) 4th rev. ed. Berlin.

Rodziewicz, M. 1987. "Le débat sur la topographie de la ville antique." *Revue des Mondes Musulmans et de la Méditerranée* 46: 39–48.

Rohde, A. 1929. *De Ovidi arte epica capita duo.* Berlin.

Romm, J. S. 1992. *The Edges of the Earth in Ancient Thought: Geography, Exploration, and Fiction.* Princeton.

Roquette, A. 1883. *De Xenophontis Vita.* Königsberg.

Ross Taylor, L. 1931. *The Divinity of the Roman Emperor.* Middletown, Conn.

Rusten, J. S. 1982. *Dionysius Scytobrachion.* (*Papyrologica Coloniensia* 10.) Opladen.

Sakellariou, M. B. 1981. "Panhellenism from Concept to Policy." In *Philip of Macedon,* ed. M. B. Hatzopoulos and L. D. Loukopoulos, 128–45, 242–45. New Rochelle, N.Y.

Schefold, K. 1989. *Die Sagen von den Argonauten, von Theben und Troia in der klassischen und hellenistischen Kunst.* Munich.

———. 1993. *Götter- und Heldensagen der Griechen in der Früh- und Hocharchaischen Kunst.* Munich.

Schoemann, G. F. 1869. *Hesiodi quae feruntur carminum reliquiae.* Berlin.

Schwartz, E. 1889. "Quellenuntersuchungen zur griechischen Geschichte." *RhM* 44: 163–93.

Scott, A. 1991. *Origen and the Life of the Stars: The History of an Idea.* Oxford.

Scott, K. 1928. "The Deification of Demetrius Poliorcetes." *AJPh* 49: 137–66, 217–39.

Sealey, R. 1993. *Demosthenes and His Times: A Study in Defeat.* Oxford.

Segal, C. 1986. *Pindar's Mythmaking: The Fourth Pythian Ode.* Princeton.

Sinclair, T. A. 1932. *Hesiod: Works and Days.* London.

Snell, B. 1975. *Die Entdeckung des Geistes: Studien zur Entstehung des Europäischen Denkes bei den Griechen.* 4th rev. ed. Göttingen.

Stewart, A. F. 1997. *Art Desire and the Body in Classical Greece.* Cambridge.

Tambiah, S. J. 1973. "Form and Meaning of Magical Acts: A Point of View." In *Modes of Thought,* ed. R. Horton and R. Finnegan, 199–229. London.

———. 1990. *Magic, Science, Religion, and the Scope of Rationality.* Cambridge.

Thomas, K. 1971. *Religion and the Decline of Magic.* London.

Thomas, R. 1989. *Oral Tradition and Written Record in Classical Athens.* Cambridge.

Tod, M. N. 1948. *A Selection of Greek Historical Inscriptions.* Vol. 2, *From 403–323 B.C.* Oxford. (Abbreviated *GHI.*)

Tuplin, C. 1987. "Xenophon's Exile Again." *Homo Viator: Classical Essays for John Bramble,* ed. M. Whitby, P. Hardy, and Mary Whitby, 59–68. Bristol.

Usener, H. 1887. *Epicurea.* Leipzig.

Van Groningen, B. A. 1953. *In the Grip of the Past: Essay on an Aspect of Greek Thought. Philosophia Antiqua,* vol. 6. Leiden.

———. 1957. "Hésiode et Persès." *Mededelingen der Koninklijke Nederlandse Akademie van Wetenschappen, Afd. Letterkunde* 20: 153–66.

Veyne, P. 1988. *Did the Greeks Believe in Their Myths? An Essay on the Constitutive Imagination.* Trans. Paula Wissing. Chicago and London.

Vian, F., and E. Delage, ed. and trans. 1974. *Apollonios de Rhodes, Argonautiques.* Vol. 1. Paris.

———. 1980. *Apollonios de Rhodes, Argonautiques.* Vol. 2. Paris.

———. 1981. *Apollonios de Rhodes, Argonautiques.* Vol. 3. Paris.

Vojatzi, M. 1982. *Frühe Argonautenbilder. Beiträge zur Archäologie* 14. Würzburg.

von Arnim, H. 1902–24. *Stoicorum Veterum Fragmenta.* 4 vols. Leipzig. (Abbreviated *SVF.*)

von Staden, H. 1975. "Experiment and Experience in Hellenistic Medicine." *BICS* 22: 178–99.

———. 1989. *Herophilus: The Art of Medicine in Early Alexandria.* Cambridge.

Wade-Gery, H. T. 1949. "Hesiod." *Phoenix* 3: 81–93.

Walbank, F. W. 1951. "The Problem of Greek Nationality." *Phoenix* 5: 41–60.

———. 1985. *Selected Papers.* Cambridge.

Walcot, P. 1966. *Hesiod and the Near East.* Cardiff.

———. 1970. *Greek Peasants, Ancient and Modern.* Manchester.

Weiler, I. 1968. "Greek and Non-Greek World in the Archaic Period." *GRByS* 9: 21–29.

Welles, C. B. 1962. "The Discovery of Sarapis and the Foundation of Alexandria." *Historia* 11: 271–98.

West, M. L. 1966. *Hesiod: Theogony.* Oxford.

———. 1978. *Hesiod: Works and Days.* Oxford.

Wickersham, J. M. 1991. "Myth and Identity in the Archaic Polis." In *Myth and the Polis*, ed. D. C. Pozzi, J. M. Wickersham, 16–31. Ithaca and London.

Wilamowitz-Moellendorff, U. von. 1884. "Antigonos von Karystos." *Philologische Untersuchungen* 4 (Berlin), app. 4: 330–36.

———. 1928. *Hesiodos Erga.* Berlin.

Winiarczyk, M., ed. 1991. *Euhemerus Messenius Reliquiae.* Stuttgart and Leipzig.

Winkler, J. J. 1991. "The Constraints of Eros." In Faraone and Obbink 1991, 214–43.

Witherspoon, E. T. 1928. *Hippocrates.* Vol. 3. London.

Wünsch, R. 1912. *Antike Fluchtafeln.* Bonn.

Wyss, B., ed. 1936. *Antimachi Colophonii Reliquiae.* Berlin.

INDEX

Abydos: 102
Acarnania: 84
Achaean League: 13
Achaemenid empire [see also s.v. Persia]: 104-5, 106, 122, 137; as the "Barbarian Other," 110-11; Greek associations of, 114-15 with n. 56, 137; satraps, 179, 190
Achilles: 6, 35, 50, 104, 251, 289
Actium: 241
Aegean: 6, 41, 43, 151 with n. 37, 177, 185, 290
Aegospotami: 144, 147, 149, 150 with n. 26, 151 n. 37
Aeneas: 46 n. 36
Aeneas Tacticus: 93 with n. 23
Aeolus: 290-91
Aeschines: 108, 166
Aeschylus: 41, 63, 72, 174, 284; *Oresteia*, 97; *Persians*, 42, 112, 113, 122
Aesop, *Aesopica*: 63
Aetolia: 84; Aetolian League, 130
Africa, N.: 23, 29, 175, 178, 190
Africa, T. W.: 210
Agamemnon: 116, 168, 289
Agesilaus: 134, 135, 138, 143
Agis II: 147, 150 with n. 34, 151, 152 n. 40, 154, 156, 158
Agis III: 178
Agis IV: 212, 213-14, 216
Agrios: 22
Aiaia: 16, 22
Aiëtes: 15, 16, 22, 23, 26, 28, 32, 200
Aison: 16, 17, 18
Aitia, Aetiologizing: 9, 28, 31, 35, 39, 198, 200, 206

Ajax: 12 n. 27, 272
Alabanda: 207
Alba Longa: 234 n. 1
Alcibiades: 90 with nn. 17-18, 91, 92, 100, 101-2, 103, 121 n. 96
Alciphron: 147
Alcmaeon (of Croton): 244
Alcmena: 255
Alexander (of Macedon): 4, 11 n. 22, 31, 37, 106, 113 n. 50, 114, 129, 131, 169, 183, 211, 224, 235, 240, 282; and Alexandria, 172-196; Cleomenes and, 188, 189, 191-92; conquest of Asia, 129, 247; deification and, 248; foundations, 177, 180; *kleos*, pursuit of, 180, 240; literary knowledge, 184; myths concerning, 175, 178 n. 33, 179, 193; Panhellenism and, 104; Pharaoh of Egypt, 179; *pothos* and, 182, 185; Regent of Macedonia, 177; religiosity, 181, 185, 186; sexual nature, 195; tomb of, 193-94; Tyre and, 182; visit to Siwah, 179, 185-88
Alexander (of Pherae): 120
"Alexander Romance," the: 172, 175, 179, 180, 182, 183-84, 186, 187, 188, 189-90
Alexandria, Alexandrians: 4, 36, 172-96, 198, 200, 206, 207, 281, 296; Alexander's foundation of, 177-90; *The Alexandrine War*, 182 with n. 61; Antirrhodos, 197; archaeology of, 175-76, 184, 193; Canopic Way, 193; Chatby cemetery, 184; Corniche, 176; court poetry of, 33;

Eleusis suburb, 205; Great Harbor, 176, 189, 192, 196; Hellenistic, 6, 33, 37, 198, 267; Heptastadion, 175, 183, 192; Lake Mareotis, 181, 184, 189; Library, 174, 192, 195, 206, 207-8 with n. 23, 208; Museum/Mouseion, 174, 192, 195, 202, 206, 208; myths concerning, 193–94; Necropolis, 184; Pharos, 174, 175, 181, 182, 183, 191, 192, 195, 197; "Pompey's Column," 186; Sema, 192–94; sewerage system, 182, 188, 189
Alexandropolis: 177
Alexias (archon): 154
Allegory: 3, 25-26, 27, 32 with n. 93, 34, 38 with n. 115
Amazons: 7, 113, 170, 175, 271
Ammianus Marcellinus: 175, 183
Ammon, oracular shrine of: 179, 185–88
Amphictyonic League/Council: 108, 109 n. 28
Amphidamas: 64, 66
Amphipolis: 84, 88, 96, 103
Amr: 174
Amykos: 20 with n. 54, 33
Amyrtaeus: 76
Anacreon: 112
Anatolia: 14
Anaxagoras: 13, 199
Anaxibios: 142
Anaximander: 11 n. 22, 287
Anaximenes: 239
Anderson, W. S.: 262
Andocides: 88, 92, 93, 110-11 n. 36, 141, 143, 144
Andromeda: 245
Andros: 42
Antagoras of Rhodes: 201
Anticleia: 290
Antigone: 294
Antigonids: 130
Antigonus Gonatas: 217, 218
Antilochus: 58 n. 47
Antimachos of Colophon: 16 n. 39, 25, 199, 200

Antiochus (Alcibiades' steersman): 102
Antipater: 104, 130
Antoninus Liberalis: 26, 255 with n. 18, 258
Antonius, M. (Mark Antony): 234–35
Aphareus: 120
Aphrodite: 19, 37
Apollo: 24, 29 n. 88, 38 with n. 115, 203, 282
Apollodorus (mythographer): 2, 255, 257 n. 39, 259 n. 49, 284
Apollonius (the Classifier): 207
Apollonius Rhodius: 15, 16, 18, 19, 25, 27, 31-39, 281; and Callimachus, 31, 197-209; life, 34, 205-6; religion and, 36-37
Apsyrtos: 24 n. 70, 30, 37
Aratus of Soli: 217, 245
Arcesilas IV of Cyrene: 23
Archaic age: 12, 38, 101, 113
Archidamus II, King: 83, 86
Archidamus III, King: 120, 124
Archilochus: 48, 108, 198, 206
Archimedes: 97, 276 n. 69
Architecture: Parthenon, 77-78
Ares: 24, 256
Arginusae: 101
Argo: 5, 11, 16, 18, 19, 20 with n. 54, 25, 29, 31, 33 n. 97, 35-36 with n. 105, 37, 39; speaking beam of, 32 n. 95
Argonauts, Argonaut myth: 1, 6, 8, 10, 15-39, 200
Argos: 27, 88, 89, 90, 215; Argive League, 87
Ariadne: 16, 41, 251, 284
Aristarchus: 106 n. 8, 207 n. 23
Aristobulus: 187 with n. 99, 188
Aristophanes: 85, 97, 98, 122, 124, 127, 164; *Acharnians*, 109, 122 with n. 106, 167; *Birds*, 122; *Clouds*, 56, 85, 166; *Lysistrata*, 109, 167; Panhellenism and, 109, 110, 118; *Peace*, 87 with n. 15, 109; *Thesm.*, 122 with n. 106
Aristotle: 7, 14, 26-27, 113, 195, 244;

Ath. Pol., 145, 156, 176 n. 69; *Constitution of Athens*, 95; *De Caelo*, 239; [*Oeconomicus*], 191 with n. 123; *Politics*, 65, 113 n. 50, 226 with n. 2
Aristoxenus of Taras: 276–77 n. 70
Arrian: 41, 179–80, 182, 184, 187, 191–92
Arsinoë II: 247–48
Artaxerxes II Mnemon: 122, 128, 133, 135, 137, 140, 147
Artaxerxes III Ochus: 178 with n. 33
Artemis: 188, 257, 258
Artemisium: 110
Ascra: 53
Ashcroft, J.: 223 n.1
Asia Minor/Anatolia: 104, 112, 113, 124, 134, 135, 137, 150, 177, 178
Asklepiades of Samos: 204
Assinaros R.: 91, 92
Astypalaea: 42
Atheism: 29 n. 85
Athena: 19, 32 n. 95, 35, 36 n. 112, 37, 45, 292
Athenaeus: 161
Athens, Athenians: 7, 11 n. 23, 12 n. 24, 25, 36, 41, 42, 44, 73–74, 76, 79, 87, 114, 128; Academy, 246; Acropolis, 36 n. 112, 40, 144; Areopagus, 258; and Argos, 87, 90; Attic dialect, 131; bribery and, 129 with n. 144; cavalry, 93, 94, 98, 137 n. 16, 138–39, 140, 143 with n. 47; class-divisions, 77 n. 8, 90, 95–96 with n. 31, 97–99, 102, 121, 124, 138–39, 160–61, 163, 231, 276 with n. 69; cleruchies, 125; Congress Decree, 119; Council of 500, 139; democracy, 97–98, 101–2, 114; economics of, 94–97; *eleutheria* and, 107, 129, 130, 131; euphemisms of, 12 and n. 26; Euripides on, 116–17; exiles, 148–49; farmers, 109–10; foreign policy of, 84, 94–95, 111, 127, 133, 137, 140; Four Hundred & Five Thousand, 99, 102; gods and, 240; grain-supply and, 94–96; *Hellenotamiai*, 118–19;

Hermocopids, 91–92; Herodotus on, 108; imperialism of, 97–98, 118–19; *isonomia*, 98; Kerameikos, 218; late, 131; Long Walls, 77, 88, 144, 145, 148, 151, 153; market inspectors, 164; Melos and, 63 with n. 53; metics, 144; modern, 160–61; Munychia, 139, 146; ostracism, 90 with n. 19; Panathenaic procession, 36 n. 112; Parthenon and, 73, 78, 97, 170; Phaleron, 45; Piraeus, 45, 88, 96, 130, 139, 144, 145, 146, 147, 148, 150 n. 28, 151 n. 37, 153, 155, 156–57, 158; plague and, 83, 85, 86; Second Athenian Confederacy, 120 with n. 85, 125, 127; sexual habits, 165–69, 170, 287; Sulla's sack of, 130; terms of surrender, 148–49; thalassocracy, 98; the Thirty, 101, 121 with n. 93, 139, 140, 142, 144–59; tribute-lists, 80; war-profiteers, 87
Athos, Mt.: 189
Attalids: 116; Attalus I, 131
Attica: 41, 43, 44, 45, 51 n. 21, 77, 125, 136, 137, 142, 145, 254, 255, 258; *kouroi*, 97; literacy in, 100; Phyle, 139, 145; Spartan raids in, 83, 86
Auden, W. H.: 221
Augustine, St.: 222
Augustus/Octavian: 46, 187, 193; apotheosis of, 234–36 with nn. 5, 8 and 10, 237, 240, 243–44, 247
Aurelian: 193
Aurora: 254, 255–56, 257, 258; sexually insatiable, 256 n. 27, 258 with n. 48
Austen, J.: 295, 296
Autolycus: 273
Ayrton, M.: 285, 286

Babylon, Babylonia: 137, 177
Bacchus, Bacchants: 251, 284
Badian, E.: 104 with n. 2, 122 n. 98, 129 n. 148
Bagoas: 19
Bakker, J.: 223
Balkans, Balkan peninsula: 107, 131

Barbarians: 69, 112, 120; Achaemenids as, 115, 123, 129; as the Other, 29, 30 n. 90, 31, 76, 110, 111–12, 113, 121–22, 125, 126–27, 128, 129, 165; despotic *mores* of, 114; Gauls as, 131; Greeks as, 116; Macedonians as, 115, 128, 129, 131; Romans as, 115, 130
Battos I of Cyrene: 23
Bellerophon: 15 n. 37
Beloch, K. J.: 81, 106, 107, 127, 146
Bennett, W.: 222
Benson, E. F.: 192
Berenice II: 248
Bergman, I.: 296
"biographical fallacy," theory of: 197–99
Black Sea (Euxine, Pontos): 10–11, 16, 21, 22, 28, 29, 31; grain-route, 151 n. 37
Blossius: 211
Blum, R.: 207
Boeotia, Boeotians: 45, 87, 88, 134; Lake Copaïs, 88
Boreads: 16, 18 n. 46, 20, 30
Bosworth, A. B.: 180
Brasidas: 83, 103
Bronze Age: 6, 32, 282, 288–89
Brown, B.: 189
Browning, R.: 59
Brutus, M.: 234; the tragedy *Brutus*, 234 n. 4
Bulwer-Lytton, E.: 296
Burgess, A.: 162, 222
Burke, E.: 71
Busolt, G.: 79, 88, 146–47 with n. 14
Byron, G. G., Lord: 102
Byzantion: 29, 151 n. 37, 177

Cabiria: 296
Cadmus: 162–63, 286, 287
Caius Caesar: 250
Calasso, R.: 281; retelling of Greek myths by, 281–87
Calidonian boar-hunt: 20 n. 54
Caligula: 193
Callibius: 155 n. 55

Callicles: 63 with n. 53, 79
Callimachus: 29, 31, 39, 174, 195, 197–209, 247–48; *Aitia*, 202, 203, 204–5; *Epigrams*, 283; Florentine scholia to, 204; *Hekale*, 204; *Hymn to Apollo*, 202, 203; *Ibis*, 201–2, 204–5; life, 205, 207–8; "Telchines," 202, 203, 204
Calymne (Kalymnos): 42
Calypso: 251 n.2, 293–95
Cambridge Ancient History: 67–78
Cameron, A.: 198–209
Camillus: 155
Campania: 40, 42, 43
Campbell, J.: 283
Canopus: 191
Capua: 230
Caracalla (emperor): 193
Caria, Carians: 112
Carroll, L.: 291
Carthage, Carthaginians: 111, 179
Caspian Sea: 11 n. 22
Cassandra: 25, 116
Cassirer, E.: 2, 283
Catasterism: 4, 234–49, 282; astrology and, 248–49; astronomy and, 245, 247–48
Cato, M.: 272
Catullus: 248
Caunos: 206
Cavafy, C. P.: 130, 172 with n. 4, 173 with n. 6, 174, 195, 296
Cavalry: Athenian, 93, 94, 98, 137 n. 16, 138–39, 140, 143; Persian, 178; Syracusan, 93
Cecrops: 204
Celsus (medical writer): 280
Centaurs: 113
Cephalus: 251–63
Ceramic ware: Attic vases, 17, 19, 20–21; Theban, 17
Cercidas: 217
Chabrias: 155
Chaeronea: 129
Chalcedon: 151 n. 37
Chaos: 10 and n.18

Charon of Lampsacus: 69
Charybdis: 35, 291
Cheiron: 16, 35
Chersonese, Tauric: 29
Chesterton, G. K.: 43
Chimaira: 11, 14
Chios: 107-8 n. 21, 120
Chremonidean War: 130 with n. 153, 211, 216
Christianity: 79, 162, 226, 238, 245, 249, 286; the Virgin Mary, 248
Chronology: 7-8, 25, 28, 39 n. 116, 144-59, 186, 187 with n. 98
Chrysippos (mythical): 8
Chrysippos (Stoic philosopher): 27, 218, 227, 228, 244
Chrysostom, John: 193
Cicero, M. T.: 225, 228-29, 230, 231, 234 n. 4, 240-41 with n. 47; *De Finibus*, 229; *Somnium Scipionis*, 246-47
Cilicia: 178
Cimon s.o. Miltiades: 72, 88, 98, 155; Eurymedon victory, 168; philolaconism of, 118
Circe: 16, 20 n. 54, 22, 251 n. 3, 257, 288, 293-94
City-state (*polis*): 70, 76, 114, 138, 142, 217, 218, 282; Euripides on, 116-17 with n. 69; Hellenistic, 211-12; Isocrates and, 126
Clarendon, E. H., Earl of: 71
Clashing Rocks (*Symplegades*): 22, 26, 28, 32 with n. 94, 35 with n. 105, 37, 200
Claudius (emperor): 238, 245
Cleanthes: 218
Cleidemus: 41
Cleisthenes: 90 n. 19, 97, 98, 161, 216
Clement of Alexandria: 27 n. 81
Cleomenes (of Naucratis): 173, 181, 188, 189, 190-92, 194
Cleomenes III, of Sparta: 119, 211, 212, 213-15, 216, 218
Cleon: 77 n. 8, 79, 83, 85, 86-87, 95, 98, 103

Cleopatra VII: 173, 175, 195, 196
Cleophon: 98, 99, 151, 153
Clinton, H. R.: 228 n. 4
Clinton, W. J.: 222 n. 1, 228 n. 4
Cnidos: 206
Colchis: 10, 22, 23, 28, 35, 38
Colonization, colonialism: 11, 22, 30, 113, 124-25, 162, 180; cannibalism and, 209
Comets, eclipses: 235-37, 242-44 with nn. 55, 60, 61; Chinese records of, 243 with n. 61
"Common peace" [*koine eirene*]: 110-11 n. 36
Conon (Athenian admiral): 120, 137, 153
Conon (court astronomer): 248
Constantine (emperor): 238; Baths of, 290
Corcyra: *stasis* on, 83
Corinth, Corinthians: 12, 18, 23, 30 n. 91, 87-88, 89, 107-8 n. 21, 114, 139 with n. 31, 143, 160; Corinthian war, 100, 119, 137; Gulf of, 83; League of, 216
Cornford, F.: 2, 72, 91
Coronea: 133, 134, 137, 138, 139 with n. 31, 143
Crassus, M.: 230
Craterus (of Olynthus): 188
Crete, Cretans: 40, 45 n. 30, 257, 260; Minoan civilization, 184 with n. 70
Critias: 79, 100, 101, 146, 217
Cumae: 45
Cunaxa: 140
Curtius Rufus, Q.: 179, 184 with n. 81, 187 with n. 99, 190 with n. 116
Cybele: 282
Cyclopes: 113, 200, 291
Cyme: 45
Cynics: 34, 228; as *kosmopolitai*, 174
Cynossema: 102
Cyrene: 23, 24, 178, 185
Cyrus the Younger: 133, 135, 137, 140, 142, 143, 158
Cyzicus: 102

Daedalus: 3, 40–46, 226 n. 2, 251, 285
Danaë: 114
Danaïds: 13 n. 28
Dante Alighieri: 288
Danube R. (Ister): 29
Darius II: 147
Darius III: 177, 178
Davidson, J.: 160–71
Da Vinci, L.: 292
Dawson, D.: 220
Dean-Jones, L.: 273 n. 51
Decelea: 150, 154, 156, 158
Deidameia: 251
Deinocrates: 188, 189
Deion[eus]: 255
Delbrück, H.: 84, 86 with n. 12
Delium: 83, 84
Delos: 3, 42, 43, 45; Delian league, 98
Delphi: 23; aphorisms of, 166; the
   Pythia, 25; Sikyonian treasury, 20
   n. 54
De Man, P.: 121 with n. 95
Demaratus: 114
Demeter: 25 n.74, 203
Demetrios of Phaleron: 217
Demetrios Poliorcetes (the Be-
   sieger): 36, 160, 240 with n. 31, 282
Democracy, Greek: Athenian, 97–
   98, 101–2, 114; opponents of, 79;
   Thucydides and. 78–79
Democritus: 239
Demophoön: 251 n. 3
Demosthenes (4th cent. orator):
   105 with n. 6, 111, 114, 129, 191 with
   n. 123, 248; and Panhellenism, 115,
   118, 125, 126–29; *Philippics*, 127
Demosthenes (5th cent. general):
   77 n. 8, 83, 84
Derow, P. S.: 211
Derrida, J.: 171
Deukalion: 7
Dexileos: 139 n. 31
Diana: 257
Dicaeopolis: 109, 167
Didacticism: moral, 9
Dikaiarchos: 14

Dike: 48–49 n. 9, 56–57 with n. 42,
   61–65
Dio Cassius: 235 with n. 5, 236 with
   n.10
Dio Chrysostom: 135
Diodorus Siculus: 6, 28 n. 82, 85, 89
   with n. 15, 93, 146, 147, 150 with
   nn. 26 and 34, 153 n. 47, 175 with
   n. 20, 156, 179, 188, 201
Diogenes Laertius: 135, 227 with n. 3
Diogenes of Sinope: 26, 30
Dionysios I of Syracuse: 111, 120, 126
Dionysios of Halikarnassos: 28
   n. 82, 111, 216, 241–42 with n. 48
Dionysios Skytobrachion: 6, 15 with
   n. 36, 27–32, 38 n. 115, 39, 201, 204
Dionysodorus: 148 n. 20, 153, 191
Dionysovouni: 44
Dionysus: 44, 240, 282, 284, 286
Dioscorides: 265
Dioscuri: 20, 29
Disraeli, B.: 121, 189
Dobesch, G.: 119
Dodds, E. R.: 78
Dostoevsky, F.: 288
Douglas, K.: 288
Dover, K. J.: 165, 166, 168
Dreamchild: 291
Drögemüller, H.: 75
Droysen, J. G.: 127
Dryden, J.: 261
Dumbing Down of America, The: 295
Durkheim, E.: 2
Durrell, L.: 172, 173, 174, 191, 195

Eagleton, T.: 163, 171
Ecbatana: 104
Eclectics: 228
Economics and trade, ancient: 7 n.7,
   11, 74–76, 77 n. 8, 86, 136, 173, 191;
   Sicilian Expedition and, 94–97
Edelman, M.: 106 n. 14
Edmonds, J. M.: 82
Egesta/Segesta: 76–77, 94, 96
Egypt, Egyptians: 8, 76, 178, 208,
   266; Alexandria and, 173, 177–78,

182, 190, 202; Greek ambiva-
lence to, 8 n.13, 173; Heliopolis,
179; Karnak, 290; magic in, 266;
Nofret, 292; Pharaohs, 175, 183,
266; Rahotep, 292; Saïte dynasty,
76
Ehrenberg, V.: 194
Ekali: 44
Eleusis: 141, 142
Eleutheria [freedom]: 107, 129
Eliot, T. S.: 25, 35, 286; *The Waste
Land*, 290
Elysium, Elysian Fields: 245
Empedocles: 86, 276
Empson, W.: 14 n. 33
Ennius, Q.: 240
Eos: 17, 255
Ephesus: 188 n. 107
Ephoros of Cyme: 88, 146, 153 n. 47
Epidaurus: 228
Epic poetry, Hellenistic: 31–32, 39,
198–209
Epicurus, Epicureanism: 223–24,
226, 227, 228, 282
Epigraphy: 76–77, 80, 82
Epimetheus: 56, 60
Erasistratos: 174, 273
Eratosthenes: 206
Erechtheus, Erechtheïds: 41, 255
Erichthonios: 204
Erigone: 45
Eriphyle: 255
Eris: 51, 53
Erskine, A.: 210–21
Eteonicus: 150 n. 28
Etna, Mt.: 243 with n. 61
Etruscan mirrors: 17
Euboea: 42, 45
Euboulides (archon): 136
Euboulos: 136
Euclid: 276 n. 69
Euhemeros, Euhemerism: 13, 14, 36,
37, 39, 240, 244, 247, 282
Eumelos (mythical character): 16
Eumelos of Corinth (poet): 12, 18
n. 45, 23 with n. 64

Eunomia: 105
Euphemos: 20 n. 52, 23, 24
Euphrates, R.: 203
Euripides: 38, 117, 174, 184, 263, 281,
282; *Andromache*, 117; *Bacchae*, 162–
63; *Hel.*, 116 n. 67; *Iph.Aul.*, 113
n. 50; *Iph. Taur.*, 116 with n. 61;
Medeia, 25, 116 n. 67; *Orestes*, 116;
Phoen., 116 n. 67; scholia, 44, 45;
Supplices, 108; *Trojan Women*, 91
n. 20
Europa: 257 n. 41
Eurotas R.: 86
Eurymedon: 168–69
Eurymedon R.: 168
Eusebius: 8, 28

Falwell, J.: 222 with n. 1
Farming, archaic: 47–54 with n. 32
Faye, M.: 222
Fehling, D.: 70
Feminists, feminism: 162, 166
Finley, M. I.: 74, 84, 107, 114
Flamininus, T. Quintius: 130
Folk-tale motifs: 20–21, 32 n. 94;
liminality, 22 with n. 61
Fontenrose, J.: 262–63
Forrest, G.: 85, 211
Forster, E. M.: 172 with n. 3, 174, 194,
195
Foucault, M.: 162, 164–65, 166, 167,
168
Fowler, A.: 167
Frankfort, H.: 239
Fraser, P. M.: 176 with n. 24, 194
Frazer, J. G.: 2
French, A.: 84
Freud, S., Freudianism: 2, 283

Galen: 265, 268, 280
Games, Roman: *Ludi Apollinares*, 234;
*Ludi Veneris Genetricis/ Victoriae
Caesaris*, 235
Gaul, Gauls: 131
Gaza: 178
Gellner, E.: 173 n. 6

Genealogies: 12, 16, 25
Geography: 10–12, 14–15, 21–22, 26, 31, 38–39 with n. 116, 44, 84, 113; environmental influence on character, 113; sphericity of globe, 239
Ghosts: 11 n. 23
Gibbon, E.: 71
Gide, A.: 173
Gladstone, W. E.: 121
Glaucon s.o. Ariston: 95–96 with n. 31
Gods, Greek: 7, 14, 36, 37–38, 50, 182, 240; anthropomorphism of, 37; arbitrary power and amorality of, 9–10, 78, 282; epiphanies, 38 with n. 115; Euhemerus on, 240; Hellenistic, 281
Gods, Roman: divinization of mortals as, 234–49; Quirinus, 241; Roma, 237
Golden Fleece: 19, 20, 22, 24, 26, 28, 38
Gomme, A. W.: 84–85
Gorgias: 111; *Helen,* 265 with n. 10
Gorgons: 20 with n. 53, 113
Gratian (emperor): 238
Graves, R.: 166
Greco-Roman period: 6
Greece, modern: 53–54 with n. 32, 55 with n. 37, 60–61 with n. 52, 69, 88, 106, 129 with n. 148, 130, 131, 160–61, 260 with n. 54, 290; Bavarian monarchy of, 131; the colonels' Junta, 228; *ethnikismós,* 288; occupation of, 114; Turks and, 114, 131
Greene, G.: 174
Griffith, D. W.: *Intolerance,* 296
Grote, G.: 5, 79, 105 with n. 7, 126–27
Grundy, G. B.: 84
Gryllos: 138, 143 n. 47
Gylippos: 93, 150 n. 26

Hades: 239, 245, 288–89
Halicarnassus: 177–78

Hall, E.: 76
Hammond, N. G. L.: 84
Hardy, G. H.: 276 n. 69
Harpies: 16, 18, 20 with n. 54, 30, 32 n. 93, 290
Harrison, J. E.: 2
Hector: 272, 273
Hecuba: 6
Hegelochus: 185
Heinze, R.: 253
Hekataios of Miletos: 16, 69
Helen: 18, 170, 289, 291
Helios: 22
Hellanikos of Lesbos: 25, 69
Hellas: 107, 108, 117, 118, 129
Hellenistic Age: 6, 9 n.15, 15, 27; art of, 36, 170, 244, 247, 281; literature of, 5–39, 197–209, 255, 286
Henley, W. E.: 71
Hephaestion: 191, 194
Hephaestus: 226 n. 2, 257 n. 41, 289
Hera: 16, 18, 27, 35–36, 37, 39; the Heraea, 158
Heracleitus/Heraclitus: 79, 112–13, 160, 211, 287
Heracles/Hercules: 14, 15 n. 37, 21 with n. 56, 25 n. 74, 26 with n. 75, 29, 30, 38 n. 115, 240, 245, 281, 282, 284; appetites of, 32–34 with n. 97, 281; as civilizer, 29, 30, 34; claimed as ancestor by Ptolemies, 33; Pillars of, 21
Heraclides Ponticus: 246
Hermes, Herms: 91–92, 289, 294
Hermocrates: 93
Herodas: 172, 174
Herodoros: 26 with n. 75, 29
Herodotus: 3, 8 n.13, 9, 11 n.23, 14, 22, 29, 100, 122, 184, 198, 239, 284; on *eleutheria,* 107, 114, 115; Herodoteans, 3, 70–71 with n. 5, 78; historiography of, 68–70, 198; hostility to, 69–70; Ionic dialect, 70–71; *philobarbaros,* 69, 115; praise of Athens, 108 with n. 27; rejection of Ocean, 11 and n. 22, 16, 39; style

of, 70–71; and Thucydides, 68–71, 81; translations, 70–71 with n. 4

Heroic Age: 6–7, 8, 12, 27, 32, 33, 35

Herophilos: 174, 273; use of metaphor, 276–77 n. 70

Hesiod: 3, 8, 16, 22, 26, 45, 53 with n. 31, 58–59, 60–62, 65–66, 108, 123, 198, 206, 245, 254, 281, 285; anti-war, 108 n. 24; "barons" and, 47–48, 54 with n. 33, 55, 61, 63; divine law and, 52 with n. 28; fable of the Hawk and the Nightingale, 12, 61–65; family lawsuit, 47–57; *Theogony*, 17, 22, 47, 55, 63, 64, 256; *Works & Days*, 3, 47–66

Hesione: 29, 30 n. 88

Hesperides: 21, 33

Hesychius of Miletus: 201

Hipparchus (astronomer): 237

Hippocrates, Hippocratic medicine: 71, 86, 113, 271, 275, 280; *Airs Waters Places*, 113–14, 122; *Ancient Medicine*, 273; *Aphorisms*, 280; *The Art*, 274; *The Physician*, 272; *Regimen IV*, 270; *Sacred Disease*, 276; *On Wounds in the Head*, 272–73, 280 n. 89

Hipponax: 202

Historicism: 3, 6, 79

Historiography: 75–76, 79–103, 113; Hellenistic, 43; Herodotean, 68–70, 198; historicist, 79; and myth, 79, 83, 199–200; *Quellenforschung* and, 81; rational, 81 with n. 9; Thucydidean, 68–73, 78–79

Hobbes, T.: 71, 78–79, 86

Hogarth, D. G.: 186, 192–93 with n. 131

Homer, Homeric epics: 5, 6–7, 22, 24, 26, 29 n. 88, 35, 36, 38, 63, 69, 70, 106, 108, 112 with n. 45, 131, 168, 184, 198, 199, 200, 203, 206, 272, 281, 283, 285, 289, 291; Alcinoös, 292; Arete, 292; Eurymachus, 293; Homeric Question, 71; *Iliad*, 16, 26, 38 n. 115, 58 n. 47, 60, 61 with n. 52,

65, 106 n. 8, 170, 200, 226 n. 2, 284; Melantho, 293; moly, 289; Nausicaä, 292; *Odyssey*, 16, 20 n. 54, 26, 34, 35–36 with n. 108, 45 n. 30, 112, 181, 200, 288–96; Penelope, 288, 292; Telemachus, 289, 290, 291

Homonoia: 115, 125, 127

Hopkins, Gowland: 276 n. 69

Hoplites: Athenian, 77, 94, 98; Spartan, 77 n. 8, 86

Horace (Q. Horatius Flaccus): 240

Housman, A. E.: 43, 89

Hume, D.: 276 n. 69

Hutchinson, G. O.: 202

Hyccara: 94

Hyginus, Gaius Julius: 252, 256, 257–58, 259

Hylas: 33

Hymettus, Mt.: 254, 256, 257, 260 with n. 54

Hypatia: 227

Hyperbolus: 90, 95, 98

Hyponomos: 188

Hypsipyle: 16, 18, 23

Icaria/ Icarion (Attic deme): 44; Dionysus of, 44

Icaria (island): 41, 42, 44

Icarius: 45

Icarus: 40–46, 251, 284

Iconography/Visual Arts: 17, 19, 21, 25, 36, 163, 168, 170; Aphrodite, 170; of Daedalus and Icarus, 40 with nn. 3 and 4; Esquiline *Odyssey* paintings, 288–89; "Eurymedon" RF vases, 168, 169; Gorgons in, 170; of Herodotus and Thucydides, 72–73; *kouroi*, 170; Minoan, 170; Pergamene, 116, 131

Imbros: 149

Inaros: 76

Industrial Revolution: 226

"Inherited Conglomerate," the: 7, 36

Intellectual tradition, Greek: conservatism of, 7; hubris in, 39

Intertextuality: 35, 253, 262–63
Io: 114 n. 56
Iolkos: 16, 17, 20 n. 51, 30
Ionia, Ionians: 6–7
Iphigeneia: 116
Iris: 32 n. 93
Iron Age: 61–62
Isis: 182, 247–48
Islam: 174
Isocrates: 7, 25 with n. 74, 107; *De Bigis*, 121; *Führer*, quest for, 120, 128; *In Lochitem*, 121; life, 119 with n. 80, 120–21, 124; *Panegyricus*, 119, 120, 121, 122, 123–24, 128; on Panhellenism, 105, 112, 115, 119–126; *Philippus*, 119, 121; preoccupation with peace, 124 with n. 111
Issus: 177, 179
Istros: 136
Italy: 22, 29, 175, 242, 283

James, H.: 295, 296
James, W.: 3
Janus: 245
Jason (mythical): 5, 10, 15–16, 17, 18, 19, 20 with n. 51, 21 n. 55, 23–25, 28, 29, 30 n. 91, 34, 37, 38, 199, 225
Jason of Pherae: 125, 126
Johnson, S.: 210
Julian (emperor): 285
Julius Caesar: 193; apotheosis of, 234–49; murder of, 234
Julius Obsequens: 242
Jung, C.: 283
Jupiter, Jove: 236, 245
Justin: 179, 188
Juvenal: 199, 261

Kaerst, J.: 127
Kagan, D.: 79–97
Keos (Kea): 42
Keuls, E.: 2
Keynes, J. M.: 171
Khedive Ismail: 176
Kingship: 38
King's Peace: 111–12 with n. 39, 119, 121–22 with n. 98, 126

Kipling, R.: 8, 273 n. 51
Kirk, G. S.: 1–2, 4
Kleos, klea: 6, 9, 123, 125, 180
Knossos: 42, 184, 288
Kretheus: 16
Kypselos: 18, 23
Kythnos: 42

Labyrinth: 46
Lacan, J.: 162; "glance and gaze" theory, 169–70, 171
Lacedaemon: 213
Laïos: 8
Lamachos: 92, 109
Lamian/Hellenic War: 107, 130
Lang, A.: 1
Laocoön: 290, 291
Laomedon: 29–30 with n. 88
Larkin, P.: 162
Latinos: 22
Lawrence, T. E.: 141
Laws, legal codes: 12, 47–66, 101, 136, 163–64
"Leaina": 160
Leake, W. M.: 44, 84
Leavis, F. R.: 208
Lebynthos: 42
Lefkowitz, M.: 197, 198, 205, 286
Lemnos: 16, 23, 29, 34, 149
Lenin, V.: 193, 221, 227
Lenz, F. W.: 253, 261
Lesbos: 149, 150 n. 28
Leuctra: 213
Lévi-Strauss, C.: 2, 283
Lévy-Bruhl, L.: 2
Libya: 16, 24, 25, 32 n. 93, 185
Lindblom, G.: 296
Lister, J.: 273
Literacy: 12–13, 100
Livia: 237
Livy (T. Livius Patavinus): 242, 243
Lloyd, G. E. R.: 267 n. 19
Lotze, D.: 148
Lucan (M. Annaeus Lucanus): 245, 250
Lucian: 285; *Icaromenippos*, 238
Lucretius T.: 14, 225, 230, 232

Luther, M.: 79
Lycambes: 48
Lycurgus (Spartan): 212, 215
Lysander (Spartan commander):
102, 121, 144, 145, 146, 147–48 with
n. 20, 149–50 with nn. 26, 28, 37,
151, 152 with n. 40, 153–54 with
n. 47, 155, 156–58 with n. 62, 214;
the Lysandreia, 158
Lysias: 111, 120, 144, 146, 151, 152, 153
n. 47

Ma: 282
Macaulay, T. B.: 71, 170
Macedonia, Macedonians: 69, 106,
118, 127, 129, 130, 178, 179, 184, 195,
214, 216, 218
MacNeice, L.: 1, 169, 291
Magic, ancient: 4, 6, 20–21 n. 55,
24, 32, 36, 38; accuracy condition
of, 267; affective theory of, 266–
67; amulets, apotropaics, 269, 274
n. 56, 278, 288; astrology, 230, 268;
binding spells, 268, 279; control
and power in, 266–68; *Ephesia
Grammata*, 269; erotic, 24–25;
Magi and, 264–65 with n. 2, 269
with n. 28; medical, 30, 264–65,
267–80; miracles, 29 n. 85; papyri,
269, 270, 271, 279, 280; Pliny's
Natural History and, 264–80; of
poetry and rhetoric, 265 with n. 10;
sex and, 267–68; spells, incantations, 264, 265, 266, 269, 273
with n. 52, 278; sympathy, *similia
similibus*, 269, 277–78 with nn. 73–
74
Magna Graecia, S. Italy: 22, 45, 245
Mahmoud Bey: 192–93
Manticores: 113
Mantinea: 90, 138
Marathon: 19, 44, 45 with n. 30, 108
Marmor Parium: 7 n. 10, 28
Mars: 245
Martinez, D.: 266
Marvels (*thaumata*): 11, 15, 28 with
n. 84, 32, 36, 39

Marx, K., Marxism, Marxists: 161,
212, 220, 225, 226
Mattingly, H.: 82
Mazaces: 179
Medeia: 12, 16 with n. 37, 17, 18, 19,
20–21 with n. 55, 23–24, 32, 34, 37,
224; immortality of, 17, 24; magic
and, 20, 24–25, 30, 32, 270; murderer, 24, 30, 32 n. 95 (Apsyrtos),
25, 30 n. 91 (children); rationalised,
30
Medeios: 17
Medicine, ancient (see also s.v.
Hippocrates): apparent causality, principle of, 270–75, 279;
Asclepiad, 276; Athenian plague
and, 85, 86; cooking analogies, 276;
Dogmatists, 228; Empiricists, 228;
experiment, social suspicion of, 276
with n. 69; Four Humors, 229, 274,
276–77; fractures and dislocations,
treatment of, 271–72; Hellenistic,
174; *incubatio*, 275; magic and, 267–
80; metaphor in, 276–77 n. 70;
Methodists, 228, 274; microscopes,
lack of, 273 with n. 51; Plato and,
274; Pneumatists, 228; public hy-
giene, 77, 86; Sacred Disease, 229;
sepsis, 272–73, 280
Medism: 107
Mediterranean: 10, 16, 22, 23, 39, 43,
96, 176, 177, 178, 205; cults of, 282
Megabyzus (temple warden): 134,
135 with n. 5
Megalopolis: 224
Megara: 12 n. 27, 87; Nisaia, 87
Meiggs, R.: 80
Melos, Melians: 63, 73, 89, 158
Memnon: 114 n. 56
Memphis: 173, 179, 180, 183, 187
Menander: 286
Menelaus: 289, 291
Mercenaries: 135, 137, 141, 142, 178
Mercury: 245
Messenia, Messenians: 86
Messina, Straits of: 290
Metrodorus: 227

Metternich, Prince K. von: 106
Meyer, E.: 81
Miletus, Milesians: 113, 177, 245
Military affairs, misc.: aberrations of, 93; fifth-column tactics, 93; siege-warfare, 93 with n. 24
Mimnermos: 22
Minos: 16, 41, 257 with nn. 39, 41
Minotaur (Asterius): 27, 46, 284
Mitchison, N.: 212
Mitford, W.: 79
Mithridates VI of Pontus: 278
Mohammed Ali: 173, 176
Momigliano, A.: 71 n. 5
Montgomery, R.: 170
More, St. Thomas: 79
Morgan, K.: 253 n. 11
Morris, W.: 1
Moses: 290
Muggeridge, M.: 85
Müller, M.: 38 n. 115
Munn, M.: 99–103
Munro, J. A. R.: 148
Murray, G.: 7
Muses: 64 with n. 57, 66
Mycenae, Mycenaean Age: 2, 5–6, 288
Mysia: 33 n. 97, 34
Mysteries: Eleusinian, 25 n. 74, 92
Myth: 1–4, 79; aetiology and, 200; Alexandria and, 173 ff.; allegorization of, 13–14, 200; ancient revaluation of, 5–39; apotheosis as, 234–49; Argonautic, 15–39; Daedalus and Icarus, 40–46; functions of, 9; geography and, 11, 21–23, 113; genealogy and, 8–9; historicity of, 6–7, 8, 26–28; historiography of, 6, 79; Holocaust Myth, 2; irrational treatment of, 43 with n. 20; Macedonian "non-Greekness" and, 129 with n. 148; modern treatments of, 281–87; mythos and logos, 3–4, 6–8, 10, 11, 13, 199–200, 287; Ovid's use of, 250–63; Persian Wars and, 112; rationalization of, 14–15, 200; religion and, 9–10, 79, 283; Spartan, 213–17; systematization of, 12–13; theories of, 1–2; Trojan War and, 112
Mytilene: 27, 65, 73

Nabarzanes: 178
Nabis: 213
Naples: 22
Narratology: 35
Nasser, G. A.: 174
Naucratis/Naukratis: 180–81, 205, 206
Naupactus: 86
Naxos: 42, 155
Nazism: 220–21
Nectanebo (Nekht-har-hebi) II: 175, 178 n. 33, 179
Neobule: 48
Nephele: 254
Nereïds: 32, 37
Nero (emperor): 245, 266
Nestor: 168
Nicias: 72, 87, 88, 90–91, 92, 93; Peace of, 74, 83, 87–88, 96, 103; proxenos of Syracuse, 94; slave-dealer, 94; superstitious, 239
Nicocles: 124
Nietzsche, F.: 83
Nikidion: 227, 233
Nile, R.: 178, 179; Canopic branch, 180, 181; Delta, 179, 183, 190, 192
"Noble Savage," concept of: 116, 131
Nonnus of Panopolis: 284, 285
North, O.: 222
Nubia, Nubians: 281
Numenius: 188
Numerius Atticus: 237, 244
Nussbaum, M.: 223–33

Ocean: 11 and n. 22, 16 with n. 39, 21, 22 with n. 59, 39
Odysseus/Ulysses: 11, 16, 22, 35, 39 with n. 116, 65, 251 nn. 2–3, 273 with n. 52, 288, 289–96

Ogygia: 294
Oita, Mt.: 38 n. 115
"Old Oligarch," the: 98
Olympia: 134, 135 n. 5, 284
Olympian pantheon: 14, 200, 240, 244, 246, 247, 281, 282, 287
Olympic Games: 30, 111
Olympus, Mt.: 245
Orality: 8, 21
Orestes: 16 n. 37
Origen: 27 n. 81
Orion: 245, 256
Orwell, G.: 221, 251
Ostracism: 90 with n. 19
Ovid (P. Ovidius Naso): 40, 41–42 with nn. 14–17, 43–44, 107, 127, 143, 236–37, 241 with n. 41, 270, 283; *Ars Amatoria*, 250–69; Augustus and, 251; *ekphrasis*, 251; intertextuality, use of, 253, 262–63; magic and, 265 with n. 11; *Metamorphoses*, 251, 256, 257, 258, 259 n. 48, 260, 282; as *praeceptor amoris*, 46 with nn. 36–39, 251–63; on Procris, 250–63; *relegatio* of, 134; *Remedia Amoris*, 251; Sabine women, rape of, 250; structural patterns in, 250 n. 1

Paglia, C.: 225, 288, 289, 290–91, 292, 293, 294–95
Palaiphatos: 14, 38 n. 115
Pandora: 56, 60
Panhellenism: 3, 29, 31, 76, 104–31, 216; cults of, 78; Panhellenic Games, 107
Pannonia: 244
Papadopoulos, Col. G.: 228
Papyri, papyrology: 82
Paraetonium (Mersa Matruh): 186, 187 n. 99, 188
Paralia: 44, 45
Paris: 18
Parker, D.: 225
Parmenides: 287
Paros: 42

Pascal, B.: 246
Pasiphaë: 41, 46, 250–51, 257, 258, 281, 284, 285
Patrios politeia ["ancestral constitution"]: 105, 149
Paul, St.: 108
Pausanias (Agiad King of Sparta): 139, 140, 150
Pausanias (Spartan Regent): 109 n. 28
Pausanias (travel-writer): 19, 103, 135, 137
Pelagius: 222
Peleus: 20 n. 54
Pelias: 16, 17, 20 nn. 51, 54, 30, 37
Peloponnese: 214, 215
Peloponnesian War: 74–75, 77 with n. 8, 79–97, 108, 109, 115, 120, 124, 135, 136, 140, 147; Archidamian War, 77 with n. 8, 83, 85–87, 103, 116, 119; economics of, 94–97; First, 81; Ionian-Decelean war, 87 n. 14, 100, 102, 103; Peace of Nicias, 74, 83, 87–88, 96, 103; Persian involvement in, 115; Sicilian expedition, 89, 91–93, 100, 103
Pelops: 24 n. 70, 287
Pelusium: 178, 183
Pendéli: 44
Pentekontaetia: 81, 83
Penthelidae: 65
Pepys, S.: 175
Perdiccas (Alexander's marshal): 190
Pergamon: 36, 116, 131
Pericles, Periclean age: 36, 38, 67–78, 85, 97, 98, 99, 101–2, 119, 170, 238, 245; Archidamian war-policy and, 77 with n. 8, 85–87; Funeral Oration of, 70, 72, 162; nicknamed "the Olympian," 85; Samos and, 150 n. 31; Thurii and, 106
Perinthos: 177
Persaeus: 217
Perses: 47, 48, 49; bribery by (?), 49 and n. 16, 50–58

Perseus: 15 n. 37, 114, 245
Persia, Persians: 76, 98, 107, 111, 114
n. 56, 130, 133, 168, 178; empire of,
105, 112; Magi, 264-65 with n. 2,
269 with n. 28; Panhellenic crusade
against, 123, 127, 128, 177
Persian Wars: 31, 98, 108, 111, 112,
113-14, 125, 128
Peters, B.: 294
Pfeiffer, R.: 202
Phaeacia, Phaeacians: 22
Phaëthon: 254
Phasis R.: 16
Pherecydes: 254, 255, 258
Philip II of Macedon: 94, 105, 106,
110, 114, 120, 125, 127 with n. 121,
126, 216; alleged Heraclid ances-
try, 105; bribery, use of, 129 with
n. 144; Demosthenes on, 111;
Perinthos campaign, 177; victory at
Chaeronea, 119
Philip V of Macedon: 146
Philippides: 36 with n. 112
Philistus of Syracuse: 88, 89 with
n. 16
Philocrates, Peace of: 105
Phineus: 16, 20 with n. 54, 29-30, 38
Phoenicia, Phoenicians: 178; fleet,
177, 178, 187, 287
Phoenix: 50
Phormio: 83
Phrixos: 16, 20, 28
Phyllis (mythical character): 251 n. 3
Pindar: 6, 9, 16, 23, 24 nn. 69-70, 25,
32, 39, 78, 98; anti-war, 108-9 with
nn. 27-28; Fourth Pythian, 6, 15,
16, 20 n. 52, 22 with n. 61, 23 with
n. 63, 24-25
Pinney, G. F.: 168
Plataia: 11 n. 23
Plato, Platonism: 7, 26-27, 37, 79,
97, 99, 102, 161, 164, 217, 220,
228, 231, 244, 245, 276; [Epi-
nomis], 246; Gorgias, 63 with n. 53;
Laws, 98, 233, 245; Meno, 226 n. 2;
Neoplatonism, 285; Nocturnal

Council of, 79; Phaedrus, 246;
Republic, 63 n. 53, 97, 107, 231-32;
Seventh Letter, 101, 231; Timaeus,
274 with n. 56; on war and stasis,
127, 231
Pleistoanax, King: 87
Pliny the Elder (C. Plinius Secun-
dus): 11, 235 with n. 8, 237, 238; on
magic and medicine, 264-80
Plutarch: 89, 93, 144, 155, 159; Agis,
212; Alexander, 179-80, 181; Camil-
lus, 155; Cleomenes, 214, 215; Lysan-
der, 147, 148, 150 n. 26, 153 n. 47,
155, 157; Moralia, 177; On the Mal-
ice of Herodotus, 69; Romulus, 241;
Solon, 215-16
Pluto: 283
Poias: 21 n. 55
Pol Pot: 227
Polyaenus: 93 with n. 23
Polybius: 129, 133, 146
Polydeuces: 33
Polyphemus: 291
Polyxena: 116
Po R. (Eridanos): 29, 39
Pöschl, V.: 253, 256, 260
Poseidon: 16, 20 n. 51, 29 n. 88, 248,
290
Posidippus (playwright): 131
Potidaea: 93 n. 24
Pound, E.: 286
Powell, J. E.: 71 n. 4
Praxiteles: 170
Priam: 17
Pritchett, W. K.: 84
Private Eye: 224
Procris: 250-63
Proculeius Julius: 241, 244
Prodikos: 14, 34 n. 104
Prometheus: 286
Propaganda: 12
Protagoras: 37, 73, 239, 281, 282
Proteus: 179, 186
Proxenos (friend of Xenophon): 137,
140
Prusa: 135

Ptolemaic/Lagid dynasty: 173, 183, 206, 266; gigantism of, 188, 195, 196; luxury of, 195
Ptolemy I Soter: 180, 190, 193, 197
Ptolemy II Philadelphos: 30 with n. 90, 31, 176 n. 23, 196, 205, 206, 247–48, 273–74
Ptolemy III Euergetes I: 174, 205, 206, 248
Ptolemy X Alexander I: 193
Pylos: 77 n. 8, 83
Pyrrhus: 126
Pythagoras, Pythagoreanism: 244, 245–46
Pythodorus (archon): 145 with n. 8, 154

Ranke, L. von: 91
Rashomon: 2, 4
Rationalism, rationalizations: 4, 6–7, 8, 25–26, 28–29, 30, 32, 36–37, 38, 41, 201, 238, 244
Red Sea: 290
Religion, Greek: 9–10, 12, 37, 78, 100; anthropomorphism of, 244; *asebeia* trials, 106–7 with n. 15, 141; burial customs, 41; Hellenistic, 36, 174, 281–82; Lysander, divine honors to, 158; pollution (*mivasma*), 10, 78; ruler-worship, 36, 160, 240 with n. 31, 282; superstitions, 92, 238, 239
Religion, Roman: 247; prodigies, portents, 242; ruler-worship, 234–49; Vestal Virgins, 265
Renault, M.: 195
Rhacotis: 182, 183, 184, 186, 187, 194
Rhianos of Crete: 201
Rhodé: 205
Rhodes: 205, 206, 207, 208
Rhône R. (Rhodanus): 29, 39
Riddle, J. M.: 268
Rieu, E. V.: 32, 295
Robespierre, M. F.: 221, 227
Rohde, E.: 253
Roisman, J.: 136
Rome, Romans: 6, 22, 46, 205, 210,

218, 230, 247; apotheosis and, 248; Campus Martius, 237, 240; Senate, 237
Romulus: 237, 240–42, 244
Rosselini, I.: 292
Rostropowicz, R.: 205
Rutherford, E.: 276 n. 69
Rutilius Rufus, P.: 217

Salamis: 12 n. 27, 98, 108, 131, 155
Sallust (Roman historian): 74, 285
Sallust/Saloustios (Neoplatonist): 285
Salt Lake City: 189
Samos: 42, 93, 146, 149–51 with nn. 28, 30; Pericles' siege of, 150 n. 31, 152–53, 154, 155 n. 55, 156–58 with n. 62
Samothrace: 29; mysteries of, 29 n. 85
Sappho: 82
Sarakatsani: 55
Sarapis: 182, 186, 187, 192
Saronic Gulf: 87
Sartre, J.-P.: 169, 171
Scholars, psychology of: 3–4, 69–73, 82–83, 106, 159, 197, 202, 207
Scott, A.: 245 n. 70, 246
Scylla: 35, 290, 291
Scyros: 149
Scythia, Scythians: 122 with n. 106, 168
Searle, J.: 162
Segal, C.: 262–63
Seneca, L. A.: 223, 225, 233; *Apocolocyntosis*, 238; *Medea*, 224
Seriphos: 42
Servius: 243, 252, 256, 258 with n. 48
Sestos: 151 n. 37, 158
Seuthes: 135
Sex, Sexuality: 24 with n. 69, 25, 29, 30, 46 nn. 36–37, 110, 160, 162–63, 286; Alexandria and, 172, 195; contraception, 257 with n. 39; economics of, 165; Homer and, today, 293–94; homosexuality, 76, 162,

164, 166, 172, 258, 261; magic and, 267; Ovid on, 251-63; pederasty, 34 n. 102, 76, 170; penetration theory, 162-63, 165-69, 171, 258; pornography, visual, 170; Presidential, 222 n. 1; prostitution, 165-66; satyrs and, 166; venereal disease, 257 with n. 39

Sextus Empiricus: 225
Shakespeare, W.: 296
Shaw, G. B.: 212
Shelley, P. B.: 210
Shiftlessness (*amechania*): 10, 16, 19, 20, 37, 199
Sibyl, the: 46 n. 36
Sicily: 22, 42, 43, 45, 91 n. 20, 175, 217; alliance with Egesta, 76-77; Sicilian Expedition, 74-75, 89, 91-93, 100, 103, 239; wealth and resources of, 96
Sidon: 178, 284
Sigeion: 29
Silleus: 205
Siphnos: 42
Sirens: 6, 252, 295
Siwah Oasis: 179-80
Skeptics: 228
Skiapods: 113
Skillous: 134, 135
Slater, P.: 2
Slaves, Slavery: 76, 165-66, 226, 230, 232
Snow, C. P.: 106 n. 14
Socrates: 7 n.9, 10, 85, 91 n. 20, 95, 97, 102, 140, 141, 142, 228, 276 n. 69; trial and execution, 100, 141, 143, 214
Solon: 51 with n. 21, 53, 63, 212, 215-16
Sophists, Sophistic movement: 70, 76, 79, 118, 238
Sophocles: 7, 21 n. 55, 26, 87 n. 13, 174; *Antigone*, 7
Sounion: 45 n. 30
Sparta, Spartans: 76, 77, 79, 86, 107, 109, 110-11, 121-22, 124, 127, 130, 133, 135, 155, 287; ephors, 148, 152,

156 n. 59, 159 n. 79; Euripides on, 117 with n. 72; Hellenistic, 119, 212-16; helots, 86; Homeric, 291; Laconism and, 133, 135, 137, 142; Messenians and, 118; military training, 213; occupation of Athens, 144; relations with Persia, 115, 122, 140; sodomization of brides, 287; war party and peace party, 84

Spartoi, the: 32
Spencer, H.: 219
Speusippus: 120
Sphacteria: 77 n. 8, 84
Sphaerus: 211, 214, 215, 216, 218
Stasis: 107, 111, 142
Ste. Croix, G. E. M. de: 80, 16
Stevens, W.: 225, 233
Stevenson, R. L.: 71
Stewart, A.: 160, 169-71
Stoa, Stoicism: 4, 26, 34, 222, 228; astrology and, 248-49, 268; *ataraxia*, 224, 226, 232; cosmology, 220, 222, 248-49; ethics, 224, 226; Hellenistic, 210-21, 223-33; magic and, 268; Middle Stoa, 211, 217, 218; *sympatheia* and, 249, 265; Rome and, 210, 211, 216, 218-19; Spartan influence on, 216
Strabo: 9 n.15, 21, 28-29, 42-43 with n. 19, 112 n. 45, 175, 183 with n. 68, 184 with n. 76, 196, 239
Strepsiades: 56
Strombichides: 148 n. 20, 153
Successors, the (*Diadochoi*): 37, 193-94, 211
Suda/Souda, the: 201-2, 206, 207
Suetonius: 235-36
Suez: 1956 war, 173
Sulla, L. C.: 130
Susa: 137
Switzerland: 39
Sydow, M. von: 296
Syracuse: 93, 96; Epipolae, 92; Gamoroi, 93; and Nicias, 94; siege of, 92
Syria: 188; Third Syrian War, 248

Tallis, R.: 162

Talos: 20, 21 n. 55, 32, 41

Tambiah, S. J.: 267 with n. 19

Tanglewood Tales, The: 1, 284–87

Tantalus: 287

Taras, Tarentines: 126

Tartaros: 238

Taurians: 28

Tegea: 11 n. 23

Teiresias: 162–63

Textual criticism: 44, 57 with n. 44, 146–47 with n. 12, 206

Thasos: 158

Thatcher, M.: 95

Thebes, Thebans: 13 n. 28, 98, 109, 258; Alexander's destruction of, 104, 130; Medism of, 109 with n. 28

Themistocles: 90 n. 19, 106 n. 14, 153

Theocritus: 37, 203

Theognis: 97

Theophilos of Alexandria: 27 n. 81

Theopompos: 118

Thera (Santorini): 23, 42, 290

Theramenes: 121, 139, 144, 147–48 with n. 20, 150–51, 152 with n. 40, 153

Thermopylae: 110

Thersites: 61, 65

Theseus: 16, 26, 41

Thespiae: 56, 58, 66

Thespis: 44

Thessaly: 107

Thetis: 35–36 with n. 108

Thibron: 135, 140, 142

Thirlwall, C.: 79

Thorikon: 45, 255, 258

Thrace, Thracians: 28, 135, 141, 150 n. 28, 158 n. 76, 177, 244, 281

Thrasybulus: 102, 144

Thrasymachus: 63 n. 53

Thucydides: 3, 12 n. 24, 14, 72, 79–97, 131–32, 133, 147, 153, 162, 184, 216–17 with n.18; and Alcibiades, 92 n. 22; chronology of, 77, 99; cult of, 68 with n. 1; Egesta and, 77; historiography, 77 with nn. 7–

8, 78–79, 102–3; life, 72, 103, 132; Melian Dialogue, 63, 73, 89, 158, 216; on Peace of Nicias, 87 with n. 14; *Realpolitik* and, 118; style of, 70–71; Thucydideans, 3, 71–72, 77 with nn. 7–8, 99

Thucydides s.o. Melesias: 99

Thurii: 106

Thyestes: 287

Thynias: 37 with n. 115

Tiber, R.: 130

Tiberius (emperor): 6, 238, 252, 262

Tiberius Gracchus: 211, 218

Timokrates: 227

Timon (of Phlius): 195 with n. 143, 202

Timotheus: 120

Tiphys: 46

Tissaphernes: 10

Titans: 113

Tithonos: 17 with n. 42, 256

Toynbee, A.: 106

Travels of Sir John Mandeville, The: 11

Triballians: 122 with n. 106

Trigaios/Trigaeus: 87 with n. 13

Triton: 20 n. 52, 37

Trojan War, Troy, Trojans, Troad: 1, 7, 25, 29 with n. 88, 35, 104, 112, 114 n. 56, 116, 289, 290, 291, 292

Tylor, E.: 2

Tyranny, *tyrannoi:* 111, 120

Tyre: 178, 182

Tyro: 16

Tyrrhenia, Tyrrhenians: 22

Tyrtaeus: 215

Under Milk Wood: 295

Urbanism: 12

Vandiver, E.: 1

Varro, M. T.: 273 n. 51

Velleius Paterculus: 237, 238

Venice: 205

Venus: 236–37, 245

Vergina: 38

Versailles, Treaty of: 83
Vespasian: 238
Vessey, D. W.: 201
Viet Nam: 292
Virgil: 40 n. 3, 42, 45, 250–51; *Aeneid*, 46 with n. 36; *Georgics*, 243 with n. 61
Vitruvius: 188

Wade-Gery, T.: 86 with n. 12
"Wandering Rocks" (*Planktai*): 35–36 with n. 106
War and warfare (misc.): 108 with nn. 24, 26; atrocities, 112; naval, Arab distrust of, 174; siege-warfare, 150 and n. 31, 152; *stasis*, 127
Watts, G. F.: 285
Webb, S. & B.: 212
Welles, B.: 180, 186
Westlake, H. D.: 86 with n. 12
White, S. A.: 211
Wilamowitz-Moellendorf, U. von: 207, 256
Williams, V.: 294
Woodhead, A. G.: 85

Xenocrates: 246
Xenophanes of Colophon: 37, 244, 281
Xenophon: 34 n. 104, 95 with n. 31, 101, 115, 144–45, 146 n. 12, 152; *Anabasis*, 115, 135; *Cyropaedia*, 115; exile, 133–43; *Hellenica*, 144, 148, 150 n. 26, 151, 153 with n. 47, 157; *Poroi*, 136; Ten Thousand and, 135
Xerxes: 104, 114 n. 53

Young, B.: 189

Zeno (of Kition): 2, 210, 211, 220, 227; Athenian attitude to, 218; *Politeia*, 2, 211–12, 216, 217–18
Zenodotos: 206
Zeus: 9, 13, 17, 27, 29 n. 88, 37 with n. 114, 245, 248, 257 n. 41, 281, 284; in Hesiod, 50, 52, 59 n. 50, 60, 61, 63 n. 54; weather-god, 282
Ziegler, K.: 201
Zimmern, A. E.: 118 with n. 75